Hotel Design

Planning and Development

SECOND EDITION

Hotel Design
Planning and Development

SECOND EDITION

Richard Penner, Lawrence Adams
and Stephani K. A. Robson

Routledge
Taylor & Francis Group

NEW YORK AND LONDON

Second edition published 2013
by Routledge
2 Park Square, Milton Park, Abingdon, Oxon OX14 4RN

Simultaneously published in the USA and Canada
by Routledge
711 Third Avenue, New York, NY 10017

Routledge is an imprint of the Taylor & Francis Group, an informa business

First edition published by Architectural Press, an imprint of Elsevier Science
© 2001 Walter A. Rutes, Richard H. Penner, and Lawrence Adams

British Library Cataloguing in Publication Data
A catalogue record for this book is available from the British Library

Library of Congress Cataloging in Publication Data
CIP data has been applied for

ISBN: 978-0-08-096699-1 (hbk)
ISBN: 978-0-08-096700-4 (ebk)

Acquisition editors: Nancy Green, Liz Burton, and Wendy Fuller
Editorial Assistant: Laura Williamson
Production manager: Alfred Symons
Book designer and typesetter: Alex Lazarou

Printed by Everbest Printing Co. Ltd, China

Contents

Acknowledgments

This book is the result of many decades of experience in the specialized field of hotel architecture and interior design—the experience of the scores of people who generously provided us with their insights about design and with examples of their work. We credit the architects, designers, photographers, and others who encouraged us and provided us with material about their projects—there are many more than we can suitably acknowledge here.

We owe a special debt to three giants in the industry: architect Michael Graves, designer David Rockwell, and developer Barry Sternlicht, who agreed to introduce the book with personal observations about their distinguished careers and about the future of hotel architecture, design, and development. Also, to their assistants who helped with the work: Ben Wintner at Michael Graves & Associates, Joan MacKeith and Maggie Hartnick at Rockwell Group, and Beth Shanholtz at Starwood Capital. In addition, sincere thanks to Robert E. Kastner, Ian Schrager, John C. Portman, Jr., Stephen Perkins, Roger Thomas, Howard J. Wolff, Steve Rushmore, Jim Anhut, and Sara Schoen for providing a series of sidebar commentaries for specific chapters.

We cannot offer enough thanks for the patience and enormous good judgment of the editors at Taylor & Francis and W. W. Norton: Laura Williamson, Wendy Fuller, and Nancy Green, and, especially, Ruth Mandel of Images Sought and Found, without whose assistance this book would not have been possible.

Also, over the past few years, students at Cornell and other universities took on individual research projects or assisted with the many drawings that illustrate the book. These include Katie Kozarek, Jerome Chen, Eduardo Quintero, and Carla Moulton. Their interest and enthusiasm for the details of hotel planning issues are infectious.

Our own associations with many good friends provided helpful comments throughout the writing of the book, and others went far beyond the call of duty in providing resources. There are too many individual contributors to acknowledge each one. We want to thank, however, the many hotel executives who identified their company's most exciting new properties and the many media services and marketing people who provided us with images and drawings, all of whom willingly met our endless request for additional information. Most of all, we must recognize the sacrifices made by our families, friends, and colleagues who have provided incredible support and encouragement to complete this project. Thank you all.

Foreword

The Architect's Perspective

Michael Graves, FAIA, and Patrick Burke, AIA
Michael Graves & Associates
Princeton, New Jersey

Business hotels and resorts compete for today's sophisticated global travelers, and their developers and operators often look to architects and interior designers to create new and interesting "experiences" for the guest. For decades, the hotel industry had been focused primarily on functionality and operations, and hotel design became formulaic. For business hotels, the predictability that came with standardization was often a virtue. For resorts, however, the trend resulted in a proliferation of hotels across the globe that looked as if they could be located anywhere in the world. Hotels in Egypt could have easily been built in Costa Rica, or in Miami.

All that has changed over the past 15 years as leisure travelers seek unique experiences connected to local culture and context. As architects and designers, we ask ourselves, "What is special about this place, and how can we capture that spirit?" The sense-of-place influences every scale: from the landscape and buildings, to the interiors and the smallest details of their furnishings. Thus, a resort in Costa Rica might be designed as a series of ecologically friendly, small-scale, semi-open-air pavilions, creating the feeling of being immersed within the tropical landscape. Or a spa resort in Switzerland may incorporate restorative natural thermal baths and grand fireplaces within architecture that is contemporary in design but constructed according to local craft traditions.

Urban hotels too can reflect local culture. For example, The St. Regis Cairo embodies the worldly character of the hotel's brand while conveying the ambience of the host country through details, materials, colors, and patterns inspired by the context and intended to be locally sourced. Going local is just one component in the prevalent interest in environmental responsibility. The hospitality industry increasingly recognizes the benefits of building and operating hotels that are efficient in their use of water and energy. This requires integrative thinking among members of the design team and a commitment from developers and operators. Significant technical inroads have been made not only in building envelopes and mechanical systems but also in the hotel kitchen, laundry, and waste management. We believe that guests appreciate the healthful aspects of environmentally responsible places, as much as they appreciate good design.

Good design, long associated with luxury and boutique hotels, today brings fresh and sometimes innovative solutions to three-star and four-star properties as a way of differentiating brands, providing value, and attracting guests. In creating operator standards for these hotels, many of which cater to the business traveler, we have learned that the attributes must be adaptable to different building layouts and designs since many of such hotels are conversions of existing properties and not always new construction. Like their higher-end counterparts, these hotels recognize the guests' expectations for services that meet today's needs.

Hotels, like other customer-oriented institutions, continually evolve in the services they provide and how they provide them, creating a gradual change in the building type. What hotels offer the public today meets the expectations and needs of business and recreational travelers, from express grab'n'go food to Internet access and programmable technology for everything from hotel check-in to controlling light, sound, and temperature in the guestrooms.

Despite the importance of the public spaces in hotels—the lobby, lounges, restaurants, spas, and fitness center—guests' satisfaction is ultimately judged by their experience of the living accommodations. In many of today's higher-end developments, the guestroom may be a traditional hotel room or a serviced apartment, a phenomenon that has transformed the standalone hotel to a mixed-use mini-community. For the architect, the guestroom, or the apartment unit, is the essential building block that sets the module for the building. It's the place where one gets to think through who the guests are and what they need; guests may be a group gathering to play golf, a family on vacation, or a solo business traveler using the room as a temporary office. While some hotels once thought they had "perfected" the guestroom, today, just as in the technology industry, there is an impetus to innovate. The guestroom is being rethought in terms of its aesthetics, functions, and features. As savvy travelers, we have embraced the idea of traveling to different places and enjoying great guest experiences, and a well-designed guestroom is a measure of success.

As architects who have been involved in hospitality projects for decades, we know there is simply no "one size fits all" in this industry. Therefore, a book like this is very helpful as a comprehensive reference guide to hotel design, planning, and development. We are honored to have been asked to offer a few comments on today's hotel world and look forward to reading the insights of our colleagues.

The Interior Designer's Perspective

David Rockwell
Founder and CEO
Rockwell Group
New York, New York

Today's hotel is not merely a destination, but is also a convergence of an incredible array of experiences. The moment guests enter, they become part of a vibrant microcosm, a carefully crafted environment that provides both a thrilling escape and domestic comforts. While the hotel's calendar of events may change with the seasons, the value placed on small, everyday rituals is a constant. This is the very nature of the new hotel: its ability to be both up-to-the-moment with the latest trends, yet reassuringly personal and accommodating to a broad spectrum of guests.

The hotel itself is a hybrid linking two worlds: home and destination. In terms of design, this idea is most clearly represented by the hotel's entrance, which becomes a celebratory focal point of the lobby space. Although the hotel is itself a dynamic environment, it is also situated within a larger set of attractions and cultural milieu. Hospitality environments today must engage and reflect local context, forging a symbiotic relationship with the cities and neighborhoods beyond their walls. By joining in the celebration of local festivals or assimilating regional ingredients in their culinary offerings, authentic flavors of the world can permeate the hotel in myriad ways. An East Asian hotel might offer a traditional tea service, for example, and staff uniforms may be designed by an emerging fashion star. Fostering a rich sense-of-place can transform a fleeting hotel stay into an enduring, memorable experience.

Through innovative uses of technology, hotels are able to reflect the interconnectedness of our lives today. From the moment you step into a hotel, smartly integrated, cutting-edge tools can transform and heighten previously tedious chores. Check-in desks are becoming a thing of the past. With advanced data-management systems, greeters can personally welcome each guest at the door by name. A cumbersome process becomes convenient, even leisurely, as travelers check in via iPad over a gin-and-tonic in the lounge. These are the least of the possibilities that our information age offers us. Rooms are equipped with a range of customizable features with which to personalize your space: at the touch of a button guests can control the lighting, changing the room's entire mood, select a special aromatherapy-infused shower to shake off the drag of jet-lag, or conjure up a concealed high-end entertainment system.

This flexibility translates into a warmth and openness towards individual needs that complements the distinctive character of a hotel. Each guest brings with him or her a personal routine of comforts, which the hotel should respond to attentively with a fine-tuned menu of services. Quotidian rituals are enabled by diverse, dynamic spaces. In common areas, purposeful design can set the scene for spontaneous encounters and reveal unexpected and delightful details; everyone can find a favorite gathering spot—a lounge that allows intimate conversations, a lobby where you can go to see and be seen, or a comfortable corner to curl up with a book.

In tune with the tempo of the individual and resonating with multiple rhythms, the hotel environment today presents an inviting, comfortable haven. The most successful hotel interiors transform a sojourn into an unforgettable experience, however brief, and position guests as the curators of their own journeys.

The Developer's Perspective

Barry Sternlicht
Chairman
Starwood Capital Group
Greenwich, Connecticut

My mother is an accomplished artist. During our childhood, many of her paintings hung in the hallway of our home and in the living room. I loved the colors she used, the texture of her knife, and the calmness and feelings they evoked in me. Most of all, I marveled at the creative process, how on a blank canvas one could create such emotion and beauty. In high school, I took several art classes where I focused on painting. Good artists understand the delicacy of composition of the canvas … still lifes arranged just so—work … and others don't. A picture taken at one angle tantalizes the viewer, but seen from another it is boring. The juxtaposition of one color against another is complementary and soothing, or dark, disturbing, and uncomfortable. While my parents suggested I not become an artist, I love design and architecture and so, for me, marrying design and real estate in the form of hotels was not work but the fulfillment of childhood ambitions.

Over the years, I bought an immense amount of property in many product types such as office, retail, golf courses, senior housing, and, of course, hotels. I marveled at design that worked, that powered occupancy, and achieved great rents versus that which did not. For example, when I lived in Chicago, I worked across the street from the Water Tower, perhaps America's most successful vertical mall. The center was always busy and it felt busy. The mall was designed with anchor stores at either end, but in the center was a circular space four or five stories high in which were the glass elevators and all the escalators. You saw everyone in the mall! It was always busy and going up and down the escalators you could see all the stores you forgot were tenants or new stores you wanted to be sure to visit before you left.

What I noticed about the hotel industry in 1995, the year I decided I would do a national "boutique chain" that I named W Hotels, was that the industry had spent decades dumbing down the product, and competed on price but not on aesthetics. We had a $79 a night chain, followed by those at $99, $109, $139, and $179. My theory was that we could build a chain where we would compete on design: that design matters, that consumers would not only pay more for great design but that it would build an emotional attachment with them, that they might define themselves by our aesthetic and we would build brand loyalty and, therefore, give ourselves pricing power. In hotels, the product had become commoditized. One could not tell the brand by looking at the room. It seemed that interior designers had gone to the "one size fits all" box, like the failed K car of Chrysler where someone had the brilliant idea of building multiple bodies on the same chassis and engine. Consumers saw right through it and so, by trying to be all things to all people, you appealed to almost no one. Or, at least, we can say you built no brand loyalty.

There are certain spaces you walk into that put you at ease and make you feel comfortable. These are spaces that work:

proportions that are elegant, furniture that is sized appropriately for the space it occupies, pieces that speak to each other and enhance each other with their presence. We react to texture, to proportion, to color, and the immense talent of great interior designers is that they take the complex and make it look effortless, just as great athletes seem to hardly be trying when they are in their zone. A space may be filled with numerous wonderful textures, vibrant color, and surprising and dynamic innovative products. It simply feels right and yet it is, in my mind, just as hard as the great painter's compositions executed in the physical space. Sometimes design makes you nervous, is unsettling, and you simply want to leave; sometimes you don't even know why. And then there is design for design's sake.

If you are working in hotel design, you can't forget it's about people, customers, and that they are going to be part of your "composition" when it is complete. Great designers can deftly edit a space, modify its contents, work across all the dimensions of design—scale, color, texture, lighting—in their heads, and the result will be spaces that work, that make people feel good, that are inviting. If the artist can execute this with great originality, it becomes memorable, a classic. To me, it's about the human experience for, after all, hotels are meeting places for weary travelers. Why not dazzle them and amaze them and leave them yearning for one more night's stay? Just as Apple, Samsung, and Aston Martin have created loyal customers through innovative industrial design, so too can great designers influence, strengthen, and even define a great brand.

Preface

Development and Design Interact

For their kind Foreword illuminating the timeless goals of the world's largest industry, we immensely thank Michael Graves, David Rockwell, and Barry Sternlicht, who represent the major disciplines involved with hotel development and design.

Much has changed about hotels and the hospitality industry since the 2001 edition of *Hotel Design, Planning and Development*. In just over a decade, the Internet has risen to being the key form of communication for our guests and development teams alike and shapes how everyone does business everywhere in the world. Rapidly advancing technology is supporting the application of sustainable principles in design and operations. Robust growth in hotel supply during the 2000s reflected new segments, new markets, new lodging products, and new approaches to financing in a difficult economy. Today there are more hotel brands than ever, each demanding a specific set of design and operational requirements that make an integrated effort among the developer, operator, and design team paramount in order to ensure a successful outcome. In 2001, most hotel development was still taking place in North America. Now, Asia is the engine of much of the industry's growth and other parts of the world are poised to follow suit. There has never been a more exciting or more challenging time to create hotel assets.

This book is intended to serve as a practical guide to the hotel building type for practitioners and students alike. Our inquiry begins with the word "hotel" itself, meaning mansion, borrowed from the French soon after the American Revolution in an effort to express the sophistication of the new multifaceted inns that then appeared. From their onset, these novel mixed-use establishments served the varied needs of a rapidly expanding society by freely adapting new residential, commercial, and industrial features to hotel use. These include the first grand ballroom in New York, an atrium and Merchants' Exchange in Boston, a domed European lobby in New Orleans, and a theater, shops, and laundry in London. Their competitive nature meant that hotels were among the first buildings in most cities to incorporate the newest technologies such as gas and electric lighting, central heat, telephones, and elevators.

Such creative responses to consumer needs and desires more than ever drive hotel design and development today. There is no such thing as a "generic" limited-service or full-service hotel anymore. Ever-greater segmentation means that hotels need to be keenly focused from the very start of the development process. The specific requirements of the road-warrior business traveler, the design-savvy boutique guest, the family on vacation far from home, the meeting planner and corporate travel coordinator, as well as the hotel management company and the selected brand, all require careful consideration throughout the planning and design stages. And as digital technology continues to evolve at breakneck speed, developers and designers must constantly adapt to make sure that the amenities and infrastructure in all new projects keep pace.

In the following chapters we expand upon the practices, features, and trends that shape the hotel development industry. So sophisticated are today's markets that certain once-popular concepts have faded into oblivion while some previously negative traits are now considered attractions. Therefore, we are pleased to be able to interpret today's design, technology, and creative concepts which continue to offer such bright prospects for the future.

Richard H. Penner
Lawrence Adams
Stephani K. A. Robson

We dedicate this book to the memory of **Walter A. Rutes**, FAIA, our late coauthor and mentor. Wally for many years was a hotel architect and corporate executive, responsible for many of the innovations in the last quarter of the twentieth century. We miss his spirit and good sense.

PART 1

Hotel Types

Overview

Arriving in Esfahan, Iran, centuries ago, you could stay outside the city gates at a roadside caravansary now called the Sha Abbas. Or desiring better service, you might continue to the Khan, an in-town hotel. As a "frequent traveler" journeying to Rome, you could stay at a downtown *mansione*, a boarding house on the Appian Way, or at a spa resort.

While the quality of hotels has advanced immeasurably over several centuries, especially their services, the basic functional elements remain almost as simple and familiar as in ancient times. But with increasing guest sophistication—and imaginative development and design—we anticipate growing demand globally for increasingly diverse and customized hotels, resorts, and related leisure-time amenities for the world's largest industry. The first part of this book discusses and illustrates scores of different types of hotels and considers how their design is being refined and their markets reassessed. They range from sensible extended-stay residential units to lavish super-luxury urban suite hotels. Hotel developers are reconsidering the design and character of all hotel types, from ecotourist retreats to the adaptive reuse and restoration of existing urban infrastructure. The latter provides a variety of finely detailed hotels and entertainment amenities that dramatically upgrade inner-city environments. And family-oriented theme parks continue to serve as multi-resorts for major corporate trade exhibitions and conventions as well as for advanced leisure-park communities.

The explosive growth of our global economies has generated extravagant architectural and engineering accomplishments around the world: in the Middle East, China, India, and Russia, as well as in Europe and the United States. Such major resort destinations as the Palm Islands in Dubai have sprouted dozens of hotels featuring all the leading brands with luxury accommodations and residences. Resort World Sentosa, off the coast of Singapore, City of Dreams in Macau, and CityCenter in Las Vegas represent massive investments in multi-hotel, residential, retail, entertainment, gaming, and conferencing developments. Extraordinary hotel architecture continues to amaze travelers with such exceptional structures as the Marina Bay Sands in Singapore and with such iconic mixed-use developments as the Elbphilharmonie in Hamburg, Germany, which includes a philharmonic hall wrapped with hotel rooms. Design hotels extend the boutique fascination by emphasizing great architecture combined with chic interiors and now include fashion designers entering the fray with their own brands, such as Armani Burj Khalifa and Missoni Edinburgh. Fashionable downtown hotels such as Hotel Gansevoort and The Standard in New York's Meatpacking district bring new vitality to dormant neighborhoods and serve as place-making destinations.

W Dallas Victory Hotel and Residences, Dallas, Texas
With 252 guestrooms and 94 luxury residences, this 33-story hotel and condominium tower is the centerpiece of the 72 acre (29 hectare) Victory master-planned development in Dallas. Designed by HKS Architects, the hotel includes a 10,000 sq ft (925 sq m) spa, pool, and fitness facility, 11,000 sq ft (1,020 sq m) of meeting space, and Ghostbar, a sleek and stylish rooftop venue.

Environmental responsibility has taken on new dimensions worldwide in all segments of the hotel and resort industry as new properties seek LEED certification or similar recognition by a number of other international green-design rating systems.

Other major prototype developments include hotels with themed shopping and entertainment atriums, all-villa enclaves, various types of vacation ownership resorts and spas, as well as vertically integrated mixed-use high-rise towers combining hotel functions with offices and trade centers incorporating flex-suites affording virtual officing. One type that has seen major growth in the past decade is multi-branded hotels, where one site or building houses two or more competing brand hotels. The next several chapters illustrate a wide range of the era's most significant hotel types, from future concepts for world-class multi-resort destinations to the most innovative and cost-effective limited-service prototypes. While the opening chapters discuss the latest examples in each category, and describe the different features of each type of hotel, the Design Guide, Part 2, provides information on how to program and design the hotel guestroom, public, and back-of-house areas.

With concepts ranging from airport conference center hotels to exotic eco-tourist lodges and from high-fashion design hotels to gigantic casino hotels, Part 1 reviews more than fifty different types of hotels now flourishing in today's increasingly customized marketplace. Separate chapters are devoted to each of 11 major categories. For example, suburban hotels offer many choices ranging from office-park hotels to country inns, while resorts encompass an ever-widening array from luxury wilderness lodges to remote island resorts. The repositioning of countless downtown and suburban properties is accomplished by innovative renovations, restoration, additions, or adaptive reuse. The conference center hotel, which significantly differs from the urban convention hotel, is discussed in terms of design options, planning, and development considerations, as well as social and cultural implications. Highly imaginative future hotel and resort development concepts are summarized in the final chapter. A continuing theme is the emphasis on carefully targeting specific market segments so that the hotel may better fulfill its function. For example, luxury resorts and super-luxury hotels need small, superb restaurants and health spas to maintain their clientele.

In industrialized nations, familiarity with new types of hotels is essential for developers to plan their expansion strategies and devise more imaginative prototypical features that attract new customers to hotels. Some types of hotels are as different as is a single-family home compared to a high-rise apartment tower in the residential field; it is essential for the designer to understand the variations in facilities, program areas, and circulation patterns required for each new form of hotel designed to serve a particular market niche. Also, an overall familiarity with diverse types encourages cross-fertilization of ideas, as, for example, introducing larger health spas to fill relaxation needs at conference centers, adding meeting rooms to turn country inns into instant conference retreats, and borrowing attributes of super-luxury hotels, such as original artwork, to better upgrade other types of hotels. New ideas for better hotels come from each member of the design team, ranging from market researchers to food and beverage (F&B) consultants, and include a variety of specialized disciplines from high-tech systems experts to talented landscape architects and

environmental designers. Chapter 19, Technical Coordination and Construction, discusses the development areas in which consultants are recommended—even required.

Classifications

Since hotels generally are classified by location, function, and other special characteristics, a given hotel may fit more than one category—for example, Ames Hotel in Boston is both a design (boutique) hotel and an example of adaptive reuse. A number of airport hotels could also be considered conference centers or convention properties. However, the overlap should not impair the usefulness of the classification system referenced in this book, which permits easy access to information by subject headings generally used in the hotel field and clear to the public.

While hotel classifications are necessary for purposes of organizing and referencing information, they are by no means perfect and no substitute for specific knowledge of the individual character and detailed ingredients of the hotel. As a writer in the *New Haven Register* lamented:

> Along with new hotel types and almost infinite combinations and varieties, it is increasingly difficult for guests to select a hotel when labels are inadequate or misleading. Downtown hotels have as many tennis courts, pools and saunas as resorts. Resorts have as many convention or conference guests as downtown convention hotels or airport meeting centers. Motor inns are not necessarily superior to motels. And "inns" are not necessarily old. "Lodge," "spa," "guest ranch" also are unclear labels. Price is no indicator—expensive hotels may have small rooms, while budget hotels have larger, better appointed rooms. Buying on the basis of ingredients looks like the new wave.

Our late coauthor, Walter A. Rutes, FAIA, at the turn of the century wrote:

> It is likely that today's oxymoron marketing mantra of "mass customization" is increasing in the hotel field, after bringing gold to industries ranging from clothing to personalized vitamins. It responds to the consumer's desire for individual treatment in an increasingly impersonal world. If the typical guest buys designer clothes and made-to-order music CDs from a long questionnaire, why not a virtual Ritz at Times Square?
>
> (Rutes, Penner, and Adams, 2001, p. 6)

Therefore, in this book guest perceptions are emphasized as much as the actual differences among types of hotels. In other words, what's "in" at the inn is even as important as what's in it.

Planning and Design Considerations

Since each type of hotel seeks different kinds of guests, its planning requirements will vary by its location, quality level, size, image, space standards, circulation, and other characteristics. For example, convention hotels and conference centers require closeness to airports, while vacation villages and ski lodges do not. Airport hotels and roadside motels need high visibility and good highway signage, while conference centers, country inns, vacation villages, and ecotourist retreats seek seclusion. And while super-luxury hotels must be small to create an intimate atmosphere, upscale hotels must be large enough to justify the greater number of restaurants, lounges, and banquet rooms required by first-class or five-star international standards.

Design considerations also vary by hotel type. For example, resorts require larger rooms and more closet and drawer space than downtown hotels due to the longer stays of their guests and the higher number of occupants per room. Some roadside inns may require larger restaurants than other hotels for peak periods such as breakfast, yet offer no room service. Casino hotels require a glittering design, while conference center décor needs to be more understated. Also, similar design concepts are expressed differently in each type of hotel. For example, the social pastime of people-watching in the downtown or suburban hotel is accommodated in its lobby or atrium space. The same purpose is served by the pool deck at the resort, the sun deck at the ski lodge, the commons area at the conference center, the outdoor bar at the vacation village's piazza, the tea lounge of the luxury hotel, or the high-fashion lobby of the boutique hotel.

While the specific facilities, area programs, and technical requirements are discussed in Part 2, Design Guide, this first section summarizes the main variations in planning and design for each distinct type of hotel.

Table 1.1 Hotel milestones

Biblical times	Boarding houses existed
500 BC	First resorts at mineral and hot springs in Greece
	Mansiones built along Roman roads to lodge government-sanctioned travelers; some inns existed for others
	Romans spread spa resorts to England, Switzerland, and the Middle East; introduced campona (inns) in England. Riviera popular with Phoenician and Greek traders
	Caravansaries, cloistered courtyard caravan stops, provided by government along roads in the Middle East
	Khans, small inns, established in Middle East towns
Middle Ages	Manorial lords, abbeys, and monasteries sheltered some travelers
	Monastic inns run by religious orders. Hospices built as hospitals and shelters for travelers
	Some inns developed in larger towns (no meals)
	Rooming houses used as relay stations for mail, government transport, rest stops, changing horses
	Hospitalers created shelters for Crusaders and pilgrims traveling to the Holy Land
1100s	Travel became safe in Europe. Inns prospered with freedom and right to travel, declined in times of lawlessness
	The European inn gradually developed
	The Three Kings Inn opened in Basel, Switzerland—earliest inn still operating
1200s	Guest houses, courier mail stations opened in China and Mongolia
	Rooming and relay stations for mail, government transportation, rest stops
	Cour St. Georges Inn opened in Ghent, Belgium
	Angel Inn opened in Grantham, Lincolnshire, England
1300s	The English country inn developed; some inns in London
	Castle Inn founded in Taunton, Somerset, England
	French law required innkeepers to replace stolen property plus pay victims three times as much in damages
1400s	French law required hotel register
	English law established regulations for inns
	The Krone Inn in Solothurn, Switzerland, is earliest adaptive reuse—converted from residence
1500s	European spas revived in Carlsbad, Marienbad
	Stagecoaches developed, using Roman road system; teams changed, carriages checked, and travelers rested at posting houses
	English innkeepers set pattern for Europe and America to follow; 6,000 inns in England
	Inn plan took form of enclosed courtyard with arched entrance, rooms along two sides, kitchen and public rooms at front side, stable and storage at rear
	First travelers' guide rating inns in France
1600s	Hotel industry developed in Europe with well-placed and reliable cuisine "at sign of insignia on a metal plaque, grating its rugged hinges in every wind"
	Seaport inns developed in American cities: for example, the Blue Anchor in Philadelphia
	Village inns developed as required by Massachusetts law in all towns: for example, the Old Yarmouth Inn at Yarmouthport
	First scheduled coach service established in England

Table 1.1 continued

1700s	Clubhouses similar to British clubs and Masonic lodges developed in America
	Spa resorts developed in Yellow Springs, Pennsylvania, and White Sulphur Springs, West Virginia
	Boodles and Coventry clubhouses opened in London
	Market Square Taverne founded in Williamsburg, Virginia
	Place Vendôme in Paris is first mixed-use complex
1780s	Dessien's in Calais, France, was early large inn
	Covent Garden Inn in London was early large inn
1790s	Industrial revolution stimulated hotels in England, Europe, and America; resorts developed
	Corre's Hotel and City Hotel in New York were first downtown hotels
	Saratoga Springs, New York, developed as spa resort
1800s	White Hart Hotel opened in Salisbury, England
	Royal Hotel founded in Plymouth, England
	Luxury "swagger hotels" established in major cities
	Early resorts built along French and Italian Riviera
	Imposing clubhouses built
	Fulton's steamship Clermont launched on Hudson River
	Exchange Coffee House in Boston was first atrium hotel
1810s	Ryokan guest houses developed in Japan
	Dak bungalows, 24-hour guest stops, run by government of India
1820s	Catskill Mountain House in New York State was early major resort
	City Hotel in Baltimore, Maryland, was first with partial gaslight
	B&O Railroad began passenger service
	Tremont House in Boston was first luxury downtown hotel with indoor toilets, locks on guestroom doors, and à la carte menu
1830s	Saratoga Springs Hotel opened in New York State
	American Hotel in New York City was first with gaslight throughout
	Astor House opened in New York City
	St. Charles and St. Louis Hotels established in New Orleans, Louisiana
	Holt's Hotel, opened in New York City, was first with an elevator for baggage
	Reform Club in London had courtyard roofed in to become an early atrium
	Euston Station Hotel, opened in London, was early example of railroad hotel
1840s	Railroads replaced coaches; coach-route inns declined
	Shepheard's Hotel, opened in Cairo, was early major adaptive reuse
	Hotel des Trois Couronnes founded in Vevey, Switzerland
	Bar au Lac Hotel opened in Zurich, Switzerland
	New York Hotel in New York City was first with private baths
	Planter's House Hotel founded in St. Louis, Missouri
	The Homestead established in Hot Springs, Virginia
	Resorts developed in Coney Island, New York
1850s	Spa resorts reached height of popularity
	Resorts developed in Niagara Falls, New York, and New Jersey shore
	Mills House opened in Charleston, South Carolina (rebuilt in 1970)
	Parker House established in Boston (rebuilt in 1927)
	Fifth Avenue Hotel in New York City was first with passenger elevators
1860s	Railroad terminal hotels such as Charing Cross in London were main type of hotels developed 1860s through 1920s
	Mohonk Mountain House established in the Catskills in New York State
	Central and Union Pacific Railroads were joined
1870s	Coney Island in New York was themed seaside resort with Queen Anne and Oriental-style hotels and amusement park with roller-coaster
	Fashionable Vendome Hotel built in Boston
	Palmer House opened in Chicago was largest of time and first built with a fireproof structure (rebuilt in 1925)
	Palace Hotel opened in San Francisco was earliest hotel with a large atrium
	Sherman House founded in Chicago
	Grand Hotel built in Point Clear, Alabama
	Continental opened in Paris (restored in 1970 by InterContinental)

1880s	Hotel Del Monte established in Monterey, California
	Hotel Everett in New York City was first with partial electric lights
	Sagamore Hotel at Lake George in New York State was first with electricity in all rooms
	Chelsea Hotel in New York City was first large residential hotel
	Mountainview House established in Whitefield, New Hampshire
	Ponce De Leon Hotel in St. Augustine, Florida, was first built of concrete
	Grand Hotel in Mackinac Island, Michigan, had largest veranda
	Victoria Hotel in Kansas City, Missouri, was first with baths in all rooms
	Hotel Del Coronado, opened in San Diego, California, was largest resort of its time
	Whiteface Inn and Golf Club founded in Lake Placid, New York
	The Savoy in London was first hotel with theater, chapel, print shop, laundry

1890s	The Broadmoor opened in Colorado Springs, Colorado
	Brown Palace in Denver, Colorado, was earliest hotel atrium still operating
	Copley Square Hotel opened in Boston
	Ecole Hotelière in Lausanne, Switzerland, was first hotel school
	Hotel Netherland in New York City was first with phones in all rooms
	The Breakers opened in Palm Beach, Florida (rebuilt in 1906, again in 1926)
	Lake Placid Club established in Lake Placid, New York
	Original Waldorf=Astoria built in New York City, tallest of its time, at 17 stories (later site of 102-story Empire State Building)
	Wentworth-by-the-Sea opened in New Castle, New Hampshire
	Claridge's, Berkeley, Connaught all opened in London

1900s	The Ritz founded in London
	The Willard opened in Washington, DC
	The Plaza, St. Regis, and Astor built in New York City
	Taj Mahal Hotel opened in Bombay (restored in 1972 by InterContinental)
	Statler in Buffalo, New York, established main principles of modern multi-story hotel and circulation flow
	First cross-country U.S. auto trip

1910s	Grand Central Terminal in New York City was early mixed-use complex
	Boarding-house resorts developed in Catskills in New York State
	Bellevue Stratford opened in Philadelphia
	Copley Plaza built in Boston
	Beverly Hills Hotel established in California
	The Greenbrier opened in White Sulphur Springs, West Virginia
	Asilomar near Carmel, California, was first non-profit conference center
	Kahler Hotel in Rochester, Minnesota, was first medical hotel
	First trans-Atlantic flight and first scheduled airline
	Hotel Pennsylvania in New York City, at 2,200 rooms, was largest of its time

1920s	Hotel boom #1 generated by economic prosperity
	Grand Central District in New York City was example of further developed hotel complex connecting five hotels
	Miami Beach developed with Mediterranean-style architecture; for example, Flamingo, Pancoast, and Roney Plaza hotels
	School of Hotel Administration established at Cornell University
	First non-stop cross-U.S. plane flight
	Baker and Adolphus hotels opened in Dallas, Texas
	Royal Hawaiian established in Honolulu
	Prohibition caused decline of hotel/restaurant business
	The Ritz-Carlton opened on the Boston Public Gardens
	The Statler in Boston was first mixed-use hotel/office building
	Ahwahnee Hotel built in Yosemite National Park in California
	Biltmore founded in Santa Barbara, California
	Stevens Hotel in Chicago had 2,700 rooms—largest of time
	The Cloister opened in Sea Island, Georgia
	Arizona Biltmore built in Phoenix

| 1930s | Depression forced many U.S. hotels into receivership |
| | The new Waldorf=Astoria in New York City, largest of its time, built during Depression |

1940s	Statler in Washington, DC, was one of few hotels built during World War II
	Flamingo in Las Vegas was first casino hotel
	Statler Hotels in Los Angeles, California, Hartford, Connecticut, and Dallas, Texas, first post-war hotels
	San Souci in Miami was first new post-war resort

Table 1.1 continued

1950s   Hotel boom #2 generated by expanded education and mass travel
Resorts developed in Caribbean
Vacation village concept developed by Club Med
Holiday Inns was first motel chain with large rooms
Casino hotels developed in Las Vegas, Nevada
Fontainbleau opened in Miami Beach
First commercial trans-Atlantic jet service
Airlines began developing hotels

1960s   23,000 hotels, 40,000 motels, and 170 chains operated in the U.S.
Resorts developed in Spanish Mediterranean, Portugal, Balearic Islands, Scandinavia, Greece, and Yugoslavia
Hyatt Regency in Atlanta, Georgia, reintroduced atrium concept
Arden House of Columbia University, Tarrytown House in Tarrytown, New York, and General Electric Co. in Crotonville, New York, were first conference centers used extensively by businesses
Sheraton at Prudential Center in Boston was first major hotel/mixed-use complex
Hilton Palacio del Rio Hotel in San Antonio, Texas, was first built with prefabricated concrete modules

1970s   Boeing 747 introduced; airlines became active in hotel development through subsidiary chains
New hotel expansion took up slack caused by demolition and conversions of hotels to apartments and office buildings
Walt Disney World Resort near Orlando, Florida, opened as first major hotel/amusement destination center
Extensive hotel development in the Middle East generated by oil prosperity
Luxury condominiums developed offering hotel services
Hotel restorations extensively developed
First suite hotels converted from condos
Time-sharing and condominium resorts developed
MGM Grand casino hotel fire in Las Vegas caused changes in building and fire codes
Outbreak of Legionnaires' Disease at Bellvue-Stratford Hotel in Philadelphia caused bankruptcy of hotel and changed engineering and maintenance operations
No-smoking rules took effect in federal buildings
Peachtree Plaza in Atlanta, Georgia, had 70 stories—tallest hotel
Multi-resort complexes developed in Maui, Hawaii, and Cancun, Mexico
China opened to foreign tourists; international hotel experts invited to participate in development of facilities
Middle East investments in U.S. real estate increased values of hotels and resorts

1980s   Hotel boom #3 generated by innovative marketing and development of specialized types of hotels, many combined with large-scale commercial complexes such as Copley Place and Lafayette Place in Boston
Airport hotels, conference centers, all-suite hotels, vacation villages, health spas, marina hotels, ski lodges, time-sharing and condo resorts developed rapidly
Casino hotels developed in Atlantic City, New Jersey
Condominium hotels developed, such as The Ritz-Carlton and Four Seasons in Boston and UN Plaza in New York City
Limited-service budget motels continued rapid growth
Popular revival of country inns
Marriott Marquis in Atlanta was largest convention hotel
Marriott Marquis in Times Square in New York City was highest-cost hotel project
Hyatt and Marriott open mega-hotels in Orlando, Florida
Hotel boom in China; 50 major hotels under construction or design including 2,000-room Lidu in Beijing; visitors increased from 200,000 at beginning of decade to 5,000,000 per year expected by end of century
Embassy Suites and Crowne Plaza by Holiday Inn, Courtyard by Marriott, and Residence Inn debut
Japanese investments in U.S. real estate increased values of hotels and resorts
Dow-Jones average of New York Stock Exchange plunged 508 points, or four times previous record one-day drop
Americans with Disabilities Act became law, affecting broad areas of hotel design and operations
Electronic key-card for hotel rooms was introduced by Ving
Resolution Trust Corporation sold off hotels as required due to failing savings and loans
First baby-boomers turned 50, Generation X gained economic power
Disney licensed operation of Tokyo Disneyland, east of the city in Urayasu, Chiba, Japan, the first Disney park outside the U.S.

1990s	Gulf War slowed tourism
	Recession of 1991 resulted in lowest financial record in hotel history, with majority of hotels not meeting debt service
	Growth through conversions became more prevalent
	Over 75 percent of top 25 U.S. chains engaged in global hotel development
	Casinos and hotels on Native American reservations gained acceptance
	Riverboat gaming on Mississippi River and Gulf Coast
	Budget hotels were industry's leading money-makers
	Disney opened Disneyland Paris in Marne-la-Vallée, France, the second park outside the United States, with seven hotels and 5,800 rooms
	Palace of the Lost City in Sun City, South Africa, based on a fantasy lost African tribe, was most costly casino resort
	Wall Street–REIT investments in as many as 15 percent of all U.S. hotels turned back financial recession, with hotel values at levels higher than paid by previous waves of international investors in the 1970s and 1980s
	Vacation ownership booming, with five million members investing record annual $6 billion at 7 percent yearly growth rate forecast
	Regent Four Seasons built in New York was highest-cost hotel project
	Mega-casino themed resorts rapidly expanding in Las Vegas, including New York, New York, Bellagio, Mandalay Bay, The Venetian, and Paris, increasingly attracting family market
	Better shower offered at Holiday Inn in place of standard tub/shower combination
	Cruise ships booming owing to unmatched appeal to affluent elderly population
	Self-service business centers widely available to hotel guests
	Hotel schools at Cornell University in Ithaca, New York, New York University, and the University of California at Los Angeles expand their role in international conferences and research activities in hotel, resort, travel, and leisure-time field, now the world's largest industry
	Universal Studios opens major resort theme park including first mega-hotel in Orlando
	Disney announced expansion of its luxury resort, retail, dining, and entertainment center at Disneyland in Anaheim, California
	Atlantis mega-hotel opened on Paradise Island, Bahamas
	Internet, incorporating console control of lighting, temperature, security monitoring, non-disturb, maid, large-screen interactive info-entertainment centers with multiple language and time zone displays, city guide, speaker/video phones, data port, and speed dialing to home and office installed in hotels by INNCOM, SeaChange, GTE, TCI, LodgeNet, On Command, ViaTV, Travelers Telecom, Zenith, Panasonic, Thomson, Phillips, etc.
	Hotel boom #4 generated by advanced technology, imaginative design, and the successful marketing of mass customization of hotels, resorts, and leisure-time amenities
	Spas booming as baby-boomers perceived them as essential to health
	Boutique hotels popular with business travelers; such developers as Ian Schrager, Bill Kimpton, and W brand by Starwood all converted older hotels or developed new properties
	First billion-dollar Native American mixed-use casino complex completed in Connecticut, catapulting the region into a major gaming center
	Entertainment hotels introduced in downtown areas, including New York City
	Hilton Hotels acquired Promus, owner of Embassy Suites/Doubletree, making it the third largest global hotel company
	Over 250 luxury and upscale hotels were announced for development worldwide
	Ultra-high-rise mixed-use hotels developed in Shanghai, Bangkok, and other major Asian cities
2000s	*Hotel Design, Planning and Development*, first comprehensive book on hotel, resort and leisure-time field by Rutes, Penner, and Adams, published by Architectural Press and W. W. Norton
	Pod hotels developed in urban business centers and airports throughout world
	Many chains developed boutique (or "lifestyle") hotel brands to compete with independent design-centric hotels
	Urban hotels introduced massive spas, for both guests and city residents
	Hotel chains introduced the lobby "great room" concept, encouraging socialization among guests
	Guestroom layouts increasingly used stall showers in lieu of the tub/shower combination
	Hotel operators frequently outsourced restaurant operations to independent operators or brands
	Suites became more common, especially in resort destinations
	All developers took greater interest in sustainable design, for operational efficiency, lower costs, and marketing reasons
	Hotels co-brand with fashion houses
	Increasing activity among niche brands of all types
2010s	Hotels introduced smartphone applications for check-in/out and use as room key
	Greater customization of guestrooms common
	Developers sought out carbon-neutral designs for hotels
	Enhanced in-room entertainment systems became popular
	Hotel companies achieved more efficient operations and economies by co-locating two or more of their brands on one property
	Modular construction using factory-built components became commonplace

Urban Hotels

The City Hotel, built on lower Broadway in New York City in 1794, trumpeted a new form of hospitality building distinct from European inns and American seaport and village inns or taverns of that period. Larger than any inn, the five-story City Hotel had 73 guestrooms but, most significantly, housed a ballroom and banquet hall—public spaces that forecast the new role that hotels would play as the center of downtown social and business life for centuries to come. Expanding on that new role in 1809, the Exchange Coffee House in Boston featured an assortment of public social and business functions including a ballroom, a restaurant, a coffee room, and a Merchants' Exchange floor beneath a 100 ft diameter (9.2 m) sky-lit dome, making this the first atrium hotel and further defining this new urban business and leisure hotel genre.

In this chapter we will examine a variety of urban hotels and the factors that influence their development and design. Dense downtown urban settings present numerous challenges and opportunities that must be accommodated and exploited for the hotel to be successful. In focusing on the characteristics inherent on downtown locations we will look at noteworthy examples of business and leisure, waterfront, entertainment, and super-luxury hotels.

Urban Business and Leisure Hotels

It was the Tremont House in Boston that established hotels as enduring monuments in the cityscape. Clad in Quincy granite, the Tremont was the most costly building in the United States in 1828. It earned the title "The Adam and Eve of the Modern Hotel Industry" by setting the standard for deluxe innovations including private locked rooms, indoor (although not private) bathrooms, *à la carte* menus, the first bellboys, and an annunciator system that allowed guests to call the front desk from their rooms. Architect Isaiah Rogers devised an ingenious floor plan of crossing corridors that splayed the public rooms across the front of the building with courtyards in the back and an intersecting guestroom wing that separated the public and private realms. Envious of the Tremont's stature, John Jacob Astor hired Rogers seven years later to design the Astor House in New York City as the new best hotel in the country. Other U.S. cities joined the competition as each major city sought to own the most prestigious hotel in the land. In New Orleans, the French citizens boasted the St. Louis Hotel while the English had the St. Charles.

Innovative design continued to flourish as each new hotel vied to outdo previous ones with such amenities as hot and cold running

Andaz and Langham Xintiandi, Shanghai, China
Located next to the Xintiandi district, which is a redeveloped nightlife neighborhood populated by restaurants, outdoor cafés and nightclubs, the two luxury-class hotel towers are joined by a dramatic curving pedestrian bridge. The façade of the 309-room Andaz is animated by multi-colored LED lighting activated into a random pattern once guests close their blackout shades. The façade of the 357-room Langham is inspired by traditional Chinese latticework (see pp. 47–49).

water in the rooms, bathrooms on each floor, gas lighting, steam heat, and room service. But no invention had a greater effect on future hotels and indeed the very skyline of the city than the passenger elevator, first used in 1859 in the Fifth Avenue Hotel in New York City. Locals referred to the elevator as a "vertical screw railway" while the English called it the "ascending room."

By the turn of the century most major cities had at least one prestigious hotel. The Waldorf and Astor hotels were developed on New York's Fifth Avenue. The Palmer House and the Sherman House, the largest hotels of their time, became the pride of Chicago's State Street, while the Palace on San Francisco's Market Street and the Brown Palace in downtown Denver displayed impressive atriums. Feeding off the frenetic growth in U.S. cities, The Savoy in London advanced the mixed-use nature of hotels by including a theater and a chapel. The Savoy had its own in-house laundry and, with 67 bathrooms to its 400 guestrooms, the builder was prompted to ask the developer if he was catering to amphibian guests.

Perhaps no hotel exhibited the extraordinary role that they would play as epicenters of the urban social, political, and business activity as the original Waldorf=Astoria. Designed by Henry J. Hardenbergh as two separate hotels for the feuding Astor cousins, the eventual reconciliation led to one of the prize public concourses of the day as Peacock Alley married the two hotels and was permanently symbolized in the hotel's official spelling with the equal mark between Waldorf and Astor. As the "Unofficial Palace of New York," The Waldorf=Astoria's huge ballroom and 40 public rooms were used for the most important social and political events of the day. Peacock Alley was a fashionable runway where elegant gowns and the latest attire were on display for those who came to see and be seen. The Bull and Bear men's café was where J. P. Morgan and Henry Clay Frick met to cut deals after the close of the New York Stock Exchange.

The early twentieth century saw the advent of the modern commercial hotel: Ellsworth M. Statler established the main principles of modern high-rise hotels when the Buffalo Statler was built in 1908 in western New York State, bringing the service departments up to the ground floor, surrounding them with restaurants, bars, and banquet facilities, and connecting them to the guestroom floors by means of service elevators. Though The Ritz in Paris was the first grand hotel to provide each guestroom with its own private bath, The Statler introduced the model for today's bedroom and bathroom set and exemplified efficient planning with its double-loaded guestroom floors. (See Chapter 15 for a discussion of planning the guestroom floor.)

Statler's innovative prototype proved monumental as it defined a model of business-tourist hotels in cities for decades to come. Still evolving through the downtown hotel boom of the post-war 1920s and 1930s, its influence continues today, finding new forms in the rapid expansion of new types such as design hotels, downtown entertainment hotels, and mixed-use complexes. And technological advances have allowed hotels to soar to incredible new heights, once again dominating the skylines of major cities around the globe.

Planning and Development Considerations

Rail travel in the early twentieth century fostered development of hotels near city railroad terminals. Many hotels took advantage after the New York Central Railroad made acres of prime sites available along Park Avenue in the Terminal City development around Grand Central Terminal. Even after the decline of rail travel many of these locations remain viable hotel development sites since they have evolved into centers of concentrated business and retail activity and the terminals themselves have become commuter rail stations. In fact, restaurants and bars of hotels built near commuter train stations are usually at their peak performance just after quitting time.

The location of a hotel in the city in many ways defines its market and its character. In addition to rail terminals, urban hotels have gravitated to locations in close proximity to active business centers and fashionable shopping districts such as New York's Fifth Avenue, Chicago's Magnificent Mile, or Tokyo's Ginza Strip. The Grand Hyatt Tokyo at Roppongi Hills is located in the heart of Japan's largest private-sector urban redevelopment project near the famous Ginza shopping district comprising the world's highest-priced real estate.

High-end residential neighborhoods with fashionable shops, museums, and art galleries often provide a magnet for luxury hotels whose character borrows from the residential surroundings. Some

The Grand Hyatt Tokyo at Roppongi Hills, Tokyo, Japan
Fusing art and intelligence, the Roppongi Hills development is known as the "Artelligent City." It includes the 54-story mixed-use Mori Tower, also designed by the hotel's architect, KPF. With 380 guestrooms, 10 restaurants and bars and 13 banquet rooms, the hotel serves a pivotal role in the livelihood of the development.

Jumeirah Frankfurt Hotel, Frankfurt, Germany
As a central component to the PalaisQuartier, a major leisure and retail project
in downtown Frankfurt in close proximity to the Stock Exchange and the popular
MyZeil shopping mall, the Jumeirah Frankfurt provides accommodations
for both business and leisure travelers, with 218 guestrooms and suites,
six multi-purpose meeting rooms, a 4,306 sq ft (400 sq m) ballroom and a
world-class Talise spa.

hotels are identified with major city plazas and parks such as the Plaza Hotel on New York's Central Park, the St. Francis on San Francisco's Union Square, and the former Ritz-Carlton (now Taj Hotel) on Boston's Public Gardens (see Urban Super-luxury Hotels, pages 44–51).

Urban renewal redevelopment efforts often seek hotels as a catalyst to attract other real estate development or to provide a necessary ingredient for the success of a project. The Jumeirah Frankfurt Hotel is a central component to the PalaisQuartier, an important leisure and retail project in downtown Frankfurt, Germany, in close proximity to the Stock Exchange and the famous MyZeil shopping mall.

A new wave of urban entertainment venues led by the resurgence of center-city neighborhoods such as the burgeoning Downtown Miami Metropolitan district, New York's Meatpacking District, Melbourne's Crown Entertainment complex, London's Leicester Square, and Singapore's Bayfront Avenue Marina have provided fertile ground for a new type of hotel, exemplified by the dazzling Marina Bay Sands hotel development in Singapore (see pages 208–211)

W London, London, United Kingdom
Evoking the cinematic legacy of Leicester Square, the hotel is wrapped with frameless glazing suspended from the face of the building like a floating sheer veil, etched with an undulating pattern like the folds of a theater curtain. Hundreds of energy-efficient light fixtures set into the outer main wall provide an infinite number of combinations and effects, controlled by sophisticated electronics from within the hotel, allowing the presence of the building to alter as day turns to night.

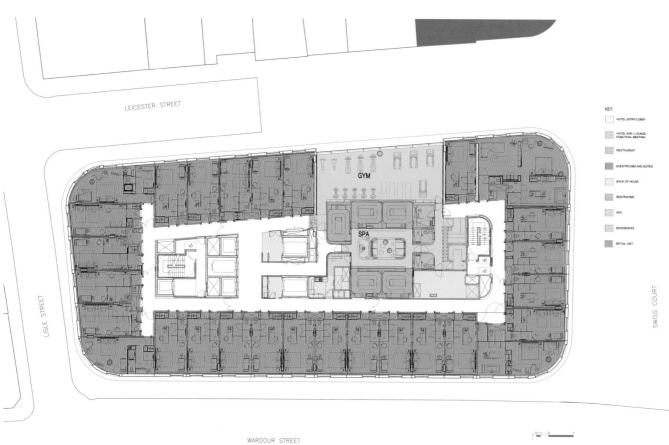

KEY:

HOTEL ENTRY/LOBBY

HOTEL BAR / LOUNGE / FUNCTION / MEETING

RESTAURANT

GUESTROOMS AND SUITES

BACK OF HOUSE

RESTROOMS

SPA

RESIDENCES

RETAIL UNIT

across the harbor from the city's central business district. As cities are realizing the value of their waterfronts after long periods of neglect, mixed-use developments that include hotels are prospering in the context of cruise ship and ferry terminals, waterfront recreation facilities, and the air, light, and spectacular views afforded by the open expanse at the water's edge (see Urban Waterfront Hotels, pages 36–43).

Boutique hotels originated in marginal neighborhoods where inexpensive and obsolete buildings were transformed into high-fashion lodgings. With their explosive popularity and heavy investment from major chains, boutique hotels (variously referred to now as design, fashion, or lifestyle hotels) have expanded to more central upscale locations in the city (see Design Hotels, Chapter 3). Other markets that drive location in the urban center are for hotels located near major medical centers, government centers, convention centers, financial markets, courts, universities, and city halls.

Place-making: Hotels that Transform and Define Neighborhoods

Pioneering developers boldly pursuing their visions by investing in risky real estate transactions can transform quiet underserved neighborhoods into dynamic center-city destinations. As we have seen in New York City with the Mercer Hotel in SoHo or the Tribeca Grand, hotels as leading-edge urban interventions become a catalyst for place-making and defining the character of neighborhoods.

The trailblazing development of the Gansevoort Hotel in the drowsy Meatpacking District in Lower Manhattan was without question a key ingredient in transforming an obscure light-industrial neighborhood of a few bistros and boutiques scattered among beef-filled warehouses into a thriving and fashionable residential, commercial, and entertainment destination.

The Gansevoort, The Standard, and The James Hotel demonstrate that the most undeveloped real estate in urban areas is often their rooftops. In multi-story hotels structural loads require a tight

Gansevoort Hotel, New York, New York (top)
Beyond catering to its sleep-over guests, the hotel-as-nightclub model of the pioneering original Standard on Sunset Boulevard endures with the Gansevoort Meatpacking NYC Hotel. With 187 guestrooms and 23 suites, the 14-story hotel features lively rooftop amenities that attract guests and non-guests to its heated 45 ft pool with underwater music, "Plunge" Bar and Lounge, landscaped garden, and 360 degree panoramic views of New York City and sunsets over the Hudson River.

Gansevoort Hotel, New York, New York (bottom)
Once a thriving hotel district in the early twentieth century, Park Avenue South has long been underserved by luxury hotels. As those early hotels were epicenters of social life in the city, the Gansevoort Park presents a new standard of hotel luxury and destination-gathering for the area. Trumping the extravagance of the Gansevoort downtown rooftop, the Park Avenue hotel's 20,000 sq ft triple-level complex features an indoor/outdoor heated pool with underwater music and multiple connected nightlife venues.

grid of columns on most floors but rooftops can be relatively column-free, providing guests with open space, abundant light and panoramic views. Views from mid-rise buildings are different from rooftop observatories on high-rise structures like the Empire State Building or Sears Tower, which provide sweeping vistas of the entire region.

Building on the successful formula of their earlier hotel on the lower West Side, the Gansevoort Park Avenue expanded the concept of urban resort with extravagant rooftop venues by creating a new entertainment destination and breathing new life into the previously lackluster Park Avenue South neighborhood in New York City.

Style and Theater

As an outgrowth of the exploding popularity of boutique hotels and an intense interest in cutting-edge design by brand-name architects, hotel developers are finding high-style design to be a significant advantage in achieving notoriety and resultant market value. Technological advances in building systems and applications of amazing new computer design programs are resulting in fantastic forms and building envelopes in all types of buildings. The hospitality industry is realizing that investment in avant-garde architecture pays off in marketing appeal.

Dubai, Abu Dhabi, and Shanghai have become virtual laboratories for ultramodern hotel buildings where construction budgets are aimed at daring experimentations of architectural fancy. Hotels are part of bold and extravagant mixed-use buildings such as Burj Khalifa, Marina Bay Sands, Meydan Grandstand and Hotel, India Tower, Crystal Island Tower, and the Shard in London. Other examples of extraordinary super-modern design include the Renaissance Paris Arc de Triomphe Hotel, the Silken Puerta América Hotel, The Address Hotel, and Frank Gehry's remarkable Marqués de Riscal Hotel in the Spanish wine region.

Renaissance Paris Arc de Triomphe Hotel, Paris, France
Atelier Christian de Portzamparc designed a striking façade for the hotel with undulating horizontal glazed bands. The undulations become bay windows in the guestrooms, affording views up and down the avenue toward the Arc de Triomphe and Place des Ternes. The hotel has direct and exclusive access to Salle Wagram, the famous banquet and event venue built in 1865, which has been fully restored according to Portzamparc's design.

The Shard, London, United Kingdom (top)
At 1,016 ft high, Renzo Piano's Shard is one of the tallest buildings in Europe and one of the most ambitious architectural achievements in the United Kingdom. The deluxe 195-room Shangri-La Hotel, at the Shard, London, is accessed by a dedicated entrance at street level and occupies floors 34 to 52 of the iconic London Bridge Tower.

Innside Premium Hotel, Munich, Germany (left)
As one part of a four-piece architectural ensemble which includes two office towers and a low-rise office building designed by Helmut Jahn in Munich's burgeoning urban redevelopment project, Parkstadt Schwabing, the Innside Premium Hotel caters to the design-conscious business traveler with 160 guestrooms and suites, a restaurant, fitness club, and conference rooms.

Celebrity architects or "starchitects" are in high demand as developers and hotel companies seek the wow-factor and media attention they bring to their hospitality developments. Michael Graves, Tadeo Ando, Norman Foster, Renzo Piano, Frank Gehry, Kengo Kuma, Rem Koolhaas, Arata Isozaki, Enrique Norton, Jean Nouvel, I. M. Pei, and Helmut Jahn are among those whose celebrity and critical acclaim have transformed them into idols of the architectural world. They are eagerly sought after by hotel developers to bring status and value to their projects.

Place and Tradition

In the Imperial Hotel in Tokyo, Frank Lloyd Wright demonstrated early in the twentieth century that hotels must reflect place and tradition. Hotels that establish their primary aesthetic identity by creating a contextual fit to the architectural heritage of the city they inhabit reflect this same sensitivity and provide real value to preserving a sense of place in the city.

Only a few doors down from the original site of the famed Tremont Hotel, Kimpton's Nine Zero Hotel is surrounded by the rich history of Boston Common, Beacon Hill, Faneuil Hall, and Quincy Market. The architects faced the rigors of the Boston Redevelopment Authority and Boston Civic Design Commission in delivering an appropriate contemporary building design in the heart of one of the oldest cities in the United States.

Beyond hotels that contain facilities for performance and entertainment (see Urban Entertainment Hotels, pages 31–35) there is a fundamental quality of downtown hotels that provides a setting where the theater of human life is played. Morris Lapidus laid bare the theatrical aspect of hotels in the 1950s with his designs for the Fontainebleau and Eden Roc hotels in Miami Beach. Here guests were cast as performers while dining in an elevated stage-like restaurant or while climbing up and down grand stairs that might have been built for Loretta Young or Scarlett O'Hara. From the Astor in New York to the Hotel Ritz in Paris, hotels have long embodied an architecture of theatricality defining a place for the drama of human activity and experience.

The prestige of Atlanta, Georgia, soared after its first atrium hotel, Hyatt Regency Atlanta, triggered a wave of new development and catapulted the city into the future, further defining its role as capital of the New South. The symbolic image of Quebec City has long been shaped by the commanding presence of the Hotel Frontenac high above the bluffs on the St. Lawrence River. Hotels as highly visible monuments and prized trophies have elevated the self-esteem of cities since the architect Isaiah Rogers produced the Tremont House in Boston and the Astor House in New York City in the early 1800s and the stately Taj Mahal Palace hotel overlooking the Arabian Sea in Mumbai opened in 1903.

Making a dominant visual statement on the skyline has long been a goal of hotel owners, supported by architects and developers alike. The majestic domed roof of the St. Louis Hotel in early nineteenth-century New Orleans could be seen miles away on the Mississippi River, and the superb twin copper spires of The Waldorf=Astoria have adorned New York City's skyline for seventy years.

The current title-holder for tallest hotel in the world is the Rose Rayhaan Hotel in Dubai superseding the former champion, the nearby Burj al Arab Hotel. The 72-story Rose tower soars to a height of 1,100 ft (333 m), offering a sleek icon on the Dubai skyline.

Mixed-use towers allow hotels to bask in the glory of magnificent skyscrapers while occupying only a fraction of the floor area. The Park Hyatt Shanghai in the World Financial Center and the neighboring Grand Hyatt Shanghai in Jin Mao Tower both once claimed to be the "highest" hotel. Surpassing both, the Shanghai Tower J-Hotel is the centerpiece of the stunning 121-story Shanghai Tower being constructed in the hub of the central business district of Lujiazui, shoulder to shoulder with the other two towers. (See Mixed-use Developments, Chapter 6)

Nine Zero Hotel, Boston, Massachusetts
In combining traditional red brick and limestone with sleek nickel, chrome, stainless steel, and glass, the façade of this 190-key downtown hotel echoes the timeless use of materials of its surrounding classic architecture, punctuated with an elegant modern style.

Rose Rayhaan by Rotana Hotel, Dubai, United Arab Emirates
The slender steel and glass tower rises from a relatively small footprint of 10,000 sq ft (929 sq m), requiring the architects and engineers to incorporate the latest structural and architectural solutions in skyscraper design for this 482-key hotel, the tallest all-hotel building on the planet.

Shanghai World Financial Center, Jin Mao Tower, and Shanghai Tower, Shanghai, China
Within a tight three-block area of downtown Shanghai, the three dueling sky-scrapers each boast first-class hotels as their crowning elements. In Gensler Architects' Shanghai Tower, the lobby of the J-Hotel is located on the 101st floor of the building and the hotel itself includes 258 guest rooms within floors 84–110.

Public Spaces

Since a hotel's architecture is often obscured and overwhelmed by its dense urban surroundings, the entrance lobbies in downtown hotels must make bold statements and lasting impressions. More than any other element, the lobby quickly sets the hotel's tone and ambience.

The grand hotels of the 1920s and 1930s saw dramatic swings in size and extravagance of their public spaces. The original Waldorf=Astoria on Fifth Avenue was rendered obsolete by the Plaza Hotel when it opened offering New York society its immense ballroom and its sumptuous palm court, parlors, and lobbies. The New Netherland built in New York in 1926 during Prohibition avoided lavish public halls and placed its emphasis on luxurious appointments in the private realms of guestrooms and suites where many guests availed

themselves of room service with bootleg trimmings. Then the new Waldorf=Astoria emerged on Park Avenue in 1931 to reclaim the title as the "Unofficial Palace of New York," as vast lobbies and ballrooms returned *en vogue.*

In the late 1960s, Hyatt Regency Atlanta expanded on such historic models as San Francisco's Palace Hotel and Denver's Brown Palace and set a new pace with its towering atrium offering a bold new dramatic form for downtown hotel lobbies. With or without atriums the trend in the 1970s and early 1980s was for large impressive lobbies. That trend has taken on new dimensions with brands such as Gaylord Hotels, where huge atriums cover acres of landscaped gardens and terraces and enclose a wonderland of restaurants, lounges, shopping streets, and performance venues. In reaction to the expense and perceived lack of warmth, many developers returned in the twenty-first century to more intimate interior spaces

Gaylord Texan Resort and Convention Center, Dallas, Texas
With 4.5 acres (1.8 hectares) of indoor gardens and winding waterways, the 1,500-room hotel boasts over 400,000 sq ft (37,150 sq m) of flexible meeting space, including the 180,000 sq ft (16,700 sq m) Longhorn Exhibit Hall. The hotel's 165 ft (50.3 m) high glass-framed atrium houses a San Antonio-themed Riverwalk complete with replicas of the Alamo and other Spanish missions.

called floor area ratio or FAR. FAR is a multiplier used to calculate the amount of floor area that can be built on the site. For instance, a site of 10,000 sq ft with a mandated FAR on the site of 15 allows a maximum of 150,000 sq ft gross (10,000 x 15) of zoning floor area to be built above grade. (Cellars and sub-cellars usually are unlimited.) If that turns out not to be enough area to make the hotel project fly, then other options may be available, such as an FAR bonus or the purchase of air rights (also called unused development rights) from an adjacent property owner. The New York City zoning map describes a theater sub-district that, in order to encourage construction and renovation of theaters, provides a floor area bonus to developers who build or renovate legitimate theaters in that district, in addition to building their own project.

City zoning regulations may also control the shape of the building in order to define view corridors, street walls, and building height. But most often bulk regulations are aimed at preventing dark stagnant streetscapes and are designed to permit light and air to penetrate down to street level and make it a healthier environment. These

and focused interior budgets on high-quality materials, lighting and artwork to achieve the sense of grandeur.

Planning Controls

A deciding factor in hotel location is very often the influence of city zoning regulations that regulate use, density and bulk on any given development site. City guidelines may also offer zoning bonus or tax incentive programs that are aimed at fostering the beneficial qualities a hotel brings to a neighborhood. Zoning constraints can rule out a site for hotel development by not permitting transient use, not allowing sufficient floor area to be built for the project to become feasible, requiring immense amounts of parking, or through some other regulation that checkmates the developer's goals. For example, one prime downtown site could not be developed as a hotel because, though city zoning regulations required two loading berths based on the proposed size of the hotel, another regulation prohibited curb cuts along the avenue frontage, thereby precluding the required loading dock and thus preventing hotel development. In order to solve the dilemma the developer had to acquire an adjacent parcel that fronted on another street that did allow curb cuts so that the hotel could build the required truck docks.

Land values in urban areas are normally so high that development calls for building the maximum allowable floor area that a site can bear. City planners regulate density in different areas of the city based on the desire to keep the character of a neighborhood low-scale and residential or to encourage large-scale development and high-rise construction. Density, therefore, is regulated by a formula relating the area of the building lot with a density factor sometimes

Kimpton Palomar, Chicago, Illinois
Shaping their design within the stringent regulations of the River North zoning district in the heart of downtown Chicago, GREC Architects sculpted the Palomar's glass and concrete envelope with an array of purposefully placed building set-backs in response to zoning requirements for sufficient light and air. Notwithstanding the restrictive zoning constraints, the limited views caused by the adjacent American Medical Association tower, and the miniature size of the property, the architects managed to incorporate a great deal of building onto the site.

Many cities now have commissions and agencies whose duty it is to oversee construction on or near its historic buildings and landmarks. In many cases whole neighborhoods are designated landmark districts so any new building must be scrutinized for its contextual appropriateness. Architects and developers often must conduct exhaustive research and prepare convincing documentation to present to the landmarks authority for approval before construction can begin. The degree to which faithful reproduction of details and design is required usually depends on the value and status of the landmark itself.

Site Factors

In any hotel development a survey of elements surrounding the site is as important as surveying the site itself. The density of urban settings presents a multitude of special problems. Placing your entrance next to an adjacent property's loading dock may be worse than putting it next to your own. Also, care should be taken when locating close to a movie theater, where long ticket queues and exiting crowds may disrupt your entrance. Some cities have regulations that prohibit alcoholic beverages being served within a certain distance of a church or school, making a liquor license impossible to obtain. Due diligence to avoid these types of surprises is essential.

Views add real value to a hotel property. Hotels routinely demand higher rates for rooms with great views of the skyline, the waterfront, or a park than for those facing an adjacent office building. Therefore, it is important to know about and even to predict where views will exist. It may govern decisions on how high to build to assure that upper-floor specialty suites gain a spectacular view over surrounding buildings. A developer may be faced with the economic decision to build a 40-story hotel with 15 guestrooms per floor as opposed to a more efficient and less costly 20-story hotel with 30 keys per floor. The added expense of building the taller structure must be weighed against the potential of higher room rates for the added value of spectacular views and the intangible value of a more significant presence on the city's skyline.

In designing a hotel in New York City, the developer and architects for the RIHGA Royal (now The London Hotel) were aware of plans for a large bulky office tower directly across the street that would limit views towards the south. In response they devised a system of bay windows so that every room had views looking east and west. Similarly, sunlight and shadows are another consideration when designing a hotel in the urban landscape. Whenever possible, roof terraces and main entrances should be arranged to receive maximum sunlight.

Space Maximization

The density of urban sites requires much tighter control over matters of efficiency and layout. The designer must make every square foot count to a degree not usually required in other hotel types such as resorts and suburban hotels where space is not such a premium.

The Nines Hotel, Portland, Oregon
In converting the 1905 vintage Meier & Frank building in downtown Portland to The Nines Hotel, SERA Architects worked closely with the Portland Development Commission in carefully maintaining the building's historic character, allowing it to maintain its status on the National Register of Historic Places (NRHP). The project won a National Preservation Award from the NRHP.

regulations are sometimes referred to as height and set-back rules and are best illustrated by New York City's 1916 Zoning Resolution that prescribed specific set-backs from the street based on sun angle studies. The result of that law defined the character of skyscraper design for decades to come, as illustrated by the remarkable renderings of Hugh Ferriss. The Shelton Hotel, the world's tallest hotel when built in 1923 with 34 floors and 1,200 rooms, was a beautifully proportioned response to 1916 zoning and set the tone for many of New York's great buildings of the 1920s and 1930s.

Use regulations can also have important ramifications in the design and development of hotels. Retail continuity was a requirement for the New York Four Seasons, built on a fashionable shopping street. According to the zoning regulation only 20 percent of the street frontage could be anything other than retail use. Therefore, the hotel entrance became very narrow, contradicting the developer's wishes for the hotel to have great presence on 57th Street. The architects, thus, were compelled to raise the lobby to the second level above the stores that flanked the entrance.

The James Hotel, SoHo, New York, New York
The locally popular rooftop venue, which accommodates up to 140 guests, is accessed from a separate entrance on a side street in order to avoid interference with hotel operations. Careful engineering and placement of rooftop mechanical systems was required in order to accommodate this exceptional rooftop setting. A colossal flying beam encircles the pool deck, framing the outdoor terrace and crowning the building with an architectural halo.

Where FAR limits the amount of area that can be built on a particular site and since cellars and sub-cellars are usually excluded from FAR calculations, components of the hotel that do not require natural light and air should be located below grade. This usually includes such back-of-house functions as laundry, kitchen, storage, engineering, housekeeping, and employee areas, in addition to mechanical spaces. Even executive offices, meeting rooms, and health clubs may be located below grade to allow valuable floor area to be utilized for additional guestrooms. The high cost of excavation is offset by the value added to the property by utilizing the allowable space for revenue-producing functions. The Jumeirah Frankfurt utilized four subterranean levels for back-of-house and parking. The Chambers Hotel in New York City needed to resort to leasing three levels beneath the sidewalk from the city in order to fit their basic program into the hotel. There are locations where cellars are not possible, such as New Orleans, where much of the city is below sea level and the water table is near the surface. Also, many of the hotels around New York's Grand Central Terminal, such as the Biltmore and The Waldorf=Astoria, were not able to utilize basement levels because the hotels were built above subterranean railroad tracks.

A convention hotel presents a particular design challenge for a tight urban site in that the tower columns and elevator core must be kept away from the clear-span ballroom. This generally means that the site must be large enough to contain both elements independently, because otherwise enormous structural gymnastics must be called upon to pick up and transfer the massive loads from the guestroom tower to avoid columns in the ballroom. In many cases the use of huge transfer girders and mechanical offsets are required in order to transfer tower columns and shear walls and to provide a feasible column placement in the public areas of the hotel. It's all part of the expense of building downtown.

Fierce competition in many cities for the limited supply of developable hotel sites coupled with extraordinary revenue growth due to increased room rates downtown has developers scrounging for all types of odd-shaped sites. Brand standards often must be compromised or abandoned in order to adapt to odd-shaped sites in dense urban settings. Today, hotels designed as narrow sliver buildings—tall buildings wedged into small, mid-block sites—are on the upswing as large sites are increasingly scarce.

Located on a tiny corner site in SoHo near the entrance to the Holland Tunnel, the 110-key guestroom tower of The James Hotel is cantilevered over a multi-level podium that includes a third-floor sky lobby. The lobby is accessed from a discrete ground-floor street entrance by a grand stair and glass-enclosed elevator that passes through richly landscaped terraces and an urban garden.

Postage-stamp-sized sites combined with security concerns because of the overcrowded streets in New York's Times Square have prompted several hotels in that area to raise their lobby above street level. These hotels must necessarily employ additional reception staff at ground level to ensure that the guests are greeted appropriately and ushered up to the lobby safely with their luggage and to prevent unwanted sightseers from wandering in and out.

Traffic, Parking, and Service

Parking is less of a requirement in downtown hotels than in most other hotel types since there is an abundance of public transportation and taxicabs and many of the city's great restaurants, museums, retail stores, and office buildings are within walking distance of the hotel. Guests arriving at a city hotel very often leave their cars parked for the entire stay, since driving on the city's congested streets and trying to find parking is far less desirable than calling a cab, hopping on a bus, or using underground transit. Many cities now discourage the construction of parking garages in order to encourage use of public transportation, thereby cutting down on congestion and pollution. This presents a problem for new hotels since a moratorium may exist on creating new parking. In fact, most city hotels lease parking from a nearby facility and use valets to park the guest's car upon arrival. Where possible hotels should provide 0.4 to 0.8 parking spaces per room in large cities, and 1.2 to 1.4 spaces in smaller cities where guests rely more on their automobile.

Entrance courts and porte cochères are rare in dense urban settings. Exceptions include the New York Hilton Hotel, with its block-long covered entry drive on the Avenue of the Americas, and

The Ritz-Carlton San Francisco on Nob Hill. The Grand Hyatt Tokyo at Roppongi Hills provides a spacious porte cochère for the main lobby entrance beneath the overhang of a large circular volume containing banquet rooms and a terrace overlooking the street. More common is a hotel drop-off zone where taxis and limousines are permitted to stand in line for hotel customers; in some cities these drop-off zones require a special permit. One important consideration when evaluating a site on a busy urban street is to make note of bus stops, fire hydrants, and other features that could prevent the creation of a passenger drop-off area for the hotel.

While building signage is of utmost importance for many hotel types including roadside and suburban lodgings that depend on recognition from a speeding automobile, in downtown locations the building itself is often relied on for identification. Critics historically have feasted on hotel architects who due to their lack of imagination in giving the building personality and identity resorted to large signs at the top. However, it is critical for hotel restaurants, if they are to survive, to have some identifying feature in the way of a sign, canopy, or marquee to identify the outlet for pedestrians; a separate entrance to a restaurant in an urban hotel is a distinct advantage. Hotel restaurants do not share the luxury of a captive audience that resort restaurants or even suburban and airport hotel restaurants have. The city is full of great restaurants, many within walking distance, so the hotel restaurant must compete at literally the same level, at street level. Without establishing a reputation by having a noted chef or spectacular décor, a restaurant that is tucked away in the public areas of a hotel will be compromised.

As indicated above, off-street loading docks are needed and frequently mandated in city hotels. The problem that arises on tight urban sites is in locating the loading area with its odors and noise as far away from the hotel entrance as possible. In the case of sites that front on more than one street, provided that curb cuts are permitted, this shouldn't be difficult. One hotel in Times Square with enormous site constraints opted for a 40 x 14 ft (12.2 x 4.2 m) hydraulic truck elevator that led to a sub-cellar loading facility, which included a giant turntable so that the truck could back up to the underground dock.

Garbage collection presents many special challenges in an urban setting, not least of which is noise. Because of traffic, collection is usually done in the middle of the night. Noise from the trucks may echo back and forth off of surrounding buildings, frequently disturbing guests. Many luxury properties go to the expense of providing high-quality sound-resistant window systems such as triple-glazing on lower floors where ricocheting sonic energy is worst.

Back-of-house Efficiency

Back-of-house operations in downtown hotels present many challenges not usually encountered in other hotel types where space is less constrained. Often relegated to cellars where valuable above-grade areas are limited to guest use, many functions have to operate with clockwork-like precision to ensure that services are provided to the guests in a timely and efficient manner. Following E. M. Statler's lead in the back-of-house design of the earlier Buffalo Statler, Warren and

Wetmore designed New York's Biltmore Hotel in 1913 with excellent functional organization. Statler's theories on hotel organization have withstood the test of time as architects such as William B. Tabler have advanced his approach, improving on efficiency and economy in hundreds of hotels and widely influencing functional design.

Some hotel chains have resorted to centralizing off-site such back-of-house functions as the laundry, operating several properties in a geographic region. This has proven of particular benefit to urban properties where space can be recaptured and reassigned, freeing up floor area for much needed administrative functions or allowing for additional function space or guestrooms.

Hilton centralized its laundry facility for a large region that included New York City, western Connecticut, and northern New Jersey. This allowed many properties within the region to free up much-needed space for back-of-house functions, administrative offices and, in some cases, additional guestrooms and meeting space. Centralization of administrative functions such as accounting and reservations may be possible through increased computerization and Internet capabilities.

Size

Following the introduction of elevators to hotels, Americans developed the large hotel in the mid-nineteenth century while Europeans cherished their small hotels, resisting the construction of major hotels over 500 rooms until well into the 1960s. Completing the circle in the 1990s, U.S. cities embraced the boutique hotel by returning to a model that provides a European level of personalized service and atmosphere (see Design Hotels, Chapter 3, pages 53–67).

The optimum-size hotel is often determined by "threshold" factors, or points beyond which:

- additional rooms are needed to offset the high land costs
- an extra elevator or second bank of elevators must be added
- an additional restaurant is needed
- the extra building height requires a more sophisticated structural system
- the added structural loads dictate more complex foundations
- another cooling tower, chiller, or boiler becomes necessary
- structured parking is needed.

But while such elements influence optimum sizing within a range of 50–100 rooms, they are relatively minor factors when compared with the inherent administrative efficiency of small versus medium- and large-size hotels.

Two hundred rooms is a threshold beyond which management begins to shift from a direct hands-on style operation to a more intricate system of multiple department heads and assistant managers. In hotels with fewer than 200 rooms, the management style can be more personal, with fewer supervisors required, more productive and happier employees, better satisfied guests, and lower operating expenses. Any economies of scale to offset this are not usually achieved until a size of 500–600 rooms is reached. In other words, labor productivity peaks at 200 rooms, declines, and is not overtaken by size economy until there are at least 500 rooms.

Note that among independent non-branded hotels, most are under 200 rooms. This proves their size is basically efficient and profitable even without the marketing and reservation-system advantages of the large chains. Moreover, large hotel restaurants tend to be overstaffed and have oversized, over-equipped kitchens, while small hotels often lease out their restaurants to more effective individual operators.

Chain-affiliated, limited-service properties under 200 keys are finding good occupancy rates and healthy RevPAR (revenue per available room) in a formula that provides limited in-house food and beverage (perhaps complimentary breakfast buffet and hors d'oeuvres and cocktails in the evening), minor meeting space, and lower staff levels.

Although less efficient to manage, hotels in the 200–500 key range are often more convenient to market and finance; for example, lending institutions often prefer to invest in two 500-room hotels in different cities than in one more efficient 1,000-room facility, no matter how great the market demand. But midsize hotels need to economize more on their capital costs to offset their lower efficiencies. Conversely, the more optimum-size hotels can translate their superior profitability into more attractive designs, whether an atrium or more elegant décor.

Guestrooms

The size of hotel guestrooms is difficult to quantify in the downtown context since there are so many sub-types to consider: The adaptive reuse of office buildings may generate very deep room layouts; design hotels often charge top dollar for small rooms; pod hotels provide minimal accommodations to those on a tight budget; and even standard rooms at super-luxury hotels may be huge. (The Setai Fifth Avenue boasts the largest rooms in Manhattan, the smallest over 450 sq ft or 42 sq m). Guestroom size only becomes a constant in the major chains where the result is similar to the suburban hotel types.

Since the average length of stay and number of occupants per room are similar, guestroom sizes in downtown hotels are equivalent to those in suburban and airport hotels. The basic 12.5 ft x 18 ft (3.8 x 5.5 m) net living room dimension varies only within about 10 percent, based on special preferences of owners or operators who believe a slightly larger room will give them a significant competitive advantage. Experience has shown that a foot of width is less important in making the room seem larger than a lighter color or other decorative scheme. For example, in the restoration of New York's InterContinental Hotel, a mirrored wall was installed in one 11.5 ft (3.5 m) wide room. Most guests felt the room was larger and preferred it to the standard 12.5 ft (3.8 m) wide guestroom.

While increased width provides minor additional space between the foot of the bed and the dresser, this space does not allow for additional furniture, whereas increased length can provide for a larger desk, extra chair, or convertible sofa. Also, increased width adds more cost than length, since it increases structural spans,

YOTEL, New York, New York

Following the success of its airport properties the Yotel developers opened a 669-room hotel near Times Square in New York City as part of a 1.2 million sq ft (111,484 sq m), 60-story LEED-Silver complex which will include residential units and the Frank Gehry-designed Signature Theatre. Proffered as affordable luxury with cutting-edge technology, the flagship Yotel urban property will feature a restaurant, bar, meeting rooms, a club lounge, and the largest hotel terrace space in Manhattan.

slab thickness, non-saleable corridor area, and exterior façade. Therefore, lengthening the room is less costly and more beneficial to the guest than widening it (see discussion on guestroom layout, Chapter 16).

No hotel prototype expresses the density and crowding issues faced by downtown hotels more than the capsule hotels in Japan. The Japanese, whose population density is 10 times greater than that of the United States, have a long history of inventing ingenious ways of utilizing minimal space. The primary market for capsule hotels is young professionals who live in the outer suburbs of Tokyo where rent is cheaper than in the city. Often kept late working or in meetings and dreading the long train ride home only to turn

around a few hours later to return, they frequently seek inexpensive overnight lodging. Conveniently located near the railway stations these hotels can contain up to 1,000 units, or capsule rooms. A capsule is a sleeping compartment, not unlike those found on trains, except they are usually entered from one end rather than from the side. Approximately 6.75 ft (2.08 m) long by 3.5 ft (1.08 m) wide by 3.5 ft (1.08 m) high, the molded plastic capsules are stacked two high along double-loaded corridors. For 4,000 yen ($35) per night one can rent a private capsule equipped with a firm mattress, TV mounted to the ceiling, radio, alarm clock, reading light with dimmer switch, mirror, corner shelf, and controllable ventilation nozzle similar to those found on airlines. Men and women are placed on separate

(continued p. 30)

—— Case Study ————————————————————————————————————

The Standard Hotel, New York, New York
Architect: ENNEAD Architects
Interior Designer: Roman and Williams

Located in Manhattan's Meatpacking District, an energized neighborhood just west of Greenwich Village bordering on the Hudson River, the 18-story, 337-room Standard Hotel brings luxury and panache to a rapidly developing part of New York. Once a light manufacturing district of nineteenth-century warehouse buildings, the Meatpacking District recently transformed into a center of high fashion, nightclubs, boutiques, gourmet restaurants, and high-end retail. The hotel literally straddles a unique and very popular linear park converted from an abandoned 75-year-old elevated railroad line known as the High Line which meanders north from Gansevoort Street to West 34th Street.

Hotelier extraordinaire Andre Balazs, creator of the Mercer Hotel in SoHo and the original Standard in West Hollywood, California, engaged the services of his college friend Todd Shliemann, FAIA, of Ennead Architects (formerly Polshek Partnership) to collaborate with interior designers Roman and Williams and set designer Shawn Hausmann in the design of the hotel. Unique among owner–developers, Balazs collaborated closely with the design team in establishing a program and design vocabulary for the project. Andre Balazs Properties

manages operations for the hotel along with six other hotels in the Balazs portfolio.

The architects maximized the development potential of the site, located in a light industrial manufacturing zone, by utilizing zoning incentives including a plaza bonus and by placing administration offices and back-of-house functions below grade to avoid using the limited zoning floor area (FAR) of approximately 200,000 sq ft (18,500 sq m). The design strategy called for leaving much of the ground-floor area unbuilt by creating an open-air urban plaza as a forecourt to the hotel entrance. The open-air seating areas of the ground-floor restaurants also do not count against the allotted floor area. Like the older structures that were built over the railroad tracks decades earlier, zoning restrictions only required that new construction over the elevated railway essentially be a box with a hole in the middle to allow the tracks to pass through. Since the city's development of the High Line into a popular public park, The Standard will likely be the last building permitted to span across it.

Situated at the collision of two distinct urban geometries, the Lower Manhattan street grid and the non-orthogonal rail

The Standard and the High Line

The Standard, lobby

The Standard, guestroom (left) and guest bathroom (above)

line that cuts across it, the building form responds with its bent double-loaded slab perched on massive concrete piers 57 ft (17 m) above the horizontally scaled industrial landscape. Drawing inspiration from French architect Le Corbusier in works such as *Unité d'Habitation* in Marseilles, the composition is one of rugged poured-in-place concrete supporting a delicate grid of super-clear water-white glass lifted above the pedestrian zone by muscular pylons, allowing natural light to penetrate to the street. The hotel's street-level restaurants reflect the neighboring historic warehouse buildings by use of reclaimed brick, steel frame windows, and metal canopies surrounding an airy open plaza.

In planning the hotel Balazs programmed a large assortment of public spaces throughout the building, continuing the long tradition of downtown hotels that serve as centers of city social life. The ground floor includes a complex series of interlinked public venues, both outdoor and indoor. Guests enter the hotel off the Grand Plaza through a day-glow yellow revolving door, arriving at an intimate reception lobby with a mirrored ceiling and a continuous light strip that visually bisects the room. The Living Room is an indoor–outdoor lobby lounge and bar off the front desk. The Standard Grill spills out onto the Grand Plaza and Washington Street and includes a less formal bistro-type bar/grill area and a separate more formal dining room. The Biergarten is a 4,000 sq ft (370 sq m) outdoor café tucked beneath the High Line. The Wine Room is a tasting room accessible from the Standard Grille and Biergarten. Opening onto the Biergarten, the Garden Room is a 1,250 sq ft (115 sq m) dividable event space that can be leased for private parties.

On the second floor the High Line Room is a 1,400 sq ft (130 sq m) dividable meeting room with high ceilings and wall-to-wall glass at both ends; one faces the river, the other faces the High Line. The adjacent pre-function lobby opens to the 2,400 sq ft (220 sq m) High Line Terrace. The 18th floor contains two flashy nightclub venues, so exclusive that neither is advertised on the hotel's website. The Boom-Boom Room, a lavish party lounge with a spectacular bar, shares the floor with Le Bain, a bi-level nightclub with a small indoor pool and access to an open-air rooftop lounge. The popularity of the two clubs has created a challenge for hotel staff since long lines form in the lobby on club nights, obstructing circulation for hotel guests. On crowded weekend nights management uses the service elevator to transport club-goers, which brings another line through the back-of-house with its predictable negative impact on room service. Newer hotels have learned to provide a dedicated elevator and entrance lobby to such popular rooftop venues.

The 337 guestrooms and suites range in size from the Standard Queen at 250 sq ft (23 sq m) to the Empire Suite at 875 sq ft (81 sq m). The typical guest floor is a variation on the double-loaded slab configuration (see The Guestroom Floor, Chapter 15), with rooms on the south side oriented with the long dimension open to more expansive views. Guestrooms have floor-to-ceiling windows and clear-glass showers offering guests views of the city while bathing.

Most back-of-house and administration offices are located on the ground floor (loading dock on West 13th Street, employee entrance, housekeeping, and main kitchen) and in the basement (administration offices, storage, and mechanical equipment).

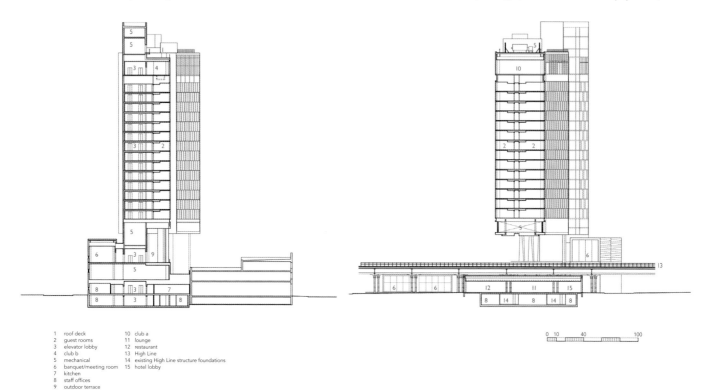

1	roof deck	10	club a
2	guest rooms	11	lounge
3	elevator lobby	12	restaurant
4	club b	13	High Line
5	mechanical	14	existing High Line structure foundations
6	banquet/meeting room	15	hotel lobby
7	kitchen		
8	staff offices		
9	outdoor terrace		

The Standard, N–S section (looking east)

The Standard, S–N section (looking west)

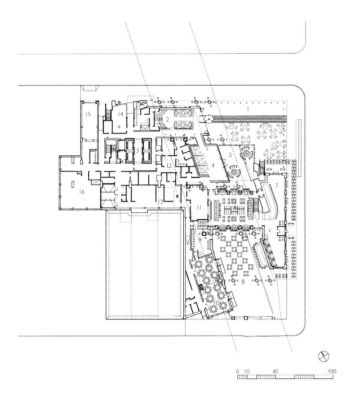

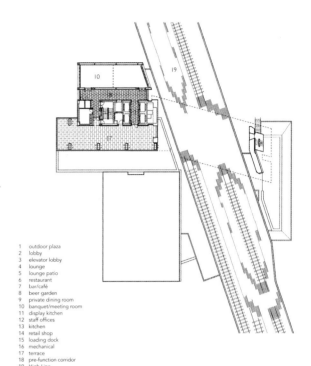

1   outdoor plaza
2   lobby
3   elevator lobby
4   lounge
5   lounge patio
6   restaurant
7   bar/café
8   beer garden
9   private dining room
10 banquet/meeting room
11 display kitchen
12 staff offices
13 kitchen
14 retail shop
15 loading dock
16 mechanical
17 terrace
18 pre-function corridor
19 High Line

The Standard, level 1

The Standard, level 3

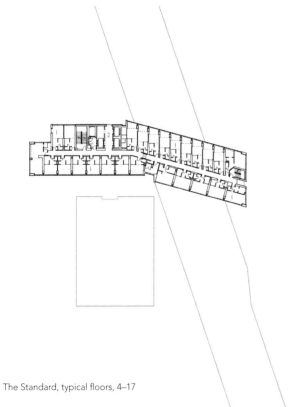

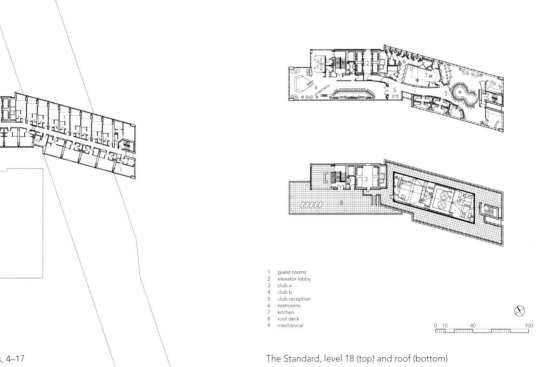

1   guest rooms
2   elevator lobby
3   club a
4   club b
5   club reception
6   restrooms
7   kitchen
8   roof deck
9   mechanical

The Standard, typical floors, 4–17

The Standard, level 18 (top) and roof (bottom)

floors; the public areas of the hotel usually include a cafeteria and a bathhouse with a communal pool, both of which are open all night. This epitome of no-frills accommodation serves an important market in a uniquely vibrant metropolis.

Following the model of the capsule hotel several new products offer similar, though somewhat larger, accommodations in dense urban locations to serve much the same traveling market. New micro-brands including Qbic, Trocadero, and Yotel, each opening its first properties at airports, have found a thriving new market in urban settings such as New York's Times Square, London's Westminster, and Amsterdam's World Trade Center. The market for affordable luxury lodging in dense urban locations has yielded a formula blending elements of capsule hotel, luxury train cabins, and first-class airline suites with boutique-style design and fashion.

Adaptive Reuse

The last few decades have seen a number of urban office buildings converted to hotels. Hotel chains are showing strong interest in establishing new properties in downtown areas, but suitable sites for new construction are scarce and expensive. At the same time, older office buildings are becoming functionally obsolete and devalued in a competitive office-space market. Converting older office buildings to hotels has proved to be an attractive development opportunity. In most cases the cost of acquisition and renovation has been less than the cost of new hotel construction. The feasibility often depends on several factors including zoning, building footprint, window spacing, building façade, floor-to-ceiling height, and the structural system. (See Chapter 12 for more discussion on adaptive reuse.)

Sustainable Urban Hotels

No longer are environmentally responsible design principles and procedures for the hospitality industry limited to eco-resorts. Developers and hotel companies are embracing sustainable principles for all types of properties including urban hotels. The hospitality and travel industry is finding that ecological responsibility both has marketing value and can actually boost profits. Many urban hotel properties seek to achieve LEED (Leadership in Energy and Environmental Design) designation from the U.S. Green Building Council by providing energy savings, water efficiency, CO_2 emissions reduction, improved indoor environmental quality, better stewardship of resources, and greater sensitivity to their impacts.

Designed to become Marriott's first LEED Gold-certified property, the environmentally focused Ritz-Carlton in Charlotte, North Carolina, features a green roof vegetated with 18,000 plants which insulates the building, slows rain runoff, and cools the air through evaporation of water. In addition, the hotel utilizes a water purification and container system that will divert 73,000 plastic bottles from landfills, save more than 104 barrels of oil, eliminate nearly 49 tons of CO_2 emissions, and save almost 605 million BTUs of electricity each year.

W Minneapolis–The Foshay, Minneapolis, Minnesota
Once the tallest building west of the Mississippi, the Foshay Tower, built in 1929, was modeled after the Washington Monument. Listed on the National Register of Historic Places and the Minneapolis Heritage Preservation Commission as a designated landmark, the building has been converted to a stylish W Hotel. The relatively small footprint permitted an easy adaptation to hotel, with 10 rooms per floor at the lower level and two suites per floor at the apex.

Meydan Grandstand and Hotel, Dubai, United Arab Emirates
Curving around the racetrack with single-loaded corridors, all 290 rooms and suites in the hotel enjoy an unobstructed view of the races. The expansive hotel incorporates high-end restaurants, the Meydan Museum and Gallery, a spa, an IMAX theater, and the Meydan Marina.

Urban Entertainment Hotels

Personifying the theatricality of the "Great White Way," the Astor Hotel built in Times Square in 1904 was a vast amusement palace with early themed restaurants, elaborate banquet halls and a famous rooftop wintergarden that brought a festive presence to Broadway. The Astor was a rousing forerunner of downtown entertainment hotels whose lobby included many theatrical and thematic elements, the most dazzling of which was the Orangerie, a restaurant with amazing scenographics and lighting effects that provided guests with a virtual apparition of the Mediterranean. Hot summer nights in New York City rendered the un-airconditioned Broadway theaters so uncomfortable that many closed their doors for the season. Outdoor performances, however, were staged in the cool night air of the outdoor rooftop theater of the Astor Hotel wintergarden. The wintergarden roof was encircled in sparkling lanterns adorning the building's cornice line and presenting a spectacle to merrymakers of the night, foretelling the glittering light show that plays today in Times Square.

Entertainment as a focus market for a downtown hotel can take many forms including music, art, gaming, sports, museums, theater, cinema—even high-tech virtual interactive media. Accommodations for such a wide variety depend on the nature of the entertainment venue being offered. Hotels near sporting events, such as the SkyDome Renaissance Hotel in Toronto, actually orient guestrooms' views to the playing field. Or at the Meydan Grandstand and Hotel in Dubai guestrooms are oriented to views of the horse-racing track below.

Hotel public spaces often actually contain the entertainment venue. The public spaces of the 21c Museum Hotel in Louisville

21c Museum Hotel, Louisville, Kentucky
The hotel itself is a giant interactive work of art, using its guests as obligatory participants. The urinal in the men's public restroom faces the clear side of a two-way mirror that is cleverly placed in the hallway leading to the women's restroom, where women often stop to fix their hair or make-up in the reflection, not knowing what stands on the opposite side.

Jumeirah Himalayas Hotel, Pudong, Shanghai, China
Architect Arata Isozaki designed the podium of the Himalayas Center as an "organic forest," with amorphous concrete pillars that mimic trees and form an open 103 ft (31.4 m) high central court connecting the box-shaped retail and hospitality wings.

Hard Rock Hotel, Chicago, Illinois
The hotel is housed in the historic Carbide and Carbon Building in the heart of downtown
on Michigan Avenue. Designed in 1929 by the sons of famed Chicago architect Daniel
Burnham, the 40-story Art Deco landmark is appropriately shaped like a champagne bottle,
with a terracotta exterior corresponding to the green glass bottle and an illuminated
golden tower alluding to the shiny foil top.

Hard Rock Hotel, Macau, China.
Occupying a circular tower reminiscent of a stack of vinyl records, the Hard Rock Hotel and Casino Macau is part of the City of Dreams Casino and Entertainment Resort Complex located on the Cotai Strip in Macau, China. Designed by Arquitectonica as part of a complex of four hotel towers, the Hard Rock Hotel sits above a mega-casino, a major high-end retail venue called the Boulevard, and two state-of-the-art high-definition multi-media theaters providing incredible sound and explosive visual effects.

immerse its hotel guests and other visitors in a plethora of artistic installations that often entice the guest to interact. On the floor next to the front desk a video-art installation called *Sleepers* projects a life-size video stream of a man and woman sleeping in bed. The position of the image is such that the guest must partially stand on the bed when checking in; guests often are startled when one of the sleepers turns over or adjusts their pillow.

As part Himalayas Center, a cultural and entertainment complex designed by Arata Isozaki in the heart of Pudong Shanghai, the Jumeirah Himalayas Hotel, incorporates the "edutainment" mission of the project throughout its public spaces. The lobby has a ceiling height of 52.5 ft (16 m) and features the "Thousand Character Essay," a spectacular display of 1,000 Chinese characters that tells a 5,000-year-old story of Chinese cultural evolution.

Few hotel companies are more purely dedicated to the art of entertainment than the Hard Rock Hotel brand. The venture started as Hard Rock Café, opening restaurants in London, New York, and Las Vegas with authentic rock-and-roll memorabilia adorning its walls and ceilings and thumping drums and electric guitar riffs filling the air. With "party hard" as its mantra, the creators soon realized that its customers could use a place to crash after dinner and drinks and so expanded the concept to include Hard Rock Hotels and Casinos. Today, the party never ends, and no one has to go home.

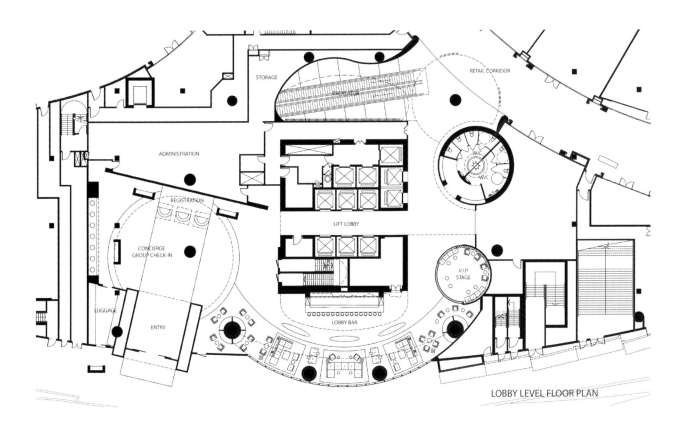

LOBBY LEVEL FLOOR PLAN

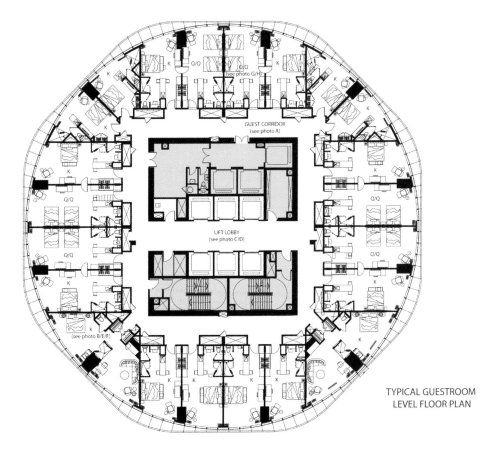

TYPICAL GUESTROOM
LEVEL FLOOR PLAN

Urban Waterfront Hotels

The first hotels in North America were seaport inns located in the harbor districts of cities along the Atlantic coast. During colonial times before the increase in travel by stagecoach, private carriage, and horseback that resulted in the construction of inns and taverns along the post roads, ships from Europe were the most important means of travel and seaport inns catered to the needs of intercontinental travel and commerce.

In the world's seafaring towns waterfronts have long been utilized for commerce relating to waterborne foreign trade. Technological developments in the shipping industry such as containerization coupled with expansion of trucking on the interstate highway system rendered obsolete many port-city waterfront dock neighborhoods that depended on overseas maritime commerce for their prosperity. Urban renewal efforts now seek to reclaim the city's waterfronts

for recreation and leisure-time enjoyment. Waterfronts in many ways have become the city's last frontier. New York City alone has 578 linear miles (930 km) of waterfront, most of it inaccessible or underutilized.

Developers and designers of downtown waterfront hotels maximize the potential of their unique sites by addressing opportunities for expansive views, shoreline access, proximity to water transportation, a dominating presence on the skyline, historic vistas, and the overwhelming sensation of being connected to a larger world. Often such hotels find synergistic benefit from being part of a complex of waterfront development such as the Fairmont Pacific Rim in Vancouver, Canada, adjacent to Canada Place including Vancouver's Cruise Ship Terminal, the World Trade Center, and the Vancouver Conference and Exhibition Center.

Waterfront properties provide ample opportunity to arrange hotel public spaces to take advantage of the spectacular views

Fairmont Pacific Rim Hotel, Vancouver, Canada.
With unobstructed views of the north Shore Mountains, Stanley Park, and Coal Harbour, guests are treated to the vistas that have transfixed travelers since Captain Vancouver arrived in 1792.

Hyatt Regency, Dusseldorf, Germany (facing page, top)
Set on a dominant promontory in trendy Media Harbor, which spills into the Rhine River, the Hyatt Regency Dusseldorf is afforded unobstructed visibility while achieving a commanding presence on the city's waterfront. Linked by a pedestrian bridge to the opposite side of the harbor, the hotel's public spaces pour out onto a festive public plaza at the tip of the headland, with views of the Old Town and the Rheinturm telecommunications tower.

Nhow Hotel, Berlin, Germany (facing page, bottom)
Built right up to the banks of the river and fitting with the surrounding industrial-style dockside buildings, the hotel, designed by NPS Tchoban Voss Architects, is composed of two U-shaped blocks, forming terraces at the second level opening to views over the water and crowned with a three-story cantilevered section conveying the image of a "crane house," echoing Berlin's old city port area. The entire overhanging soffit of the cantilevered section is a huge polished mirror, creating a dazzling visual effect reflecting the colorful river terrace below.

and refreshing breezes on the shoreline. The architects for Hyatt Regency Dusseldorf took advantage of its site on a promontory of the Rhine River by designing its lobby and restaurants to open out onto a festive public plaza at the tip of the headland.

To maximize the expansive views the orientation of the guestroom tower should allow for most of its rooms to have at least a partial view towards the water. The wedge-shaped footprint of the W Barcelona tower orients nearly all of its guestrooms toward views of the Mediterranean Sea. Likewise, the guestroom floors of the Nhow Hotel on the River Spree in Berlin is configured as a double-U plan, providing its rooms with views out across the old city port area.

Urban hotels on the waterfront can offer guests amenities that are not available at inland properties, such as waterfront cafés, boat rentals, water taxis and beaches. Korean architect Changki Yun's design for the Abu Dhabi Mirage Hotel includes a marina club, a floating theater, a cruise terminal, an artificial beach, a sailing school, and glass floating suites.

(continued p. 44)

Abu Dhabi Mirage Hotel, Abu Dhabi, United Arab Emirates
Changki Yun's nautically themed design for this urban marina hotel is composed of three buildings: the residential hotel that faces the city, the marina hotel that has an artificial beachfront, and the marina club located in the inner cove of the resort. The bridge that connects the two hotel wings contains a presidential suite and the lower deck connects them to the observation tower.

W Hotel Barcelona, Barcelona, Spain

Architect and Interior Designer: Ricardo Bofill, Taller de Arquitectura

Few urban hotels embrace and exploit their position on the waterfront as well as the W Barcelona. Nearly every significant feature of the hotel is designed by renowned Spanish architect Ricardo Bofill to capitalize on its superb coastal site overlooking the Mediterranean Sea.

Located at the new entrance to Barcelona Harbor on a 25 acre (10 hectare) plot reclaimed from the sea, the hotel is part of an ambitious urban renewal plan for Barcelona's coastline. The iconic tower is sited at the beginning of the world-famous boardwalk, La Barceloneta, that connects the hotel and the Olympic Village. The closest beach to Barcelona's city center, Barceloneta Beach, was featured on a popular travel TV program as the "Best Urban Beach in the World."

The sail-shaped tower mast of the hotel is pushed to the edge of the sea and clad in a silvery glass curtain wall reflecting the motion of blue ocean waves and colorful sky. With its commanding presence against Barcelona's magnificent waterfront and skyline, the slender 26-story guest tower is set perpendicular to the dock and shoreline affording virtually every guestroom unlimited views of the sea and city. The guestroom floor corridors and elevator lobbies are provided with floor-to-ceiling windows framing spectacular views. The Bofill design team chose red stucco walls and carpet for the corridors to contrast and enhance the rich blue of the water below. The guestrooms are designed with the bed floating in the middle of the room facing the window. Efficient use of guestroom space is sacrificed for dramatic effect.

W Barcelona

W Barcelona, lobby

W Barcelona and Barceloneta beach

W Barcelona, guestroom

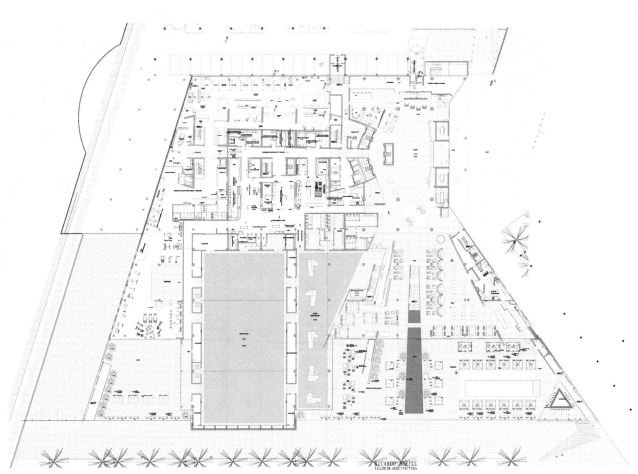

W Barcelona, ground floor plan

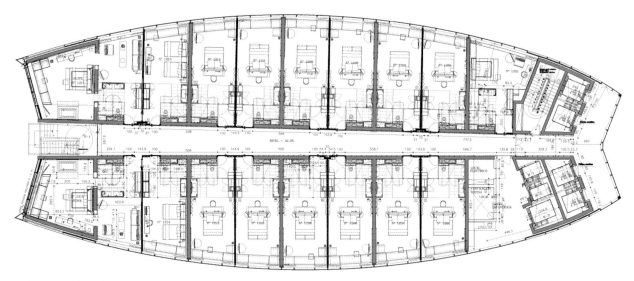

W Barcelona,typical floor plan

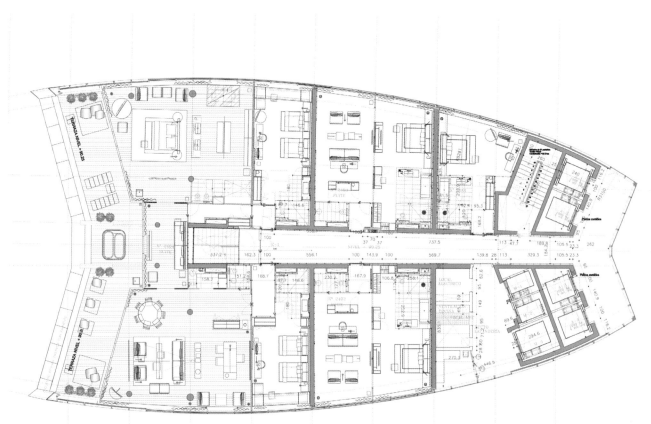

W Barcelona, suite floor plan

W Barcelona, longitudinal section

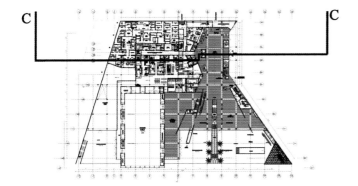

The tower volume is wrapped on the dock side by a low-slung podium containing the hotel public spaces and forming two expansive terraces overlooking the water. Awash with reflected light from the sparkling water, the hotel lobby and public spaces open out onto these sunny piazzas. One wall of the hotel's largest ballroom is constructed of floor-to-ceiling glass providing a spectacular maritime backdrop for banquets and conferences.

Urban Super-luxury Hotels

One day a guest [at The Ritz Hotel Paris] demanded sea-urchins for dinner, or she would leave the hotel on the spot—unfortunately, sea-urchins were completely out of season at that time of year. Charles, the room-service maître d'hôtel, put in a call to an independent fisherman on the Côte d'Azur. Once the precious sea food was tracked down, Charles laid on an air-taxi to fly the consignment up to Paris. A short while later, ushered in by the maître d'hôtel wearing a mischievous smile, the entire room-service team paraded into the room bearing a dozen sea-urchins on a bed of crushed ice.

(From Ritz Hotel Paris archives)

Impeccable service, urbane management, sumptuous décor, and elegant architecture are the hallmarks of a rare breed of small super-

Growing Affluence and the Diversity of Luxury

Stephen Perkins, AIA, ISHC
ForrestPerkins
Washington, DC

In the middle of the Indian Ocean, Four Seasons Maldives operates three luxury destinations: Landaa Giraavaru, Kuda Huraa and the luxury dive ship, the 40-meter Four Seasons Explorer. Out there, Four Seasons has bet on a location that could be easily swept away by the rising oceans of global warming. But more importantly, Four Seasons has bet on the insatiable travel aspirations of its guests. The settings are unique, but the high standards are the same with regard to spa, cuisine, and service. On balance, Four Seasons has created learning and conservation programs in the Maldives, and has vigorously pursued an ecologically-sensitive approach to its operations that also become part of the allure of its unique offerings.

In the early twenty-first century, as in the late nineteenth century, global transportation has inspired the affluent to go wherever they want and to stay as comfortably as they could stay practically anywhere in the world. The means to travel luxuriously is equally met by the means to luxuriate in seamless and boundless comfort in an unbroken chain of service whenever and wherever.

The difference between then and now is that today the traveler is as likely to be an affluent Turk, Russian, Chinese, Indian, or Brazilian as an American or Western European. The globalization of affluence has changed not only the patterns of luxury consumption, but also its language and desires. The modern, and in many cases, newly affluent traveler is as likely to explore those historic sites that have intrigued travelers for centuries as he or she is to look for the unique travel experience for which access may only be gained by that same affluence.

For centuries purveyors have packaged unique experiences, whether for adventure, romance, or natural beauty. Now those desires are fueled by an Internet-charged fire hose of information, largely in English, that allows the affluent traveler to search both broadly and specifically for types of lodging, and indeed, the luxury chain of unique travel experiences that cohere transportation, lodging, shopping, and highly exclusive access to rare experiences. It is this constellated chain of exclusive experiences that will increasingly attract the affluent traveler.

As affluence spreads around the world, the desire for a luxury travel and lodging experience will begin to generate much larger demand than any ever experienced before. The globalization of affluence will also result in a wide array of narrowly-focused opportunities to meet the growing passion for luxury travel. The difference in the future is that these opportunities will be increasingly enjoyed at a scale which may seem burdensome to those seeking the quiet and solitary enjoyment of rare beauty or the exhilarating thrill of physical challenge.

In 2011, 57 million Chinese tourists were expected to travel abroad and spend approximately U.S.$55 billion. In future years, large numbers of Indians and Africans will seek the novel experience that has driven travel for thousands of years. The challenge will be the protection of the novel and the accommodation of numbers almost unimaginable in our time. The risk of environmental degradation is high and, indeed, the spoiling of those attractions that generate travel will require national protections to ensure both their long-term life as well as the viability of the tourism industry.

As the unique becomes mundane, luxury entrepreneurs will test the limits of the imagination and the resources of those most able to enjoy the rarefied experience of sub-sea or space tourism. In the near-term, the quest for the rare solitary luxury-travel experience will likely be met by Sir Richard Branson's Virgin Galactic, a sub-orbital space flight available to six luxury astronauts aboard the *Spaceship Two*. At a cost of U.S.$200,000 and booked through Virgin Galactic or Accredited Space Agents, approximately 430 astronauts have signed up for space tourism.

Underwater, the growth of submarines and the abilities to inhabit the vast and largely unexplored majesty of the shallow and deep will become attractive destinations for those seeking a unique and memorable—and expensive—holiday.

The affluent traveler will always seek the unique, and with a greater diversity of travelers seeking ever-unique experiences, fragile landmarks and ecosystems must be protected from the threat of overuse. Affluent travelers are emboldened to excuse their zeal for the exceptional in all things pleasurable. And, given the heightened numbers of these travelers, national interests may require federal protection to preserve the experiences for posterity.

luxury hotels that uniquely cater to royalty, foreign dignitaries, captains of industry, celebrities, and cultural leaders. The most prestigious major chains have endeavored for decades to emulate, but have rarely been able to accomplish, the sophisticated charm and posh accommodations of the world's most exclusive closely-managed hotels. Such hotels provide a private world of rare and refined beauty where the art of personal service is practiced with efficiency and aplomb.

As with any hotel which provides a high level of personalized service, the virtues and reputation of super-luxury hotels largely are dependent on the management style of the hotel owner and staff. The owner often is very well known to the hotel's elite clientele and a copy of the managing director's impressive resume sometimes can be found in the literature describing the most important features of the property. But, most often, the leading force on which the style of service is defined is by the ever-resourceful concierge. Erudite and multilingual, the concierge commands a carefully selected, highly trained professional staff to fulfill any guest requirement, no matter how capricious, with verve and flare. For example, a concierge in one deluxe hotel was called upon to shop for and deliver an elaborate stereo system to the room of a famous conductor, who needed to rehearse for an upcoming performance.

It is not uncommon to find the staff at these hotels outnumbering guests by three to one. Some super-luxury hotels provide 24-hour personal butlers who, in addition to the more mundane duties of packing and unpacking luggage, or drawing baths, might be called upon to hand-deliver an important document across town, have a suit tailored for an important meeting, iron newspapers to prevent ink from rubbing off, or provide a stenographer for dictation at two o'clock in the morning. In addition to a personal butler, one European hotel provides its guests with a chauffeured Bentley.

Of course, the management staff must keep a detailed dossier on the predilections and idiosyncrasies of all repeat guests so that they know, for instance, that one guest sleeps until noon and must have a very quiet room shielded from morning sunlight, or that another requires a special brand of pet food for her temperamental cat.

Perhaps the most important aspect of super-luxury accommodation is the privacy, discretion, high-level security, and inconspicuous service sought by its most distinguished and prestigious clientele. "Our staff knows when it's appropriate to introduce two heads of state, or when they should blend into the Aubusson rugs," says Dan Camp, president and managing director of The Carlyle in New York City.

Design Considerations

Most super-luxury hotels derive much of their opulent character from the superb historical buildings they occupy. In fact, many such as the Hotel de Crillon in Paris and Hotel Danieli in Venice inhabit national landmarks.

Occupying a magnificent Renaissance palace—the fifteenth-century Palazzo della Gherardesca—and a beautiful former convent building—the sixteenth-century Conventino—the Four Seasons Firenze is set within a lavish 11 acre (4.5 hectare) private garden, Giardino

Four Seasons Firenze, Florence, Italy
The public spaces of the palazzo are replete with frescoes, bas-reliefs, stuccoes, and silk wallpapers, all carefully restored to bring forth their original vivid detail. The courtyard lobby is surrounded by porticoes and barrel vaults, decorated with a coffered ceiling comprising thousands of painted sunken panels. Each of the hotel's 117 guestrooms and suites is unique in dimension and character, with original friezes and fireplaces, skylights and staircases, ceiling art, and antique stoves.

Aman Hotel, New Delhi, India
The super-lux urban resort is spread over 7 acres (2.8 hectares) with two sandstone-clad wings: the nine-story Aman wing, with 31 rooms and 8 two-bedroom suites, and the five-story Lodhi wing, with 14 suites and 7 three-bedroom suites. The organization of the public spaces frames a long courtyard with water, columns, and jaali screens referencing the traditional Mughal architecture surrounding the hotel.

della Gherardesca, in the heart of Florence. It took seven years of painstaking restoration to create this stunning property which is as much a living art museum as it is a hotel. The developers hired interior designer Pierre Yves Rochon along with architects Studio Noferi and Magris & Partners to restore this opulent complex and convert it to a hotel masterpiece of unparalleled opulence. The meticulous restoration was carried out under the watchful eye of Florence's Superintendent for Artistic Historical Patrimony, the Ministry for Fine Arts and Culture, and the Department of Fine Arts.

(continued p. 50)

Andaz Shanghai Hotel and The Langham Xintiandi Hotel, Shanghai, China

Architect: KPF Architects
Associate Architect: Leigh & Orange
Interior Designers: Remedios Siembieda and Super Potato

Perhaps no two hotels more clearly demonstrate the distinction in design and service to the luxury leisure and business traveler than Andaz Shanghai Hotel and The Langham Xintiandi Hotel. The 309-room Andaz Hotel appeals to leisure travelers through its resort-style amenities, such as a rooftop wedding chapel and nightclub. Alternatively the 357-room Langham Hotel accommodates business travelers, offering meeting rooms, atrium lounge, and international dining selections.

Located in the award-winning and highly successful Xintiandi redevelopment district, the leisure-oriented Andaz Shanghai and the business-oriented Langham Xintiandi are connected by a dramatic curving pedestrian bridge that spans over Huangpi Road, which separates the two towers. With the project as centerpiece of a larger redevelopment project in downtown Shanghai, the developers of Xintiandi's North Block sought to celebrate the city's past while, through selective demolition and modern interventions, incorporating it with the commercial realities of contemporary urban living. Recognizing the value of its historic character the developers of Xintiandi reinvigorated a declining community with its 1920s gray-brick townhouses and carved-stone gates, in collaboration with the local Lu Wan District government and a consortium of banks to breathe new life into the neighborhood.

The original developer for the hotel project sought approval from city officials for a pedestrian bridge connecting the two hotels as the original plan called for both hotels to be under one management company, thereby permitting shared amenities and services. The city approved and, in fact, encouraged more bridges as city planners sought to expand the substantial underground network in central Shanghai with level-2 pedestrian connectivity. There were plans to have another bridge between the Andaz and a retail building to its south. The idea was to create a pedestrian network lifting pedestrian circulation above busy vehicular traffic, emulating the pedestrian network in Central Hong Kong that covers 4.3 miles (7 km) and connects 40 buildings. Ultimately it was determined that in the Xintiandi district ground-level circulation was far more important and so the network of bridges connecting this project was cancelled. The developer, however, having obtained approval for the bridge, decided to keep it even though it was decided that the two hotels would now be operated by two competing hotel companies. The bridge encouraged a dynamic synergy that benefited both hotels, linking the leisure-oriented public spaces of the Andaz with the business-focused function spaces of The Langham on level 2. Symbolically the bridge had value since it increased long-distance visibility of the project at street level.

Andaz Shanghai Hotel (left) and The Langham Xintiandi (right)

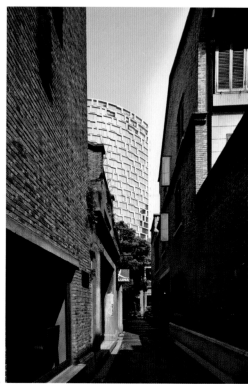

Langham Xintiandi, dining room

Andaz Shanghai, guestroom

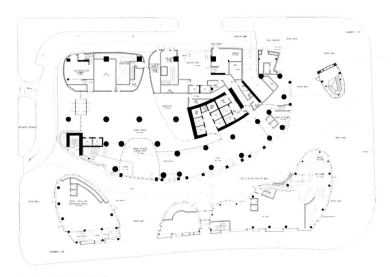

Langham Xintiandi (left)

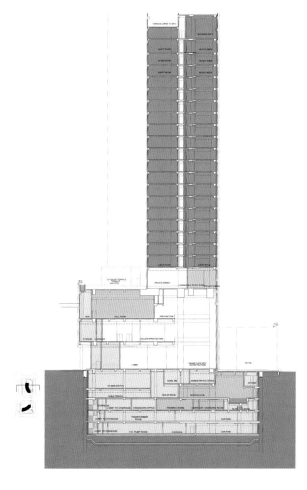

North–South Building, cross-section

The two hotels stand over 325 ft (100 m) tall with 79 ft (24 m) high podiums containing lobbies, restaurants, fitness centers, retail and meeting space. The challenge for the architects was to orient the towers to the smaller-scale two- and three-story buildings to the south. Like the 1920s townhouses the towers are clad with gray stone with fenestration patterns fashioned after Chinese latticework. The mass of the project steps down on the south to a grouping of two-story retail pavilions tempering the contrast in scale and density. The composed massing of the two towers is reminiscent of two sisters, graceful young ladies of the 1920s that strolled Shanghai's streets in pairs, symbolically holding hands through the bridge.

Far more rare, however, than historic restorations or adaptive renovations are hotels of this high stature designed as new buildings. Located in the heart of the city, the Aman New Delhi provides a superb example of cool contemporary architecture supporting superior luxury hotel service in an urban setting. Combined with an exceptional level of service, the hotel design promotes an air of sophisticated calm combining the privacy and exclusivity expected by Aman guests with the varied public facilities and social engagement demanded in a contemporary city hotel.

Public Spaces

Entrance lobbies most often are elegantly small and distinctly residential in character. Registration may occur at a small front desk or, sometimes, at private desks where the guest is invited to be seated. At The Carlyle, located in New York City's most exclusive residential area and for many years the only five-star hotel in the city, a quiet side entrance away from the hustle and bustle of Madison Avenue leads visitors into a luxuriously intimate lobby that feels more like the entry hall of a stately home than the center of a busy hotel. From the understated elegance of the hotel lobby guests may enter the Gallery for afternoon tea, have drinks in the renowned Bemelmans Bar, with its 1940s murals by Ludwig Bemelmans, or find top-name entertainment served up at Café Carlyle, well known among New York's elite as the premier cabaret room in the country.

Guestrooms

In developing the New York Regent hotel, later the New York Four Seasons, over a million dollars were spent on the construction of fully detailed guestroom mock-ups that were torn apart and rebuilt several times in perfecting the design. Early in this process the decision was made to extend the floor-to-floor height of the building to yield 10.5 ft (3.2 m) ceiling heights for every room, and to bear the exponential construction cost increase to achieve this grand scale. The rooms were equipped with bedside controls allowing the guest to open and close the drapes, turn on a discreet privacy sign, or call for maid service at the push of a button.

Bathrooms in many luxury properties now exceed one third of the overall room size. The recent renovation of a hotel in Beverly Hills, California, reduced the number of guestrooms from 253 to 184, primarily to increase the size of the bathrooms. Ultra-luxury bathroom design may now include multiple-head showers with 10-button controls and automatic temperature settings, marble vanity with two porcelain basins and brass fittings, heated fog-free mirrors, a deep cast-iron soaking tub with adjustable hand spray, three-stage mood lighting including a reading light over the tub and toilet, remote control TV with steam-free screen, "hands-free" two-line speaker phone with special digital circuits that minimize the sound of running water and automatically lower the volume of the radio or TV when a call comes in, a compartmentalized water closet, heated marble floors, heated towel bars, heated toilet seats, and bidets with hot-air drying functions. Specialty suites may offer deep whirlpool baths with windows facing

Burj al Arab, Dubai, United Arab Emirates
The lavishly decorated 8,400 sq ft (780 sq m) duplex two-bedroom royal suite on the 25th floor includes a private elevator, a private cinema, a library, a rotating four-poster canopy bed, a marble and gold staircase, leopard-print tufted carpets, and Carrara marble floors. The suite comes with a chauffeur-driven Rolls-Royce and private helicopter service.

out onto a spectacular view. But for all the bells and whistles, the most prized luxury item—and sometimes the most expensive to build—is good water pressure, a feature that is harder to achieve in new-build projects because of new regulations on water-saving devices and low-flow requirements. This is not a problem for the Four Seasons Hotel New York, which has to "warn" its guests that the deep soaking tub fills in less than 60 seconds.

Back-of-house

The design of the New York Four Seasons called for staff to take the guest's luggage upon arrival into a special luggage elevator adjacent to the entrance, carry it to a room in the sub-cellar where it was tagged and logged into the computer, and then transport it by high-speed service elevator to the guestroom before the guest entered the room.

Oberoi Udaivilas, Udaipur, India
Inspired by the majestic palaces of Rajasthan, architects Nimish Patel and Parul Zaveri of Abhikram created a luxurious masterpiece based on the rich heritage of the Mewar region with its domed pavilions, rambling courtyards, gentle rippling fountains, reflection pools, and verdant gardens.

first-class service. Employee lockers, showers, dining rooms, and lounges are often 1.5 to 2 times larger than those of less luxurious establishments and are treated as part of the hotel's basic décor rather than given the usual sterile finishes found in most back-of-house facilities.

Security and privacy continue to be essential features of super-luxury hotels and technological advances will produce ever more sophisticated systems. Such high-tech systems as electronic door locks that alert security upon entry of a room, surveillance cameras, and window sensors add to the guest's peace of mind.

In one London hotel, state-of-the-art electronic heat and motion sensors are wired from each room into the butler's pantry—a space somewhat closer to Mission Control. The butler knows whether guests are in their room so he won't disturb their privacy but is always close at hand to answer a call. In addition, the electronic key systems permit the butler to coordinate with housekeeping, engineering, and other hotel services to prevent guests from being disturbed.

The Four Seasons went through over 50,000 resumes and selected only one staff member for every 10 that were invited to be interviewed. Highly prized as they are, facilities for the staff in super-luxury hotels most often are on a level well above employee facilities in other hotel types. Super-luxury hotels pamper their employees not only to foster a sense of loyalty but to create a feeling of high esteem commensurate with the behavior and attitude required in delivering

Design Hotels

For the purpose of this chapter we will use the term "design hotels" to encompass the wide range of hotel types that are most frequently referred to as boutique hotels, lifestyle hotels and design hotels. Later in this chapter we will discuss the somewhat minor differences perceived between these three labels but for the sake of simplicity, unless discussing those differences, the term "design hotels" will be used for all three.

With the explosive popularity of design hotels over the last three decades there has been somewhat of a feeding frenzy within the industry as hundreds of new properties lay claim to the design hotel characterization, a number of design hotel chains have emerged, established hotel companies have entered the fray with their own design hotel brands, and established design hotel brands have expanded their range dramatically. Developers have realized the uncontested fact that, just as Madison Avenue ad agents discovered in the 1950s with sex-appeal, "design" sells. This phenomenon has spread to nearly all segments of the hospitality industry and we find incredibly interesting and unique design showing up at airport hotels, mixed-use projects, office-park hotels, ski resorts, casino hotels, marina hotels, etc. This chapter will limit the scope to those hotels whose most salient characteristic is a dedication to immersing the guest in a world of exquisite and interesting design featured both in its architectural innovations and unique interiors.

Hotels have been trendsetters in design and lifestyle for centuries. The grand hotels of the eighteenth and nineteenth centuries featured a very high level of individualistic interior and exterior design. The list of historic hotels that featured extraordinary and provocative design as a fundamental component would include The Ritz in Paris, The Vendome in Boston, The Savoy in London, The Waldorf=Astoria in New York, The Breakers in Palm Beach and The Del in San Diego, to name but a few.

During the post-war days of the 1950s, standardization of products and services began to emerge and hotel brands and chains became the prevalent trend in the United States and Europe. This trend was epitomized by the famous line from Holiday Inn founder Kemmons Wilson when he coined the slogan: "The best surprise is no surprise."

In reaction to the mediocrity and dreary uniformity of conventional hotel design, a few innovative developers in the 1980s realized that unique and provocative architecture and design could be a very fertile marketing asset. Anouska Hemple with her exotic Blakes Hotel in London, Ian Schrager and Steve Rubell with the ground-breaking Morgans Hotel in New York City, and Bill Kimpton with the trend-setting Bedford Hotel in San Francisco were the early pioneers of this genre. A substantial market was discovered for fashion-minded

Le Royal Monceau Raffles, Paris, France
Philippe Starck's sophisticated, irreverent design approach, with his use of bold color, unexpected materials and textures, and idiosyncratic high-quality custom furniture, completely transformed Le Royal Monceau, helping it regain its popularity with artists and celebrities.

travelers seeking an atmosphere in which they could enjoy an artistic lifestyle: a setting that immersed them in the avant-garde where they could feel they belonged to a community of insiders whose taste was impeccable.

With Morgans, arguably the progenitor of the species, Ian Schrager and Steve Rubell transformed a seedy hotel in an unstylish midtown location into a lodging that attracted movie stars, entertainment moguls, models, and designers. With designer Philippe Starck, Royalton and The Paramount soon followed in Manhattan, and some years later, Los Angeles' Mondrian and Miami Beach's Delano. Schrager and Rubell were able to address this untapped market by instilling in their lodging properties the same theatrical magic and glamorous mystique that succeeded for them at their legendary nightclub, Studio 54. Like Studio 54, these properties depended on hip cachet and chic renown for their popularity.

More Than a Place to Sleep

Ian Schrager
Chairman
Ian Schrager Hotels
New York, New York

I believe that the hotel business has become predictable, banal, conformist, marbleized, and computerized—it is too generic and has descended to a commodity business. The only opportunity for distinguishing your product from another company's product is on price, like all commodities. The industry has lost touch with its customers. Its traditions and formulas have become outdated. We have the same dislocation and void in the market as twenty-five years ago when my late partner, Steve Rubell, and I reacted to cultural shifts that were emerging at the time and conceptualized Morgans, the first boutique hotel. There was a huge opportunity to create a new genre of hotel that could not be pigeon-holed into a specific and traditional business classification. There is something wrong when you stay at a hotel in Los Angeles and it is exactly the same hotel as when you go to London or Miami. A hotel should have a sense of time and place, and that was our opportunity. There hadn't been a new idea in the hotel business, I think, since Statler invented the modern hotel room a century ago and Portman developed the atrium hotel fifty years ago.

Boutique or lifestyle hotels have become trivialized by their explosive growth. The industry has created a Frankenstein. The idea behind the boutique hotel, as I saw it, was meant to touch people emotionally and viscerally and offer guests a truly unique experience. The idea has been lost with the huge number of watered-down versions we have today. I want to bring it back in an updated version and elevate it to a cultural experience for the modern-day traveler. These travelers now expect truly unique experiences and not merely a place to sleep.

My new venture, PUBLIC, is a new breed of hotel. Its fundamental attributes are an innovative, sophisticated, and authentic style; personalized, empathic, and "essential" service that makes people feel special; lasting comfort with complete functionality; all at a tremendous value. For the first time, this type of hotel experience will be available to everyone and anyone who wants it. What is unusual is that it is inclusive, rather than exclusive. I have taken the best from the luxury segment, the best from the boutique/lifestyle set, and the best from the limited-service model and created a new kind of hotel where everything has been rethought and every original idea updated. This brand will be defined by the unique experience it creates rather than by a business classification or price point.

PUBLIC will offer both great value and service. With no traditions to uphold and a new set of priorities, I will start with a blank canvas and push the industry in a new direction. Hotels have been predicated upon the mass market model. There was a virtue in everything being the same; in coming up with an idea and "cookie-cutting" it across the country. Holiday Inn advertisements a few years ago had Kemmons Wilson's tag line: "The best surprise is no surprise." For me, there is nothing better than a good surprise when you go into a hotel and can have fun there. Well, that is what we're trying to do, come up with something that hasn't been done before. Treat a hotel as more than just a place to sleep—a place for somebody to have fun, a visual feast. Walk inside and see something that you haven't seen before. Walk in the lobby and excite people, be able to cut the electricity in the air. Offer something indefinable, the same kinds of things that make you want to purchase a car or buy a house or pick a mate. I wasn't looking to do a hotel for 100 million people. I was looking to do a hotel that I would like and, by chance, there would be other people out there who also would like it.

My hotels never were about design. Instead, they are about an approach, an experience. It's something the industry never understood. I have seen far too many over-designed and overly self-conscious hotels in the marketplace; instead, I opted for a restrained, refined, and classically cool approach to PUBLIC's design. It's a new simplicity—a "new chic," a more "sincere chic"—tasteful and understated without attitude. At PUBLIC, service matters most. But the key point of differentiation is in the kind and quality of services it offers. The brand will only offer services that matter, those that guests really want and need rather than an array of superfluous services they do not use. This marks a new approach devoid of excess and a rejection of the old-fashioned idea of what "luxury" means to people. There is no pretense here, just effortless, timeless, purist design providing a relaxed vibe and familiar atmosphere that feels like home.

Table 3.1 Distinction among boutique, design, and lifestyle hotels

Key features	Boutique hotels	Design hotels	Lifestyle hotels
Size	Below 100–150 rooms, although number is increasing (important feature)	"Smaller" than large chain hotels (feature not critical)	"Smaller" than large chain hotels (feature not critical)
Location	Mainly urban and city-center locations, but can be anywhere	Mainly urban and city-center locations, but can be anywhere	Mainly urban and city-center locations, but can be anywhere
Type of building	Most have historic element (conversion)	Most have historic element (conversions), increasingly also greenfield projects	Most have historic element (conversions), increasingly also greenfield projects
Design	Individual design (any style)	Individual, contemporary and modern design	Individual, contemporary design
Ownership/ management	Rather owner-operated	Rather owner-operated, increasingly also chain-operated	Rather owner-operated, increasingly also chain-operated
Quality level	Upscale to luxury	Anything between budget and luxury	Anything between budget and luxury
Facilities, services	Diverse facilities (small scale), personal service	Depending on quality level/category, personal service	Depending on quality level/category, personal service

Source: L. Hochedlinger, "Are design hotels more attractive real estate investments than traditional hotels?" unpublished Master's thesis, Danube University, 2010.

Attracting trendsetters and celebrities, design hotels have ushered in the return of the hotel lobby as a downtown social gathering spot, an important urban function on the wane since the grand hotels of the Golden Age, when hotels were a city's epicenter of fashion, politics, and high society. Grand hotels have long been associated with their stylish interiors. Although at a different scale but in greater quantity, this new attention to innovative style in many ways is a return to the grandeur of nineteenth-century hotels: cosmopolitan, elegant, and distinctive; a culture of design.

In the 1980s and 1990s, the term that was most often used to describe these hotels was "boutique hotels." But by Webster's definition a boutique is "small, fashionable, and independent." Dissatisfied that the implication that you had to be small in order to be considered a boutique hotel, many developers sought other terms more appropriate to their enterprises.

Fashion hotels, architecture hotels, and avant-garde hotels are just some of the terms applied to the burgeoning segment; however, the two most common substitutes for boutique hotels became lifestyle hotels and design hotels.

A number of theorists claim that there really is no difference between these three categories; however, others do find the terms useful in defining sub-segments of the genre. For instance, some claim the following distinctions (see Table 3.1):

- *Design hotels* tend to focus on innovative, experimental, or unconventional design. They can position themselves in the market anywhere from budget to luxury.
- *Boutique hotels*, though tasteful, are less unconventional in design and tend toward smaller renovated properties. They mostly cater to the upper-upscale segment.
- *Lifestyle hotels* may have qualities of both design or boutique hotels but differentiate themselves by paying particular attention to delivering an entertaining atmosphere and personalized service.

Development and Planning Considerations

Beauty as we feel it is something indescribable: what it is or what it means can never be said.

(George Santayana)

Researchers have found a high correlation between properties that profess to focus on architectural design and their profitability. The conclusion they reach is that investment in sophisticated architecture and design pays off. Even though operating costs exceed industry standards, design hotels still achieve higher revenues and profit levels than non-design hotels. Still, analysts seeking to quantify the level of *design-ness* of a property are stymied by the intangibles, attempting to answer questions as impossible to answer as "What is art?" or "What is beauty?"

"Architecture, design, service, gastronomy and lots of intangible qualities must come together like pieces of a puzzle to create a coherent picture. That is what distinguishes it from just any boutique hotel" (Carl Sendlinger, founder of Design Hotels AG).

"Atmosphere" and "ambience" are terms that have particular meaning for this segment, since they imply more than just physical design attributes and expand to include sound, scent, emotion, and, very importantly, interaction. Public spaces in design hotels take on particular importance for this reason. Restaurants and bars are very important features. They are places to see and be seen. While design hotels showcase the personal tastes of the hotel owners, the architects, and the designers behind them, they also define the guest's personality and preferences and facilitate projecting an image for the guest that they wish others to perceive.

Size

The term "boutique" connotes smallness and has been most often used to refer to small, intimate hotels. While many automatically use "boutique" to refer to a hotel with fewer than 100 rooms, this does not accurately portray the genre. Three forerunners of this burgeoning hotel type in New York City opened larger: Morgan's Hotel with 113, Royalton with 170, and The Paramount with 600 keys. Hence, from inception, design hotels have had much more to do with avant-garde design and stylish cutting-edge operation than size. The original W Hotel on Lexington Avenue in Manhattan, the first of a rapidly expanding global brand, sought to capitalize on the design hotel mystique while achieving the economies of scale in both development and operation that larger hotels generally enjoy. The challenge for developers of large design hotels is to maintain the high level of personalized service characteristic of this segment.

With 814 rooms, Bella Sky Hotel located in Ørestad, a progressive new town development near Copenhagen, is the Nordic region's largest hotel and among the largest design hotels internationally. To avoid the impersonal and formal impression associated with most large hotels, 3XN Architects incorporated a classical Scandinavian design approach where simplicity, functionality, and high quality are the hallmarks.

With Zen-like simplicity, the Kimber Modern Hotel in Austin, Texas, represents the opposite end of the size spectrum for design hotels, with only five guestrooms and one suite. Burton Baldridge Architects tailored the micro-hotel to a sloping site, tucking a few parking spots beneath the guestrooms and incorporating a lushly landscaped courtyard.

While design hotels have been thought of generally as upscale properties, many developers find opportunity at the economy end of the market. In converting an original YMCA building to the 1,000-room Hudson Hotel in New York, the developer made the decision not to gut the interior in order to combine rooms, thereby keeping the original tiny 136 sq ft (12.8 sq m) room configurations intact and construction costs low in order to create an affordable alternative

Bella Sky Hotel, Copenhagen, Denmark
Leaning 15 degrees in opposite directions, the twin towers of the Bella Sky Hotel in Copenhagen's Ørestad region give dramatic expression to what 3XN Architects refer to as the "New Nordic Cool." The hotel is built next to the largest conference center in Scandinavia.

Kimber Modern Hotel, Austin, Texas (top)
Perfectly tailored to its sloping triangular site, the minimalist hotel comprises five rooms and one suite, with simple common areas opening to a lushly landscaped courtyard.

Missoni Hotel, Edinburgh, United Kingdom (right)
Missoni's fashion trademark of colorfully patterned fabrics and prints defines the interior of the hotel, while Matteo Thun's architecture renders a playful weave of fenestration and simple yet elegant form.

hotel. Drawing inspiration from a private cabin on an upscale yacht, the Philippe Starck–designed hotel delivers high-style and panache to budget travelers. A number of economy brands have emerged to capture this market with design-centric, albeit no-frills, offerings including Yotel, citizenM, Motel One, Big Sleep, and Roomz.

Design hotels on the luxury end of the segment cater to an upscale clientele desiring a high degree of luxury and personalized service. Fashion hotels, those that bear the name of top-of-the-line fashion houses, are priced at the top end of the luxury segment as exemplified by the super-deluxe Palazzo Versace on Australia's Gold Coast. Missoni, Armani, and Bulgari all have branded properties and are expanding rapidly in the luxury sector, where luxury consumers are invited to buy not only the product but the way of life associated with it. They are encouraged not only to wear the brand but to live the lifestyle corresponding to it.

Housed in a skillfully designed but understated modern building by the Milanese architect Matteo Thun, the Missoni Hotel Edinburgh interiors are adorned from top to bottom with the colorful patterned fabrics that are the signature of the fashion design giant. As if inserting a bit of the Milan fashion scene into Edinburgh's Royal Mile, the hotel's Cucina and Bar serves as an Italian café by day and cocktail bar by night.

New Construction and Renovation

Historically, the attraction to develop design hotels may be at least partially attributable to the number of older hotels that could be refurbished for far less construction cost than building from scratch. Part of the reason that many cities have so many of these hotels is a large inventory of older hotels that could be cheaply acquired and upgraded. In the absence of suitable hotels to renovate, developers have also turned to adaptive reuse of outmoded downtown office buildings and other industrial buildings. However, the towering success of the segment has led many developers to construct hotels from the ground up. New design hotels promote the architecture itself as integral to, or in many cases the essential element of, the design concept.

Conversion of an existing hotel or adapting another building type for hotel use is often met with necessary compromise to the hotel program due to inherent flaws such as small slow elevators, inadequate back-of-house area, irregularly spaced windows and columns, and antiquated building systems. These inefficiencies can ultimately affect guest satisfaction and profitability. On the other hand, in a new building the programmed elements can be accurately planned for and properly tailored to hotel operations and, as increasingly called for, to brand standards. These advantages, coupled with the opportunity to create dynamic and exciting new architecture, help explain the increasing number of new-build design hotels.

Once the tallest office building in Boston, the nineteenth-century 14-story Ames Building was converted by the Rockwell Group to a 120-room design hotel. The designer merged historical elements of the existing structure with dramatic new lighting, furnishings, and finishes to achieve a unique and unusual composition that complements the historic fabric of the building while introducing theatricality and innovative design.

Ames Hotel, Boston, Massachusetts
Built in the nineteenth century, the 14-story office building of the railroad magnate was once the tallest building in Boston. Rockwell Group drew inspiration from the building's rich industrialist history in transforming it into a fashionable 120-room design hotel.

Hotel OMM, Barcelona, Spain
In contrast to the sensuous modulations of the front façade, shown here, the rear façade is composed as a rigid geometry of retractable horizontal metal bars, supporting a curtain of vegetation in front of private balconies.

The developers and architects for the Mondrian SoHo, faced with a tight urban site, high land costs, and onerous zoning restrictions, created a hybrid scheme where the existing 12-story load-bearing brick and riveted steel manufacturing building was partially demolished and structurally reinforced to support 13 new guestroom floors in order to fit the requisite program for the hotel. The resulting polished 25-story steel and white metal-clad tower houses the surprisingly sumptuous and thematically exotic interiors.

Forming an important new component of the historic urban street wall, the artistic expression of the newly constructed 91-room Hotel OMM is borne on its articulated façade. Its skin is made up of curved stainless steel modules clad with limestone appearing to

have been cut to create a number of slits which have been "peeled back," curling outwards like the pages of a book. The direction of the opening takes account of both the view and the proper orientation to the mid-day sun. It also serves as a screen that keeps the interior private and acts as an acoustic barrier against the considerable traffic noise from the street.

An early new construction design hotel, Chambers, a 77-room luxury hotel on West 56th Street in New York City, metaphorically captures the ambience of a renovated SoHo loft building with exposed sprinkler pipes and track lighting against raw concrete ceilings and polished concrete bathroom floors. Even as a new building meeting the exacting demands of the facilities program, the appealing character of adaptive reuse was accomplished.

(continued p. 62)

——— Case Study ———

Chambers Hotel, New York, New York
Architect and Interior Designer: Rockwell Group
and Adams Soffes Wood

Chambers has the distinction of being one of the earliest new-build boutique hotels. With the term "boutique" primarily associated with avant-garde transformations of dreary underperforming hotels or the stylish adaptive reuse of existing buildings, but with all of the design fireworks happening on the interior, Chambers led a trend that also emphasized avant-garde design of the building exterior as an important element in a genre we now refer to as design hotels.

Situated on a narrow mid-town site in Manhattan, the 15-story building steps back from the street in response to the city's strict zoning parameters, resulting in private terraces for several of the hotel's 77 guestrooms and suites. The building's façade is clad in Macedonian limestone and punctuated by brushed-aluminum French doors opening to stylized glass and blackened steel balconette railings. At street level the lobby is a double-story space with a vaulted ceiling and wrapped with a mezzanine library that is accessed by a sculptured stair that winds around a glass-enclosed fireplace. Four stout leather-clad columns modulate the space. The tableau of activity in the lobby is on display to the street through a sleek two-story transparent glass façade. Conversely the street life is made part of the lobby. The visitors' arrival experience is choreographed as they enter through a pair of colossal walnut doors carved in a basket-weave pattern, into a dark, compressed vestibule before emerging into the small but surprisingly spacious-feeling lobby. Guests are brought to their rooms via one of two glass-enclosed elevators that look out onto the raw concrete shaft with counterweights and traveling cables.

The lobby and mezzanine library function also as an art gallery as the walls are filled with original and site-specific artwork. The hotel itself exhibits over 400 pieces of art by some 100 artists. Each of the 12 guestroom-floor corridors is a commissioned work of art. Artist and film-maker John Waters filled one corridor with life-size photos of women's shoes hung only inches above the floor. Each of the guestrooms is fashioned as an artist's loft containing a minimum of three original pieces per room. The guestroom design evokes the rough-rich urban vibe of SoHo loft-living with raw concrete ceilings, exposed sprinkler pipes, and track-lighting.

The architects, Rockwell Group and Adams Soffes Wood, collaborated on fitting the owner's ambitious program onto a very restricted site by carefully budgeting the limited available zoning floor area (ZFA). To avoid using up valuable allotted floor area, the restaurant and boardroom were placed below grade in a double height sky-lit space beneath the rear yard. The saved ZFA permitted an additional four guestrooms in the tower. In order to provide the necessary back-of-house and mechanical spaces, three cellars were required. But that was not enough. The architects were able to gain an additional 2,000 sq ft (186 sq m)

Chambers Hotel

Chambers Hotel, lobby entrance

Chambers Hotel, bar and lobby

in the basement by utilizing a little-known provision that permits owners to lease space beneath the sidewalks from the city for a small annual rent. Space utilization in the hotel tower was also optimized with a tight core and stairs at the ends of a short corridor leading to eight rooms per floor on the lower floors and a single duplex penthouse unit occupying the top two floors. The award-winning Chambers penthouse opens to a generous private terrace overlooking West 56th Street.

Chambers Hotel, lobby

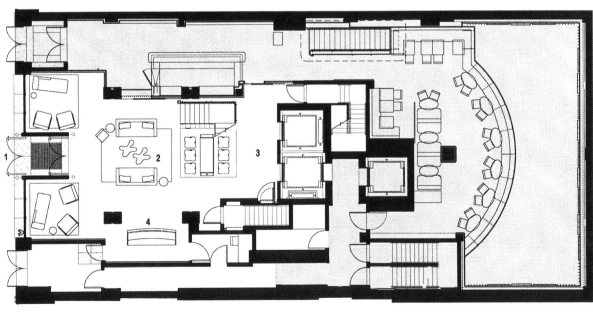

Ground Floor Plan

1- Hotel Entry
2- Lobby Lounge
3- Elevator Lobby
4- Check -In Desk

0 1' 5' 10' 20' 30' 40'

Independent to Chain

In response to the overwhelming success of the design hotel segment, international hotel companies entered the market with a number of new design brands that profess to offer the same attractive elements as independent hotels but with the advantages that come with being affiliated with a major hotel company, i.e., synergies in purchasing, marketing, sales, and staffing. Starwood's W brand boasts over sixty luxury properties worldwide, operating or planned, and continues to expand. In addition to W, Starwood has Aloft and Element to capture the limited-service side of the design hotel market. Other major hotel companies with design hotel brands include IHG with the Indigo brand, Hyatt with the Andaz brand, and Marriott with the Edition brand.

To maintain a competitive advantage with the chain-operated design hotel brands, independent hotels have flocked to consortia and online platforms that specialize in design hotels and can expose the independent properties to a wider market. Consortia such as Tablet Hotels and Design Hotels AG represent and market curated selections of hundreds of independent design-centric hotels around the world by emphasizing their cultural authenticity, thought-provoking design, and extraordinary architecture.

Semiramis Hotel, Athens, Greece
Entering the hotel, guests pass through a glowing colored-glass cube that leads into the lobby, where color-changing glass walls radiate with subtle motion. The Rashid-designed interiors are filled with vibrant colors of pink, lime green, orange, and yellow on a white background, with colored terrazzo slabs, glass tiles, teak wood, epoxy floors, custom-printed carpet, colored glass, Rashid-patterned wall coverings, and printed laminate surfaces.

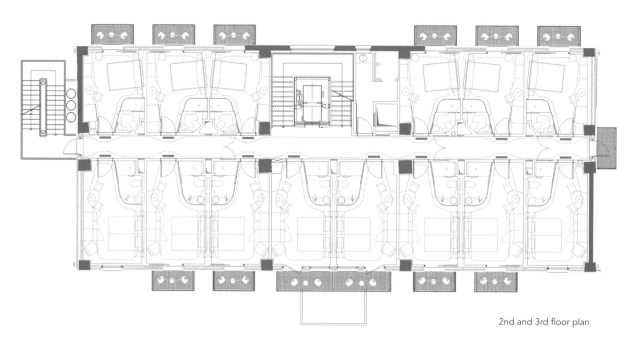

2nd and 3rd floor plan

The wonderfully eccentric, quirky and artistic creation of Karim Rashid for the Semiramis Hotel in Athens, Greece, while an exciting and stylish design hotel, still benefits from the widened market and reservation calls through its listing consortium, Design Hotels AG. Raffles Hotels, with its rich history in super-luxury hotels and resorts, expands that legacy in the design hotel segment with Philippe Starck's reinvention of Le Royal Monceau. And a small-town Mississippi manufacturer, Viking Stoves, creates a masterpiece—unaffiliated and independent—design hotel with ForrestPerkins's creation of The Alluvian in Greenwood, Mississippi.

Modern and Traditional

While one of the earliest examples of design hotels, Anouska Hemple's Blakes Hotel in London, was decidedly traditional in style, her treatment of the style was so eclectic and eccentric one would hardly recognize it as traditional design. It was, in fact, the very inventiveness with which she interpreted traditional elements that drew attention to it as unique and cutting-edge. On the other hand the skillful period renovation of New York's Algonquin Hotel by Alexandra Champalimaud, while highly creative in capturing the unique spirit of that famous hotel, through its high-style atmospherics and fashionable ambience could easily fit the design hotels' *leitmotif*.

Far more prevalent, contemporary design motifs are the palette of design hotels. The segment is replete with examples of those that embrace modernism in their architecture and interiors and establish a new and fresh imagery. Lukas Hochedlinger and Susanne Kraus-Winkler propose that design hotels can be divided into three basic groups as follows:

- *Type A:* Unique hotels that are fully designed by one designer from the outside to the inside. (Example: the Loisium Hotel in Langenlois, Austria, architecture and interior design by Steven Holl.)
- *Type B:* Hotels that are designed by multiple well-known designers who contribute their names like brands. (Example: the Silken Puerta América Hotel in Madrid, Spain, architecture by Jean Nouvel, interior designs by Zaha Hadid, Sir Norman Foster, David Chipperfield, Arata Isozaki, Richard Gluckman, and others.)
- *Type C:* Hotels that offer a modern and contemporary atmosphere through furniture, staff, etc. The name of the designer is not important, if there is one at all. (Examples: Roomz hotel Vienna, Motel One, and citizenM hotels.)

The Alluvian, Greenwood, Mississippi
ForrestPerkins served as design architect and interior designer in transforming a group of small-town buildings into a fashionable 50-room hotel. The original four-story Hotel Irving was combined with two adjacent retail buildings. Two additional floors were added to the retail buildings and a courtyard was carved out at the rear of the complex, providing necessary light and air to the guestrooms.

Le Royal Monceau, Paris, France
Philippe Starck's design for Le Bar Long in the heart of the hotel is a high, long, narrow, and luminous bar. The bartenders move behind the bar as customers sit face to face.

2. OBERGESCHOSS

0   1   5   10 m

Loisium Hotel, Langenlois, Austria
For this site in a gently south-sloping vineyard on the edge of the picturesque town, one hour west of Vienna, architect Steven Holl designed a new wine center and hotel. The project is composed of three parts: the existing 900-year-old wine vaults, which were made accessible to visitors, the Wine Center, and the Loisium Hotel Wine and Spa Resort. The ground-floor public spaces of the 82-room hotel are spatially transparent and flow to a generous courtyard oriented to views of the vineyard.

Silken Puerta América, Madrid, Spain
While the façade of the hotel was designed by the French architect Jean Nouvel, each of the hotel's 12 floors contain guestrooms, elevator lobbies, restaurants, furniture, and accessories designed by world-renowned architects and design studios, including Arata Isozaki, Norman Foster, Marc Newson, Ron Arad, Richard Gluckman, Javier Mariscal, Victorio & Lucchino, and Zaha Hadid. Appropriately, Puerta América bills itself as "12 floors with 19 stars."

Design and Planning Considerations

The value of good hotel design is no longer equated with use of expensive materials. Design hotels with linoleum floors and chrome-plated fittings are getting the same average daily rate (ADR) as conventional luxury hotels with marble floors and brass fittings. Quality design and architecture are essential values of the service that the design hotel must deliver. Notwithstanding the old adage, good design doesn't cost more to build—it may in fact cost more in design fees as developers compete for celebrity designers to add market appeal to their properties and to stay ahead of the fashion curve. Frank Gehry, Philippe Starck, Christian Liaigre, Rafael Viñoly, David Chipperfield, David Rockwell, Richard Meier, Jean Nouvel, and others are in high demand to provide prestige value as well as originality and vision. Even fashion design giants Sonia Rykiel, Todd Oldham, and Giorgio Armani are courted for exclusive designs in this domain.

As we have seen, design styles for this niche segment are as varied as the markets they serve. Whatever the market, the hotel designer's mandate is to bring to the project a high level of creativity and originality; to design an ambience that makes guests feel that they are staying in an exciting place where sleeping is the last thing on their minds. There is, however, a danger of letting innovative design approaches overshadow other fundamentals of hotel design. Some fall into the trap of style over substance. In one example, guestrooms were designed with the bed floating in the middle of the small room with a long narrow ledge very close to one side. Unfortunately this unique layout gave no room for the housekeeping staff to make the bed and resulted in the threat of a strike by the hotel union.

Historically, design hotel properties have had sub-functional back-of-house and administration areas with all emphasis going to visual pyrotechnics and hip persona. Since most early boutiques were renovations, they often inherited poor conditions from the start. Cramped basements, slow elevators, and lack of loading facilities are inherent conditions that cause undue hardship to the operation of these properties. The experimental nature of this type of hotel also presents unusual design challenges for operations and back-

Hotel Marqués de Riscal, Elciego, Spain
Located in the vineyard of the medieval town of Elciego, the 43-suite hotel was designed by Frank Gehry as a series of rectilinear elements, clad in sandstone, combined with spectacular curving panels of gold and pink titanium, and with mirror-finish stainless steel reflecting the colors of the winery. The hotel's guestrooms are distributed across two wings connected by a stunning glass bridge.

of-house areas. Both an all-white guestroom décor and bellmen in Armani suits place added burdens on the housekeeping department. Fresh exotic fruit in the room requires specialized food and beverage (F&B) service. Pet goldfish for the guests may require an aquarium department for one chain of boutiques. Demand for high-level personalized service in luxury boutiques normally requires a much higher staff-to-guest ratio that impacts all employee areas. Like any hotel, the back-of-house and administration areas need to be tailored to the operational style of the hotel. With boutiques this can be in many ways as unique and original as the physical design.

To remain economically viable, design hotels are finding it important to adopt and promote principles of environmental responsibility

Hotel Palomar, Philadelphia, Pennsylvania

The Architects Building was designed in 1929 by French-American architect Paul Philippe Cret, along with a group of 20 other architects and firms. The 24-story building is Kimpton Hotels' first LEED-certified hotel. A striking example of Art Deco architecture, the building was thoughtfully renovated by Gensler, with its historic elements incorporated into the design.

Bardessono Hotel and Spa, Yountville, California (right)

Designed to achieve LEED Platinum, the highest standard for environmental design, the 62-room luxury resort was conceived by architects at WATG with a number of sustainable methods, including gorgeous woods used throughout the hotel that were milled from salvaged trees, geothermal heating and cooling, rooftop solar panels, and occupancy sensors in the guestrooms. Operationally the hotel continues its environmental responsibility with sustainable practices including use of organic linens and cleaning supplies, recycling and composting, carbon-fiber bicycles, and on-site productive organic gardens .

and to institute green initiatives in the development and operation of their properties. One of the pioneering design hotel companies, Kimpton Hotels, earned the Governor's Environmental and Economic Leadership Award from the California Environmental Protection Agency for its sustainable initiatives. And the Kimpton Hotel Palomar in Philadelphia became one of the first design hotels to achieve LEED Gold certification in its adaptive reuse of Philadelphia's historic Architects Building. The Bardessono Hotel and Spa in California's Napa Valley, designed by WATG Architects, is a new-build 62-room luxury design resort hotel that was the third hotel in the world to achieve LEED Platinum certification. The architects integrated advanced environmental technology including geothermal heating and cooling, rooftop solar panels, and occupancy sensors in the guestrooms. With the highest achievement in sustainable accomplishment Bardessono has set the bar for environmentally responsible design hotels.

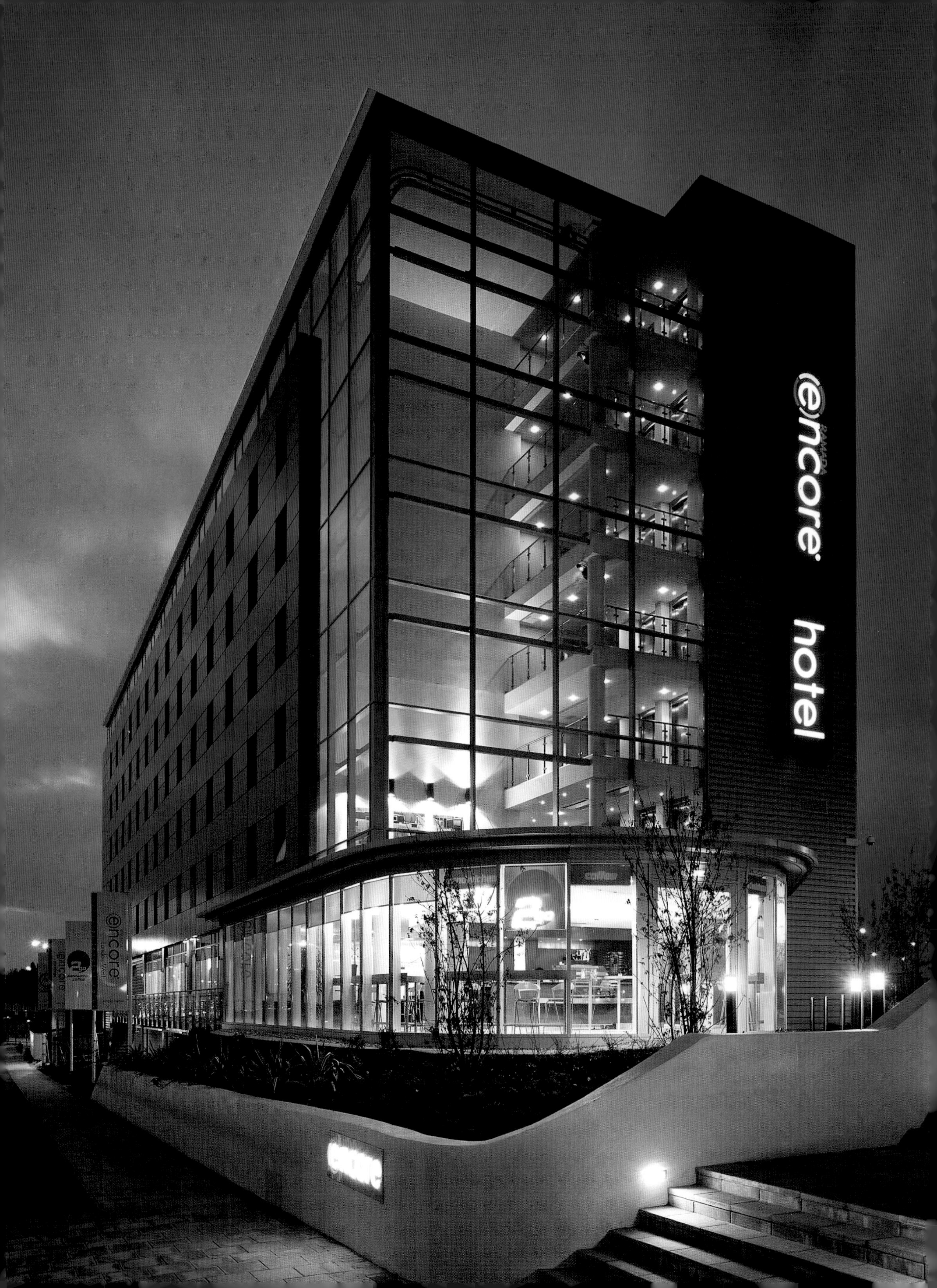
encore
hotel
encore

Suburban Hotels

In his 1898 treatise, *Garden Cities of Tomorrow*, Sir Ebenezer Howard described three options for living in the industrial age: town, country, or town-country. In promoting his utopian model he noted that cities had become alienating, unsanitary, and unlivable while the country, offering natural beauty, fresh air, and healthfulness, lacked the social advantages of city life. Early suburban or pseudo-urban development sought to offer a refuge from the noise, dirty air, crime, and congestion of late-nineteenth-century urban life while mitigating the cultural deficiencies of the countryside.

The Riverside Hotel, possibly the first suburban hotel, was built in 1870, 9 miles (13 km) west of downtown Chicago in Riverside, Illinois, an early commuter suburb planned by Frederick Law Olmsted and Calvert Vaux. Riverside was built in 1868 as a new suburban community combining "the beauties and healthy properties of a park with the conveniences and improvements of the city." Overlooking the Des Plaines River, the hotel was designed by noted Chicago architect William LeBaron Jenney, who also designed most of Riverside's houses. Even though this elite suburban development was tied directly to downtown Chicago by the Burlington Railroad line and a limited-service parkway also designed by Olmsted and Vaux, the developers went bankrupt, as it was considered at that time to be too far out of town.

Following World War II major investment in the interstate highway system and billions of dollars made available through the U.S. Federal Housing Administration and the Veterans Administration for suburban home development fueled explosive suburban residential development. By 1950, 1.5 million new house starts per year in the United States were spurred on by the post-war suburban baby boom. With expansive residential suburban development came the growth of the large-scale regional shopping center, drawing patrons from a wide geographic area and further fueling suburban expansion.

In the 1950s, industry and commerce began relocating near major highways in the suburbs as trucking superseded railways. Suburban sites with good highway access, lower land costs, plenty of parking, attractive landscaping, and nearby services spurred development of industrial parks and research and development centers. Eventually corporations began to realize advantages in decentralizing and relocating to the suburbs that were cleaner, less congested, less expensive, and safer than the city.

By the 1970s, mid-rise apartment buildings, business and science parks, shopping malls, satellite universities, sports complexes, airport commercial developments, entertainment centers, theme parks, research institutes, industrial parks, medical complexes, and a wide variety of hotels made up the rich fabric of suburbia. As commuting patterns changed to accommodate the increasing population who

Ramada Encore, London West, United Kingdom
Today's suburban hotels are incorporating the same high-style exterior design elements that have been more typical of boutique urban properties.

live in one suburb and work, shop, and play in another, highway interchanges became the epicenters of commercial development. No longer just an interchange, the highway cloverleaf had become a destination in and of itself. Naturally a strong demand arose for hotels near this burgeoning suburban business energy.

With the exception of resort hotels, prior to the 1940s most hotels were located in cities and towns. As highways superseded railroads the market for accommodations along the roadways and near residential suburbs vastly expanded. Early hotels in suburbia took the form of motels and motor inns catering mostly to the needs of highway motorists. Motels located near airports served airline crews and stranded passengers and also provided an inexpensive alternative to downtown lodging. As business activity in the suburbs increased, suburban hotels took on a different role and began to resemble downtown hotels with meeting rooms, restaurants, shops, fitness facilities, and other full-service amenities. In some suburban markets, these projects have come to resemble the mixed-use developments common in downtown areas, combining residential, office, retail, and hotel space in a single development.

Expansion of suburban growth, especially around airports, malls, and business parks, generated a multitude of user segments and price categories. To a large extent the broad-reaching market segmentation that now defines the hospitality industry grew out of the diversity reflected in the suburban hotel markets. Some hotel chains have as many as nine separate brands tailored to sub-segment markets all found with suburban applications. The chains, through extensive market research, have customized their products for wide-ranging cost categories and fine-tuned market targets beyond leisure and business travel definitions to create highly specific niche products. They have even found that some of these brands that were born in the suburbs can be applied in urban markets where there is demand for relatively inexpensive, quality lodging at a room rate that supports the higher development costs of these locations.

Selecting What Goes Into "Select Service"

Jim Anhut
Chief Development Officer, Americas
InterContinental Hotels Group (IHG)
Atlanta, Georgia

The term "select service" began cropping up among hotel developers in the first decade of the twenty-first century, marking another evolutionary milestone for our business. After essentially solving the problem of inconsistency that plagued the industry through the mid-twentieth century, hoteliers first expanded their offerings, trying to be all things to all travelers. By the early 1990s, attention had shifted to designing different properties for different travel occasions. If a significant segment of the traveling population doesn't want a restaurant, lounge, or meeting space, why not build a hotel without those things? And the "limited-service" concept took form.

This idea was refined to create the "select-service" designation—that is, a hotel without a food and beverage outlet, or with a very restricted offering, and a small amount of meeting space. The nomenclature, though, is unfortunate. We are in the service business, after all. Which part of "service" are we choosing to select or limit? Perhaps "focused service" or "brand-appropriate" hotels might be better, more accurate monikers.

The challenge for the architect and designer, therefore, is to go beyond yesterday's thinking about generally accepted constraints of this segment. Instead, first peel the onion all the way back to the product and service elements. Then examine these within the context of the constituencies for whom the hotel is being designed: guest, brand, owner, employees, and environment.

Clearly the guest is in first position. It's critical to accommodate this segment's mainstream customer needs and expectations: restorative sleep, an invigorating shower, and breakfast to get the day started right. Brand considerations take this a step further, addressing the consumer's emotional as well as practical expectations—"I feel smart that I stayed here last night. I feel good about what I paid." The sweet spot over-indexes on what matters to guests and delivers nothing that doesn't.

That brings up the owner perspective. There's a reason select-service hotels are a popular concept that continued to be developed even when the economy fell into crisis. They are efficient to build and generate a good return on investment (ROI). Solid design supports this, weighing service levels and price points against total investment.

An often-overlooked constituency are the employees. The hotel's design should take into account the multi-tasking required of the people who deliver the service, especially since select-service staff-to-guest room ratios are usually 1:3 rather than the 1:1 common in big full-service properties. Making task areas proximate in the lobby, selecting easy-to-clean fabrics and finishes, ensuring employee break rooms and restrooms are not an afterthought—all belong in the design consideration set.

The final element is the environment. As developers and designers, we're just beginning to push the envelope in this arena, through technology and materials selection that produce efficient, sustainable, user-friendly buildings that conserve natural resources while accomplishing their purpose.

Effective designers and architects think holistically about the needs of all five constituencies. They continually challenge themselves to find better ways to solve these needs within the select-service format and to create good design that produces a solid ROE: that's return on equity, employees, effort, and environment.

General Design and Planning Considerations

The design of suburban hotels in many respects is less challenging than it is for their downtown counterparts. Lower real estate values and better land availability result in significantly larger building sites. Larger parcels of land and less restrictive zoning in most cases allow for more flexibility in massing and make functional layouts easier to achieve than can be done on tight urban sites. The larger, less restrictive sites have many advantages, including better vehicular arrival and departure areas, convenient and plentiful parking, sensible lobby layouts based on optimum elevator core position and column spacing, the ability to arrange for circulation of service vehicles and loading facilities out of view from the main guest entrance and outdoor areas, and room enough for outdoor recreation facilities.

Zoning regulations in the suburbs often mandate height and density restrictions appropriate to the regional architectural character. The ability to spread out over the site lends itself to lower-rise construction and therefore less expensive building methods, further reducing project costs. For larger properties, less restrictive regulations governing the placement and configuration of the guestroom tower favor a more logical column grid which frees up long span areas suitable for lobbies, function space, and indoor pools. More flexible tower placement also permits the guest elevator core and service core to be located in closer proximity to their related functions and leads to a more efficient back-of-house configuration.

While the standard 2 acre (0.8 hectare) site remains typical for most select-service properties, designs that work on sites as small as 1.3 acres (0.5 hectare) provide developers with a broader range of options for small or costly markets. Economy hotels may require a slightly smaller site, while office-park sites may be substantially larger to accommodate extensive landscaping and outdoor recreation.

Visibility, Accessibility, and Signage

Because walk-in guests without reservations account for a higher proportion of sales at suburban hotels than is typically the case for downtown and resort hotels, prominent visibility to travelers from surrounding roads continues to be a feature of successful suburban, airport, and roadside properties. Potential sites must be evaluated for their natural contours, visibility of building signage, or other alternatives to freestanding signs, particularly in communities where there are strict signage laws. For similar reasons, entrance approach patterns providing for ease of auto access and flow for the traveler including adequate deceleration lanes, stacking space, and turning radii are equally essential.

Parking

With almost total reliance on car access, a suburban location's ability to develop its full potential for occupancy and outside business for the food and beverage outlets and function spaces is often governed by its ability to provide adequate on-site parking.

(Peak parking needs for guests, visitors, and employees may be established for each hotel based on formula given in the Design Guide, see p. 369).

Suburban hotels generally require about 1.2 cars per room or about 50 percent more parking than that of the average downtown property. Parking facilities should be sized to meet peak-hour requirements, which will vary depending on the hotel's concept and market. Properties that cater primarily to business travelers will see their busiest parking hours late on weekday evenings whereas extended-stay hotels in leisure-oriented markets tend to have peak parking demand on weekend nights. One of the advantages of mixed-use developments is that some of the parking space assigned to the office buildings can be used by the hotel during the overnight peaks, reducing overall requirements by up to 15 percent. However, peak parking hours for apartments and shopping malls prevent overlapping or significant sharing by a hotel.

Guestrooms

Guestrooms and their associated circulation and support space make up 75–85 percent of the total built area of most suburban hotels. Guestroom sizes for most select-service properties average about 325 sq ft (30 sq m) for transient hotels and 425 sq ft (39.5 sq m) for extended-stay concepts. By contrast, budget chains have reduced room sizes to roughly 230 sq ft (21 sq m) or less: Accor's "etap" brand has a standard guestroom size of only 135 sq ft (12.5 sq m) and a total build-out of 240 sq ft (23 sq m) per key. In Europe, it is not uncommon for select-service properties to have a room size as small as 235 sq ft (22 sq m), particularly if the hotel is an older building. Full-service airport and office-park hotels have similar space requirements to their urban location counterparts, namely guestrooms of 300–400 sq ft (27–37 sq m) and a total build-out of at least 575 sq ft (53 sq m) per key. The highly segmented suburban category gives travelers a choice depending on what they want to spend and how they want to spend it and provides a wide range of products for hotel developers with suburban sites of almost any size.

Increasing technical sophistication of business travelers and the explosion of information technology have produced a dramatic new emphasis in suburban hotels of all types. Guestrooms and public areas are made to function as office workspaces and wireless networking is an expected amenity at all price points. Guestroom furnishings are being designed to be reconfigured as needed to accommodate different work preferences. Guests also demand printing facilities, mobile device charging, easy connection to the in-room television to take advantage of its larger screen for work or presentations, and convenient spots at the bedside to place a tablet computer or e-reader.

Other Spaces

To be competitive and to meet the continually escalating demands of travelers, many suburban hotels have added amenities approaching those found in downtown hotels. At major airports, or regional shopping center or office-park hotels, food and beverage facilities and retail areas may be equivalent to those of the downtown hotel, while their meeting and function spaces average about 20 percent less and their lobbies and circulation spaces approximately 25 percent less than a full-service urban property. Lobbies, circulation space, and retail areas in small town and roadside hotels and motels are generally 50 percent less than those same spaces in suburban and airport hotels.

Sizing food and beverage facilities in suburban hotels is driven by the market and the brand or category. Food service is rarely offered at all in economy properties, but if provided it generally is a self-service breakfast with minimal hot offerings. In the select-service category, some brands have introduced a more sophisticated food and beverage program that offers light fare all day and, in some cases, alcohol in the evenings as a way of generating additional revenue and providing more upscale amenities, which allows these hotels to drive up the room rate. Full-service properties at airports and in office parks generally have only one table-service restaurant and one bar or lounge and sometimes supplement these with a self-service grab'n'go outlet to help handle peak demand for breakfast. Some properties have elected to forgo food and beverage operations altogether and lease portions of their sites to fast-food chains or freestanding restaurants to provide for guest needs at minimal cost or effort to the hotel.

Full-service airport and office-park hotels typically have 40–50 sq ft (3.7–4.6 sq m) of meeting space per key although properties in Asia tend to have much more. Select-service hotels may have only a fraction of this amount and roadside hotels require a great deal less meeting space—usually one small meeting space (less than 500 sq ft or 46 sq m) is all that is included in the program—and their administrative and service areas are about 20 percent smaller than those of other types of hotels since fewer guest services generally are required. Detailed space requirements and planning information are included in Chapter 14, pp. 305–311.

Roadside Hotels and Motels

Following World War I, when Americans first took to the road in great numbers, the need for roadside accommodations expanded dramatically. The majority of motorists were in search of convenience, economy, and informality not offered by the more upscale downtown hotels and so would choose from a variety of roadside inns, tourist cabins, and motor courts lining the major thoroughfares. These facilities often were a series of detached cabins operated by a family whose nearby home served as the registration office. Located on the outskirts of town, most offered a casual atmosphere, the convenience of parking next to your door, paying in advance, and leaving at any time without the check-out ritual or the need to tip.

Individual cabins of tourist courts were often dressed up in a variety of fanciful ways to catch the eye of passing motorists and to tantalize their imagination and fantasy. Wigwams, log cabins, igloos, adobe huts—these storybook cabins were perhaps hotel design's earliest examples of theme architecture. Less flamboyant cabins simply donned brightly colored roofs to be easily seen. In 1926, Arthur Heineman opened the Milestone Motel in San Luis Obispo, California, as a series of California-style bungalows and Mission-inflected services buildings, and immediately claimed credit for inventing the word *motel* by combining "motor" and "hotel" into a single memorable term.

The dollhouse-like freestanding cabins of early roadside hotels were eventually replaced by linear one-story structures housing rooms under a single continuous roof. This evolution of the building form might be traced to early prototypes of the 1930s where a guest's automobile was sheltered beneath a roof spanning between two cabins. Eventually, as lodging demand increased, these carports were closed in to make additional rooms, forming a string of connected rooms facing an open parking lot. Later, as the significant economies of construction and maintenance of this new form were realized, a second floor was added.

By the early 1930s many of these roadside lodgings gained unsavory reputations as lodgings of ill repute. "Hot sheet motels," as they were called, were rented by the hour, no questions asked. In a 1940 article titled "Camps of Crime," FBI chief J. Edgar Hoover declared that many motels were dens of vice and corruption that harbored "gangs of desperados who prey upon surrounding territories."

Following World War II, the expansion of the interstate highway system created an explosive demand for safe, clean, comfortable en route lodging. The potential of this lucrative market quickly drew the attention of hotel entrepreneurs like Kemmons Wilson, who developed a respectable chain of family-styled motels that he named Holiday Inn, after the popular Hollywood movie. Holiday Inn's chief innovation was the inclusion of a restaurant which made the facility more hotel-like, thus completing the evolution from tourist court to motel to motor hotel. By the late 1950s an explosion of motels, motor hotels, and motor inns were developed with chains such as Howard Johnson's, Travelodge, and Ramada Inn finding key locations on the new interstate highway system. By 1954 there were more motel rooms than hotel rooms in the United States and by 1972 the number doubled.

To differentiate themselves from one another, the major chains began to develop more elaborate suburban properties, adding swimming pools, coffee shops, gift shops, meeting rooms, and amenities normally associated with full-fledged hotels. This capital-intensive competition drove most of the mom-and-pop operators from the field but left a gap in the economy market. By the early 1960s a whole new generation of budget motels began to appear as stripped-down versions of the big chain products. Motel 6 rented, appropriately, for $6 per night. Days Inn advertised "luxury" budget rooms for $8 per night. By the mid-1970s segmentation and branding had rendered the word "motel" obsolete. No longer described in terms of their location on the highway, such products were now referred to by categories such as "limited-service budget hotels" or "mid-priced full-service," with new brand names ending with "Inn," "Lodge," "Hotel," or "Suites," but not "Motel." Advertising wizards produced a profusion of euphemisms to label budget/economy sector products, proffering "affordable, low-cost value" for "price-sensitive" customers.

Ace Hotel and Swim Club, Palm Springs, California
This innovative conversion of a 1965 motor hotel into a popular lifestyle destination for young travelers in the twenty-first century demonstrates the potential of the large amount of aging suburban hotel stock throughout the United States. The project combines vintage mid-century architecture with design elements from a variety of periods and styles.

Unfortunately the corporatization of the motel resulted in a bland uniformity of design that prompted *New York Times* critic Ada Louise Huxtable in 1973 to write *Hospitality and the Plastic Esthetic*, in which she condemned "the totally uniform and cheap consistency of taste and manufacture" of "the ubiquitous plastic room." But today a new appreciation of the unique design styles of early roadside motels has emerged. Entrepreneurs are trying to save some of the more architecturally interesting motels along historic Route 66, and a number of restored or replicated vintage motels such as Kate's Lazy Meadow in the Catskill Mountains of New York attract customers with a fondness for mid-century retro design. Others are converting aging roadside properties into high-style but low-cost lodging for young travelers.

To recapture markets turned off by both the higher prices of the more elaborate inns and the cheap, unimaginative designs of most budget motels, a new wave of well-managed economy lodging chains has unveiled inventive designs combining low rates with a fresher, more sophisticated ambience. New economy brands like the Tata Group's Ginger in India and Accor's HotelF1 in Europe feature very small rooms with carefully planned built-in furnishings that offer all the amenities of higher-end hotels in a very simple form, punctuated by bright colors on walls or bedding. Established U.S. brands have adopted a similar strategy. Motel 6's most recent look, dubbed "Phoenix," borrows the colors, materials, and filleted forms of mid-century design that were popular in upscale boutique hotels in the late 1990s and early 2000s.

One step above the economy brands are what are currently termed "select-service hotels." These are properties that offer higher-quality guestrooms and more public amenities than the economy brands but typically do not provide a table-service restaurant or other features of a full-service hotel. The select-service segment has seen tremendous growth in the past decade as developers have embraced the relatively low development and operating costs of

these properties relative to the rate they can command in many markets. Select-service hotels are commonly located in suburban locations because their smaller size allows them to remain profitable in markets with lower demand and their low-rise design fits into the suburban context effectively. However, developers have been having good success in creating high-rise select-service properties on tight urban sites as well.

In the past, select-service brands de-emphasized public spaces but the newest generation of these properties have multi-purpose lobbies that combine the check-in function with communal workspaces, quick-service dining and bar seating, a small retail area that sells sundries and ready-to-eat foods, and self-service business facilities such as printers, workstations, and interactive "concierge" screens. The designs of these lobby spaces are intended to support guest interaction and offer a high level of service with fewer employees. For example, Marriott re-envisioned its Courtyard by Marriott brand to make the lobby the functional as well as physical center of the hotel for guests. Four distinct guest activity zones—semi-private seating areas with dedicated televisions, a casual counter-service restaurant and bar, a business library with computers and printers, and a high-top communal table for group activity—combine in a single space that also offers a direct connection to an outdoor lounge area. A traditional check-in desk was replaced with short podiums intended to encourage employees to stand with the guest during interactions, and racks of brochures and area information were eliminated in favor of a wall-mounted touch-screen that guests can use to check weather and flight information, find local restaurants, or order ground transportation.

Today the select-service segment has also incorporated a more sophisticated visual style in the guestroom and public space interiors, and in some cases, on the building exterior. The low-rise, "residential"

(continued p. 76)

Motel 6 "Phoenix" Design Scheme
Design elements once associated solely with urban boutique hotels are now demanded by a broader market, including the suburban chain-hotel guest. Motel 6's current design scheme incorporates streamlined furniture, saturated colors, and rounded forms, a significant departure from earlier brand styles.

─── **Case Study** ──────────────────

Jupiter Hotel, Portland, Oregon
Architect: Skylab Architecture

Hotel development that recycles existing structures tends to adapt other building types to lodging uses. But developers Tod Breslau and Kelsey Bunker had a different vision: to rework a run-down 1960s motor lodge in a marginal Portland neighborhood and turn it into a "cultural boutique hotel." The site was within easy reach of the newly expanded Oregon Convention Center and its affordable environs attracted unique local shops, restaurants and entertainment that appealed to young creatives who appreciated the area's inexpensive and atmospheric housing. A hotel that spoke to this market and respected Portland's sustainable ethos was likely to be a success.

Jeff Kovel and his firm, Skylab Architecture, recognized that the target market was looking for an upbeat social experience on a budget. He transformed the motor lodge's central parking area into courtyard lounge space and gave the 81 exterior-corridor guestrooms a modern and playful look featuring low platform beds and wall-sized photomurals of American landscapes and cultural icons. The on-site 24-hour restaurant was given a radical makeover to create the Doug Fir Lounge, a popular restaurant, nightclub, and music venue. Fire pits in the courtyard extend the social atmosphere beyond the lounge and give the hotel "people buzz." The result has been a high-profile project that has received multiple design awards and achieves a higher average occupancy and room rate than its competitive set.

Jupiter Hotel, courtyard

Jupiter Hotel, guestroom

Jupiter Hotel, Doug Fir Lounge

Courtyard by Marriott "Refreshing Business" Lobby
The redesigned Courtyard lobby space serves as a social hub for guests, who can choose to use the dining areas, the communal table, or the popular "media pods" (shown at far right), either for interaction or for doing independent work in a shared environment.

style that was popular in the 1980s has been replaced by a cleaner, more geometric appearance. Starwood's aloft brand uses a distinctively shaped roof element—sometimes repeated on the porte cochère or inside the public spaces—as part of its trade dress, while the Hyatt Place and Ramada Encore brands have used a higher proportion of glass and exterior color in their façades to appear more modern and to increase visibility. Upgraded design features that are becoming more common in these properties and beginning to appear in the economy segment as well include:

- Self-service kiosks and business facilities;
- Flatscreen TVs in guestrooms and lobby spaces;
- Built-in work surfaces with high-quality wireless internet access;
- Improved bed linen programs;
- Bold color applied to interior walls and accent pieces;
- Minimal patterns on materials or finishes;
- Bed runners rather than bedspreads;
- Rounded shapes in furniture and fixtures;
- LED and colored lighting in public spaces and on the building exterior.

Efficiency of planning is important to profitability and about 80 percent of the built area is dedicated to rooms. Back-of-house areas rarely exceed 7 percent of gross hotel area because of the limited services offered in these properties. Recently, lobbies have grown slightly to accommodate seating areas and space for self-service breakfast or snacks but are still streamlined and need to be able to be operated with a minimal staff.

Airport Hotels

Airport terminals have been transformed from purely functional waystations to multi-use centers of commerce and culture, incorporating extensive malls, food and beverage outlets well beyond the traditional fast food kiosks, corporate meeting facilities, art galleries, museums, and, more than ever, elaborate and sophisticated hotels.

Some of the most interesting hotels built in recent years have been at or near airports. Formerly, most airport hotels were dowdy, inexpensive, and often noisy, catering to unlucky passengers on layover, pilots and airline personnel too tired to go into the city or with early morning departures, and guests avoiding the hassle and expense of staying downtown. While airport hotels still serve these markets, they have seen vast growth in business and leisure segments that now represent 85 percent of their guests. Today most hotel companies wouldn't dream of building a full-service airport hotel without significant meeting facilities (usually including a ballroom), self-service check-in kiosks, 24-hour business support, a health spa and fitness facility, upgraded rooms on a concierge or club level, at least two restaurants, and other upscale amenities previously limited to downtown hotels and resorts.

Much of the explosive growth in airport hotel development can be attributed to busy corporate executives asking, "When you only go from the airport to the hotel and the hotel back to the airport why would you want to stay anywhere else?" The international corporate world has come to favor meeting at airports where the location is ideal for business guests to fly in from different cities, hold their sessions, and be off in minutes, avoiding long trips into and out of downtown traffic congestion. As globalization of industry continues to fuel the pace and reach of business travel, amenities for the individual business traveler to work and meet on site are rapidly expanding.

Every major city airport now has a major "airport city" next to it. Architect Helmut Jahn noted that airports "in addition to their role of moving people and freight, have become self-sufficient economic and cultural nodes, micro-cities that are no longer dependent satellites of the old downtown."

Airport cities such as the 2.1 million sq ft (200,000 sq m) Circle at Zurich Airport in Switzerland are intended to maximize the potential of airport real estate. At the Denver International Airport, expanding demand has driven development of a second phase of what is the largest airport in the United States. Designed by Santiago Calatrava, this new mixed-use facility will incorporate a 500-room hotel and conference center, a large retail and concession plaza, and a rail station that will connect the airport with downtown Denver. In addition, Gaylord has announced it will build a 1,500-room convention hotel nearby.

Conversely, because of the high land value of many airport sites, projects with small footprints have become increasingly prevalent. Select-service hotels continue to be effective airport properties because of their low-rise structure and lower development costs, but full-service hotels are still being created in airport locations and are more likely to be physically connected to the terminal areas in an effort to maximize land use. The Fairmont Vancouver Airport is directly

Yotel, Heathrow Airport, London, United Kingdom
Tiny rooms inspired by the design of aircraft allow travelers to rest and recuperate between flights. More like cruise ship staterooms than traditional hotel rooms, the units lack windows to the outdoors, which helps control noise and light.

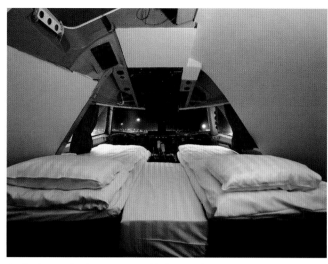

Jumbo Stay, Arlanda Airport, Stockholm, Sweden
A retired 747, mothballed for six years, now serves as a hostel for adventurous business and leisure travelers on a budget. Many of the original aircraft features were retained in the conversion of the fuselage into guestrooms and public space. Room 747, depicted here, is the most coveted sleeping room onboard.

connected to the airport's international departure hall and has all the features of an upscale business hotel including concierge floors, a health club and spa, and 8,700 sq ft (800 sq m) of meeting space. At London's Heathrow, Yotel in Terminal 4 goes the other direction, providing 75 sq ft (7 sq m) "cabins" with "monsoon" glass-enclosed showers, fold-away workstations, fully adjustable mood lighting, and, in the premium rooms, a couch that expands into a full-size bed at the touch of a button, all inspired by first-class accommodations in aircraft. Guestroom windows look into the corridors, which helps minimize outside noise. The hotel keeps costs down and revenues up by offering only self-service check-in and by selling rooms on an hourly basis, yet is able to provide 24-hour room service from staffed galleys on each floor. Similar "pod" concepts from emerging brands like Citizen M, easyHotel, and Qbic are appearing at busy airports worldwide, some only offering sleeping and work facilities but no individual bathrooms. A particularly innovative example of a high-design, low-cost airport hotel concept is the Jumbo Stay at Stockholm's Arlanda Airport: guests sleep in a retired and repurposed 747 jumbo jet with a view of the airport out each aircraft window.

The sky-lit lobby atrium, while no longer popular for downtown locations due to their high cost, finds good use in airport hotels as a comfort to guests who have arrived on long flights in cramped aircraft cabins and hunger for expansive space and air. These atriums provide a sense of light and transparency and of being closer to the sky, maintaining the milieu of flight. The atrium also contributes to noise control for rooms that face the interior. Extensive plantings in these spaces also dampen noise and provide welcome natural views to weary travelers.

The historically high guest turnover rate characteristic of airport hotels and the need to respond to full occupancy immediately due to severe weather or other travel interruptions place specialized

(continued p. 80)

Crowne Plaza Changi, Changi Airport, Singapore
The property was designed to be an oasis for tired long-distance travelers and to provide a taste of Singapore for those who may not be venturing further into the country. Designed by WOHA, the hotel is enclosed in a filigree "cage" that softens light and sound and offers passersby a framed view of the lush interior plantings that bring the Singaporean jungle indoors.

77

——— Case Study ———

Sheraton Milan Malpensa Airport Hotel and Conference Center, Milan, Italy
Architect: King Roselli Architetti
Interior Designer: Saporiti Design Hotel

Airport hotels that connect directly to air terminals face perhaps the highest number of design constraints of any hotel type: they must be low-rise, high-security, soundproofed, restful, and highly functional. The Sheraton Milan Malpensa Airport Hotel and Conference Center achieves all of these in style, with an innovative exterior that references Italy's refined design culture while responding to some challenging site issues including a roadway on one side, passenger loading and unloading facilities on the other, a railway underneath, and an existing parking garage below. King Roselli Architetti's unique proposal for a long, slender building punctuated with guestroom blocks facing a series of interior courtyards and wrapped in a sleek shell won a design competition for the building's exterior and has quickly made the Sheraton Milan Malpensa an architectural landmark.

At 433 keys, the hotel has many of the features typical of large airport hotels. Although there are relatively few multi-bay suites, a club floor with 58 rooms and a 2,100 sq ft (195 sq m)

club lounge allows the hotel operator to obtain a higher room rate from close to 18 percent of the keys. There is a generous 21,000 sq ft (1,951 sq m) of meeting space allocated among 22 function rooms as well as over 12,300 sq ft (1,150 sq m) of spa and fitness facilities and two food and beverage outlets. Of particular note is the crew lounge, a dedicated 4,300 sq ft (400 sq m) space for flight crews to relax away from other travelers. Large windows along the west façade offer spectacular views of the Italian Alps to the northwest.

While the mountain view may be unique, what makes this hotel truly stand out is its stunning exterior that wraps around the guestrooms on the terminal side of the project to create a series of seven curved forms. This fiberglass-reinforced composite membrane presented some construction challenges as architect Ricardo Roselli insisted upon a seamless appearance. By stretching long 4.6 ft (1.4 m) wide panels of the exterior material over a steel and composite frame, the designers were able to fully unify the east façade with the

Sheraton Milan Malpensa

Sheraton Milan Malpensa

roof, making it appear to be another façade to those passing overhead. Another benefit of this solution is that it blocks views into the guestrooms from Malpensa's Terminal 1, which is connected to the hotel via a tunnel.

The interiors were designed by Saporiti Design Hotel. The use of intense color as a highlight in the sleek, minimalist interior makes the lobby spaces pop while the meeting-room color scheme is much more neutral. The curves of the hotel's exterior are referenced in the lobby and ballroom ceilings, giving the hotel a streamlined and retro feel.

Sheraton Milan Malpensa, reception lobby

demands on the hotels' administrative areas and the back-of-house. Rooms division, accounting offices, front desk areas, housekeeping, food service, and engineering divisions are all heavily impacted by the operational needs unique to airport hotels.

Most airport hotels are affiliated with chains which require that their branded hotels be within 3 miles (5 km) or 10 minutes of terminals and offer food service 24 hours a day, free airport vans, same-day laundry and pressing service, business centers, and multilingual receptionists. With a new focus on the individual business traveler and corporate meeting groups, design requirements suitable for conference centers and flex-office guestrooms discussed in other chapters should be reviewed. Airport hotel guestrooms should be equipped with large work desks with ergonomic seating, WiFi and "jack packs" for connecting multiple devices to the television and to building systems.

Height restrictions for all buildings in the vicinity of airports are based on the approach angle of arriving and departing aircraft and are strictly regulated by government agencies such as the U.S. Federal Aviation Administration. Noise obviously plays an important role in site selection for a hotel, so planning should account for the air traffic patterns including arrival and departure routes around the airport. Sophisticated noise-reduction technologies are available and should be employed during construction, including the use of triple-glazed windows, noise-reduction wall finishes and foam membranes, vibration isolation springs, and sound-cancellation systems. For hotels that are physically connected to air terminals, the increased security needs of today's transportation infrastructure require special consideration. Screening checkpoints with imaging and sensing equipment as well as bollards to keep vehicles away from buildings and a profusion of security cameras inside and outside the hotel are among the standard design responses to high-security locations.

and split off entire new divisions to other suburban locales across the United States. Other major corporations followed suit in their exodus from downtown.

In Europe, British developer Stuart Lipton created Stockley Park adjacent to Heathrow Airport as a U.S.-style "business park." Lipton's emphasis was on landscape design and quality architecture as essential amenities offered to its tenants. According to Lipton, "It was all about PhDs rolling in the grass." The theory was that fertile minds function better in the pleasant open environment of a business park rather than the crowded cacophony of a city office block.

Office parks usually fall under the control of a single entity that sets out a master plan and defines development guidelines and restrictions. Amenities are important to tenants and their employees and if not available in the immediate area must be provided on-site. These include good parking, attractive landscaping, daycare facilities, food and beverage outlets, fitness centers, outdoor recreation, business support centers, meeting and conference facilities, and overnight accommodations. Since hotels can provide many of these amenities under one roof, they are a natural fit for office parks. One such property is the Westin Hyderabad Mindspace Hotel, part of the Mind Space IT Park in the massive HITEC City information technology and office complex in Hyderabad, India. Mind Space IT Park has over 4,000,000 sq ft (370,000 sq m) of office space spread over 110 acres (44 hectares) occupied by companies like Accenture, Amazon, IBM, and several banks, with the plan to eventually support 55,000 technology professionals and support staff. The Westin Hyderabad Mindspace has all the traditional features of an upscale downtown hotel but also hosts an evening social hour and provides access to a nearby golf and country club as ways to foster professional networking among its guests and clients in the surrounding businesses.

Another style of office-park hotel has much more of a suburban conference-center feel. The Hyatt Lodge at McDonald's Campus in Oak Brook, Illinois, is this kind of property: designed to emulate

Office-park Hotels

Office parks started in the United States as a natural outgrowth of suburban expansion. Many of the same qualities that attracted residential development to the outer boroughs—green space, lower costs, easier access, and safety—also attracted business development in the form of suburban office complexes. The rapid decentralization of central business districts to perimeter developments was a necessary phase in the evolution of the modern city as major office tower tenants moved to the suburban office market.

While industrial parks were the precursors of the genre, high-tech industries led the way to early office-park development. Silicon Valley, California, was an early manifestation of a modern office/science park. In the early 1960s the environs around Stanford University became a haven for computer science graduates wanting to establish their businesses in close proximity to the university's research facilities. Hewlett-Packard was the first major company to locate its California headquarters in Silicon Valley to take advantage of its research-rich environment. In the 1970s corporate giant IBM moved from its Manhattan office towers en masse to suburban Armonk, New York,

Umstead Hotel and Spa, Cary, North Carolina
Set on 12 acres (4.9 hectares) alongside a small lake, The Umstead Hotel and Spa incorporates natural materials and museum-caliber artwork throughout the 150-room luxury property. The hotel serves the adjoining corporate campus of SAS as well as other business and leisure travelers visiting the Raleigh area.

Frank Lloyd Wright's "Prairie" style, the 218-room Hyatt Lodge is low and spread out along the edge of a private lake and connected to nearby buildings via a network of bucolic walking paths. A 5,100 sq ft (474 sq m) ballroom overlooking the lake makes it a popular wedding location, giving the hotel a valuable revenue stream on weekends when corporate business may be slower. Because many of the hotel's guests stay for extended periods while attending McDonald's nearby training center, Hamburger University, the hotel has extensive fitness and recreational facilities that go well beyond the typical hotel workout room.

As with any hotel that caters to business travelers, office-park hotels must be equipped with state-of-the-art technology in guestrooms and in the conference space. These properties may have the same or more function space per key than a downtown hotel because of the demand for meeting space generated by businesses in the park. For example, the five-star Umstead Hotel and Spa in Cary, North Carolina, has 66 sq ft (6 sq m) of function space per key as well as a fine-dining restaurant and a luxury spa, giving the Umstead the feel of a beautifully landscaped destination resort despite its business-oriented location on the suburban campus of SAS World Headquarters.

Country Inns and Bed-and-breakfast Inns

Descended from eighteenth-century English and European inns, one of the oldest forms of hospitality has endured to become an important component of the leisure lodging industry. In 1980 there were approximately 1,000 inns serving about one million guests in the United States. Current industry estimates place the figures close to 17,000 inns that drive a U.S.$3.4 billion industry. International figures are harder to find but thousands of bed-and-breakfast lodgings can be found all over Europe and in locations as diverse as French Polynesia, Turkey, Panama, and even in Africa where B&Bs offer accommodation to both NGO workers and tourists.

The traditional qualities inherent in country inns and home-style bed-and-breakfasts remain central to their appeal: generous hospitality, personal attention, owner involvement, architecturally interesting or historic structures, individually decorated rooms, comfortable ambience, and unhurried surroundings. Though endless variety exists with these hostelries, most guests envision a quaint country cottage or farmhouse with a wide front porch full of comfortable seating, a cozy fireplace, a floral-wallpapered bedroom furnished with antiques and heirlooms, claw-footed bathtubs, and delicious "slow food" cooking all served up by a charming and gregarious host. The personality of the innkeeper is often tantamount to the character of the inn itself and the quality of the stay. Some referral organizations actually suggest a phone chat with the prospective host to confirm personal compatibility before booking.

The trend towards high-quality personalized service is evident in many hotel segments, and, as with the expanded development of luxury properties and the growth of boutique hotels in urban areas, is reasoned to be in reaction to the impersonal service of the large corporate hotel trade. The friendliness and authenticity of country inns and B&Bs are often preferred over the grand impressions and commercial approaches followed by other types of lodging.

Despite their popularity, inns face stiff competition and increasing costs. It no longer is sufficient to have a charming residence and a website: inns of all types must offer many of the amenities that travelers expect from any hotel—WiFi and spa-style bathrooms—as well as personalized experiences that cannot be duplicated by the chains. Properties that cater to particular niches have become more prevalent: bed-and-breakfast inns along the scenic California coastline offer special packages to biking and motorcycling enthusiasts, and fans of the macabre can stay in the room where Lizzie Borden allegedly murdered her parents in Fall River, Massachusetts. The diversity of country lodging is matched by the cultural diversity of the patrons as younger, more sophisticated, and more ethnically diverse travelers are changing the market. Some of these travelers are turning to online resources such as Airbnb.com to find inexpensive home stays, which gives additional exposure but also competitive pressure to urban B&Bs.

Individually themed guestroom designs have long been a feature of country inns and B&Bs; in fact the appeal is greater if no two rooms are alike. The Sylvia Beach Hotel in Newport, Oregon, has 20 literature-themed rooms named for famous authors from Shakespeare to J. K. Rowling, each lined with well-loved volumes to peruse. Guests at the Chateau de Tennessus in Poitou Charentes, France, can stay in an authentic medieval castle with arrow slits overlooking the moat and drawbridge. Accommodations at country inns cover a very broad range of economic categories, from simple rooms for under U.S.$50 to the elegant luxury of the five-star Twin Farms Country Estate in Vermont where rates begin at U.S.$1,300 including meals.

The ever-broadening diversity of types of country inns and B&Bs has led the Professional Association of Innkeepers International (PAII) to codify the varieties of inns based on type of building, type of ownership and operation, size, location, services, and amenities. In general, the larger the property and the less the owner is involved with day-to-day operations and interacting with the guests, the more the property is perceived as a hotel instead of an inn by the traveler. Any facility with more than 30 rooms is generally considered a bed-and-breakfast hotel.

One commonly thinks of country inns or B&Bs as restored historic buildings or renovated farmhouses where the charming characteristics and fine craftsmanship of past eras are essential values of the experience. Creating a B&B/country inn from a historic structure usually means carving out guestrooms and baths where none existed before or adding wings. It is important when undergoing renovations of this kind to maintain the style and quality of workmanship original to the building. Housing of administration and back-of-house functions, such as laundry/housekeeping, food preparation, or repair shops is often accomplished in cellars, outbuildings, or off-site.

Many country inns are designed to capture a sense of history and regional personality by employing the architectural styles, detailing, workmanship, materials, traditional furnishings, and artifacts of an earlier period, but contemporary approaches to the design of country inns have produced some dazzling new architecture and interiors. In stark contrast to the traditional notion of a country inn, the View Sunset Monzen Family Inn, sited in the Japanese countryside overlooking the Sea of Japan, represents a hyper-modern evolution of the genre. Its

The Inn at Middleton Place, Charleston, South Carolina
Unlike most country inns, The Inn at Middleton Place has a distinctly modern aesthetic. Concrete, wood, metal, and glass follow a formal grid pattern in the L-shaped block of low-rise buildings facing an expansive green courtyard and the Ashley River beyond.

Special-purpose Hotels, Hybrids and Other Suburban Hotel Types

The explosive development and expansive diversity found in the suburbs has led to a wide variety of hybrid hotel types that cater to an even wider variety of markets. These hotels are characterized as accommodating a multitude of regional functions including shopping malls, universities, museums, amusement parks, medical centers, restaurant villages, and even small towns in addition to the larger audiences discussed above such as airports and office parks. Most suburban hotels accommodate more than one geographical market, so it is not surprising to find a major chain hotel serving a small university town near an airport "fly-in" business park and close to a major regional shopping center. In addition to satisfying price category requirements, these hotels must provide a variety of amenities and facilities that satisfy all potential user types.

Suburban Mixed-use Developments

Combining hotels with office space, residences, shopping, and entertainment has been a popular development strategy for decades. Although many mixed-use developments are built in urban settings

futuristic architecture demonstrates a new and unique approach to lodging with guestroom pods strung along a pedestrian deck that frames a carefully crafted garden overlooking the sea and leads to the lobby and a lookout tower. In the south of France, Michel and Sebastien Bras created a strikingly modern hotel and a restaurant with three Michelin stars in the hills outside Laguiole, featuring a glass-walled dining room cantilevered off the hillside to maximize the views over the rolling Aveyron countryside. The building is composed of three parallel tiers that step downhill to give all guestrooms a western exposure.

At 55 rooms, The Inn at Middleton Place outside Charleston, South Carolina, is perhaps best defined as a small hotel. Its rustic setting alongside a nationally registered historic plantation transports guests to the eighteenth century but the inn itself was built over 250 years later and earned an AIA Honor Award for distinctive architecture in 1987. An ivy-covered concrete shell provides circulation and connects the modern room blocks that face a pristine courtyard and the Ashley River beyond. Inside, the guestrooms offer all the comforts of a luxury country inn—wood-burning fireplaces, window shutters, braided rugs, and handcrafted furniture—but with a clean-lined, contemporary feel.

As the country inn continues to evolve as one of the hospitality industry's most enduring forms, it will be the homelike atmosphere that will continue to draw guests to the tranquil ambience and gracious welcome that it offers.

Hotel Habita, Monterrey, Mexico
This suburban hotel, designed by architect Agustín Landa, sits in a residential neighborhood and features a solely black-and-white interior. The curved 10-story tower is topped with a pool and open-air bar with expansive views of the surrounding city and mountains.

to maximize the use of expensive real estate, there are also suburban mixed-use projects that incorporate striking hotels. The Hotel Habita in the San Pedro neighborhood of Monterrey, Mexico, stands at the junction of two curving structures that contain office space and apartments. Landa Arquitectos designed a unique ovoid concrete ten-story tower that creates unusual and dramatic floor plans for each of the hotel's 39 sleek luxury guestrooms.

Suburban mixed-use developments in the United States often emphasize the pedestrian experience. Hotels may not be fully integrated with retail or commercial areas but will be an easy walk along attractively planned outdoor pathways. A major connection to public transit is becoming a common component of these projects, with light rail or subway stops incorporated into the design as a way of increasing the appeal and hence the value of the residential units and commercial space. The specific needs of the market determine the precise mix and proportion of uses, and local climate has a lot to say about how these uses are physically connected.

Marriott's Renaissance Club Sport is a hotel concept designed for these kinds of suburban mixed-use locations. The hotel combines guestrooms and dining with a 50,000 sq ft (4,645 sq m) high-quality fitness, spa, and sports club that drives revenue in the form of community memberships. Sport club members also dine in the hotel and are a source of "VFR" roomnights (visiting friends and relatives) that supplement lodging demand from nearby office buildings.

Mall Hotels

Shopping malls reached their peak in the late 1970s as the natural result of residential suburban growth and served as a potent catalyst for further residential and business expansion. Suburban hotel development gravitated to these locations, lured to the crossroads by the same magnetic attraction that fused new residential, retail, and business projects. For example, the area surrounding King of Prussia Mall outside of Philadelphia, Pennsylvania, has grown to include a wealth of office parks, recreational facilities, and housing developments which in turn has driven the development of a cluster of hotels that range from smaller economy and all-suite properties to hotels with four-star service. One of these properties, the Dolce Valley Forge, offers all the features of a downtown business hotel—24,000 sq ft (2,200 sq m) of meeting space, a business center, and 24-hour fitness facilities—with an outdoor pool and garden that attract leisure travelers who have come to spend a day or two at the nearby regional shopping complex.

Mall areas can attract large numbers of family travelers, and some projects have directly targeted this segment by offering unique features. The Great Wolf Lodge Grapevine opened in 2007 about 2 miles (3 km) from the 1.6 million sq ft (147,200 sq m) Grapevine Mills Mall outside of Dallas, Texas. The lodge offers family-friendly recreational facilities centered on an 84,000 sq ft (7,725 sq m) waterpark with multiple indoor and outdoor play areas as well as a children's club, interactive role-playing game spaces, an arcade, a teens-only social room with the latest in online and video gaming, a children's spa, and, at a peaceful remove from all the activity, a full-service spa for adults. However, the property also sports a

20,000 sq ft (1,840 sq m) conference center, a useful amenity given its location relative to the Dallas–Fort Worth Airport 10 minutes away. Partnerships with well-known, kid-friendly food and beverage brands both simplify and promote on-site dining.

University Hotels

Universities have always provided a profitable market for the hotel industry for housing families and friends who are visiting students, prospective students or professors, invited lecturers, conference attendees, visitors on research-related or administrative business, sports fans, and others. Many universities worldwide operate their own hotels on campus, in some cases integrating these hotels with hospitality management programs and utilizing students of the schools as industry trainees. The substantial demand for meeting space from campus activities makes conference facilities a significant part of any university hotel. For example, the J. Willard Marriott Executive Education Center at the Statler Hotel at Cornell University provides nearly 20,000 sq ft (1,840 sq m) of conference space within the hotel itself and is physically connected to the School of Hotel Administration with its own auditoria, amphitheaters, and flat-floored classrooms which can all be used for group events when classes are not scheduled.

University hotels often have a relatively high proportion of suites as a result of the high number of VIP guests and families who come to campus. Designers of these hotels often are charged with making the property connect both physically and emotionally to the university; campus views are very important, as is the incorporation of university iconography and donor recognition.

(continued p. 86)

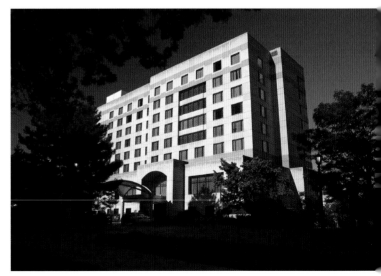

Statler Hotel, Cornell University, Ithaca, New York
The 150-room campus hotel and executive conference center serves the diverse university market of alumni, recruiters, speakers, trustees, and families of students. It features a wide range of meeting rooms, including a 94-seat amphitheater, used for management training programs and academic conferences.

─────── **Case Study** ─────────────────────

The Study at Yale
Architect: Kuwabara Payne McKenna Blumberg

Like the Jupiter Hotel profiled earlier in the chapter, The Study at Yale in New Haven, Connecticut, is a conversion of a 1960s motor hotel, but that ends the similarities between the two projects. Intended to be the first hotel of a new brand, The Study at Yale aims to reflect the unique character of neighboring Yale University and to establish an emotional and intellectual bond with its guests and the surrounding cultural community by fostering a strong sense of place. The result is a gently quirky concept that uses the art of reading as a motif for the hotel's comfortable, contemporary style.

In order to increase the room count in what had been most recently the Colony Hotel from 86 keys to a more profitable 124, developers Hospitality 3 and Toronto architects Kuwabara Payne McKenna Blumberg added two new floors to the existing building. The guestrooms in the original building had large picture windows with stunning views of the Gothic academic buildings of Yale's campus so this feature became the focal point in the redesign: a narrow desk that runs the width of the room faces the window, and in the suites—or "studies"—a cozy reading nook is also oriented toward the view. Each guestroom also features a leather chair and ottoman with a reading light to encourage perusal of the hundreds of books and periodicals available in the hotel's public spaces. Even the room-service menu, labeled "Food for Thought," refers back to the hotel's academic setting.

On the top floor, a new 1,200 sq ft (112 sq m) Penthouse Lounge also has a panoramic view of Yale and generates additional revenue as event space for smaller gatherings. This space supplements a further 1,800 sq ft (167 sq m) of meeting space on the ground floor. Also at ground level, the Library/Living Room features a café with coffee and light snacks, and the on-site restaurant and lounge emphasizes local, contemporary cuisine. Together these spaces push The Study at Yale's total allocation of food and beverage space beyond what a typical 124-key boutique hotel might have in order to attract custom from the entire Yale community, not just from hotel guests.

An immediate hit, The Study at Yale sets a new standard for upscale university hotels and demonstrates how aging hotel stock can be effectively reborn provided that there is a strong fit among the project's location, design, and intended market.

The Study at Yale, Chapel Street façade

The Study at Yale, Penthouse lounge

The Study at Yale, lobby

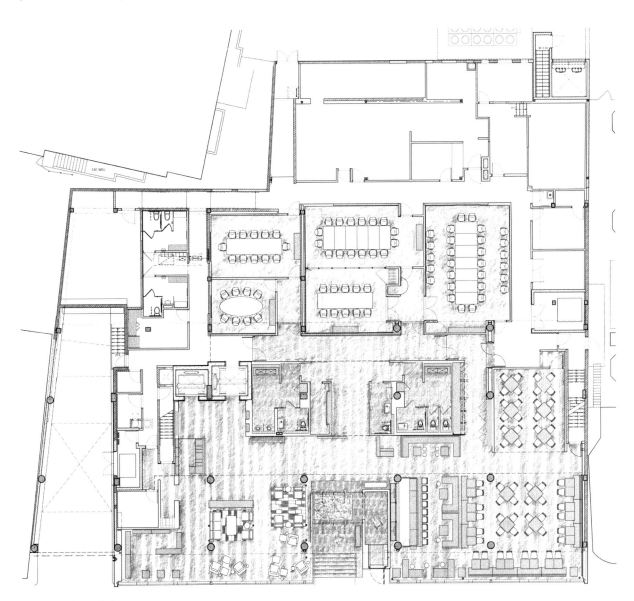

The Study at Yale, lobby level plan

Medical Hotels

During the early twentieth century, with the dawn of advanced medical services, the citizens of Rochester, Minnesota, were solving a community-wide problem. Annually, the Mayo Clinic medical phenomenon was attracting more than 60,000 patients to a city with a population of only 15,000. Hospital waiting lists were long, and hotel accommodations were in short supply. To serve the growing demand, in 1907 John H. Kahler built his first hotel with 60 rooms. Part convalescent hotel and hospital unit, it contained an upper-floor surgical and obstetrical suite and nursing school. It soon became grossly undersized for its market and, after numerous additions, operates today as the Kahler Grand Hotel with 624 rooms and 30,000 sq ft (2,750 sq m) of meeting space connected to a further 100,000 sq ft (9,250 sq m) of conference facilities in the neighboring Mayo Civic Center. Today 50 hotels with over 5,000 rooms now serve the Mayo Clinic and achieve robust occupancy rates.

Table 4.1 Suggested medical hotel program features

Adjacency	Separate short-term guest stays and residential-style rooms to allow for greater patient privacy and restful ambience.
Public amenities	Public amenities (e.g., restaurants, deli/convenience store, gift shop with a section for special needs items, and beauty and barber shops).
	Patient center that provides facilities where guests can use an exercise room, medical library, lounge, card, and video room, or catch up on work at a complimentary business center, patient/guest relations program including counseling and other specialized services.
	Fitness and rehabilitation center.
Room amenities	Shower stalls in each bathroom.
	Large easy chairs for daytime lounging.
	Rooms equipped for long-term living including DVD player, kitchenette with microwave ovens, refrigerator, dishwashers, and tableware.
Access	Enclosed connection to the adjacent medical building.
	Oversized elevators, hallways, and guestrooms to accommodate for movement of stretchers and wheelchairs.
	Extra-wide hallways and doors for easy wheelchair access.
Medical	Emergency response system monitored 24 hours a day by medical personnel.
	Medical waste disposals in each room.
	Special consultation and private meeting spaces for group and individual counseling.
Design	Patient-friendly interior design improves appetite and flatters complexion.
Others	Accommodate needs of local and visiting medical community.

Innovations in medical care and the increasing emphasis on outpatient services have spurred significant growth in hotels associated with hospitals and medical centers around the world. These properties offer accommodation to patients before and after tests and outpatient procedures as well as to family members and to health-care professionals who are on site only for short periods of time to conduct research or participate in conferences. This diverse client base means that medical hotels must offer an array of design features that have high functionality as well as aesthetic appeal. A growing source of international demand for medical hotels comes from

"medical tourists," generally affluent travelers who seek medical care outside their home nation at greatly reduced cost when compared with U.S. medical expenses. Costa Rica, Thailand, India, and Israel are all leaders in this area with many more countries rapidly increasing their medical capacity to attract this lucrative market. Singapore's Connexion development represents the latest thinking in providing hotel services on a health-care campus, in this case the cutting-edge "mediplex" of Farrer Park Hospital, Farrer Park Medical Center, and One Farrer Hotel, all elements of the same massive, mixed-use building. The hotel component provides accommodation for

Connexion Integrated Health Centre, Singapore
A 250-room full-service hotel is just one component of this single structure, which contains hospital facilities for in- and outpatient care, physicians' offices, a conference center, a medical school, and recreational facilities, all connected to a commuter rail station below grade.

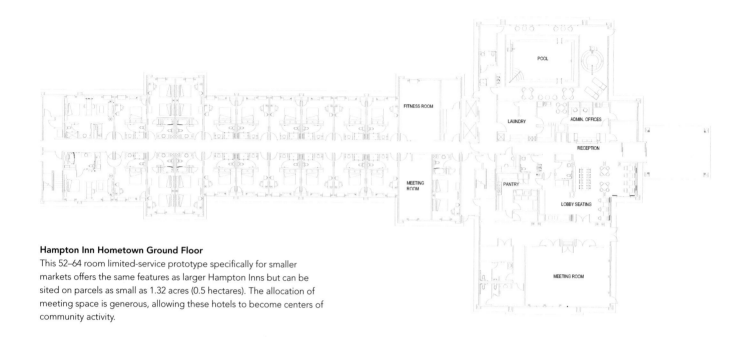

Hampton Inn Hometown Ground Floor
This 52–64 room limited-service prototype specifically for smaller markets offers the same features as larger Hampton Inns but can be sited on parcels as small as 1.32 acres (0.5 hectares). The allocation of meeting space is generous, allowing these hotels to become centers of community activity.

outpatients and for visitors to the complex as well as meeting space to support the hospital, medical center tenants, and the graduate school of medicine that is incorporated into the complex. On five floors of the hotel are the specially designed "hospitel rooms" featuring oversized bathrooms and separate sleeping areas for family members who may be sharing the room with the patient. These rooms can also be converted to hospital beds as the need arises. In all other respects, One Farrer Hotel looks and feels like an upscale boutique hotel with 120 "typical" hotel rooms, rooftop tropical gardens, indulgent spa facilities, retail shops, restaurants, and conference spaces. This integrated approach offers operational synergies that make this model likely to become more common for new-build health centers worldwide.

In developing the medical hotel's room mix, it is important to recognize the phases of recovery that many patients may experience as they relate to guestroom needs. When first released from the hospital the patient may need to be attended to closely by a private nurse or family member. The patient will not be mobile and may not feel presentable enough to mix with other guests, preferring to stay in his or her room. A full kitchenette may be required as well as adjacent accommodations for attending family members or nurse. Once patients become ambulatory, they may enjoy moving about on the floor and so may be able to use a central kitchen area with a small dining room, TV lounge, or sunroom on the same floor. Patients near the end of their stay may be able to enjoy the public spaces and hotel lobby, restaurant, and exercise facilities as available. Table 4.1 outlines some of the design features and services that these hotels can provide.

Small-town Hotels

Small-town hotels represent perhaps the most cross-bred of all hybrids. Regarded by the large chains as a tertiary market, small towns offer lodging in the form of unbranded motels, bed-and-breakfasts, country-style inns, or smaller versions of well-known branded suburban hotels. These hotels often lack the regimentation characteristic of larger, more urban accommodations. Small-town properties may take a prominent role in community affairs and often are the setting for wedding receptions, high school reunions, local awards ceremonies, beauty pageants, bingo nights, fraternal club meetings, seasonal festivals, and other community functions. Swimming pools and health clubs often are open to locals for a modest fee. Upscale restaurants in small-town hotels are sometimes the best dining option in town and naturally become a local social epicenter.

Hilton has created a "hometown" prototype of its Hampton Inn brand for these smaller markets, allowing developers to create a hotel with all the benefits of brand affiliation but at a size that makes sense for locations that cannot support a large number of rooms. At no more than 64 keys, Hampton Inn Hometown hotels are designed to be built faster on a smaller site than typical Hampton Inns.

New Suburban Brands

Suburban hotels continue to be a laboratory for new prototypes and hybrids. Just as the diversity reflected in suburban markets has led to the development of new lodging products, the evolution of suburban and exurban life is driving the creation of ever more niche hotel brands with unique design features.

One fertile area of development is in the all-suite segment. Originally "one size fits all," today's all-suite brands offer an array of suite types and amenities targeting both professionals on assignment and weekend leisure guests. Marriott's TownePlace Suites is a recent example of the trend toward studio suite brands with much smaller guestrooms and public spaces than the all-suite concepts that were developed in the 1980s. In their typical rooms, these hotels feature a small kitchen area (although with minimal cooking facilities beyond a microwave), a pull-out sofa, a generous and customizable working space, and a single king bed, all in a space of roughly 330 sq ft (30.6 sq m). The current fashion to use bright blocks of color in high-contrast interiors is reflected in the brand décor as is the provision of a communal table in the lobby space to support working alone but in the company of others—now a hallmark of the younger traveler's working style.

Targeting a similar demographic such new brands as Hyatt Place, aloft, and NYLO have all entered the market with modern designs that emphasize the lobby "great room" where guests can work, eat, drink, and socialize. Hyatt Place properties can be either new-builds or renovations of properties formerly under other flags, but aloft and NYLO were planned as entirely new constructions.

Looking forward, it is clear that the economy and select-service brands will continue to develop upscale-like amenities but in a smaller space or with minimal hotel labor in order to provide a higher-quality experience at a price more in keeping with suburban demand. Even if they are not staying in gateway cities, twenty-first-century travelers will expect all hotels to have a comfortable room, the latest technology, and high style.

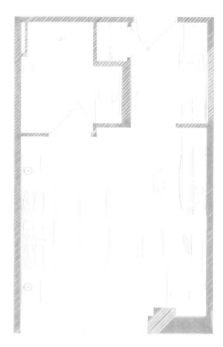

TownePlace Suites Typical Room
Designed with business travelers on longer-term assignments in mind, this studio unit offers a second, rolling work surface that can be positioned anywhere in the room and a small kitchen area with full-sized appliances.

Multi-branded Hotels

Developers seeking to build branded lodging in urban areas often find it difficult to acquire suitable property due to the high cost of land. Building more than one brand on a single site, however, can create more feasible economies-of-scale and result in a number of development, marketing, and operational advantages. The concept of dual-branded properties began with projects where two brands from the same hotel company were built on the same site but in separate buildings. The concept has expanded to include a wide variety of configurations including multiple brands in a single building or complex.

Planning and Development Considerations

Multi-branded hotel developments benefit from the following advantages:

- There is reduced initial construction cost per room with smaller program areas due to shared public space, meeting space, recreation, administration, and back-of-house. Savings can be as much as 30 percent.
- Hotels have reduced operating costs and greater efficiency with shared services and a centralized staff under one general manager.
- Meeting space becomes more cost-effective. A ballroom might not be feasible to build and operate for one hotel alone but when shared by two, it becomes viable.
- Blended product provides more options for the customer; for example, the extended-stay guestroom has a kitchen while the upscale transient brand has a restaurant for guests who don't feel like cooking.
- Blended product captures a broader market in multiple demand segments (transient plus extended-stay or mid-price plus economy brands)
- Right-size the project to the property. Investment in a site that should support 400 keys can now support two hotels at 200 keys.
- There is reduced risk to the investor. If one brand doesn't attract customers, the other one might.
- There is increased brand loyalty. One brand generates interest in the other. Guests get exposure and become attracted to an unfamiliar new brand.
- Operators can adjust the guests to the product that best suits them. If guests are booked long-term in a transient hotel but

JW Marriott and Ritz-Carlton at L.A. LIVE, Los Angeles, California
Gensler's sleek glass tower tapers outward to accommodate the larger footprint of the Ritz-Carlton guestrooms and residences, presenting a striking architectural profile to downtown L.A. and reflective of the hotel's program. The dual-branded hotel complex is remarkable in offering two superb luxury brands within a single property.

are better suited to the extended-stay product, they can be moved over.

- Cross-selling becomes easier without competing sales forces.

A developer in São Paolo, Brazil, sought to reposition a 600-key downtown hotel with a branded product but the building was too large for the particular brand. Instead, the hotel was split between two distinct but compatible brands each capturing a substantial share of its respective market. Similarly, a developer in Silver Spring, Maryland, sought to adapt an office building in a prime location to a single focused-service brand but realized the building was too large for just one hotel, and the commercial office market was flat. The zoning in that neighborhood had been changed to restrict high-rise building so the developer was not permitted to build from the ground up. Working with Hilton, the company ended up developing a dual-branded project that housed two hotels within the former office building. The Silver Spring property became a co-branded Homewood Suites and Hampton Inn.

Homewood Suites and Hampton Inn, Silver Spring, Maryland
Developers converted a 150,000 sq ft (13,935 sq m) underachieving office building into two Hilton brands, each sized appropriately to their market share and achieving mutual efficiencies in shared administration and back-of-house areas.

It is a frequent problem for developers, seeking the advantages of a dual-branded property in a dense urban area, to find a site large enough to accommodate two separate freestanding buildings. The most common solution has been to design the two brands within a single new structure with shared amenities and services.

A common formula for dual-branded properties is to marry an extended-stay product with a mid-priced transient product, each at approximately the same price tier. For example a Hilton Garden Inn is combined with a Homewood Suites (also by Hilton) or a Residence Inn with a Courtyard (both by Marriott). Other combinations include products at different price tiers, such as a mid-priced brand with a budget brand. Another formula combines a brand focused on the leisure market with one serving the business market. There are even dual-branded properties where two hotel brands from different and sometimes competing hotel companies occupy the same building. The Four Seasons Hotel in Las Vegas occupies the upper floors of the Mandalay Bay Resort and Casino although the two hotels are managed independently. Likewise Andaz Shanghai Hotel by Hyatt and The Langham Xintiandi Hotel (see pages 47–49) are physically connected by a sky bridge and have a synergistic relationship but are operated independently.

Design Considerations

There are a number of building configurations that we find in multi-branded hotel projects. The earliest model is simply having two stand-alone buildings that share the same lot. In the case of the Hyatt Place and Hyatt Summerfield Suites at Fort Lauderdale Airport in Florida, the developers preferred seeing the success of the Hyatt Place before committing to the second hotel. The two hotels benefit from certain operating cost savings as one general manager runs both properties and cross-selling is a significant advantage.

The more substantial economic and operational benefits of multi-branding come when the hotels are physically connected. Only then can they truly share the construction cost savings and operational efficiencies inherent in the multi-branding concept. To a large extent the form that these combined properties take is driven by site constraints. If the site is large enough, the preferred configuration is to have two towers connected at the base with public and back-of-house space and two separate entrance canopies. The risk for hotel companies when the hotels are connected is maintaining brand identity and avoiding brand confusion. Most brands have architectural prototypes that have been carefully developed to provide an identifiable image representative of the brand. Marrying two brands within a single building presents a challenge to architects to blend these images effectively so that the building does not evoke Frankenstein, yet maintains a clear representation of the prototypical building elements. Two towers connected at the base with separate arrival areas lends itself very well to this goal since each separate tower can follow the brand prototype. More difficult is a smaller site which can only accommodate a single tower. The brand-confusion issue is exacerbated if the site can only allow for a single entrance canopy. In some cases signage becomes the only vehicle to brand identity.

Homewood Suites and Hampton Inn, Toronto, Canada
Located within minutes of Toronto's Pearson International Airport, the two buildings boast 126 Hampton rooms and 128 Homewood brand suites and are joined by a shared common area, pool, and fitness center. The developers realized a need in both the upscale extended-stay and mid-priced transient hotel segments in the growing Toronto Airport Corporate Centre area.

Hilton Garden Inn and Homewood Suites, Jacksonville, Florida
On a tight downtown site, Bounds and Gillespie Architects placed an L-shaped tower on the site, leaving only one quadrant for open space. The clever site plan utilizes the open space for two incompatible functions shared by the two brands. The swimming pool is nicely screened from the entrance court but becomes a vibrant element to view from both hotel lobbies.

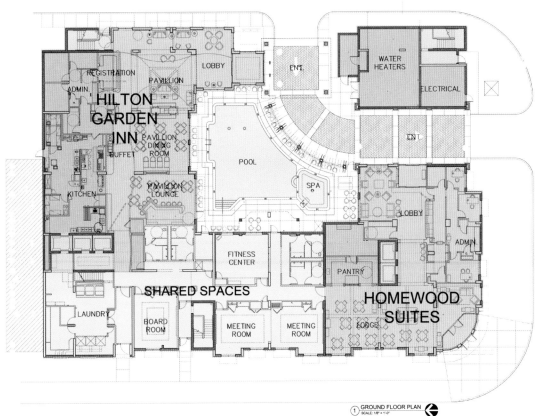

① GROUND FLOOR PLAN
SCALE: 1/8" = 1'-0"

HOMEWOOD SUITES

HILTON GARDEN INN

LEVEL 1

0 5' 10' 20' 30' 40' 50'
North

Key
1 Porte-cochere
2 Vestibule
3 Hilton Lobby
4 Homewood Suites Lobby
5 Reception
6 Private Dining
7 Sales Area
8 Office
9 Pantry
10 Food Preparation
11 Hallway
12 Service Entry
13 Lounge
14 Bar
15 Kitchen
16 Ballroom
17 Meeting Room
18 Board Room
19 Business Center
20 Bar Lounge
21 Kitchen
22 Terrace
23 Pool
24 Fitness Center
25 Employee Break
26 Laundry

A single tower can be divided either horizontally, where guestroom floors of each hotel brand are on one or the other side of the tower, or vertically, where guestroom floors of one brand are built above the other. In either case each brand needs to have its own entrance, lobby, and passenger-elevator core, though they can share emergency exit stairs and service elevators if carefully planned. In horizontally divided projects, since guestrooms and corridors of each brand share the same floors, it is necessary to create a break in the corridor so that guests do not circulate to the other brand's side of the floor. Brand standards should be maintained in the décor of each brand's corridors. The Hilton Garden Inn and Homewood Suites in Jacksonville, Florida, is designed as an L-shaped tower with each leg

Hilton Garden Inn and Homewood Suites, Bossier City, Louisiana
Faced with Holiday Inn's new brand standards for eliminating exterior corridors, the owners decided to demolish the existing building and reflag the site with two Hilton brands. Mathes Brierre Architects designed the first low-rise dual-branded property, with two independent four-story wings formed around a courtyard and swimming pool and linked at the entrance by a single-story public space podium. A single porte cochère leads to the two branded lobby elements: Hilton Garden Inn's iconic "Pavilion" and Homewood Suites' recognizable "Lodge." The two hotels share administration, back-of-house, recreation, and meeting spaces.

dedicated to a brand. The ground floor of this tight rectilinear site is cleverly arranged with a shared arrival court leading to separate entrances. The common swimming pool is tucked neatly between the two wings adjacent to but screened from the arrival court.

In addition to the brand confusion issue there are functional problems to solve when combining two or more hotels within a single building envelope. Circulation requirements connecting each brand's lobby to shared meeting space or recreational amenities often mean that the lobbies become connected by a corridor or pre-function space. This allows for guests from one hotel to easily visit the lobby of the other. While this has the advantage of giving the guest exposure to the other brand, it can have functional disadvantages as well. For instance, Hilton Garden Inn serves its guests a free hot breakfast while Homewood Suites does not; care must be taken in the plan layout to discourage the Homewood customers from availing themselves of the free meal intended for the Garden Inn guests.

If the goal is to have a cohesive exterior tower design, the architect must sometimes address the fact that the typical guestrooms of each brand are of different widths and sometimes have different window sizes and patterns. This difference will become evident on the building's façade. In addition, each brand prototype might have different exterior material and color palettes. Or they may have different cornice, pilaster, roof gable, or other architectural details; one prototype might have a flat roof and the other a pitched roof. Fortunately, many brands offer the developer more than one prototype to choose from. Others allow the architect latitude to creatively interpret the prototypical elements, thereby making the process of blending styles less of a challenge.

At the corner of West 54th Street and Broadway in New York City a 67-story mixed-use building was designed by architect Nobutaka Ashihara with 30 floors of a Residence Inn above 25 floors of a Courtyard by Marriott. This rather extraordinary example of a vertically stacked dual-branded property includes a six-story podium containing retail stores, restaurants, and other public space.

Ibis is a European budget brand by Accor that is often joined with an upscale brand such as Mercure or a Suite Hotel (also by Accor). When designing a hotel with brands at different price points, the more upscale brand guestrooms should be oriented toward the better views. This is the case with the Coeur Mediterranée in Marseilles, France, where the guestrooms of the more upscale Suite Hotel have a covered loggia that faces north with views of the sea, while the budget brand Ibis faces away from the view.

Marriott Place Indianapolis is a true multi-brand complex featuring four individual brands on a single city block connected to the Indiana Convention Center: JW Marriott Downtown Indianapolis (see pages 192–195), Courtyard by Marriott Downtown Indianapolis, Fairfield Inn & Suites Downtown Indianapolis, and SpringHill Suites Downtown

Residence Inn and Courtyard, New York, New York
In creating this 67-story dual-branded hotel on a narrow 10,000 ft sq ft (925 sq m) lot, developers of the 340,000 sq ft (31,500 sq m) building utilized air-rights purchased from adjacent properties and from the renovation of a theater in Times Square, exploiting a zoning incentive granted to promote the restoration of historic Broadway playhouses.

95

Indianapolis. While the JW Marriott and the Fairfield Inn are separate hotel buildings joined at the base, the Courtyard and SpringHill Suites follow the model of the Jacksonville project with the two brands housed in a single L-shaped tower with a shared arrival court and separate entrances covered by a sweeping semi-circular canopy.

An exceptional variation to the L-shaped tower model of dual-branded hotels is the 123-key Ritz-Carlton and 878-key JW Marriott Hotel, the centerpiece of the $2.5 billion L.A. LIVE entertainment development district in downtown Los Angeles. The twist to this luxury dual-brand is the inclusion of the 224-unit Residences at The Ritz-Carlton on the upper floors of the 54-story tower. With both brands at the highest price tier, they differentiate themselves by the markets they serve. The JW Marriott Hotel will serve the convention, group meeting, and tourist market, while the five-star accommodations of The Ritz-Carlton Hotel will be ideal for headline performers, visiting sports teams, and executives doing business at L.A. LIVE and downtown.

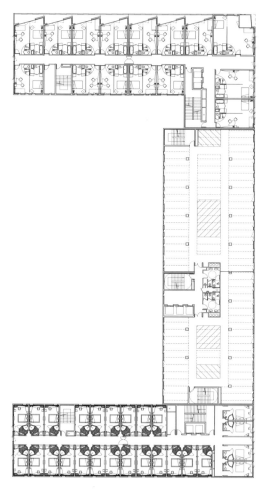

Coeur Mediterranée, Marseilles, France
The mixed-use building is organized as a U-shaped plan consisting of an Ibis Hotel in the south wing and a Suite Hotel in the north wing, with office and commercial space in between. The building skin is like a continuous ribbon, pierced by stylized trapezoidal-shaped windows. The north-facing Suite Hotel façade contains a covered loggia with views of the Mediterranean Sea.

Ibis and Mercure Salvador Rio Vermelho Hotel, Salvador, Brazil
In Brazil, many dual-brand hotels have been successfully developed, a large majority of them using the brands of the Accor Group. The first dual-brand hotel of the country, using the brands Mercure and Ibis, was inaugurated in the city of Salvador. The hotel, a concept conceived by HVS São Paulo, is today delivering excellent results to its investors.

Marriott Place, Indianapolis, Indiana
Three separate arrival courts on two streets greet guests at the four Marriott brands in a remarkable ensemble serving a variety of markets in this vibrant downtown area. One block away, the 622-room Indianapolis Marriott Downtown Hotel is connected to the Marriott Place hotels via a series of bridges, which in turn connect all five hotels to the Indiana Convention Center.

Courtyard and SpringHill Suites, Indianapolis, Indiana
While it is essential to take care to avoid the problem of brand confusion that arises when co-locating hotels on a single property, the benefits of shared administration and back-of-house and the synergy of cross-selling prove to outweigh those concerns. The Courtyard and SpringHill Suites manage to share a single porte cochère that leads to separate brand-identifiable entrances.

Crowne Plaza and Staybridge Suites, Abu Dhabi, United Arab Emirates
Set along the Yas Links Abu Dhabi and the turquoise Arabian Gulf, all 428
rooms and suites of the Crowne Plaza and 164 suites of the Staybridge feature
magnificent views and are within walking distance of the Yas Marina Circuit
and the Ferrari World Abu Dhabi theme park. The two hotels, while housed in
separate towers and serving different markets, are connected at two basement
levels and share extensive back-of-house facilities and below-grade parking.

Case Study

JW Marriott and Ritz-Carlton, Los Angeles
Architect: Gensler
Interior Designer: Gensler

As the centerpiece of the $2.5 billion L.A. LIVE entertainment development district, the 54-story dual-branded hotel is the first skyscraper to be built in downtown Los Angeles in nearly two decades. Anchored by STAPLES Center, AEG's development includes 5,000,000 sq ft (464,500 sq m) of entertainment, hospitality, and office amenities, which annually bring more than 600 live sports, concerts, major award telecasts, family shows, and corporate events to its 35 acre (14 hectare) campus. The hotel complex is located on a super block with the Nokia Theater, Club Nokia and the ESPN Broadcast Facility, all connected through a series of pedestrian plazas. STAPLES Center and the Los Angeles Convention Center are across 11th Street to the south.

Although the L-shaped massing of the hotel tower and the representative building signage gives the impression that the JW Marriott occupies the shorter leg and The Ritz-Carlton the taller, the organization of the building actually has the 879-room JW Marriott hotel on floors 4 through 21 and the 123-room Ritz-Carlton hotel on floors 22 through 26. Floors 27 through 52 hold 224 Ritz-Carlton Residences. Architects at Gensler created a 31 ft (9.4 m) deep standard room bay for the JW Marriott guestrooms and suites and sited them on the lower floors of the building. The shape of the tower flares outward as it ascends, starting at the Ritz-Carlton floors to accommodate the luxury hotel's larger rooms while maintaining the column grid bay dimensions. The widening tower footprint also provides the greatest floor area for the valuable Ritz-Carlton Residences towards the top of the building. To create this profile the architects placed curved steel columns near the top of the tower, facilitating installation of the giant glass curtain wall.

The earthquake-resistant structure was designed with a thin, steel-plate shear wall system instead of thicker concrete shear walls which reduced the weight of the tower's structure by 35 percent. In addition to savings in construction cost, this system resulted in energy savings by reducing the quantity of materials for the structure and foundations.

Gensler's design for the hotel building gained LEED certification through a series of sustainable features including drought-tolerant landscaping and light-colored paving at the pool decks, single-ply roofing to help create a cool roof, and low-water-consumption bathroom fixtures and waterless urinals to reduce water usage. California's Title 24 energy requirements code mandates a maximum transparency of 60 percent on building façades. The architects used computer modeling to develop a system to reduce transparency on the lower hotel floors and to gradually increase transparency on the upper floors in response to marketing demands for greater access to views for the high-end residences. This was achieved using glazing types

.JW Marriot and Ritz-Carlton at L.A. LIVE

with a variety of transparency and reflectivity. Ceramic fritting on the glass allows light penetration to be modulated while reducing heat gain. In order to promote a sense of unity for the building's façade, the architects used a random dimensional pattern and alternating blue, silver, and gray-colored glass to address the different-sized openings and higher floor-to-floor heights as the building ascends.

JW Marriot at L.A. LIVE, lobby

The Ritz-Carlton has a discreet entrance court off a relatively quiet side street that leads to an intimate chandelier-lit and mahogany-paneled reception lobby for hotel guests and an adjacent equally intimate lobby for The Ritz-Carlton Residences. By contrast the JW Marriott's entrance is off bustling Olympic Boulevard and leads to a dramatic triple-story lobby that has become a popular public gathering spot and teems with life, especially before and after events. The south side of the lobby opens to a small public plaza that leads to the larger Nokia Plaza, which is ringed by a series of video screens and ties the complex to the STAPLES Center.

The third floor looks down to the huge lobby and contains meeting spaces and a small ballroom. A bridge at the third level connects across Georgia Street to the JW Marriott Conference and Banquet Center with over 80,000 sq ft (7,400 sq m) of function space, including a 25,000 sq ft (2,300 sq m) ballroom.

JW Marriot at L.A. LIVE, swimming pool

The conference center is ideally located to connect in the future to a planned expansion of the Los Angeles Convention Center to the south.

On the fourth floor, directly above the JW Marriott lobby, there is a 4,000 sq ft (370 sq m) fitness center opening to a large pool deck that can accommodate up to 1,000 visitors and guests, providing an ideal downtown party venue. While guests of the JW Marriott have access to The Ritz-Carlton's 8,000 sq ft (740 sq m) spa, guests of The Ritz-Carlton have exclusive rights to the 3,400 sq ft (315 sq m) Club Lounge, rooftop pool, and private fitness center on the 26th floor. A double-story restaurant located on the 24th floor offers exceptional views of Los Angeles.

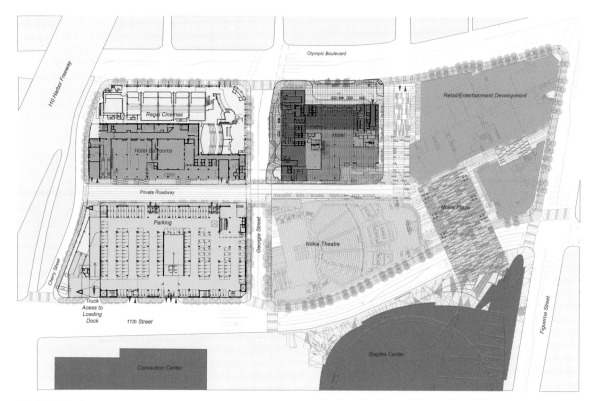

L.A. LIVE, site plan

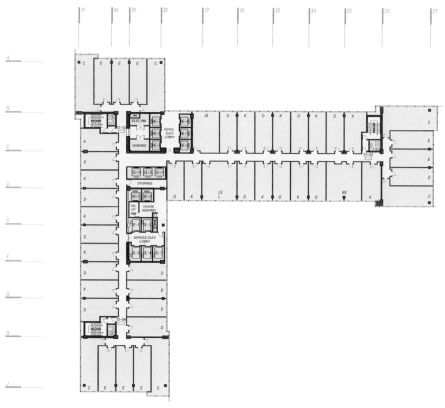

JW Marriot at L.A. LIVE, typical guestroom floor

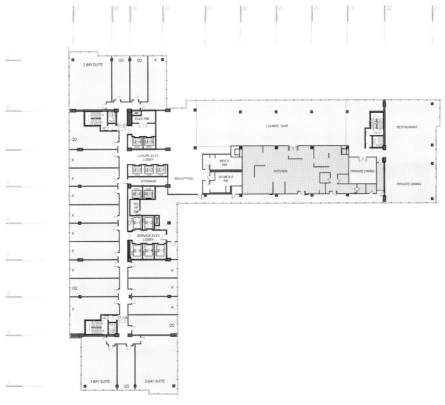

Ritz-Carlton at L.A. LIVE, 24th floor plan

Ritz-Carlton at L.A. LIVE, 26th floor (fitness center and pool) plan

Mixed-use
Developments

Each element of the mixed-use complex, including its hotel, office building, condominiums, and shopping mall, benefits from integration with a larger, more prestigious project. With its higher visibility and more ambitious overall planning concept, the impact of the entire development is far greater than the sum of its parts. In addition to its more efficient methods of land use, assembly, construction, and financing, the mixed-use complex encourages innovative design, often overriding outdated zoning regulations, improving traffic circulation patterns, and initiating planning variances beneficial to both the community and the developer.

The Exchange Coffee House Hotel, built in Boston in 1809, was one of the earliest hotels to provide ample public spaces that ushered in a new era of hotels as downtown social and political epicenters. In addition, it is one of the earliest examples of a mixed-use hotel building. The Merchants' Exchange, located under the giant sky-lit rotunda of the hotel's main floor, provided a market not only for the 200 guestrooms but also for the ballroom, coffeehouse, and dining rooms that were the very public spaces that defined this new genre. It set an early example for the synergistic advantages that result from combining diverse functions into mixed-use developments, especially when the hotel is a central component of the mix.

The end of the nineteenth century saw tremendous building development around major railway stations, including hotels, office buildings, retail, and other uses. The large and lavish hotels offered so many special amenities and public functions that they often were spoken of as "cities within cities." In Chicago one of the most spectacular of these developments was the Auditorium Building, which combined three types of public use. Designed by Adler and Sullivan, it combined an office block, a luxurious 400-room hotel on Michigan Avenue, and an acoustically perfect 4,300-seat theater, the world's largest when it opened in 1889. Except for the entrance, the theater was almost completely enclosed from the street by the hotel. Created to provide a permanent home for Chicago's opera, symphony, and other performing organizations, the multi-use commercial components—the hotel and commercial office space—were included in order to offset possible losses from the operation of the theater. The complex rose 16-stories, the tallest in Chicago at the time, in part by adapting innovative structural systems to allow the hotel ballroom to span the theater. More than a century later, mixed-use projects continue to be in the forefront of structural innovation and the competition to have the tallest building.

Pioneer of the modern downtown hotel, Ellsworth M. Statler constructed The Park Plaza Hotel, the first major mixed-use development combining hotel and office building, covering a full

W Mumbai at Namaste Tower, Mumbai, India
Following the great tradition of Indian architecture, W. S. Atkins's design of the striking 62-story tower reflects the namaste yoga gesture of hands clasped together, symbolizing a greeting to the city of Mumbai. Incorporating a W hotel, office, and retail space, the building will be topped by a quadruple-height atrium space, which will enclose a restaurant and bar with stunning views of the busy city.

Armani Hotel, Burj Khalifa, Dubai, United Arab Emirates
Soaring high above downtown Dubai in the iconic Burj Khalifa is the world's tallest building, Armani Hotel Dubai, the first hotel designed and developed by Giorgio Armani. The fashion designer's signature style is evident in the interiors, with sophisticated colors, clean lines, and unique textures that blend together seamlessly with the tower's stunning architecture.

block in Boston in 1927. Two years later, on the day before the stock market crash in 1929, a $42 million construction contract was signed for The Waldorf=Astoria, a monumental hotel/residential complex that represented the last major hotel project to be built until after World War II. Major mixed-use projects that contained hotels did not appear again until the government-sponsored urban renewal efforts of the 1960s prompted such huge developments as

Place Bonaventure in Montreal and Boston's impressive Prudential Center. These key projects set the pace for downtown revitalization by attracting both regional and international clientele to their large convention facilities, office structures, and impressive malls and by providing the latest in recreation and entertainment amenities for the city. The Prudential development, the largest complex of its kind up to that time, included a 50-story office tower with a popular

Kingdom Tower, Jeddah, Saudi Arabia
The immense tower will be the centerpiece and first phase of a $20 billion proposed development known as Kingdom City, located along the Red Sea on the north side of Jeddah. The tower's primary uses will be hotel and residential, with most of the floor area going to a Four Seasons hotel and residences and luxury condominiums. The tower will also include office space and the world's highest observatory.

India Tower, Mumbai, India
Designed by Foster and Partners, the spectacular 125-story India Tower is located on Marine Lines, named after the Marine Battalion Lines, a military establishment built by the British in south Mumbai. The tower is planned to house the 255-key Park Hyatt Mumbai, which will also include 55 apartments serviced by the hotel and exclusive banqueting and meeting facilities.

visitors' observation center at its top, a 5,000-seat civic auditorium, a 1,500-room twin-tower Sheraton hotel, two apartment towers, and a 3,000-car underground garage.

In the 1970s John Portman's designs for Embarcadero Center in San Francisco and Renaissance Center in Detroit demonstrated the use of huge atriums to provide the focus and organizing elements of mixed-use developments which included offices, retail, and hotels. Other significant complexes facing more stringent site limitations relied on stacking of functions vertically such as Water Tower Place

in Chicago, with its Ritz-Carlton Hotel topping a multistory shopping mall, and Araldo Cossutta's cylindrical hotel occupying the upper floors of the Credit Lyonnaise office building in Lyons, France.

Two major mixed-use projects, the Houston Galleria and Boston's Copley Place, highlighted the public's infatuation with shopping malls; here, the hotels supplied potential shoppers while the malls provided hotel guests with a wealth of extra amenities. In these pioneering developments, which included office buildings and convention facilities, corporate travelers and executives could

Shanghai Tower J-Hotel, Shanghai, China
Shanghai Tower J-Hotel of Jin Jiang International Hotels will span the
84th to 110th floors of the tallest of a group of three supertall buildings
in Pudong, the other two being the Jin Mao Tower and the Shanghai
World Financial Center. The hotel will feature 258 luxury guestrooms,
with the hotel lobby located on the 101st floor.

bring their families on business trips to enjoy the array of shops and
recreational facilities, while many tourists were drawn to the hotel-
in-mall concept, providing instant activity for their vacations.

Two major mixed-use developments of the early 1980s signified
the explosive business growth and rapid expansion of tourism in
Singapore during that period. Raffles City, designed by I. M. Pei and
taking its name from the world-famous Raffles Hotel, borders on
downtown Singapore and contains two major hotels and an office
tower connected by a seven-story podium containing retail and
restaurants. Both hotels are operated by Westin and therefore benefit
from certain shared back-of-house and administrative functions. The
Westin Stamford Singapore, at 71-stories, was the tallest hotel in the
world when completed. John Portman's Marina Square convention
complex in Singapore included an even higher ratio of hotel space,

offering three major hotels each focused around a major atrium
space with restaurants, cinemas, shopping, office, and recreational
facilities clustered at their bases.

Stretching ever skyward there is a developing breed of mixed-use
super-towers that house luxury hotels, expensive condominiums,
and premium office space, lending dominant visibility and global
notoriety to those users. Burj Khalifa, the world's tallest building
(as of this writing) stands at 2,717 ft (828 m) with 163 habitable
floors, not including mechanical floors. As the flagship of a larger
mixed-use development called Downtown Dubai that includes Dubai
Mall, the world's largest shopping mall, and the spectacular Dubai
Fountain, Burj Khalifa houses the fashionable Armani Hotel with 160
luxury guestrooms and 144 signature Armani Residences. The hotel
occupies the lower 39 floors while the upper floors contain luxury

condos, corporate suites, a restaurant, and a public observatory. An engineering marvel designed by Adrian Smith of SOM Architects, the building's Y-shaped floor plan configuration is ideal not only for structural stability but also for the hotel and residential usage, with the wings allowing maximum outward views and inward natural light.

Not to be outdone and bearing a strong resemblance to Frank Lloyd Wright's Mile High building, Kingdom Tower is designed by Adrian Smith to be 568 ft (173 m) taller than Burj Khalifa. With 5.7 million sq ft (530,000 sq m) of floor area, Kingdom Tower will feature a Four Seasons hotel, Four Seasons serviced apartments, Class A office space, luxury condominiums, and the world's highest observatory. With 210 floors the massive tower will be served by 59 elevators. The three-petal footprint is ideal for hotel and residential units and the tapering wings produce an aerodynamic shape that helps reduce structural wind loading. The stunning tower is the centerpiece of a major mixed-use development by Prince Al-Waleed bin Talal. Named Kingdom City, it will include residential, commercial, and entertainment uses along a pedestrian-friendly waterfront promenade. The developers of Kingdom Tower regard it not only as a symbol of economic strength but as a cultural icon marking Jeddah's historic importance as the traditional gateway to the holy city of Mecca.

Development and Planning Considerations

Because of their size and complexity and their potential and projected impact on surrounding communities, large mixed-use projects are very often made part of a more comprehensive urban master plan, and therefore are subject to the goals and guidelines set forth by the local planning authority. For the same reasons, these large projects are often subjected to intense scrutiny by local communities and civic groups and can be the source of heated debates over economic, social, and environmental benefits and drawbacks. Many projects, such as the Elbphilharmonie in Hamburg, Germany, require huge capital commitments and can drag on for years until a consensus is reached with regard to the scale and composition of the project. Because of the beneficial influences that a hotel provides, incentives are very often offered in the form of zoning variances and bonuses, as well as tax abatements and other economic incentives meant to encourage developers to include hotels in their schemes. Hotels often act as catalysts, promoting other more lucrative surrounding development, and are as essential as residential development for a balanced community.

In the same mold as Louis Sullivan's Auditorium Building, the Elbphilharmonie, designed by Herzog & de Meuron, brings an iconic cultural building to a prominent site on Hamburg's harbor. And just as with the Auditorium Building, a major performance space will synergistically cohabit the building with a significant hotel. Buried deep in the heart of the stunning glass form that emerges from the historic warehouse building, the 2,150-seat philharmonic hall is wrapped on all sides by 250 hotel rooms and 47 apartments. Coming off a broad waterfront public plaza adjacent to the hotel lobby, the entrance to the performance hall is via a breathtakingly long escalator that runs diagonally across the warehouse, transporting

Westin Elbphilharmonie, Hamburg, Germany
The 250 guestrooms and 47 serviced condominiums of the Westin Hamburg will wrap around a new philharmonic hall with spectacular views of the sprawling Hamburg harbor. Architects Herzog & de Meuron designed this complex mixed-use project placing a dramatic mirror-glass-skinned wave-inspired form on top of an existing red-brick building, formerly a cocoa bean warehouse.

visitors up to a spacious public terrace with spectacular views of the city and harbor.

The key goal to a successful mixed-use development must be for each component of the development to benefit from its inclusion with the overall project and to draw significant advantages from its interaction with other components. For that to happen, a synergy must exist between its various uses, such as hotels, office, retail, residential, and entertainment, to produce a positive confluence where the entire development becomes far greater than the sum of its parts. The W Mumbai Hotel brings the W brand's prestigious international reputation and design hotel cachet with 350 rooms in the 62-story Namaste Tower designed by WS Atkins. Hotel, office, and retail uses are synergistically woven with multiple shared amenities, including a top-floor quadruple-height atrium space which will enclose the Sky Restaurant and Bar with stunning views of south central Mumbai. Advantages of mixed-use projects include:

- Higher visibility as a result of being part of a larger more prestigious project
- More efficient methods of land use, assembly, construction, and financing

- Greater built-in market demand
- Adjacency to a captive audience
- Certain shared operating costs
- Combined efficiency of a central energy plant serving the entire complex
- Combined loading facilities
- Better control over and improved traffic circulation patterns
- Combined comfort and security of an enclosed development
- Shared parking where different peak business hours allow for a reduction in spaces
- Insulation against market fluctuations of any one component

Shangri-La Hotel at the Shard, London, United Kingdom
Renzo Piano's beautifully conceived contribution to the London skyline in the London Bridge Quarter will include 538,000 sq ft (49,950 sq m) of office space and a 195-room Shangri-La Hotel. Two sky gardens are located on each office floor to help improve indoor air quality as well as naturally ventilate the work areas.

Just as a hotel's success is based on the right mix of facilities, the viability of a mixed-use development depends upon the optimum combination of uses it offers. A market analysis and feasibility study may provide a rational evaluation of the proposed uses and indicate the profitability of the overall project as well as each component by itself. It is difficult to find building types or uses that are not on some level compatible with hotels or for which some historic precedent can't be found. One might think of factories or prisons, but it doesn't take much imagination to realize that a hospitality market could exist even for these functions.

Major mixed-use projects can revitalize a section of a city by delivering its amalgamation of compatible businesses in the form of a spectacular architectural statement. Renzo Piano's Shard at London Bridge Quarter does just that and more. As the tallest building in Western Europe, the 72-story building is an iconic symbol of economic growth for central London. A 195-room Shangri-La Hotel shares this magnificent edifice with offices and luxury apartments, along with a public viewing gallery at the top. The development of the Shard included major improvements to a vital public transportation hub that includes London Bridge Station, with over 350,000 journeys through the station daily.

Design Considerations

Whether connected through a mall, an atrium, a central lobby, or some other pedestrian circulation element common to other primary functions in the mixed-use development, the hotel lobby should be designed as an extension of the overall development. In most cases, because of greater circulation resulting from traffic of adjacent uses, the hotel lobby should be 20 percent larger than those of other downtown hotels with comparable guestroom capacity. Hotel restaurants and lounges should have entrances directly on the common circulation where possible, with open cafés on the center's atriums. Their restaurant and bar seating should be 30 percent more than in conventional downtown or suburban hotels, reflecting the greater built-in demand for lunch and dinner, drawing from the center's retail, entertainment, residential, and office areas.

With a bridge connecting the development to Air Canada Centre, home to the Toronto Raptors (basketball) and the Toronto Maple Leafs (hockey), the Maple Leaf Square mixed-use development includes two slender residential towers above a nine-story podium containing retail, office space, entertainment venues, a daycare facility, and a 167-room Le Germain Hotel. The roof of the podium will be landscaped into a series of courtyards and terraces for hotel, daycare, and residential uses.

In high-rise mixed-use complexes where uses are divided vertically and hotel guestroom levels are located on upper floors over office, retail, or residential levels, a hotel "sky lobby" may be required if adequate space is not available in the building's podium. A porte cochère and a well-defined street-level hotel entrance lobby must be provided, and should be separate and distinct from the office, residential, or retail entrances. The entrance lobby must be staffed by doormen and a reception desk, where guests are greeted and

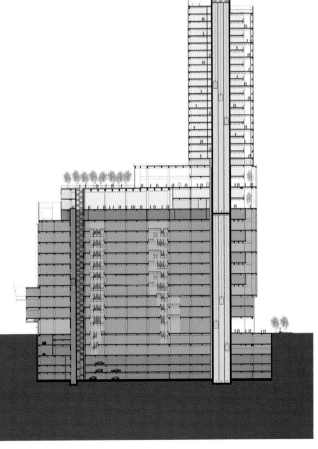

Le Germain Hotel at Maple Leaf Square, Toronto, Canada
Connected to the Air Canada Centre, Maple Leaf Square is an
energetic 24-hour sports, entertainment, and residential development
in downtown Toronto. Twin residential towers with 900 condominium
units rise above a nine-story podium containing the 167-key Le Germain
Hotel, a daycare center, a 40,000 sq ft (3,716 sq m) Longo's supermarket,
sports bar, and fine-dining restaurant, with additional office and
commercial space.

Grand Hyatt Chengdu, Chengdu, China
The 450-key Grand Hyatt hotel is designed on 25 floors above the
12-story, 120,000 sq ft (11,148 sq m) Chicony Plaza Department Store,
on a full city block adjacent to a vibrant public square in the central
business district of Chengdu. The two primary masses of podium and
tower are unified by a series of stepped gardens that are accessible
from the hotel's sky lobby, ballrooms, and dining facilities.

directed to express elevators that take them directly to the sky lobby floor. This should contain all of the ingredients normally found in a downtown hotel lobby: reception desk, lobby lounge, restaurants and bar, and access to function rooms and health clubs. From the upper lobby, guests gain access to a separate set of elevators connecting to the guestroom floors. Sky lobbies have the potential for great drama as they may open up to a dramatic panoramic view. The Ritz-Carlton at the International Commerce Centre in West Kowloon, Hong Kong, is (as of this writing) the current title-holder as the world's highest hotel. Occupying floors 102 to 118, the hotel also boasts the world's highest swimming pool on the 118th floor. In a new meaning to the term "sky lobby," guests are whisked by express elevators in 50 seconds up to the 103rd floor main hotel lobby, with astonishing views of the harbor and city skyline. KPF Architects' design for the ICC tower was originally taller but Hong Kong zoning regulations require building heights to be less than the surrounding mountains.

To determine the number of parking spaces required in a mixed-use complex, a study of peak-hour business of all major uses should be conducted to determine the crests and valleys of parking requirements for each use at different times during the day. For example, since the peak business hours of retail malls and hotels overlap, separate additional parking is normally required to accommodate both functions. A specific parking area should be set aside for hotel use to ensure space for its guests. With underground garages, a separate shuttle elevator between the garage and the

(continued p. 116)

Radisson Blu Hotel, Chicago, Illinois
The undulating concrete slabs of the 86-story tower, with resulting odd-shaped projecting balconies, provides a strong connection to outdoors and forms an unexpected community of adjacent users. Hotel guests enjoy participating in this high-rise vertical neighborhood while delighting in its spectacular views.

Solis Hotel, Shenzhen, China
Conceived as a floating horizontal skyscraper, Steven Holl's design for the headquarters building of Vanke, China's largest residential real estate developer, will include a 200-room Solis Hotel, an 86,000 sq ft (8,000 sq m) conference and exhibition center, serviced apartments, and small restaurants and cafés scattered throughout a tropical park.

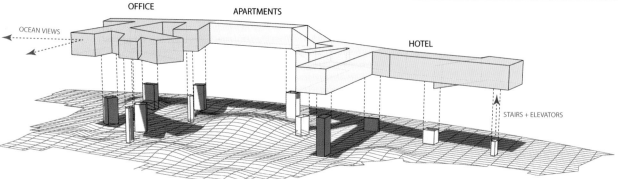

The Ritz-Carlton at the International Commerce Centre (ICC), West Kowloon, Hong Kong, China

Architect: KPF Associates and Wong & Guyang
Interior Designer: LTW Design Works

Union Square in West Kowloon, Hong Kong, is a massive mixed-use development project on 33.5 acres (13.54 hectares) of reclaimed land. The development is ringed with 17 high-rise buildings with 11,732,940 sq ft (1,090,026 sq m) of commercial, residential, and leisure uses, including the 890,700 sq ft (82,750 sq m) Elements shopping mall with 123 high-end stores, an ice skating rink and the 1,600-seat Grand Cinema, the largest cinema complex in Hong Kong. Built on top of Kowloon Station of the Hong Kong Mass Transit Railway, the complex includes some of the tallest buildings in Hong Kong, including the tallest residential tower—the Cullinan—and the tallest commercial building—the 118-story International Commerce Centre (ICC), designed by Kohn Pederson Fox Architects (KPF). In addition to private residences, the twin-tower Cullinan houses the 393-room W Hong Kong Hotel and the 266-suite HarbourView Place. The pinnacle of the development is the ICC, which houses the "highest hotel" in the world—The Ritz-Carlton Hong Kong.

KPF designed the tower with tapered inverted corners and with gently sloping curves at its base to optimize the building's structural performance. Its triple-glazed curtain wall curves outward at the base, forming entrance canopies on three sides, with a dynamic atrium on the north side that provides a public connection to the public transit station, Elements Mall, cinema, and the rest of Union Square.

The Ritz-Carlton Hong Kong occupies floors 102 to 118 of the ICC tower, with 312 luxury guestrooms including a 30,000 sq ft (2,750 sq m) presidential suite on the 117th floor. Guests enter the hotel's arrival lobby in the building podium and are taken in high-speed express elevators 1,394 ft (425 m) to the Sky Lobby on the 103rd floor. Three restaurants, Tosca, an Italian restaurant,

(top) Ritz-Carlton at ICC, sky lobby (103rd floor)
(bottom) Ritz-Carlton at ICC, guestroom

Ritz-Carlton at ICC

Ritz-Carlton at ICC, swimming pool (118th floor)

Ritz-Carlton at ICC, dining room

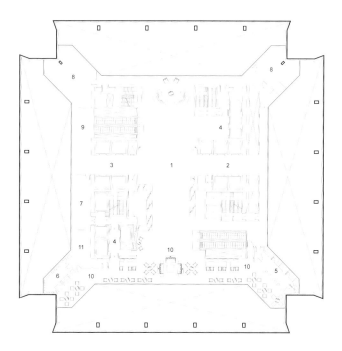

HOTEL RECEPTION LEVEL

1. RECEPTION HALL
2. HOTEL LIFT LOBBY
3. HOTEL SHUTTLE LOBBY
4. LIFT LOBBY
5. FEMALE WC
6. MALE WC
7. OFFICE
8. ANCILLARY OFFICE
9. HOTEL GIFT SHOP
10. LOUNGE
11. STORE

Ritz-Carlton at ICC

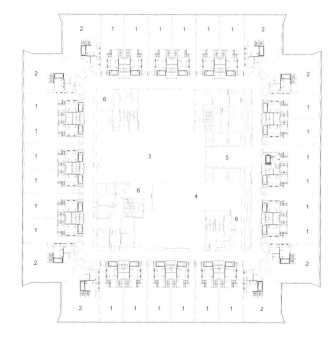

HOTEL GUEST ROOM LEVEL

1. STANDARD ROOM
2. EXECUTIVE SUITE TYPE 1
3. AHU ROOM
4. SMOKE MAKE-UP FAN ROOM
5. HOTEL LIFT LOBBY
6. BACK OF HOUSE

a Chinese restaurant, and the main restaurant, are all located one floor below reception on floor 102. Guests need key-cards in order to use the hotel elevators to access the hotel rooms on floors 104–117. The 118th floor includes a dazzling infinity-edge swimming pool, along with the Ozone Bar. The 116th floor houses the 9,250 sq ft (860 sq m) Ritz-Carlton Spa by ESPA, with nine deluxe treatment rooms and two couples' suites, all with floor-to-ceiling windows overlooking the harbor. Near the arrival area in the building podium, The Ritz-Carlton operates 14,000 sq ft (1,300 sq m) of meeting space, including one of Hong Kong's largest ballrooms at 10,000 sq ft (925 sq m).

KPF collaborated on ICC with Hong Kong Polytechnic University in the design of an innovative energy-optimizer air-conditioning system that monitors consumption, storing data for further analysis. Other sustainable features of the building include elevators with a smart-card system that puts passengers heading to similar destinations together to reduce the waste associated with vertical travel, as well as reusing the water from the air-conditioning unit for use in the cooling towers and toilet flushing.

lobby is preferable for security purposes, rather than extending the central elevator bank directly to the garage levels.

Service entrances may be combined for all facilities in the complex, and located underground on tight urban sites. Special security practices must be provided at the loading docks and receiving offices in this type of shared arrangement.

A wide variety of configurations are employed when combining uses within a single building or complex, and the hotel's interactive role is defined by its position in the composition. Hotels can be the dominant component of the mixed-use complex, such as with Grand

Hyatt Chengdu, where the hotel is the larger of the two uses in the building, or may represent a relatively small part of the development, as with the Radisson Blu Hotel in the Aqua Building in Chicago, where the hotel occupies only 18 out of 86 floors.

Within a single building a mixed-use complex is normally divided vertically with the hotel at the top, middle or bottom of a tower. The vertically separated hotel must be served by its own ground-level entrance canopy and a dedicated bank of elevators. Where the site is large enough to permit a horizontal arrangement of uses, the hotel may be located on the same floors as the other uses but in a separate wing of a single building, such as the Solis Hotel at Steven Holl's Vanke Center in Shenzhen. Alternatively, it may be a separate building linked by common spaces, as with Holl's Linked Hybrid Hotel in Beijing, which is literally linked with a bridge at an upper level and at grade by common circulation.

The Crystal Towers Hotel and Spa in Cape Town is an example of a mixed-use complex where each element—hotel, residential, and commercial office—is expressed as a separate architectural form within the overall ensemble. The hotel and residential towers share a common promenade that links the two uses at grade.

Linked Hybrid, Beijing, China
Steven Holl's design for the mixed-use complex comprises 650 apartments in eight towers ranging from 14 to 21 stories that are connected near their tops by one- and two-story bridges. The bridges form a "sky loop" that provides programmed space for art galleries, shops, cafés, and even a fitness club with a swimming pool. A cylindrical hotel and an angular multiplex movie theater rise from a large reflecting pool at the heart of the complex.

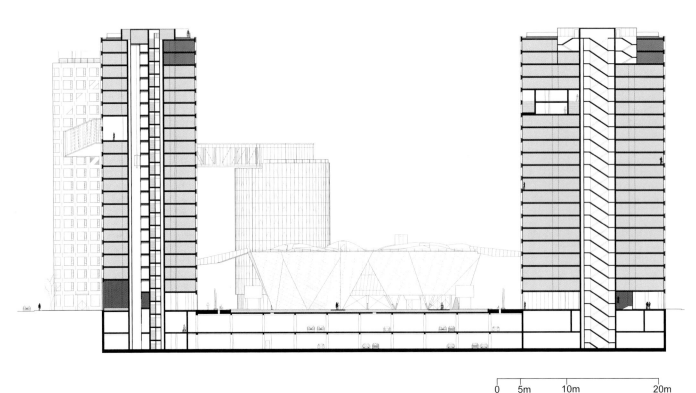

0   5m   10m   20m

116

What pressures specific to the twentieth century does the combination of program impose on architectural form? Concentration of many social activities within an architectural form distend and warp a pure building type. Certain previously neglected forms of associations have been wrenched together in the modern city so as to generate buildings which might stand as an anti-typology, if examined under current theoretical preoccupations. Building functions are mixed, disparate uses combined, structures collected here are "Hybrid Buildings" with respect to use. Although there are examples of combined function buildings throughout history (the house over the shop is prevalent in many ages and cultures), Hybrid Buildings developed most rapidly in the twentieth century. The modern city has acted as fertilizer for the growth of architectures from the homogeneous to the heterogeneous in regard to use. Urban densities and evolving building techniques have affected the mixing of functions, piling one atop another, defying critics who contend that a building should look like what it is.

(Steven Holl, quoted in Joseph Fenton, *Pamphlet Architecture 11: Hybrid Buildings*, Princeton: Princeton Architectural Press, 1984, p. 3)

Crystal Towers Hotel and Spa, Cape Town, South Africa
The mixed-use development is composed of three building components. The 12-story, 180-key hotel tower and 90-unit residential tower are joined at the base by a common retail promenade. The free-standing six-story commercial office building completes the ensemble and shares access over the canal by a distinctive steel suspension bridge.

Resort Hotels

The first resorts were seaside spas in ancient Greece and Rome, a concept which soon advanced throughout the Roman Empire (see the list of hotel milestones in Chapter 1). After their decline in the Middle Ages, spas were revived along with the flourishing of the arts and sciences during the Renaissance, and returned to prominence throughout Europe. For example, the most famous of ancient spa destinations, Germany's Baden-Baden, has over fifty hotels to cater to the thousands of visitors who come each year to enjoy the town's natural mineral springs, a draw since the time of Roman emperor Aurelius Severus. Following similar origins, the earliest North American resorts were spas, starting in the 1750s in White Sulphur Springs, West Virginia, and in the resort community of Saratoga Springs, New York, which reached the height of its popularity as a national social center in the 1850s.

During the early years of the industrial revolution, resorts remained the province of the well-to-do. Fashionable hotels, such as Mohonk Mountain House in upstate New York and the Hotel del Coronado in San Diego, California, prospered in diverse scenic mountain and seaside settings. But the twentieth century saw the resort become increasingly accessible to the middle class through steadily rising disposable income and paid vacations, particularly following World War II. This included dramatic increases in leisure travel by Europeans and Asians, primarily Japanese, as well as Americans. Resorts experienced a sustained growth boom, eventually evolving into highly customized categories serving many different types of vacationers.

Beyond basic property type, location is a prime influence on resort development. In established resort regions such as Cancun or Phuket, resort amenities—spas, sports and recreation facilities, and related retail—are provided in virtually all hotels, for required market flexibility and because they are preferred and expected by most travelers. Also, resort amenities often are added to non-resort properties because of the continued growth of health consciousness and fitness megatrends. Resort programming, site layout, and hotel design are all vitally influenced by such cultural and market trends.

It's not just vacationers who seek out resorts: the MICE segment (meetings, incentives, conventions, and events) increasingly looks to these properties to attract participants and add value to meetings and events. The needs of the leisure and MICE markets, combined with cultural and environmental considerations in a given location, determine whether the resort buildings are designed in low-rise structures to sensitively blend with the traditional community and landscape, as at the Qasr Al Sarab Desert Resort by Anantara, or in striking, highly conceptual buildings like the innovative Yas Viceroy

Qasr Al Sarab Desert Resort by Anantara, Abu Dhabi, United Arab Emirates
This property's strong sense of place was inspired by Bedouin fort architecture and local building techniques, including earthen retaining walls and a stucco exterior that resembles traditional mud construction.

Hotel in Abu Dhabi. But regardless of the building type, resort guests demand a strong sense of place.

While most vacation spots are places guests travel to, new types of in-city resort-like hotels are designed to advance weekend or other non-traveling "stay-cations." Often located on the urban waterfront or in the heart of the city near upscale shopping and offering elaborate spa facilities, these hotels effectively function as urban resorts, designed for tourists as well as local guests preferring convenient close-by vacations that save on travel time and expense.

This chapter is organized into nine basic categories reflecting the wide range of resort types, from secluded beach resorts to vast multi resort destination complexes. While casinos and vacation ownership properties have many resort-like qualities, these hotel types have special design requirements and will be discussed in their own chapters.

General Planning and Design Considerations

The primary function of a resort is to offer an escape from everyday life. Environments that are highly evocative of a specific place, time, or culture are appealing to resort travelers, who want experiences that they cannot get at home. Many successful resorts emphasize vernacular architecture and materials as a way of transporting guests to what is often an idealized version of a destination, but one that assures that the vacation will be memorable. This requires careful consideration of local building styles and relationships to the geography. Landscaping takes on much more importance in resorts, as guests tend to spend more time outside at these properties, which means attention to detail during the design phase to create pleasing outdoor experiences and to provide the means for operators to maintain them.

Resorts are subject to fluctuations in demand that are somewhat predictable: ski resorts will be busiest in the snowy months, while the lakefront resort peaks in the summer. Planning a hotel that can handle high volumes of guests during the peak season but will still be profitable in the shoulder seasons presents challenges. A common approach is to divide guestroom areas into blocks or wings that can be opened and closed as demand dictates, and to do the same with amenities such as food and beverage outlets and recreational spaces. Designing with seasonality in mind is also helpful in the event of unforeseen dips in demand due to natural or political upheaval. Conversely, the developer and designers need to consider how the property will grow as a destination becomes more popular.

In recent years the trend has been toward more family and extended-family resort travel, pushing up the demand for suites and self-contained villas or cabins. Today's resort may have as many as 25 percent of its keys allocated to suites, and many luxury properties are made up largely of standalone villas.

Length of stay influences the number and size of hotel amenities. Resorts tend to have many more food and beverage seats per key than other types of hotels, because offering dining variety keeps guests on the property throughout their stay. The provision and placement of sports and recreation facilities has the same goal: to enhance the guest experience while generating additional revenue, either directly through user fees or indirectly through food and beverage or retail purchases. Length of stay also should be noted when planning the guestroom, as larger closets and more storage space in general will be necessities.

Just as guests have higher storage needs in resorts, so do hotel operators. Depending on the setting, a resort may receive less frequent deliveries of some or all supplies, so adequate back-of-house storage is key. Maintenance facilities for golf courses and boat docks, as well as shops and storage for recreational equipment and outdoor furnishings, all add to the resort's support space, which can be as high as 15 percent of the hotel's total built area.

Each kind of resort hotel has specific and unique planning and design requirements. The following sections describe nine major types of resort and illustrate some of each type's important development, planning, and design issues.

Seaside Resorts

From the Sardinian coast to the Gulf of California, from Cape Town to the Canaries, and from Key West to Kauai, most vacationers head for the seaside, where seemingly endless beachfronts continue to supply idyllic sites for most new resorts. Views and water sports, including underwater scuba trails (and schools for certification), as well as imaginative accommodations, keep the second-oldest form of resort, after the health spa, the most popular of all. Major seaside resorts also provide golf and tennis facilities matching those of scenic mountain and desert resorts, as much as those specializing in golf or tennis. They emphasize sports and spa facilities as well as convention and conference centers for business groups. Such resort amenities also attract the typical business traveler, who often chooses them, where available, over downtown or suburban hotels. And corporate groups increasingly prefer resorts for business gatherings, as their more relaxed atmosphere promotes teamwork and closer personal contacts. "Even when people play a bad round of golf together, it brings them closer," one manager observed. Corporate meeting planners feel that resorts:

- Combine the most effective training atmosphere, with a touch of reward added as motivation.
- Are self-contained, with conference and recreational amenities closely integrated, making it easier to keep a group together in a more productive series of meetings.
- Go all out to please aesthetically, with imaginative design, lush scenery, and recreational features that leave groups with a sense of reward for their working meetings.

But the above factors apply only if the resort provides the highest quality conferencing technology, uppermost in the meeting planners' requirements. Of equal importance, to attract both family and business groups resorts must provide the widest and most imaginative array of sports and recreation activities, from golf to aerobics and teen activities, to ensure satisfying all members and guests of the typical group.

St. Regis Sanya Yalong Bay Resort, Sanya, China
Set within a wetlands sanctuary, the 400-room resort's main building is completely surrounded by water, including a lagoon, a private marina, and two landscaped swimming pools. Against a mountainous backdrop, this aquatic setting enhances the hotel's relationship to its 800 ft (244 m) of pristine beachfront.

Four Seasons, Bora Bora, Tahiti
Overlooking the cerulean waters of Bora Bora lagoon with sensational views of Mount Otemanu, each of the 121 beach and over-water bungalows is styled after classic Polynesian bungalow architecture featuring traditional teak-wood furnishings, high ceilings, and thatched roofs made from pandanus leaves.

Planning Considerations

Although closeness to the water is the essential ingredient of the seaside resort, environmental regulations in many areas, particularly those lacking comprehensive master plans, mandate large set-backs of 200 ft (61 m) or more from the shoreline. While guestroom balconies and full exterior window walls help dramatize beach views, designers add such water features as canals and decorative pools to enhance the hotel's relationship to the shoreline and to compensate where the hotel is off the beach. This is done at the Kahala Hilton in Honolulu, Hawaii, which has its own large lagoon and dolphin pond, and the St. Regis Sanya Yalong Bay Resort, which is entirely surrounded by water.

Alila Villas Uluwatu, Bali, Indonesia

Perched high above limestone cliffs on a dry elevated savannah, 84 villas are tucked into the gently sloping landscape, each with a private pool and cabana overlooking the sea. WOHA Designs employed sustainable principles throughout the complex, including careful placement of structures with minimal disruption to the existing vegetation and to the natural contours of the site.

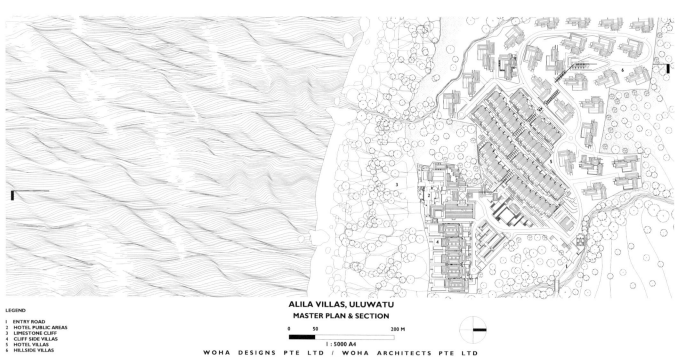

LEGEND

1 ENTRY ROAD
2 HOTEL PUBLIC AREAS
3 LIMESTONE CLIFF
4 CLIFF SIDE VILLAS
5 HOTEL VILLAS
6 HILLSIDE VILLAS

ALILA VILLAS, ULUWATU
MASTER PLAN & SECTION

0   50   200 M

1 : 5000 A4

WOHA DESIGNS PTE LTD / WOHA ARCHITECTS PTE LTD
2008
© WOHA Pte Ltd DEC 2003. All rights reserved.

Shade structures, whether moveable, trellised, or landscape types, increase comfort along beaches, and are essential at swimming pools and other water-sports facilities, whirlpools, bars, and food-service areas. Siting the hotel at or close to the shoreline, or in a lagoon, becomes more interesting and exciting when environmentally compatible, such as at Four Seasons Bora Bora or Beach House Maldives, where bungalows are built out over the water, strung along a serpentine boardwalk.

Hotels built into shoreline bluffs or cliffs can be strikingly effective, as at the Alila Villas Uluwatu on the dramatic southern cliffs of the Indonesian island of Bali. As with Uluwatu, care must be taken to plan around important landscape features such as large boulders or mature trees when siting cliff-side villas.

Resorts provide ocean views for virtually all rooms. The more efficient double-loaded corridor designs are oriented perpendicular to the shoreline, allowing interesting 90-degree views of both land and water. Single-loaded hotel wings provide the guest with a 180-degree water view, but the construction costs are about 15 percent higher, since they require twice the normal corridor space, plus additional exterior walls with windows in the corridors and related air-conditioning. Known as "cost guzzlers," they are not only wasteful of energy and land, but require additional staff due to the structure's increased servicing distances. But a small percentage of single-loaded spaces can often be most cost-effective, particularly where this helps provide an economical solution to an otherwise unusable site or building orientation problem. However, where climates

W Retreat Kanai and Spa, Riviera Maya, Mexico
Views of the ocean and mangrove landscape define the building forms in Richard Meier's design for the 180-room W Retreat Kanai, located on the Yucatan Peninsula near Cancun. The strong T-shape geometry of the main hotel building surrounds the main pool, maximizing daylight with its southwest orientation and engaging spectacular views. A single-loaded guestroom wing is intersected by parallel wings that run perpendicular to the shoreline, with guestrooms that angle out toward the sea.

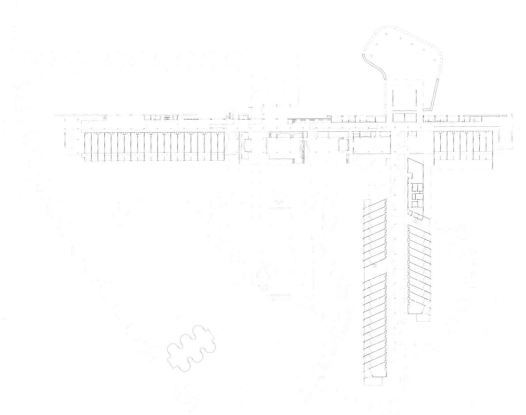

Ground Floor Plan
Kanai

5 m   35 m

Richard Meier & Partners Architects LLP
January, 2011

Paradisus Resort, Punta Cana, Dominican Republic
The all-inclusive 537-deluxe suite resort, located on world-famous
Bavaro Beach, allows guests to enjoy unlimited meals and snacks,
beverages, entertainment, sports facilities, services, and amenities.
Situated on 96 acres (38.8 hectares) of beachfront property in Punta
Cana, the resort is designed to blend 35 two-story bungalows and
a spectacular lake-style swimming pool in perfect harmony with the
natural beauty of the exotic environment.

permit the single-loaded hotel to have an open-air balcony-type
corridor, it costs about the same as the double-loaded scheme, and
may present a viable solution.

As with other types of lodging, architects can plan resorts in a
variety of ways. Atriums with single-loaded interior balcony corridors
may be justified in luxury resorts with the highest rates. For example,
if the architect locates guestrooms on three sides of the major lobby
space, all oriented toward the ocean, the guests are rewarded with
views of the crashing surf. The total land area requirement for a luxury
resort, however, depends on larger considerations than the coverage
or bulk of its buildings. For example, a 500-room mid-rise beachfront
hotel generally requires about 10 acres (4 hectares), including a
swimming pool and related landscaping, with most parking placed
below grade. However, the total land development for the resort
depends on the extent of major recreational components such as
golf, tennis, and other such amenities. For instance, a tennis center
with 10 courts would require an additional 3 acres (1.2 hectares),
and an 18-hole golf course approximately 110 to 160 acres (45 to
64 hectares).

An important planning consideration for resort developments,
particularly for those in remote locations or on uninhabited islands,
such as the Beach House Maldives and Mandarin Oriental Dellis
Cay in Turks and Caicos, is the availability and accommodation of
employees. Often a developer will look for a village or a number of
villages within the vicinity of the resort site that can supply a large
portion of the resort's labor pool. Training programs are set up for

the purpose of employing locals to serve the resort; however, skilled
positions may need to be filled by importing experienced personnel
and accommodating them in or near the resort. Transportation to
and from the resort must also be considered. In some cases, in larger
resorts, an employee village may be planned for this purpose and
could include housing, basic retail, child care, and entertainment
facilities for its inhabitants. Higher-echelon staff might be given small
villas or other more upscale lodging. Employing local residents has the
benefit of providing an economic improvement aspect to the project
and can facilitate approvals and acceptance of the development
by local government authorities. Investment in the infrastructure,
housing, and schools within an established nearby village can also
be a viable option to insuring the availability of quality personnel.

The variety of accommodation offerings at individual seaside
resorts has reached a new apex with the Water Cay Baccarat Resort
in Turks and Caicos. When it is completed, visitors will be able to
book a variety of room types in the main hotel building, an over-
water bungalow, in-water bungalow, overland tree-house, inland
tree-house, cliff villa, beach villa, marina condo unit or ocean condo
unit. That's not to mention several varieties of seaside single-family
villas offered in the rental pool.

In the early stages of seaside resort planning, it is important to
identify plant materials for the project and to initiate a site nursery
so that new plantings are somewhat mature by the opening of the
resort. Without a nursery the resort may take several years to look
complete, as vegetation needs time to fully develop.

All-inclusive resorts provide guests with a wide range of amenities
and food and beverage venues as part of the vacation package.
These types of resorts require major back-of-house and support
spaces beyond normal operations. The Paradisus Punta Cana Resort
in the Dominican Republic boasts "ultra-inclusive" amenities, with
12 restaurants, seven bars, 24-hour room service, nightclub acts,
unlimited golf, tennis, horseback riding, and spas, and even includes
Dominican cigars. Guests at these resorts are required to wear digital
wrist-bands or other devices to prove that they are legitimate users
when they avail themselves of the inclusive amenities.

Design Considerations

Architect Marcel Breuer pointed out that the main visual features
people focus on are the landscaping and the building finishes. But
while building materials may vary in their appeal, proper landscaping
always receives praise, and this is never more true than at a resort.
Landscaping also relates the development to its natural environment,
whether coastal, mountain, or desert.

Architects and interior designers appropriately draw on the beauty
of the natural landscape as a vital theme of the resort's design. Since
guests are drawn to their favorite environments, such as the Caribbean
for the beach and the sun, or mountain locations for scenery, such
natural attractions are reinforced by both the architecture and interior
design through color, form, and materials. For example, earth tones
and rugged finishes often psychologically blend with mountain resorts,
while pastel colors more closely recall beach locations, green interior
accents complement forest settings, and natural sandstone finishes

(continued p. 128)

Park Hyatt Maldives, Hadahaa
Architect: SCDA Architects
Interior Designer: SCDA Architects

Park Hyatt Maldives, Hadahaa, is situated on a small pristine island 250 miles (400 km) south of Male on the Gaafu Alifu (North Huvadhoo) Atoll, believed to be one of the largest and deepest atolls in the world. Designed by Singapore architect Chan Soo Khian of SCDA Architects, the resort opened as an Alila resort but a few years later was rebranded as a Park Hyatt.

Guests arrive via speedboat from the airport and are greeted on the arrival jetty by resort staff and taken to a sheltered reception area, whose design was derived from the distinctive timber-ribbed hull of the traditional Maldivian *dhoni* boat, used for inter-atoll navigation. Metaphorically, the guests arrive to an overturned boat, as if cast away to an enchanted island. Local craftsmen were used to create the dhoni hull, ensuring authenticity in the details. From reception the guests are taken to one of the 50 villas, offered in three types.

There are 14 Aqua Villas, which are 1,200 sq ft (110 sq m) and built over the water along the jetty; 20 Island Villas, which are 1,300 sq ft (120 sq m), built along the beach, and include a private plunge pool; and 16 Island Villas, which are 1,100 sq ft (102 sq m), are nestled among the natural vegetation of the island, and include a private deck. The orientation of each villa was carefully arranged to take best advantage of the tropical climate, utilizing high open ceilings, cross-ventilation, deep roof overhangs, and window-shading devices.

The resort includes a PADI five-star diving water sports center, offering guests the opportunity to dive amidst undisturbed reefs and sites in this untouched atoll, where the marine life is more abundant and varied than anywhere else in the Maldives. Other facilities include a tropical island garden spa, a fully equipped fitness and health center, two specialty restaurants, a rooftop lounge, and a library with a star-gazing roof.

The architect took great care in the design of the resort to preserve the natural vegetation, in order to maintain the ambience of the island and minimize its environmental footprint. Green Globe certification was achieved by utilizing sustainable design principles, including rainwater harvesting, waste treatment plants, solar shading, cross-ventilation in all indoor spaces, and bio-diversity protection of native species. The resort's close proximity to the equator makes it less susceptible to tropical storms, so precautions for storm-surge and wind-resistant structures were less of a concern than for resorts in more vulnerable locations.

Park Hyatt Maldives Hadahaa, aqua villas

Park Hyatt Maldives Hadahaa, reception dhoni

Park Hyatt Maldives Hadahaa, island villa

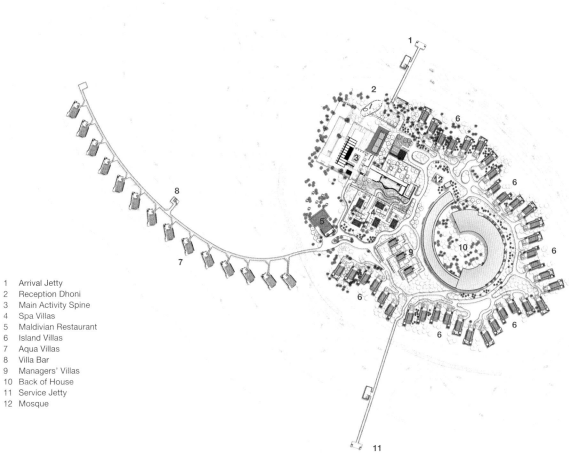

1   Arrival Jetty
2   Reception Dhoni
3   Main Activity Spine
4   Spa Villas
5   Maldivian Restaurant
6   Island Villas
7   Aqua Villas
8   Villa Bar
9   Managers' Villas
10 Back of House
11 Service Jetty
12 Mosque

Park Hyatt Maldives Hadahaa, site plan

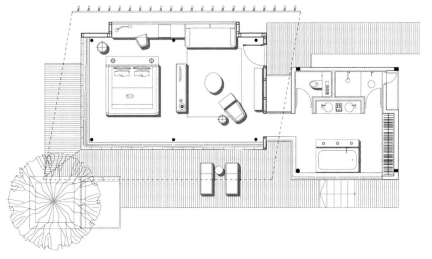

Park Hyatt Maldives Hadahaa, island villa floor plan

Four Seasons Resort, Republic of Seychelles
Built on a rugged site on Mahe Island, the resort exemplifies the principles of designing in harmony with the existing terrain. The development was carefully crafted onto this sensitive site, which stretches from a coral beach to tropical hillsides and rock outcrops. To minimize disturbance to the natural beauty and the ecological balance of the site, individual structures were painstakingly located and then adjusted at micro level to ensure existing rock outcrops and vegetation were least disturbed and the natural flow of rainwater was not adversely affected.

Viceroy, Anguilla, British West Indies
Set on rocky bluffs overlooking Meads Bay, the Viceroy casts strong geometric lines against the subtle natural beauty of the Caribbean beachscape. WATG Architects crafted an elegant ensemble of stark modern structures to house 166 villas, townhomes, and resort residences with a 140-seat restaurant and an 8,000 sq ft (743 sq m) spa at this luxury seaside resort.

harmonize with desert sites. In addition, local artwork and decorative motifs recall and inform the guest of the area's traditions.

Besides natural and traditional beauty, resorts emphasize comfort and luxury. Historically, for the well-off, resorts are generally expected to be more lavish in amenities and décor, even when informal in mood. Lobbies should be 30 percent larger than those of suburban or airport hotels, and 10 percent greater than those of downtown hotels of comparable size. This also reflects the additional time guests spend lounging and socializing in lobbies at resorts. Since many guests like to shop on vacations, 50 percent larger retail space should be provided than in downtown or suburban hotels. Complete space requirements are provided in Chapter 14.

Since both the average length of stay and the number of occupants per room are greater in resorts, guestrooms should be at least 10 percent larger. In areas with higher family occupancies, such as in Orlando, near Walt Disney World Resort and Universal Studios Escape, the guestroom length should be increased from the standard 18 ft to 21 ft (5.5 to 6.4 m) for ease in accommodating required roll-away beds and cribs. Closets should be at least 4.5 ft (1.4 m) long, since vacationers pack more clothing and sports equipment. Guests expect larger bathrooms, with dressing areas and additional amenities provided, as in the more luxurious resorts. Balconies should be at least 5 ft (1.5 m) deep, furnished with a table, chairs, and at least two chaises, essential for lounging and sunbathing, as well as enjoying views and relating to the outdoors.

A full-height window wall may be provided at the balconies to enhance guestroom views, with interlocks recommended on the doors, so that if they are left open the cooling system will automatically shut down. In addition to conserving energy, this avoids the possibility of mildew, which would cause discomfort in the guestroom. Some otherwise fine resorts experience this condition, particularly where care is not taken to vent wall cavities that may cause in-room condensation.

Exterior back-of-house areas, particularly loading docks and service drives, should be concealed by retaining walls, trellises, and landscaping. Truck docks must be roofed and enclosed to prevent unsightly views, noise, and odors. Where visible from upper levels, roofed areas should be terraced and decoratively landscaped to ensure pleasant exterior views from all guestrooms.

But no element sets the ambience of the resort more than its pool area. Since guests spend more time there than in any other public space, it affects their overall impression of the resort more than any other element and provides the same memorable experience as the main lobby in the downtown hotel.

Guests expect imaginative pool designs, which often provide a transition between the building and its surrounding natural land forms. Fanciful elements such as bridges, islands, grottos, and waterfalls, as well as totally abstract free forms, provide decorative photo backgrounds most often sought by guests at the pool. However, the overall pool size and shape must allow for swimming laps, group play, wading, and, with today's accent on fitness, sports such as water polo. Nevertheless, diving boards should be avoided, since they are a prime cause of accidents. The design must also maintain sight lines for lifeguard surveillance of all areas. A whirlpool at least 8 ft (2.4 m) in diameter should be located adjacent to the

**Anantara Desert Islands Resort and Spa by Anantara,
Abu Dhabi, United Arab Emirates**
Set on the island haven of Sir Bani Yas, a nature reserve just off the coast
of Abu Dhabi, the luxury Desert Islands Resort sits on a pristine beach
surrounded by the warm waters of the Arabian Gulf. The shoreline
infinity pool forms a breezy backdrop to a romantically lit outdoor
seafood restaurant.

swimming pool, with a second whirlpool near the beach. Wave-
pools, waterslides, and pools with spray fountains and related play
equipment are particularly important for resorts with high family
occupancy, but a separate adult pool must be provided in such cases.
Children's wading pools, where desired, should be located close to
the main pool for purposes of surveillance by parents.

However, pool design is subject to regional and cultural differences.
For example, in China a separate pool for younger children generally
is not desirable, because the Chinese believe that families should
treasure swimming together and be encouraged to do so. In various
Middle East areas, communal bathing is not permitted in public.
Local health and safety regulations also may vary. For example, while
popular with many guests, ramped pools, allowing bathers to wade
in from one end as at a beach, are prohibited in some areas because
of their lack of safeguards against entry by small children.

Pools must be located to obtain maximum sunlight exposure, but
in equatorial climates shading such as trellises must be designed
over a part of the pool, for relief from the sun. For example, at a

Hilton Sanya Resort and Spa, Sanya, China
Nestled amongst tropical gardens that stretch along 840 ft (256 m)
of pristine oceanfront beach, WATG's design for the 500-room resort
features a dramatic 25 acre (10 hectare) aquatic landscape that includes
nine swimming pools.

Ritz-Carlton Sanya, Sanya, China
Located on 37 acres (15 hectares) of the most secluded area of Yalong Bay, Sanya, this hotel's destination is known as the "Oriental Hawaii," as well as being China's only tropical seaside tourism resort. For the 450 guestrooms, suites, and villas, architects at WATG drew influence and inspiration from the classic building design of Beijing's Summer Palace, with high-pitched ceilings, dark rich wood, intricate carvings, and mosaic detailing, coupled with grand water features and opulent furnishings.

resort in Sharjah, along the Arabian Gulf, a tensile fabric structure is provided over the pool during the day, to reduce the intense sunlight, yet the pool must be heated at night.

And for one of the resort's most popular vacation sports, people-watching, for which more guests use the pool deck than the pool, adequate chaise-longue space must be provided. More than any other area, the pool deck encourages socializing, and many guests make friends there. Therefore, provide area for at least 1.5 chaises per room. Satellite bars often are built into or contiguous with the pool as convenient outdoor snack, juice, marina, or *tiki* bars, providing food and beverage service to virtually all outdoor areas.

Environmental Technology

With rare exceptions, the hotel industry fully understands the folly of any lack in preserving the environment, if for no other reason than to avoid problems which could diminish the guest appeal of the region. As Scott Berman, partner in the hospitality and leisure group of PricewaterhouseCoopers, warns: "Limpid, turquoise seas sell. Polluted waters and destroyed reefs don't."

Yet examples persist of inadequate protection, bureaucratic authorities, improper actions by developers and builders, and lapses in enforcement of standards posing potentially incremental as well as irreversible effects on total communities and business economies. For example, in an 80 mile (129 km) stretch along the east coast of Mexico's Yucatan Peninsula, extending from the fully developed Cancun area to the protected Mayan archeological sites of Tulum, one of the largest resort construction programs in history started with over 9,000 resort rooms and condominiums, to be followed by another scheduled 15,000 resort units over a five-year period—expansion that took fast-growing Cancun 20 years to develop. Dubbing it the Riviera Maya, developers proceeded, in many cases without approved permits, paving hundreds of acres of mangrove swamps, the crucial plant-life responsible for nourishing ocean reefs as well as wildlife. Such natural phenomena, properly protected, can preserve an ancient geographic area such as the Yucatan as a continuing attractive and viable ecotourist paradise, no matter how fragile it may be. But radical land-use changes require adequate study and respect for sound technical judgment. Only through alert international news reporting was the above critical condition exposed, publicly condemned, and corrected by the developers. Hopefully,

such publicity encourages proper legal reforms in other delicate environmental areas.

Acapulco, former Mecca to the jet set and popular resort, suffered serious long-term environmental damage from over-development, which, along with severe crowding and related social problems, resulted in a major decline in its tourism. Not surprisingly, some of our most superb resort areas, those best able to attract natural and historic interest and favored by sunny climates and convenient airline connections, may be lured into developing unreasonable resort densities. Therefore, for any large new resort development, studies should include an assessment of the eventual total capacity and an analysis of alternative physical concepts. These need to offer the developer a fair return, provide the guest with a vacation experience, and protect and preserve the environment and community. Frequently, developers run into legal difficulty by not being familiar with the local requirements. It is important that developers work within the system to:

- Prepare environmental and other analyses and keep clear documentation at each stage.
- Identify the government agency responsible for approving various aspects of the project.
- Acquire copies of all legal requirements, necessary permits, or technical standards applying to the project.
- Monitor construction and proactively seek government inspection and approval at each stage.

Waldorf=Astoria Maldives, Republic of Maldives
With a rich history stretching as far back as 2,000 BC, the Maldives formed part of a thriving trade route for the ancient Egyptians, Romans, Mesopotamians, Chinese, and Indians. Located on the pristine, lagoon-ringed Haa Alifu Atoll, which is fringed by powder-white beaches and has a leafy jungle at its center, the 35 acre (14 hectare) resort comprises 83 Maldivian-style villas, three restaurants, four bars, and a luxurious spa.

Island Resorts

The benefits of clean environments to islands have not escaped savvy vacationers, who by the planeload choose them as preferred getaways. Call it the "island phenomenon," but with economics amiable to leisure travel, land values of island resorts compared to those on other sites may soon exceed megatrend proportions.

In the mid-twentieth century, the Big Island, Hawaii's largest and most unique lava-based geological formation, began establishing the era's largest group of environmentally motivated, experimental, and ultimately successful resorts. Respected environmentalist Laurance Rockefeller, founder of RockResorts, and his highly dedicated architect, Nathaniel Owings (the O in SOM), created the Mauna Kea Beach Hotel: "one of the world's finest resorts, with Polynesian art displayed throughout, and its residential wings elevated to permit the landscaped grounds to freely flow into its interior gardens and courtyards further enhancing the resort experience" (Rutes and Penner, 1985). The design was far ahead of its time: the developers tested mock-ups of villa units, which decades later became a popular environmental

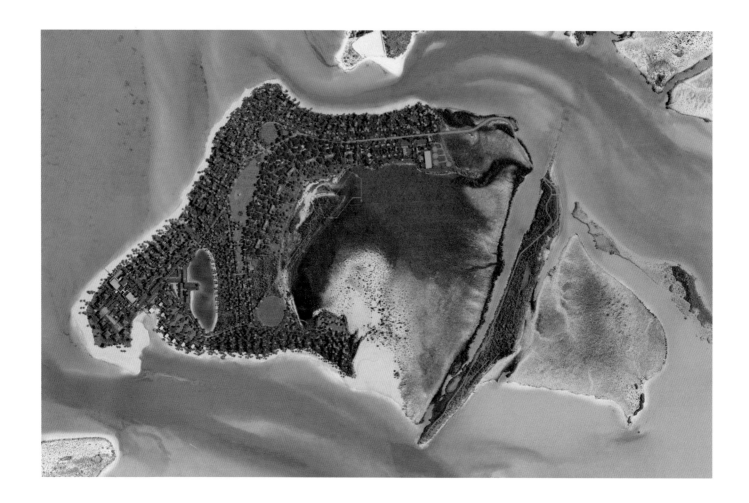

Mandarin Oriental Dellis Cay, Turks and Caicos Islands
Master-planned for an uninhabited island with building designs by seven of the world's foremost architects—David Chipperfield, Zaha Hadid, Kengo Kuma, Piero Lissoni, Shigeru Ban, Chad Oppenheim, and Carl Ettensperge—this 560 acre (227 hectare) island resort is planned to include 71 luxury waterfront and over-water villas, a 30,000 sq ft (2,750 sq m) spa, gourmet restaurants, retail, recreation and entertainment venues.

concept. Also, they made a noble effort to preserve the natural lava surface on the golf course; however, resort guests, wearing cleated golf shoes, voted to banish the hazardous slippery surface.

Planning a resort on an uninhabited island, such as the Dellis Cay resort in Turks and Caicos or the Beach House Maldives, presents many challenges and opportunities. Investment in basic infrastructure alone can make such developments prohibitively expensive to build. Special systems are often called for, such as wastewater-treatment plants, desalinization or reverse osmosis equipment, and electrical power generation through solar, tidal, or fuel-driven devices. Garbage collection must be planned, considering prevailing winds, for the use of clean-burning incinerators and compost areas. Fire stations and medical clinics are also important considerations for the more remote locations. Depending on the location, it might be necessary to include a cell phone tower on the island.

Water Cay Resort guests arrive at a small dock near Providenciales and are greeted in a simple lounge building, where they check in, hand over their luggage, and board a sleek speedboat for the 20 minute ride to Water Cay. The arrival experience is carefully choreographed as the boat enters a narrow channel leading past the marina village through thick native vegetation and up to the main hotel building, where an electric cart awaits, ready to whisk the guests on to their private over-water bungalow. Services of a coastal engineer become important for the planning of such resorts,

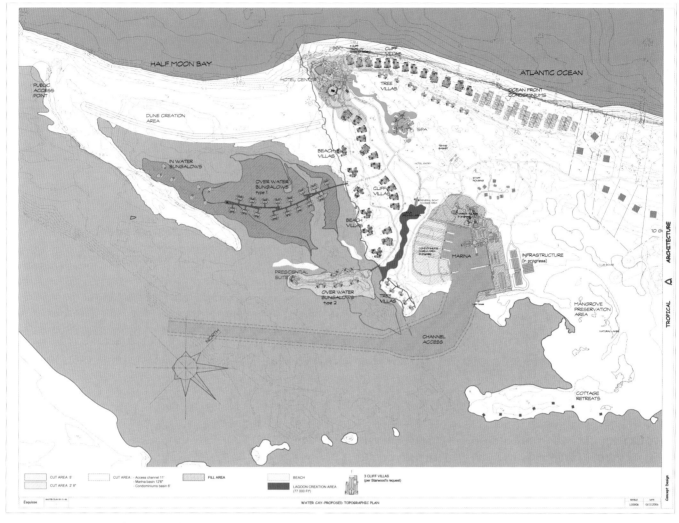

Water Cay Resort, Turks and Caicos Islands

Tahitian architect Pierre Lacombe of Tropical Architecture worked closely with coastal engineers in expertly sculpting this uninhabited island to its maximum potential for resort development. The 400 acre (160 hectare), 110-key resort includes 16 over-water bungalows, seven in-water pavilions, 28 tree houses, 26 cliff villas, and six beach villas. The hotel center includes multiple restaurants, bars, and lounges. The resort also includes a luxury spa, a marina village, a sports complex, and housing for 40 employees.

WaterColor Inn and Resort, Santa Rosa Beach, Florida

WaterColor is a 499 acre (201 hectare) master-planned community located on the northwest Gulf Coast. Planned by Cooper, Robertson & Partners, under the direction of the St. Joe Company, the resort exhibits vernacular architecture and many of the same new urbanism principles as its predecessor, Seaside Florida, which lies directly to the east. Fitting it perfectly to the milieu, Rockwell Group designed a 60-room beachfront hotel that combines the luxury of a Southern grand hotel with the casualness of an unpretentious beach cottage.

with dredging canals for sea craft movement and analysis of wave action and bathymetric and hydrology studies to determine the flow of tides into and out of arrival channels. Tidal range and storm surge determine the height of buildings above mean sea level and instruct engineering of structures to withstand impact during tropical storms and hurricanes. Jetties and artificial reefs are sometimes needed for beach protection and construction, and can even be used to construct small islands.

In the Caribbean islands, Florida, the Gulf Coast, the U.S. East Coast and Baja California, resort structures must be designed to withstand hurricane-strength winds of 150 mph (240 kph), as called for in the South Florida Building Code, and to withstand impact from large and small airborne missiles. Wooden structures are often better suited to these conditions through their ability to flex in strong winds, while more rigid structures such as steel or concrete may reach a failure point before bending. The corrosive nature of salt sea air must be considered when using steel for construction or when using metal finishes on the interior or exterior of the buildings.

Desert Resorts

In the early 1900s, the dry climate in desert communities began attracting visitors seeking its health benefits. A number of desert lodges sprang up around the Coachella Valley near Palm Springs, California, specializing in asthmatic and respiratory care. In 1909 Nellie Coffman created the famous Desert Inn in Palm Springs as a health-care hostelry. Early hotel operators seized the opportunity to attract wealthy Easterners afraid to travel to Europe during the war and attracted to the subtle beauty and serenity of the "Land of Eternal Sun." La Quinta Hotel, the desert's oldest resort, built its first 56 guest casitas in 1926 and quickly became a retreat for Hollywood stars looking for tranquility and seclusion. The city of La Quinta was named after the resort in 1982.

Attracted to the majestic beauty of ancient sand dunes, deep canyons, towering plateaus, looming buttes, mesas, and other mighty rock formations, travelers to desert resorts seek out the elemental harshness and solitude of the desert landscape.

Planning and Design Considerations

Were it not for the Palm Springs aquifer, Coachella Valley would have stayed raw desert, suitable only for a few drought-tolerant animals and plants. All drinking and other domestic water comes from the aquifer, a source usually referred to as groundwater. Water from the Colorado River recharges the aquifer via the 122 mile (196 km) Coachella Canal. It is also naturally recharged by rain and melted snow from nearby mountains. Many desert-resort locations are not so fortunate as to have a ready source of potable water. Developers face a formidable challenge, as this limited resource must often be pumped from great distances at a great cost. Acquiring water-source access rights from public utility companies can also be quite challenging.

Golf courses at desert resorts are in high demand, and they require huge amounts of water to operate and maintain. Water-treatment plants must be considered when planning resorts where water is scarce. Treated wastewater, or graywater, can be used to irrigate the resort's landscape and golf-course fairways. Advances in water filtration systems, including microfiltration, ultrafiltration, reverse osmosis, and ultra-violet disinfection, can now successfully render even sewer water safe to drink. However, the psychological barrier to using filtered wastewater remains an obstacle, especially in luxury-resort locations where just finding odor-free graywater in their toilet bowl is objectionable to many guests.

Desert-resort developments must also be planned carefully with natural drainage systems in mind. The parched soils of desert landscapes are easily saturated with rain and shed large proportions of groundwater along the paths of least resistance. The seemingly innocuous river beds that may remain dry for months can become pathways for flash floods after a rainfall or mountain snowmelt.

Landscape design principles for desert resorts range from preserving the existing desert ecosystem to complete transformation of the landscape into a desert oasis. Indigenous plants require significantly less water than non-indigenous species. Native species are durable, require less attention, and stabilize soils against erosion. Xeriscaping is a landscaping approach that reinforces the natural equilibrium of the ecological system, an integral aspect of eco-resort developments that emphasize the uniqueness of the desert, particularly its diverse ecology.

Located in Canyon Point, a beautifully austere desert in a remote area of Utah just north of the Arizona border, the Amangiri Resort has been designed to embrace the rugged ecology that for centuries has been home to the native Navajo and Hopi tribes. Dinosaurs are known to have flourished in the region and footprints and fossils dating back 160 million years are common. True to the principles of ecotourism, the 34 private guestrooms are housed in a compact cluster of low-profile buildings representing a minimal invasive insertion into the arid landscape. In deference to the harsh Utah terrain and in order to blend the hotel in with the area's Entrada Sandstone, the architects devised a unique concrete mix of local sand, cement, and aggregate that approximates the coloration and density of the surrounding geological formations.

Practically all the precipitation that falls in the most arid areas is returned to the atmosphere by evapotranspiration. Clear skies and low humidity cause extreme daily and seasonal temperature ranges as the sparsely covered land surface is heated quickly by solar radiation and then rapidly cools at nightfall. Adobe construction is extremely durable, sustainable, and accounts for some of the oldest existing buildings in the world. In hot climates, adobe buildings offer significant advantages compared with wooden buildings, because of their greater thermal mass. Adobe walls provide a heat reservoir that levels out the heat transfer through the wall to the living space. The massive walls require a large and relatively long exposure to heat from the sun before they warm through to the interior and begin to transfer heat to the living space. After the sun sets and the temperature drops, the warm wall will then continue to transfer heat to the interior for several hours, due to the time-lag effect. Thus, a well-planned adobe wall of the appropriate thickness is very

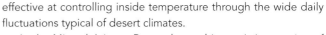

effective at controlling inside temperature through the wide daily fluctuations typical of desert climates.

At the Miraval Arizona Resort, located in a pristine portion of the Sonoran Desert near Tucson, Arizona, sustainable elements are inherent throughout the design. Adobe brick and rammed-earth walls provide a thermal mass that collects heat and cools interiors during the day and then re-radiates it to warm the interiors at night. A highly reflective high-albedo roof coating reduces the absorption of solar energy and heat transfer into the buildings. In planning the resort, native plant species were selected to match the unique Sonoran habitat and do not require irrigation. The architects carefully located the low-profile buildings to preserve the existing landscape, which is covered with old-growth saguaro cacti. As this grows only one inch per year, the largest on site, with eight arms, has been estimated to be more than 120 years old.

Amangiri, Canyon Point, Utah (left)
Located within the Grand Circle, surrounded by the Grand Canyon, Monument Valley, Grand Staircase, and Zion National Parks, the 600 acre (240 hectare) site for this luxury desert resort supports a harsh but austerely beautiful ecosystem, encompassing a remarkable diversity of plants and animal species. The owners engaged three inventive Arizona architects to collaborate on the design—Marwan Al-Sayed, Wendell Burnette, AIA, and Rick Joy, AIA. For this particular project, the trio of friends formed a company, I-10 Studio, named after the freeway that connects their offices in Phoenix and Tucson.

Miraval, Tucson, Arizona (below)
Coyotes, rabbits, javalinas, snakes, raptors, and dozens of other bird species make their home here. At the base of the Catalina mountain range, 35 miles (56 km) north of Tucson, a vast watershed drains the central valley, passes through the site and continues south. Ocotillo, saguaro, and barrel cactus mix with acacias and mesquite. Mithun Architects' LEED-Silver certified resort balances intimate luxury with rugged surroundings using simple, durable, and natural materials suited to the arid climate.

Qasr Al Sarab Desert Resort by Anantara, Abu Dhabi, United Arab Emirates
Constructed next to a 200 ft (61 m) high sand dune on the largest uninterrupted sand desert in
the world, the 206-key resort serves as a luxurious oasis in the midst of an extraordinarily hostile
environment. The architects, Dubarch, specified traditional desert building systems, such as rope
joints between the walls to allow them to expand and contract in the heat.

Equally remote but in stark contrast to the compact array of
contemporary low-lying structures of the Amangiri, the 206-key
Qasr Al Sarab Desert Resort is relatively massive, measuring 2.5
km end to end and populated with towers, turrets, and serrated
roofs of distinctly Arabic architectural style. The resort is located
in the Liwa Desert, part of the Empty Quarter, the world's largest
uninterrupted body of sand and one of the earth's hottest, driest,
and least hospitable environments. It is difficult to imagine a more
difficult place to build a hotel. Taking cues from the indigenous
architecture of the Bedouin fort structures of the Abu Dhabi region,
the design of the hotel complex reinforced local building design and
traditions while delivering extravagant luxury and superbly opulent
accommodations in one of the harshest deserts on the planet.

Golf Resorts

Introducing golf courses to new resorts can significantly improve
their overall perception and bottom line, beyond golf's own direct
contribution. For example, while golf is preferred over other resort
activities by one out of six vacation travelers, its value is far greater in
relation to the aura it brings to the resort and increased occupancies
through cross-marketing the hotel with the popular sport. The benefit
of the "golf touch" to the resort is analogous to what the "boutique
touch" is to the urban makeover. In some cases these two ideas
are combined, as seen in the Finca Prats Hotel Golf and Spa. This
environment provides the intimate experience of a boutique hotel
that also includes the golf experience as one of its amenities.

Golf: invented by the Romans, named by the Dutch, and born of
Scottish working classes, its dedicated enthusiasts span every level
of skill and background, increasing the game's grip to megatrend
status. While practiced and played as vigorously as any sport, for

Finca Prats Hotel Golf and Spa, Lleida, Spain
The 40-room design/golf hotel includes a fully equipped spa, two
restaurants, indoor pool, and a playroom for children. Guestrooms are
on the top floors of the buildings, providing views of the first tee and
18th green of 18-hole Raimat Golf Club.

many golf is more of an experience than a game, which reinforces
its role as a key element in the planning, marketing, and design of
upscale and luxury resorts. Golf components increasingly attract
extended-stay and limited-service hotel brands—small wonder,
given that there are over 16,000 golf courses in the United States
and approximately 30,000 worldwide.

Although golf may be virtually non-existent in some global markets,
it is omnipotent in many of the most lucrative, and has a large
development potential in many of the world's expanding markets.
The presence of golf in North America has become saturated with
the expectation that golf course development will slow significantly
in this geographic area. Cuba, South America, Portugal and Spain,
Vietnam, India, and China are all considered prime areas for golf
course development, which would in turn provide ample opportunities
for a variety of golf-centered resorts for the upscale and luxury
markets.

Research shows that many of the best links now are at luxury
resorts. While the venerable early Scottish courses once boasted
dormitories ("dormies") for their employees, few golf clubs provide
guestrooms for members or guests and fewer public courses provide
overnight lodging, an early exception being one of the world's most
admired courses, Torrey Pines in La Jolla, California, and its superb
hotel resort. The potential exists for golf club resorts, including
their application to golf developments, in uncharted regions. The

expanding interest in golfing across a wide range of socioeconomic
backgrounds may provide a fertile market for golf resort developments
that center around public courses with moderate to lower-priced
accommodations.

Design and Planning Considerations

Program elements of golf course facilites and hotel facilities are
highly complementary and provide ample opportunity for synergistic
design. The golf clubhouse is best located near the hotel lobby and
should contain or be adjacent to a cocktail lounge and restaurant
overlooking the course. Public space should spill out onto a viewing
platform in clear sight of the first tee and the eighteenth-hole green.
The size of the viewing platform should be determined according to
the number and frequency of high-profile tournaments held at the
course. The retail store of the pro shop located near guest circulation
provides an excellent opportunity to attract impulse purchasing.

Golf clubhouse, locker rooms, cart and bag storage must be
carefully planned so that circulation to other hotel amenities is not
disrupted by cross-traffic. These facilities need to be located at
ground level or even below grade, where gentle ramps lead up to
the golf trails. Sufficient accomodations for golf staff and caddies
need to be provided.

Abu Dhabi Golf Club Resort Hotel, Abu Dhabi, United Arab Emirates
Designed by GREC Architects, the luxury golf resort hotel is set within an award-winning 27-hole course just outside the UAE capital. The main facilities of the resort focus on the world-renowned tournament golf course, but amenities are not limited to golf-centered activities. Several themed restaurants, ballrooms, business and meeting facilities, pools, and an extensive spa form a small resort campus.

Front desk check-in will involve separating the guests' golf bags and gear from their other luggage by bringing them down to the cart and bag storage area. An additional 40 percent of area in the luggage room should be provided. Locker rooms and showers for guests are less important, since the hotel guestrooms serve that need, but some may be provided for the purpose of ambience.

In addition to the accommodations and conveniences provided for the guests and the ecological impact of the facility, consideration for the necessities of the grounds and equipment maintenance and storage are integral details for the development of golf resorts. Providing for both convenient and efficient access to the supplies and equipment needed while considering the impact of these structures on the overall aesthetic of the design can be significant contributing factors to the success of a golf resort. Golf course maintenance facilities must include a cart "barn" for storage and maintenance of vehicles such as tractors, mowers, and pick-up trucks in addition to the golf carts. Access and storage areas for mulch, specially formulated sand, and soil and grass pallets must also be included, together with a chemical storage area with all safety features as may be required, such as explosion-proof light fixtures, emergency eye-wash fountains, and good ventilation.

There is a growing interest in creating golf resorts that reflect a direct relationship to the surrounding environment. In some cases, as with the Steigenberger Golf Resort and Hyatt Regency Tamaya

Resort and Spa, the grounds and buildings replicate a historical and cultural reference that enhances the overall experience of the guests during their stay. In other instances, as with the Hersham Golf Club, this relationship is considered from the perspective of the ecological impact of the facility itself. Design considerations reflect the designer's intention to conserve natural resources and to be sensitive to the surrounding ecosystem.

Architect Michael Graves's design for the Golf Resort El Gouna displays an architectural character that is inspired by the essence of rural Egyptian buildings. The result is a resort that blends with its natural surroundings. Home of an 18-hole golf course, this resort has 208 guestrooms, suites, and villas. A unique feature is the hotel lagoon, which is available for dives.

Embracing the rich history of the Tamayame, with 350 pueblo-style guestrooms, the Hyatt Regency Tamaya Resort and Spa is situated at the base of the Sandia Mountains in New Mexico. Designed by HKS Architects, the resort is situated in the landscape to maximize views of the nationally ranked golf course and the mountains, cottonwood groves, and the Rio Grande River beyond.

In one of the more unusual and creative golf resort designs, Reardon Smith Architects have created a 198-room luxury subterranean resort hotel as an addition to the existing Hersham Golf Club in Surrey, England. The design features three garden courtyard areas set beneath the ground surface. Appearing as large sand-traps, these

Steigenberger Golf Resort El Gouna, El Gouna, Egypt
Architect Michael Graves's design for the El Gouna Golf Hotel displays an architectural character derived from the cultural context of Egyptian rural buildings. Surrounded by a broad lagoon that falls between the hotel and the 18-hole championship golf course, the resort offers 208 guestrooms, suites, and villas. The main building steps down toward a long lap pool with wide terraces, orienting views of the golf clubhouse and pyramid-shaped restaurant on the other side of the lagoon. Clusters of guestrooms are built around the edge of the peninsula and overlook the golf course.

Hersham Golf Club Hotel, Walton-on-Thames, United Kingdom
Designed to be the world's first underground luxury hotel, the 198-room property was subject to strict planning guidelines within London's Green Belt. As an addition to the existing golf club, this unique approach to sustainable development sets back from local residential areas and is positioned within an enclave of existing woodland to further obscure it from view.

Hyatt Regency Tamaya Resort and Spa, Santa Ana Pueblo, New Mexico
HKS Architects' layout for the hotel guestrooms and public spaces was driven by the site's bountiful views of the mountains and the Rio Grande River. Twin Warriors Golf Club, the resort's nationally ranked Gary Panks–designed golf course, was routed in and around 20 ancient cultural sites.

serve as light wells, allowing an abundance of natural light into the hotel guestrooms. Hotel facilities include restaurants, bars, business amenities, underground parking, and, of course, the golf clubhouse. The carbon footprint of this hotel is reduced through combined heat and power generation, heat exchangers, ground source heat pumps, graywater recycling, and rainwater harvesting.

Spa Resorts

Spas are the oldest form of resort. Bathing in natural springs for the purpose of ritual purification, healing specific ailments, inspiring visions, or relaxing the body and spirit has roots in dozens of cultures worldwide. Today, "taking a cure" is more than just a soak in a mineral bath: the International Spa Association reports that in 2009 there were 143 million visits to spas, generating over U.S.$12 billion in revenue from treatments as diverse as mud wraps, hot bamboo massages, Vichy showers, Turkish steam baths, and sitting in salt caves to relieve bronchitis. In the United States alone, the number of spas has grown by almost four times since 1999 and spa development has exploded on five continents, particularly Asia where spa growth is projected to be in the double digits. Spa resorts are clearly big business.

Spas' overriding virtue of providing psychological as well as physical restoration is unquestioned. This has long been recognized, from the Baths of Caracalla in ancient Rome to hip retro Palm Springs. In addition, many guests select spas because of their health education programs that focus on total wellness. Destination spas—those operations that make such programs the primary focus of multi-day stays—combine state-of-the-art wellness treatments and education with luxurious accommodations and first-class healthy cuisine. Hotel amenity spas are more focused on day use only, and while they may offer an educational component to their services, they primarily offer one- to two-hour treatments by appointment to hotel guests, and in many cases to the general public.

In the early days of the twentieth-century spa resort boom, spas tended to have a strong thematic component evocative of a real or imagined warm-weather setting. Spas being developed today are much more diverse in design and attempt to capture a strong sense of place by relying on vernacular ingredients, techniques, and architecture. An excellent example of this approach is the Hotel Therme Vals at the foot of Alp Vallatsch in Switzerland. Although there was a long history of a spa in this location, the resort struggled until the 1980s, when the village of Vals bought the property, with its utilitarian 1960s hotel rooms. Eventually architect Peter Zumthor was retained to transform the spa facility into a site-specific setting that, according to Zumthor, "focuses on the quiet, primary experience of bathing." The spa's roof, jutting out from the side of the mountain below the main hotel block, forms an extension of the lawn and opens up to reveal the pool below in a way that resembles an archeological dig and invites exploration. The overall effect is dramatic yet calming, the perfect ambience for a mountain spa.

Hotel Therme Vals, Vals, Switzerland
This striking destination spa was designed by Peter Zumthor. Sixty thousand carefully cut pieces of local quartzite stone were employed to form a serene enclosure for the mineral spring pools.

Development and Planning Considerations

Spa resorts are primarily considered part of the luxury segment, although spa-going is becoming more prevalent with a broad range of travelers. The luxury brands Four Seasons, Aman, Oberoi, Mandarin Oriental, and Ritz-Carlton have all incorporated award-winning spas in their resorts, and now upscale chains such as Sheraton and Hilton are rapidly rolling out house-brand spas in their properties worldwide. Spa concepts managed by third-party operators like ESPA, Steiner Leisure, Clarins, and Red Door have strong brand recognition outside the hotel brands with which they are affiliated, and new spa brands are entering the market every year.

In addition to the spa facilities themselves, the spa resort provides luxury accommodations, including outdoor recreational features similar to beach, golf, and tennis resorts. But spa resorts may also serve outside members and visitors as well as hotel guests. Therefore, their reception facilities and parking areas may be up to twice the size of those at other resorts.

The spa resort often requires a separate reception area for the health spa, which should be easily accessible to guests from the hotel lobby. A special spa elevator may be provided, serving the guestroom floors and allowing guests to move freely between their room and the spa without moving through the lobby. However, in some properties the formal check-in desk is being eliminated in favor of a more intimate and personalized approach. St. Regis' Iridium spa concept has taken this a step further and no longer includes locker rooms in its program: guests are escorted from a pre-treatment lounge to a private spa where they change, store their possessions, have their treatment, and may shower afterwards, all in the same suite. Gender-specific spa areas should each have access to shared spaces where couples can lounge together and proceed to couples' treatment rooms. The growing popularity of groups attending spas together has inspired special areas for these guests so that they do not disturb other spa-goers. There are even children's spas, where kids can get treatments on their own or side by side with a parent.

The space allocation for the spa is largely a function of the hotel size and type as well as the intended market. Spa resorts that encourage day use of their facilities tend to have 150–250 sq ft (14–23 sq m) of spa space per guestroom key. Destination spas have much more because of the wider range of treatment options and other amenities that these properties provide: 600 sq ft (56 sq m) or more per key is typical. Urban hotels with amenity spas tend to allocate only about 50–60 sq ft (5–6 sq m) per key to the spa. The number of treatment rooms varies as well: resort spas average about one treatment room for every 10–20 keys, whereas destination spas may have as many as one for every three guestrooms.

Providing retail space associated with the spa is a vital component of a successful spa operation. As much as 40 percent of a hotel spa's revenue can come from the sale of skin- and hair-care products and spa-related clothing items.

Design Considerations

Spa facilities are designed for multi-sybaritic experiences ranging from tension-relieving massages to progressive-resistance exercising and health and beauty consultation. Dressing areas should be spacious, comfortable, and safe underfoot, generously mirrored, and luxurious, with ample backup areas for storing and issuing robes, slippers, soaps, hair-dryers, and so on. In many spas, the dressing area for each gender will have dedicated sauna, steam, and whirlpool facilities. The central wet areas containing hot and cold plunges and hydro-massage spa baths should bring in natural light whenever possible and be surrounded by other hydrotherapy features to simplify plumbing. The cost of these areas continues to increase, so many properties are downsizing or eliminating pools and providing chilled lounges instead of cold plunges. Dry treatment

Enchantment Resort and Mii amo Spa, Sedona, Arizona
Gluckman Mayner Architects relied on the colors and light of the famous Sedona landscape in the design of this destination spa, which is routinely ranked as one of the world's best.

The Lodge at Woodloch, Hawley, Pennsylvania
This luxury destination spa and resort by architecture firm Cooper Carry makes use of soaring windows to capture natural light and highlight the changing seasons in the surrounding Pocono Mountains.

Banyan Tree Sanya, Sanya, China
The resort's 3,980 sq ft (370 sq m) two-story spa pool villas each offer a 600 sq ft (55 sq m) private pool and a second-story outdoor massage area that overlooks a manmade lagoon.

areas for massage, facials, and nail services should be kept separate from wet areas. Proper detailing of the finishes and equipment throughout the spa requires expert consultation. Examples of these design details include: (1) designing tiled ceilings at a slight slope to properly carry off condensate; (2) providing screened terraces or pavilions for outdoor massages for singles and couples, where the climate permits; (3) building sophisticated temperature and humidity management, lighting, and music systems so that the operator can carefully control and customize the ambient environment; (4) incorporating hospitality support spaces for making and serving hot and cold infusions and light snacks; and (5) planning for administrative and back-of-house functions within the spa footprint to facilitate third-party operations.

The Marina Hotel

Since its debut in the early 1980s, the marina hotel has advanced greatly in technology and amenities. But interest in expanding knowledge of the oceans promises to be the key impetus to future development. "Our marina teaches the guests and visitors valuable information about the oceans," observes the dock master of Atlantis, one of the world's premier marina hotels.

Case study examples envision resorts with marinas and marine habitats, many of which may be booked through vacation ownership exchange privileges. Research indicates that yachts and second homes remain the leading status symbols. The boom in luxury marinas is due to the increased number of yachters, just as the boom in vacation ownership, to a large extent, is aided by the symbolism of the second home. While vacation ownerships are limited second homes, they are close enough to satisfy the typical buyer.

Mid-market marina development is slowed by improved dry-storage technology as well as by people moving up to larger boats, causing vacancies in slips 20–30 ft (6–9 m) long. But larger boats are more efficient and provide greater satisfaction. As a solution, developers propose new waterfront hotels for places such as Marina del Rey in Los Angeles, and larger mixed-use marina, hotels, and additional recreational amenities for areas near the approaches to New York City's suspension bridges, which still await City approval.

Planning and Design Considerations

Developers try to closely integrate hotels with marinas wherever possible. This is important to ensure convenient access to the marina, provide efficient catering to boats, and better dramatize the marina and water themes in the hotel. Whether a boat rental facility and starting-out point for sports sailors, stopover resort for inter-coastal boating excursions, or convenient vacation center for water sports enthusiasts, the marina hotel hosts local boaters from surrounding communities who sail or motor over to dine out or spend the weekend. Others dock boats permanently at the marina, driving to the resort to use their yacht for weekend sailing.

Planning the hotel location in relation to the marina is of prime importance. At the Tianjin East Point Sheraton, architects Woods Bagot situated the two towers to maximize views of the marina and the seaside. The hotel is connected to the marina via a seaside promenade and a string of retail outlets and restaurants. The Marina + Beach Towers project, designed by Oppenheim Architects, literally spans the narrow spit of land between the oceanfront and back bay, where the hotel integrates with the marina.

As a destination resort for yachters, the marina hotel is more luxurious than beachfront developments, as well as extended-stay hotels and some vacation ownership sites. This should be reflected by 25 percent more luxury suites and a higher standard of furnishings. In addition, marina hotel guestrooms should have balconies overlooking the water. The ultimate size of the dock is a function of the local boating market. For example, in a coastal resort area with a tropical climate, the marina should contain at least two boat slips for every five guestrooms. Full access to golf and tennis is required to attract

Sheraton Tianjin Hotel, Tianjin, China
As the first phase of a master-planned redevelopment project for East Port of Tianjin, the complex includes a 630-room Sheraton hotel, a destination retail/ entertainment complex, a yacht club, and a marina. The sweeping form of the yacht club opens up to the marina and twists up to form an iconic beacon.

Marina + Beach Hotel, Dubai, United Arab Emirates
Twin hotel towers lean together, sheltering a richly landscaped botanical garden that opens to restaurants and entertainment venues and leads to the beach on the ocean side and to the marina on the bay side.

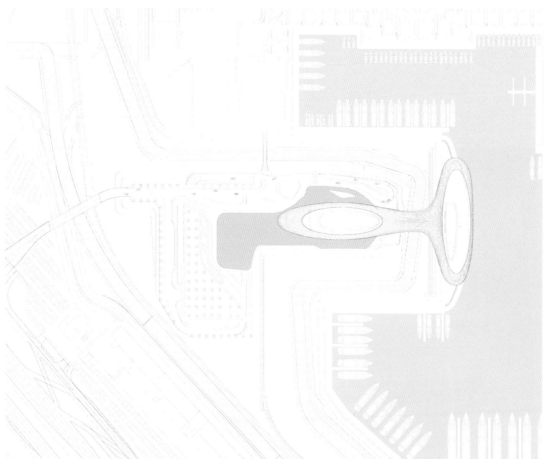

Viceroy Hotel, Abu Dhabi, United Arab Emirates
Set half on land and half on water, with two 12-story towers under a spectacular glass sheath, Asymptote Architecture's design for the 499-key hotel includes eight restaurants, a rooftop cabana, a business center, a spa, a gym, and two rooftop swimming pools. A steel and glass bridge passes over the racetrack, connecting the Formula 1 race circuit to the Yas Marina and Yacht Club.

Viceroy Hotel, Abu Dhabi, United Arab Emirates

vacationers, satisfy all members of a group or family, and provide destination attractions for yachters. The marina facility must include retail shops for boating supplies, fishing and water sports gear, groceries, a clothing boutique, and self-service laundry, as well as fuel supply and repair shops. Large complexes may decide to include a major boat overhaul facility if none is available nearby.

The marina administration office provides navigational facilities and expert personnel to assist guests. Its docks are equipped with standard boat-servicing outlets for electricity, communications, water supply, and waste, as well as general boat maintenance if not otherwise available in the vicinity. Some developers may test the feasibility of building a private yacht club adjacent to the hotel, to create another visual element and amenity for guests.

On Yas Island in Abu Dhabi, Yas Marina is operated by world leader in luxury marinas, Camper & Nicholsons Marinas. Located at the heart of Yas Marina Circuit, the marina has a capacity for 143 yachts from 33 ft to 295 ft (10–90 m), and additional visitor berthing for super-yachts up to 492 ft (150 m). Yas Hotel has two 12-story towers: one is built over a Formula 1 race track, the other over the Yas Marina. The towers are linked by a steel and glass bridge that passes over the race track and by a spectacular curvilinear glass sheath that spans the two towers with more than 5,000 diamond-shaped glass panels.

Since technical advances have reduced demand for boat slips under 30 ft (9 m), adversely affecting revenue at many marinas, long-range trends at marina hotels are toward larger boats because of their ease of maintenance and provision of greater satisfaction. A form of "shared-yacht" ownership, paralleling vacation ownership, may make yachting dramatically accessible to the vast number of middle-class boaters.

W Singapore Sentosa Cove, Singapore
Situated on the eastern end of Sentosa Island, the 290 acre (117 hectare) Sentosa Cove development offers Singapore's only true oceanfront residences. At the heart of the development lies One15 Marina Club, a mega-yacht marina club with moorings for some 204 yachts. With 320 hotel rooms and 236 signature residences, the W Singapore is set on a 6 acre (2.4 hectare) peninsula with yachts moored on two sides. A shell-shaped roof hovers above rooftop garden terraces on the retail and entertainment center, while the bowed form of the six-story hotel anchors the peninsula.

Ski Resorts and Mountain Resorts

Following the development of efficient snow-making equipment and safe, user-friendly ski gear in the 1970s, interest in cross-country and downhill skiing continued to climb each season. And with consistent demand, ski lodges matured into full-fledged, year-round hotels, complete with spas, gourmet food, entertainment and conference centers. These, increasingly, were managed by upscale brands, happy to maintain the ski lodge's traditional ambience. With the introduction of retail base camps needed at large-scale resorts, the original ski lodge has become a "village resort for all seasons." These newer ski resorts match the full range of comforts and services offered by other types of resorts, including indoor–outdoor pools and whirlpool baths, tennis courts, trails for hiking, mountain biking, and scenic excursions. Also, they increasingly attract summer and shoulder-season tourists and conference attendees, as well as many non-skiing guests in the winter.

In addition, the major hotel companies are expanding in the vacation ownership arena, including at sites suited to the needs of skiers and their families who are attracted to the vacation ownership concept. While the slopes and the larger resort environment generally are high quality, what attracts buyers most is the value of the residential unit, along with the economic advantages and pride of ownership. Not surprisingly, the first of the new "buttoned down" family vacation prototypes at ski areas were launched by Hyatt, Ritz-Carlton, and Four Seasons at the long-established Lake Tahoe, Vail, and Aspen ski resorts.

Planning and Development Considerations

Because of valid concerns regarding natural preservation in rapidly expanding ski areas, strict planning and environmental controls are the rule in new developments. At the same time, larger-scale ski resorts are needed to satisfy the increasing demands for recreation as well as to meet complex ecological requirements. But most agree that large-scale developments can be planned better to blend in with the natural landscape. Also, through phased development, authorities can more easily monitor the development against exceeding approved densities or ignoring environmental controls. For example, The Ritz-Carlton Highlands, Lake Tahoe, in Truckee, California, requires no more than 20 acres (8 hectares) to create a village setting including retail, dining, entertainment, and service facilities for guests and visitors.

As most guests travel by air to ski resorts, lodges should be located within a two-hour drive of a major airport and, better, close to a commuter airport. While the majority of guests complete their journey by van or tour bus, up to 40 percent drive or rent cars at the airport. Because of heavy snow conditions and to avoid the negative visual impact of unrestricted open parking, developers generally provide parking below the hotel, thereby preserving the views and contours of the natural terrain.

At ski resorts, as at an ecotourist retreat, vacation village, or country inn, one of the most inviting elements of the lodge's arrival experience is its natural unspoiled environment. Therefore, parked

buses and building signage which intrude on the natural landscape should be avoided. As guests arrive, skis are checked outside the lodge and routed directly to a central ski-storage area, often by a special outside ski elevator. The lodge generally is located on a sloped site, with its ski facilities, including storage, service, and ski shop areas, on a lower level accessible to the ski run-out and remount area behind the lodge. A 200–300 ft (61–91 m) wide area at the base of the chairlift is needed to accommodate any waiting lines to assemble classes.

Ski slopes usually are located on the shaded side of the mountain for maximum retention of hardpack snow base, with the lodge oriented so that guestrooms have maximum sun exposure and views of the ski slopes. While balconies and roof terraces are popular at ski lodges, as they are at beach resorts, they are more costly to construct owing to snow loads and the greater waterproofing required. Guests strongly prefer upper-floor rooms with panoramic views. Wherever possible, rooms with dormer windows and sloped ceilings should be designed into lodges, as market research indicates that such features are highly desired.

Design Considerations

Designers of ski lodges find rich inspiration in traditional mountain vernacular architecture. The prevalent architectural style of Rocky Mountain ski resorts follows the characteristics of U.S. rustic tradition, with such noted landmarks as the Ahwahnee Inn in Yosemite Valley, Old Faithful Lodge in Yellowstone Park, Timberline Lodge on Mount Hood, and Paradise Lodge on Mount Rainier. Architect Robert Stern, in his design of the Aspen Highlands Village, adopted the style and employed native stone, logs, and rough clapboards to form solid walls and broad eaves to shed Aspen's powdery snow and protect residents from the strong Colorado sunlight. By contrast, in the Goldenkey Ski Hotel in Turkey we find a contemporary interpretation of a classic alpine lodge with steeply pitched—albeit bright red-painted metallic—roofs to shed the build-up of heavy snow. In a similar yet more sophisticated mode, architect Matteo Thun crafted a wonderfully modern interpretation of a traditional Bavarian wooden lodge in his design of the Vigilius Mountain Resort in northern Italy.

Arrival at a mountaintop ski resort and circulation from the resort to the ski slopes can take many forms, usually dictated by location and terrain. At the St. Regis Deer Crest in Park City, Utah, guests arrive by car or taxi at a generous porte cochère, check in at the arrival pavilion, and ride up a steep incline in a funicular to the main hotel building. They then travel back down to the arrival complex to access the ski slopes, which are within a short walk or ski ride.

A very popular concept that has gained significant weight in the marketing of resorts and mountainside condominiums, as exemplified by The Ritz-Carlton Bachelor Gulch resort, is the provision of ski-in/ski-out access. Guests are attracted to the pure notion that they can don their skis at the lodge and ski directly to the slopes and back, without having to board a crowded bus or some other mode of intermediate transportation. The Ritz-Carlton Lake Tahoe, with its slope-side location mid-mountain on Northstar Resort, provides

Ritz-Carlton Club, Aspen Highlands, Colorado
Designed in traditional mountain vernacular architecture, the ski lodge sits below a 12,500 ft (3,800 m) mountain with stunning vistas and 125 challenging trails. This ski-in/ski-out resort is just 8 miles (13 km) from the spectacular peaks of the Maroon Bells, part of the White River National Forest with six peaks rising above 14,000 ft (4,350 m).

Goldenkey Kartalkaya, Bolu, Turkey
Architects LEA Invent designed a contemporary interpretation of an alpine ski lodge with three wings set around an inner garden, and positioned to take maximum advantage of daylight and the view of the Köroglu mountains. Each of the 41 guestrooms was carefully placed with a different relationship to the views.

Vigilius Mountain Resort, San Vigilio, Italy
On a pristine Vigiljoch peak in South Tyrol with views of the Dolomite Mountains, the eco-resort is only accessible by cable car or on foot. With 36 guestrooms, six suites, two restaurants, a library, a lounge, conference rooms, and a spa, the design of this exclusive mountaintop refuge employs sustainable principles, including an accessible landscaped roof, and adjustable shutters on the façade control solar energy.

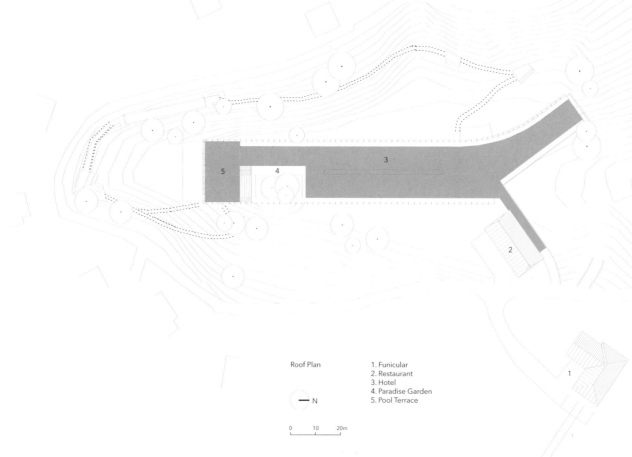

Roof Plan

N

1. Funicular
2. Restaurant
3. Hotel
4. Paradise Garden
5. Pool Terrace

0   10   20m

St. Regis Deer Valley, Park City, Utah
Employing a pair of 15-passenger cable-hoisted tram cars on steel rails, the funicular is based at the resort's Snow Park Building and ascends over 230 ft (70 m) in just 90 seconds to the primary hotel building, which houses the majority of resort's amenities, guest rooms, and private residences, with convenient slope-side access directly on to the Deer Hollow ski run.

Ritz-Carlton Bachelor Gulch, Avon, Colorado
The 237-room ski lodge includes a 21,000 sq ft (1,950 sq m) spa, restaurants, a meeting space, and a 54-unit Ritz-Carlton Club comprising of two- and three-bedroom residential units. The building is constructed with 7 miles (11 km) of logs and 6 million lb (2.7 million kg) of moss rock, recalling the iconic architectural traditions of the grand National Park lodges of the Rocky Mountains, such as the historic Old Faithful Inn at Yellowstone.

Montana Trails Lodge, Big Sky, Montana
Located at the gateway to the celebrated Big Sky Ski Resort near Yellowstone National Park, where snow enthusiasts see 400 inches (10 m) of annual snowfall, Bitnar Architects' design for this 52-room mountain resort hotel took inspiration from the great traditions of 1920s National Park architecture.

skiing guests with perfect ski-in/ski-out access, complete with luxury "ski valet services" by the resort's "mountain concierge."

The mountain location and ski focus help determine many details of the design solution. Developers and operators prefer fireplaces in the main public spaces and also, as practicable, in hotel suites and condominium and vacation ownership units. However, the number of fireplaces in some locations may be restricted by environmental regulations, which might limit them, say, to a few specific suites. Air-conditioning, on the other hand, may not be required if summer temperatures are comfortable, as is often the case at higher elevations. In the rooms and suites, showers might be substituted for bathtubs in some units. Durable-finish materials must be used throughout the interiors to avoid the damaging effect of ski boots. Hard-surface stone flooring should be used at entrance areas because of heavy boot traffic and dampness. However, for acoustical reasons, dense carpet is required in other public areas, to cushion the boot steps.

Bar and lounge areas should be designed to enhance the unique camaraderie that flourishes at ski lodges among skiers of all ages. But multiple outlets may be necessary to meet the differing needs of diverse age groups. The main cocktail lounge or a lobby bar, offering a fireplace, comfortable furnishings, mountain views, and entertainment generally is for more affluent middle-aged guests. But another bar nearby may attract the more raucous skiers. It has a dance floor and popular music, and doesn't absolutely require

(continued p. 154)

Ritz-Carlton Lake Tahoe, Truckee, California
Hornberger + Worstell Architects designed the resort as a series of linked pavilions tucked into the contours of the hillside. Each pavilion steps down with the hillside, terminating with a grand octagonal lobby at the center of the massing. Great care was taken to protect the natural form of the landscape and to integrate the building seamlessly into its forest setting.

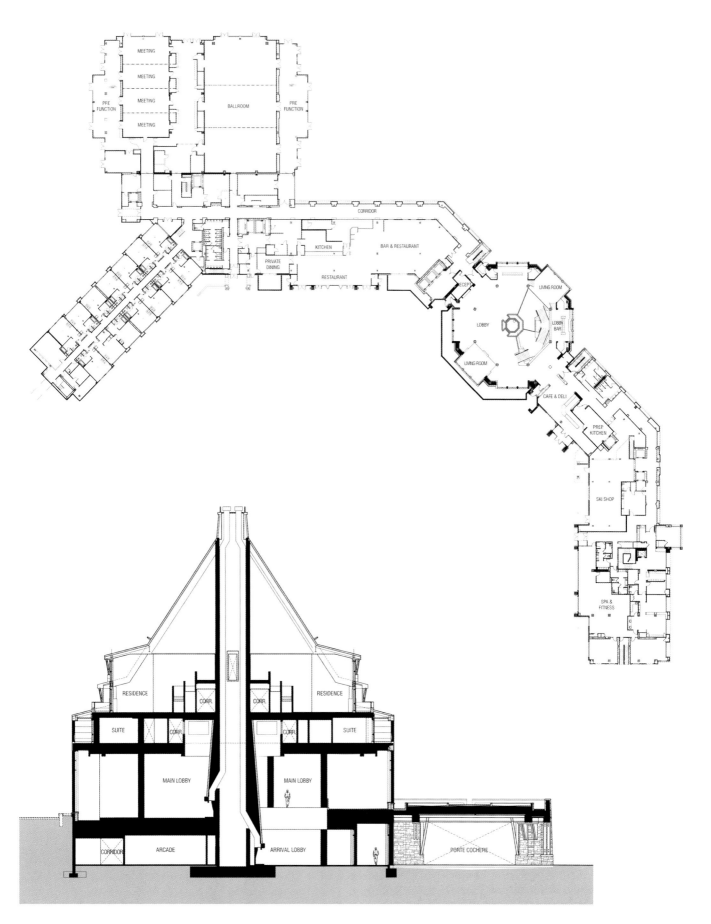

Case Study

The Arrabelle at Vail Square, Vail, Colorado
Architect: 4240 Architecture Inc.
Interior Designer: Slifer Designs

Located in the heart of Vail Square at Lionshead Village, Vail, Colorado, the Arrabelle ski resort hotel is situated at the base of Vail Mountain and Ski Resort, a short hop from the Eagle Bahn gondola, which transports skiers to the crest of the mountain. Founded in the early 1960s by veterans of the U.S. Army's 10th Mountain Division, which once conducted survival training there, Vail has grown into one of the world's best-known ski resorts. But the aging village was not keeping pace with Aspen, its more glamorous rival. As a central component to a redevelopment project totaling a quarter of a billion dollars, The Arrabelle at Vail Square is the focal point connecting the ski slopes to the cafés, galleries, and boutiques in a European-style village setting. The Arrabelle complex includes a 36-room hotel, 66 condominiums, a spa, and a conference center, in an assortment of connected buildings clustered around a series of narrow plazas lined with shops and restaurants. The composition, designed by 4240 Architecture Inc., is reminiscent of streetscapes you would find in Innsbruck, Prague, or Salzburg. Separate buildings with a variety of Bavarian-themed façade treatments are all connected by a series of bridges and tunnels. An oval ice-skating rink links the complex to the village square and opens vistas to the slopes above. A third-floor bridge arches over the ice rink and frames a picturesque view from the square to the mountainside. In the summer, the ice-skating rink becomes a public plaza with fountains and is used as an outdoor concert area. The first level of the southeast quadrant of the ensemble, the section closest to the gondola, is dedicated to ski activities, with a ski shop, ski club, and café. Skiers can pick up their gear at the ski shop and make their way directly to the slopes without having to board a crowded bus, making the Arrabelle a true ski-in/ski-out destination, but with the unique attribute of also being an integral part of a lively resort village.

(from top)
The Arrabelle, entrance court
The Arrabelle, lobby
The Arrabelle, guestroom

The Arrabelle, Lionshead Village

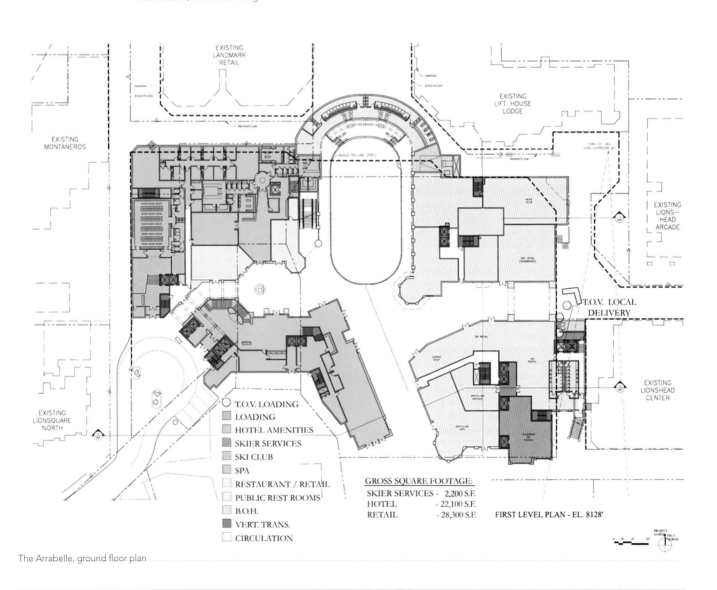

T.O.V. LOADING
LOADING
HOTEL AMENITIES
SKIER SERVICES
SKI CLUB
SPA
RESTAURANT / RETAIL
PUBLIC REST ROOMS
B.O.H.
VERT. TRANS.
CIRCULATION

GROSS SQUARE FOOTAGE:
SKIER SERVICES - 2,200 S.F.
HOTEL - 22,100 S.F.
RETAIL - 28,300 S.F.

FIRST LEVEL PLAN - EL. 8128'

The Arrabelle, ground floor plan

Hotel SnowWorld, Landgraaf, Netherlands
The 100-room ski resort, located in the hilly landscape of South
Limburg, is directly attached to the world's largest indoor ski slope.
SnowWorld Landgraaf has five slopes with nine lifts. The longest
ski slopes in Landgraaf are 1,700 ft (520 m) and feature a six-seater
chairlift.

outside views. Finding ways to combine the diverse age groups, as
they review the day's ski runs, contributes to the lodge's pleasant
atmosphere.

While lunch is at most a light snack, dinner at ski lodges is
considered an important social occasion for more discussion of skiing
experiences and re-energizing for the next day. Restaurants should
have natural light, with outdoor decks for daytime use, and raised
interior levels to enhance views. An ideal restaurant mix includes
an upscale restaurant, a three-meal café, and an optional self-serve
indoor–outdoor kiosk for light daytime snack service.

The Ecotourist Resort

> Clearly the problem of man and nature is not one of providing a
> decorative background for the human play, or even ameliorating
> the grim city; it is the necessity of sustaining nature as source
> of life, milieu, teacher, sanctum, challenge and, most of all,
> of rediscovering nature's corollary of the unknown in the self,
> the source of meaning.
> (Ian McHarg, *Design with Nature*, New York: Doubleday/
> Natural History Press, 1969, p. 19)

The world's heightened concern for the survival of the planet and
a new awareness of the preciousness of threatened ecosystems
and cultures have fueled the global emergence in the past decade
of ecotourism as one of the strongest growth areas in the travel
industry. Travelers range from passionate advocates of ecological
responsibility to those wanting to experience unspoiled nature, its
wildlife, and indigenous cultures up close. Most travelers are eager
to escape their homogenized settings and experience the local
environment or its people. Therefore, ecotourist resorts specialize
in catering to these needs in varying degrees.

Interest in sustainable principles has taken on new proportions in
nearly every segment of the hospitality industry with LEED certification
through the United States Green Building Council (USGBC) and
BREEAM certification through the World Green Building Council
(WorldGBC). Environmental sustainability is now regarded as an
essential element in exhibiting to travelers that the hotel company
is fulfilling its obligation to be environmentally responsible. The
movement reaches its apex with ecotourism and is manifested in
the design of eco-resorts.

The International Ecotourism Society (TIES) was founded in 1990
and defined ecotourism as "Responsible travel to natural areas that
conserves the environment and improves the well-being of local
people." TIES promotes the principles of ecotourism in order to:

- Minimize impact
- Build environmental and cultural awareness and respect
- Provide positive experiences for both visitors and hosts
- Provide direct financial benefits for conservation
- Provide financial benefits and empowerment for local people
- Raise sensitivity to host countries' political, environmental, and
  social climate

Ecological Responsibility

Ecotourism, sustainable development, and green architecture in
many ways are descendants of the environmental movement of the
1960s and 1970s when "back to nature" was the call. Over thirty years
ago, *The Whole Earth Catalog* provided a sourcebook of tools for
living off the land for a generation who embraced the principles of
ecological responsibility. It provided detailed technical information
on alternative energy and fuel sources, recycling, organic agriculture,
and other non-polluting, eco-friendly technologies. Stanley Selengut,
a civil engineer who has been called the godfather of ecotourism

resort development, utilized many of the ecological principles of sustainable design in the creation of an experimental resort called Harmony in the U.S. Virgin Islands. Harmony was designed to run on solar and wind power and to leave its hilly oceanfront site as undisturbed as possible. Floor tiles were made from slag and discarded glass, carpeting from last month's plastic bottles. Rooftop solar panels provide hot water, and photovoltaic collectors, augmented by windmills, provide power. Passive systems such as cross-ventilation, heat-resistant glazing, and a wind-scoop at the roof peak help to make the interiors comfortable. Gutters catch rainwater, which then is stored in cisterns built into the foundations and available for later use. Interior wallpaper is made from recycled newsprint. Occupancy sensors detect lack of motion and turn off power in unoccupied rooms. Selengut maintains that ecotourism has much to do with providing a valuable educational experience to the traveler. According to him, "The qualities needed for successful ecotourism are more attuned to the entertainment industry than real estate development. Most resorts try to protect guests from experience, but we try our best to put them into the experience."

With ecotourism also referred to as "soft-path tourism," an important goal is to provide experience without disruption. There is a responsibility incumbent on both the developer and the tourist to prevent damage to fragile ecosystems and to avoid negative influence on indigenous cultures. For such conservation groups and trade organizations as The International Ecotourism Society, the goal is to set the standards of ecotourism, and to support responsible travel to natural areas where the environment and its wildlife is being conserved and the well-being of the local population is being sustained. This usually means encouraging resorts that utilize recycled or locally produced building materials, employ solar or alternative energies, provide environmental education, are designed to blend in with their surroundings, donate part of their profits to local conservation efforts, recycle waste and wastewater, serve locally grown and produced food and beverages, and sell and display handicrafts of local artisans.

"Ethnotourism" or "eco/ethnotourism" are terms used to emphasize the cultural and spiritual dimensions of sustainable development and to promote the experience and conservation of regional culture and heritage. Consequently, archeologists and anthropologist have become important consultants of the eco/ethnotourist resort's design and development team.

Site Considerations

At the Amandari Resort in Bali, Indonesia, the designers transformed a deforested mountain area into a beautiful Balinese romantic courtyard and garden, utilizing a design principle called Site Repair, as delineated by Christopher Alexander in his pioneering book on design methodology, *A Pattern Language*. In proposing the concept of Site Repair, Alexander states:

> Buildings must always be built on those parts of the land which are in the worst condition, not the best. And, on no account place buildings in the places which are most beautiful. In fact, do the opposite. Consider the site and its buildings

as a single living eco-system. Leave those areas that are the most precious, beautiful, comfortable, and healthy as they are, and build new structures in those parts of the site which are least pleasant.

(C. Alexander, S. Ishikawa, and M. Silverstein, *A Pattern Language: Towns, Buildings, Construction*, Oxford: Oxford University Press, 1977, Pattern No. 104—Site Repair, p. 567)

Saffire Resort, Coles Bay, Australia
Echoing Christopher Alexander's design pattern for Site Repair, the luxury eco-resort has been built using core principles for "the protection of healthy sites" and the "healing of damaged sites." The original site was a caravan park that had suffered a great deal of degradation and erosion. Drawing from the concept of Coastal Sanctuary, the site was restored with 30,000 native plants to encourage a return to its natural form. The resort employs the ecological practices of bushfire management, collection and conservation of rainwater, and minimal use of night lighting of landscaped areas.

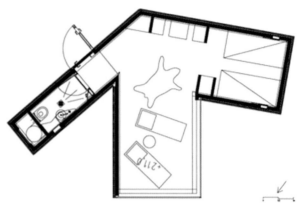

Juvet Landscape Hotel, Alstad, Norway
Architects Jensen & Skodvin designed a masterpiece of modern architecture, harmoniously situated in the midst of a rugged natural landscape. Set on a sheer river bank, among birch, aspen, pine, and nature-sculpted boulders, each of the seven rooms is a detached structure with one or two walls constructed of floor-to-ceiling glass. Every room design is unique and gets its own individual view of a dramatic piece of landscape, yet all are perfectly private as no room looks at another.

Great (Bamboo) Wall, Beijing, China
Architect Kengo Kuma explored the metaphorical qualities of bamboo in a 10-room eco-resort in a forest adjacent to the Great Wall of China. In sharp contrast to the Great Wall's brick and stone, a material manifestation of severing ties with outside civilizations, bamboo is a symbol of cultural exchange, perfectly suitable for the work of a Japanese architect in China.

156

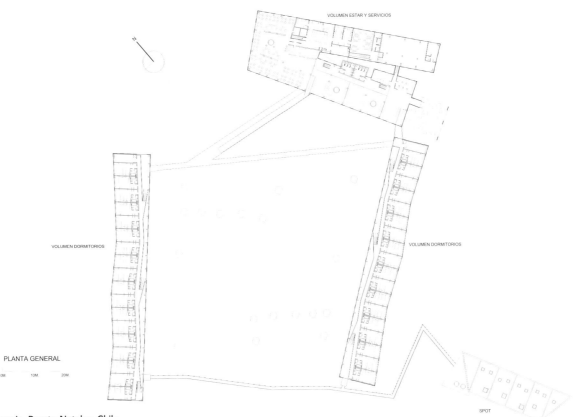

Hotel Remota, Patagonia, Puerto Natales, Chile
The 72-room eco-resort hotel lies at the base of the Patagonian
Mountains on a sea channel 125 miles (201 km) from the Pacific Ocean.
The main hotel building is flanked by two guestroom wings forming an
elegant grassy courtyard and framing a magnificent view out over the
water to the vast rugged peaks of Torres del Paine National Park.

Arrebol Patagonia Hotel, Puerto Varas, Chile
Situated on a sloping, forested hill along Llanquihue Lake, this building, designed by architect Harald Opitz Jurgens, is clad in alerce wood cut into rugged brick-like shapes to fit in unobtrusively with the surrounding woodland. With two volumes, one public and one private, the 22 guestrooms are placed on the uppermost part of the site with views of a lake, while the public spaces, the lounge, restaurant, and meeting rooms are located on the main level.

Tierra Atacama Hotel and Spa, San Pedro de Atacama, Chile
Located on the Altiplano of the Atacama Desert, within view of the Licancabur volcano, the 32-room eco-resort displays an architectural vocabulary that recognizes the precarious balance between nature, design, and the needs of travelers. Sustainable systems emphasize the value of water by recycling wastewater to supply the hydroponic garden, an irrigation system that follows ancient techniques for supporting local plant-life, and a desalination plant to supply potable water to the hotel.

Architect Kengo Kuma designed a 10-room boutique eco-resort in an ecologically sensitive forest near the Great Wall of China. The Great (Bamboo) Wall Hotel straddles two hills and conforms to the intricate undulation of the terrain, nestling comfortably into a shallow swale. The resort "wall" is made of vertical stalks of bamboo permitting light and wind to pass through with minimal interruption.

A special breed of ecotourist resorts are located in the most remote and extreme environments and, therefore, for the more adventurous tourists often are the most beautiful to visit. The Hotel Remota was designed by Santiago-based architect Germán del Sol in a rugged and remote Patagonian landscape, outside Puerto Natales, Chile, at the base of the Patagonian Mountains, a range with giant majestic horn-shaped peaks, glacier-fed lakes, and primordial forests. Weather in Patagonia can be quite intense, with sustained winds sometimes reaching in excess of 70 mph (113 kph). The hotel serves as a base camp for explorations into the spectacular surrounding wilderness of the nearby Torres del Paine National Park. The orientation of the building means that the guestroom wings frame the view over the sea channel to the vast peaks beyond. In another example of Site Repair, the original grass that was removed to make room for the hotel footprint was retained and reinstalled on the building roofs, in a 24 inch (61 cm) insulating layer.

The Tierra Atacama Hotel and Spa is located in the Atacama Desert in northern Chile, one of the driest places on earth, with relative humidity often as low as 2 percent and occasionally approaching zero. As a result, the sky is remarkably clear and the sunlight very strong. Building orientation and wide overhangs are necessary to

Anantara Xishuangbanna Resort and Spa, Xishuangbanna, China
Nestled along a sweeping curve of the Luosuo River and surrounded by verdant tropical landscapes, the 103-room luxurious eco-resort is designed in a contemporary interpretive style integrated with the rustic natural beauty of its exotic rainforest locale.

shield the guests from the intense sunlight. Appropriate to these intense site conditions, the design of architects Rodrigo Searle y Matías González uses stone, mud brick (adobe), and rammed earth, utilizing one of the oldest and most sustainable and ecological building systems ever devised. In his book *Earth Architecture* Ronald Rael says, "It is assumed that earth is a fragile, ephemeral material, while in reality some of the oldest extant buildings on the planet are made of earth" (Princeton: Princeton Architectural Press, 2009, p. 9).

Luxury Ecotourism

At the luxury end of the ecotourism spectrum, we find finely crafted resorts which practice good principles of eco-sensitive construction and fulfill many of the credentials recommended by The International Ecotourism Society but are, nevertheless, primarily luxury resorts where the guest is pampered and there is little sense of roughing it with nature. Not all visitors to ecotourist resorts wish to be thrust into the teeming wilderness or to be immersed in the customs and

rituals of a distant culture. Many want the stimulating and illuminating exposure to the wonders of nature without compromising the creature comforts of a luxury resort.

Anantara is a hotel company, founded in 2001, whose portfolio includes a number of luxury resorts that draw their strength from the rich cultural traditions, historic heritage, and natural beauty of their destinations throughout Asia and the Middle East. The Anantara Xishuangbanna Resort and Spa is set on the banks of the Luosuo River in the midst of the Hengduan Mountains, in Yunnan province, an idyllic mountainous setting fringing northern Laos. The region is home to the indigenous Dai people, who are renowned for their folklore and colorful festivals such as the water-splashing celebration called Songkran. Xishuangbanna is rich in nature, including rainforests, rare plants, and wildlife such as the Asian elephant, which is still found in the wild. The resort draws its architectural inspiration from traditional Dai architecture, with simple clean lines and use of bamboo throughout. Visitors enjoy comfortable contact with the rainforest from covered porches while pampered with luxury amenities or, if they wish, avail themselves of a deeper experience on guided tours into the rough.

(continued p. 164)

—————— Case Study ——————

Southern Ocean Lodge, Kangaroo Island, South Australia
Architect: Max Pritchard Architect
Interior Designer: Max Pritchard Architect

On a remote south-coastal plain of Australia's exotic Kangaroo Island, architect Max Prichard designed a sinuous string of 21 guestrooms perched 130 ft (39.5 m) above sheer limestone cliffs overlooking the Southern Ocean. Widely acclaimed as Australia's Galapagos, Kangaroo Island is home to an abundance of native wildlife including koalas, sea lions, fur seals, ospreys, parrots, penguins, wallabies, and, of course, kangaroos, making it a favorite destination for ecotourism.

Respectful of the ecologically delicate setting, the composition of structures is purposefully low-scale, tucked neatly into the scrubby coastal bush. The material palette was kept simple, with locally quarried limestone, glass, and blue-gray steel. The main lodge is an organic-shaped pavilion at the crest of a hill and includes the reception lobby, restaurant, bar, and "Great Room," with floor-to-ceiling windows opening to dramatic views

Southern Ocean Lodge, ocean suite

Southern Ocean Lodge, Kangaroo Island beach

Southern Ocean Lodge, terrace

Southern Ocean Lodge, lounge

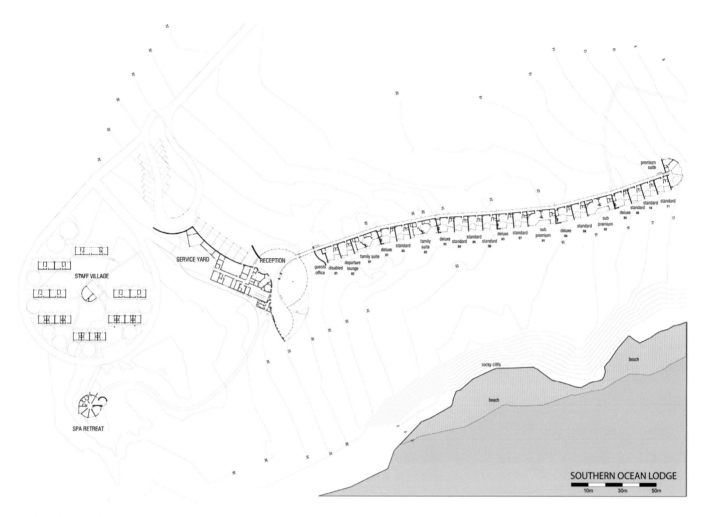

Southern Ocean Lodge, site plan

of the rocky coastline. The guestrooms are connected to the east by a 600 ft (180 m) long single-loaded breezeway, ensuring that each room has an unobstructed view of the ocean. At the far end of the breezeway is the Osprey Pavilion. With 1,300 sq ft (120 sq m), this deluxe suite enjoys 180-degree views, an open fireplace, and a plunge pool with a terrace. To the west of the main lodge, accessed by a winding boardwalk, is a freestanding cylindrical structure housing the spa retreat.

The architects held a series of public forums with local residents to allay concerns about a resort development on their unspoiled landscape and to reassure them that use of eco-friendly materials and construction methods would have minimal environmental impact on the site. A number of sustainable features were incorporated into the development, including rainwater harvesting, rooftop photovoltaic panels, and hot water provided by geothermal energy. Wastewater and sewage are treated by an organic, worm-based system and dispersed through an underground irrigation system. Owing to the remote location, employees are housed in an on-site staff village with seven freestanding cabins, each containing four bedrooms and clustered around a commons building.

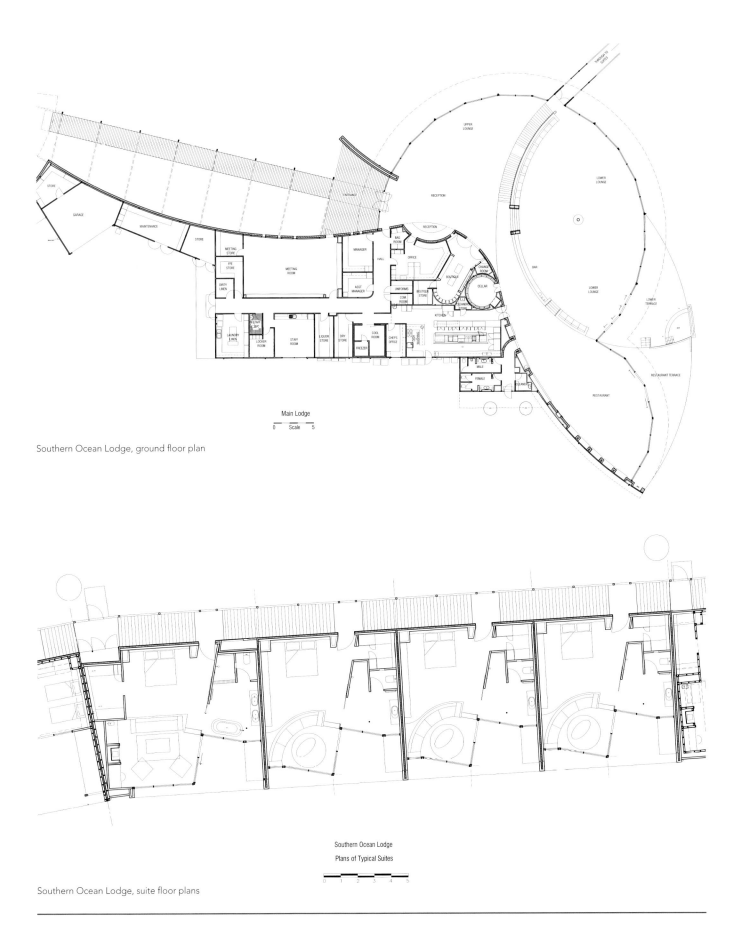

Southern Ocean Lodge, ground floor plan

Main Lodge

0   Scale   5

Southern Ocean Lodge

Plans of Typical Suites

0   1   2   3   4   5

Southern Ocean Lodge, suite floor plans

The hotel industry continues to expand its long-term worldwide interest in advances in green architecture and eco-sciences such as hydroponics, as exemplified by the CuisinArt Resort and Spa's hydroponic farm established on the Caribbean island of Anguilla. The state-of-the-art hydroponic process provides fruits, vegetables, and edible flowers free from pollutants and pesticides, produce used for preparing meals in the resort's restaurants.

There are still great realms of empty ocean, deserts reaching to the curvature of the earth, silent, ancient forests and rocky coasts, glaciers and volcanoes, but what will we do with them? In the quest for survival, success and fulfillment the ecological view offers an invaluable insight. It shows the way for the man who would be the enzyme of the biosphere—its steward, enhancing the creative fit of man-environment, realizing man's design with nature.

(Ian McHarg, *Design with Nature*, New York: Doubleday/ Natural History Press, 1969, p. 19)

Wilderness Lodges and Wildlife Reserves

A special breed of ecotourism seeks to provide its guests with unforgettable adventure by thrusting them into dense primeval jungles and exotic rainforests where they interact with tigers, bears, rhino, and elephants, or onto rugged coastlines populated by migrating whales and dolphins. With overpopulation and depletion of natural resources plaguing our fragile planet, such wilderness resorts provide an increasingly rare opportunity to enjoy the pristine beauty of the wilds. Many visitors to wilderness resorts are looking for a sense of adventure and an element of danger, with the wonder of riding an elephant through a bamboo jungle or the rush of a long-tail boat ride up a winding rainforest river.

Singita was founded in 1925, by James Fawcett Bailes, who bought a large piece of land in Mpumalanga province, South Africa, with the goal of preserving it and protecting its magnificent wildlife. It is now known as the Sabi Sand Game Reserve, on the western border of the Kruger National Park. In 1993, his grandson built Ebony, the first Singita property, on that site, as an exclusive game lodge offering unsurpassed luxury and wildlife experiences.

Singita Pamushana Lodge in Zimbabwe is a mission-oriented luxury eco-lodge dedicated to saving endangered species within the Malilangwe Wildlife Reserve. These include the roan antelope, the sable antelope, and the black rhino, which is on the verge of extinction. The lodge comprises six luxury suites and one villa, each offering spectacular views of the Malilangwe Dam. Each suite features en suite bathroom and shower, as well as an outdoor shower, private plunge pool, double-sided fireplace, mini-bar and fridge, room safe, air-conditioning, overhead fans, private lounge, direct-dial telephones, and game-viewing deck with Swarovski spotting scope. The main lodge area offers an indoor dining room, open dining room, teak-deck dining areas, bar, library, open-air lounge, wine cellar, two heated swimming pools, and a Jacuzzi, all overlooking the Malilangwe Dam and sandstone hills.

Anantara Golden Triangle Resort and Spa, Golden Triangle, Thailand
Guests of this wilderness resort, perched high in the lush hills of Thailand's border, may choose to spend the day pampered at the luxurious accommodations of the main lodge or experiencing the more adventurous elephant camp, designed along the lines of the traditional mahouts' villages, found in the hills of northern Thailand in the days when logging employed the majority of Thailand's elephants.

The Princesse Bora Lodge and Spa, located on Sainte-Marie Island off the coast of Madagascar, is involved in the observation of humpback whales and works closely with CetaMada, an association concerned with the protection of these marine mammals. Thanks to this collaboration, CetaMada has acquired unique knowledge concerning humpback whales. The Princesse is committed to the economic well-being and social life of Sainte-Marie Island. Most of the staff (approximately 90 employees) come from nearby villages. The resort favors the use of local products to sustain the local economy and is also involved in educational projects, in particular with the local school of Vohilava.

Singita Pamushana Lodge, Malilangwe Wildlife Reserve, Zimbabwe
Set within a remote wilderness bounded on the west by the rich riparian
woodland flanking the Chiredzi River and on the east by Gonarezhou
("place of the elephants") National Park, the seven-key lodge incorporates
the natural environment and the forest-like architecture, with spectacular
views of the lush gardens and lake below.

Princesse Bora Lodge and Spa, Sainte-Marie Island, Madagascar
Built along a white-sand beach lined with coconut palms and facing a
beautiful lagoon, the 20-key eco-lodge offers executive beach, luxury,
and comfort villas, all interspersed in a tropical garden.

Planning and Design Considerations

As with island resorts, the remoteness of these eco-adventure
lodges requires special consideration to provisions, access, staffing,
and infrastructure. It is characteristic of many of these resorts to
be very small and provide fewer than 20 guestrooms or tents. The
back-of-house and staffing requirements are therefore relatively
small compared to most isolated island resorts, although the
remoteness may require significant storage capability. If possible,
it adds to the ambience and guest experience if qualified staff can
be found in nearby villages, as with the Princesse Bora Lodge. A
significant investment can be bringing sufficient electrical power
to the resort, since the noise of a generator would disturb the
local wildlife.

Getting the guests to and from the resort can be a challenge
but can also contribute to a significant part of the guests' eco-
experience. Whether arrival is by Jeep or Range Rover on a narrow
mountain road or by longboat up a jungle-lined river teeming with

Multi-resort Destination Complexes

According to a 2011 Marriott survey for its SpringHill Suites brand, 89 percent of U.S. travelers choose a vacation destination first and then go looking for the right lodging package, so it is logical that resort hotels tend to cluster around beautiful and popular settings. When this clustering happens in a strategic and planned way, the result is perhaps best described as a multi-resort destination. The best-known of these is Orlando, Florida. When Walt Disney started acquiring property in the area in 1963, he envisioned a sister theme park to his successful Disneyland in California and a novel "Experimental Prototype City of Tomorrow." Almost fifty years later, Orlando has become a vacation behemoth, with over 51 million visitors in 2010 alone, coming from all over the world to visit dozens of theme parks, shopping malls, and other attractions, spending close to U.S.$30 billion in the process. On the Disney property itself there are 31 hotels (eight of which are operated by a third party), all carefully planned to attract different market segments and offer unique—but all very "Disneyfied"—vacation experiences.

While the Orlando model may not be replicable or even desirable in many markets, the idea of developing a series of resort properties in a single location has caught on, particularly in the Middle East and Asia. One good example is the Palm Jumeirah in Dubai, which is the most massive land-reclamation project to date, creating a 9.6 sq mile (25 sq km) mega-resort with hotels, attractions, entertainment venues, retail, and a large variety of residential developments. Pressure for more beachfront development because of the phenomenal growth of Dubai inspired developer Nakheel to make more beach by dredging up sand from the Persian Gulf to create the palm-shaped project. A 6.8 mile (11 km) outer crescent serves as a breakwater to protect the 16 residential "fronds" and is the site of much of Palm Jumeirah's commercial development, which is connected to the mainland by a 3.4 mile (5.4 km) monorail. Already huge on its own, Palm Jumeirah is actually just a small part of a planned 2 billion sq ft (185.5 million sq m) of new development that Nakheel intends to build in Dubai. There are also dozens of other mega-resort complexes being proposed for this small emirate, now the business and tourism hub of the Middle East.

On the other side of the Asian continent is Resorts World Sentosa. Master-planned and designed largely by architect Michael Graves, the project includes six hotels and a wealth of entertainment options in three distinct zones on Sentosa Island, off the coast of Singapore. Resorts World Sentosa attracts families to its theme parks and shopping, gaming enthusiasts to its casino, and conventioneers to the 7,300 seat underground Compass Ballroom and 25 other meeting rooms. The designers made every effort to highlight the natural beauty of the island and the project has earned a BCA (Building and Construction Authority) Gold Green Mark rating for its environmental initiatives.

A multi-resort destination on a smaller scale is Mayakoba on the Riviera Maya in southeastern Mexico. Developers OHL wanted to protect the mile-long beach and retain the pristine jungle setting, and therefore constructed most of the project's infrastructure about a third of a mile (500 m) back from the shoreline. Three low-rise luxury hotels flank a Greg Norman–designed championship golf

Four Seasons Tented Camp, Golden Triangle, Thailand
Amid exotic bamboo jungles, where the borders of Thailand, Laos, and Burma converge, the luxury resort offers 15 tented accommodations that allow adventurous guests to immerse themselves in a wilderness experience, recalling the romantic spirit of nineteenth-century explorers.

crocodiles and piranha, the opportunity to set the stage for great adventure should not be overlooked.

Buildings and structures at jungle lodges tend to be very sparse and simple, aiding the perception that this is an encampment that can be picked up and moved to another location at a moment's notice. It is important that support facilities are kept out of sight. The Four Seasons Tented Camp Golden Triangle, located in dense jungle overlooking the Ruak River where the borders of Thailand, Laos, and Burma converge, offers 15 tented accommodations, each named after local hill tribes. The resort is designed to echo the romantic spirit of nineteenth-century explorers. Each tent is interwoven with indoor and outdoor living areas. An outdoor deck measures 398 sq ft (37 sq m) and features a daybed and two massage beds built on a wooden platform, covered by the extended roof. A luxurious sleeping area features a bed with mosquito net. An open-plan bathroom is incorporated into the living area, featuring a custom-made, two-person, hand-hammered copper bathtub with hand shower in the center of the tent. An outdoor rain shower and separate WC are adjacent to the living area. In an effort to preserve the sounds of nature and the forest environment, televisions, DVD players, and radios are not provided.

Resorts World Sentosa, Singapore

Resorts World Sentosa is a strong example of an Asian integrated resort which combines lodging, entertainment, gaming, convention and retail space in a single complex. The development targets multiple markets through the six different hotels on site, from the art-themed Hotel Michael—named for project architect Michael Graves—to an invitation-only, luxury all-suite property.

Mayakoba, Riviera Maya, Mexico

Three luxury hotels, high-end residential villas, championship golf facilities, and a flawless stretch of Caribbean beach make up this carefully planned destination resort along the southeastern shore of the Yucatan. The development was the first project in Latin America to be recognized as a Rainforest Alliance Verified Destination in light of the development team's care in respecting the many natural attributes of the 600 acre (240 hectare) site.

course that winds sinuously around the property. Two of the hotels also have villa components, located along the beach and separated from the main hotel areas by dense forest and manmade lagoons that tap into underground water already on the site. Local materials form an important element of the design that Three Architecture, designers of two of the project's hotel properties, calls "a resort in and of the jungle."

Large resort projects like these are complicated to plan and execute, particularly because of the varying nature of the design criteria for each component of the complex. Lodging and attractions have their own planning requirements and must be well integrated into the master plan from the beginning of the development process.

Master-plan Design Considerations

Multi-resort destinations can vary as much as do any individual resorts. These developments can provide needed expansion of recreation amenities as well as benefits to local economies. They extend the existing social and physical infrastructure by contributing vital support to airport development as well as roads and necessary services. However, sound guiding principles must be followed to avoid overcrowding, congestion, and cultural and environmental problems. This can be accomplished by designing large-scale master plans which preserve and enhance the regional ecology, maintain reasonable density standards, and mitigate vital concerns for traffic, utilities, clean air, pure water, and natural landscaping.

A major destination resort needs a vast site with adequate space to allow future growth, including resort hotels, and to protect itself from competitive businesses in the vicinity and within the region. The master plan confirms the sites of the resorts and limits their size, number, height, and the maximum volume of future developments. It also establishes a model system of architectural controls, based on historic inspiration, environmental goals, and research, so that the project's design balance between architectural variety and contextual unity will be continued in any new developments. Master-planning a multi-resort destination offers the advantage of a single-minded direction for the entire project. The alternative is to break large projects into numerous sites, each under a different ownership, with no central strategy or possibility of reaching agreements on design guidelines, for example, or when and whether to expand.

Accommodation Planning Considerations

There is usually a variety of types of lodging at multi-resort destinations, reflecting the diversity of the resort's visitors. Many prefer the total experience and convenience of staying within an integrated resort, offering easy access, longer hours, and package pricing. Walt Disney's original concept of providing the most desirable themed lodging concepts "inside the gate," to enhance and be enhanced by the resort, ultimately proved the most successful course. Each multi-resort destination development company needs to consider its strategy for creating lodging within the complex and whether to establish its own management company.

The decision on what type of resorts to build, the number of rooms, rate class, and operational policies will vary depending on the market study for the complex as well as a separate analysis of each of its elements. Familiarity with new hotel types will assist the developer in determining the most appropriate concepts and brands for a given project.

As with any resort, lodging that is part of a multi-resort destination project needs to offer a transporting experience. Landscaping, views, the arrival sequence, and access to widely dispersed amenities within a given hotel's grounds all require detailed consideration as part of the master plan. Although there may be opportunities for shared support resources across several hotels within the destination, the trend toward having different operators for each hotel component makes true economies difficult. Brand identity needs to be carefully married to the overall vision for the development, emphasizing the value of having recognized hotel brands on board sufficiently early in the development process.

One of the boldest and most influential approaches to multi-resort destination lodging, the "vacation village," introduced a super-casual atmosphere reflecting the socioeconomic changes of the mid-twentieth century, when Club Med introduced the concept with the following entreaties: "an antidote for civilization …"; "respite from the frantic pace …"; "an avenue to other civilizations …"; and "hotels offer you a room, Club Med gives you an entire village!" The vacation village model has influenced all hotel design, even outside the resort category. A strong sense of place, multiple on-site amenities to keep guests on the property, the bundling of features into single-price vacation packages, and a carefully orchestrated guest experience from booking to departure are hallmarks of the original vacation village concept which have been adopted by other kinds of hotel developments.

Long walking distances, normally a source of guest complaints in spread-out low-rise hotels, can become an architecturally exciting, enjoyable experience in the context of a village design approach. Planners can make walking a feature of the resort and encourage it by planning the facilities in the same way that anchor stores are positioned in a large mall. For example, if the entrance lobby is at one end of the resort, a campanile might be designed to create interest at the opposite end, with pools, snack bars, and sports and other activity centers widely spaced en route. A central plaza is the meeting place and focal point, with dual areas, one shaded and trellised for daytime use, and another more open to the sky for the evenings. With the village broken into varied courtyards on different levels, even an 800-room resort can easily maintain a smaller-scaled, more personal atmosphere.

To further enhance walking experiences, the design needs to provide more than beautiful vistas, lush indigenous landscaping, and authentic statuary. Since smooth walkways bear urban connotations, surfaces are given varying textures appealing to the tactile senses. For ambient sound, cooling fountains are mounted on walls at turns in walkways or set freestanding in courtyards. Outside illumination is provided by wall sconces and path lighting, rather than high-intensity floodlights, to avoid harsh shadows. Earthy colors are used with bright accents that reflect local decorative themes and artwork. In these idyllic surroundings, guests are made more aware

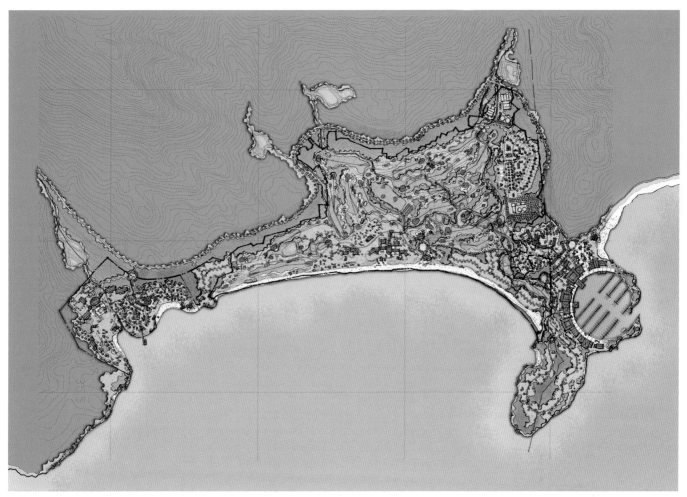

Binh Tien Resort, Nha Trang, Vietnam
This multi-destination resort features over 800 keys across four different hotels, 161 residential villas, and a wealth of recreational facilities including a casino, two beach clubs, and a large marina. As an additional amenity, an 18-hole golf course was positioned as a buffer between the resort and the adjacent nature reserve but still offers at least one beachfront hole.

of their senses, becoming more responsive to aesthetic themes and detailing.

Multi-resort destination complexes increasingly will include village-inspired designs as essential elements to maintain variety and reduce density, as required in large-scale integrated beachfront developments.

Attraction Development and Planning Considerations

A key component of many multi-resort destinations is one or more theme parks. Research comparing a theme park to a non-themed amusement park of the same size and capacity shows that a theme park is superior in attracting visitors, generating revenue, and enhancing satisfaction. Theme parks exhibit these attributes:

- Greater geographical attraction
- Longer length of stay
- Enhanced food and beverage sales
- Enhanced retail, logo, and themed merchandise sales
- Improved overall experience and increased repeat business.

Spending on retail items and food and beverages, when appropriately themed, increases in proportion to the length of stay, with higher-quality theming capable of significantly increased margins. Similarly, the number of days visitors spend at a park is proportional to the distance they travel for the unique experience. Not surprisingly, asset values of theme parks are positively affected by the quality of the themes. As leisure venues and vacation destinations, theme parks offer an escape from the routine. Thus Universal Studios' multi-park resort stated the obvious when naming its venture "Universal Escape."

Themes for most leisure parks and resorts fall within one of the following categories:

- *Historic places and cultures* are normally readily researched and widely appreciated. Depending on the theme, it can be costly to achieve quality and authenticity. Site conditions may require extensive area development of landscape, hardscape, topographical, and visual site control. The Tivoli Gardens in Copenhagen is a very early example of this type of park; others include World Showcase at EPCOT in Orlando, Disney's California Adventure, Taiwan Folk Village, Port Aventura, and the Polynesian Cultural Center in Hawaii.

- *Fantasy characters and places* provide flexibility to create a unique atmosphere for escape from reality. Beloved characters from fiction or animation serve as a springboard for design ideas, and fantasy locations offer tremendous freedom to the design team for creating ever more elaborate environments. Some of the most prominent parks in the world fit into this theme category: Islands of Adventure, Florida; Caribbean Bay, South Korea; Parc Astérix, France; and the Magic Kingdom at Walt Disney parks worldwide.

- *Subject-focused themes* are always strong when well defined and clearly identified. The subject of the park establishes the architectural vocabulary and thematic atmosphere. It is important that the theme subject should not be too trendy or quickly outdated. For example, parks with a future theme often are out of date by the time the project gets off the drawing-board and is constructed, although Disney has celebrated the "retro" aspects of its 1955 vision of Tomorrowland in today's park. Prominent subject-focused theme parks include Universal Studios (films), SeaWorld (oceans), Ferrari World Abu Dhabi (luxury cars), and Disney's Animal Kingdom at Walt Disney World Resort, Florida (animals).

- *Activity-focused theme parks* often have a limited theme, and in those cases it could be argued that activity alone does not justify the theme. However, the general media and public perceive most amusement parks and waterparks as theme parks. Certainly, activity-focused parks can be themed as an enhancement for the activity. Enormous waterparks like Wet'n'Wild in Australia or the indoor ski hills at SnowWorld in the Netherlands or Ski Dubai are prime examples of these kinds of parks.

Within these four theme categories are a vast number of theme park types which, when appropriately combined, can attract and even develop new target markets.

Ideation begins with a series of brainstorming sessions between the developer and the design and economic consultants specializing in themed entertainment experiences. Practiced interdisciplinary consultants explore the project's objectives and a myriad of potential solutions, including details such as how to encourage different age groups to benefit from each other's presence. This think-tank method is also used in developing trend analyses.

Once the concept is approved in sufficient detail, including a workable budget and source of financing, the full technical team of specialists turns the desired concept into reality. Throughout the design and planning process, the key factor for success is to focus the product on the best guest experience within realistic budget parameters. To do this, the design team must have a clear definition and understanding of the target markets, including seasonal shifts and related promotional and yield management systems. The park should be designed to allow flexibility of live show content and capacity levels, as well as shifts in merchandise content and food and beverage selections. The greater the ability to satisfy the market, the longer that market group will be in the park and the more they will spend.

The key to a positive guest experience is the attraction mix. The attractions, whether shows or rides, are measured in several ways beyond the given expectation of being a quality entertainment experience. The team considers: the mix of attraction types, so that a good variety of experiences is provided; the attraction's age group appeal; and how many people per hour the attraction can accommodate, measured by its hourly entertainment capacity units (ECUs). The calculation of ECUs is most readily understood by using a theater attraction as an example. A theater that can seat 500 people and process the guest entry, seating, safety orientation, film presentation, and guest exit in a total of 20 minutes has an hourly ECU of 1,500 (500 people x 3 cycles/hour = 1,500 ECU). At times, new attraction concepts have to be significantly modified to achieve overall ECU demands, because guests will only tolerate queues of a certain duration. Designing attractions within attractions is one way of addressing long queues.

Another measurement of overall park capacity is based on the average density of guests per acre or hectare. One rule-of-thumb is 700 to 1,000 guests per acre (0.4 hectare) of actual park area (excluding parking). If park area densities fall too far below 400 guests per acre, this may generate an impression of the park being unsuccessful or having a less energized atmosphere. Indoor theme parks normally become a unique challenge, with economically driven demands for around 1,500 visitors per interior acre. The market in Japan seems to have the record, with popular expo parks reaching average attendance densities of up to 2,000 guests per acre.

Daily guest attendance is never consistent. Even in major year-round tourist destinations such as the parks in and near Orlando, Florida, attendance patterns fluctuate within seasonal markets. With the given fluctuation of daily attendance, parks are planned and designed based on the "design day" and "design hour." The design day is neither the annual average daily attendance nor the peak day average attendance; rather, it is a more sophisticated figure based on an analysis of critical attendance days within the annual attendance pattern. Sometimes, a rule-of-thumb of the 10 to 15 busiest days can provide a preliminary design-day number. The design-day attendance is then used to establish the design hour, which is a function of the park's operating hours and the visitor's average length of stay, based on the park's overall ECUs. The tighter the margin between park operating hours and guest length of stay, the closer the design-hour attendance is to the design-day attendance.

The design-hour attendance is the primary park sizing guide. Everything, from the more macro figures such as in-park acreage/density, total park ECUs, restaurant and retail mix to micro measures such as restroom capacities and wheelchair/stroller rentals, is sized based on the design-hour attendance.

The park's size and attraction mix has the most to do with determining a guest's length of stay. Attractions with extremely high ECUs may process guests too quickly and reduce length of stay, whereas attractions with too limiting an ECU will create congestion and result in such a negative guest experience that visitors may leave early out of frustration. Another rule-of-thumb is that guests should visit about 1.5 attraction experiences per hour; therefore, to generate an eight-hour length of stay, each guest should see about twelve attractions in addition to food and retail experiences. If the park's design hour is 10,000 people, then the overall park's hourly ECU would be 15,000 to 18,000, depending on the overlapping age appeal of the attraction mix.

After the development and design team have established the major capacity and overall use characteristics, they proceed with the preliminary conceptual plan for the park. One of the most critical success factors is the placement of attractions within the park. Some common strategies include:

- Locate some of the most appealing "must see" attractions on the extreme edges to draw guests through the park past impulse retail, and less popular attractions.
- Offer within each sub-theme area attractions which appeal to a variety of age groups.
- Place the attractions so that the overall hourly ECU count is evenly distributed, to avoid congestion and ensure an even distribution of guests throughout the park.

The physical layout of the park is strongly influenced by site conditions, theme parameters, operational policies, and cultural differences. There are several overall planning models commonly used in theme park design.

- *Hub and spoke plan:* This was developed by Walt Disney for Disneyland in Anaheim, California, and is still considered one of the best models for theme park planning. In its original form it had the entry/exit spoke flanked with appropriate retail shops. This spoke channeled all arriving guests to the center of the park, where a visual icon punctuated the hub and became an orientation element seen from multiple vantage points in the park. At DisneySea in Tokyo, this element is Mysterious Island. From the central hub, each of the other spokes are circulation gateways to the various sub-theme zones of the park. The advantage of quickly bringing visitors to a central location and then exposing multiple gateway options is excellent for swift and even distribution of guests into all sub-theme areas. Often included with the hub and spoke plan is an outer-rim circulation loop connecting the sub-theme zones.
- *Loop plan:* This plan is used at Islands of Adventure (IOA), Universal Escape, Orlando, Florida. In the case of IOA, the loop surrounds a central water amenity; however, some loop plans place general service and maintenance functions in the center, for ease of operations. A major challenge of loop parks is that once visitors establish a direction of travel there is no choice, whether they

might want to revisit a favorite attraction or jump across the center. Where there is a single entry to the loop, attractions opposite the entry point (regardless of popularity) often do not operate at full capacity during the opening hour, and somewhat later they have extensive queues because both circulation directions converge. Some parks with the loop layout try to move guests to sub-theme zones beyond the entry point by using various modes of group transportation, but that is rarely as effective as a central pedestrian entry point to all sub-theme zones.

- *Figure eight plan:* Essentially two loops, this plan has many of the attributes of the hub and spoke. Generally, designers make the crossover of the figure eight—where the two loops connect—the entry point, where it acts as a central hub to distribute guests in four directions through the sub-theme zones.
- *Random plan:* Unconventional or random plan strategies are often a result of unusual site conditions or external planning forces which dictate an unusual approach to park planning design. An example of this is the Fantasy Island Water Park on Sentosa Island in Singapore, in which an irregular site had several utility easements cutting across it. Planning was further complicated by the requirement for both a primary entry and a secondary gate for a future monorail station. Designers determined that the random plan would integrate the lost-civilization theme and archeological-dig storyline.

While economic viability remains the key threshold factor, high-profile attractions with accompanying lodging are a continuing megatrend in an industry where attendance numbers are rebounding strongly from the 2008–2010 recession and new projects of all types are being proposed worldwide.

Casino Hotels

While the Broadmoor resort in Colorado Springs, Colorado, briefly experimented with gaming at the turn of the nineteenth century, it wasn't until 1947 that the first successful casino hotel, The Flamingo, was built in Las Vegas. It was reputed to be owned by the underworld, but from this dubious start gaming developed into one of the most popular segments of the U.S. hotel industry. Over a span of seventy years, the U.S. casino hotel industry transformed the Las Vegas desert into the world's largest multifaceted resort. It conceived theme parks laced with hotels and tied to convention centers, shops, and shows by a variety of arcades, skyways, and people-movers, traversing geographic themes from New York to Paris, Rome, Venice, Egypt, North Africa, and Mandalay, and in recent years has moved towards modernist developments that combine traditional casino entertainment with dramatic residential space. This "integrated resort" development trend has since expanded to new markets worldwide, particularly in Asia. The Cotai Strip in Macau is planned to connect as many as 20 hotel projects from many of the world's leading luxury hotel brands, interspersed with expansive retail, entertainment, and dining facilities.

New gaming licenses have made Singapore a destination for international casino guests, while South Korea, Taiwan, and Vietnam lead six additional Southeast Asian nations that have recently introduced casino gaming. There is also substantial gaming growth in Europe, Australia, and Latin America.

Despite this explosion in international casino development, the United States still has by far the largest number of gaming properties. Las Vegas alone has an inventory of over 145,000 hotel rooms, 7.5 million sq ft (700,000 sq m) of meeting space, and over 2 million sq ft (185,810 sq m) of gaming areas, along with hundreds of other demand-generating attractions. However, significant international developments are challenging Las Vegas for gaming supremacy in a single location. Today, the second-largest gaming market in the world is Macau, with over 25 million visitors annually, 90 percent of whom come from China. In 2011, gaming revenue in Macau was more than double that of Las Vegas.

Native American tribes also continue to be a development force, with over 400 casinos in 28 U.S. states. Many tribal casinos are limited to a Class II gaming license, which restricts them to games of chance played against others, such as bingo and poker, rather than against the house. However, Class III licenses have become more common and many of the major casino-operating companies have formed partnerships with Native American groups to create casino resorts that rival any in Nevada or Atlantic City in terms of casino floor space, restaurants, and entertainment.

City of Dreams Resort, Macau, China

This $2.1 billion development features over 2,200 rooms in four hotels—Crown Towers, Hard Rock Hotel Macau, Grand Hyatt Macau, and an apartment hotel—as well as a 420,000 sq ft (39,000 sq m) casino and an elaborate array of entertainment, dining, and retail facilities on its 28 acre (10.6 hectare) site. The project joins as many as 11 additional casino, lodging, and entertainment developments proposed for the Cotai Strip integrated resort.

173

Revel, Atlantic City, New Jersey
Built on one of the largest beachfront sites in Atlantic City, Revel features
the tallest hotel tower in its market. The exterior was designed by
Arquitectonica.

Most casino hotels in the past have focused heavily on simulacra of the exotic. But the opening of CityCenter in Las Vegas in late 2009 and Marina Bay Sands in Singapore in 2010 has shifted development impetus away from heavily themed casino resorts toward cutting-edge design; these hotels represent the vanguard of a current trend for involving world-class architects in new gaming developments. Casinos are now taking more design cues from the boutique hotel segment than from the theme park industry. The goal for many projects built in the second decade of this century will be to create an aspirational environment that will both age well and appeal to a broad market.

Development Considerations

The strong economy and favorable financing opportunities in the early 2000s led to an explosion of casino development in major gaming markets and on tribal land in the United States. Locations that had previously restricted gambling were spurred by this growth to change legislation to permit a variety of gaming options, a situation that presented casino projects with significant competitive pressure. The deep recession of 2008–2009 offered additional challenges to casino developers. In many markets there is now an oversupply of lodging capacity that keeps room rates down and discourages new development.

Because of this oversupply, many developers are turning to the acquisition and repositioning of existing properties. This development approach is particularly attractive in markets like Atlantic City, where declining gaming revenues have made new casino construction difficult to finance. Casinos being created today need a broad range of on-site demand generators—lavish retail complexes, spas, multi-pool outdoor recreation areas, and large nightclubs and show lounges—to offset reductions in gaming revenues and to fend off competition from non-hotel gaming sites in neighboring markets and a burgeoning online gaming culture. These elaborate facilities have pushed casino hotel development costs ever higher, making it difficult for all but the largest development groups to get projects built. Some projects

Vdara, Las Vegas, Nevada
Unlike most other Las Vegas hotels, the Vdara condo-hotel does not have a casino. The tower, designed by Rafael Viñoly, is made up of three nested arcs that appear to slide past each other.

have included a condominium component as an additional source of financing and to grow demand for the casino's revenue-generating amenities, although this strategy became problematic during the mortgage crisis in the late 2000s.

Not surprisingly, lucrative gaming revenues often enable casino hotels to offer guestrooms at highly competitive rates, thereby attracting not only more gaming customers but a variety of other guests as well. Elaborate entertainment and some of the world's finest resort facilities act as magnets to international tourists and convention groups and provide an attractive discounted vacation for families. However, these features make major casino projects an enormously expensive proposition, and have led to the development of non-gaming hotels that offer far fewer amenities than a typical casino but are still within easy reach of other properties' offerings. These hotels often are less expensive to build because they have minimal investment in such high-cost spaces as food and beverage outlets and entertainment facilities. One example of this approach is Vdara at CityCenter, a 1,495-room condominium hotel that has only one lounge bar and restaurant, one fast–casual food outlet,

and no casino space, yet is physically connected to Bellagio and ARIA, both massive full-service casino hotels. The resulting high proportion of guestroom space relative to total building area allows Vdara to reduce operating expenses and offer an alternative to those travelers who prefer to stay in a quieter location but still be close to gaming, dining, and entertainment facilities.

The management of casino properties is dominated by a small group of specialized operators, limiting the number of traditional hotel brands that have a presence in gaming locations in the United States. Some of these operators have developed brand identities of their own and are capitalizing on their name recognition as they expand into new markets, while Asian casino development often features a combination of such well-known gaming brands as Sands and MGM with luxury lodging brands including St. Regis, Four Seasons, and Grand Hyatt.

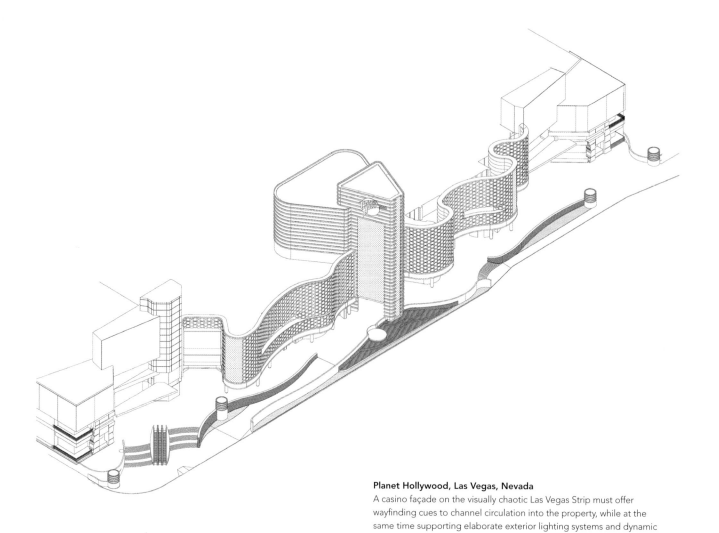

Planet Hollywood, Las Vegas, Nevada
A casino façade on the visually chaotic Las Vegas Strip must offer wayfinding cues to channel circulation into the property, while at the same time supporting elaborate exterior lighting systems and dynamic promotional signage. Planet Hollywood's façade—retrofitted onto an existing building—adds visual interest to the casino exterior while achieving all of these functional goals.

Planning and Design Considerations

Because casino hotels need to provide many additional amenities to promote the gaming operation, these projects require a greater ratio of non-revenue-producing space than any other hotel type. In addition to more traditional non-revenue-generating spaces in the back-of-house, additional resources that upscale casino hotels must provide to be competitive include elaborate "high-roller" suites and villas traditionally furnished free to high-stake players, star suites for big-name entertainers staying at the hotel, and gourmet "hold tables" in restaurants on or near the gaming floor permanently reserved for quick service to high rollers who want to spend the maximum time at the tables. To compensate, casino hotels typically are models of functional efficiency in planning the hotel operational areas, and are designed to minimize construction and operating costs in the back-of-house as well as in some of the public areas. Here, quality concepts and attention to design detail are vital elements in the hotel's success. Because guests spend a much longer time in hotel public areas in casino properties than in most other types of lodging operations, floor plans should encourage and reward guests' exploration and finishes must enhance the sense of place evoked by the overall project theme. In some markets, visiting a variety of hotels' public spaces is a big part of the casino vacation experience and the public has increasingly high expectations for the quality of casino design.

The Casino Gaming Floor

The amount of gaming space provided in a casino hotel varies, depending on the market. In locations that have a high proportion of day-trippers who do not stay overnight, 250 sq ft (23.2 sq m) or more per key of casino floor is typical, whereas in Las Vegas this number is much lower—roughly 30–40 sq ft (2.7–3.7 sq m) per key—due to

Designing Casino Hotels

Roger Thomas, Executive Vice President—Design
Wynn Design and Development
Las Vegas, Nevada

In the beginning, the casino was the driving force behind the hotel—everything was designed and pricing was gauged to feed the casino. But with the advent of the Mirage in 1989, the rooms, restaurants, bars, retail, and entertainment ceased to be adjuncts to the casino and in today's resorts carry equal weight in the design process and in the revenue stream.

At Wynn, we don't think these are different aspects—they are all integrated parts of the resort experience. The balance and flow of the parts is paramount in everything we do.

As designers, our job is to create memories and places of possibility. I call what we do "evocatechture." For each project we don't do a theme or replicate something that's been done before. Instead, we develop our own unique design vocabulary to create drama, mystery, wonder, delight—emotions that you'll remember and tell others about.

We design our projects from the guest's point of view, considering the experience from the entrance all the way to the arrival at the most intimate space: the guestroom. We think hard about the way each area is used, how it should look, how the guest gets there. In our designs, we like to create "neighborhoods," each with a specific focus of gaming, food, beverage, retail offerings, and other services, everything that our guests need and want within easy access of their hotel elevator.

From the guest's point of view, wayfinding can be a real problem in a large casino resort, and we spend a lot of time and effort in anticipating questions about directions before guests ask them, and in creating legible, clear signage placement accordingly.

We also consider all the practical aspects of casino and resort operations. Our table-game areas are intimate and personal, owing to many factors including ceiling height and individual chandeliers over each table. This created the problem of obstacles to security cameras, which we overcame through research and development in a full-scale working model of the casino for Wynn. We were able to test our ideas and prove that all aspects of the design worked for licensing officials. It was expensive, but worth it for the unique look and better patron experience.

In designing something as massive and expensive as a casino resort, we do not follow trends; if you are capturing the latest design trend, you're already out of date by the time it is built. Casino resorts have a development time frame of three to five years, so their design needs to be classic and unique, revealing new thought rather than following others' innovations.

the high proportion of convention and family vacationers who visit the city but may not participate in gaming. Casino space is generally contiguous rather than dispersed throughout the property.

The casino floor has to balance excitement and engagement with security. The goal is to create an open area with good sight-lines while offering a wide range of playing locations to suit the preferences of all types of players: some prefer more personal space while others thrive on the energy of close quarters, while still others may want a smoke-free environment. Slot machines typically are clustered in a small configuration of not more than 10 machines each, and table games are generally laid out in groups of 8 to 12, with each group centered around a supervisor or "pit boss." The growing popularity of poker has made tournament space an important consideration; many casinos have a flexible area on the gaming floor that can be roped off and set up for temporary events. Finally, high-limit gaming areas, where the minimum bet can be $5,000 or more, need to be conveniently located for VIP guests but separated from the main casino. In most jurisdictions, these areas must be visually open to limit the possibility, or even the perception, of illegal activity.

No other building contains security monitoring systems equal to those of a casino. Called the "live peek" in Atlantic City and the "eye-in-the-sky" in Las Vegas, the system of concealed pan-and-tilt cameras is monitored by security guards in a special screening room. It also records the gaming action at each table so that events can be closely reexamined if any complaints or suspicions of cheating arise. Recent improvements in camera technology have given the designer more freedom in ceiling height, with ceilings as high as 40 ft (12 m) now possible, whereas earlier cameras could not perform accurately at this range. In addition, the layout of the gaming tables is carefully designed to facilitate surveillance of the dealers and players by non-uniformed security guards, or "floaters," generally positioned at the ends of each line of tables. Smaller European-style casino hotels often are less security-conscious, with less extensive digital surveillance; these hotels exhibit a more casual arrangement of tables rather than the straight-line layout favored by U.S. gaming operators. Overall security usually is maintained jointly by a government agency and the casino management, with control offices located in the main cashier station (the "cage") and in a high-tech monitoring room. A security cell must be provided on the premises for detaining suspects. Some properties provide special back-of-house break facilities for the dealers, containing men's and women's restrooms, dressing facilities, and a private dining room adjacent to the gaming area.

One of the largest design constraints on the casino floor is the "money path," which leads from the cage, to "hard" and "soft" counting rooms for coins and paper money, respectively. The money then proceeds to a special money-truck loading dock via a heavy-load elevator under rigorous surveillance. Because of the tremendous weight of coinage in slot machines, the gaming floor itself used to have special structural needs. However, today's slots are primarily digital and coins rarely are seen, making the machines lighter in weight; this offers the operator additional flexibility to modify the layout as playing patterns change. Highly themed slot games that use multimedia to generate interest and encourage play are becoming more popular and can be used strategically to draw users to particular parts of the casino floor. The placement of

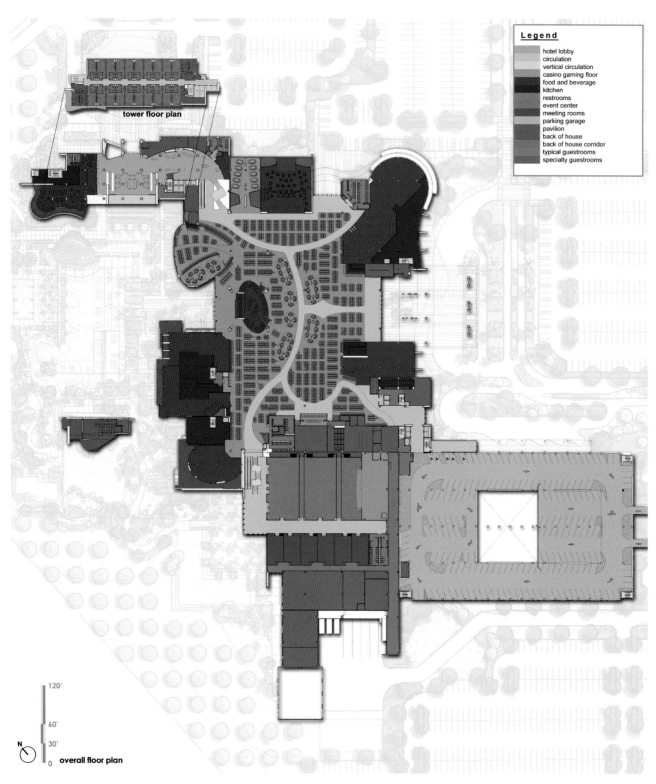

tower floor plan

Legend

- hotel lobby
- circulation
- vertical circulation
- casino gaming floor
- food and beverage
- kitchen
- restrooms
- event center
- meeting rooms
- parking garage
- pavilion
- back of house
- back of house corridor
- typical guestrooms
- specialty guestrooms

120'

60'

30'

0

N

overall floor plan

Casino Public Area Schematic

This plan illustrates many of the design issues that designers face when planning a casino hotel. Usually the hotel is attached at one end of the casino floor, oriented to allow unobstructed views over a landscaped area or pool. The convention space or meeting rooms are located at the opposite end to draw traffic back and forth through the gaming areas. The food and beverage venues are strategically located around the perimeter of the floor to create activity around the edges. These are serviced from a service level below.

City of Dreams Casino, Macau, China
Dedicated gaming floors such as this VIP gaming lounge for high-limit and high-profile guests are standard in most casinos. Local gaming laws may require that a visual connection between these spaces and the main gaming floor be maintained, so designers must develop creative solutions to balance privacy with clear views of play.

Crown Casino, Macau, China
The interiors for this 180,000 sq ft (16,725 sq m) casino were designed by Remedios Studio and won the first annual International Gaming Award for Best Casino Interior Design.

The Venetian, Las Vegas, Nevada
The Venetian and its sister hotel, The Palazzo, represent the epitome of the themed Las Vegas mega-resort: over 7,000 oversized keys, a 120,000 sq ft (11,100 sq m) casino, more than 500,000 sq ft (46,500 sq m) of high-end retail, and over 1.8 million sq ft (167,000 sq m) of convention space, when combined with the adjacent Sands Expo Convention Center. The design reflects the architecture and culture of Venice while supporting the operational needs of the largest resort of its kind in the world.

the cage, traditionally near the middle of the floor, is no longer so important, as slot winnings are redeemed at freestanding kiosks that double as bill-changers and ATMs.

Because some guests prefer to play slot machines alongside the gaming floor and others prefer them in dedicated areas, slots usually are located fairly evenly in both places. Slot areas should have ceiling heights of at least 12–16 ft (3.7–4.9 m) to accommodate promotional signage above some of the games. Carousels with circular groups of slot machines occupy about 20 sq ft (1.9 sq m) per machine as opposed to 10 sq ft (0.9 sq m) for conventional linear layouts. In some markets, additional space also must be provided for poker tables and sports-book betting operations. Such traditional games as keno and roulette have been converted to digital form and are now interspersed with slot machines. It is likely that more interactive digital games will continue to develop and will substantially influence future casino-floor design.

The number and type of table games varies with the location. In a casino hotel in the United States, a ratio of about five blackjack tables to each roulette and craps table is average. Typically, baccarat and high-stakes poker and blackjack tables are provided in a high-limit room, with more added at a ratio of about one for every 50 other gaming tables. While blackjack and roulette tables may be combined in any grouping, the other gaming tables are located in separate groups. Based on the above ratios, the area required for the gaming floor will average approximately 250 sq ft (23 sq m) per table. Hotel casinos planned with more widely spaced table layouts have, with few exceptions, proven less inviting to gaming customers, who generally prefer a more crowded atmosphere; of course, the tighter

spacing also saves on construction and operating cost. In Asian and European hotel casinos, the ratio of types of games changes, with the number of card game and baccarat tables generally doubling and craps games cut by about half. Tribal casinos may offer a bingo facility as well as more typical casino games.

Dining, Lounge, and Entertainment Facilities

To keep players on property and to attract other guests to the hotel, casino hotels typically have a much higher number of food and beverage outlets than traditional hotels. In Las Vegas, one food and beverage operation for every 150–160 rooms is typical. Casino hotels in Asia generally have an even higher number of food and beverage outlets. For example, Galaxy Macau has over 50 restaurants and lounges, about half of which boast Asian themes.

Bars and lounges should be well integrated directly with the gaming floor to enhance the ambience of both areas and stimulate business from one to the other. This also simplifies bar service to the gaming tables. Restaurants also should be convenient to the gaming area and, if on a different level, accessible by escalator, with good visibility from both the gaming and entrance lobbies. Cafés, grab'n'go outlets, and buffet dining areas should be open to the main public spaces, with entrances to the signature and specialty restaurants directly off the main lobbies and circulation concourses. Famous entertainers and elaborate dinner shows are expected in the largest casino hotels, but major show rooms are usually impractical for small- or medium-sized casino hotels, which generally provide cabaret entertainment lounges rather than the more costly dinner shows.

Convention Facilities

With the trend toward combining large trade shows with related corporate and association conventions, today's 1,000-room and larger casino hotels more than meet the requirements of the convention market. These groups, including family incentive groups, increasingly seek out resort locations for their events; in recent years, about 10 to 15 percent of visitors to Las Vegas have been convention participants. Therefore, the casino hotels' additions of luxury spas, chef-driven signature restaurants, and sophisticated entertainment programs position casino hotels to increase their penetration of the convention market.

Although meeting space requirements should be driven primarily by market needs, properties like The Venetian Macau that cater to large conventions can have over 300 sq ft (27.9 sq m) of meeting space per guestroom key. A more typical ratio for resort-type casino hotels is between 25 and 40 sq ft (2.3–3.7 sq m) of meeting space per key. As with other convention hotels, casino projects with significant meeting space typically have a dedicated porte cochère for the arrival of convention attendees, as well as loading facilities on the same level as the primary event spaces.

Guestrooms

Casino hotel rooms are larger and more luxuriously planned and appointed than those in suburban or downtown hotels. Guestrooms in casino properties built in the first decade of the twenty-first century average about 550 sq ft (50 sq m), with many five-star properties boasting typical rooms of over 700 sq ft (65 sq m). Because of its gaming revenue, the casino resort can provide greater luxury in every room compared with non-casino properties at the same price point. Soaking tubs, large stall showers, floor-to-ceiling windows, and sophisticated in-room technology for controlling lighting, window treatments, and entertainment systems have become standard in higher-end projects. Even though most casino guests are traveling for leisure purposes, the provision of adequate workspace with internet capability remains important, particularly in properties with substantial meeting space, as guests alternate work with leisure activities.

Casino guestrooms typically receive heavy usage, so material choices should be able to stand up to considerable traffic and abuse as well as engage a range of age groups. Depending on the market, a high proportion of queen-queen or double-double rooms may be appropriate. For these high-occupancy rooms, luggage storage and closet space need to be carefully planned.

High-roller or VIP suites are a typical addition to the casino room mix, giving these hotels a high percentage of suites relative to other types of properties. Suites may offer two or three bedrooms attached to a large central living space, as well as the potential to connect to smaller facilities accommodating a high-profile guest's entourage. Amenities might include dual rainfall showers, freestanding tubs,

in-room dining supported by a substantial wet bar, and a powder room off the living space. These units typically are restricted to key-access floors and supported by dedicated guest services and housekeeping staff.

At the very highest level of accommodation are luxury villas, which have been added to several of the most prominent casino properties at costs well above U.S.$1,000 per sq ft (U.S.$10,750 per sq m). While these villas may sometimes be rented, more often they are provided as an incentive to very high rollers. Enormous balconies, private pools, saunas and hot tubs, movie theaters, billiard rooms, and 24-hour butler service are just some of the features that make these villas—some well over 10,000 sq ft (925 sq m)—the ultimate luxury experience.

Greater guest sophistication and increasing expectations will continue to put pressure on casino hotels to incorporate up-to-date designs and amenities and remain current as technology changes. Casinos are becoming segmented psychographically rather than demographically. Efforts to appeal to a younger clientele while still attracting older gaming customers will present design challenges. Sustainable initiatives are likely to grow beyond the high-profile LEED-certified flag-bearers, such as CityCenter and The Palazzo in Las Vegas, to become a factor in planning any casino project. Guests increasingly will demand smoke-free areas, hypoallergenic guestrooms, and transparent sustainability efforts on the part of the operator that do not compromise the excitement or escapist atmosphere that gaming customers seek.

Flamingo Hotel, Las Vegas, Nevada
One of older properties on the Las Vegas Strip, the Flamingo received a mid-century modern update in 2007. The resulting "GO" room concept, designed by Cagley & Tanner, features a brown, white, and flamingo pink color scheme that makes witty reference to the swinging heyday of Vegas while offering twenty-first-century amenities.

───── Case Study ─────

The Cosmopolitan, Las Vegas, Nevada
Architect: Arquitectonica

Most Las Vegas casinos are erected on vast sites with plenty of working room. The 2,995-key Cosmopolitan has more in common with a city hotel than a classic Vegas mega-casino: the tight 8.7 acre (3.5 hectare) site forced the design team to make some unorthodox space-planning decisions. Unlike most casino hotels, the project is long and narrow, with two guestroom towers sitting on top of a five-story podium that contains 300,000 sq ft (27,870 sq m) of retail, dining, and entertainment space and 150,000 sq ft (13,935 sq m) of meeting facilities, topped by three elevated pool areas and several outdoor lounges.

The tight site forced back-of-house functions to be even more efficient than they are in a typical casino. Several administrative functions are housed off-site in leased space 3 miles (2 km) from The Strip. Uniform-issuing is completely automated to reduce labor and space. Valet-parking areas make use of vehicle lifts to maximize all three dimensions of space in the underground parking garage; valet drivers bring each vehicle to a camera station, where the car is measured and the appropriate available space for that particular car is identified by computer.

Even though space was at a premium, standard guestrooms start at a generous 610 sq ft (57 sq m), made visually larger in many cases by 6 ft (1.8 m) wide exterior terraces, a rarity in the Las Vegas market. The project was originally envisioned as primarily a residential development with a relatively small number of hotel rooms, but the market crash of 2008 and a change in project ownership just as interior finishing on the building was beginning prompted the move to an all-hotel model and explains the large bay size and many of the room configurations. Remnants of the original condominium building program are

The Cosmopolitan, guestroom

The Cosmopolitan

The Cosmopolitan, Chandelier bar

apparent in the limited porte cochère area and a more intimate feel to the hotel lobby. These tighter spaces set the hotel apart from other large casino projects on the Las Vegas Strip but introduce functional challenges for the operator.

The exterior was created by Arquitectonica, and features a 52-story angled double-loaded tower on the west side of the podium and an equally tall rectangular tower on the east side. A host of designers participated in the interior design of the hotel and restaurants—Bentel & Bentel, Jeffrey Beers, David Rockwell, and Adam Tihany among them—under the coordination of the Friedmutter Group, who served as executive architects. Contemporary art is featured throughout the hotel, and nowhere more strikingly than in the main lobby, where eight

6 ft x 6 ft (1.8 m x 1.8 m) columns delineate the queuing space while displaying continuously changing digital art commissioned by the hotel.

Most of The Cosmopolitan's 14 restaurants share a circulation "hub" that acts as a gathering place and waiting area with a neighborhood atmosphere. This space evokes a retro-classic Vegas feel through vintage artwork and furnishings along with black-and-white photos of 1960s Vegas personalities, a pool table and football game, and lounge-style seating that encourages interaction. On a lower level, more dining options share space with a retail complex that features eclectic brands not available elsewhere in Las Vegas. Each food and beverage operation, including the buffet, has its own dedicated kitchen area. Several

The Cosmopolitan, lobby

lounge bars are divided between the casino floor and the main pool area, a space that can be configured to double as a venue for outdoor concerts and special events. A rooftop nightclub and dayclub, featuring its own outdoor lounge space and pool scene, sits on the top of the podium.

The ground-floor casino is nearly 100,000 sq ft (9,290 sq m), more limited in space than casinos in other hotels of similar size, and unique in that it has floor-to-ceiling windows looking out onto the famed Las Vegas Strip. Its centerpiece is the Chandelier, a multilevel bar designed by David Rockwell, with over two million beaded crystals and housing three unique lounge experiences offering cocktails prepared using molecular gastronomy techniques. A further innovation is The Cosmopolitan's "casino cabanas," semi-private rentable units with plush lounge furniture, separated from the casino floor by drapery.

Completed at the end of 2010, The Cosmopolitan is likely to be the last major casino development on The Strip for several years.

Convention Hotels

Among the largest lodging properties today are those hotels and resorts which are designed to host conventions and other national and international meetings. In North America, most of the larger cities have several hotels in the 750 to 1,500 guestroom range, while surprisingly few international cities outside Asia boast even one hotel of this size. In the United States and Canada, the foundations for group business are the large corporate, association, and SMERF (social, military, educational, religious, or fraternal) meetings, while in Europe, for example, the convention market focuses on the international trade shows held in such cities as Berlin and Milan. These major industry events often occupy more than one million sq ft (92,900 sq m) of exhibit space and fill every hotel in the city—many of them older, relatively small properties—but don't require the kind of meeting and banquet space that is the essential characteristic of a major convention hotel. However, with the growth of professional associations worldwide, there should be a dramatic increase in the demand for larger convention hotels.

The French philosopher Alexis de Tocqueville, among the first to identify the United States' appetite for group participation, would not be disappointed by the mass-meeting activity held in today's convention-oriented hotels and conference centers. Cities such as New York and Las Vegas, for example, host about four million convention guests every year and, worldwide, the number of people attending meetings and conventions is well in excess of 100 million. Even resort areas, such as Orlando or Scottsdale, have become major convention destinations. In addition, smaller standalone resorts find that they need to cater to meeting and group business in order to fill guestrooms mid-week and in the shoulder and off-season. In major cities, on the other hand, the convention market extends year-round, with the few slow periods around the main holidays.

Given the increasing importance of the group market, and the ability to attract meetings at a wide range of locations—downtown, suburban, airport, and resort, for example—the early 2000s saw the explosion of a variety of distinctly different convention hotel types. Smaller cities of up to 250,000 people may have a convention-oriented hotel in the range of 300–400 rooms, with a ballroom for 800–1,000 people. Major cities push these numbers much higher, and most hoteliers would define a convention hotel as having a minimum of 500 rooms, for regional and small national meetings, up to 1,500 or more rooms at major destinations or for headquarters hotels adjoining the largest convention centers. With the development of airport hubs around the world, developers have built convention-oriented properties outside the major cities, to ease the burden on travel into center-city and because large sites are more available

JW Marriott, Indianapolis, Indiana
The Marriott hotel, one of five corporate properties adjoining the convention center, dominates the Indianapolis skyline (see pages 192–195).

Table 9.1 Orlando, Florida, selected convention hotels

Location	Hotel	Guestrooms	Number of meeting rooms	Ballroom area in sq ft (sq m)
Hotels adjoining the Orange County Convention Center	Rosen Shingle Creek	1,500	68	95,000 (8,825)
	Hilton Orlando	1,417	63	48,100 (4,470)
	Rosen Centre Hotel	1,334	33	35,000 (3,250)
	Peabody Hotel	891	32	26,700 (2,480)
	Rosen Plaza Hotel	800	22	26,000 (2,415)
Convention hotels within Walt Disney World	Walt Disney World Swan and Dolphin*	2,265	83	54,300 (5,045)
	Disney Coronado Springs	1,967	46	60,200 (5,590)
	Disney Yacht and Beach Club*	1,217	21	38,000 (3,530)
	Disney Contemporary	1,041	33	44,800 (4,160)
	Grand Floridian	877	16	18,200 (1,690)
Convention hotels within Universal Studios	Loews Royal Pacific Resort	1,000	22	41,500 (3,855)
	Loews Portofino Bay Hotel	750	23	15,000 (1,390)
Other Orlando convention hotels	Orlando World Center Marriott Resort	2,000	73	105,000 (9,750)
	Gaylord Palms Resort and Spa	1,406	61	46,700 (4,340)
	Hilton Bonnet Creek and Waldorf= Astoria*	1,001	68	36,000 (3,345)
	JW Marriott Orlando Grande Lakes Resort	1,000	46	29,600 (2,750)

* Two hotels marketed and operated together.

Estrel Hotel & Convention Center, Berlin, Germany
The 1,125-room Estrel Berlin is the largest convention, entertainment, and hotel complex in Europe. With suites as large as 970 sq ft (90 sq m), and divisible convention hall of 50,500 sq ft (4,700 sq m), few venues in Europe can compete for the largest or most important meetings. The complex can accommodate 3,500 people for a banquet, or 1,000 people at the Festival Center, directly connected to the hotel by a glass-enclosed bridge.

outside the downtown areas. And, increasingly, conventions are held at resort areas, where guests can take part in non-meeting activities or where families can spend a day on vacation while one parent is busy.

There are many examples of convention hotels which combine these elements. For example, in Orlando, Florida, which after Las Vegas has the second-largest number of hotel rooms in the United States, the Orange County Convention Center is immediately surrounded by several large hotels with 800 or more guestrooms, all within a few minutes' walk. Each one alone might host a substantial meeting, but together they provide a sufficient base of overnight rooms for nearly any major convention. And within miles, both Disney World and Universal Studios continue to expand their convention-oriented properties, in order to attract groups who find it appealing to combine meetings with the theme-park experience. Historically, hotels in Orlando had catered to the family market, but with the substantial expansion of the convention center in 2004 more luxury hotels opened. Table 9.1 suggests how large these clusters of major convention-oriented hotels may be, especially when the destination is widely favored.

As Table 9.1 shows, the number of hotel rooms is only part of what defines today's convention hotel. In addition, the property requires a major ballroom and substantial amounts of exhibition and multi-purpose meeting space, totaling some 50–100 sq ft/ guestroom (4.6–9.3 sq m), or about three to four times the amount of meeting space that is normal for most business-oriented hotels. In addition, these hotels offer multiple food and beverage outlets, expanded health and fitness facilities, and a much higher number of suites, typically about 3 percent but sometimes approaching 5–8 percent of the total number of guestrooms.

Table 9.2 Convention hotels operating data

	Number of rooms		
	<500	500–1,000	>1,000
Average size (rooms)	298	751	1,423
Occupancy (percent)	59.6	66.8	69.8
Room revenue	$28,097	$38,505	$43,611

Source: PKF Consulting. *Trends® in the Hotel Industry*, USA Edition. New York: PKF Consulting, 2010.

Table 9.3 Full-service hotels operating data

	Number of rooms		
	<150	150–300	>300
Average size (rooms)	119	214	440
Occupancy (percent)	63.0	62.7	66.2
Room revenue	$23,890	$30,283	$35,058

Source: PKF Consulting. *Trends® in the Hotel Industry*, USA Edition. New York: PKF Consulting, 2010.

A large convention hotel today requires a minimum of 1,000 rooms committed to the convention, without which large groups may not consider booking a hotel. Management companies insist on another 200–400 rooms to avoid turning away repeat transient travelers during peak convention periods. Secondary cities may have convention-oriented hotels about half this size. The convention hotel's smaller counterpart, the conference center (see Chapter 10), caters to smaller groups who require only 50–200 guestrooms and who prefer single-purpose conference and training rooms. While the convention hotel can accommodate varied meetings of all sizes, it focuses primarily on larger groups, whereas the conference center provides a more intimate atmosphere, and such dedicated spaces as an amphitheater and dozens of breakout rooms needed by smaller groups.

Many older convention hotels, unable to expand, have been made obsolete because of the growth in the size of association and other large organizational meetings. Increasingly higher attendance at conventions and trade shows—especially at the popular destinations—often spills over into several hotels clustered around a "headquarters" hotel. This has created opportunities for larger-capacity meeting and exhibit halls in such lead hotels, in some ways duplicating or replacing the older city convention centers and municipal auditoriums.

The interest in convention hotels is easy to understand. Group business, and especially the large meetings market, grew at over 5 percent a year in the late 1990s; data from *Meetings and Conventions* magazine show that the total number of meeting attendees nearly doubled from 1985 to 2009. However, the economic downturn in the early twenty-first century slowed growth dramatically. According to STR, the number of group rooms sold actually declined from 2002 to 2010. And convention-hotel room occupancies in 2010 were about 5 percent below those of a decade earlier. Still, cities and hotel companies seek to develop convention-oriented hotels

because not only do they greatly increase tourism business, but both occupancy percentage and room revenue in large convention hotels generally outpace those of smaller properties. Tables 9.2 and 9.3 report 2009 data, from the height of the recent economic recession (note that the number of rooms differs in the two tables); industry experts project that guestroom occupancy and revenue numbers will grow dramatically in the second decade of the century.

Planning and Design Considerations

Convention hotels are among the most difficult building types to plan and design because the usual complex functional requirements are exacerbated by the size of the program—1,000 rooms or more, substantial public areas including a large clear-span ballroom, and increased back-of-house spaces. In urban downtown locations this is made even more difficult by small sites and restrictive zoning. In selecting a site, the development team needs to recognize the major planning considerations for a successful convention hotel and test the site against these key criteria:

- Test the site for FAR (floor area ratio) to accommodate total hotel area at program ratios such as 850–900 sq ft (80–84 sq m) per room.
- Separate hotel entrances including main lobby, ballroom and exhibit hall, restaurants, employees, hotel receiving, and exhibit unloading.
- Provide sufficient public arrival space for cars, taxis, and shuttle buses.
- Provide sufficient service space, including for unloading of exhibits.
- Create a lobby space of sufficient size for the market and appropriate to the site.
- Allow sufficient clear-span for the hotel ballroom, often as much as 125 ft (38 m) or more, outside the guestroom column structure.

Because of the scale of new convention hotels, these criteria, while similar to those for smaller downtown or airport hotels or for larger resorts, create new challenges for the development team. In addition to many more guestrooms and suites, the total amount of public and support space, the size of the ballroom, and the number of elevators often are two to three times those of other major hotels which don't focus on the convention market.

Urban Convention-center Headquarters Hotels

As the major destination cities build new convention centers or expand older ones (see Table 9.4), many with one million sq ft (92,900 sq m) or more of exhibition space, they also provide one or more sites for an adjacent "headquarters" hotel, usually connected directly to the convention center. Because they operate at relatively high occupancies and rate compared with other first-class hotels in the same market,

Table 9.4 Major American convention centers

Name	City	Exhibition space in sq ft (sq m)	Number of meeting rooms
McCormick Place	Chicago, IL	2,600,000 (241,500)	173
Orange County Convention Center	Orlando, FL	2,500,000 (232,200)	84
Las Vegas Convention Center	Las Vegas, NV	2,150,000 (199,700)	144
Georgia World Congress Center	Atlanta, GA	1,600,000 (148,600)	106
Morial Convention Center	New Orleans, LA	1,500,000 (139,300)	140
Sands Expo and Convention Center	Las Vegas, NV	1,300,000 (120,700)	25

Source: Cvent.

these projects often are awarded on a competitive basis. These hotels, connected to the convention center, don't need as much dedicated function space, because they benefit from the symbiotic relationship with the public facility next door. In Atlantic City, New Jersey, the city provided a site for a new 500-room headquarters hotel adjacent to the new convention center. The Sheraton Hotel was designed to complement the exhibition and meeting facilities in the convention center and therefore has a relatively small 27,000 sq ft (2,500 sq m) of its own ballroom, banquet, and breakout rooms, in addition to other amenities.

Looked at closely, most city convention centers don't generate sufficient operating profit to stand on their own. Instead, the case for a public convention center is usually made on the basis of visitor spending—on hotels, restaurants, transportation, and retail shopping, and the related sales and other taxes generated—as well as the many thousands of jobs created in the community.

Boston opened a new convention and exhibition center in 2004. The city held a competition to identify an operator for a convention

Westin Boston Waterfront, Boston, Massachusetts
After Starwood won the competition for the convention headquarters hotel in South Boston, it redesigned the project, reducing the number of guestrooms and ballrooms, and reflagged the hotel from Sheraton to Westin.

headquarters hotel, to be built adjacent, won by Starwood's Sheraton brand. Architects initially designed a 1,200-room hotel with two gigantic ballrooms but, when it appeared that the project was too large for the demand, Starwood reduced the program to about 800 rooms and eliminated the larger ballroom, intending to build a second phase later; they also rebranded the project as a Westin Hotel, assuring higher room rates.

Often, cities partner with hotel companies to build a hotel connected to the public convention center. The original McCormick Place South Hall opened in Chicago in 1996 with 3 million gross sq ft (containing 840,000 sq ft of exhibition space and 143,000 sq ft of meeting space, including two ballrooms). Two years later the city opened the 800-room Hyatt Regency nearby, and in 2001 the convention authority added a 24,400 sq ft (2,260 sq m) conference center, serviced and controlled by the hotel and connected to it by a pedestrian bridge. In 2007 the city nearly doubled the size of McCormick Place, adding the 2.3 million gross sq ft (213,677 sq m) West Hall (containing 470,000 sq ft [43,664 sq m] of exhibition space and 240,000 sq ft [22,297 sq m] of meeting space), maintaining its standing as the largest convention facility in North America,. To keep pace, by 2013 they will add 470 keys to the hotel, including 10 new suites. Because of the great size of McCormick Place and its extensive meeting space, the Hyatt Regency required very little function space of its own. While a convention hotel in every respect because of its market orientation, and with great demand for breakout rooms, the hotel space program was much closer to that of a transient hotel. (And building the additional conference center increased the availability of smaller meeting rooms.) However, the hotel suffered from several operational problems: high occupancies were hard to maintain because of the convention booking cycle at McCormick Place, which differs from those of hotels; some concessionaries in the convention center didn't provide a "hotel-quality" experience for guests; and labor union issues arose over the use of space.

The public–private partnership is often difficult to navigate, and the economic downturn beginning in 2008 hasn't helped. Both residents and competing hotel owners are vocal in not wanting to provide public financing for private development, yet cities need to initiate convention-center and hotel construction several years ahead of any economic upturn. Although the Oregon Convention Center Urban Renewal Area plan was adopted in 1989 and the convention center opened in the early 1990s, Portland has struggled for over two decades to develop a headquarters hotel. Initially intending to provide at least 800 rooms, more recently the city has sought a

Table 9.5 Convention-center headquarters hotels

Hotel	City	Guestrooms	Number of meeting rooms	Ballroom area in sq ft (sq m)
Hilton Americas	Houston, TX	1,203	43	39,100 (3,600)
Hilton San Diego Bayfront	San Diego, CA	1,190	56	34,100 (3,150)
Marriott Marquis	Washington, DC	1,175		30,000 (2,750)
Hyatt Regency	Denver, CO	1,100	35	30,000 (2,750)
JW Marriott	Indianapolis, IN	1,005	54	40,500 (3,750)
Grand Hyatt	San Antonio, TX	1,003	29	31,000 (2,850)
Omni Dallas	Dallas, TX	1,001	24	31,700 (2,900)
Marriott Marquis	Nashville, TN	1,000		40,000 (3,700)
Sheraton Phoenix Downtown	Phoenix, AZ	1,000	17	29,000 (2,650)
Westin Boston Waterfront	Boston, MA	793	22	15,000 (1,350)
Baltimore Hilton	Baltimore, MD	757	44	26,700 (2,450)
Westin Convention Center	Pittsburgh, PA	616	23	11,000 (1,000)
Hilton Omaha	Omaha, NB	600	21	10,000 (900)

Hyatt Regency McCormick Place, Chicago, Illinois
The Hyatt Regency attached to McCormick Place has gone through many renovations and expansion projects since first built, to keep the hotel facilities current with the needs of the market.

phased development starting at 400 rooms. Over the same time, Virginia Beach, Virginia, among other locations, has been vainly trying to develop its convention headquarters hotel. Cities recognize that they lose convention business by not having a headquarters hotel, yet the projects continue to be difficult to finance. Even with the meetings industry in turmoil, cities regularly announce major

expansion plans to existing centers—several have been expanded 10 times, or more. Recently opened or announced headquarters hotels are listed in Table 9.5.

Many experts believe that the number-one factor in attracting conventions to a city is having a good headquarters hotel convenient to the convention center. Many cities face the question of whether they should provide public financing for a convention center and/or convention headquarters hotel. For example, the question became a major campaign issue in the last mayoral election in Kansas City, Missouri: some candidates believed that providing assistance for a 1,000-room headquarters hotel involved too much financial risk, while others saw the hotel as being crucial to attracting outside visitors and a primary catalyst in dramatically boosting convention business. It seems clear that a large, well-designed hotel convenient to a convention center offers a substantial value to visitors that can't be overlooked.

Urban Convention Hotels

The traditional convention hotel is a major chain–operated property in one any of the large convention cities—New York, Chicago, Washington, San Francisco, and so forth—many with 1,000–1,500 rooms or more. While they may be convenient to the convention center, these projects aren't usually directly adjacent to the city facility and don't depend only on that business, but market to midsize groups (500–1,000 or more people) who need large amounts of meeting, dining, and breakout space. Based on the projected growth of the convention market, new convention hotels with over 1,000 rooms and over 50,000 sq ft (4,640 sq m) of meeting and exhibit space are being announced in major cities. If sites weren't so difficult to acquire, operators would consider doubling the meeting space by providing a second major ballroom and additional breakout rooms. If still more site area were available, many would add a major exhibit hall.

Ideally, convention hotels are better located on large sites where most of the function space spreads out over only one floor. Therefore, the goal at airport and suburban locations, or in major urban renewal sites, is to acquire a parcel four or more times the size of the largest

(continued p. 196)

─────── Case Study ───────────────────────────────────

JW Marriott Hotel, Indianapolis, Indiana
Architects: HOK Group and CSO Architects
Interior Design: Simeone Deary Design Group

The new 34-floor JW Marriott hotel, fondly known as "Big Blue," in Indianapolis is a visible marker on the city skyline. The 1,005-room property, at 34 floors the tallest hotel in Indiana, features the largest ballroom in the Midwest, 40,500 sq ft (3,700 sq m). One stated goal for the hotel design was to help make Indianapolis one of the largest convention destinations outside Las Vegas and Orlando. The iconic JW Marriott anchors the 7 acre (2.8 hectare) Marriott Place development, a collection of five Marriott properties offering business and leisure travelers multiple lodging options—the JW Marriott Indianapolis, plus a Courtyard, SpringHill Suites, and Fairfield Inn, as well as the renovated Marriott Indianapolis Downtown. This gives a total of 2,248 rooms connected by skywalks to the expanded Indianapolis Convention Center and close to the Lucas Oil Stadium, home to the NFL Indianapolis Colts, and Conseco Fieldhouse, home to the NBA Pacers and frequent NCAA games. The hotel includes two major ballrooms, the larger on the third floor, and 54 meeting rooms totaling over 104,000 sq ft (9,600 sq m) of flexible function space. The elegant hotel tower, a gently curving double-loaded slab, includes 980 king and double-double rooms plus 25 suites, featuring 40 inch high-definition plasma-screen televisions and an ingenious plug-in panel designed to reduce clutter on the desktop.

JW Marriott

JW Marriott, lobby

JW Marriott, lobby lounge

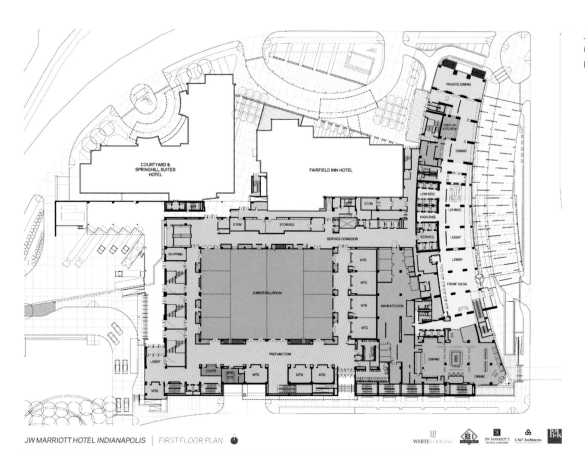

JW Marriott, ground floor
(lobby and junior ballroom)
plan

JW MARRIOTT HOTEL INDIANAPOLIS | FIRST FLOOR PLAN

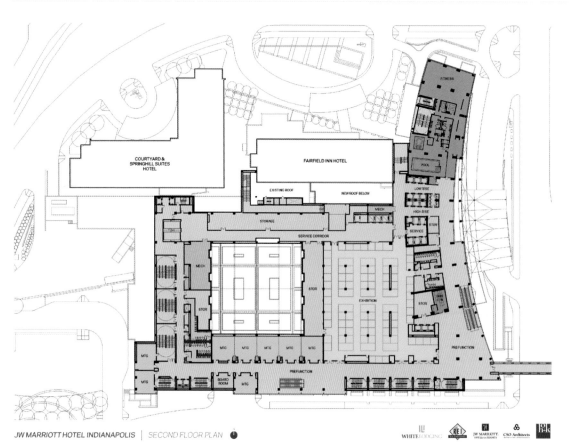

JW Marriott, second floor
(exhibit hall) plan

JW MARRIOTT HOTEL INDIANAPOLIS | SECOND FLOOR PLAN

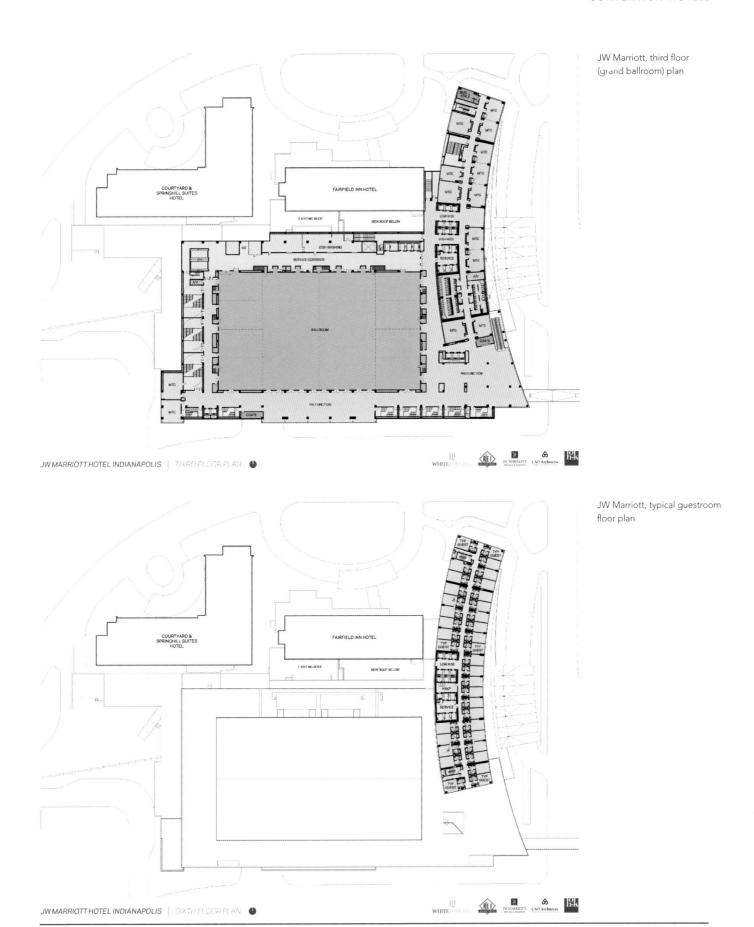

JW Marriott, third floor
(grand ballroom) plan

JW MARRIOTT HOTEL INDIANAPOLIS | THIRD FLOOR PLAN

JW Marriott, typical guestroom
floor plan

JW MARRIOTT HOTEL INDIANAPOLIS | SIXTH FLOOR PLAN

Marriott Marquis, Washington, DC
The new 1,175-room Marriott Marquis, attached to the Washington Convention Center, includes a 30,000 sq ft (2,750 sq m) grand ballroom, plus 75,000 sq ft (6,950 sq m) of additional meeting rooms, and a major indoor event terrace, and expects to qualify for LEED-Silver certification.

Table 9.6 Gaylord entertainment convention hotels

Hotel	City	Guestrooms	Meeting rooms	Ballroom area in sq ft (sq m)
Gaylord Palms	Orlando, FL	1,406	61	46,700 (4,330)
Gaylord Texan	Dallas, TX	1,511	70	50,000 (4,645)
Gaylord National	Washington, DC	2,000	82	50,000 (4,645)
Gaylord Opryland	Nashville, TN	2,881	102	55,300 (5,130)

ballroom. A compromise may be possible, for large projects, to put some smaller meeting rooms, as well as food and beverage outlets and back-of-house areas, on another floor, but the major function space should be configured as compactly as possible. In addition, both cities and private developers are creating downtown entertainment districts (see pages 31–43) which further fuel tourist and convention activity. Sites near the waterfront, shopping, cultural attractions, or new entertainment districts offer alternative sites for convention-oriented hotels, despite their distance from the convention center.

The Gaylord Entertainment Company operates four major convention hotels throughout the United States (Orlando, Dallas, Washington, and Nashville), ranging from 1,406 to 2,881 rooms, with ballrooms between 46,000 sq ft and 55,000 sq ft (4,330–5,130 sq m), and recently announced a new 1,500-room project in suburban Denver (see Table 9.6). The Gaylord National, outside Washington, DC (see pages 197–199), features 470,000 sq ft (43,600 sq m) of flexible convention, banquet, meeting, and exhibit space, plus additional terraced function lawns overlooking the Potomac River. A self-contained hotel and convention center, it doesn't rely on major meetings held at the Washington Convention Center, where a new Marriott Marquis Hotel has been constructed.

Downtown sites large enough to support major convention hotels of over 1,000 rooms are rare. Consider that the hotel requires a clear-span ballroom and adjoining pre-function areas, placed where they do not fall beneath the guestroom structure. Therefore, a site to accommodate a major ballroom of 120 x 250 ft (36 x 76 m) and public and service functions that surround it, in addition to the guestroom tower, may require a site of more than 60,000 sq ft (5,500 sq m), or half a full New York City block. In fact, a normal rule-of-thumb in urban locations is to seek a site that is at least 2.5–3 times the size of the largest ballroom. While careful planning at the schematic stage may allow the developer to build on a smaller site, this requires the architect to place the ballroom on an upper or lower level, requiring additional elevators or escalators, and a junior ballroom on still a

(continued p. 206)

Gaylord National Resort and Convention Center, National Harbor, Maryland

Architect and Interior Designer: Gensler

Because so many national associations are headquartered in Washington, DC, it is among the largest meeting destinations in the country. Gaylord, which also operates gigantic self-contained convention properties in Nashville, Dallas, and Orlando, opened a 2,000-room hotel and convention center at National Harbor, on the Potomac River outside Washington, DC, in 2008. The property includes a massive 178,000 sq ft (16,500 sq m) exhibit hall, four ballrooms ranging between 51,000 and 8,800 sq ft (4,700 and 800 sq m), with 28 to 20 ft high (8.5 to 6 m) ceilings, as well as 112 other rooms for small meetings and breakout sessions. The facility includes 17 covered loading bays and extensive communications connections throughout the meeting and exhibit space. The ballroom pre-function areas add nearly an additional 50 percent.

The hotel's design is an H-shaped guestroom tower centered around a terraced atrium lobby with views across gardens and the Potomac River. Immediately next to the hotel is the convention center, with its exhibit hall on the ground floor and two huge ballrooms above. Additional ballrooms are on the second level of the hotel; smaller meeting and conference rooms are spread throughout the lower three floors. The seven restaurants and lounges provide guests with a wide variety of dining options, and retail outlets are spread throughout the property's public areas.

Gaylord National (below and top right)
Gaylord National, lobby atrium (right)
Gaylord National, ballroom (bottom right)

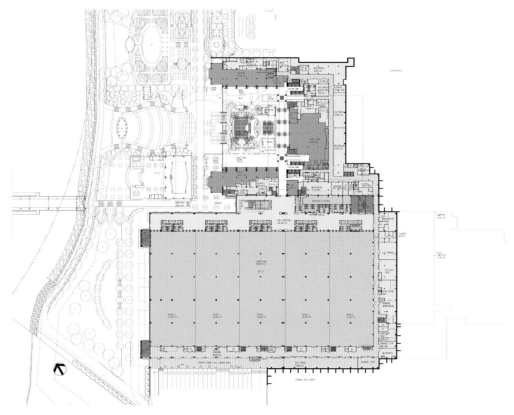

Gaylord National, ground floor plan

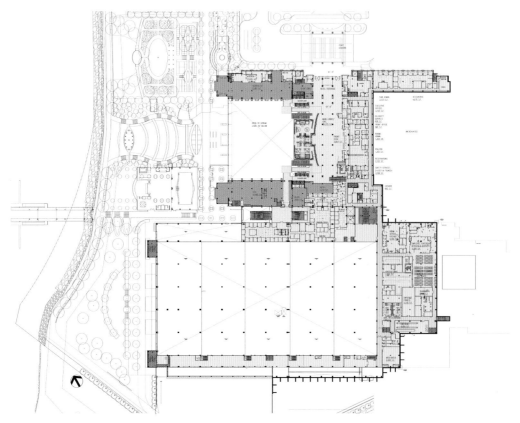

Gaylord National, second floor (lobby and exhibit hall) plan

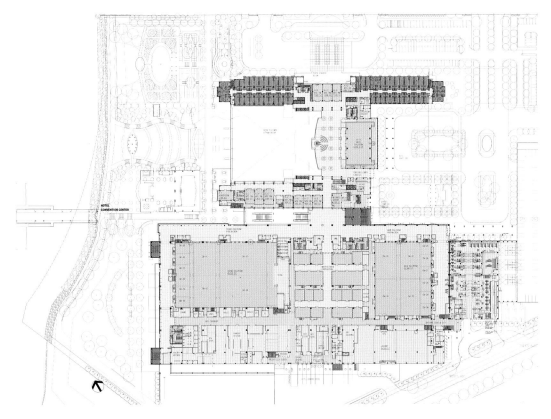

Gaylord National, third floor (ballrooms) plan

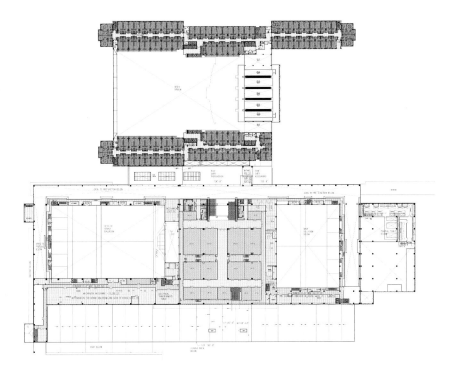

Gaylord National, typical guestroom floor (and meeting rooms) plan

─── **Case Study** ───────────────────────────────

Hilton San Diego Bayfront Hotel, San Diego, California
Architect: John Portman & Associates
Interior Designer: Joseph Wong Design Associates

The hotel, an urban resort located directly on the waterfront and adjoining the city convention center, features a public promenade that connects it to the bay. Both the bayfront setting and warm climate permit the activation of landscaped outdoor terraces, available for private parties, adjacent to each level of the function space. The hotel entrance is elevated one level above grade, providing heightened views of the bay, a 4.3 acre (1.7 hectare) public park, and the city skyline. Public art is featured, from the porte cochère through the lobby ceiling sculpture, to the F&B outlets, function areas, and guestrooms. The steely blue palette of the tower glazing reflects the color of the bay.

The 1,190-room hotel contains 50 meeting and breakout rooms on four floors, including ballrooms of 34,000 and 24,000 sq ft (3,150 and 2,200 sq m). Oversized freight elevators and wide doors allow vehicles to reach the fourth-floor Sapphire Ballroom. The well-zoned hotel has two restaurants on the lower floor and a bar on the lobby level, each with its associated outdoor seating—the casual restaurant terrace featuring a fire pit—that overlook the boat activity on the bay. The ground floor also includes a full-service spa/health club and outdoor pool and deck.

Hilton Bayfront

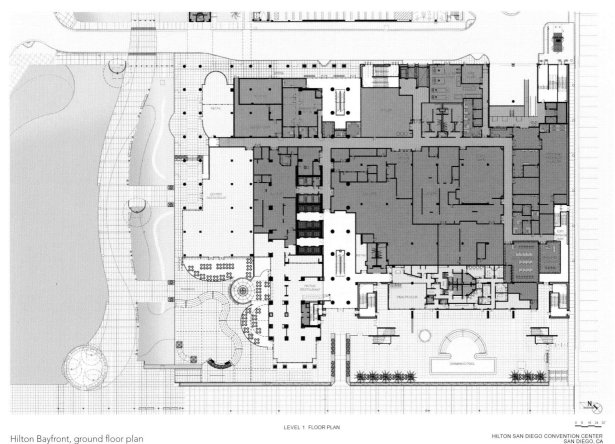

LEVEL 1 FLOOR PLAN

HILTON SAN DIEGO CONVENTION CENTER
SAN DIEGO, CA

Hilton Bayfront, ground floor plan

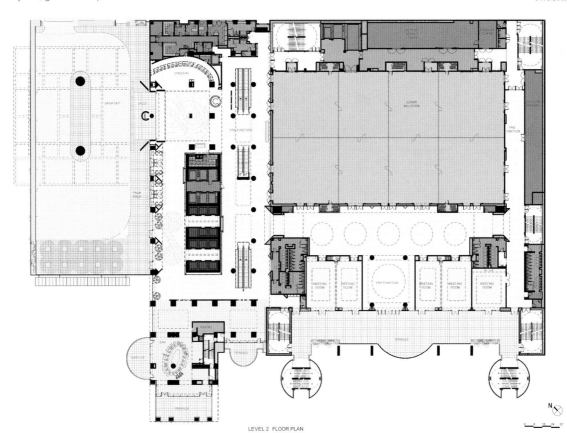

LEVEL 2 FLOOR PLAN

HILTON SAN DIEGO CONVENTION CENTER
SAN DIEGO, CA

Hilton Bayfront, second floor (lobby and junior ballroom) plan

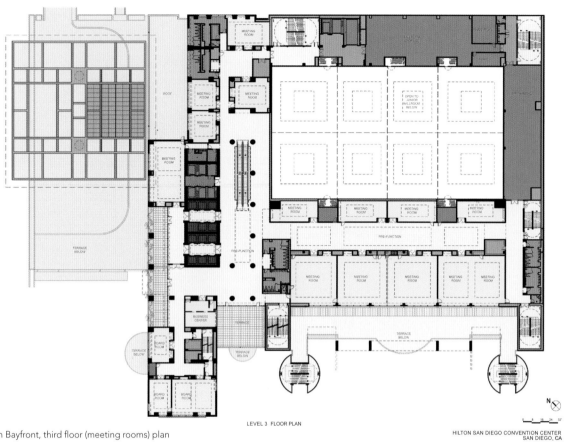

Hilton Bayfront, third floor (meeting rooms) plan

LEVEL 3 FLOOR PLAN

HILTON SAN DIEGO CONVENTION CENTER
SAN DIEGO, CA

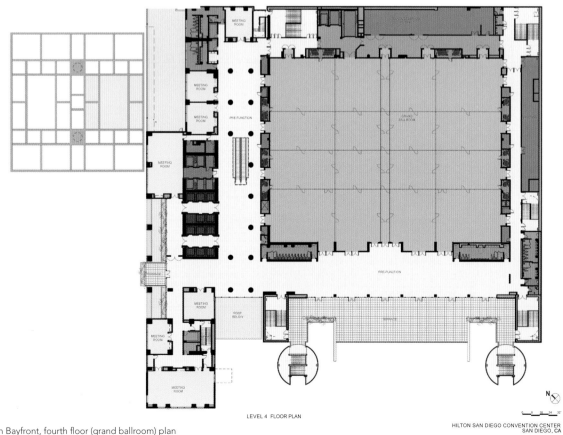

Hilton Bayfront, fourth floor (grand ballroom) plan

LEVEL 4 FLOOR PLAN

HILTON SAN DIEGO CONVENTION CENTER
SAN DIEGO, CA

Hilton Bayfront,
typical guestroom floor plan

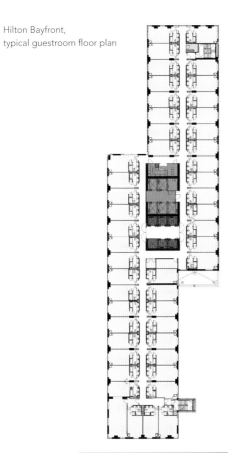

Hilton Bayfront, lobby

Hilton Bayfront, swimming pool

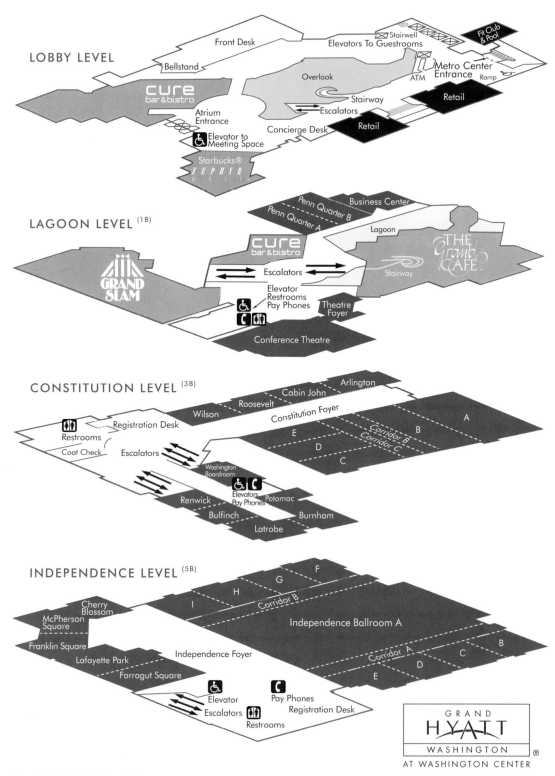

Grand Hyatt, Washington, DC

With building heights limited in Washington, DC, by ordinance, architects struggle to organize the hotel elements in a compact mid-rise building. The exploded diagram illustrates how the 900-room Grand Hyatt's atrium lobby, with restaurants and lounges overlooking the central water feature, covers two floors of underground convention space, cleverly solving the structural tension between large-span meeting rooms and the guestroom structure. The smaller meeting rooms and support functions fill the zone around the ballrooms, where the guestroom structure does not permit a major column-free space.

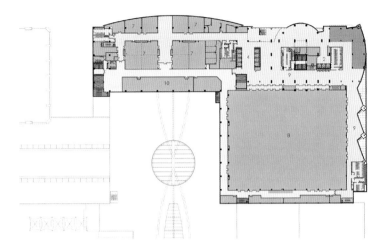

1. Hotel Lobby
2. Guest Elevator
3. Convention Center Lobby
4. Convention Center Elevator
5. Garage Entry
6. Garage
7. Meeting Room
8. Exhibition Hall
9. Prefunction Area
10. Back of House
11. Ballroom
12. Void
13. Sky Lobby Lounge
14. Bar
15. Restaurant
16. Office
17. Roof Garden
18. Spa
19. Pool Deck
20. Guestroom
21. Guestroom Type A
22. Guestroom Type B
23. Guestroom Type C
24. Guestroom Type D
25. Dynasty Suite
26. Presidential Suite
27. Royal Suite
28. Roof Top Restaurant
29. Outdoor Dining
30. Roof

Level 12 Floor Plan - Exhibition Hall

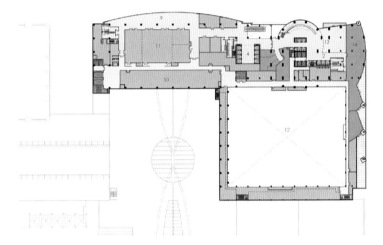

Level 13 Floor Plan - Ballroom

Centara Grand, Bangkok, Thailand

The luxury 505-room hotel and convention center retain their own identity within the larger CentralWorld Plaza development. The podium contains several levels of parking, the hotel convention facilities, and other public spaces. The iconic hotel tower unfolds into a lotus flower-like crown, serving as a dramatic landmark on the urban skyline.

205

different level. This stacking of the function rooms complicates the design of the vertical circulation, requires additional egress stairs, and forces duplication of back-of-house service areas.

Building in Washington, DC (and many other cities) is further hindered by strict height limitations. Many hotel developers, therefore, excavate two or three levels underground in order to provide enough floor space to make a project feasible. The Grand Hyatt Washington, with 900 guestrooms and 58 suites, has about 40,000 sq ft (3,700 sq m) of function space, including two midsize ballrooms, reached by escalators leading down from the lobby entrance to basement floors. The ground-level hotel atrium essentially falls directly above the ballroom space, with guestrooms ringing it on four sides filling the city block. Many Washington, DC, hotels have function space on lower levels.

In the late nineteenth century, the first urban convention hotels, such as the Willard in Washington and The St. Regis in New York, were able to provide open, column-free ballrooms only by placing them on the top floor. This approach was structurally efficient, and the rooftop ballrooms it produced are still much admired for their dramatic views. But with the increased capacities of today's meeting and banquet facilities and the extensive elevators and egress stairs that now are required, this solution is no longer practical. Wisely, cities are implementing special zoning districts to help developers assemble the larger sites needed to satisfy the demand for major new convention-related hotels.

Orlando World Center Marriott, Orlando, Florida
The 2,000-room resort sprawls over many acres; it features 10 restaurants and lounges and 450,000 sq ft (44,550 sq m) of event space on one level. The 105,000 sq ft (10,350 sq m) Cypress Ballroom is the largest column-free resort ballroom in the country.

Suburban or Resort Convention Hotels

Suburban, airport, and resort destinations also offer the opportunity to capture convention business. Frequently, these projects are physically removed from nearby attractions and, as a result, need to be fully self-contained. The Hyatt Regency at O'Hare Airport, one of the early John Portman–designed atrium hotels, has seen the market grow up around it, including the suburban Donald E. Stephens Convention

Center in Rosemont, Illinois, but originally it was a dedicated airport convention hotel. More descriptive of this type are resort projects in such cities as Palm Springs, California, and Orlando, Florida.

Among the largest and most successful is the Orlando World Center Marriott, which added 500 guestrooms and the mammoth Cypress Ballroom, 105,000 sq ft (9,750 sq m), with a 145 ft (44 m) clear-span, in the early 2000s. The Cypress Ballroom, often used as an exhibit hall, is the largest column-free resort ballroom in the country. The hotel features three other ballrooms, as well as many small meeting and breakout rooms and extensive pre-function areas, many outdoors. While both Orlando and Las Vegas continue to offer opportunities for large convention hotels, many with themed designs, these projects cannot universally be applied to other locations.

Each of the principal hotel management companies tries to have a presence in each of the major markets. While some chains traditionally may have been oriented more towards resort or downtown or airport locations, as they have matured the companies have become more similar in the distribution of their properties. That is, each of the major companies—Marriott, Hilton, Hyatt, Sheraton, Westin, and so forth—includes a blend of resort, business, and convention hotels and competes head-to-head in most locations, including for the convention market. In some cities they collaborate. In New York, for example, where none of the biggest hotels is particularly close to the Javits Convention Center, the Hilton (2,086 rooms), Marriott Marquis (1,946 rooms), Sheraton (1,746 rooms), and Grand Hyatt (1,336 rooms) frequently work together, along with other hotels, to attract and serve major city-wide conventions.

Planning Public Areas

As with every hotel, planning the public space begins with thinking through the arrival sequence. In planning major convention hotels, architects need to consider the volume of arrivals or departures likely at peak times, as well as the need to accommodate shuttle buses to the convention center or other attractions. Therefore, for a 1,000-room hotel it may be necessary to have as many as four lanes at the porte cochère, in order to avoid congestion.

In fact, all spaces need to be somewhat oversized: lobbies must accommodate greater numbers of guests checking in or out; elevators must transport guests within confined periods of time; restaurants and lounges experience dramatic peaks around the convention schedule; and recreational facilities are taxed when sessions are not being held. Lobby planning guidelines of 15 sq ft (1.4 sq m) per guestroom may be 1.5 times the norm for suburban or small city hotels, which don't generate substantial group business. Restaurant capacities increase because of high double occupancy in the guestrooms, and lounges are oversized to accommodate demand in the late afternoon and evening from meeting attendees. Guests are more likely to shop during a convention than they are on other business trips, so retail space may approach the amount found at resorts.

Of course, the main feature of convention hotels is the function space: exhibit hall, ballrooms, meeting and banquet rooms, and small breakout rooms must be designed to meet very particular needs of a wide range of business and social activities. Convention hotels don't do the same amount of social business that smaller city hotels do, so the rooms can be designed more fully for meetings. And, unlike conference centers which provide very purpose-specific meeting space for their guests, convention hotels generally provide more generic, multi-purpose rooms, with a high number of subdivisible walls creating flexible arrangements of space.

While the program is different from other hotels, the planning principles are much the same: creating a sense of arrival, separating public and service activities, making spaces and functions easily locatable, and so forth. The interrelationship of the key convention spaces must encourage the flow of attendees mainly between the ballroom and the exhibit hall, or between the ballroom and the meeting and breakout rooms. If any of these elements is on a different floor, the architect must provide an open stairway or escalators and a visual connection between their pre-function areas. Where the climate offers the opportunity, foyer spaces must open onto plazas and pool decks, and small and midsize rooms, especially, might have their own access to outdoor terraces. Resort convention hotels might be designed with one side of the ballroom featuring a series of sliding panels that can open the space fully to the foyer, and to a terrace beyond.

Experienced architects know that early schematic designs must look forward and incorporate features to protect hotel operations from modifications during later design development which will reduce the functionality of the project. For example, in the schematic design of the ballroom area, there are essential considerations for the architect:

- Provide extra-wide service corridors. During later design development, the usable width of the corridors is reduced by the partition storage areas, banquet-service equipment, audiovisual equipment, egress requirements, structure, and mechanical/electrical provisions.
- Provide an oversized pre-function area. Later additions of such support functions as public toilets, coat rooms, grand stair or escalators, and meeting registration, etc., reduce the usable space.
- Provide sufficient structural support for hanging divisible partitions.
- Provide oversized back-of-house support space. Most programs underestimate the space required for furniture storage, audiovisual storage, pantry/prep areas, back-of-house staff space, partition storage, and so forth.
- Plan two-story or higher space. Consider such impacts of the high-ceilinged ballroom as blocking windows in the surrounding areas on the next level. Allow for a deep roof structure.
- Provide control rooms for projection and lighting, with direct views to the front of the ballroom, perhaps by using the mezzanine space above the pre-function area.
- Provide additional service/freight elevators. Banquet service places high demands on service flow, and the service elevators supporting the guestroom tower are insufficient for banquet service.
- Provide truck space for loading and unloading of exhibits. Any use of the ballroom or meeting space for exhibits requires truck

(continued p. 213)

Case Study

Marina Bay Sands, Singapore
Architect: Safdie Architects
Interior Designers: CL3 and Safdie Architects (hotel atrium and corridors)

The Marina Bay Sands, an integrated resort developed on Singapore harbor by the Las Vegas Sands convention and casino operator, is a wildly extravagant U.S.$S8 billion development. In what is now the largest hotel in Singapore, the 2,561 guestrooms are organized into three 56-story towers, capped by an iconic SkyPark with its infinity-edge pool overlooking the distant city and harbor. The entire project sits above a convention podium, its five floors containing over 1.2 million sq ft (111,000 sq m) of exhibition and meeting space. (See other images on the front of the dust jacket.) Additional public amenities in the podium include a casino, the ArtScience Museum, two 2,000-seat theaters, over 50 different dining outlets—from casual to gourmet in a range of cuisines—and several hundred retail shops, as well as an outdoor-event plaza overlooking the water.

The Marina Bay development draws on the company's experience in Las Vegas and Macau, and redefines Singapore's standing among the major meeting destinations in Asia. The project was developed within guidelines established by the government to assure orderly growth of the entire site, maintaining aspects of the city grid, establishing lower buildings along the waterfront, and sustaining view corridors between the high-rise hotel towers, set back from the harbor edge.

Five floors of high-ceilinged convention and exhibition space anchors one end of the podium; at the opposite end are the lotus-inspired ArtScience Museum, with its retractable roof, and the two theaters; the central section is a Las Vegas-style casino plus arcades of retail shops and restaurants. The water edge is animated with an event plaza and "floating" crystal pavilions—one a nightclub, one a retail store. The three hotel towers are capped by the SkyPark, a huge cantilevered platform containing two rooftop restaurants, a nightclub, an executive lounge, landscaped gardens, and an observation deck with 360-degree views of the city skyline and harbor. The principal feature of the SkyPark is the 480 ft (145 m) infinity-edge pool, engineered to withstand high wind forces.

Marina Bay Sands

Marina Bay Sands

Marina Bay Sands, lobby atrium

Marina Bay Sands, infinity-edge swimming pool

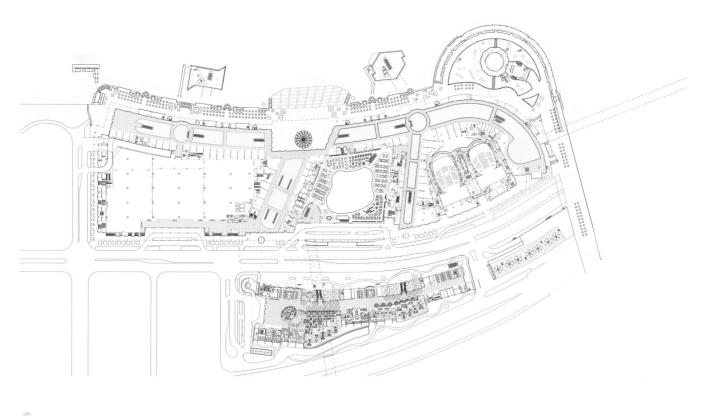

Scale 1:1000   0 10 25   50 m
Moshe Safdie and Associates, Inc. ©

Marina Bay Sands, ground floor plan

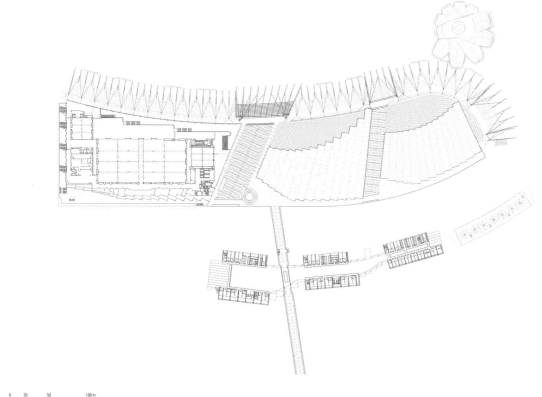

Scale 1:2000   0 20 50   100 m
Moshe Safdie and Associates, Inc. ©

Marina Bay Sands, fifth floor (ballroom and guestrooms) plan

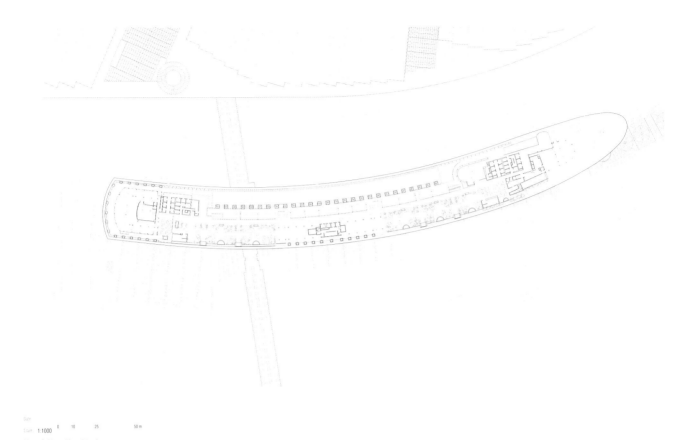

Scale 1:1000   0   10   25   50 m

Moshe Safdie and Associates, Inc. ©

Marina Bay Sands, rooftop (SkyPark) plan

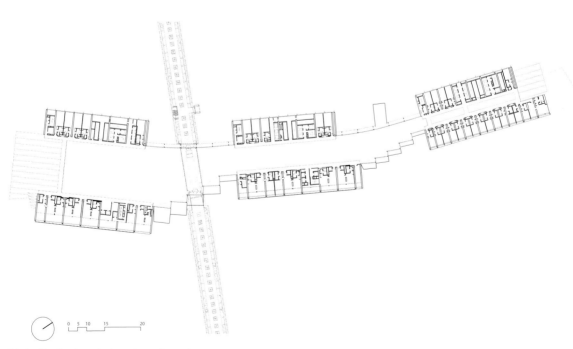

0 5 10   15   20

Marina Bay Sands, typical guestroom floor plan

A

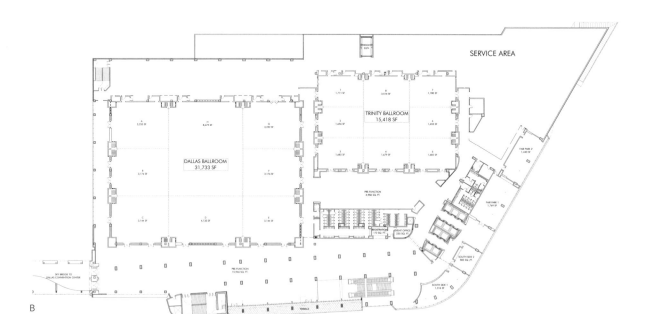

B

Omni Hotel, Dallas, Texas
(A) Following an often acrimonious debate, construction has begun on the city-owned convention-center hotel in Dallas, expected to open in early 2012. (B) The 23-floor 1,000-room Dallas Convention Center Hotel features 110,000 sq ft (10,200 sq m) of event space in 39 meeting rooms.

space far in excess of what usually is available at the hotel receiving area. Plan for easy display access to the ballroom through full-height garage doors.

Convention hotels require the latest in computer networking and audiovisual technology, including teleconferencing capability throughout the function space, in part to meet the special needs of customers when they launch new products. The hotels generally require projection booths, sophisticated sound systems, flexible lighting, and soundproof movable partitions to subdivide function rooms. Where there is demonstrated demand, convention hotels may need to include such additional features as space and equipment for simultaneous translation and a movable stage in the ballroom.

Food and beverage operations need to be flexible to serve meeting attendees and their families throughout the day. Many convention hotels feature multiple F&B outlets, including celebrity chefs or specialty restaurants. The 2,561-room Marina Bay Sands integrated resort complex in Singapore has over fifty dining options, most in the adjoining convention, casino, and retail complex; the 2,000-room Gaylord National in Washington has seven outlets, many more than most urban hotels in the United States. Even with the frequent banquet events, there is high demand on food and beverage facilities at convention hotels. The high number of people and the restricted schedules place an especially high burden on outlets to improve their ability to serve guests quickly and increase turnover. This creates special demands on the food-service consultants and hotel architects to conceive outlets to meet the guest needs and plan the back-of-house areas appropriately.

Conference Centers

To the layperson, one of the more confusing distinctions about hotels is between the related terms "convention" and "conference." But to a hotelier, a convention attracts several hundred to many thousands of attendees, while a conference caters to relatively small groups seeking a more intimate venue and close personal interaction. Although a few important conference properties were established in the early twentieth century—Asilomar was founded on the northern California coast in 1913—it wasn't until the second half of the last century that major universities and corporations saw the need for dedicated educational or training centers. Even then, the movement started slowly with Arden House, initially operated by Columbia University in Woodbury, New York (1950, now operated by the Open Space Institute), among the first, followed by such notable examples as the Harrison Conference Center in Glen Cove, New York (1968) and Doral Forrestal in Princeton, New Jersey (1979, now operated by Marriott). By late in the century, conference centers had demonstrated a successful product that was widely accepted and offered promise for continued growth.

Distinct from other types of lodging properties that cater to groups, a conference center is designed, first and foremost, to provide an environment conducive to effective meetings, especially for groups of fewer than 50 people. (In Europe the conference center may be much larger, intended for international meetings of several thousand people, much like convention centers in the United States.) In the United States, conference centers provide a dedicated, distraction-free, comfortably furnished, and technologically equipped facility with, importantly, the added feature of a professional staff to provide a high level of service both to the meeting planner and the conference attendees. At such a center, all aspects of the facility design, conference support services, food and beverage program, and recreational amenities enhance and further the goals of a meeting.

The rapid development of conference properties paralleled a corresponding period of substantial growth in the number of (and attendance at) meetings, from the smallest workshops to the largest national conventions. Various studies by the trade press and independent research organizations show that, although all segments of this market were increasing, the smaller corporate management, training, and sales meetings were growing the fastest. For example, while the number of association meetings—usually the meetings with the largest attendance—actually decreased over the last few years of the twentieth century, corporate meetings in the United States increased by nearly 10 percent, to about 835,000 annually, with an attendance of over 50 million people and expenditures in excess of $10 billion.

IBM Palisades, Palisades, New York
With over 48,000 sq ft (4,450 sq m) of function space, including 43 conference rooms, a ballroom, and tiered classrooms and amphitheaters, the IBM Palisades complex offers the perfect distraction-free learning environment for strategic planning, management development, and training sessions.

The Small Meetings Market

The conference center industry is at a point where its specialized lodging product has gained wide acceptance; the positive experience from the 1980s into the early 2000s has educated both meeting planners and attendees. At the same time, the demand for venues for small conferences is rapidly increasing. Recent studies of the number of small corporate and association meetings estimate that there were 800,000 small conferences, with fewer than fifty people, held in the United States in 2000, plus an additional 50,000 held by U.S. organizations overseas. One operator saw an increase in 2010 of outbound bookings by British companies of 50 percent to continental Europe and 25 percent to North America. In addition to these small meetings, which ideally are held in the more intimate, better-serviced conference centers, the properties frequently accommodate groups as large as 200–300 people. Most experts anticipate that the number of small conferences and training programs will continue to grow, even during periods of economic downturn, for several key reasons:

- Corporations are facing an increasingly competitive environment, and their employees are being challenged to understand new manufacturing, marketing, and financial techniques and concepts.
- The growing trend toward consolidation in many industries requires that company management meet to meld cultures and business practices.
- Omnipresent legal and regulatory issues necessitate frequent educational seminars.
- Increasing reliance on technology and computerization makes it necessary for businesses to continually train and update employees.

Conference and educational planners struggle to find the ideal meeting or training environment for their particular program. They increasingly find that dedicated conference centers or hotels at universities offer a setting and services that can't be matched by traditional multi-purpose hotels and resorts. These new facilities must be programmed and designed to accommodate a particular mix of conference sessions.

- *Training programs* are the most common type of small meeting, often incorporating a high level of audiovisual support. Some companies may feature fairly standard video presentations, while others involve the trainees in intensive role-playing exercises and group sessions, which may be videotaped and played back for critique and discussion. While these events average only a few days, many training programs can last several weeks. Although a typical class size is about 20, many training meetings include as many as 30–50 people. Depending on the degree of involvement of the corporate human resources and training staff from a particular company, the training site may be selected because of its proximity to the corporate headquarters. As companies in the early twenty-first century recognized the increasing importance of training, many bypassed the proximity issue by building their

own dedicated training center, complete with guestrooms and extensive classroom and meeting support areas.
- *Management meetings* include executive conferences and management development sessions. These generally range from about two days to five days and are designed for groups of 10–50. The meetings often are very intensive, and planners may schedule recreational and social activities to offer an opportunity for relaxation. As a result, organizers usually select resort or suburban conference centers with extensive recreational facilities.
- *Professional and technical meetings* are similar to the training and management sessions in many ways but may only run two to three days. The size of the meeting depends largely upon the topic and sponsor. Many are held at universities, where the faculty of business, management, or engineering schools serve as workshop instructors; however, all types of conference centers attract at least some small number of technical meetings.
- *Regional and national sales meetings* ideally are held at conference centers because of the need for highly sophisticated audiovisual presentations and the desire to keep the attendees focused on the session theme. These meetings generally last three to four days and vary in size, with national meetings reaching as many as several hundred attendees. Sales meetings have many objectives, among them increasing employee motivation and enthusiasm, familiarizing employees with new product lines or sales strategies, and reasserting corporate goals and philosophies. Many larger sales meetings are held in hotels and resorts, but the small and midsize regional meetings are ideal for conference centers.
- *Incentive trips and other types of meetings* are also good candidates for using conference centers. Incentive trips, which usually last about a week, generally are held at major resort hotels or popular destinations. Companies that offer incentive trips as a reward to sales or management personnel tend to include business meetings during the event, although their intensity and rigor varies. Resort conference centers, especially those with on-site golf or skiing, and those properties near popular destinations are best positioned to attract this business.

Product introductions, smaller association meetings, and other specialized types of conferences are a less important part of the conference center market—these often involve hundreds of people, may be fairly short in duration, and do not generate the food and beverage and rooms revenue essential to supporting the more expensive conference center operations.

Types of Conference Centers

Conference centers fall into distinct categories. These distinctions are based for the most part on the ownership, market orientation, and usual mix of facilities. Of course, many conference centers exhibit the characteristics of several different categories; many of the corporate conference centers, for example, compete with executive properties by soliciting general meetings. Also, like other lodging properties, an older conference center may find that its market

Table 10.1 Conference-center characteristics

Type of center	Typical meeting uses	Facility characteristics
Executive	Mid- and upper-level training and management development; management planning; sales meetings	Suburban locations; 200–300 midsize to large guestrooms; multiple dining and beverage outlets; moderate number of midsize conference rooms; large number of breakout rooms; moderate recreational facilities.
Resort	Mid- and upper-level management meetings; incentive trips; sales meetings	Resort destination or suburban locations; 150–400 large guestrooms; multiple dining and beverage outlets; small to moderate number of conference rooms; additional banquet rooms; extensive recreational amenities (especially outdoors).
Corporate	Technical and sales training for low- and mid-level employees; management development meetings; outside conferences if company policy permits	Suburban or headquarters locations; 150–400 guestrooms (size varies); limited dining alternatives; extensive training or conference rooms to meet corporate objectives; specialized rooms; auditorium; moderate to extensive recreational amenities.
University	Executive education for middle managers; scientific meetings and continuing education programs	On-campus location; 100–200 midsize guestrooms; limited dining and beverage options; small to moderate number of conference rooms; amphitheater; auditorium (at continuing education centers); recreation usually located elsewhere on campus.
Not-for-profit	Religious, educational, and government staff training; association and foundation meetings	Often at remote locations; 25–100 rooms; single dining room; small to moderate number of generic conference rooms; large multi-purpose room; limited recreation (primarily outdoors).

Table 10.2 Facilities comparison by conference-center type

	Executive conference centers	Resort conference centers	Corporate conference centers	University conference centers
Guestrooms	Average to large-size rooms, few suites; club floor	Large to very large rooms, 5–10 percent suites	Small to average-size rooms; few or no suites; commons area on each floor	Average-size rooms; few suites; case study or commons area on each floor
Public areas	Large lobby with lobby lounge; conference dining and specialty restaurant; entertainment lounge and game room	Average lobby with view over grounds; conference dining, specialty restaurant, and recreation dining; entertainment lounge	Lobby size highly variable; lobby lounge if corporate policy permits; conference dining and private dining; game room	Small to average-size lobby; reading room or quiet lounge; conference dining and private dining; cocktail lounge
Conference areas	Ballroom; large variety of conference rooms and many breakout rooms; boardroom	Large ballroom; moderate number of meeting and breakout rooms; amphitheater	Auditorium; large number of similar classrooms; computer or special-purpose rooms; offices for trainers	Executive education: amphitheaters, breakout rooms and faculty offices Continuing education: auditorium and many classrooms
Recreation areas	Swimming pool; racquet courts; health club/spa	Many outdoor facilities; pool; health club/spa	Gym or pool; racquet courts; health club	None (use university facilities)

matures and may need to reposition itself to continue to attract business. Doral Arrowwood, for instance, north of New York City, was conceived as a corporate center by the financial giant Citicorp in the early 1980s. It then evolved into an executive facility (late 1980s), added a strong resort orientation (early 1990s), and in 2001 opened new guestroom and meeting wings dedicated to the training needs of Pfizer, a leading pharmaceutical company, thus reverting to its original corporate heritage. Table 10.1 identifies the principal types of conference centers, the typical meetings they attract, and their general physical characteristics. Tables 10.2 and 10.3 compare the space program and conference facilities among the four major conference center categories.

Table 10.3 Schematic design program by conference-center type

	Executive conference centers	Resort conference centers	Corporate conference centers	University conference centers
Guestrooms				
Number of rooms	225–300	150–400	125–400	100–200
Typical net area*	325–375 (30–35)	325–400 (30–37)	275–350 (26–32.5)	275–350 (26–32.5)
Gross area*	525–600 (49–56)	525–625 (49–58)	450–550 (42–51)	450–550 (42–51)
Percent of total	50–55	45–55	35–45	45–55
Public areas				
Number of restaurants	2	3	1–2	1
Number of lounges	2	2–3	1	0–1
Gross area*	90–125 (8–12)	90–125 (8–12)	60–200 (6–19)	85–115 (8–11)
Percent of total	8–12	8–12	7–12	9–14
Conference areas				
Number of ballrooms	1	2	0	1
Number of auditoriums/ amphitheaters	0–1	1	1–4	2–3
Number of meeting rooms	10–20	6–15	6–40	4–10
Number of breakout rooms	6–20	4–8	4–20	6–15
Gross area*	175–225 (16–21)	125–190 (12–18)	250–400 (23–37)	175–300 (16–28)
Percent of total	16–22	8–20	20–35	20–35
Recreation areas				
Gross area*	15–50 (1–5)	50–200 (5–19)	35–90 (3–8)	0–20 (0–2)
Percent of total	2–6	4–15	3–5	0–2
Administration/service				
Gross area*	125–175 (12–16)	140–190 (13–18)	200–300 (19–28)	125–200 (12–19)
Percent of total	13–18	14–17	15–25	12–15
Total gross area*	950–1,150 (88–107)	1,000–1,250 (93–116)	1,100–1,500 (102–140)	850–1,100 (79–102)

* Floor area figures are provided in sq ft (sq m) per room.

Executive Conference Centers

The executive conference center presents the most typical facility and usually falls in either the mid- or high-price category. Oriented toward corporate meetings, including both training and management development sessions, the executive centers feature a relatively large number of conference rooms—as many as 20–30 meeting rooms for 200–300 guestrooms. Most executive centers are located in the suburbs around the larger cities, such as New York, Washington, Atlanta, and Chicago, or close to a major airport hub. The late 1990s saw similar growth of executive conference facilities in the major business centers of the U.K., Scandinavia, Japan, and Australia. With increasing competition and land costs, the main concern of both developers and operators should be whether a proposed facility has the potential to attract weekend conferences or social business, both of which are necessary to ensure profitability.

The late 1990s saw growth in executive conference centers when several major urban convention hotels added a wing or renovated one or two floors to create the more intimate conference environment that their otherwise extensive function spaces failed to provide. The Sheraton New Orleans, with 1,100 rooms and 90,000 sq ft (8,360 sq m) of function space, constructed a five-story addition to house a new executive conference center. The facility offers eight additional high-quality meeting and boardrooms, totaling 17,000 sq ft (1,580 sq m), with added conference services and amenities typical of the best conference centers:

- Flexible controls for lighting, power, audiovisual components, and climate
- Comfortable ergonomic chairs and oversized tables
- State-of-the-art high-speed communications capabilities and multiple dataport outlets
- Tackable walls and presentation railings
- Permanent walls rather than divisible partitions for superior acoustics
- Support functions including private group office space, conference concierge, refreshment kiosks, upgraded restrooms, and public telephones

(continued p. 222)

The Alexander, Indianapolis, Indiana
Architect and Interior Designer: Gensler

Dolce Hotels and Resorts, the major New Jersey-based conference center operator, is developing a 157-room center-city lifestyle hotel and conference facility in downtown Indianapolis, Indiana, a model it expects to be a prototype for future development in other locations. The property, located on a parking lot between the headquarters of Eli Lilly (and several other large employers) and the city's retail and commercial core, is expected to attract a mix of individual business and leisure guests, along with meeting groups. In addition to the guestrooms, the public–private joint venture includes 57 extended-stay units in a second building, 15,000 sq ft (1,390 sq m) of meeting space, a major-branch YMCA, and additional office, retail, and parking space.

The well-zoned building features largely commercial space on the ground floor, lobby and conference space on the second floor, and four levels of guestrooms. The center will include a Cisco TelePresence video-conference room, to connect with people in other locations, and a boardroom with its own private balcony overlooking the city skyline. The four restaurants, including the second-floor bar with its several terraces, are unusual for a conference center of this size, but should attract local customers in addition to the hotel guests and conferees. The hotel's own small fitness facility will complement the state-of-the-art YMCA.

The striking building, designed around a downtown brick plaza, incorporates an efficient double-loaded-slab guestroom structure above two floors of modern hotel facilities. The glass-walled lobby incorporates large comfortable seating groups and a stone fireplace.

The Alexander

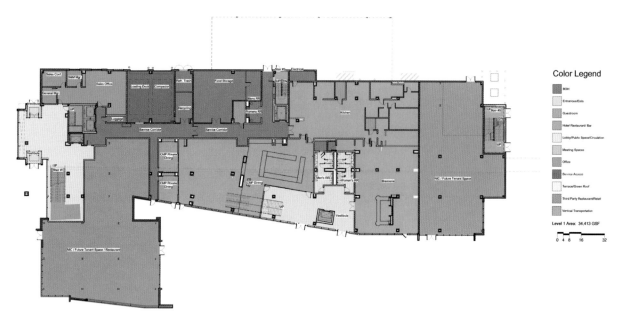

The Alexander, ground floor plan

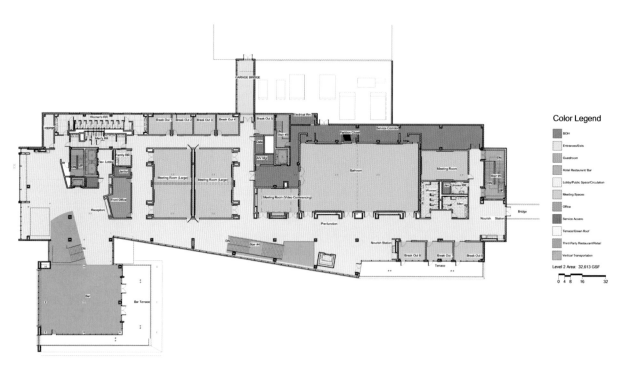

The Alexander, second floor (lobby and meeting rooms) plan

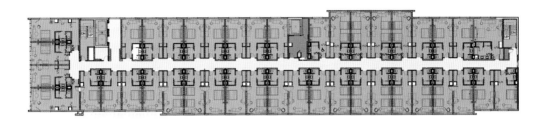

Color Legend

BOH
Entrances/Exits
Guestroom
Hotel Restaurant/ Bar
Lobby/Public Space/Circulation
Meeting Spaces
Office
Service Access
Terrace/Green Roof
Third Party Restaurants/Retail
Vertical Transportation

Levels 4-5 Area: 20,965 GSF

0 4 8   16   32

The Alexander, typical guestroom floor plan

The Alexander, lobby

The Alexander, bar

The Dolce management company is developing a prototypical executive conference hotel in Indianapolis. Located just east of Conseco Fieldhouse and within a short walk of the convention center, surrounded by four of the city's largest employers, the 157-room boutique hotel is expected to operate as a specialized meetings venue and social hangout for local professionals. Part of a much larger development, the hotel includes retail, a full-service brasserie restaurant, and 15,000 sq ft (1,400 sq m) of function space on the second floor, including a subdivisible ballroom and eight breakout rooms.

Resort Conference Centers

The resort conference center has grown in prominence in two distinct and opposite ways: many evolved from executive properties by marketing and promoting their expanded recreational facilities, while other centers changed from a resort by adding a meeting complex to better fill low shoulder and off-season periods. The resort centers are designed for the same type of management meetings, as well as for sales and incentive groups. Resort conference centers vary in size: many new properties have approximately 300–400 rooms, in order to support the recreational infrastructure, but a more recent trend is for projects to have only 150–200 traditional hotel guestrooms but include nearby time-share rental units (see Residential Hotels, Condominiums, and Vacation Ownership, Chapter 11). The resort centers usually have somewhat less meeting space than do executive centers, but offer more food and beverage choices and substantially larger recreational facilities. New resort centers are being built in suburban locations where there is sufficient land, and in the more traditional resort destinations, such as the Arizona desert and along the California coast.

Corporate Conference Centers

The corporate conference and training center is the largest physically—in the late 1980s a few corporations opened properties with more than 1,000 rooms. However, these became tremendously difficult to fill during recessionary periods and were expensive to maintain; also, corporate consolidations made many of these obsolete. Although some corporations now are building facilities with 150–250 rooms, new projects tend to be in the range of 250–400 rooms. Corporate centers contain much more meeting space than do other conference center types because of the need to meet very specific training needs. Many major corporations, especially those in telecommunications, insurance, pharmaceuticals, and financial services, struggle with the decision of whether to build their own suburban residential center (or urban day-meeting complex), or to rent space at executive centers or at another site. Fortunately, they all realize the importance of training and employee development to their success.

The major distinction among corporate centers is whether the facility will be used for training or for management development. Training centers may be very large, with many hundreds of guestrooms,

or companies may build a series of smaller centers for different product lines or service needs. The training centers tend not to have a ballroom or even many large meeting rooms, with perhaps only one room larger than 2,000 sq ft (185 sq m). They do, however, feature a large number of mid- and small-size conference rooms: the 233-room Dolce Atlanta-Peachtree center, originally built by Pitney Bowes, has over 60 small training rooms. Management development centers, on the other hand, have more midsize and large rooms, fewer small conference rooms, a high number of breakout rooms, and one or more amphitheaters for special presentations, equipped with the latest audiovisual technology, including distance learning capabilities.

At Dolce Palisades, IBM built a customer education center to train and update users of major IBM systems. Now open to the public, its 50,000 sq ft (4,650 sq m) of conference space includes a main auditorium with rear-screen projection, 24 additional meeting rooms, and 34 breakout rooms. Major spaces include three multimedia amphitheaters with touch-screen controls and response keypads, another dozen rooms with fixed tables, two computer labs, and smaller flexible meeting rooms. Ten elegant, glass-enclosed refreshment pavilions overlook a large pond in the center of the site.

The 206 guestrooms are organized along wide, multi-story galleries in a serpentine structure somewhat removed from the rest of the complex. The oversized single-occupancy rooms feature a wood-grille divider between the bed area and the dressing room, and all are equipped with personal computers. The project is beautifully sited and detailed, with stone, metal, and wood trim throughout the lobby, dining and lounge areas, recreational center, conference and training core, and guestroom wing.

University Conference Centers

The university conference center meets three different needs: the more luxurious facilities are designed for dedicated business or medical school executive education programs; some provide lodging for campus visitors and educational conferences; and still others cater for growing continuing education programs, one of the principal missions of public universities. The university centers generally are no larger than 150–200 rooms and feature amphitheaters or a large auditorium, as well as the more typical conference rooms. These centers exist because the large research universities realize that their reputations depend, in part, on the types of executive and adult education programs they run, and on their ability to bring business executives to campus on a regular basis. In addition, the more progressive colleges and universities attempt to keep in close touch with alumni and prospective donors.

In a few cases, the university will partner with a local corporation to create a special educational conference center, intended partly for the university and partly for the use of the company. At the University of Texas, AT&T, as a communications partner, helped fund the construction of a campus hotel and executive education center that has become a major contributor to a vibrant campus/business exchange in central Texas. One opportunity of university centers is

IBM Palisades, Palisades, New York

Top: The guestroom areas, in a separate four-story serpentine wing, are organized around a large circulation atrium encouraging participants to leave their rooms and socialize.

Bottom: The 206 guestrooms, the majority overlooking the wooded site's artificial lake, feature a handsome wooden grille dividing the bed area from the dressing room.

just this—to enhance the educational mission of the institution and drive both economic and social progress in the region. In other cases, a company will offset some of the construction cost in return for naming rights; The Statler Hotel and J. Willard Marriott Executive Education Center at Cornell University is of this type.

Not-for-profit Conference Centers

The not-for-profit conference center is the most variable conference center category. It may be owned by a religious or educational organization, association or foundation, research center, or private humanitarian or arts group. The facilities reflect the particular mission of an organization and may offer the public or specific interest groups the opportunity to meet in a spectacular mountain setting, for example, or near a historic landmark. For example, the National Arbor Day Foundation's 144-room Lied Lodge and Conference Center in Nebraska is dedicated to environmental stewardship: the American Hotel and Lodging Association (AH&LA) has honored the center for "a culture of integrating environmental management practices that improve everyday operations and the bottom line, while maintaining quality service and meeting guest expectations." The center features a fuelwood plant for heating and cooling, and is open as an educational demonstration site.

(continued p. 228)

Lied Lodge and Conference Center, Nebraska City, Nebraska
Operated by the Arbor Day Foundation, the center focuses on forestry management and the exposed timbers in the lobby reinforce this theme. The Adirondack-style 144-room Lied Lodge hosts programs emphasizing conservation and environmental stewardship.

—— Case Study ——

AT&T Executive Education and Conference Center, University of Texas, Austin

Architect: HKS and LakelFlato
Interior Designer: Wilson and Associates

The 297-room AT&T Executive Education and Conference Centre (EECC), including 21 oversized suites, has become *the* place to hold business or educational meetings in central Texas. The block-square conference center, fully accredited by the International Association of Conference Centers (IACC), is located at the southern edge of the Austin campus, within sight of the State Capitol and the university's carillon tower. Not only is it convenient to the university, state government and agencies, and corporations in downtown Austin, but it is an attractive destination for both leisure guests and conferees. The LEED Gold-certified hotel, featuring many specialized high-tech meeting spaces, also includes many sustainable features. For example, the courtyard functions as a green roof above underground parking, and the landscape drip-irrigation system reduces potable water consumption; native plant species use little water.

As with other university-based conference centers, the EECC offers visitors the chance to interact with university experts from all departments. The Courtyard Gallery regularly presents a wide range of artwork produced by faculty and alumni from the College of Fine Arts. The building also houses the Campus Club, the university faculty club, whose dining room fills the east side of the lower-lobby level. Other food and beverage outlets include the Carillon, a conferee and public dining room along the north edge of the complex and accessible from the courtyard, a sports lounge near the entrance, plus a quick-service coffee bar in the lobby.

The flexible 40,000 sq ft (3,700 sq m) of meeting space offers 37 rooms ranging from a 300-person multimedia amphitheater and divisible ballroom to tiered and traditional flat-floor classrooms with superior connectivity, plus 12 breakout rooms to support small-group work. The hotel guestrooms, many overlooking the central courtyard and others with rooftop terraces or balconies overlooking University Avenue and the carillon, feature wireless internet and other technology touches that guests now expect and depend on.

Local Austin graphic designer fd2s provided directional and destination signage and, in addition, provided graphic identities for the several food service outlets. They also created custom carpet patterns for the ballroom, incorporating elements from Texas history and the university.

AT&T Executive Education Center

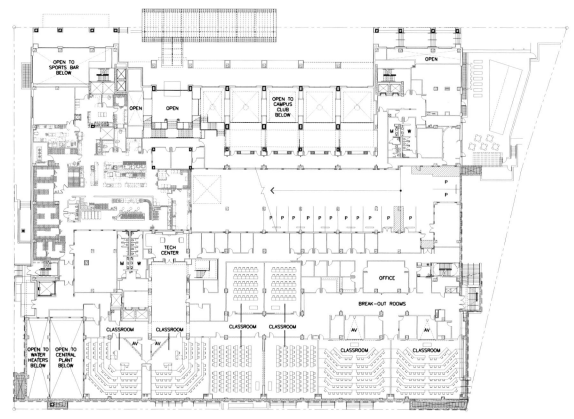

AT&T Executive Education Center, second floor (lower lobby) plan

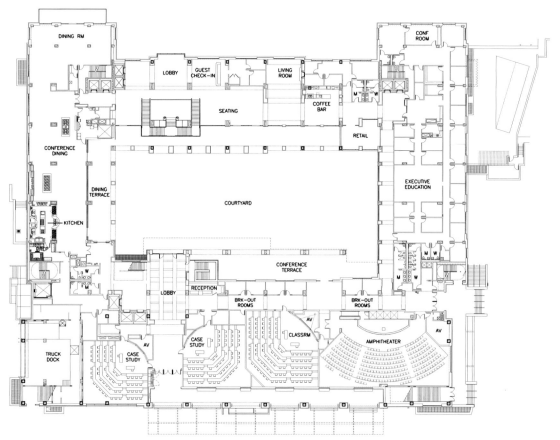

AT&T Executive Education Center, third floor (lobby) plan

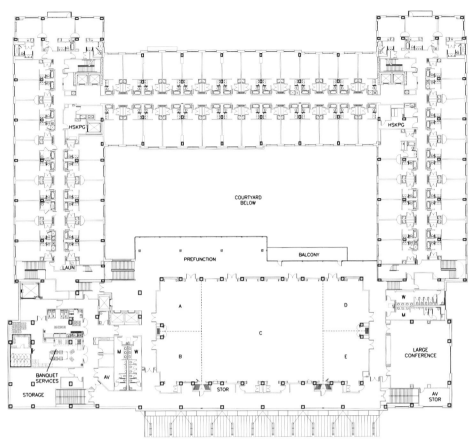

AT&T Executive Education Center, fourth floor (guestrooms and ballroom) plan

AT&T Executive Education Center, conference room

AT&T Executive Education Center, boardroom

Joint-venture Conference Centers

Hybrid centers should appear in the future as corporations, government, and education look for collaborative opportunities. Florida's historic Biltmore Hotel developed the Conference Center of the Americas, in a joint venture with the city of Coral Gables and the University of Florida system. It adds 40,000 sq ft (3,700 sq m) of meeting space, including two tiered amphitheaters and 15 other conference and breakout rooms, to the older resort facilities. One emphasis is expected to be conferences focused on doing business in Latin America, in addition to statewide and regional government conferences, executive education programs, and a variety of non-degree courses.

Planning and Design Considerations

There are significant differences in the physical organization of conference centers and those of more traditional hotels and resorts. Many of these differences are related to the conference center's principal planning objective: to separate the conference and training areas from the other functions in order to eliminate distractions and intrusions during a meeting. Dining, lounge, banquet, and recreational areas usually are located away from the meeting wing, in connecting structures, or even in separate buildings. Other objectives include the architectural massing and careful siting of the facility to enhance the residential scale and create a feeling of closeness with the environment. Roadways, parking areas, and surrounding activity are screened. Moreover, the architects must design a particularly efficient building. Given the additional floor area programmed for meeting and recreational facilities, it is essential that architects keep non-essential space to a minimum.

Planning the Guestroom Areas

Because of the major focus on the public areas and, especially, on the conference core, the architect must deal with the guestroom areas in a straightforward manner. For example, the usual program for the guestrooms calls for fairly standard rooms of 300–350 sq ft (28–32.5 sq m), typical three-fixture bathrooms, a small number of suites, and few extra amenities. The architect should attempt to organize the guestroom wings along double-loaded corridors to reduce the amount of public circulation space (see Chapter 15).

The rooms at the smaller end of the range are in facilities designed for single occupancy, generally at the more price-sensitive corporate and university centers, but this may be shortsighted in that they are less adaptable for more upscale markets in the future. These facilities also have few suites, certainly no more than three per 100 rooms, and no "club floor" or executive level, as do upscale business hotels. On the other hand, the executive and resort centers, as well as the management-oriented corporate centers, provide rooms fully competitive with those in the best hotels at 350–400 sq ft (32.5–37

sq m), include four-fixture bathrooms, allocate up to 5 percent suites (resort centers as many as 10 percent), and feature additional amenities in order to meet the demands of the non-conference guests throughout the year. The layout of these guestrooms must recognize the need for meeting attendees to work on case studies or other training materials in their rooms, often involving group discussion. University centers may provide group study rooms on the upper floors, just for this reason, to accommodate the focus on group discussion and project work. Often, these rooms are treated similarly to suite living rooms, but with the focus on working space rather than lounge or entertainment activities.

Planning the Public Areas

In contrast to their fairly typical guestroom areas, conference centers are far from typical when it comes to planning the public areas and, especially, the function space. Like convention hotels, the conference facilities frequently provide two major entrances, one the lobby entrance for the overnight guests, the other the function entrance, here intended for the day conferee. Unlike many hotels, conference centers generally do not market or position their food and beverage operations to the general public but prefer to reserve them for the conference attendees, to support the learning objectives of the meeting. Beverage outlets are common, but understated. Many university and some corporate centers, as a general policy, do not provide any bar or lounge spaces, although these may be found as part of a game room or informal pub operation.

The emphasis, of course, is on the meeting areas. The planning and design objectives specific to the conference core include the following:

- Locate the conference core, whether in the form of classrooms, breakout rooms, amphitheaters, or other special-purpose rooms, away from other public functions to minimize distractions.
- Dedicate the conference core to the meeting functions; provide a separate area for such social activities as banquets and receptions in the general vicinity of the food and beverage operations.
- Provide a conference foyer, with direct access from outside or from the main hotel lobby.
- Incorporate necessary public support functions, including meeting registration, conference concierge, restrooms, and coat and phone areas.
- Design and equip each conference room to enhance the meeting purpose. In general, provide spacious, brightly daylit, high-ceilinged rooms which incorporate flexible lighting and audiovisual systems, comfortable furnishings, and individual climate control.
- Place assembly and refreshment areas throughout the conference core to provide opportunities for frequent informal gathering and to allow greater flexibility in scheduling breaks. Include outdoor terraces where the site and weather permit.
- Locate service-support functions such as conference services offices, pantry space, and audiovisual equipment, furniture, and other storage rooms nearby.

Conference center operators demand that the architect design the other principal areas to support the meeting focus. For example, most facilities include a dedicated dining room for the conference attendees. This is designed to allow clusters of people coming out of a session, often groups as large as six to eight, to find a table and seat themselves, serve themselves from a lavish buffet, and leave as they are ready—in contrast to guests waiting for a host to seat them (often at a number of small tables), then waiting for the server and the meal and the check. Larger conference centers, and most executive and resort properties, usually provide a more upscale specialty restaurant and, increasingly, an additional, more casual room with an informal snack or grab'n'go menu.

The recreational areas are considerably more extensive than in most hotels: the typical conference center will include an indoor pool, health club with exercise and aerobics rooms, basic spa facilities, and, frequently, racquetball courts. University-based centers may have limited recreational amenities, given budgetary constraints and the knowledge that nearby on campus are myriad recreational facilities. Resort and some executive conference centers may have multiple golf courses, extensive tennis facilities, and other recreational amenities to rival the best in the country.

Planning for Operations

Equally important to the success of a conference or meeting are the types of services that the conference center provides: a conference coordinator assists the meeting planner with arrangements during the weeks leading up to the conference; the conference concierge provides the meeting participants with information, messages, and such business-center services as typing, faxing, copying, and express mail; audiovisual technicians not only provide and, if necessary, operate the audiovisual equipment but may even produce a custom videotape or CD-Rom for a particular session or as a record of the meeting; and many centers have their own closed circuit television production studio, graphics print shop, and photographic darkroom.

Most conference centers price their facilities based on the "complete meeting package," or CMP. This offers the meeting planner a single daily rate, including lodging, three meals in the conference dining room, 24-hour use of conference rooms, refreshment breaks, and standard audiovisual support. The only extras are for special event dinners, such specific audiovisual requests as the production of a tape, and golf greens fees. The CMP also includes continuous refreshments, permitting the instructors increased flexibility in scheduling a break. The refreshment centers generally feature a wide selection of hot and cold beverages, pastries and fruit in the morning, and various snacks in the afternoon. This typical arrangement of the conference dining room and continuous breaks necessitates fewer decisions by the meeting planner in terms of cost, schedule, and exact number of attendees. It also offers more flexibility and choice to the attendees themselves, and gives the operator greater certainty in planning staffing and food purchasing.

Residential Hotels, Condominiums, and Vacation Ownership

Since their inception, the grand downtown hotels have attracted a number of affluent guests who, being able to afford the luxurious service and carefree lifestyle offered by these exquisite facilities, chose to make their accommodations more or less permanent. The hotels in turn welcomed these often-prestigious residents, as having them enhanced the hotel's image and ensured occupancy. That trend of special guests staying for months, even years, in the comfortable security and pampered luxury of their favorite suite at their favorite hotel has carried through even today, while at the same time the market for permanently owned residential apartments with luxury hotel services has flourished.

Built in 1884 as one of New York City's first cooperative apartment houses, the Chelsea was later converted to a hotel, yet has maintained a high ratio of permanent residents to this day. The hotel has a long, rich history of former residents who were celebrated writers, artists, and performers: Thomas Wolfe, Dylan Thomas, Brendan Behan, Mark Twain, Tennessee Williams, Sarah Bernhardt, Arthur Miller, Jackson Pollock, Bob Dylan, Leonard Cohen, Patti Smith, and Dennis Hopper—even Sid Vicious of the Sex Pistols. Many were said to have drawn a special inspiration while living at the Chelsea Hotel. Arthur C. Clark and Stanley Kubrick chose a room in the Chelsea as their workshop when writing the screenplay for their movie, *2001: A Space Odyssey*.

Residential hotels reached their peak of fashion in major U.S. cities during the Roaring Twenties, with affluent celebrities, artists, and others who could afford to savor hotel services. Examples in New York City include the St. Moritz, Hampshire House, Ritz Tower, New Netherland (now the Sherry Netherland), and Hotel des Artistes. With a few exceptions, such as The Pierre, these hotels had small exclusive lobbies and limited public space, setting themselves apart from hotels that primarily catered to transient guests and had grand public rooms. What these hotels lacked in their public spaces they made up for in the large opulent private suites in the tower. Considered one of the last gasps of the Great Boom, The Carlyle was built as a residential hotel just before the stock market crash of 1929 and followed the same formula, with its opulent but residential-scaled lobby, designed by Dorothy Draper. Composer Richard Rodgers was The Carlyle's first permanent resident and U.S. Presidents Truman and Kennedy made the hotel their New York headquarters.

The Waldorf=Astoria was the first hotel to separate residential and hotel components in a major mixed-use building, creating the concept of luxury towers within a hotel and serving as a model for many contemporary developments. The Waldorf Towers section of the building was accessed by private elevators from an elegant

Exclusive Resorts, Papagayo, Costa Rica
Each of Exclusive Resorts' 19 private Poro Poro residences on Costa Rica's Peninsula Papagayo was meticulously designed and finished to make the most of the cliffside development's breathtaking ocean views, blend seamlessly with the surrounding landscape, and provide a wealth of resort-style amenities including private pools, hot tubs, and more.

residential-scale lobby off East 50th Street and from the mid-block driveway that tunnels through the building. Housing large luxurious apartment suites which today are sold as "boutique" hotel rooms, the Towers was architecturally sculpted to resemble the notable twin-tower residential buildings that line Central Park, but actually was a single tower that rises to a height of 625 ft (190 m) over the 25-story base of transient hotel rooms and sumptuous public spaces. Service elevators thread through the base to the hotel's vast system of kitchens and back-of-house areas bringing services to the Towers. Famous former residents of The Waldorf=Astoria include General Douglas McArthur, the Duke of Windsor, Henry Kissinger, and President Herbert Hoover, who, in 1931, delivered a radio address from there on opening night.

Hotels with residences are once again popular with developers, and several different models have been created in response to specific tax laws and market conditions. The financial structure of these projects is attractive to residents, hotel owners, and operators for the following reasons:

- *Developers:* The developers can leverage the appeal of the hotel brand to help finance the hotel from the sale of the residences, thereby avoiding direct interest charges, including those accrued during construction, if the units are pre-sold.
- *Residence owners:* The residence owners can take advantage of normal personal-tax write-offs for interest and real estate taxes or depreciation of rental property.
- *Operator:* The hotel operator can manage the residences efficiently for the owners, while gaining additional revenue for the hotel company in the form of management fees and user fees.

During the housing boom of the early 2000s, many older hotel properties were converted to or replaced with condominium developments. Smart developers retained hotel functionality in these projects, as the overbuilding of condos and a lack of new supply of hotel rooms in markets like New York are now making condo-to-hotel conversions more attractive.

Hotels with Condominiums

The mixed-use development model, in which condominiums are built above, below, or beside transient hotel rooms and sold to individuals who may use hotel services such as housekeeping or room service, remains the most prevalent approach to combining residential and hotel uses. As with other mixed-use projects, the components of the complex benefit synergistically in their interaction with each other and add value to the project as a whole. But the key to the success of the development is the inclusion of a five-star hotel chain. Many luxury brands have embraced this approach to extend their presence in high-profile markets. Most of these projects are in either urban centers—largely in the U.S., Middle East, and Asia—or exclusive resort destinations.

Ritz-Carlton Club and Residences, San Francisco, California
The transformation of the former San Francisco Chronicle Building into luxury residences involved stripping off white enamel siding, added in the 1960s, to reveal the original Burnham & Root façade dating from 1889. A new tower addition was clad in a contrasting material, increasing the building area while maintaining the focus on the beautiful sandstone and brick of the older structure.

Four Seasons Resort, Vail, Colorado
Referencing classic European mountain resort design, the property features a separate entrance for owners and guests using its two-, three-, and four-bedroom private residences.

232

In San Francisco, Ritz-Carlton has its luxury residences located a few blocks from the main Ritz-Carlton San Francisco hotel in a classic Burnham and Root building, providing a more intimate and exclusive setting for these high-end units. Four Seasons uses a more common approach to combining a hotel with residences in Vail, Colorado: the property there has private residences and hotel rooms in the same building, with condominiums available to purchase whole or through a fractional ownership arrangement.

Planning and Design Considerations

Mixed-use projects that combine hotel and residential space with other uses are among the more complicated structures being built today. Highly complex programmatically, the circulation between hotel guests, condominium owners, office occupants, sports club goers, shoppers, and those attending special events requires careful, detailed planning on a grand scale. Residential condominiums that share a tower with hotel rooms usually have a dedicated entrance and elevator lobby for condominium owners that is separate from the main hotel lobby. This entrance may have a staffed door and reception area and will certainly offer owner-only services like mail handling, storage lockers, and in some cases valet parking. The

Ritz-Carlton Guangzhou has a residents' lounge and business center that is separate from those available to hotel guests, and, like many luxury developments in Asia, has a VIP elevator that is distinct from the condo-only elevators, for the sole use of those owners with the most prestigious units. Offering dedicated elevators for residents is generally a requirement for projects like these, which often means that the hotel's core is considerably larger than would be the case for a transient-only hotel of the same type and size.

Early on, the developer needs to decide what level of finish to provide in the residences. The advantages of providing fully furnished units versus raw empty space, where owners can design and custom-build their own unit, will have to be carefully weighed and will depend on the particular market.

Residence owners usually are given access to hotel services like housekeeping, room service, and concierge on a fee-for-use basis. Therefore, the connection between the hotel's back-of-house spaces and the residential core requires consideration. Basic services like waste collection, exterior landscaping, security, and common-area maintenance are handled by the hotel and included in monthly or annual fees.

The market for luxury living accommodations continues to grow as consumer preferences gain in sophistication, leading to increased demand for the type of personalized service offered in serviced

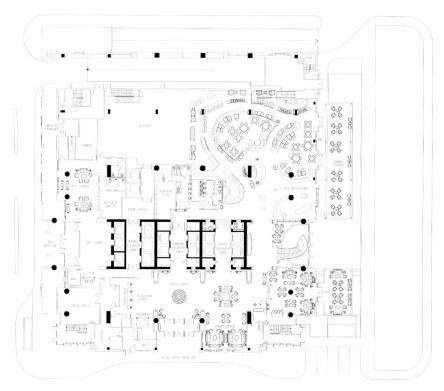

Ritz-Carlton Hotel and Residences, Guangzhou, China
Apartment residents and destination-club guests have their own auto drop-off, lobby, front desk, lounge, and elevator bank in this combined five-star hotel and luxury residential building. Residents can easily access hotel services while at the same time enjoying dedicated facilities well away from busy public spaces.

St. Regis Hotel and Residences, Singapore
Two 23-story crescent-shaped residential towers flank a 299-room five-star hotel
in a clever reflection of the Singaporean national flag.

W Hollywood, Los Angeles, California
In what is arguably the most iconic location in its market—the corner of
Hollywood and Vine—the W Hollywood was designed to reflect the movie
industry and celebrity culture in a modern way: even the façade plays a role, as
it can be used as a projection screen. The hotel and residences are housed in
separate towers but residents have full access to hotel services and amenities.

luxury apartments in prime markets. Global economic growth will
also drive travel demands of major corporations, who will look to
residential hotel products to house staff on long-term temporary
assignments; these companies may purchase blocks of condominiums
in strategic locations.

Condominium Hotels

Another model that combines hotel rooms with condominiums is
the condo hotel. In condo hotels, residential owners allow their
condominiums to be rented out as hotel rooms when they are not
in residence. The hotel operator maintains the condos as part of the
hotel's room inventory and provides housekeeping and other typical
hotel services to the guests using the unit. Any revenue from guest
use of the condo, after the hotel operator's expenses and fees are
deducted, is shared with the condominium owner.

The advantages of these kinds of properties are similar to the
traditional residential condominium model: developers can get cash

The Signature at MGM Grand, Las Vegas, Nevada
This three-tower condo-hotel development offers exclusive non-smoking guest accommodations and access to all the amenities of the nearby MGM Grand, but with a quieter and more residential setting. Each condominium in The Signature at MGM Grand is privately owned and is included in the hotel's inventory when the owner is not in residence.

up front from condo buyers to help finance the project; condo buyers get an asset that they can use and sell; and hotel operators can earn fees and offset some costs through assessments on condo owners. The difference here is that in a condo hotel the condominiums are considered part of the hotel's inventory, whereas in the pure residential model those units remain the sole purview of their owners.

Condo hotels may have many of the same mix of amenities and design features as hotels that offer residential condominiums: a separate entrance, reception, and parking area for condo owners and a mail room and storage areas for condo owners' use. However, in order to facilitate guest use of the condominiums when they are in the hotel's overnight inventory, condo elevators must be accessible to regular hotel guests.

Condo hotels enjoyed a building boom in the 2000s but many projects foundered in the economic crisis. Developers are required to promote these projects as second homes for personal use rather than as investments, but many speculators purchased units in the hope of making more than enough to cover their mortgages and carrying costs. These buyers were often disappointed, as hotel

occupancy and rates in some markets dropped precipitously and a huge number of condominiums flooded the market. It will take substantial economic recovery before these kinds of projects are likely to become common once again.

Vacation Ownership Resorts

Introduced in Europe in the 1960s and named for a resource-sharing practice in the information technology industry, "time-sharing" was a simple economical method of easing family vacation costs by sharing beach or mountain apartments in blocks of two to four weeks. But as the concept spread, it fell prey to unbusinesslike promotions and aggressive sales tactics which disaffected consumers for years. Eventually, when regulated, marketed, redesigned, and managed by experienced hotel companies and renamed "vacation ownership" in the 1990s, blocks of time in resorts that could be pre-purchased and traded once again became a popular and viable lodging option.

West 57th Street by Hilton Club, New York, New York
This 161-room hotel in the very heart of Manhattan is newly constructed and combines mid-city convenience with a more intimate and homelike atmosphere than a typical New York transient hotel. Like many other urban vacation ownership properties, West 57th Street by Hilton Club does not offer a restaurant on site but does have its own spa, fitness facilities, and business center.

Marriott Vacation Club Grande Vista, Orlando, Florida
With over 1,600 units, this vacation ownership resort is near to major demand-generators in the southwestern Orlando area but offers a quieter, more residential feel than many regular hotel properties in its market. The units include one-, two-, and three-bedroom villas with fully equipped kitchens and in-room laundry to support family vacation travel.

Developers appreciated the cash flow, while buyers liked locked-in vacation prices as well as having the potential to trade for alternative destinations, especially since the introduction of "points" systems for these kinds of transactions. Even with the global recession that softened resort demand in the late 2000s, vacation ownership has retained much of its appeal. A 2011 Ernst & Young research report noted that there are over eight million vacation intervals owned in the U.S. alone, and 45 percent of recent buyers are repeat customers who purchase additional units from the same developer or chain. The prospects for vacation ownership projects look strong, particularly as markets like China and India benefit from rising incomes and a growing middle and upper class.

For operators, the primary advantage of the vacation ownership system is that time-share properties enjoy significantly higher occupancies than other resorts: in 2009, time-share resorts had an average occupancy of 80 percent, compared with typical hotel occupancies of 58 percent. Therefore, hotel chains can improve their occupancy figures by converting units in desirable destinations that have lower than normal usage into vacation ownership properties. Consequently, hotels consider vacation ownership as being complementary to their business rather than competing with it.

It is important to note that the term "vacation ownership" can incorporate various types of shared-ownership resorts. Most often, "vacation ownership" refers to a time-share, but some use the phrase to describe any lodging that has pre-sold, shared usage. Table 11.1 provides a guide to the various forms of residential and shared-usage lodging products and how they typically differ.

Development and Planning Considerations

The most successful vacation ownership projects affiliate with an established hotel chain: some of the biggest names in the vacation ownership field are familiar hotel companies such as Hilton, Hyatt, Marriott, Starwood, and Wyndham. Many consumers do not have the time or inclination to independently research their purchase and feel safer choosing a well-known brand. It also may help the buyer understand the product better and faster. Vacation ownership developments are ideal for combining with mixed-use commercial or resort projects since their owners typically visit more often, bring family members or friends with them, stay longer, and spend more per unit than regular hotel guests. It is no surprise, then, that Disney has made vacation ownership a significant component of its development strategy.

Obtaining development financing is easier for vacation ownership projects: they are considered safer investments than hotels, since the

Table 11.1 Categories of shared-usage lodging products

Attribute	Residences/condominiums as part of mixed-use hotel project	Condo hotel	Fractional ownership	Vacation ownership/vacation club/time-share*	Residence club*	Destination club*
Buyer's equity in real estate	Yes: Deeded ownership of unit	Yes: Deeded ownership of unit	Yes: Deeded ownership of a portion of the unit	Usually none	Usually yes	Usually none
Cost structure	Initial purchase + annual fees + assessments	Initial purchase + annual fees + assessments	Initial purchase + annual fees + assessments + usage fees	Initial purchase + annual fees	Initial purchase + annual dues + service usage fees	Initial deposit + service usage fees
Buyer's investment potential	May be rented to third party; may have income from sale of property	Participation in hotel revenues; may have income from sale of property	May have income from sale of interest	Minimal; may have income from sale of contract	May earn income from appreciation at sale of membership; membership fee may be partially refundable	May earn income from appreciation at sale of membership; membership fee may be partially refundable
Property type	Luxury units; studio to 4+ bedrooms	Upscale to luxury units; studio to 2+ bedrooms	Luxury units; 2+ bedrooms	Midscale to upscale units; studio to 2+ bedrooms	Luxury units; studio to 4+ bedrooms	Luxury units; 2+ bedrooms
Services	Basic maintenance and doorman services included; five-star hotel services à la carte	Basic maintenance included; hotel operational services included when unit is in hotel pool	All maintenance services included; five-star hotel services à la carte	Basic maintenance included	All maintenance services included; five-star hotel services à la carte	All maintenance services included; five-star hotel services à la carte
Type of location	Major urban centers; resort destinations	Major urban centers	Major urban centers; resort destinations	Primarily resort destinations	Major urban centers; resort destinations	Major urban centers; resort destinations
Main target markets	Empty-nesters and recent retirees; corporate executives	Individuals	Affluent families; empty-nesters and recent retirees	Families; older retirees	Affluent families; empty-nesters and recent retirees	Affluent families and recent retirees
Roomnights available to general public	No	Yes	No	Often	No	No

* Terms used inconsistently across the industry.

construction loan is often paid back by the development company from the sales of the units. This often occurs before the property fully opens. Long-term hotel debt, on the other hand, is paid back over many years from the property's cash flow. Operating profits are more predictable for vacation units, whereas hotel occupancy is subject to greater variation. And while hotel rooms must be sold every night, vacation ownership units are sold in advance for longer blocks of time; in many time-shares, unaffiliated overnight guests are welcomed on a space-available basis as an additional source of revenue.

Vacation ownership resorts share many planning characteristics with transient resorts, including a strong sense of place or theme, multiple on-property food-service and recreation options, and an emphasis on attractive views and landscaping, while urban locations have very similar public spaces and back-of-house areas to those found in city hotels. Where vacation ownership projects differ from transient hotels is in the room size and amenities. Because of the longer length of stay typical of the time-share guest, vacation ownership units are designed more like condominiums, often with full kitchens, two or more bathrooms, balconies, and more generous storage space. Many have multiple bedrooms or connecting "lock-off" suites to accommodate extended families and friends traveling together. In the luxury segment, these units may be indistinguishable from a high-end, standalone vacation home. With landscaped balconies, irregular façades angled toward the views, and stepped low-rise building forms, vacation ownership resorts emphasize the individuality and privacy of the units to an even greater extent than do other resort designs.

Fractional Ownership, Residence Clubs and Destination Clubs

In the classic time-share model, buyers purchase blocks of time but do not have any equity in the properties themselves. Fractional ownership is the practice of buying a deeded share in an expensive asset, originally aircraft but today applied to a vacation home or desirable city apartment. In a fractional ownership resort, buyers have a fee-simple interest in a portion of a condominium or home and may use the unit for a predetermined number of days or weeks each year, negotiated in advance with the other owners. Typically, these units are scheduled and maintained by a luxury hotel operating

company in exchange for annual owners' fees. Owners can purchase individual services during their stay, such as housekeeping, catering or kitchen-stocking. Fractional ownership is generally less costly than owning a vacation home outright but still offers the benefit of being able to sell one's interest in the property at market value.

A residence club takes the fractional ownership idea one step further. Residence club buyers purchase membership in a club that owns a number of vacation homes, and with that membership obtain the right to stays in any of the club's destinations, which are usually in luxury resort or sought-after city locations. Developers are careful to make these properties look and feel as residential as possible and to incorporate top-of-the-line furnishings and amenities, as

Lower level

Upper level

Costa Rica - Poro Poro - Upper (Residence type 4)

Exclusive Resorts, Papagayo, Costa Rica
Inspired by the idea of "luxury living in the treetops," the spacious Exclusive Resorts residences at Peninsula Papagayo offer private infinity-edge pools, hot tubs, dual master suites, sumptuous outdoor showers, expansive outdoor living areas, and fully custom interior finishes combining indigenous woods, natural stones, and the works of local artists and artisans to infuse each home with true Costa Rican style.

47 Park Street—Marriott Grand Residence Club, London, United Kingdom
This 49-suite neo-Georgian fractional ownership property is located just off
Park Lane in the desirable Mayfair district. Residences offer either one or two
bedrooms and are each equipped with spacious living areas, gourmet kitchens,
and period artwork.

fractional and residence club buyers are generally high net-worth
consumers with high expectations for luxury and service. The homes
in fractional developments are typically at least three bedrooms and
many are well over 5,000 sq ft (465 sq m), with private pools, decks,
outdoor fireplaces, and expansive gourmet kitchens. In order to
maintain a feeling of exclusivity, these developments tend to have
only a small number of units in any one location, in contrast with
time-share resorts, where there might be hundreds of condominiums
in a single resort.

Another model is the destination club, which is a non-equity
variation on a residence club. Members buy the right to book a set
number of nights in any of the club's collection of luxury homes in
resort and city destinations but do not have an ownership position
in the real estate.

Various forms and definitions of residential-style lodging are still
evolving as developers look for creative ways to finance projects
and consumers seek high-value travel experiences. For example, it
is not uncommon for the terms "residence club" and "destination
club" to be used interchangeably, or to have variations in how
projects identified as a "club" are actually structured. Limitations on
foreign ownership of real estate in some countries make time-shares,
clubs, and fractional ownership into viable alternatives to buying a
vacation home, and the potential for investment gains often adds
to the appeal of purchasing a residence for leisure or business use
within a hotel development. The challenge for designers of these
properties is to create facilities that can combine the best attributes
of a home and a resort and to be able to move between the two as
market conditions change.

Updating Existing Hotels

Hotels are continually being updated. Renovation work and refurbishing are necessary for the financial health of hotels and, each year, more money is spent on these activities than for the construction of new hotels. About every five years there is the need to replace worn-out soft goods, such as wall coverings, carpets, and drapery. Case goods, including beds, furniture, and some equipment, require replacement every 10 years. Modernized mechanical systems, up-to-date lighting, new plumbing fittings and other extensive changes are called for every 15 to 25 years.

In addition, hotels frequently alter existing spaces, such as enlarging a successful restaurant, adding an exercise facility or business center, or converting an underutilized nightclub to another use. In cases where there is no available space, owners might consider constructing an addition to the existing hotel in order to meet market demands and realize greater profits. Over time hotels lose their luster—styles need to be updated to reflect current tastes. A fresh look to an existing hotel is often essential in order to compete with a new or recently renovated hotel nearby. Targeting a growing segment of the public interested in sustainability leads to renovations that make a hotel more ecologically friendly, often with the goal of obtaining LEED certification. Improvements in operational efficiency, and to back-of-house facilities to provide better services and to boost staff morale, are also reasons to renovate.

Such work is often performed while the hotel remains in operation and with as little disruption to service as possible. All efforts should be made to keep noise, debris, and general inconvenience to guests at a minimum. Construction projects undertaken in an operating hotel are more costly than when the hotel shuts down. This is because of limited hours the crew can work, partitions required to block off areas under construction, complimentary goods and services provided to guests, and temporary facilities set up for those that are out-of-service. However, closing a hotel, or even a portion of operations, can also have drawbacks, including loss of revenue and valued employees, and making regular guests seek out competitors. Planning must be carefully done. Renovation of guestrooms often is scheduled in stages, with blocks of rooms or floors done in sequence while the rest remain in service.

Renovations of a major scale involve the complete overhaul of an existing hotel or the conversion of another building type for use as a hotel. Reflagging an existing hotel, changing from one hotel brand to another, usually requires alterations to meet a new hotel company's rigorous brand standards, which might include new bathroom configurations, additional public spaces, or upgraded back-of-house facilities to facilitate a new level of guest services.

St. Pancras Renaissance Hotel, London, United Kingdom
The original Midland Grand Hotel, designed by Sir George Gilbert Scott in 1873 for the Midlands Railway Company, is listed as a Grade 1 London landmark. The building underwent a £150 million renovation and restoration project where existing public rooms were meticulously restored, with some, like the Ladies' Smoking Room, retaining their original name but now used as a venue for private events. All details of the grand staircase with its cathedral-like ceiling were restored, down to the fleur-de-lis hand stencils, wrought-iron balustrade, and patterned carpet.

Table 12.1 Renovation cycle of existing hotel

Stage	Cost/room	Scope
6-year refurbishment	$6,000–15,000	Replace carpet, fabrics (upholstery, bedspreads, drapery), vinyl wall covering, repaint
12-year major overhaul	$25,000–40,000	Repeat above plus upgrade systems and equipment (computers, life-safety, kitchen, laundry)
50-year "gut renovation"	$60,000 +	Repeat above plus change functions, circulations, etc.; consider exterior renovation

The main factors favoring total renovation over new construction are savings in construction expenses ("gut" renovations generally cost 30 percent less than building from the ground up), the lack of prime and spacious sites (particularly in urban areas), time savings (although not always the case), and continuing appreciation for historic architecture by the public. (See Table 12.1.)

Hotel Renovation

In periods of economic downturn, hotels often postpone renovation work and sometimes defer maintenance. When good times return, cash is available to do things that have been put off or just to take advantage of having money on hand as an incentive to upgrade facilities. In order to substantially change the look of a hotel or to undertake a major renovation that requires that the building be totally emptied, a liquidation sale can be a way to generate income by selling off furniture, equipment, lighting fixtures, and other items that still have some life but will not be used in the newly renovated hotel.

The existing building places serious constraints on most renovation projects and these must be addressed during the design process. While initial building surveys strive to be as complete as possible, contractors or others on the team inevitably discover unknown existing conditions. Sometimes the builders uncover magnificent details which the owner or designer wants to incorporate into the finished project. At other times, serious deterioration is only made evident after demolition. Both budgets and schedules for renovation projects can be substantially off their initial projections as a result of these unforeseen conditions. This is a gamble for all renovation projects and contingencies must be built into design, documentation, and construction budgets to cover these possible costs. In 2007 London's Savoy Hotel closed for what was estimated to be a £100 million renovation. However, because of the need for unanticipated major structural stabilization the actual cost grew to £220 million, which was borne by the owner.

Hotels reflect the economic circumstances of their communities. Prosperity in the industrialized nations at the end of the twentieth century has brought about the transformation of many urban neighborhoods. The once working-class district of Shoreditch in London's East End has recently been gentrified by artists and web-technology industries. Many industrial buildings have been put to new use, including a formerly vacant 1893 Victorian warehouse on Boundary Road, which is now the Boundary Hotel. Designed and developed in 2008 by Sir Terence Conran with his wife Vicki, and in partnership with Peter Prescott, guestrooms have been individually inspired by Mies van der Rohe, Le Corbusier and Charlotte Perriand, Eileen Grey, the Bauhaus, Shaker design, the cartoonist Heath Robinson, and others to whom Conran pays homage, and for a clientele that is familiar with modern design. The small 17-room Boundary, with restaurants, a café, bakery, and food hall, integrates an old building into its new neighborhood.

In an effort to spur development in a certain area, to protect a historic building, or to encourage sustainable development, governments may offer tax credits for private developers to renovate an existing building. These subsidies can offset risk and help with financing. Such sites should be pursued for possible hotel development. The environmental cost of tearing down a building to construct a new one on the same site is considerable. Portland, Oregon, has an impressive record as a city committed to sustainability and green architecture. It offers financial incentives and technical assistance to developers. Sage developers were able to take advantage of this in transforming a 1980 office building that had been vacant for 17 years into Marriott Courtyard, the city's first LEED Gold-certified hotel. Being part of a public redevelopment scheme from the beginning also may include the advantage of saving time, as these projects often find it easier to secure necessary approvals from city agencies.

The individual business traveler and business conferences are primary markets for most hotels today. Many hotels are turning over more space for meeting rooms and business centers. In addition, guestrooms are being modified to be business-friendly, with two phone lines, large desks, task lighting, and flexible layouts that allow rooms to be used for small business meetings. Couples who travel often include one who uses the room to work and the other who uses the room for leisure. Converting two small rooms into a suite or providing a separate dressing area between the sleeping area and bathroom are ways that hotels today find to balance the needs of couples staying for mixed purposes. Many older hotels were built with guestrooms that are considered too small by today's standards. Detroit's 33-story Book-Cadillac Hotel opened in 1924 as the world's tallest hotel, with 1,136 guestrooms. Tough years led to liquidation in 1986, after which the building was shuttered. An infusion of $200 million allowed the Book-Cadillac, now part of the Westin chain, to reopen in 2008. The small rooms were combined to make 453 spacious new guestrooms and 67 condominium apartments on the top floors.

Hotels which need to complete the renovation or remodeling in time to meet the high season, to set new rates, or to accommodate a special event bringing in many guests now can get turn-key packages from companies that bundle together design, purchasing, and consulting services. These firms provide all items for a standard guestroom at a lower cost and in less time than can be accomplished with the traditional design process. While this might not be an option for hotel owners who take a personal interest in every detail,

Westin Book Cadillac Hotel, Detroit, Michigan
A $176 million interior makeover of the hotel was completed in 2008, designed
by ForrestPerkins. As part of the renovation, much of the original décor of
the Grand Ballroom (renamed the Venetian Ballroom) and Italian Garden was
re-created. A three-story addition with a ballroom and conference spaces was
added on a vacant adjacent site and a 13-story department store was razed for a
new 10-story parking garage.

it does answer to those who are satisfied with a good look that is
completed quickly and saves money. Working from basic choices set
up in showrooms, the owner has limited options for customization.
These are cosmetic renovations that do not involve mechanical,
plumbing, or electrical modifications or spatial changes that require
services of engineers and architects.

When hotels change possession, they are often renovated to
publicize the new ownership and appeal to a new clientele. The
16-story Gramercy Park Hotel was built in Renaissance Revival
style to the design of Robert T. Lyons in 1925 and extended in
1929 by Thompson and Churchill. With spacious guestrooms and
generous facilities, the hotel maintained an understated luxury, and
was patronized by guests from the upper-middle class and those
wanting to keep a low profile. In 2003, Ian Schrager purchased the
185-room Gramercy Park Hotel and, under the direction of artist/
filmmaker Julian Schnabel, completely transformed the interiors. The
new décor emphasizes lush materials, jewel-like colors, and custom
furniture, expressing Schnabel's play on early twentieth-century
wealthy bohemian style. Guests are still given coveted access to the
private park, which has not changed since its inception.

There are occasional renovations that do not succeed in meeting the
expectations of their patrons. Even before materials have become worn,
the owners find it necessary to make changes that would be appreciated
by their guests. New York is a city that prides itself on change. In recent
years the pace at which it reinvents itself has accelerated dramatically.
While from the exterior much of New York's building stock remains the
same, interiors are frequently being updated. This is especially true
for its hotels, which are often competing to have the latest design.
However, the one hotel that has resisted this trend is the Algonquin.
Built in 1902 on West 44th Street in midtown Manhattan, the 174-room
Algonquin Hotel did not make its reputation until 1919, when a group
of young writers and critics, known for their wit, gathered daily for ten
years at the Round Table. A 1998 renovation that bordered on the
cliché was not at all to the liking of the hotel's fiercely loyal clientele,
who do not look kindly upon tinkering with their memories. Now
part of Marriott's Autograph Collection, the Algonquin underwent its
most recent renovation in 2008. The challenge for designer Alexandra
Champalimaud was not to replicate the past, but to maintain its highly
valued character while discreetly providing up-to-date amenities and
new lighting. (See Table 12.2.)

(continued p. 252)

Gramercy Park Hotel, New York, New York
With a retractable roof 16 stories above the city, the Gramercy Terrace recalls the celebrated rooftop garden life popularized at the turn of the century in New York City at such places as Ziegfeld's Club at the New Amsterdam Theatre, Stanford White's rooftop garden at the original Madison Square Garden, and the Astor Hotel in Times Square.

Algonquin Hotel, New York, New York
A New York landmark since 1987, the Algonquin was made a National Literary Landmark in 1996 by the Friends of Libraries USA, a rare distinction for a hotel. Interior designer Alexandra Champalimaud spearheaded a $4.5 million renovation in 2008 that touched virtually every corner of the famous hotel, including upgrades of the historic lobby's furnishings, the famed Oak Room, Blue Bar, renowned Round Table Room, and all suites and guestrooms.

New York Marriott Marquis, New York, New York
The Times Square hotel undertook a $39 million makeover that included 1,900 guestrooms and suites, the Broadway Lounge, the Broadway Ballroom, and a new atrium restaurant and bar. Crossroads restaurant and bar at the base of the hotel's vast atrium includes a dazzling two-story mirrored spiral structure integrating a 20-seat bar and including a halo of color-changing kinetic lights on the top that shine down onto the bar and up at the open-sided guestroom corridors above. "The interior architecture and design we created for the New York Marriott Marquis is designed to reflect the energy and excitement of Times Square," says Stephen Perkins, AIA, ISHC, principal and co-founder of ForrestPerkins.

Table 12.2 Existing hotel checklist

Mechanical systems

Heating, ventilating, and air-conditioning systems
- ❑ Temperature and humidity control
- ❑ Fresh air control and filtration
- ❑ Mechanical noise and vibration control
- ❑ Energy efficiency
- ❑ Zone control
- ❑ Environmental systems

Life-safety systems (review updated local codes)
- ❑ Sprinklers, standpipes, hose racks, fire extinguishers
- ❑ Smoke detection, fire alarm, voice annunciation, fire command station
- ❑ Emergency power generator, lighting, fire pumps, elevator recall
- ❑ Kitchen hood protection (dry foam), computer room (halon)
- ❑ Smoke-proof exit stairs (pressurization, ventilated vestibules)
- ❑ Fire-resistive walls around guestrooms, stairs and between floors, fire-rated doors, closers
- ❑ Fail-safe locking systems
- ❑ Corridor smoke purge

Energy conservation
- ❑ Computerized energy management systems
- ❑ Heat-recovery systems (kitchen and laundry hot water and exhaust)
- ❑ Air-purifying systems (exhaust recirculation)
- ❑ Insulating windows (double and solar glazing)
- ❑ Lifecycle energy analysis
- ❑ Motion sensors, lighting controls in guestrooms
- ❑ Vestibule and revolving doors
- ❑ Alternative energy sources (solar, wind, photovoltaic)
- ❑ Variable air volume system
- ❑ Long-life energy-conserving light bulbs

Vertical transportation systems
- ❑ Passenger elevators
- ❑ Service and freight elevators
- ❑ Escalators
- ❑ Conveyors

Telephone and communications systems
- ❑ Computerized least-cost routing, accounting, wake-up call, and so on
- ❑ House and public phones, telex and fax service, cable and satellite dish, closed circuit TV, HDTV
- ❑ High-speed internet connections

Light dimming systems
- ❑ Meeting and banquet spaces
- ❑ Restaurants
- ❑ Lounges
- ❑ Lobbies
- ❑ Guestrooms

Management systems

Computerized hotel management systems
- ❑ Room status, guest histories
- ❑ Accounting, auditing, inventories
- ❑ Data storage
- ❑ Billing, point-of-sale charging
- ❑ Automatic barcode systems
- ❑ Reservations
- ❑ Safe-deposit boxes
- ❑ Time stamps

Security systems
- ❑ Card-locking systems, door peepholes, security latches
- ❑ TV surveillance of entrances, service dock, elevators, escalators
- ❑ Wireless communication
- ❑ Alarms for exit stairs, cashier
- ❑ Cashier's vault, safe-deposit boxes (front desk)
- ❑ In-room vaults
- ❑ Security lighting

Entertainment systems
- ❑ In-room movies, closed circuit TV
- ❑ Satellite TV, AM/FM bedside control, CD, HDTV, video players
- ❑ Cable

Health club equipment
- ❑ Exercise equipment
- ❑ Sauna, steam-bath, whirlpool
- ❑ Swimming pool
- ❑ Lockers, showers, plumbing fixtures

Guest bathroom accessories
- ❑ Pulsating shower heads
- ❑ Lighted makeup mirrors
- ❑ Towel warmers
- ❑ Heat lamps
- ❑ Shoe polishers
- ❑ Whirlpools and steam-baths

Audiovisual systems
- ❑ Projection
- ❑ Sound
- ❑ Translation

Movable partitions
- ❑ Meeting rooms
- ❑ Ballroom

Soundproofing
- ❑ Guestroom door gaskets
- ❑ Windows
- ❑ Meeting rooms

Repair shops and equipment
- ❑ Carpentry
- ❑ Plumbing
- ❑ Electrical
- ❑ TV, video, CD

Parking systems
- ❑ Automatic entrances
- ❑ Car elevators and ramps
- ❑ Directional signs
- ❑ Paving surfaces, landscaping, lighting

General
- ❑ Interior fixed-décor signage
- ❑ Interior furnishings
- ❑ Kitchen and bar equipment
- ❑ Laundry and dry-cleaning equipment, laundry chute
- ❑ Waste disposal systems, compactor

Rate the existing condition of each item on a scale from 0 to 3, estimating the cost of new additions or upgrades as required to meet current standards.

The Jefferson Hotel, Washington, DC
Architect: ForrestPerkins
Interior Designer: ForrestPerkins

Many buildings in the United States are named after its third president. However, perhaps none comes as close to embodying his theories on architecture and design as the Washington, DC, Jefferson Hotel, located in a quiet neighborhood just four blocks from the White House. The eight-story Beaux-Arts design of Jules Henri de Sibour was constructed in 1922 as the Jefferson Apartments and converted into a hotel in 1955.

In 2007 The Jefferson Hotel underwent a two-year complete renovation that saw most interior spaces demolished. Back-of-house operations were shifted to a newly acquired nearby townhouse, allowing for the consolidation of many small rooms into large spaces to be used for meetings and catering. Structural modifications were required to make these spaces column-free. Awkward circulation was rationalized; slow, undersized elevators were replaced; new accessible restrooms were added; the entry

vestibule was enlarged, with an air lock to conserve energy; the kitchen was expanded; and other modifications were made to improve organization, to provide new services and features, including a spa, for the hotel, and to bring it up to current building codes. Floor slabs to a previously acquired adjacent building were demolished and new slabs were constructed to align it with the main building, so that inconvenient steps between the two could be eliminated.

The peeling away of plaster on the ceiling over the existing lobby revealed a magnificent vaulted skylight, which was restored and brings natural light to what is now a dining area for the hotel's much-praised restaurant, Plume. While many public spaces have been opened up, architectural features ensure that The Jefferson Hotel retains its intimate scale. Original documents with Jefferson's signature, the presence of numerous books, plus

The Jefferson Hotel

The Jefferson Hotel, winter garden

The Jefferson Hotel, reception desks

The Jefferson Hotel, suite

The Jefferson Hotel,
typical floor demolition

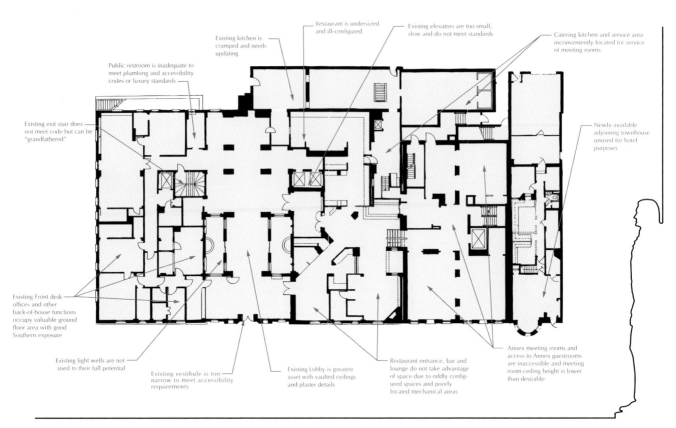

Existing kitchen is cramped and needs updating

Restaurant is undersized and ill-configured

Existing elevators are too small, slow and do not meet standards

Catering kitchen and service area inconveniently located for service of meeting rooms

Public restroom is inadequate to meet plumbing and accessibility codes or luxury standards

Newly available adjoining townhouse unused for hotel purposes

Existing exit stair does not meet code but can be "grandfathered"

Existing Front desk offices and other back-of-house functions occupy valuable ground floor area with good Southern exposure

Existing light wells are not used to their full potential

Existing vestibule is too narrow to meet accessibility requirements

Existing Lobby is greatest asset with vaulted ceilings and plaster details

Restaurant entrance, bar and lounge do not take advantage of space due to oddly configured spaces and poorly located mechanical areas

Annex meeting rooms and access to Annex guestrooms are inaccessible and meeting room ceiling height is lower than desirable

The Jefferson Hotel, existing conditions plan

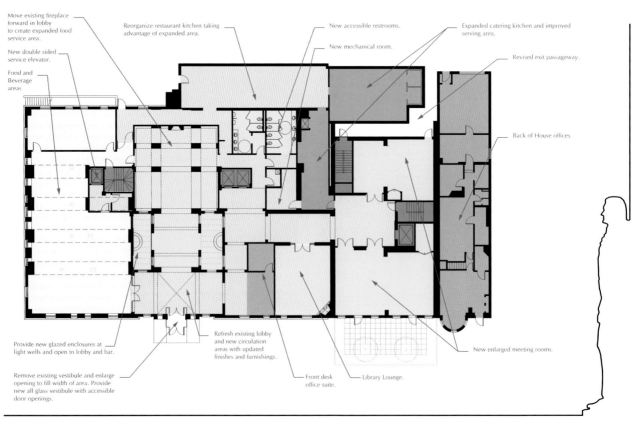

Move existing fireplace forward in lobby to create expanded food service area.

Reorganize restaurant kitchen taking advantage of expanded area.

New accessible restrooms.

Expanded catering kitchen and improved serving area.

New double sided service elevator.

New mechanical room.

Revised exit passageway.

Food and Beverage areas

Back of House offices

Provide new glazed enclosures at light wells and open to lobby and bar.

Refresh existing lobby and new circulation areas with updated finishes and furnishings.

New enlarged meeting rooms.

Remove existing vestibule and enlarge opening to fill width of area. Provide new all glass vestibule with accessible door openings.

Front desk office suite.

Library Lounge.

The Jefferson Hotel, proposed public area plan

French-style period furniture, artifacts, and fittings work together with the architecture to create an ambience that captures the spirit of Jefferson.

All 99 guestrooms and suites underwent complete transformation. The re-created rooms have been embellished with details replicating eighteenth-century design and are furnished with antiques. The intent was to re-create the hotel's interiors according to the neoclassical principles that had inspired Jefferson.

Discreet placement of new technologies to respond to the needs of twenty-first-century guests does not detract from the overall eighteenth-century character of the hotel. All efforts have been made to provide a setting where a person in Washington, DC, on business will have all that is needed to conduct his or her affairs, but will also feel welcomed as a guest in a private home, one in which Jefferson himself might have had a hand.

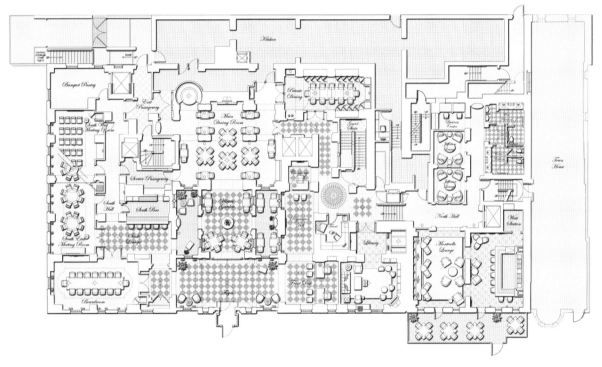

The Jefferson Hotel, ground floor plan

Restorations

Restoration is a special category of renovation in which the intent is to re-create the original structure. Original building elements are retained or, when this is not possible, they are replicated. Most legislation for landmark structures stipulates that building exteriors be restored, but allows the owner discretion with respect to the interior. Restoration work usually involves the expertise of preservation architects who prepare documentation regarding the original design, along with proper materials and methodologies needed for stabilizing, restoring, and cleaning historic buildings. Piecing together the design of a building long after its completion can be a difficult task. Usually the original architect's drawings no longer exist; if they are available, they reflect the intention of the architect and not necessarily what was actually built. Boston's Liberty Hotel, which incorporates a former jailhouse, built in 1851, as its lobby and for several public functions, has a magnificent towering central space that was once crowned by a cupola, torn down in 1949. Having access to the drawings of Gridley James Fox Bryant, architect for the jail, allowed the construction of a new cupola based upon Bryant's original design, which had been built in modified form owing to budget constraints in the nineteenth century and which only came into existence in 2007 as part of the restoration. Old photographs are helpful, but they usually document only a portion of the building and do not positively identify materials or define spaces. Probes to uncover elements hidden by subsequent renovations are a rich source of discovery—even a fragment of an original element can reveal a great deal. Still, there are frequently gaps where there is no positive evidence or clue of the original component. In these instances, the preservation architect relies on his or her knowledge of other similar buildings in order to make educated assumptions.

Once the historic building is understood and documented, the painstaking reconstruction work begins. In the past, buildings, especially those meant to last, were built by craftsmen, many of whose expert skills are no longer part of today's building industry. While the growing movement to restore historic structures has brought a revitalization of many building crafts, it can still be difficult to find qualified artisans. Because of their specialized skills and the labor-intensive nature of their work, restoration projects are usually more expensive and time-consuming than new construction. In some cases, the designers go to great lengths to find replacements for original materials, often custom-making some items, which can involve fabrication by special molds made from surviving original building elements to re-create lost ones. While much depends upon the condition of the existing structure and the elaboration of its architecture, these projects call for a strong commitment by the owner. Such undertakings have great prestige and are much appreciated by today's public, who have come to highly value historic architecture.

By a strict definition of terms, totally restoring a hotel to its original condition is rarely possible or even desirable. No matter how significant the architecture, no guest wants to be without the latest comforts and technologies. Additionally, hotels must provide new facilities to meet present-day demands. When the Dolder Grand Hotel opened in 1899, most people came for the fresh mountain air near Zurich and the disciplined regime of its Curhaus (health spa). The small ascetic guestrooms were adequate and in keeping with the character of this city resort and the cultural sensibility and economic situation of the Swiss in this era. However, restoration of the Dolder Grand in 2008 had to respond to a new wealthy clientele with a different sensibility and expectations. The hotel today caters not just to locals, but also to international travelers who come to enjoy the impressive architecture in a spectacular setting, along with a new relaxing and extravagant spa. While the exterior of the original Dolder Grand has been restored to look as it did in the first years of the twentieth century, the new rooms, which are a consolidation of smaller ones that reduce the key count by more than half, reflect the luxury and amenities of affluent guests.

The guestrooms in London's Midland Grand Hotel were not especially small and had high ceilings, fireplaces, expansive windows, and ornate details, but, as with most hotels built in the late nineteenth century, they lacked private bathrooms (there were only eight bathrooms for its 300 rooms!). Restoration of the hotel, which opened as the St. Pancras Renaissance Hotel in 2011, included guestrooms with their historic features, but necessitated the elimination of more than half of them to accommodate private bathrooms, which are large and well appointed, appealing to travelers in the twenty-first century.

Today's global economy includes many countries that have been outside the international exchange of business and culture for many years. For nearly four decades China was cut off from other nations. In 1929, when Shanghai was divided into four concessions by the British, French, Americans, and Japanese, Victor Sassoon, a British businessman, built Sassoon House on a prime location on the Bund overlooking the Huangpu River. Designed by Palmer and Turner Architects, who incorporated both European and Chinese styles and motifs, it originally housed the Cathay Hotel, the most celebrated hotel in Shanghai. The Cathay drew an international clientele and reflected the cosmopolitan character of the city at that time, when it was the cultural and commercial center of the Far East. When the People's Republic of China came to power in 1949, the hotel was used as offices, in 1956 becoming the Peace Hotel. In 2007 it was restored to its former splendor as the Fairmont Peace Hotel and is once again a part of the international life of Shanghai, though without foreign occupation in a city where China is now dominant.

If a much-loved hotel in good condition suffers unexpected damage from a fire or other disaster, people are anxious for its restoration as soon as possible. The Taj Mahal Hotel, which opened in 1903, is one of the great hotels constructed in a British colony. It was financed by Jamsedji Tata, a wealthy Bombay industrialist, as a place where Indians of all castes and Europeans could socialize at a time when most hotels and restaurants were segregated. Today, Mumbai is at the center of India's global economy and The Taj plays host to Indian elites and others from all over the world, continuing the vision of its founder. On November 26, 2008, The Taj Mahal Hotel was involved in a series of attacks in central Mumbai by armed militants who held the hotel under siege for over 60 hours. Hostages were taken and at least 167 were killed. There was extensive building damage, especially to the palace wing, where fires raged. As testament to the spirit and resilience of the hotel, which stands as a symbol of the city and of

(continued p. 260)

─── Case Study ───────────────────────────

The Liberty Hotel, Boston, Massachusetts
Architect: Cambridge Seven Associates
Interior Designer: Champalimaud Design

The south slope of Beacon Hill has always been one of Boston's most desirable residential locations. But in the nineteenth century the north slope became home to some of the city's poorest immigrants, and it is at its foot that the Charles Street Jail was constructed in 1851, in accord with the Auburn Plan, which allowed for the segregation of inmates according to sex and severity of committed offence. The original building plan was cruciform, with four wings extending from a central atrium of dramatic height. With 30 large arched windows allowing maximum light and ventilation, it was a model of enlightened prison reform.

However, in 1973, after a rebellion by inmates, the Charles Street Jail was deemed by the courts to be unfit for occupation because of overcrowding, which violated the constitutional rights of the prisoners. The final remaining prisoners were shifted to Suffolk County Jail in 1991, and Massachusetts General Hospital, which borders the site to the north, acquired the property. Their request for proposals required that historic elements of the building, which was listed in the National Register of Historic Places, be retained.

Liberty Hotel

Charles Street Jail, 1848

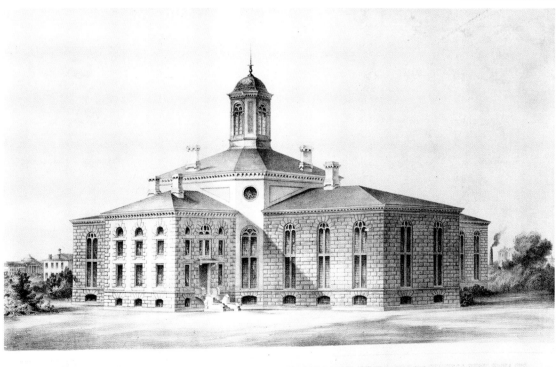

Charles Street Jail, cell

Liberty Hotel, lobby

Liberty Hotel, lobby

Liberty Hotel, guestroom

Today all of Beacon Hill is an expensive neighborhood and its proximity to Boston Common, Faneuil Hall, the financial district, the State House, and other downtown locations make it especially desirable. The jail was now sitting on a prime piece of Boston real estate. High brick security walls with barbed wire and a guards' gate had isolated the building from the neighborhood, but once these were demolished the former jail building could become an accessible part of the city.

In 2001, developer Richard Friedman initiated a project that would reuse the jail as part of a new luxury hotel. He was able to take advantage of $15 million in tax credits from the city of Boston, with approval from the Massachusetts Historical Commission. The architectural firm Cambridge Seven Associates, working closely with perseveration architect Pamela Hawkes and various public conservation agencies, was retained to balance the needs of a clientele very different from the prison's inmates with the historic 1851 building. After five years of extensive restoration and new construction, and at a cost of $150 million, the Liberty Hotel opened in 2007.

Soaring to a height of 90 ft (27 m), the octagonal atrium of the jail is a most spectacular space from which four wings radiate and which is surrounded by three levels of metal catwalks that once accessed the cells. These have been modified as balconies to reach meeting rooms, a ballroom, a restaurant, a bar, and a few new guestrooms. The atrium has been adapted to make the hotel lobby.

Select portions of the original jail were restored to give visitors an idea of what the building looked like. However, while it contains an important part of Boston's history, the Liberty Hotel is not a museum.

The furnishings in the old jail are mostly contemporary in style, with many making reference to the past. The reception desk is decorated with stencils that recall nineteenth-century lace embroidery; carpets are woven in an old New England style, with traditional patterns that are transformed in scale; a new wrought-iron chandelier and vintage lighting fixtures have been selected; and historical scenes are depicted in a ceramic art installation between the escalators leading up to the lobby.

The hotel plays with the jailhouse theme by locating its bar, Alibi, in the former drunk tank, naming its restaurant "Clink," where staff wear uniforms with prison numbers 1851 and 2007 (important Liberty Hotel dates), exhibiting fictional mug shots on corridor walls, and replacing the "Do not disturb" sign with "Solitary." A former exercise yard has become a courtyard garden for outside dining. Guests today can work out in the health and fitness center located in the new tower.

While the Charles Street Jail had 8 x 10 ft (2.4 x 3 m) cells for 220 inmates, the Liberty Hotel has significantly larger accommodations for just 18 guests in the historic structure. Abutting the north wing, an additional 280 luxuriously appointed guestrooms are located in a new 16-story tower, which offers many rooms commanding views of the Charles River and the city. The brick tower is modern in design and stands in contrast to the mid-nineteenth-century Quincy granite jail.

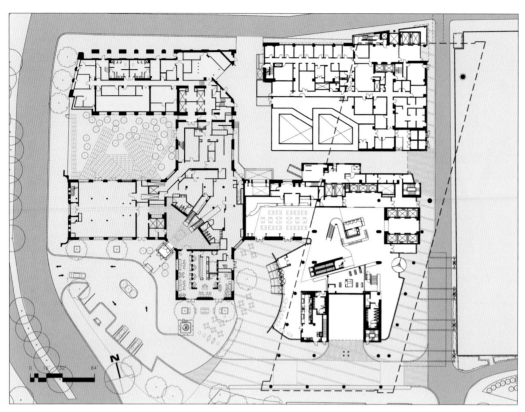

Liberty Hotel, ground floor plan

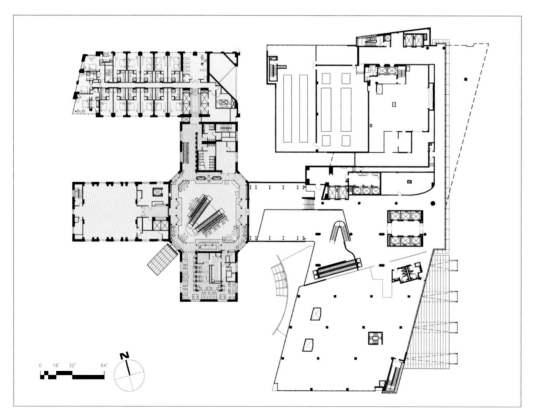

Liberty Hotel, second floor (lobby) plan

─── **Case Study** ───

Dolder Grand Hotel, Zurich, Switzerland
Architect: Foster + Partners
Interior Designer: United Designers Ltd

In 1899, the 220-room Dolder Grand Hotel and Curhaus (health spa), designed by Basel architect Jacques Gros, opened in a country setting on the Adlisberg hill, close to central Zurich. Especially popular with local residents, the Dolder Grand operated as a seasonal hotel until 1924, when it opened year-round. Over the decades there were many modifications, including the 1964 addition of a modern wing with 60 rooms, robbing the hotel of its original symmetrical design. Unable to secure needed investment, the Dolder Grand closed its doors in 1990. New owners, coming up with 80 million, commissioned Foster + Partners architects to produce a master plan.

All additions to the 1899 building were removed and the historically protected exterior of the main building, along with several public rooms, was restored. Excavation allowed for two basement levels that provide back-of-house services and an extension under the main entry driveway, which, because of the site's steep slope, offers great views for a new restaurant and function rooms. Public spaces on the main level were reorganized to work with repositioning the main entry from the north side,

where it was moved in a 1924 renovation to make room for a new restaurant, to its original south-side location, where guests can take advantage of spectacular views of Zurich, the lake, and the Alps beyond. Foster marks the new restored entry location with an immense deep-red canopy.

Foster + Partners designed two symmetrical steel-framed sinuous wings in a soft silver color to frame and highlight the old building, now restored to its original ochre and red color, with its fanciful black roof. Generous new guestrooms, all with balconies, bring the total number to 173, fewer than the number in 1899 because the original spartan rooms in the old building were consolidated to meet the needs of today's affluent guests. The all-glass triple-glazed façade of the new addition is shaded by automatically operating awnings and stencil-cut aluminum screens in a tree pattern, which link it to the surrounding woods. With 70 geothermal wells sunk nearly 500 ft below ground, Foster's 230,000 sq ft (21,368 sq m) addition, which doubles the size of the hotel, uses less than half as much energy as the original.

Dolder Grand Hotel

Also part of Foster's additions are a business center, event space, conference rooms, a ballroom, and a new 43,000 sq ft (3,950 sq m) spa with Japanese therapies, which brings the Dolder Grand back to its origin as a urban health resort. There are only 240 parking spaces, discouraging private automobiles. Guests are encouraged to make use of public transportation, including the Dolderbahn rack railway, whose upper terminus is near the hotel and which connects to the Zurich tram system. The hotel also operates a shuttle bus to downtown Zurich. Opening in 2008, after three years of construction, the Dolder Grand is once again a place where city residents can come for rest and relaxation, and it also meets the high standards of wealthy international travelers.

Dolder Grand Hotel, golf course

Dolder Grand Hotel, 1899

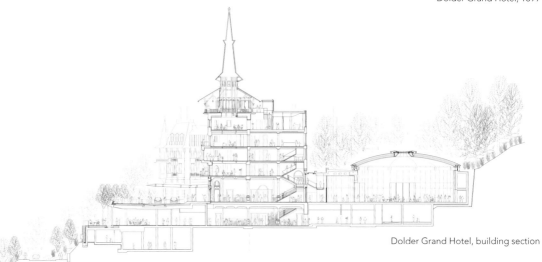

Dolder Grand Hotel, building section

258

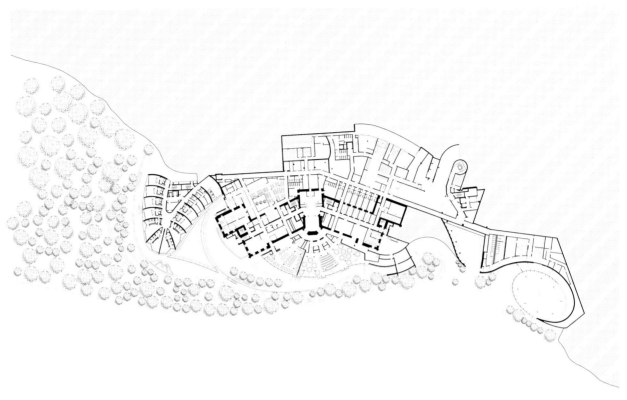

Dolder Hotel, Zurich - Lower Ground Floor

Dolder Grand Hotel, lower ground floor plan

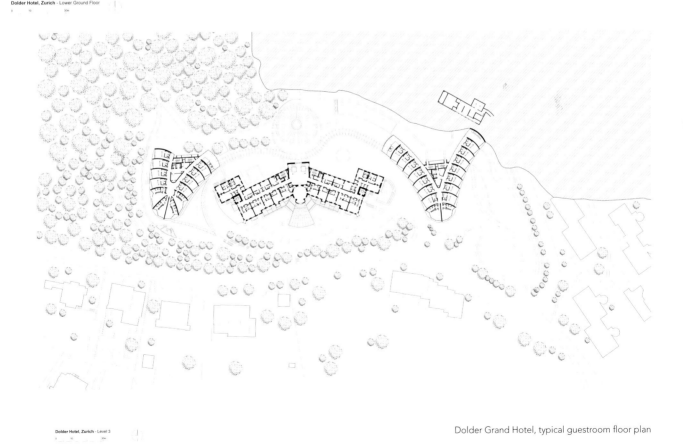

Dolder Hotel, Zurich - Level 3

Dolder Grand Hotel, typical guestroom floor plan

Fairmont Peace Hotel, Shanghai, China
The historic Cathay Hotel has been returned to its former glory. Managed by Fairmont Hotels and Resorts and designed by Hirsch Bedner Associates, the hotel's 270 guestrooms, six restaurants and Jazz Bar, once popular with the expatriate community, have been skillfully restored and once again made part of the international life of Shanghai. The Presidential Suite occupies the tenth-floor penthouse where the hotel's flamboyant creator and former owner, Victor Sassoon, once lived.

the nation, parts of the hotel were again operational in less than a month after the attack. And in August 2010, after an extensive $40 million restoration and renovation by a team of Indian and foreign design and restoration professionals, The Taj Mahal Hotel was brought back to its former glory, with expanded services and as a showcase for its extraordinary collection of Indian artifacts.

Landmark hotels are at a premium and are usually very profitable for owners, who are able to capitalize not only on the valuable historic architecture but also on a name that resonates strongly within the community. Photographs of the hotel in its heyday and a roster of famous people who once were guests can be incorporated into promotional brochures and public relations literature. They can also be displayed in the hotel to give present-day guests the feeling that they are reliving history by seeing themselves in the same spaces as existed in the past. San Diego's Hotel del Coronado has hosted 16 U.S. presidents, Prince Edward and Wallis Simpson, Thomas Edison, Babe Ruth, Charles Lindbergh, and a long list of Hollywood

stars including Rudolph Valentino, Charlie Chaplin, Esther Williams, Humphrey Bogart, Frank Sinatra, Ronald Reagan, Brad Pitt, and Madonna. The hotel has also been featured in several films, such as *Some Like It Hot*. This connection plays an important role in marketing the hotel, including publication of a book that the hotel sells. Architects Hornberger + Worstell undertook a 500,000 sq ft (15,200 sq m) renovation of the largest wood-framed structure in the United States. The project included seismic upgrades of the historic smoke stack and of the main historic building, building code upgrades throughout, the addition of double-loaded corridors to reach guestrooms, and the addition of HVAC (heating, ventilation, and air-conditioning) to guestrooms. The project also included remodeling of the poolside guestroom buildings, the 389 guestrooms in the main historic building, the International Banquet Room, and the Ocean Terrace Restaurant and kitchen.

London's Savoy Hotel opened in 1889 as Britain's first luxury hotel. Managed by César Ritz and with Auguste Escoffier, who

Taj Mahal Palace, Mumbai, India
In the aftermath of the 2008 terrorist attacks on Mumbai that left the landmark hotel badly damaged, a $40 million renovation was undertaken and the hotel restored to its historic palatial splendor. Enhanced security systems employing real-time intrusion-detection and threat-assessment technology are now in place to guard against such events in the future.

developed modern French cuisine, as chef, it was an immediate success, attracting a high-profile clientele. After years of decline, the hotel opened again in 2010 after a major restoration. The renovation sought to continue its commitment to the latest technologies, albeit in a discreet manner so as not to distract from its well-appointed new interiors. The interiors, by Pierre Yves Rochon, are in two styles that reflect The Savoy's high days of glamour. Edwardian rooms facing the Thames have suites named after well-known guests, including Winston Churchill, Maria Callas, Claude Monet, Charlie Chaplin, and Katharine Hepburn. Art Deco rooms on the Strand have suites named after Marlene Dietrich, Frank Sinatra, Richard Harris, and Noël Coward. The Savoy hopes to attract the same type of wealthy patron as it did in its early years.

One aspect of luxury hotels constructed prior to World War II is that they were built to last. Materials were substantial and details often integral to the structure of the building itself. The cost of

Hotel del Coronado, San Diego, California
Architects Hornberger + Worstell were engaged to produce a master plan that defined the hotel's future growth. The architects undertook a two-phase restoration project that included seismically upgrading the overall structure of the hotel's grand Victorian building.

The Savoy, London, United Kingdom
It has been described as "the most ambitious hotel restoration project ever undertaken in London." The hotel has been virtually rebuilt as architects ReardonSmith worked closely with the structural engineer and contractors to bring the building back to its original framework. The magnificent dome that now floods the Thames Lounge with natural light had to be uncovered and restored, and a number of changes were needed to accommodate the brand requirements of Fairmont Hotels and Resorts.

removing this work was prohibitively expensive, and renovations to these hotels in the mid-twentieth century tended to conceal this elaborate decorative aspect. For example, in an era that valued neither historic architecture nor high ceilings, designs often included dropped ceilings to permit the easy installation of mechanical systems, totally concealing the interior detail. Columns, moldings, and other elements were often encased in easily maintained materials. In peeling back these later renovations, architects can discover missing original details.

However, in many instances, such treasures are gone or damaged beyond repair. In the last twenty years many manufacturers have introduced into the general market reproductions of many historic building elements, fittings, and fixtures that have been made according to original specifications or in newer materials. This is especially important for lighting. It was not until the twentieth century that electrical lighting was commonplace. Candles gave way to gas lighting in the nineteenth century, but obviously no one now would consider lighting a hotel, even an impressive historic one, by either of these means. While electrical lighting continues to be used today, new lamps provide increased illumination and are more efficient that those of even a decade ago. There are manufacturers who make lighting fixtures that look antique but are illuminated by the latest advances. The construction industry, too, has become more familiar with working on historic structures and there are now, in almost every community, those who specialize in this field.

While it takes longer for a hotel with a name long synonymous with quality to lose its reputation, it can happen. A lax attitude toward new demands and to the quality of interiors is seriously detrimental to the financial operation of the hotel. Many nineteenth- and early twentieth-century luxury hotels were built primarily to serve the wealthy leisured class who sought to "get away from it all." Today, business is the main reason that people travel, and they have different requirements and are often able to pay a premium for quality accommodations and service. Hotels in the United States have catered to this class of traveler for some time, and now hotels everywhere are making this adjustment. New wireless technologies are able to satisfy the many needs of business travelers without making hotels over to a business-only ambience. In addition, the leisure traveler today wants to be not "away from it all" but connected, via the internet, to family, friends, hometown news, personal finances, etc. Hotels today are more and more able to accommodate both classes of guests.

Many existing buildings, even some that were originally hotels, have serious drawbacks in meeting the needs of present-day hotels. In the case of historic buildings it makes good sense to build a sound working relationship with government authorities in charge of landmark issues. Meeting the requirements of landmark authorities involves much negotiation and many compromises. Their mission is to protect the historic integrity of the building, and they can often help to secure waivers from the building department that might allow for valet parking, a curb cut for a loading dock, or other such need.

Building codes and legislation affect all renovation work. It is a challenge in a restoration to incorporate new code requirements so that they do not distract from the interior design. Life-safety codes and codes for the disabled are of foremost importance. In the United States, the Hotel and Motel Fire Safety Act of 1990 prohibits federal employees from staying in hotels which lack sprinklers and smoke detectors. For hotels with federal employees as frequent guests, this was a strong incentive to install such devices. Special provisions for the disabled have extended well beyond providing accessibility for people who use wheelchairs. The Americans with Disabilities Act of 1990 broadens the definition to include individuals with such disabilities as sight and hearing impairments, arthritis, heart conditions, emphysema, amputated limbs, and AIDS. Wide ranges of modifications are necessary to meet their requirements. While most codes only come into effect when new or renovation work is undertaken, some require that buildings comply by a certain date.

For buildings in earthquake zones, seismic upgrades are a major factor in renovation work. Many hotels on the West Coast of the United States are required to provide seismic upgrades for their buildings, including historic structures, such as the Hotel del Coronado in San Diego and The Nines in Portland, Oregon. While this is costly and time-consuming, it can be done without compromising the integrity of historic features.

Reflagging

Reflagging an existing hotel typically refers to the changing of a hotel brand to adapt to current market conditions. Rebranding can occur between two brands within the same hotel company, as with the Westin Fort Lauderdale Beach Resort and Spa, which was changed from another Starwood Hotels and Resort brand, the Sheraton Yankee Trader; or changing the franchise to a different company's brand, as with the New Orleans Roosevelt, a Hilton Hotels Waldorf=Astoria, which was rebranded from a Fairmont property following Hurricane Katrina.

In order to compete with the new upscale properties sprouting up along Fort Lauderdale Beach Boulevard, new owners and Starwood Hotels and Resorts decided to transform the underperforming though historically popular beachfront destination, Sheraton Yankee Trader.

Westin Beach Resort and Spa, Fort Lauderdale, Florida
Mathes Brierre Architects with ForrestPerkins transformed the former Sheraton Yankee Trader to meet the strict Westin brand standards for guestrooms, public spaces, and back-of-house functions. Guestroom windows were enlarged to broad full-height sliding-glass doors that open to painted steel balconette railings, giving guests the impression of standing at a private balcony overlooking the sea.

The Roosevelt New Orleans, New Orleans, Louisiana (above and facing)
After horrific conditions caused the New Orleans Fairmont to close its doors following Hurricane Katrina, developers undertook a massive renovation project and rescued this landmark hotel, bringing it back to its historic luxurious glory as part of the Waldorf=Astoria Collection. The renovation included restoring the legendary Blue Room and the trademark Sazerac Bar, made famous by the official Louisiana state cocktail.

Mathes Brierre Architects, with interior designers ForrestPerkins, were charged with redefining the twin-tower property to meet Starwood's more deluxe brand-standards for a Westin hotel, and to expand its conferencing facilities by adding two 10,000 sq ft (3,040 sq m) ballrooms and an expansive third-level outdoor "entertainment" terrace overlooking the Atlantic shoreline. The addition of a Westin Heavenly Spa was a brand-standard requirement of Starwood in the reflagging of the resort hotel.

For much of the early twentieth century, the original Roosevelt Hotel in New Orleans served as the social and political epicenter of the city. In the 1930s a twelfth-floor suite of this magnificent grand dame was the city headquarters for the legendary Louisiana governor Huey P. Long. After new owners acquired the Fairmont flag in 1965, many locals nostalgically continued to call the famed hotel "the Roosevelt," even though its official name was the New Orleans Fairmont Hotel. The dramatic events and conditions following Hurricane Katrina in August of 2005 caused severe damage to the infrastructure and resulted in contamination of every floor of the hotel. The property was in a shambles. With superb foresight that New Orleans would soon recover from the immense devastation, Sam Friedman of Dimension Development purchased the building in 2007 and courageously undertook a $170 million renovation. Two years later, it opening its doors, reflagged as The Roosevelt New Orleans, a Waldorf=Astoria hotel. The reopening of The Roosevelt

COMMON STREET

BARONNE STREET

UNIVERSITY PLACE

CANAL STREET SIDE
LEVEL 1

ROOSEVELT HOTEL, NEW ORLEANS LOUISIANA

0 5' 10' 20' 30' 40' 50'

Key
1 Entry Foyer
2 Lobby
3 Front Desk
4 Teddy's Cafe
5 Blue Room
6 Sazerac Restaurant
7 Sazerac Bar

8 Domenica Restaurant
9 Salumi Bar
10 Private Dining
11 Spa
12 Fitness
13 Retail
14 Concierge

15 Mechanical
16 Luggage
17 Service Alley
18 Loading Dock
19 Kitchen
20 Prep Kitchen
21 Human Resource

InterContinental Paris Avenue Marceau, Paris, France
The Crowne Plaza Paris Champs Elysées was reflagged following a major interior renovation. Designed by Bruno Borrione, part of Philippe Starck's team, the hotel is a mix of French classical and urban contemporary design, combining classically inspired features such as Venetian Renaissance frescos with modern furniture and décor.

became an inspiration for New Orleans's continued economic and physical recovery as the hotel has regained its prominence among the city's finest hospitality destinations.

Reflagging can also take the form of converting an independently operated hotel to a well-known hotel brand, or vice versa. For example, Le Royal Monceau, near the Champs-Elysées in Paris, was operated independently from its opening in 1928 and enjoyed a rich history of catering to artists and celebrities. Deciding that it had long ago lost its appeal to its original market base, the new owners chose to upgrade the hotel's reputation with the well-known elegance and luxurious renown of Raffles Hotels and Resorts. By hiring Philippe

Starck, designer extraordinaire, to redesign the hotel, the owners have reinvented the hotel for a new generation.

The motivation to reflag a hotel can be based on a number of reasons:

- A developer may decide to purchase a property and reflag it to a particular franchise company with which he or she has a strong relationship, based on multiple successful ventures.
- Poor performance and lack of profit is often the cause of seeking a new brand that can bring better fees, concessions, and returns.

London NYC, New York, New York

Frank Williams and Associates designed New York City's first all-suite hotel in 1985, which at that time was the tallest hotel in the city. Originally branded the RIHGA Royal by Royal International Hotel Group Associates of Osaka, the 514-suite hotel was reflagged the London NYC after a major interior renovation by London-based designer David Collins. The new name is meant to suggest an amalgam of both its namesake cities, worldly sophisticated, and with an incomparable cosmopolitan energy.

- A shift in market conditions, where a location becomes saturated with a particular segment, can prompt the need to differentiate with a fresh new brand.
- Desire on the part of the hotel company to establish its brand in a particular location may lead it to offer significant incentives to the current owner.
- Seeing the opportunity to attract an untapped market segment for a particular location may prompt the developer to find a new flag.

Branding up by converting a property from a lower price tier to an upper price tier is far more common than the reverse. Branding up can increase business because of the added services and amenities, which will appeal to a higher room-rate clientele. The 55-room Crowne Plaza Paris Champs-Elysées was reflagged the InterContinental Paris Avenue Marceau following a major interior renovation. The design, by Bruno Borrione, combined classical and modern design, each exuding a richness befitting the Comte de Breteuil, whose Paris residence is one of the three heritage buildings from different periods that share a central courtyard and make up the hotel. Public spaces and guestrooms have been refitted with luxury items that would be familiar to their affluent clientele. By upgrading the hotel to the InterContinental brand, the owners sought to associate it with the InterContinental Paris, which has always been one of Europe's great hotels.

The high cost of renovating a property to meet new and upgraded brand standards is a significant consideration when deciding to rebrand a property and requires due diligence on the part of the owners to avoid unnecessary and unexpected costs. Such costs might include: stiff termination and liquidated damages fees from the former franchisor; fees for failing to rebrand in a timely manner from the new hotel company; loss of revenue during the transition during a period of time with no affiliation; and the cost of re-identifying all logo items, including directional signs, highway signs, hotel signage, folios, stationery, and toiletries.

Additions

Small-scale additions allow hotels to meet changing demands and increase profits. The need for supplementary guestrooms, a conference facility, fitness center, or countless other items can be met by additional construction. The addition must complement the hotel's layout and organization—new public areas connected to the lobby, guestroom floors located close to existing elevators, or service areas adjoining the current back-of-house on lower floors. On urban sites, where there is the impetus to add extra floors on top of a building, one must consider the carrying loads of the existing structure, plus the capability of elevators to be extended and their adequacy to serve more guests. The original late nineteenth-century Victorian warehouse that became Terence Conran's Boundary Hotel had space for just 12 guestrooms. In order to accommodate five duplex suites, each of which is created by a different designer in their own individual style, the original mansard roof of the warehouse was

The Boundary Hotel, London, United Kingdom
The small 17-room Boundary Hotel, with restaurants, a café, bakery, and food hall, integrates itself into a neighborhood of artists and gallery patrons, who are familiar with modern design and can appreciate Terence Conran's latest endeavor. The original mansard roof of the warehouse was demolished and replaced by a two-story addition incorporating five new duplex suites.

demolished. It was replaced by a new two-story structure, faced with louvers concealing private terraces, which sits in marked contrast atop the original red-brick building, reflecting a new use for the former warehouse and the area's recent transformation. On the new roof there is a grill restaurant, set in a garden with an open fireplace and offering 360-degree views of London.

An addition can also be to an adjoining site. The combining of two buildings can give a totally new identity to an existing hotel. In 2003, the London Carriage Works, built in 1860 in the style of a Venetian palazzo, became the very successful Hope Street Hotel in Liverpool. In 2007, the owners acquired an adjacent 1960s office building owned by Merseyside Police and developed it to add 41 new guestrooms, three duplex suites, conference rooms, and a new reception area. With a modest budget of £4.5 million and a concern for the environment, it was decided to reuse the existing structure. Foundations on sandstone were sound, but the original

Hope Street Hotel, Liverpool, United Kingdom
Designed by Falconer Chester Hall, the Hope Street Hotel addition is a strong twenty-first-century presence on a very special street in Liverpool's Georgian quarter, with many listed Victorian buildings and framed by the Anglican and Roman Catholic cathedrals. The new addition calls attention to the Hope Street Hotel in a way that a more contextual addition would not.

Westin Beach Resort and Spa, Fort Lauderdale, Florida
In order to meet growing demand for meeting space in Fort Lauderdale Beach and as part of the rebranding of the hotel, a 50,000 sq ft (4,645 sq m) banquet facility was added to the south wing of the hotel, including two 10,000 sq ft (929 sq m) ballrooms and a large rooftop entertainment terrace, perfect for weddings and outdoor parties.

Table 12.3 Hotel addition checklist

Evaluate capacity of existing areas to accommodate added traffic:
- ❑ Entrance drives and parking
- ❑ Lobby and front desk
- ❑ Food and beverage outlets
- ❑ Guest circulation (including elevators)
- ❑ Service circulation (including elevators)
- ❑ Kitchen, laundry, loading dock, employees' facilities
- ❑ Recreation facilities (including health club)
- ❑ Internet service capacity

Obtain data on existing conditions:
- ❑ As-built drawings
- ❑ Site surveys including existing utilities and landscaping
- ❑ Legal and zoning restrictions
- ❑ Soil tests
- ❑ Detailed inspection of existing structural and mechanical conditions

Evaluate engineering systems to be used:
- ❑ Connections to existing structure and foundations
- ❑ Structural constraints of site
- ❑ Energy analysis, including existing mechanical and electrical systems and capacity of plant and utilities services

Reevaluate renovation needs of existing hotel in terms of matching higher standards of new addition:
- ❑ Architectural upgrading of the exterior (for example, entrance canopy, balconies, façade materials, windows, roof treatment, signage, paving, landscaping)
- ❑ Interior upgrading (furniture, furnishings, finishes, fixtures, equipment, lighting, graphics)
- ❑ Guestroom amenities
- ❑ Public space interiors
- ❑ Life-safety, security, communications, audiovisual, and computerized hotel management systems

building was four stories and in some parts only two. The five-story addition, topped by the three duplex suites and function rooms with views across the Mersey and to the Welsh mountains beyond, required that as little weight as possible be added to the existing structure. Existing reinforced concrete columns were strengthened for greater carrying capacity for the new steel extension. The mostly glass façade added less weight than a masonry one, like the 1860 building, would have done. (See Table 12.3.)

Adaptive Reuse

For a long time, buildings constructed for other purposes have been converted into hotels. Irish castles, English country manor houses, French chateaux, and Rajput palaces in Rajasthan, India, have all been adapted as hotels. These grand residential buildings lent themselves well to conversion. In fact, the intent was not to stray too far from the original. Part of the appeal of this transformation was that guests found themselves welcomed into the homes of aristocrats, gentry, maharajas, and other persons of high social rank whom they would not likely visit under other circumstances. This

helped to compensate for shared bathrooms, no air-conditioning and the lack of other amenities generally available at more typical hotels. Guests could take meals in the formal dining room, lounge in drawing rooms, read in the library, and stroll in the private grounds just as the original residents did. Guests could think of themselves as members of a privileged class enjoying themselves at home. Some hosts continued to live on premises and established these elaborate bed-and-breakfast accommodations in order to earn the monies needed to maintain their stately properties, while others ran them as businesses. Ownership often passed into the hands of other individuals bearing no relationship to the original owners, and most continue to be run as relatively small-scale operations.

Today, with a high demand for accommodation, especially in urban areas, and a dwindling number of new sites on which to build or existing hotels to be renovated, a wide range of building types are being converted into hotels. Many of these have little or no relation to lodging and some were not intended for human occupancy at all. They vary greatly in scale, category, and location.

The quality of materials and craftsmanship of landmark buildings cannot be equaled today and the grand scale of their public spaces lends itself to dramatic entrances and lobbies. Such features give these hotels a palatial presence. The lavish budgets that these hotel projects have available for renovations, especially for properties in prime locations, allow for sensitive restorations that please the city authorities who oversee landmark issues. Between 1911 and 1922, the headquarters for the Port Authority of London, which oversaw the city's ports, was constructed at 10 Trinity Square, on a 3 acre (1.2 hectare) site visible from the Thames. In 2006, Singapore-based KOP Properties acquired 10 Trinity Square with plans to adapt it into a 120-room luxury hotel, with 37 privately owned residences on the four floors above. From the exterior, this Grade II-listed building will remain as originally designed. During World War II the Port Authority headquarters was bombed, but damage was limited to the central rotunda. In 1976 a nine-story office tower was built in the court by Willis Insurance, who purchased the property from the Port Authority in 1971, when London's ports had fallen into steep decline. The new plans, by the architectural firm of Woods Bagot, call for the removal of all non-original elements, including the Willis tower, and extension of the building floor plate inward to focus on a new circular glazed atrium. The lower two floors will be capped by a suspended double-glazed skylight separating the hotel from the private apartments above. This bold intervention is called the "whirlpool" for the way the new roof canopy slopes down to the chamfered main entry-tower pavilion, and it adds two new glazed stories set back over the double mansard of the existing building. At ground level, the new construction will be barely visible. In addition to restoration of the exterior, several grand historic interior spaces of the old Port Authority will also be restored and used for new hotel functions.

Office buildings are frequently considered likely candidates for hotel conversion. The soft market for office space in many cities, compared with the tight market for hotels, makes such transformations especially attractive to developers. The most sought-after are buildings of historic value. Few office buildings of landmark status come on the market today. Most are 1950s and 1960s structures in need of overhauls, but

Kruisherenhotel–Maastricht, Maastricht, Netherlands

The Kruisheren monastery in central Maastricht, the oldest continuously occupied city in the Netherlands, was converted to a luxury design hotel. From the exterior, the buildings look untouched since the early sixteenth century. From the exterior, aside from the bold red-and-white painted shutters for the upper windows, the clue that marks the monastery's new use is the highly polished copper tunnel on a side of the church that is now the main public entrance. Inside the former church are the hotel reception area, conference rooms, library, shops, and a coffee bar. A restaurant is positioned on a constructed mezzanine in the nave, under soaring Gothic vaults with traces of original frescos, with clouds of light floating from fixtures that can change color. The hotel has 60 guestrooms, 50 in the cloister, seven in the gatekeeper's lodge and three in a small new addition.

not economically or functionally suitable to remain as office buildings. These structures often have footplates too small and ceiling heights too low to allow for renovation into office space that meets today's market demands. Yet, as hotels, these buildings sometimes can be suitable. They often have a high proportion of windows to floor area—ideal for guestroom layouts—and a ceiling height, relatively low for offices, which is entirely suitable for guestrooms. With cost savings over new construction, an obsolete office building can be the beginning of a new hotel. In 2000, Marriott expanded its Courtyard brand in Portland with a 13-story banal office building that had formerly belonged to Toronto National and had stood vacant for 17 years on a prime site in the financial district. Not only were the interiors demolished for a new use, but the façade, which had ribbon windows not suitable for a hotel building, was selectively demolished in order to install windows more appropriate for its new use. Also, the new façade design made the three additional floors match the floors below. Unlike landmark buildings, whose pedigree the hotel owners

10 Trinity Hotel, London, United Kingdom
Plans call for London's original Port Authority Headquarters to be transformed into a 120-key luxury hotel with 37 condominiums. The exterior of the building is protected under a Grade II listing by London's landmark authorities, but architect Woods Bagot's plans call for a major structural overhaul of the building interior, including the reintroduction of the original domed central rotunda.

wish to promote, the owners of hotels converted from nondescript post-war office buildings seek to conceal the use of the original building by gutting all the interior spaces in a total makeover. Such conversions have so far been limited to mid-level accommodation, unlike the five-star option that landmark buildings can offer.

Often inherent in many buildings not originally planned as hotels is the disparity between existing conditions and optimal or, in some cases, even minimal hotel standards. The guestroom is most critical. In prime urban areas, where demand for new hotels greatly exceeds sites available for new construction and few existing hotels are available for upscale renovations, many buildings which do not obviously lend themselves to hotel conversion are being considered. Many large department stores have left center-city locations for suburban malls, following their customers and wanting to take advantage of ample parking and easy deliveries. Optimally, department stores have expansive floor plans to display large qualities of goods, where views to the exterior are considered distractions to shoppers. In contrast, hotel rooms are best arranged on floors that have access to natural light and, if possible, views. The 14-story Meier and Frank flagship store in downtown Portland was built in the early twentieth century. In 1982, it was placed on the National Register of Historic

Places. After being taken over by Federated Department Stores in 2005, it was rebranded as Macy's, which occupied the lower five floors and basement. The upper floors were adapted into a hotel. A seven-story atrium was cut into the full-block building and two floors were added to create The Nines Hotel. The interior was effectively gutted in order to lay out 333 guestrooms and to provide spaces for hotel functions. A street-level welcome lobby brings guests to the seventh floor. Interior guestrooms face the 7,000 sq ft (650 sq m) lobby, with a ballroom below.

After decades of neglect and abandonment, many neighborhoods in successful cities are undergoing a renaissance, and hotels are playing a major role in this transformation. An influx of new people and money is transforming districts that had not previously been attractive to visitors, especially those from out of town. Today, some are new destinations for artists, tourists, and shoppers.

It is highly unusual to find two components of the same original building complex that are each adaptively converted to hotels, albeit ones that are not connected and not owned or operated together. The National Maritime Union, founded in 1937, commissioned New Orleans architect Albert Ledner to design a headquarters for them on Seventh Avenue and 12th Street in Greenwich Village, and a larger

Courtyard by Marriott, Portland, Oregon
After sitting vacant for 17 years, the Toronto National Building was transformed into a 256-room hotel, the first Marriott property to receive LEED Gold certification. It is a primary example of how a midscale hotel can achieve a high level of environmental performance; the entire façade was replaced, three stories were added to the building, and an adjacent building was rebuilt to become part of the hotel.

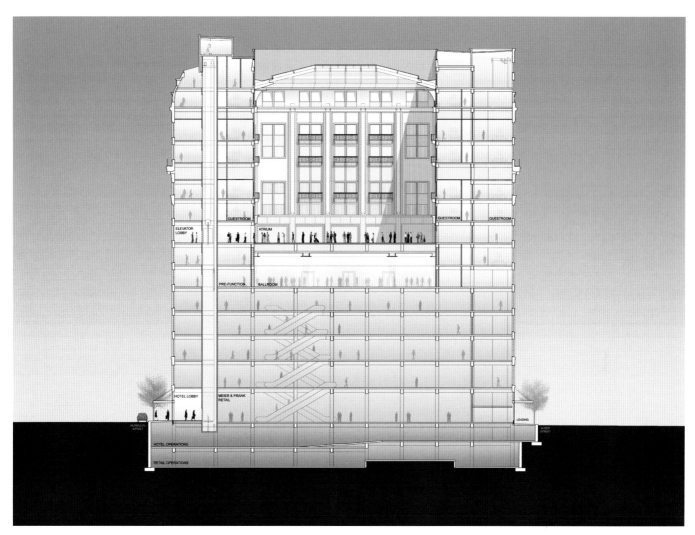

The Nines, Portland, Oregon

Many factors influenced ForrestPerkins and SERA Architects in converting the former department store to a luxury hotel, including historical considerations and related tax credits through the National Park Service; environmental approaches required for LEED certification; brand standards and expectations from Starwood Hotels and Resorts; and operational efficiency necessary to Sage Hospitality.

The Maritime Hotel and Dream Downtown Hotel, New York
The corner of 17th Street and Ninth Avenue has two adjacent yet independent hotels, once part of the same building complex that housed the annex to the National Maritime Union. The Maritime Hotel underwent a minimally invasive transformation, reusing most of the existing configurations for guestrooms and public spaces. The Dream Downtown hotel underwent a more extreme makeover involving an entirely new façade on 16th Street, a re-clad façade on 17th Street, and all-new guestrooms and public spaces.

annex, that would include dormitory rooms and other facilities for visiting seamen, on Ninth Avenue between 16th and 17th Streets in the Chelsea district of New York. The Joseph Curran Annex was completed in 1966 and faced the Robert Fulton Houses, a large public housing project that was completed in 1965. With its 5 ft (1.5 m) round porthole windows and sloping façade on 17th Street, the Annex was truly a unique building. By 2002, the neighborhood just south of the Annex, known as the Meatpacking District for its slaughterhouses and packaging plants, along with drug dealing and prostitution, had been transformed into an area with high-end boutiques, art galleries, expensive restaurants, and an active nightclub scene. In 2003, the Ninth Avenue-facing wing of the Curran Annex was converted to The Maritime Hotel, playing a part in this new downtown scene. The quirky design of the building appealed to the new owners, who wanted a hotel "not like New York's other hotels." Rather than combine the dormitory rooms to make larger ones more in keeping with the standards of hotel guests, small sailors' quarters were made over in a style reminiscent of the tight quarters one finds on luxury ocean liners. The remaining block-through part of the Annex, which spanned from 16th Street to 17th Street, continued to be operated by Covenant House, a substance-abuse support facility, until 2011, when it too was converted to a fashionable hotel. The Dream Downtown, designed by Handel Architects, accentuated the syncopated rhythm of the 17th Street façade with a seemingly random addition of porthole windows, and encased the façade with a gleaming stainless steel cladding. (See Table 12.4.)

Table 12.4 Adaptive reuse: examples of structures converted to hotels

Type of structure converted	Hotel	Type of structure converted	Hotel
Commercial		Townhouse	The Hempel, London
Office building	Ames Hotel, Boston		Blakes, London
	10 Trinity Square, London		Hotel Eden, Rome
	Marriott Courtyard, Portland, Oregon	Elderly home	The Standard, Los Angeles
	Marriott Courtyard, Washington, DC	Company housing	American Club, Kohler, Wisconsin
	St. Martins Lane, London	Dormitory	L'Hotel, Paris
	Shoreham II, New York	Farmhouse	Inn at Chester, Chester, Connecticut
	W New York–Union Square, New York	Harem	Shepheard's Hotel, Cairo, Egypt
	Loews Philadelphia Hotel (PSFS Building), Philadelphia	Hunting lodge	Oberoi Mena House, Giza, Egypt
	Hotel Burnham, Chicago		Ajit Bhavan, Jodhpur, India
	Hotel Le Germain, Montreal	Palace	Kempinski Hotel Taschenbergpalais, Dresden, Germany
	Hyatt Regency, Buffalo, New York		Marriott Cairo, Egypt
	Landmark Hotel, San Antonio, Texas		Palace do Bussaco, Portugal
	Capital Hotel, Little Rock, Arkansas		Villa d'Este, Lake Como, Italy
Shipping headquarters	Hotel New York, Rotterdam, The Netherlands		Udaipur Lake Palace, Rajasthan, India
Bank	JW Marriott, Chicago		Villa Vista Hermosa, Mexico (Cortez's palace)
	ME Hotel, London	Governor's palace	Hostal Nicolas de Ovando, Santo Domingo, Dominican Republic
	Le Meridien Hotel, Boston		
Department store	The Nines, Portland, Oregon	Private home	New York Palace, New York City
	Chateau Sonesta Hotel, New Orleans		Tarrytown House Conference Center, Tarrytown, New York
	Point Hotel, Edinburgh, Scotland		
	Canal Street Marriott, New Orleans		Schlosshotel Vier Jahreszeiten, Berlin
	Gran Hotel Cuidad de Mexico City, Mexico City		Seven One Seven, Amsterdam
	Planters Inn, Charleston, South Carolina		Hotel Qufu, China (Confucius' home)
Parking garage	Brookshire Hotel, Baltimore, Maryland		Hotel d'Angleterre, Remmen, Copenhagen, Denmark
			Holiday Inn Chateau Le Moyne, New Orleans, Louisiana
Manufacturing			
Printing company	Proximity Hotel and Print Works Bistro, Greensboro, North Carolina		Roxborough Hotel, Ottawa, Canada
			Queen Victoria Inn, Cape May, New Jersey
Automobile factory	Le Meridien Lingotto, Turin, Italy		Numerous bed and breakfast inns
Warehouse	The Mercer, New York City	Antebellum mansion	Monmouth, Natchez, Mississippi
	Adelphi Hotel, Melbourne	Maritime housing	Maritime Hotel, New York
Flour mill	Art'otel, Potsdam, Germany		Ace Hotel, Seattle
Fountain pen factory	Seidler Hotel Pelikan, Hanover, Germany	Masonic temple	Hilton St. Charles, New Orleans
Ship engine plant	Bla Hallen Hotel 11, The Netherlands		Renaissance Providence, Rhode Island
		Adobe house	Hotel Terrantai, San Pedro de Atacama, Chile
Public			
College	Ritz-Carlton, San Francisco	**Religious**	
Prison	Liberty Hotel, Boston	Church	Hilton International Budapest, Hungary
	Four Seasons Hotel, Istanbul, Turkey	Convent	Tomtom Suites, Istanbul
Waterhouse	The Waterhouse at South Bund, Shanghai		Milan Four Seasons, Milan, Italy
Customs house	Marriott Customs House, Boston		El Convento Hotel, San Juan, Puerto Rico
Pub	The Prince of Wales, Melbourne, Australia	Monastery	Pousada Santa Maria de Flor da Rosa, Crato, Portugal
City hall	Hotel de Ville, Binghamton, New York		Geneva-on-the-Lake, Geneva, New York
Fire station	Sheraton Greensboro, North Carolina	Priory	Bath Priory Hotel, Bath, England
	Hilton Hotel, Columbus, Georgia		
Lighthouse	East Brother Lighthouse Inn, Point Richmond, California	**Other**	
		Castle	Schloss Eckberg, Dresden, Germany
Railway terminal	Aloft, Dallas		Chateau de Creissels, Millau, France (built 801)
	Radisson Lackawanna Station, Scranton, Pennsylvania		Chateau de Meyrargues, Aix-en-Provence, France (built 970)
	Choo Choo Holiday Inn, Chattanooga, Tennessee		
	Hyatt Regency St. Louis, Missouri		Numerous castle hotels throughout Europe
Treasury building	Hotel InterContinental, Sydney, Australia	Water tower	Hotel im Wasserturm, Cologne, Germany
		Grain silos	Hilton Quaker Square, Akron, Ohio
Residential		Historic fortress	Mandawa Castle, Rajasthan, India
Apartment house	The Mondrian, Los Angeles		Namrana, Rajasthan, India
	Sheraton Rittenhouse, Philadelphia	Granary	Copenhagen Admiral Hotel, Copenhagen, Denmark
	Bleibtreu Hotel, Berlin	Pirate hideaway	Sam Lord's Castle, Barbados, West Indies
	Hotel Widder, Zurich, Switzerland	Ship	Queen Mary, Long Beach, California
	Hotel Lancaster, Paris	Stable	Das Triest, Vienna
	Regents Court, Sydney, Australia	Social club	Dylan Hotel, New York
	Stanford Court Hotel, San Francisco		
	Marriott Essex House, New York		
	Tremont Hotel, Baltimore, Maryland		
	Sheraton Winnipeg, Canada		

—— Case Study ——

The Waterhouse at South Bund, Shanghai, China

Architect: Neri and Hu Design and Research Office
Interior Designer: Neri and Hu Design and Research Office

Neri and Hu Design and Research Office designed a 19-room hotel adapted from a 1930s dockyard building. The hotel, named The Waterhouse at South Bund, opened in 2010 in the Shipiupu district, facing the Huangpu River, in Shanghai.

Respecting the industrial character of the area, the architects have retained the timeworn façade of the original building, onto which they placed a two-story rooftop addition clad with Cor-Ten steel, whose rusted appearance evokes old ships in the dockyard. However, overscaled minimal projecting dormers, and large cutouts at the rooftop bar that offer dramatic views of the river and Pudong, distinguish The Waterhouse at South Bund from its neighbors as the work of very sophisticated architects.

The entry is of rusted steel but in a markedly new design. Also on street level, two large portions of the original façade have been replaced with wide expanses of glass. They both offer views into the inner courtyard—one through the lounge and the other through the restaurant, where long communal dining tables draw one visually into the space. This play between inside and outside is carried on in varying ways throughout the hotel.

The inner courtyard, onto which most guestrooms face, is an abstraction of a traditional Chinese lane that has been extended vertically. The shuttered windows have inner mirror faces that heighten the fractured views guests experience throughout.

The Waterhouse at South Bund

The Waterhouse, lobby

The Waterhouse, guestroom

There has been no effort to restore this dockyard building as it was in the 1930s. Instead, the accumulated crust of eight decades remains. This is an approach that has been taken with other structurally robust old industrial and manufacturing buildings, in cities where changing economies have left many of them vacant, to adapt them into artists' studios, galleries, and museums.

The hotel interiors continue to highlight the accumulated layers of the building's past. Exposed wall surfaces are left raw, to be appreciated as one would a work of art. New materials, some of which have been recycled from demolished areas, are of muted hues that do not distract from the rough patina of the walls. A three-story space has been claimed for the lobby, with exposed structural steel reinforcement, and a contrasting clean white ribbon is formed by a bridge that crosses the space at an incline to connect unaligned guestroom corridors above. A rare appearance of strong color comes when the low sun reflects a luminous golden red-rust glow on the Cor-Ten steel, which can occasionally and unexpectedly be glimpsed from inside, in addition to from the roof.

With numerous narrow connecting stairs and several level changes, one can imagine the original hodge-podge of spaces. The architects work with this to create guestrooms that are highly individual, eccentric, yet decidedly modern. In one, a glass-enclosed tub commands the room as if part of an artist's installation. Sly insertions into the floor slab and walls of private rooms allow narrow glimpses that break down the boundary between private and public areas.

Visitors to The Waterhouse at South Bund are able to share the wonderfully excited feeling that the owner and architect found on first viewing an old building that would become their new project. Neri and Hu have used space, light, and an appreciation of the existing construction to craft a unique building of rare invention that should have strong appeal to travelers who understand and appreciate this aesthetic. It should also help to revitalize a district in a way that does not destroy its architectural heritage. (See Table 12.5.)

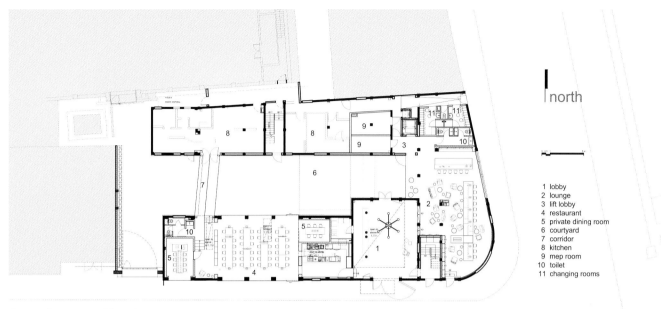

The Waterhouse, ground floor plan

north

1 lobby
2 lounge
3 lift lobby
4 restaurant
5 private dining room
6 courtyard
7 corridor
8 kitchen
9 mep room
10 toilet
11 changing rooms

Table 12.5 Ages of famous hotels

Hotels over 100 years old	Hotels over 75 years old
❑ Hotel Les Trois Rois, Basel, Switzerland	❑ The Ritz, London
❑ Cour St. Georges, Ghent, Belgium	❑ The Greenbrier, White Sulphur Springs, West Virginia
❑ Hotel Krone, Solothurn, Switzerland	❑ The Broadmoor, Colorado Springs, Colorado
❑ Hotel d'Angleterre, Copenhagen, Denmark	❑ The Copley Plaza Hotel, Boston
❑ Grand Hotel Sauerhof, Baden bei Wien, Germany	❑ The Plaza, New York
❑ Hotel de Crillon, Paris	❑ The Old Faithful Inn, Yosemite National Park, Wyoming
❑ The Continental, Paris	❑ The Fairmont, San Francisco
❑ Hotel des Trois Couronnes, Vevey, Switzerland	❑ Huntington House, Pasadena, California
❑ The Royal Crescent Hotel, Bath, England	❑ The Shelton Hotel, New York
❑ The Palace Hotel, San Francisco	❑ The Biltmore, Los Angeles
❑ The Strater Hotel, Durango, Colorado	❑ The Taj Mahal Hotel, Bombay, India
❑ Le Chateau Frontenac, Quebec City, Canada	❑ The Hermitage, Nashville, Tennessee
❑ Banff Springs, Alberta, Canada	❑ The Bellevue-Stratford, Philadelphia, Pennsylvania
❑ Chateau Lake Louise, Alberta, Canada	❑ The St. Regis, New York
❑ St. Louis Hotel, New Orleans, Louisiana	❑ The Seelbach, Louisville, Kentucky
❑ The Chelsea Hotel, New York	❑ The Mount Washington Hotel, Bretton Woods, New Hampshire
❑ The Cincinnatian, Cincinnati, Ohio	❑ The Sagamore, Lake George, New York
❑ Mohonk Mountain House, New Paltz, New York	❑ The Breakers, Palm Beach, Florida
❑ Grand Hotel, Point Clear, Alabama	❑ The Drake Hotel, Chicago
❑ Grand Hotel, Mackinac Island, Michigan	❑ The Chicago Hilton and Towers
❑ Hotel del Monte, Monterey, California	
❑ The Capital Hotel, Little Rock, Arkansas	
❑ The Jefferson Hotel, Richmond, Virginia	
❑ The Mission Inn, Riverside, California	
❑ The Brown Palace Hotel, Denver, Colorado	
❑ The Savoy, London	
❑ The Tovar Hotel, Grand Canyon	
❑ Hotel del Coronado, San Diego, California	
❑ Claridge's, London	
❑ The Connaught, London	
❑ The Willard, Washington, DC	
❑ The Ritz, Paris	
❑ The Oberoi Grand, Calcutta, India	

PART 2

Design Guide

Site and Master Planning

A hotel project becomes real once the site is selected. Up until that point, the developers and architects may have an idea of the hotel they plan to construct, but developing the exact physical concept and design cannot really begin until the property is known. Most hotels are developed on one of the following types of sites:

- Rural and undeveloped sites (usually for resort hotels or retreats)
- Suburban and provincial sites, often in small towns or along major roadways
- Urban sites in metropolitan business centers

Each type requires special and particular criteria, both for its selection and for the development of designs for the building and grounds.

Resort Sites

Modern means of transportation and longer vacation times, especially for Europeans, have made it possible for people to travel long distances for their holidays. In fact, getting as far away as possible can be a strong attraction. Exotic landscapes with pristine beaches and warm weather continue to prove popular with today's travelers, especially those suffering during the cold winter months in the northern hemisphere.

Resorts closer to home, especially those easily reachable by automobile, also are attractive. While they might not be as glamorous as the exotic resorts, they can offer their guests a rich variety of amenities in an environment which gives them an intimate experience with nature. A local attraction, such as a lake, trails for cross-country skiing, or even a top-notch restaurant, can entice non-resident visitors, especially on weekends. They can also be part of local support for a project at its planning stage.

For all resorts, selection of the site is of paramount importance. Because rural tracts of land often are large, in part to provide protection from neighboring development, a good deal of attention must go into planning the relationship among lodging, public spaces, recreational areas, and services. International and less developed areas present a special group of issues for the development team, including:

- *Transportation and accessibility*. Select a site within two hours of an international airport and readily accessible by road. Construction of new roads is expensive, in addition to the

Viceroy Miami Hotel, Miami, Florida
The hotel shares an immense 300 ft (91 m) long infinity-edge swimming pool and 80-person hot tub, on the 15th floor of the Icon Brickell mixed-use development project, with two condominium towers. Design was by Arquitectonica.

283

Terranea Resort, Rancho Palos Verdes, California
Located on the Palos Verdes peninsula and surrounded by the Pacific Ocean,
resort site design facilitates views down the Southern California coast, Catalina
Island, and the coastal mountains. The largest courtyard, the entry courtyard,
features a central cooling fountain under a canopy of date palms. With the entry
lobby and most of the public space near the top of the resort site and away from
the water's edge, the guestrooms form a gentle terrace down the site to the
Pacific Ocean.

difficulty in securing permission to pass through property not
owned by the hotel. In the more remote locations where local
roads might prove difficult for coaches, jeeps and sport utility
vehicles might be an alternative for shuttling guests from the
airport to the hotel. Road access also influences the ability to
bring in construction equipment and the delivery of supplies
once the hotel is operational.

- *Political climate.* Consider international attitudes toward the
destination. Nothing keeps guests away like the possibility
of violence. Even after major unrest has subsided and home
countries no longer place restrictions on their citizens traveling
to these spots—and even if the strife is limited to a narrow region
of a nation not affecting the resort area—the vast number of
alternatives available to tourists today make these countries
unlikely destinations. A wave of terrorist attacks in the Russian
ski resort areas of the North Caucasus Republic, near the highest
mountain in Europe, resulted in this burgeoning tourist region

being closed off to travelers indefinitely. Attacks by militants
included blowing up a tower supporting a ski gondola, which
plummeted to the ground with four passengers aboard.
- *Ownership.* Investigate local laws influencing real estate,
development, and employment. Many countries do not permit
foreign nationals to own property. Such legal restrictions can
make it difficult for hotel companies wishing to operate abroad.
Partnerships with local citizens may be necessary.
- *Community relations.* Establish good public relations with the
local community. Tourism is a major industry and hotels bring
in substantial amounts of hard currency. Often the hotel needs
to demonstrate to government officials the financial and social
benefits that the hotel will bring to the local population. The
developer may be required to improve some aspect of the local
community infrastructure, such as providing a sewage system or
constructing a new school.

Atlantis Dubai Resort Hotel, Dubai, United Arab Emirates
The Palm Monorail runs along the trunk of the Palm Jumeirah in Dubai,
connecting the Gateway station at the entry to the Palm to the Atlantis hotel at
the far end. The monorail will eventually be linked to the Dubai Metro and to the
Al Sufouh Tram, designed to be an integral part of the Dubai transport network.

In large resorts guest and visitor parking should be separated, with the guest spaces close to the building complex. In both cases, provide a landscaped and shaded walkway between the parking area and the hotel. In cases where visitors come to use a specific amenity, parking should be located near the special area and away from the guestroom reception lobby.

Most resort guests are first-time users who are there to enjoy and experience the environment. It is important that they be able to grasp the overall layout of the property in order to get around fairly easily. If possible, the main building, housing the primary reception area and other public spaces, should be prominently sited on or near the highest point of the site, visible to guests as they approach it. From here, guests can gain an overall orientation to the resort and staff can point out particular features. Special consideration should be given to views of the resort's main attractions, such as the beach, golf course, or ski lift, from the main lobby. While all the features of a site need not be evident at once, facilities should not be hidden or difficult to find.

Sites can be organized with such devices as a bell tower, fountains, sculptures, or flagpoles that stand out in the landscape as points of reference. The clues to a site's organization should be made through spatial patterns or on-site transportation systems rather than signage, which should serve only a secondary purpose. This is especially challenging on large sites with a wide range of facilities. The network of paths connecting various areas should be clear. A balance needs to be struck between the obvious, which sometimes can be boring, and variety, which may be confounding. The expert landscape designer and architect is able to offer interesting diversions while making the site understandable. The 114 acre (46 hectare) site of Atlantis Dubai stretches 1 mile (1.5 km) along the outermost arc of the Palm Resort Development and includes a complex of venues, including a vast aquatic park and three-story aquarium, 17 restaurants, luxury boutiques, nightclubs, 6,000 sq ft (5,600 sq m) of meeting and function space, and the iconic 1,539-key conjoined hotel towers, all connected by an intricate system of pathways and waterways.

Four Seasons Resort, Hualalai, Hawaii
Inspired by the architecture of traditional Hawaiian villages, the resort fulfills the concept of *kipuka*—a lushly landscaped paradise surrounded by molten lava flows. Guest suites were designed to blur the distinction between indoor and outdoor space, an elaborate system of sliding pocket doors and shutters providing the ability to completely open up many exterior walls.

Table 13.1 Recreational facilities space requirements

❑	Children's play area	1,000–3,000 sq ft (93–280 sq m); varies by age group, play equipment, etc.
❑	Swimming pool	40 x 82 ft (12 x 25 m); approximately five lanes
❑	Racquetball	20 x 40 ft (6 x 12 m); add 10 ft (3 m) at back wall
❑	Basketball	50 x 94 ft (15 x 28.7 m)
❑	Volleyball	30 x 60 ft (9 x 18 m); add 8 ft (2.4 m) around all sides
❑	Tennis	36 x 78 ft (11 x 23.8 m); add minimum of 12 ft (3.7 m) around all sides of court
❑	Soccer	225 x 360 ft (68.6 x 109.7 m); championship field
❑	Golf	160 to 180 acres (65 to 73 ha); 18 holes, including clubhouse, parking, and practice areas.

Confirm precise dimensions with local sports authority.

A major consideration in planning the landscape is maintenance. Lushly planted gardens give pleasure to all and, especially in tropical climates, offer an opportunity to exhibit local specimens that impress outsiders with their exotic character. However, manicured gardens are labor-intensive. In regions where labor costs are low, this is not a major factor and the designer can create impressive gardens, a wonderful way to embellish a special spot. Small gardens can have a strong visual presence without excessive labor and, for this reason, they often are part of most hotel landscape schemes. It is important that designers consider water conservation, especially in climates where it is a scarce resource. Recycling of wastewaters and retainage reservoirs to supply the watering requirements of the resort are possible ways to deal with this problem.

On large sites, a more practical approach is to allow nature to continue its course, or to enhance the natural experience through the introduction of a few select elements. Such areas should appear pristine and do not require excessive management. Unique attributes should be preserved and highlighted.

Both gardens and natural landscape encourage a contemplative mood. People often come to resorts in order to "get away from it all," at least for part of the time. All resorts should have some quiet outdoor places where one can be alone with nature. A simple bench with a tranquil view can be highly restorative to the human soul. Water, too, can have a calming and cooling effect. This is a major reason ocean- and lakefront properties are so popular. Long after a day of swimming, sailing, surfing, and other water sport is over, the calm that one experiences from watching the surf rush up the sand or the moonlight glisten on the water's surface is totally relaxing. Even small bodies of water can have a soothing effect. On sites lacking major water bodies, ponds can be carefully sited to create visual interest, as well as to collect surface and subsurface waters, drain swamps that breed mosquitoes, act as cooling devices for mechanical systems, or provide other useful functions.

Sporting activities are a major component of most resorts. Many recreational amenities require relatively large expanses of flat land. Table 13.1 indicates what may be considered space guidelines for different recreational features. In calculating actual space required, add as much as 30 percent for small groups of onlookers and circulation.

The natural landscape is an increasingly scarce and valued resource, helping to foster the green movement throughout the world. Today, many natural environments are protected, whether locally, nationally, or globally. It is important that resorts and even hotels on smaller parcels of land not disrupt the ecological balance. Many jurisdictions have strict legislation regulating construction and other activity on designated sites. Resorts, in particular, need to exceed the strict definition of the law. The lure of a resort comes from its natural setting, and its continued success is highly dependent upon a quality environment free from pollution. Increasingly, resort companies realize the benefits of taking leadership roles in protecting the environment by achieving LEED or BREEAM certification through the utilization of design and operational initiatives (see The Ecotourist Resort in Chapter 7).

Older travelers are a growing proportion of resort guests. With time available for extended stays, not limited to peak times, affluent

Four Seasons Resort, Bora Bora, Tahiti
Over-water bungalows, designed in the style of traditional island houses, are perhaps the most romantic and certainly the most intimate accommodations in the South Pacific. The bungalows are situated on stilts over a lagoon with relatively calm shallow water. Most have sundecks and platforms from which you can step directly into the lagoon waters for swimming or snorkeling or to contemplate the sunset. In locations susceptible to tropical storms the structures must be made strong enough to withstand storm surge.

retirees are a major source of revenue for resorts. The operator needs to meet their particular needs, including provisions for less intense activities like golf pitch, shuffleboard, pools that exclude children and fast swimmers, game rooms for playing cards, walking paths free of obstacles, and other amenities that do not demand a high level of exertion.

Where resorts are relatively remote from a community that offers an available labor supply, it may be necessary to provide housing, recreational amenities, and other services to attract staff. These employee facilities must be wholly separate from the guest areas. Another approach is to build a community for staff close by but outside the confines of the resort property. This is particularly worthwhile where staff accommodations include space for family members, offering a more stable workforce.

Often, in these remote locations, the indigenous population lives in remarkable harmony with the environment. Over centuries the people have developed a language to shape their surroundings, making use of local materials, adding unique details and embellishments, and

adapting simple technologies to their structures. Developers and designers may choose to apply features learned from this vernacular architecture. It is possible for a modern resort, with all the comforts a Western tourist expects, to fit in with its more humble surroundings, with respect to both its built form and its landscape.

In tropical climates the distinction between inside and outside is not as rigid as it is in temperate zones. The spilling out of interior functions onto adjacent exterior spaces is highly appealing and can occur through most of the year. In such instances, terraces become an outside bridge between the hotel proper and the landscape. Additionally, functions that normally occur indoors, such as meals, can be located outdoors and away from the main hotel building, perhaps in a small pavilion that might protect yet highlight food and beverage activities. Meals set in an exotic landscape can become special occasions. To provide better service, these outdoor areas need a connection to the kitchen and other back-of-house areas, ideally out of view of the guests. Setups away from the main reception areas of the hotel offer privacy and can be used by non-resident

Four Seasons Resort, Republic of Seychelles
One of Web Structures' primary goals in designing this resort was to minimize disturbance to the natural beauty and the ecological balance of the site. An existing lake on site has been rejuvenated and used as a natural retention pond to retain and filter rainwater before the overflow is allowed to enter the ocean.

groups, such as local businesses, passing tour groups, or a wedding, without disturbing resort guests.

Most resorts and large hotel complexes are built in phases. It may be difficult to raise the needed large sums of capital initially, and investors prefer to test the demand. If a project is successful, then expansion often follows. The designers should anticipate how the project might grow and adapt and plan for a range of possible future modifications. For example, the resort might add guestroom villas, or more function space, or recreational amenities. The master plan would, say, locate the swimming pool in the first phase so that it won't impede future construction of additional facilities. In addition, the early phases should provide the engineering infrastructure to facilitate later tie-ins. The most profitable expansions are of guestrooms, which are the least costly spaces to construct. However, the entire master plan must contain sufficient amenities and services to support such an undertaking.

Often, the scale of a resort hotel is overwhelming, especially where it is located in a less-developed country with a simple indigenous architecture. One way to mitigate this contrast is to situate the hotel adjacent to a prominent feature in the landscape that can help to integrate it to its environment. The Four Seasons Seychelles Resort, built on a rugged site on Mahe Island, exemplifies the principles of designing in harmony with the existing terrain. The development was carefully crafted onto this sensitive site, which stretches from a coral beach to tropical hillsides and rock outcrops. The goal of the architects and engineers was to minimize disturbance to the natural beauty and the ecological balance of the site. Careful analysis needed to be carried out in order to minimize the "cut-and-fill" earthwork necessary in the creation of approximately 6 miles (10 km) of access roads. It was important to ensure the development did not adversely affect the natural flow of rainwater on downhill slopes. Individual structures have been painstakingly located and then adjusted at micro level to ensure existing rock outcrops and vegetation are least disturbed. An existing lake on site was repaired for use as a natural retention pond to retain and filter rainwater before the overflow is allowed to enter the ocean.

Suburban Sites

Developers of hotels in suburban locations must consider the impact of adjacent properties when selecting a site. While zoning places some restrictions, largely on use (e.g., residential, commercial, industrial, etc.), too many communities are lax in their regulation of commercial strip developments, where hotels and motels might best be located. And in some communities there are no zoning ordinances. Obviously, certain ventures are less compatible than others: manufacturing businesses are surrounded by storage yards, automobile service stations may have abandoned vehicles on their sites, and nightclubs and bars generate late-night activity that could disturb guests' sleep. Before selecting a particular site, the developer needs to consider the benefits or negative impacts of the surrounding activities. Some may generate additional room or food and beverage revenues; others may detract from the experience by their appearance, or create noise or traffic congestion. The organization of the hotel on the site can help minimize these impacts. Often, suburban hotels focus both public spaces and guestrooms onto a landscaped courtyard and place the parking areas around the hotel in order to provide a buffer zone to adjacent properties.

In addition, there are landscape devices to help block out incompatible neighbors. A high wall is an extreme solution, and it places a hard confining edge at the hotel property, making it seem blocked in. Trees are a much better solution. They contribute to a positive perception of the property, provide shade in summer, protect from winds in the winter, muffle noise, and filter the air. Trees are widely used to conceal, shade, and soften the parking areas of the site. They block out car headlights that can disturb ground-floor guestrooms. The careful selection and placement of trees can create a sense of greater space, privacy, and mystery, especially if planted with consideration of foreground, middle ground, and background.

Hotels in suburban and provincial areas, especially if not near a major tourist attraction, cater to a mix of business and transient guests, in addition to people visiting residents nearby. The hotel should reflect the economic status of its community. Except in very wealthy districts, most suburban hotels fall into mid-range categories. The image of a hotel can be greatly enhanced by thoughtful landscape design. Even a small well-planted entrance court gives an essential favorable first impression to an arriving guest. An avenue of trees offers a sense of formality and importance. However, the landscape design should be appropriate to the hotel's price range or people may think that its rates are higher than they can afford.

Lower- and mid-priced roadside hotels that attract a large number of guests in transit rely largely on billboards to announce their presence. The signage should be designed to reinforce the image of the hotel and respect the environment, while complying with local restrictions. Developers should be wary of communities that ban highway advertisements because this may reduce their ability to attract guests.

The traffic generated by hotels must be acknowledged and properly managed. Traffic is a concern to the hotel's neighbors, especially where the hotel is in a residential district. Understandably, homeowners do not want the noise and pollution from guests' cars and, especially, from trucks making deliveries and removing trash. The hotel itself offers little or no benefit to local residents. These are strong arguments, often used to stop a hotel project. It is essential that early in the project an experienced traffic consultant develop a clear strategy for handling vehicles to help deflect reservations which the community might have. This also is indispensable for projects located in a town center.

With the dependence on guests arriving by automobile, it is advantageous to find a site near a major highway intersection. However, the confluence of intersecting roadways can be confusing to travelers, and access to the hotel still might be difficult. It is nearly impossible for the developer to change existing roads to accommodate the hotel, so one should clearly understand traffic patterns before selecting what might appear to be an opportune site. A site that might be difficult to reach because of a complicated nexus of thoroughfares also can be an impediment to deliveries and staff. All such judgments need to be reviewed, even before the site is purchased.

Finding an adequate labor force is increasingly difficult. Staff for suburban hotels may drive—increasing the demand for parking—but many depend on public transportation to reach the property. Therefore, finding a site close to bus or train lines is important, and this may even assist hotel guests, who can leave their car at the hotel during the day. In some locations, management may organize car pools or provide bussing from outlying areas. It is unusual, but possible, for the hotel site to be within walking distance of residential areas where staff might live. For further discussion on roadside inns and motels see Chapter 4.

Urban Sites

In the denser urban areas, virtually the entire site is covered by the hotel building. The hotel is a closed container for all its functions. Even if there is open space at ground level, it usually is reserved for a porte cochère, fountain or artwork, and incidental plantings that soften the building's edge—and possibly an outdoor space where guests can relax or dine. It is possible, in addition, to take advantage of areas where the building steps back, creating a terrace, or rooftops, for outdoor amenities. An outdoor swimming pool on the roof of a multi-story urban building can command breathtaking views. Al fresco dining on an upper-floor terrace, with its lush plantings and separation from the street noise and pollution, can provide a valuable asset and differentiate an urban hotel's lounge or restaurant from that of its competitors.

In many industrialized nations, the rural and suburban areas often are relatively homogenous with respect to income levels, while urban areas offer a striking contrast. The range of hotel types reflects this difference. The most luxurious hotels are in major cities. Upscale hotels vie for the most prominent sites, close to expensive shops, museums, concert halls, business centers, parks, and other major attractions. Their guests have access to private cars and taxis. The cities also offer a market for budget accommodations, which may be located in fringe areas but should be close to such public

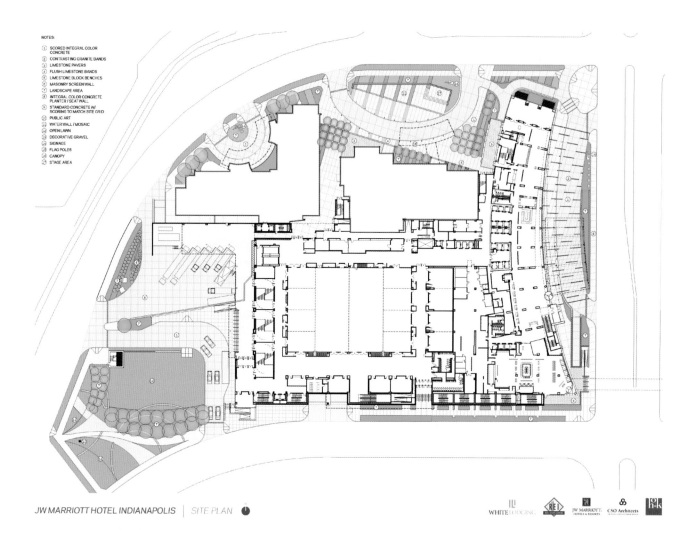

NOTES:

1. SCORED INTEGRAL COLOR CONCRETE
2. CONTRASTING GRANITE BANDS
3. LIMESTONE PAVERS
4. FLUSH LIMESTONE BANDS
5. LIMESTONE BLOCK BENCHES
6. MASONRY SCREEN WALL
7. LANDSCAPE AREA
8. INTEGRAL COLOR CONCRETE PLANTER / SEAT WALL
9. STANDARD CONCRETE W/ SCORING TO MATCH SITE GRID
10. PUBLIC ART
11. WATER WALL / MOSAIC
12. OPEN LAWN
13. DECORATIVE GRAVEL
14. SIGNAGE
15. FLAG POLES
16. CANOPY
17. STAGE AREA

JW MARRIOTT HOTEL INDIANAPOLIS | SITE PLAN

WHITE LODGING   REI   JW MARRIOTT HOTELS & RESORTS   CSO Architects   HOK

Overall A

Marriott Place, Indianapolis, Indiana
Four Marriott-branded hotels share the city block, with three entrance courts and a major loading dock. One entrance court, which serves the Fairfield Inn and has access to the Springhill Suites and Courtyard hotels, is called Art Plaza and features a 36 ft (11 m) tall red steel abstract sculpture of a cardinal, the Indiana state bird. The art-filled plaza has become a public amenity for downtown residents and employees.

transportation centers as train and long-distance coach stations, or local bus and subway stops. This convenience is especially important to travelers who carry their own baggage.

Parking in cities is increasingly restricted to limit traffic congestion, especially in the central business cores. For hotels, valet parking, using a nearby parking garage, may be an option. Parking beneath the hotel requires enormous capital investment and the integration of elevators, mechanical ventilation, and sprinklers. While underground parking can cost at least five times more than the construction of surface parking, it does provide both safety and convenience to guests. Mid-range hotels, which have the highest required ratio of cars to guestrooms, are most challenged by the need for and expense of providing parking on site.

Loading docks are a necessary component of hotels. Noisy, unsightly, and smelly, they should be located well away from public entrances to a hotel, ideally on a different street, where delivery and trash removal trucks do not meet with vehicles bringing guests to the hotel. Security demands often mean that VIP and celebrity guests, including heads of state and their entourages, enter a hotel by a back entrance, all too often via the loading dock area. Therefore, where this may occur they should be well protected from view and designed for secondary access to the public areas. For further discussion on urban hotels see Chapter 2.

Analyzing the Project Site

In understanding the larger issues that make a site suitable for a hotel or resort, the development and design team must study more fully the characteristics of the property itself—terrain, soil conditions, utility availability—as well as governmental regulations and other factors. The site information, along with the hotel program and market demand data, are the major elements which form the basis for the project design.

Site Characteristics

A first step is the topographical survey, which establishes a base map for the site. From the survey the designer may immediately identify several design opportunities, as well as a number of constraints. For example, the grade or slope of the land influences the eventual building location and its entrances, both public or service, including such details as disabled accessibility, baggage handling, and truck access to the loading areas. On a larger scale, roads and walkways must be planned for access to various site components, recreational amenities sited, and "view corridors" established. Accuracy is essential. An inaccurate survey can create innumerable problems in every aspect of the development: utilities, parking, landscaping, recreational areas, entrances, structure, zoning and building codes, and so forth. Finally, there are major cost implications in determining cut-and-fill, or the amount of excavation and grading necessary.

The survey also maps the boundary and locates features such as existing buildings, trees, and fences. War stories abound regarding

lawsuits between neighbors who accidentally, or unknowingly, build a fence or building on an adjoining site. Even government planning documents must be taken as guidelines and not accepted as gospel without careful confirmation. The site survey must prove the edges and locate all site features, natural and manmade.

The initial site survey generally does not provide information on soil type or bearing capacity. For larger projects, and those requiring extensive foundations, additional site investigations are required to understand soil characteristics such as erosion potential, acidity, porosity, plasticity, compressibility, and its richness for landscaping. In rural sites, which might need both wells for water and a septic system, the type of soil can have a great impact on the budget. Also, good topsoil should be saved and shifted, to be reused later in the landscaping phase.

The subsurface conditions, such as the height of the water table and the bearing capacity, are no less important and also have serious financial implications. Early in the project, a geotechnical engineering firm should take a set of soil borings to answer a range of questions: Is the ground rock or loose soil? Is it uniform throughout the site? Is it relatively wet or dry? What are the natural drainage patterns? What types of foundations are most suitable to the soil conditions? The geotechnical report should help the architect and structural engineers make appropriate and cost-effective design decisions

Government Regulations

A second major element affecting the site and building design is the set of government land-use and building regulations in place. Prior to acquiring the site, the developer should be familiar with the pertinent regulations and know how they will influence the project. Most people see these as constraining the hotel development in some way—limiting the number of floors, requiring a certain number of parking spaces, or establishing environmental conditions. However, the regulations also serve to protect the owner from inappropriate development on adjoining property in the future, and establish a baseline for a good-quality project. Typical regulations include the following general categories:

- Zoning
- Building and health
- Historic preservation
- Ecological conservation
- Community interests

Zoning codes establish the overriding parameters for site development by mandating what and how much can be constructed. The city (or other jurisdiction) is divided into many "use" zones (residential, commercial, industrial, etc.) with very specific regulations for each. Each of several commercial zones identified on the map, for instance, will have different requirements for set-backs (distance between the building and the property lines), height (number of feet or meters or number of floors), density (number of units per acre or hectare), parking and loading spaces, and so forth. Zoning restrictions vary widely; in rural sites, construction may be limited to

Four Seasons Firenze, Florence, Italy
The Four Seasons Firenze is set within a historic 11 acre (4.5 hectare) private garden, Giardino della Gherardesca, in the heart of Florence. Restoration of the priceless garden received nearly as much attention from historic preservation agencies as the historic buildings within it.

two or three stories, or it may not even be regulated. Urban zones may vary from a maximum height of three to six floors in residential districts to no limit in downtown business districts. In some cases, land parcels may be combined and air rights purchased, to enable a larger development than would be permitted on one site alone.

The zoning maps are based upon the desire of the community to control certain types of development and to separate incompatible uses from each other. Bonuses may be given in exchange for amenities such as public access or public space. The lack of availability of public services may limit some projects, which impose demands on the fire department, schools, libraries, road capacity, and utilities—particularly water supply and sewage. In smaller cities, developers have purchased new fire equipment, such as a ladder truck, which, in turn, removed the municipality's objection to the project and facilitated its approval.

Meeting early with the local city planning department or the building department is useful. They are the source for up-to-date information, will render preliminary interpretations of the zoning and building codes, and help identify other requirements imposed by additional regulatory agencies. Some communities require consideration by a regional planning office, or oceanfront towns may defer to a coastal commission. Projects in sensitive areas may be required to complete a lengthy environmental impact statement, which often is used by communities as a roadblock to slow down unwanted development. These sites may include wetlands and flood zones, requiring consultation with the U.S. Army Corps of Engineers. As the project moves forward, other agencies become involved, looking at such details as utility connections, waste removal, signs, lighting, and overhanging objects such as canopies.

The developer should never discount the interests of the local community. It is a good practice to draw in the community early in the planning process, to understand and address their concerns. The developer, then, can more easily apply for needed variances or exceptions, or can request special FAR bonuses if the city is so inclined.

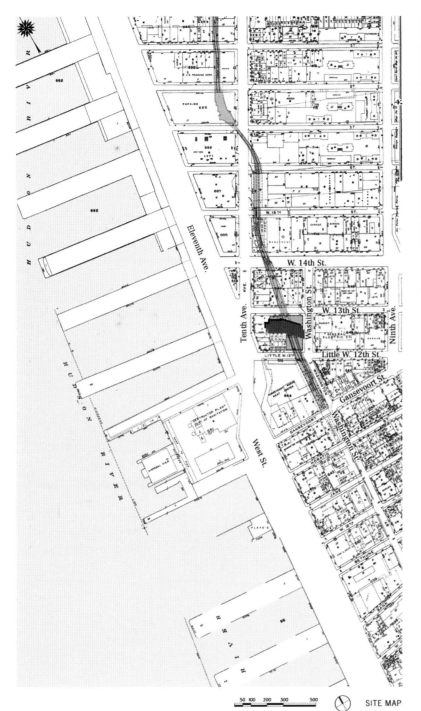

The Standard, New York, New York
The idea of urban hotels interfacing with public plazas and parks takes on new meaning when the park literally passes through the hotel. The High Line, a section of a former elevated railroad spur, has become a popular destination for residents and tourists. The hotel has become as much a part of the High Line experience as the linear park has for hotel guests.

50 100 200 300 500   SITE MAP

Developing the Project Site Plan

In establishing the concept for the site development, it is critical that the owner prioritize the program and goals. Some issues are more important than others, and value judgments must be made. Are views from the public areas or guestrooms more important? Is it necessary or desirable to separate different guest segments, say families and business travelers? How important is conserving a portion of the site for future development? Is the budget an absolute figure? And so forth.

Who has this responsibility? The project developer must prepare a statement of criteria and objectives, which becomes the guiding document for the entire project. The architect and other consultants should refer back to this overriding philosophy as they proceed, over months or years, to make countless design decisions which, together, create the resort "idea" that the guest experiences. But it is the site plan that offers one of the greatest opportunities to influence the project, its functional design, budget, customer reaction, and eventual success. Of course, a resort or other lodging type can have nearly any character, depending on the location, qualities of the site, owner's objectives, market segments, and so forth. Luxury retreats can be grand or imposing or, just as easily, homey and comfortable; resorts can be designed in the local vernacular or in a more international style; business hotels more often may have a corporate feel, but in Orlando, for example, as in other locations, the most successful hotels carry a theme. While other important operational aspects can be changed, the design is for the long term.

In addition to the character of the design feel, the architect and others need to integrate a range of practical functional objectives. The best designs accommodate these functional and operational aspects while they also create a special ambience, appropriate to the site and market. That balance is essential.

Accessibility and Circulation

Two key issues that are important to the guests' arrival at the site are visibility of the entrances and appropriate signage. This can be accomplished by any of several means, including sight lines, road-widening, lighting, divided highways, planting, and graphics. But the entrance to the site, and, specifically, the location and number of curb cuts, must be coordinated with the city or highway department. Larger projects and those in congested areas benefit from the analysis of a traffic consultant, who may lead negotiations with the local authorities to obtain highway modifications for the benefit of the project. These might include a new highway exit, turning lanes, traffic lights, or pedestrian or vehicular bridges and underpasses.

Once the guest has arrived on site, the major objectives are to separate vehicular and pedestrian routes and to conceal service circulation. Suburban sites may have limited pedestrian circulation except for movement across the parking lot, but resorts require careful study and design to protect the ambience of the locale from being overwhelmed by vehicles. All projects need to design the access to the service areas, primarily loading, trash, and employee entrance, for maximum efficiency, while avoiding cross-circulation or inconvenience to guests. During the conceptual design, the traffic consultant should study the plan and indicate possible problems caused by the location of roadways, parking, and public and service entrances.

Surface parking often is the single largest site component of a hotel development. Of course, tight urban sites may have no on-site parking, yet alternative arrangements must be considered, including valet service, and expensive on-site underground parking may be necessary. In several European cities, automated high-density parking systems exist to lessen the space requirements. In North America, about 200 sq ft (18.5 sq m) per car is typically allotted for valet parking, and up to 350 sq ft (32.5 sq m) is needed for guest self-parking, including aisles and ramps. The developer needs to consider the importance of proximity of parking to the lobby and guestrooms, and how often guests may use their cars, ranging from several trips per day in rural and suburban sites to infrequent use in urban locations (see Chapter 17, Tables 17.12 and 17.13).

View

Once guests arrive in their hotel room, among the first things that they do is to open the drapes and look out of the window to check the view. This natural instinct speaks volumes about the importance of this feature. Dealing with guestroom views is crucial in selecting the site, orienting the buildings, developing the building form, and designing the pattern of windows, or fenestration. Not every building is a high-rise, not every site is blessed with 360-degree views, so something must be done to compensate the guest. The site designer may create interesting features or manipulate the terrain in ways to enhance the views. These may be as simple as designing small gardens or pleasant landscape vistas, or directing views across the swimming pool or tennis courts or into an interior atrium. Where there is a truly special view, of mountains or the beach, for instance, and if project budget and orientation permit, the building may be constructed as a single-loaded corridor scheme, with rooms only on the view side and the hallway on the other.

Utilities

Although not a particularly glamorous aspect of project development, the impact of such utilities as electrical power, telephone, water, and sewerage must be understood early on. In urban locations these can be assumed to be present, as are, perhaps, natural gas and high-speed data lines. But rural locations and small island sites may have a limited utility infrastructure. What is the source of these services? What are the factors that govern their acquisition? Are they available in the quantity required on site, or is it necessary to upgrade existing services or bring in completely new ones? After an analysis of the costs from the local utility company, the developer may determine that it is better to have an on-site plant to take care of the project's needs. In some locations, utility deregulation has forced utility companies to compete for rates and even to purchase excess power from private users.

The cost of these services can be a major component of the operating expenses of the hotel or resort, generally falling between 3 and 5 percent of total revenues. Early investigation into the local cost of electricity, gas, fuel oil, and even solar or wind power as the predominant fuel source is necessary. Recently, and into the foreseeable future, a procedure called "peak shaving" will have an increasing impact on the bottom line. This is most effective where demand charges for electrical energy are high, and may involve the use of multiple fuel sources. During peak-rate periods for electricity, the system automatically cycles certain equipment off and on to lower demand, or shifts power to alternative sources such as gas or solar.

Four Seasons Resort, Langkawi, Malaysia
The 91-key tropical beachfront resort is surrounded by thick jungle, lush foliage, and dramatic cliffs. The guest pavilions and villas are skillfully arranged around a series of pools and lagoons, contributing to the tranquil atmosphere of the luxury resort.

Natural Landscape

Understanding how to use the natural landscape to benefit the site and building designs is important in increasing guest appreciation of the project and reducing construction and operating costs. The topographic plan identifies areas where excessive slope might mandate expensive grading and the construction of retaining walls. But, also, these areas may offer among the best for views and, with proper landscaping, can be among the memorable areas at a property.

Plants of all types—trees, shrubs, grasses, gardens, and so forth—provide obvious yet significant benefits to a site. Consider a barren site and how much more pleasant a landscaped courtyard or simple lawn is by comparison. Trees and large plants offer cooling shade and protect guests from uncomfortable glare. They offer handsome visual effects—defining views, providing a sheltering canopy and flowering buds, screening unwanted elements—at the same time as contributing to nature by sheltering small animals, encouraging ground cover, or retaining soil and moisture. Deciduous trees change with the season, offering a variety of effects, while conifers provide year-round shelter, useful as a windbreak or snow barrier in the colder months.

The soil on the site can readily support the indigenous vegetation, but the landscape architect will have to determine whether it is suitable for the new landscape plan and how well it is likely to survive the rigors of construction. Any major trees on the site may be worth

Table 13.2 Checklist of site and outdoor furnishings

❑	Seating:	Permanent, moveable
❑	Lighting:	Overhead, bollards, in ground flush, ornamental, directional, architectural
❑	Trees:	Grates, guards
❑	Bollards:	Illuminated, vehicular
❑	Fencing:	Ornamental, territorial, security
❑	Utilities:	Sewer covers, site drains
❑	Waste receptacles:	Built-in, freestanding, material choice
❑	Signage:	Directional, destination, informational
❑	Bicycle racks	
❑	Gazebos	
❑	Kiosks	
❑	Planters	
❑	Clocks	
❑	Flag poles	

Table 13.3 Security options

❑ Electronic surveillance, including intelligence-enabled camera network

❑ Emergency command station near entrances and loading dock and connected with a central command-and-control center

❑ Alarm or enunciator panel located at command station with backup panel in security office

❑ Security-guard staff

❑ Staff trained in security awareness

❑ Trained voluntary fire-protection team

❑ Fire alarm system

❑ Fire annunciation system (activated by floors or controlled by telephone switchboard)

❑ Design of site and buildings to include good surveillance and architectural barriers

❑ Site lighting

❑ Staff ID procedures

❑ Roadways with clearance for emergency vehicles

❑ Security alarms on walk-in refrigerators and freezers, liquor, golf, silver and china storage

❑ Real-time intrusion-detection and threat-assessment technology

protecting. The designer might decide to make special efforts to save unique plant specimens; otherwise, suitable replacements will have to be selected. There is an art to arranging the landscape environment, to selecting plants for particular aesthetic and functional requirements, as well as planning the circulation and building and other functional elements of the site.

One opposite but related element is the design of the small site structures and the selection of complementary site furnishings. These items, listed in Table 13.2, are best when they seem to disappear into the landscape, whether through color, material, or clever position, yet they need to be present to serve a variety of guest functional needs.

Four Seasons Resort Langkawi illustrates the goal of blending indigenous architecture with lush tropical vegetation to obtain a distinctive look. Presiding over a 1 mile (1.5 km) expanse of Tanjung Rhu cove, Langkawi's most beautiful beach, the resort is fringed by silvery sands, lush rainforests, mountain landscapes, and emerald waters. Individual pavilions are scattered throughout, with exquisite landscaped gardens in the style of a native village. The seamless blending of Asian, Indian, and Arabic influences creates a uniquely Malaysian milieu, while each pavilion offers timber floorings, soaring ceilings, open-air verandas, and views to the Andaman Sea or tropical gardens.

Security

Security threats to the hotel industry come in two basic forms: the casual petty criminal/intruder, and the more serious professional intruder, or terrorist. Terrorist attacks targeting hotels and resorts, as with the attacks on The Taj Mahal Palace Hotel in Mumbai and the North Caucasus ski resorts in Russia, have brought about a heightened concern for security against these dangerous threats in addition to the customary concerns over theft, robbery, and personal assault. This is of particular concern where the hotel or resort is a frequent host to political figures and dignitaries who are prime targets for militants. The hotel or resort operator must strive to create an environment in which the guest feels safe and secure without any security features being too obvious, utilizing cutting-edge convergent IT and security technologies. (See Chapter 19.) The developer needs to give early thought to establishing a security plan for the site, and may seek the help of a consultant to identify threats and devise strategies for control. Among the common security and safety issues which the team must address are overall guest and employee security and safety, general crime reduction, fire and life safety, and emergency medical response. Table 13.3 lists many of the specific ways in which security may be achieved. Strategies include monitoring access to the site and buildings where traffic is relatively light, and minimizing the number of entry points. The perimeter areas should be designed using the natural characteristics of the site landscaping, supplemented by walls, fences, TV surveillance, and motion detectors to discourage intruders.

Four Acres Hotel and Residences, Scottsdale, Arizona
Located along the Arizona Canal with 134 hotel keys and 46 residential units, the design by Ronnette Riley Architect and Mathes Brierre Architects called for two crescent-shaped towers connected by a broad promenade and banquet facilities. The pool deck is located over the ballroom, with fountains feeding a waterfall that cascades over the glass-enclosed promenade and into a lush garden pond below.

Professional Documentation

The site development aspects of a major project—say, a suburban hotel, conference center, or resort—plays a major role in the design studies and eventual building plans and construction documents. The previous discussion has touched on some of the types of special consultants who might be called on for their expertise—many more are needed for the hotel itself—and who contribute to the creation of a series of documents needed for construction. These include:

- Site plan showing all features
- Grading plans or contour maps
- Utility layouts
- Planting schemes
- Lighting plan
- Construction details
- Vehicular and pedestrian circulation plans

Programming
and Development

On its surface, the idea of developing a lodging property seems fairly simple: the developer conceives a new project, buys the land, hires the architect, acquires financing, builds the structure, and opens the hotel or resort—to great success. But, in reality, it is more complex and fraught with risk. Part 1 of this book describes the tremendous variety of competitive hotel types—which one is best for a particular site and market? How are the market needs assessed? Who is the customer and what facilities does he or she really need and expect? What skills are needed in the design team and what specialized consultants should be hired? And so forth.

Therefore, developing the successful hotel requires bringing together the experience of scores of professionals from real estate, finance, design, construction, hotel operations, and many other disciplines, whose work then must be coordinated and channeled to complete the project—defined by the market requirements and the architect's design—both on time and on budget. The bubble diagram (see overleaf) suggests one simple way to conceive a project: programming, design, cost estimating, construction, and operations. It is easiest to describe the development process as a linear one, complete the first step, then proceed to the next, and so forth. But it seldom happens that way. Development is messy, with lots of false starts and circling back to reassess a decision. The diagram implies just that. At each step you may need to consider altering some of the previous decisions, to change the market orientation, for example, or to reduce the project scope in order to save money. This chapter will discuss some of the key aspects of development—project sequence, feasibility, and facilities programming—and will introduce the concept of prototype development.

Project Sequence

Hotel projects follow the same general sequence as other development projects, but with some important nuances. The future hotel operator, for instance, usually is involved from nearly the first step, influencing the site selection, space program, choice of consultants, and so forth. Therefore, it is best to consider how the principal management companies or "brands," the organizations with the development and operating experience, think about a new project, and incorporate their methods.

Most of these companies have real estate professionals and architects on staff, who field perhaps dozens of inquiries a day from developers with an idea for a new hotel or the desire to reposition

Armani Hotel Lobby, Burj Khalifa, Dubai, United Arab Emirates
Located in the iconic Burj Khalifa, the world's tallest building, is the first hotel designed by Italian fashion leader Giorgio Armani. The "stay with Armani" experience is exemplified by the clean design, fine finishes, and many amenities in the luxury hotel. Guests can participate in the Armani lifestyle experience by taking home items purchased from the designer's in-house retail outlets.

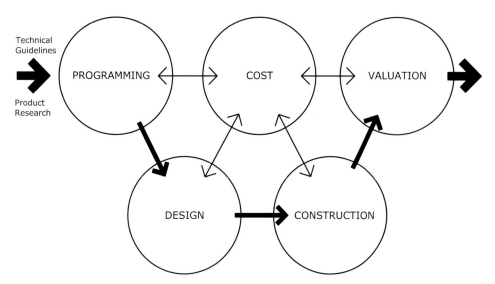

Development flow chart
Based on market data and other research, the design team continually refines program, budget, and design, utilizing development software to perfect new projects and prototypes.

an existing asset. The prospective operator needs to carefully assess the developer's experience and financial wherewithal and balance this against the company's own strategic goals. Does it have an appropriate lodging product to meet the developer's goals? Does it want to expand in that region? At that particular site (airport, downtown)? At that quality level? And so forth. If some of these can be answered in the affirmative, the technical staff from the management company may help coordinate and provide guidance and feedback during some of these basic steps:

- Evaluate the prospective site
- Complete a feasibility study
- Select the architect and design consultants
- Prepare a facilities program:
  - Concept statement
  - Area program
  - Operational description
  - Project budget
- Obtain financing
- Review the hotel design (schematic, design development, construction documents)
- Monitor construction and the hotel opening

One of the first steps, of course, is to confirm the location and particular site and assess its suitability for a hotel. This is partly carried out in the feasibility study from a market standpoint, but, equally importantly, the site needs to be evaluated from a design and construction perspective. Often, the operator's technical assistance staff will visit the site to assess its accessibility, visibility, and overall suitability for a hotel.

Feasibility Analysis

Among the first steps that the developer of a new hotel must take is to prepare a market study and financial projections. The study, usually assembled by a consulting firm and further refined by the management company's senior operations staff (if the hotel is to be chain-operated), has two key aspects. First, it assesses present and future demand for lodging and such other hotel services as meeting areas, restaurants and bars, and recreational facilities. Second, it estimates operating income and expenses for 10 years after the hotel opens.

There is no single formula for success. Projects with optimistic feasibility studies may do poorly, while occasionally those built despite a negative report do surprisingly well. However, the more successful projects combine several ingredients: good location, continuing strong demand, the proper mix of facilities, and professional management. To some extent, the prototypical feasibility study common to the hotel industry critically assesses all these factors. What these studies don't consider is the impact that outstanding design—whether architectural, interior, or landscape—can make on a future property's success.

Feasibility studies often have differing objectives. Most are used to increase the confidence of others in a project's success and to obtain permanent financing. Thus, often, it is a basic component of the developer's package to prospective lenders. But feasibility studies also may be used to obtain an operating franchise or management contract or to attract equity participation. Similar reports but with different emphases may be used in negotiations with city officials to support a developer's request for a zoning variance, or to reinforce his or her contention that the project will increase local sales and real estate taxes and add new jobs. Occasionally, in recent years, feasibility studies have been commissioned by a municipality, public

Testing Hotel Feasibility

Steve Rushmore, MAI, FRICS
President and Founder, HVS
Mineola, New York

When designing a hotel the architect and development team need to create a project that ultimately is feasible economically. Unless the hotel's owner is more ego-driven than economically motivated, most investors are looking for a substantial return on their invested capital. Since feasibility means different things to different people, let me provide my perspective, as a hotel consultant who has completed thousands of studies on this topic.

The process I like to use for determining whether a proposed hotel is economically feasible is to compare the total project cost (including land) with the hotel's estimated economic value on the date it opens. A feasible project is one where the economic value is greater than the cost. Accurately estimating the total project cost is a relatively simple process for the architect and development team. However, determining the economic value is much more complicated.

The first step in the valuation process is to perform a market study where the local hotel demand is quantified and allocated among the supply of existing and proposed lodging facilities. The allocation of roomnight demand is based on the relative competitiveness of each hotel in the market. The end result is a projection of demand captured by the proposed subject hotel, which is then converted into an estimate of annual occupancy. A similar procedure is used to project the average room rate.

The second step is to project the hotel's operating revenue and expenses based on the previously estimated occupancy and room rate, providing an estimate of annual net operating income. Most consultants use a 5–10 year period, meaning the calculation needs to be repeated for each year.

The last step is to convert the projected net operating income into an estimate of value using a weighted cost-of-capital discounted-cash-flow procedure. The end result is an estimate of economic value that can be compared to the total project cost.

Some consultants, for the last step, will substitute a net present value (NPV) calculation or determine the internal rate of return (IRR). However, I prefer using the economic value approach because you end up comparing "apples with apples"—i.e., cost with value.

As you can see, this process of determining economic value requires local market knowledge, hotel financial expertise, and experience with valuation methodology. Luckily for architects and hotel developers, there are two simple rules-of-thumb that will provide a rough approximation as to whether a project is economically feasible.

The first thumb rule tests the cost of the land to determine whether it exceeds a supportable economic land value. The following formula calculates economic land value:

$$\text{Economic land value} = \text{occupancy} \times \text{average room rate} \times \frac{\text{no. of rooms} \times 0.04}{0.08}$$

To illustrate this, assume that a proposed hotel is being considered on a parcel of land that can be acquired for $3,800,000. Zoning permits the development of 200 rooms. Basing our estimate on local market conditions, we believe the proposed hotel should achieve a stabilized occupancy of 70 percent and an average room rate of $150. Using these inputs, the economic land value would be calculated as follows:

$$\frac{0.70 \times \$150 \times 200 \times 365 \times 0.04}{0.08} = \$3,832,500$$

The calculation shows that the economic land value is above the cost of the land, so the developer is not overpaying for the land. If the land cost was $4,000,000 or above, the developer would need to reevaluate the project, because this price is not supported by the hotel's underlying economics. If additional rooms were added or a higher-quality hotel were developed, the value would perhaps be positive. This economic land value formula works well in most markets; however, for prime center-city locations the 0.04 factor can be modified upward to 0.08.

The second rule-of-thumb is the average rate multiplier formula. This is a very simple way to approximate a hotel's total economic value. The formula is as follows:

$$\text{Economic value of hotel} = \text{average room rate} \times \text{no. of rooms} \times 1000$$

Using the numbers from this example produces an economic value of $30 million. If the hotel's total development cost is much over $30,000,000, there could be a problem with its feasibility. In most cases, if the development cost is significantly higher than the economic value, it is because the local market's average room rate is too low to support the contemplated improvements. In these situations, the proposed plans and specifications need to be scaled back in order to produce a lower total project cost, which might then create a feasible project.

One additional point of reference looks at the percentage relationship between the hotel's land cost and the economic value. In this example, the value of the land is approximately

continued overleaf

13 percent of the overall economic value of the hotel ($3,832,500/30,000,000 = 13 percent). This relationship should be no more than 15 to 20 percent. In parts of the world where labor costs are much lower, this percentage relationship can be higher.

Using these hotel feasibility rules-of-thumb combined with a professionally prepared study will ensure that the architect and developer are creating an economically viable project. Of course, there are numerous exceptions that may need to be considered in the evaluation. Before abandoning a project because the rules-of-thumb don't produce the desired results, it is advisable to call in a professional hotel consultant to prepare a fuller analysis that will either verify or dispute the conclusions produced by the rules-of-thumb.

agency, or—in developing countries—the national government, in an attempt to attract new private development.

Only infrequently do these studies actually assess the feasibility of a project. This is because any calculation of relative success depends on much more than the objective analysis of the lodging market. Not only does it depend on accurate projections of future conditions, but it also must take into account such confidential factors as the developer's investment strategies and tax status.

Assuming the study doesn't go beyond projecting net operating income (NOI), or cash flow available after fixed charges (real estate taxes, property insurance, reserve for replacement, and management fee), the typical outline includes:

- *Local area evaluation:* Analyze the economic vitality of the city or region and describe the suitability of the project site for a hotel.
- *Lodging market analysis:* Assess the present demand for lodging (and other revenue generators) and future growth rates for each of several market segments; identify the existing supply of competitive properties and anticipate additions to the supply; and assess the competitive position of the subject property.
- *Proposed facilities:* Propose a balance of guestroom and public facilities, including restaurants, bars, meeting and banquet rooms, retail shops, recreation facilities, and parking.
- *Financial analysis:* Estimate income and expenses for the hotel over a 10-year period to show its potential cash flow.

However, these sections are not treated in equal detail in the typical study. The parts that have the most direct relationship to the architectural solution—the site analysis and the facilities program—are the least highly refined. The supply-and-demand analyses and the financial projections, on the other hand, are the most specific, understandably, since the study is prepared by market and economic consultants. Unfortunately, too often the study does not give full enough consideration to trends beginning to influence the market

and their possible impact on the project design. The following discussion and the accompanying tables, adapted from an actual report, highlight the principal aspects of a typical hotel feasibility analysis.

Analyzing the Local Area

As a prelude to the market analysis, most feasibility studies present data illustrating the economic climate in the area—from the entire city or region to the particulars of the specific project site. Many critics consider them no more than "boiler-plate," yet they are helpful in providing necessary background to lenders from outside the local community and in establishing a relative sense of the different lodging markets. In broad terms, the local analysis includes:

- Growth trends in population, employment, income, tax receipts, new construction, airport data, etc.
- Major public and private facilities, including those for education, health, government, transportation, religion, tourism, etc.
- Travel and visitor analysis, including volume and percentage of traffic by car, air, train, bus, and ship, as appropriate

The emphases of the study should reflect the probable type of hotel project. For example, a resort hotel would be only marginally concerned with industrial and commercial influences, perhaps as secondary markets for off-season periods. Instead, it should focus on natural attractions and recreational opportunities in the area, and on airline and highway networks from the principal feeder markets. For the same reason, area analyses for hotels sited near a university, a major medical complex, or a high-tech development should deal with trends influencing these specialized demand-generators—perhaps high-level training sessions—rather than with those of the larger industrial and commercial sector.

The area evaluation also should include a detailed site analysis. In addition to the obvious site description—size, boundaries, topography, and so forth—the analysis should emphasize visibility, accessibility, and suitability to hotel use. The first two are most critical for motel and other roadside properties that attract predominantly highway business, much of it from travelers without previous reservations. The suitability discussion may emphasize such site advantages or potential constraints as views, natural features, proximity to local attractions or businesses, adjacent uses, room for expansion, zoning, and utility availability.

Analyzing the Lodging Market

The largest part of the feasibility study is the analysis of the demand for guestrooms and other hotel services and the enumeration of existing competitive hotel rooms. The study must acknowledge future shifts in demand, as individual market segments expand or contract and as neighborhoods undergo change. Making assumptions about these future changes, as well as about growth rates, improves the sophistication of the analysis but adds considerably to its risk.

Table 14.1 Existing lodging demand by hotel and market segment

Property	Rooms	Occupancy	Commercial	Group	Leisure	Local	Total
Hotel A	200	85.01%	34,500	9,500	12,000	6,050	62,050
Hotel B	200	82.01%	29,300	8,200	14,160	8,200	59,860
Hotel C	165	74.01%	22,000	4,500	13,500	4,560	44,561
Hotel D	135	80.01%	6,200	12,800	19,340	1,190	9,530
Total	700	80.6%	92,000	35,000	59,000	20,000	206,000

Table 14.2 Future area-wide lodging demand by market segment

Market demand segment	Growth factor	Current demand	Year +1	Year +2	Year +3	Year +4	Year +5
Commercial	3%	92,000	94,750	97,600	100,500	103,500	106,400
Group	5%	35,000	36,750	38,500	40,500	42,500	44,600
Leisure	3%	59,000	60,700	62,600	64,500	66,400	68,400
Local	3%	20,000	20,600	21,200	21,800	22,500	23,200
Total demand		206,000	212,800	219,900	227,300	234,900	242,600
Competitive supply		255,500	255,500	365,000*	365,000	365,000	365,000
Estimated area-wide occupancy		80.6%	83.3%	60.2%	62.3%	64.4%	66.5%

* The competitive supply increases in Year +2 with the opening of the proposed 300-room hotel.

The growth factors represent an annual increase; current demand is the number of rooms sold by market segment (see Table 14.1).

Therefore, the developer must be prepared to analyze and review the consultant's assumptions.

The demand for lodging can be calculated in two complementary ways. In one approach, the consultant assembles estimates of the need for guestrooms from interviews and meetings with local business people representing the various generators of lodging demand: industries, government and commercial offices, universities, medical centers, amusement parks, and so forth. For the most part, the demand is separated into three major market segments: convention and other group business, individual commercial business, and leisure travelers. Occasionally, the report may identify airline crews or senior-citizen tour groups, for example, where these or other specific markets are a key component of the business. It analyzes each segment thoroughly in terms of its weekday/weekend characteristics, seasonality, price sensitivity, amount of double occupancy, and, most importantly, its anticipated growth over the succeeding several years. At the same time, the report should assess the potential for group meeting business, restaurant and spa demand, and requirements for other hotel services and amenities.

The second, and quicker, way to estimate total demand—although with important limitations—is to know the current year's occupancy rates at the competitive hotels. Totaling a simple calculation for each hotel (number of rooms x average occupancy percentage x 365 days)

results in a figure that represents the annual area-wide demand for guestrooms. Unfortunately, the use of average occupancy rates fails to take into account daily or seasonal fluctuations in demand and, importantly, does not identify the "fill days," when the local hotels are at 100 percent occupancy and must turn away potential guests. Also, not all operators are willing to provide accurate data on their business.

The consultant estimates future demand for each segment by extending the current-demand figures using various growth rates. These inflation factors—critical to the conclusions of the market study—are based on identifiable trends, economic projections, and the consultant's judgment and experience. A simplified market segment analysis, including the application of growth factors, is shown in Tables 14.1 and 14.2.

Similarly, the consultant prepares a table which sets out the competitive hotels or "competitive supply," showing their physical characteristics (number of guestrooms; capacity of restaurants, bars, meeting and banquet areas; amount of recreation facilities and parking) and fundamental operating statistics (occupancy percentage, "rack" or listed rates, average rate—the result of group discounts or promotional rates—and double occupancy). In smaller communities, or where there are few or no competitors in the subject property's class, less competitive hotels may be added to the analysis. The

Table 14.3 Future lodging demand by hotel and market segment in Year +2

Property	Rooms	Occupancy	Commercial	Group	Leisure	Local	Total
Existing total demand			97,600	38,500	62,600	21,200	219,900
Proposed hotel fair share (30%)			29,280	11,550	18,780	6,360	65,970
Proposed hotel market share			90%	120%	100%	80%	97.1%
Proposed hotel	300	58.5%	26,352	13,860	18,780	5,088	64,080
Hotel A	200	64.7%	26,718	6,675	8,940	4,865	47,198
Hotel B	200	62.4%	22,655	5,765	10,515	6,605	45,540
Hotel C	165	56.2%	17,030	3,180	9,990	3,675	33,875
Hotel D	135	59.3%	4,845	9,020	14,375	967	29,207
Total	1,000						

The existing total demand comes from Year +2 in the previous table.

The proposed hotel's fair share of each market segment is 30 percent (300 of 1,000 total rooms);

its own market share depends on its relative location, facilities, chain affiliation, etc.

This example shows that the proposed hotel will do best (120 percent penetration) in the Group segment.

consultant should adjust the supply analysis for future years to reflect the construction of additional hotels, the expansion of existing properties, the renovation and repositioning of lower-quality hotels, as well as any anticipated deletions from the market.

Next, the consultant establishes the competitive standing of the proposed hotel by assessing its location, size, facilities, rate, and quality level versus the existing properties. This part of the analysis focuses on guestroom occupancy percentage and average room rate. The concept of "fair share," which assumes that a new hotel will attract at least its proportionate share of the aggregate market demand, is at the center of the competitive evaluation. On occasion, the consultants may propose that a particular hotel will capture more (or less) than its fair share of a specific market segment because of its location, facilities, chain affiliation, or, perhaps, nothing more than its newness.

This refinement of the aggregate demand figures allows the consultant to begin to assign occupied guestrooms to area hotels in proportion to their current standing, as modified by the introduction of the new property into the marketplace. Commonly, guestroom occupancy during the first two or three years is several percentage points below a stabilized or target operating year, because the hotel needs this time to develop its full sales potential. The third year is frequently used as the standard to represent the probable operating results in a stable year. Table 14.3, carrying forward the earlier example, illustrates how hotel occupancies dramatically suffer when additional rooms are added to the market.

In addition to guestroom occupancy, the feasibility report projects estimated average room rates for the new hotel, based on existing rates at similar quality hotels inflated to "future dollars." The average rate is expanded to represent total room sales for each year, and this figure, based on numerous assumptions and estimates, provides the basis for many of the financial projections, briefly discussed later in this chapter.

Defining the Proposed Facilities

Feasibility consultants include in the body of the report a general description of the proposed facilities. As illustrated here, this description includes the following elements, outlined in only the broadest terms:

- Number and mix of guestrooms and suites
- Number of restaurants and lounges with their capacities
- Amount of meeting and banquet facilities, with their capacities or floor area
- Health club and other recreational facilities
- Parking
- Additional amenities, such as retail shops, entertainment, and any special services

The facilities description, substantially based on the supply-and-demand analysis, is the one section of the report that most directly influences the pre-design and planning phases of the hotel development project. It establishes the number of guestrooms and lists the major public facilities that provide the order-of-magnitude framework for the preliminary space program (see Table 14.4). Although the report briefly describes the public areas, it neglects entirely the back-of-house service areas and administrative offices.

Some developers feel that the typical definition of the public areas isn't detailed enough. They request that the consultants identify specific operational and design features that will help assure the hotel's

Table 14.4 Proposed facilities list

Guestrooms	Units	Bays
King	150	150
Double-double	125	125
Accessible (king and double-double)	10	10
Suite (one-bay; connects to two guestrooms)	9	9
Suite (two-bay; connects to two guestrooms)	6	12
Club-floor executive lounge	0	4
Manager's residence	0	0
Total	300	310

Food and beverage outlets	Seats
Three-meal restaurant	120
Specialty restaurant	80
Cocktail lounge	0
Lobby bar/lounge	90
Total	300

Function rooms	
Ballroom	700
Meeting and banquet rooms, total	400
Boardroom (included above)	0
Total	1,100

Other public facilities		
Indoor swimming pool		
Health club, sauna, exercise room		
Retail shops	2,000 sq ft	(185 sq m)
Parking	350 spaces	

to 30 pages of financial tables projecting income and expenses for the subject property for 10 years following its opening (see Appendix D).

The financial analysis is based on averages of hotel operations established by several major financial services and consulting firms, including PricewaterhouseCoopers, PKF Consulting, and HVS Global Hospitality Services. These and other international consulting firms, as well as Smith Travel Research, regularly publish annual statistics comparing hotels by size, region, type, age, and, for smaller properties, those with and without restaurants. The developer of a new property should be familiar with the basic organization of, and approximate values reflected in, these industry statistics.

In selecting the feasibility consultant, the developer should seek a firm with experience and high industry credibility. The consultant must be neutral and objective if he or she is to prepare an independent report that will be accepted by lenders or another audience. In addition, the developer must insist on complete documentation of sources and explanations of assumptions. The developer may provide data that is biased in favor of the project, and other people and companies interviewed for the study may purposely exaggerate or simply be too optimistic. Similarly, such assumptions as growth rates, inflation, and market penetration, if even slightly in error, can substantially alter the reliability of the study.

A well-prepared feasibility study can establish the basis, in terms of both financial and facilities goals, for a profitable and clearly defined hotel. The developer who begins the project with a relatively narrow focus, who instinctively defines the number of guestrooms, public facilities, quality level, services and amenities, etc., can better target the market analysis, select truly competitive hotels, define rate and occupancy, identify important trends, and outline the needed facilities. The developer, then, must critique the drafts of the study and insist on a clear and logical presentation of the competitive environment.

success, and that they discuss how these influence the positioning of the hotel. Many studies, though, do little more than suggest that the property "will be developed as a first-class hotel and be expertly managed and promoted."

It is common for the hotel management company, the future chain operator, to review the feasibility recommendations critically and to modify them to reflect its own operating strategies as well as its own perceptions about the local market. While depending on the feasibility report for background material and for the objective judgment of experienced hospitality consultants, some sophisticated developers may alter significant portions of the facilities outline or the occupancy and rate assumptions, to better support their own image of the project.

Preparing the Financial Analysis

In addition to the main body of the feasibility study, which analyzes the local area, identifies supply-and-demand characteristics, and proposes a project of a specific size, the full report includes a second principal part, the financial projections. This section contains 15

Facilities Programming

While the general orientation of the hotel may be known early in the project and tested during the feasibility phase, establishing the hotel program is especially important because of the highly competitive nature of the hotel business. The pre-design documentation for a new project or for the major expansion or repositioning of a hotel must fully describe and define both the space needs and the operational requirements. Without such information, the architect and design consultants are unable to fine-tune standard rule-of-thumb numbers or to create a unique hotel for a precise market. Much of this documentation is required to obtain a lender's package to finance the hotel.

Complete facilities programming is much more than a list of the space requirements; it also must address a variety of needs: location, market demand, competition, quality level, operational features, restaurant concepts, staffing, budget, and market trends. Feasibility consultants generally recommend a mix of certain facilities, but the hotel management company, working with the owner and architect,

Table 14.5 Conceptual area requirements

	Roadside inn midscale		Urban hotel first-class		Resort hotel luxury		Convention hotel first-class	
Number of guestroom keys	150		300		300		600	
Number of guestroom bays	150		315		360		650	
Net guestroom area*	325	(30)	375	(35)	450	(42)	375	(35)
Gross guestroom area*	450	(42)	525	(49)	640	(60)	525	(49)
Total guestroom area*	67,500	(6,270)	165,375	(15,365)	230,400	(21,405)	341,250	(31,702)
Guestroom percentage	80%		75%		70%		65%	
Total hotel area **	84,375	(7,840)	220,500	(20,485)	329,140	(30,575)	525,000	(48,770)
Total area per key*	562	(52)	728	(68)	1,095	(102)	807	(75)

* In sq ft (sq m).

** Total area figures exclude parking.

develop the final program. Table 14.5, illustrating four conceptually different hotels, shows how widely the program for a property can vary depending on its purpose, market orientation, and other issues. Note that hotels of different types can vary from about 550 sq ft (51 sq m) per room to over 1,000 sq ft (93 sq m), because of the substantially different mix of facilities.

The facilities program includes not only the area requirements but also a narrative discussion, which defines the project in qualitative terms and outlines many of the operational requirements and constraints.

Defining the Project

With so many designers and consultants at work on a major hotel project, it is essential to reach a consensus on the goals and objectives of the development: What market is the new hotel supposed to attract? What class and what type of hotel will it be? What services and amenities should it provide? Which public functions should be emphasized? Therefore, it is helpful to prepare a concise definition of the project to identify these issues, to outline the primary public facilities, and to provide a gross estimate of the size of the project. The paragraph below illustrates the type of statement that clearly, yet concisely, defines the project's intent.

The hotel will be a first-class, full-service, high-rise, convention hotel with 800 rooms and 50,000 sq ft (4,640 sq m) of meeting space. Located in a growing retail and entertainment district near the proposed new convention center, the project should accommodate, besides convention attendees, both the individual business traveler and weekend "vacationer." Facilities should include two restaurants, two lounges, a spa/health club, business center, ground-level retail, and parking for 600 cars.

The second part of the preliminary definition of a new or expanded hotel project is a fuller summary of guestroom mix and principal

public facilities. Before the developer's team can move on to the program and later design phases, they need a precise list of the revenue-producing areas, those on which the support and service areas are based. This list forms the core of the expanded space program. For example, even a cursory listing of the restaurant and banquet requirements influences the size and design requirements of the kitchen, food and beverage storage, and employee areas. As the developer focuses on the projections for operating income and expenses, the designers refine their summary list of major facilities to better meet the project objectives. Such a summary might include:

- Guestrooms
  - Number of room "keys" (separate rental units)
  - Number of room bays (total equivalent room modules)
  - Number and description of suites
  - Typical room and suite dimensions
- Lobby and public areas
  - Architectural image and ambience
  - Amount of retail space
- Food and beverage outlets
  - Capacity of each restaurant
  - Capacity of each lounge
  - Quality level and theme for each
- Function space
  - Dimensions of the ballroom (including ceiling height)
  - Amount of other meeting and banquet space
  - Need for exhibition space
- Recreation facilities
  - Quality level of health club/spa
  - Outline of any additional facilities
- Parking requirements
- Technical requirements
  - Special building systems and guest amenities

The early estimates of project size generally are little more than the application of basic rules-of-thumb. The experienced hotel developer and architect calculate gross project floor area from an understanding of the typical guestroom dimensions—to which they apply factors to increase the area to allow for circulation (corridors, elevators, stairs), walls, and other unsalable space—and the relative amount of public and support space required for a particular type of hotel. Until a more detailed program is established, this gross approximation of project size is the critical basis for all cost estimates. In the detailed program examples later in this chapter, the area requirements vary tremendously, depending on the type, quality level, and architectural configuration of the hotel.

Allocating Program Areas

The development of the architectural space program does not occur at one time, nor does it result in a static document. The early definition establishes an approximate total area for the project; later, the architect develops a space list at the beginning of the conceptual design phase and refines a more detailed program during the schematic and design-development phases. Because the technical-services staffs of the major hotel-operating companies have the experience to react quickly and accurately to requests for programmatic information, many developers never prepare a comprehensive space program. Instead, the detailed planning and space-use information is transmitted through a comprehensive management company design guide or bit-by-bit during the ensuing design phases, as the architect requires more specific technical information. But, with computer programs such as Strategic Hotel Area Program Estimate and Evaluation (SHAPEE) now available, detailed area information can be issued early and can be updated easily during the design phases.

The preliminary space program permits the architect to begin the schematic studies for the project. Usually, the management company staff prepare the list based on their own standards, as well as on their experience with similar projects and on the market information provided in the feasibility report. They analyze the broad guidelines established in the earlier estimates to see whether the estimates still accurately reflect the size, class, and type of hotel. The staff then expands these guidelines to include a list of the principal guestrooms and suites, as well as public, administration, and service areas.

Often, the mix of food and beverage outlets or the balance between a large ballroom and the smaller meeting and banquet rooms will be modified, to reflect the operator's knowledge of a local market or to exploit the management company's development strategies. Thus, an operator's programming and planning expertise should influence the project at the earliest date.

The space list prepared by the operating company begins to set the framework for a clear understanding of the facilities and of the image the hotel will project to the public. The operating company identifies the mix of guestrooms and suites; defines the specific restaurants, lounges, and function areas; details the amount of administrative office space; and allocates area to service functions—kitchens, receiving, storage, employee areas, laundry, housekeeping, engineering, and maintenance spaces. Table 14.6 proposes a room mix, summary space program (gross areas), and detailed space program (net areas) for hotels of three different sizes.

Development Software

Robert E. Kastner
President, 9 Tek Ltd
Email: kastner51@aol.com

Sophisticated software programs are essential in the development and construction process. Particularly useful are those systems that integrate multiple steps in hotel development and build upon each other, such as software that combines the building program, construction budgeting, and proforma financial analyses.

One example of such a program, which has been continually refined over more than twenty-five years, is the SHAPE Software System, a series of Excel templates that allow developers and consultants to generate detailed planning and analysis information for a proposed hotel or resort project anywhere in the world.

The first module, Strategic Hotel Area Program Estimate and Evaluation (SHAPEE), provides a programming template which allows the user to input such basic assumptions as typical guestroom area, number of restaurants and their capacities, and amount of function space. From this foundation the program generates a detailed area program (in either square feet or square meters), expanding these public areas and adding all the back-of-house support functions, which can be modified further as members of the design team develop a fuller sense of the hotel and its market.

The second module, Strategic Hotel Area and Project Estimate (SHAPEST), links SHAPEE to cost data, which calculates total project cost and other budget data on a per key or per bay basis. The cost estimates are dependent on such hotel attributes as quality level and location.

The last module, Strategic Hotel Analysis Program Evaluation and Proforma (SHAPEPRO), further builds on the previous modules and, by adding its own set of capital and operating assumptions, generates a 10-year cash flow projection. The developer may find most useful the integrated internal rate of return (IRR) and present value (PV) calculations, as well as a value-added (V-A) analysis which allows the user to run through any number of "what-if" scenarios: changing the space program; modifying construction, FF&E, or technical costs; or adjusting operating assumptions. Together, these programs, and others that may accomplish similar objectives, provide an essential tool to the developer and other members of the team.

(continued p. 312)

Table 14.6 Hotel area program

	Size of hotel (number of rooms)					
	200	**500**	**1,000**	**200**	**500**	**1,000**
Guestroom mix						
King (50%)	100	250	500	100	250	500
Double-double (42%)	84	210	430	84	210	430
Accessible (2–3%)	6	15	20	6	15	20
Suite (5%)	10	25	50	10	25	50
Summary hotel area program	Area in sq ft			Area in sq m		
Net guestrooms and suites area	69,125	197,000	394,375	6,420	18,300	36,635
Gross guestrooms and suites area (net area + 45%)	100,231	285,650	571,844	9,310	26,535	53,125
Lobby	2,900	6,000	12,100	270	555	1,125
Food and beverage outlets	5,600	13,750	23,200	520	1,275	2,155
Function areas	8,800	31,300	77,400	820	2,910	7,190
Recreation	950	6,550	12,050	90	610	1,120
Total net public area	18,250	57,600	124,750	1,695	5,350	11,590
Total gross public area (net area + 25%)	22,813	72,000	155,938	2,120	6,690	14,485
Administration	3,135	6,945	10,665	290	645	990
Food preparation	3,450	15,990	28,790	320	1,485	2,675
Receiving and storage	2,190	4,275	8,150	205	395	755
Employee areas	2,120	4,750	8,270	195	440	770
Laundry and housekeeping	2,100	5,900	9,990	195	550	930
Engineering	1,300	3,345	6,220	120	310	580
Mechanical (estimated)	2,850	10,600	20,300	265	985	1,885
Total net back-of-house area	17,145	51,805	92,385	1,595	4,815	8,585
Total gross back-of-house area (net area + 20%)	20,574	62,166	110,862	1,910	5,775	10,300
Total gross hotel area	143,618	419,816	838,643	13,340	39,000	77,910
Gross hotel area per key	718.1	839.6	838.6	66.7	78.0	77.9
Gross hotel area per bay	700.6	819.2	818.2	65.1	76.1	76.0
Detailed hotel area program	Area in sq ft			Area in sq m		
Guestrooms and suites						
Guestrooms @ 325 sq ft (30 sq m)	61,750			5,735		
Guestrooms @ 375 sq ft (35 sq m)		178,125	356,250		16,550	33,095
Suites (equal mix of one and two bays)	4,875	13,875	28,125	455	1,290	2,615
Support (linen storage, vending, ice)	2,500	5,000	10,000	230	465	930
Lobby						
Flow area	2,000	4,000	8,000	185	370	745
Seating	200	500	1,000	20	45	95
Retail	300	800	2,000	30	75	185
Assistant manager	0	100	100	0	10	10
Support (bellman, luggage, toilets, phones)	400	600	1,000	35	55	95
Food and beverage outlets						
Three-meal restaurant	3,000	4,800	6,000	280	445	555
Specialty restaurant	0	2,400	2,800	0	225	260
Theme restaurant	0	0	2,000	0	0	185
Quick service/grab'n'go	400	750	1,000	35	70	95
Lobby lounge	1,800	2,400	3,600	165	225	335
Cocktail lounge	0	0	1,800	0	0	165
Entertainment lounge/sports bar	0	2,400	3,600	0	225	335
Pool bar	0	0	400	0	0	35
Support (bar storage, toilets, coats)	400	1,000	2,000	35	95	185

Detailed hotel area program	Area in sq ft			Area in sq m		
Function areas						
Ballroom	5,000	12,000	30,000	465	1,115	2,785
Ballroom foyer	1,200	3,000	7,500	110	280	695
Junior ballroom	0	5,000	12,000	0	465	1,115
Junior ballroom foyer	0	1,500	3,000	0	140	280
Banquet rooms	0	3,000	8,000	0	280	745
Meeting rooms	1,400	2,400	5,000	130	225	465
Boardroom	0	800	1,500	0	75	140
Amphitheater	0	0	2,400	0	0	225
Support (function and AV storage, projection booth, toilets, coats)	1,200	3,600	8,000	110	335	745
Recreation						
Swimming pool (water surface not in total)	0	1,000	1,500	0	95	140
Pool, including deck, whirlpool	0	2,400	4,000	0	225	370
Lockers, toilets, sauna	300	600	1,000	30	55	95
Exercise room	600	1,000	1,500	55	95	140
Spa treatment rooms	0	1,000	2,400	0	95	225
Children's playroom	0	0	500	0	0	45
Reception/manager/office	0	150	350	0	15	35
Support (pool equipment and storage)	50	400	800	5	35	75
Administration						
Front office						
Reception	150	300	500	15	30	45
Front office manager	120	120	120	10	10	10
Assistant manager	0	100	100	0	10	10
Front office work area	120	240	450	10	20	40
Credit manager	100	100	100	10	10	10
Director of rooms	0	150	150	0	15	15
Reception/secretary	100	100	100	10	10	10
Reservations area	80	150	250	5	15	25
Reservations manager	0	100	100	0	10	10
Telephone operators	80	150	250	5	15	25
Telephone manager	0	100	100	0	10	10
Safe-deposit boxes	30	60	100	5	5	10
General cashier	0	120	120	0	10	10
Count room	125	150	200	10	15	20
Work area/mail/storage	80	150	250	5	15	25
Executive office						
Reception/waiting	200	250	300	20	25	30
General manager	150	200	250	15	20	25
Executive assistant manager	0	180	180	0	15	15
Resident manager	0	0	180	0	0	15
Food and beverage manager	120	150	175	10	15	15
Secretary	100	150	200	10	15	20
Conference room	0	200	250	0	20	25
Copying and storage	60	120	200	5	10	20
Sales and catering						
Reception/waiting	150	200	300	15	20	30
Director of sales	150	150	200	15	15	20
Revenue manager	100	120	150	10	10	15
Sales representatives	150	300	600	15	30	55

Table 14.6 continued

Detailed hotel area program	Area in sq ft			Area in sq m		
Director of public relations	0	150	150	0	15	15
Secretary	0	225	375	0	20	35
Catering manager	120	150	200	10	15	20
Banquet managers	100	200	400	10	20	35
Beverage manager	0	120	120	0	10	10
Convention services	100	120	240	10	10	20
Secretary	0	150	225	0	15	20
Copying and storage	60	150	300	5	15	30
Accounting						
Reception/waiting	0	100	200	0	10	20
Controller	120	150	180	10	15	15
Assistant controller/auditor	0	100	100	0	10	10
Accounting work area	150	500	800	15	45	75
Payroll manager	120	120	150	10	10	15
Secretary	0	100	300	0	10	30
Copying and storage	100	200	250	10	20	25
Computer room	0	100	400	0	10	35
Accounting records archive	100	200	400	10	20	35
Food preparation						
Main kitchen	2,000	8,000	14,000	185	745	1,300
Banquet pantry	0	3,000	6,000	0	280	555
Specialty restaurant pantry	0	1,000	1,500	0	95	140
Bakeshop	0	600	1,000	0	55	95
Room-service area	100	300	500	10	30	45
Chef's office	100	120	120	10	10	10
Dry food storage	400	1,000	1,800	35	95	165
Refrigerated food storage	200	500	1,200	20	45	110
Beverage storage	150	450	1,000	15	40	95
Refrigerated beverage storage	100	250	400	10	25	35
China, silver, glass storage	200	500	1,000	20	45	95
Food controller office	100	120	120	10	10	10
Toilets	100	150	150	10	15	15
Receiving and storage						
Loading dock	200	400	800	20	35	75
Receiving area	250	500	1,200	25	45	110
Receiving office	120	150	150	10	15	15
Purchasing office	120	175	200	10	15	20
Locked storage	100	250	400	10	25	35
Trash/recycling area	200	400	800	20	35	75
Grounds equipment storage	200	400	600	20	35	55
General storage	1,000	2,000	4,000	95	185	370
Employee areas						
Human resources						
Personnel/reception	120	150	200	10	15	20
Personnel manager	120	140	160	10	15	15
Assistant personnel manager	0	120	120	0	10	10
Interview rooms	100	100	200	10	10	20
Training room	0	250	400	0	25	35
Files and storage	100	150	200	10	15	20
First aid	80	100	150	5	10	15

Detailed hotel area program	Area in sq ft			Area in sq m		
Timekeeper	100	120	120	10	10	10
Security	0	120	120	0	10	10
Employee facilities						
Men's lockers/toilets	400	900	1,800	35	85	165
Women's lockers/toilets	500	1,200	2,400	45	110	225
Banquet staff lockers	0	400	600	0	35	55
Employee cafeteria	600	1,000	1,800	55	95	165
Laundry and housekeeping						
Laundry						
Soiled-linen room	100	150	150	10	15	15
Laundry	1,000	2,500	4,000	95	230	370
Laundry supervisor	0	100	120	0	10	10
Valet laundry	0	250	400	0	25	35
Supplies storage	50	125	200	5	10	20
Housekeeping						
Housekeeper	100	125	150	10	10	15
Assistant housekeeper	0	100	120	0	10	10
Secretary	0	100	100	0	10	10
Linen storage	500	1,500	3,000	45	140	280
Uniform issue/storage	250	500	1,000	25	45	95
Supplies storage	50	150	250	5	15	25
Lost and found	50	150	250	5	15	25
Sewing room	0	150	250	0	15	25
Engineering						
Engineer	100	125	150	10	10	15
Assistant engineer	0	100	100	0	10	10
Secretary	100	100	100	10	10	10
Engineering work area	500	1,000	2,500	45	95	230
Carpentry shop	300	400	700	30	35	65
Plumbing shop	0	200	350	0	20	35
Electrical shop	0	200	350	0	20	35
Paint shop	0	200	350	0	20	35
Energy management computer	0	120	120	0	10	10
Engineering storeroom	300	900	1,500	30	85	140
Mechanical areas (estimated)						
Mechanical plant	1,200	6,000	12,000	110	555	1,115
Transformer room	400	1,200	1,800	35	110	165
Emergency generator	300	600	1,000	30	55	95
Meter room	50	150	250	5	15	25
Fire pumps	0	150	250	0	15	25
Electrical switchboard	500	1,500	3,000	45	140	280
Elevator machine room	200	500	1,000	20	45	95
Telephone equipment room	200	500	1,000	20	45	95

Bethesda Marriott Suites, Bethesda, Maryland
Marriott has redesigned the lobby in most of its older hotels to incorporate a "great room," designed to be a flexible public space for greeting arriving guests, light eating, meeting, and general socializing. It generally incorporates reception pods, individual and group seating areas, café, and associated outdoor terraces.

- Architectural configuration (low- or high-rise, shape of guestroom tower)
- Number of floors (added floors greatly increase amount of vertical circulation)
- Location of food and beverage outlets (may require various satellite kitchens)
- Location of the ballroom (may require pantry; also establishes column-free zone that affects guestroom-tower placement)
- Availability of basement space
- Ratio of land to gross building area (affects stacking of public areas, duplication of circulation and lobbies, and need for parking structure)

Describing the Operations

The facilities program is incomplete until the future hotel operations, as well as the basic space requirements, are fully defined and described. Usually developed by the hotel operator, the description of the operations includes various checklists of guest services, proposed staffing levels, and back-of-house activities, in addition to schematic diagrams that show the designer which spaces must be adjacent to each other. Because services vary greatly from property to property, the complexity and importance of their description also differs.

Among the most challenging aspects of hotel design is the necessity to develop a plan that accommodates both the great variety of guest markets and the operational requirements of the hotel. These often are in conflict, and the cost of providing for every need is likely to be prohibitive. Architects and operators have to make countless value-judgments: for example, about whether the hotel will cater primarily to individuals or to groups, the relative prominence of the several restaurants and lounges, or the importance of direct food service to the secondary meeting rooms.

For the most part, the key planning objective is to group public functions around the lobby, to position service functions convenient to the receiving area, and to cluster food outlets and function rooms around the kitchen.

Many operating decisions are changing because of the increased automation and computerization of the hotel industry. Its labor-intensive character forces hotel management to create innovative procedures and systems to reduce the necessity for repetitive staff work while maintaining a quality level of service. Table 14.7 identifies the range of the necessary operational program decisions that management must make, which influence the planning and design decisions.

One area that directly affects the guests' perception of the entire hotel is the food and beverage operation. The operator or a qualified restaurant consultant must provide highly detailed descriptions of each individual restaurant and lounge so that the architect, interior designer, and kitchen planner can develop a unified design and operation. The description of the food and beverage concept should detail every aspect of the operation, including capacity, floor area, name and graphics, menu, theme, hours, staffing, special equipment, uniforms, and table-service requirements. Starwood Hotels developed a series of restaurant concepts for their hotels, some of them brand-

Operating companies issue their programming material in a variety of forms. Many hotel companies have developed extremely detailed space programs for different-sized hotels and for different locations or markets. These programs specify precise area requirements. For example, the lobby program may list area requirements for public seating, bell stand, luggage storage, sundries shop, house and public phones, and so forth. Global Hyatt, among other operators, provides a moderately detailed list of most functional areas and their space requirements, but simply states that the lobby should be a "function of the architectural design, of ample space and character appropriate to its function of welcoming guests and serving as a popular meeting place." These two approaches illustrate the different development strategies of today's management companies. Still, all brands regularly modify and update their standards to introduce new ideas and accommodate growing market trends. For example, Marriott recently has changed its lobby concept in most corporate hotels, establishing a "great room," a more open space that encourages guests to work, plug in, socialize, and relax.

Therefore, a precise program depends on understanding the interconnection between a variety of planning and design aspects of hotels. It is clear that the relative size of the guestroom is a major determinant of total project area; it is less obvious that the eventual choice of a particular configuration for the guestroom structure (see Chapter 15) can influence the project's total size and budget by 15 to 20 percent.

Developing a clear project statement may help to define some of the quality, facilities, and architectural alternatives that are basic to establishing an accurate program. The following factors, many of which are undetermined until the schematic design phase is complete, greatly influence the space requirements for hotels and resorts:

Table 14.7 Operational program decisions

Guest services

Parking	Valet or self-park? Garage or on-grade?
Luggage handling	By guest or bellman? Use public or service elevator?
Front desk procedures	Safe deposit?
Guestroom food service	Hours, menu, cart or tray service?
Restaurant service	Hours, types of service, theme dining, retail operations, outdoor, etc.?
Recreation	Hours, open to public, children, lockers nearby, food service?
Guestroom communications	Telephone(s), TV cable/movies, wired, wireless Internet, etc.?
Guestroom amenities	Coffee maker, iron/ironing board?
Guestroom services	Evening turndown, concierge floor or butler?
Guest security	Cardkey system, fire alarm and evacuation procedures?

Staff operations

Employee entrance	Timekeeper, security?
Employee uniforms	Issuing, laundering, storage?
Employee facilities	Cafeteria, lounge, recreation, housing?
Staff communications	Cell phone, pager?
Information technology	Property management system, revenue management, point of sale, etc.?
Accounting/controls	F&B control, purchasing/receiving, drop-safe, closed circuit television?
Food preparation	Central or decentralized?

Material handling

Receiving area	Weather protection, separate from trash, security?
Trash and garbage	Holding, compactor, recycling?
Laundry	In-house, guest valet, hours/shifts?
Vertical circulation	Stocking of linen rooms, rooftop restaurant, linen/trash chutes?

specific, others internal signature concepts or third-party operator concepts. Chapter 17 includes basic outlines for food and beverage concept checklists (see page 349).

The description of the hotel operations also should include a complete staffing program. The number of employees and their assignments affect the space requirements in three primary areas: administrative offices, employee lockers and toilets, and employee cafeteria. In resorts and some international hotels, staff housing may even be required; and in Muslim countries, prayer rooms are standard in the back-of-house and appear in some public areas. In addition, the staffing program dictates the need or desirability for different systems and equipment in the numerous office and back-of-house areas.

Preparing the Project Budget

A final part of the facilities program is the preparation of an outline budget summary (see Appendix C). Because total project cost varies

10-fold or more—from less than $60,000 for small inns to well over $600,000 per guestroom for the finest luxury hotels—strict budget control throughout the entire design and construction process is critical. Budgeting is made more difficult by the common practice in hotel work of using separate architectural and interior design firms. Therefore, the developer must define precisely the design and budget responsibilities of the architect, interior designer, and other consultants, for example differentiating between the general construction budget and the furniture, fixtures, and equipment (FF&E) budget. This is further defined in the sample budget coordination matrix, in Appendix E.

In addition, the entire FF&E category, with which the architect and many developers often are unfamiliar, frequently approaches 20 percent of the total project budget. It is important that the FF&E and pre-opening budgets are developed collaboratively by the consultants and hotel operator, to assure that sufficient amounts are allocated to these key lines. In addition to the FF&E budget, the operator is responsible for operating supplies and equipment (OS&E) and needs to develop that budget. The extraordinary total amount of non-bricks-and-mortar dollars required to equip and open a hotel emphasizes the need to establish sound budgetary controls at the outset.

Prototype Development

The growth in hotel prototypes began in the mid-1980s and continues today as an approach for hotel chains to launch new brands. Many of the major management companies, such as Marriott and Holiday Inn, realized that they were saturating their traditional downtown or roadside locations, and needed new products in order to continue to grow. Marriott launched its Courtyard brand, to compete with mid-price roadside properties; Holiday Inn countered with Embassy Suites and Crowne Plaza, which, although very different in their physical characteristics, appeal to the business market, and, more recently, the mid-tier Holiday Inn Express. In every case, the new products were based on imaginative and well-studied designs and market concepts. The list of significant brand prototypes that are becoming virtual household names includes:

- Embassy Suites, the largest of the early upscale all-suite prototypes; the two-room suites initially were designed around an atrium.
- Residence Inn, the leading extended-stay prototype, acquired by Marriott.
- Courtyard by Marriott, initially developed as a roadside inn and organized around a central landscaped courtyard, but so successful that Marriott now builds many urban high-rise "courtyard" projects.
- Hilton Garden Inn, intended to match the success of Marriott's Courtyard developments; also frequently developed as an urban "garden inn."
- Crowne Plaza, Holiday Inn's most successful response to the franchisees' requests for an upscale prototype for a downtown or suburban business hotel.
- Home2 Suites, Hilton's new mid-tier extended-stay product, with large public gathering areas, complimentary breakfast, retail market, large studio and one-bedroom suites, and including several "green" initiatives.
- Ian Schrager's one-off boutique hotels, followed by Bill Kimpton's Palomar and Chip Conley's Joie de Vivre brands, all early boutique hotel chains (see Design Hotels, Chapter 3).
- W Hotels, the first boutique brand by a major chain (Starwood), intended to dominate the segment.
- Formule 1, the economically innovative product from the French operator Accor, its rooms typically furnished with both a double bed and loft bed; it has shared public showers and toilets in Europe but private facilities in other regions.
- Element, Westin Hotel's environmentally conscious new brand, with mandated LEED certification, full guestroom kitchens and spa-like bathrooms.
- Hotel Indigo, IHG's entry into the mid-price boutique segment, offering the reliability of a branded hotel.

- Pod Hotel, in New York and being developed in other North American cities, with private bathrooms and outstanding in-room technology, for the spartan business customer.

Creating a new lodging prototype has several obvious advantages. First, the company can focus greater research and design resources on developing one superior concept, adaptable to a wide variety of conditions and sites. Many prototypes feature low- and mid-rise options, sometimes with both indoor and outdoor corridor schemes, or with an atrium alternative. Also, they may include different public area options: one version may have no F&B areas, another a small breakfast lounge or gourmet grab'n'go pantry, while others feature a full-service restaurant, the decision depending on the size of the hotel and its immediate surroundings. Accor's budget-brand Formule 1 incorporates private bathrooms in most world regions, but has shared showers and toilets in Europe.

Second, the product, through repeated analysis, should be able to better meet the customers' expectations. The construction of the physical asset is the largest single investment over the life of a hotel or inn, and it is imperative that it be "right" from the start.

Third, prototype development saves reinventing the wheel on each new project. The company should be able to test-market its new concepts and closely monitor the customers' reactions, fine-tuning the project in its successive versions.

Companies developing different prototype lodging products may proceed along either of two separate paths. One is to develop a standard property design, and to expand it in a "cookie-cutter" approach across a region or country. Often, the prototype includes a series of design options to overcome excessive standardization, but the basic goal must be justified by substantial savings in project cost or design and construction time that otherwise could not be achieved. One example is La Quinta Inns' early prefabrication system. Very different but equally viable is the "protopart" or kit-of-parts approach, as illustrated by Embassy Suites' partial plans of buildings, from typical guestrooms and suites to health center, kitchen, and laundry layouts—as well as scores of standardized details.

In the first case, the prototype system should not dictate a standardized appearance to the extent that its usefulness is diminished. Therefore, it must provide flexibility for site differences and alternate designs appropriate to different regions. The second example, the "protopart" system, encourages greater flexibility for adapting the program and design to meet the requirements set out by local authorities that, to their credit, may require the design to blend in with its surrounding environment. Some of the original cookie-cutter products completely reversed their initial strategy to one of encouraging flexibility in their exterior designs. Table 14.8 lists many of the significant examples of major prototypical developments in the twentieth century, often illustrated throughout the book. Many of these don't incorporate "cookie-cutter" design solutions; rather, they are innovations in architectural design or hotel management that have had a major impact on the lodging industry.

Table 14.8 Influential hotel prototypes of the past century and into the future

Design concept	Major originator	Hotel design
The modern multi-story hotel	Ellsworth M. Statler	Statler Hotel, Buffalo, New York
The mixed-use hotel–office building	Ellsworth M. Statler	Park Plaza Hotel and Statler Office Building, Boston, Massachusetts
The family roadside hotel	Kemmons Wilson	Holiday Inn, Memphis, Tennessee
The super-budget motel	Jean-Marc Espalioux	Formule 1 prototype, France
The airport terminal hotel	Conrad Hilton	Hilton Chicago O'Hare Airport, Chicago, Illinois
The medical hotel	Kahler Corporation	Kahler Hotels, Rochester, Minnesota
The modern convention headquarters hotel	Tisch Brothers and architect Morris Lapidus	Americana Hotel, New York City
	Uris Brothers and architect William B. Tabler	New York Hilton, New York City
The modern atrium hotel	John C. Portman, Jr.	Hyatt Regency Hotel, Atlanta, Georgia
The conference center	Walter Green	Harrison Conference Center, Glen Cove, New York
The extended-stay hotel	Jack DeBoer	Residence Inn, Wichita, Kansas
The all-suite hotel	Robert Woolley	Granada Royal, San Antonio, Texas
	Walter A. Rutes	Embassy Suites prototype
The modern beach resort	Morris Lapidus	Fontainebleau, Miami Beach, Florida
	Carl Fisher	Development of Miami Beach, Florida
The fantasy resort	Chris Hemmeter	Hyatt Regency Hotels, Kaanapali, Waikaloa, and Kauai, Hawaii
The modern spa resort	Allard Roen and Ward Hutton	La Costa, Carlsbad, California
The eco-resort	Stanley Selengut	Harmony Bay Camps, St. John, U.S. Virgin Islands
The environmental resort	Laurance Rockefeller and architects Nathaniel Owings and Charles Bassett	Mauna Kea Beach Resort (RockResorts), The Big Island, Hawaii
	George (Pete) Wimberly	Intercontinental Hotel, Tahara'a, Tahiti
The vacation village	Serge Trigano	Club Med, France
The resort theme park	Walt Disney	Polynesian Resort, Walt Disney World, Orlando, Florida
The boutique hotel	Steven Rubell, Ian Schrager, and designer Philippe Starck	Morgan's and the Royalton, New York City
	William Kimpton	Vintage Court, San Francisco, California
The entertainment hotel Show business themes	John L. Tishman and architects Arquitectonica and D'Agostino Izzo Quirk	Westin New York (Times Square), New York City
	Forrest City Ratner and architect Beyer Blinder Belle	Hilton Times Square, New York City
	Madison Equities and architect Frank Williams	W Times Square, New York City
Educational themes	The Moody Foundation and Morris Architects	Moody Gardens, Galveston, Texas
	Bayindir Holding and architect Oktay Nayman with HHCP Design International, theme park consultant	Bati Tourism Center and Tatilya Theme Park, West Istanbul, Turkey
Downtown resort and sports and event center	Tankanaka Corp. and architect César Pelli	Sea Hawk, Fukuoka, Japan
Sports stadium hotel	Wright Adjeleian Allen Rubell and NORR Partnership	Renaissance Hotel at Toronto SkyDome, Toronto, Canada
The chain hotel with a super-luxury rating	Four Seasons Hotels and architects Pei Cobb Freed and Frank Williams	Four Seasons Hotel, New York City
The mega-hotel	William J. Marriott	Orlando World Center Marriott Resort, Orlando, Florida
The ultra-tel	John C. Portman, Jr.	The Westin Peachtree Plaza, Atlanta, Georgia
	I. M. Pei	Westin Stamford Hotel, Raffles City, Singapore
The spacetel	International consortia	NASA, Houston, Texas
	Design Studies	WATG, Irvine, California
	Design Studies	Space Island Group, Los Angeles, California
Luxury boutique resort	Adrian Zecha	Amanpuri, Phuket, Thailand, and Amandari, Bali, Indonesia
Lifestyle chains	Barry Sternlicht	W New York, New York City
Pod hotels	Simon Woodroffe and Gerard Greene	Yotel, Gatwick Airport, London, U.K.
Co-branding with fashion	Gordon McKinnon	Hotel Missoni, Edinburgh, Scotland
		Bulgari, Milan, Italy
Multi-branded hotels	Al Gulamani	Hampton Inn and Homewood Suites, Toronto Airport, Canada
	Bruce White	Marriott Place, Indianapolis, Indiana

The Guestroom Floor

The planning of the typical guestroom floor presents one of the greatest challenges in hotel design. Because the guestrooms and suites generally represent between 65 and 85 percent of the total floor area in a hotel or resort, any savings in the planning of a single level are multiplied many times. Therefore, a major planning goal in every lodging project should be to maximize the amount of salable guestroom space and keep to a minimum the vertical core, horizontal circulation, and necessary support areas.

In addition, there are several important architectural objectives. The architect should select a particular plan configuration and orient the building to enhance the appearance and visibility of the structure, to reduce energy costs, and to better accommodate possible future expansion. As lodging demand increases the developer may want to add rooms, either by extending the guestroom wings, adding additional floors, or constructing a new tower structure. For many projects, depending on the location, the architect needs to consider a configuration and orientation to take advantage of views from the guestrooms. In developing the plan itself, the designer should reduce as much as possible the walking distances for both the guest and the housekeeping staff, provide the support functions, and seek ways to reduce construction cost and non-salable space. Table 15.1 lists the principal guestroom-floor planning objectives.

The program requirements for the guestroom floors are relatively few: a designated number of guestrooms or suites, conveniently located public and service elevators, exit stairways to meet the building code and provide safe egress, adequate linen storage and vending areas, and small electrical and telephone equipment rooms.

The analysis of alternate plan configurations for the guestroom structure is one of the earliest design studies for a hotel, even before the exact guestroom mix is confirmed. The conceptual program may call for, say, 300 rooms including 15 suites, at a typical size of 350 sq ft (32.5 sq m). The architect starts with the objective of providing a specific number of guestroom bays of a particular size and, taking into account constraints and opportunities of a particular site, may initially select a double-loaded corridor configuration, or a more compact vertical tower, or a spacious atrium structure—each with its myriad variations. Low-rise properties generally are planned using a double-loaded corridor and may be shaped into L, T, or another configuration. High-rise buildings may follow similar patterns, can be terraced into pyramid-like forms, or can adjoin a large lobby space so that some of the rooms look into the hotel interior. The tower plan, where the guestrooms surround a central core, can be rectangular, circular, or practically any shape. And the atrium configuration, in early hotels such as the Hyatt Regency Atlanta a basic rectangular plan, in

Gaylord National, Washington, DC
The hotel has efficiently planned guestroom floors in double-loaded wings surrounding the lobby atrium, some rooms overlooking the activity in the lobby space (see pp. 197–199).

Table 15.1 Guestroom-floor planning objectives

Siting and orientation

❑ Site the guestroom structure to be visible from the street.

❑ Orient guestrooms to enhance views.

❑ Assess the relative visual impact and construction cost of various guestroom plan configurations.

❑ Position the guestroom structure to limit its structural impact on the ballroom and other major public spaces.

❑ Consider solar gain; generally north–south is preferable to east–west exposures.

Floor layout

❑ Organize the plan so that the guestrooms occupy at least 70 percent of the gross floor area.

❑ Locate elevators and stairs at interior locations to use maximum of outside wall for guestrooms.

❑ Develop the corridor plan to facilitate guest and staff circulation.

❑ Place the public elevators in the middle third of the structure.

❑ Provide service elevators, linen storage, and vending in a central location.

❑ Plan corridor width at a minimum of 5 ft (1.5 m); 5'–6" (1.65 m) optional.

❑ Design guest bathrooms back-to-back for plumbing economies.

❑ Locate disabled-accessible guestrooms near guest elevators.

more recent projects has taken on numerous complex shapes. These various configurations are illustrated with selected plans throughout this chapter; a fuller discussion of the design of individual guestrooms and suites appears in the next chapter.

What is the most appropriate configuration for the guestrooms? In densely populated urban areas, where land costs are high and the site may be relatively small, organizing an ideal arrangement of public and support spaces on the lower floors may be the most critical consideration. Two major planning requirements, the preferred location of the public and service elevators and of the column-free ballroom, often dictate both the placement of the guestroom structure on the site and its shape. At resort properties, on the other hand, the opposite is true: the internal functional organization of the hotel elements is secondary to the careful siting of the buildings to minimize their impact on the site and to provide views of the surrounding landscape, beach, or mountains. Many newer resorts feature not a single building but, instead, provide a number of villa structures that greatly reduce the perceived scale of the project and give the guest a greater connection to the site and the recreational amenities, as well as an enhanced sense of privacy. At airport sites, height limitations often dictate the choice of a specific plan, one that packages the rooms into a relatively low and spread-out structure. The earlier chapters illustrate scores of hotels and resorts and make clear the great variety of possible guestroom-floor configurations.

While the choice of a plan type is the result of a balanced consideration of site, environment, and program requirements, the architect must realize that a particular configuration will shape the economics of the project. In addition to these budgetary issues—the initial construction and FF&E costs, as well as ongoing energy and payroll expenses—plan type also influences the more subtle aspects of guest satisfaction. The most economical design may not provide the best design solution. Thus, a less efficient plan type may offer more variety in room types, a more interesting spatial sequence,

shorter walking distances, or other advantages that affect the guest's perception of the value of the hotel experience.

Analyzing Alternative Plan Configurations

In order for the operator to realize profits, the design team must attempt to maximize the percentage of floor area devoted to guestrooms and keep to a minimum the amount of circulation and service space (service elevator lobby, linen storage, vending, and other minor support spaces). Although the architect and developer must not ignore aesthetic and other functional issues, a simple comparison among the alternative plans of the percentage of space allocated to guestrooms versus non-revenue-producing space can suggest more efficient solutions. The major alternatives among plan types are described in Table 15.2.

An analysis of the plans of more than 100 different guestroom floors shows that some patterns yield more cost-effective solutions than other types. The choice of one configuration over another can mean a saving of 20 percent in gross floor area of the guestroom structure and of nearly 15 percent in the total building. For example, the three principal plan alternatives—the double-loaded slab, the rectangular tower, and the atrium—when designed with identical guestrooms of 350 net sq ft (32.5 sq m) yield final designs that vary from about 470 to 580 gross sq ft (44 to 54 sq m) per room.

The study also indicates the effect of subsequent minor decisions on the efficiency of the plan—pairing two guestrooms back-to-back, choosing a double- or single-loaded corridor, grouping of public and service elevators, and planning efficient access to end or corner rooms. Because guestrooms account for such a major part of the total hotel area, the architect should establish a series of quantitative benchmarks for the efficient design of the guestroom floors.

The relative efficiency of typical hotel floors can be compared most directly by calculating the percentage of the total floor area devoted to guestrooms. This varies from below 60 percent in an inefficient atrium plan to more than 75 percent in the most tightly designed double-loaded slab. Clearly, the higher this percentage, the lower the construction cost per room, which, in turn, offers the developer a range of options. He or she may choose to build additional guestrooms, provide larger guestrooms for the same capital investment, improve the quality of the furnishings or of particular building systems, expand other functional areas, such as meeting space or recreational facilities, or simply lower the construction cost and project budget.

The following sections describe, for each of the basic guestroom configurations, the planning decisions that have the most influence on creating an economical plan. In some cases, it is the number of rooms per floor; in others it is the location of the elevator core; or in another it may be the shape of the building that is most critical. In general, the most efficient configurations are those where circulation space is kept to a minimum—either the double-loaded corridor slab or the compact center-core tower.

Table 15.2 Guestroom floor analysis

Configuration	Rooms per floor	Dimensions ft (m)	Guestroom (percent)	Corridor sq ft (sq m) per room	Comments
Single-loaded slab	Varies 12–30+	32 (10) x any length	65	80 (7.5)	Vertical core usually not affected by room module
Double-loaded slab	Varies 16–40+	60 (18) x any length	70	45 (4.2)	Economical length limited by egress stair placement to meet building code
Offset double-loaded slab	Varies 24–40+	80 (24) x any length	72	50 (4.6)	Core is buried, creating less perimeter wall per room; more corridor because of elevator lobby
Rectangular tower	16–24	110 x 110 (34 x 34)	65	60 (5.6)	Planning issues focus on access to corner rooms; fewer rooms per floor make core layout difficult
Circular tower	16–24	90–130 diameter (27–40)	67	45–65 (4.2–6)	High amounts of exterior wall per room; difficult to plan guest bathroom
Triangular tower	24–30	Varies	64	65–85 (6–7.9)	Central core inefficient owing to shape; corner rooms easier to plan than with square tower
Atrium	24+	90+ (27)	62	95 (8.8)	Open volume creates spectacular space, open corridors, opportunity for glass elevators; requires careful engineering for HVAC and smoke evacuation

Each guestroom floor configuration has certain characteristics that affect its potential planning efficiency. The table shows the basic building width or dimensions, the usual percentage of floor area devoted to guestrooms, and the amount of area per room needed for corridors. For example, the table shows that the offset double-loaded slab is the most efficient in terms of maximizing guestroom area and that the atrium configuration is the least economical, largely because of the high amount of corridor area required per room.

Slab Configuration

The "slab" configuration includes those plans that are primarily horizontal, including both single- and double-loaded corridor schemes (see plans above). The few planning variables are concerned primarily with the building's shape (straight, angled, L-shaped, or other), the layout of the core, and the placement of the fire stairs. The architect must answer the following questions:

- *Corridor loading:* Given site conditions, are any single-loaded rooms appropriate?

- *Shape:* Which particular shape (straight, "offset," L, "knuckle," courtyard, or other configuration) best meets site and building constraints?
- *Core location:* Should the public and the service cores be combined or separated, and where in the tower should they be positioned?
- *Core layout:* What is the best way to organize public and service elevators, linen storage, vending, and other support areas?
- *Stair location:* How can the egress stairs best be integrated into the plan?

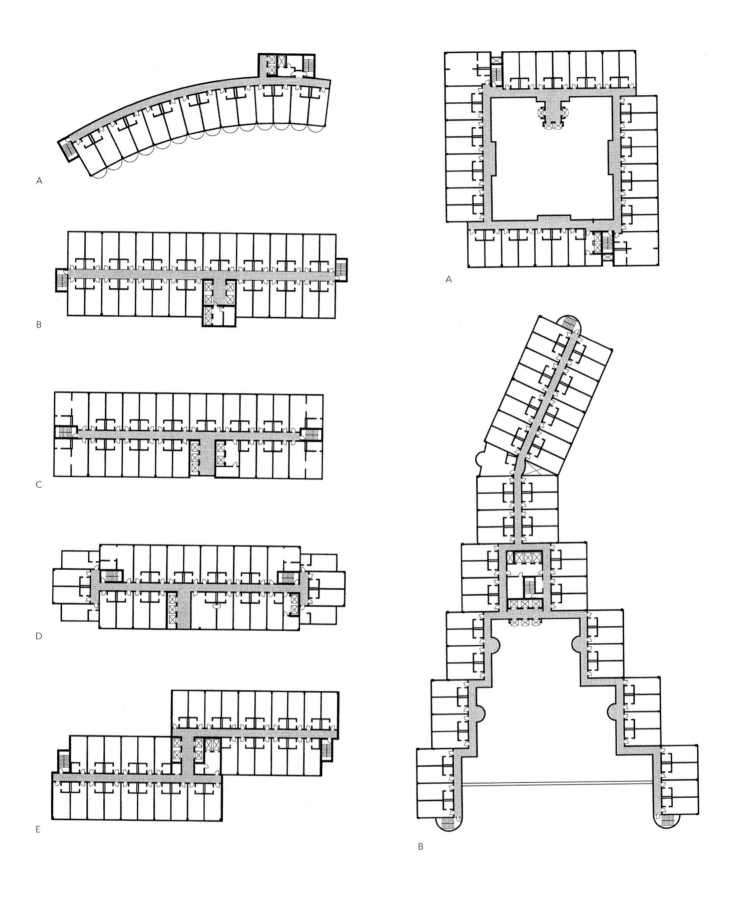

A

B

C

D

E

A

B

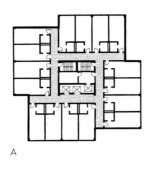

A

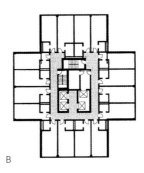

B

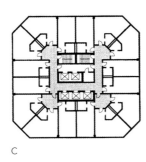

C

D

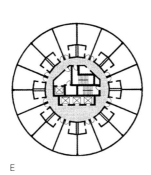

E

F

Tower configurations
(A) Pinwheel plan accommodates all typical rooms but requires extra corridor area. (B) Cross-shape plan reduces corridor but increases building perimeter. (C) Square tower features efficient circulation and back-to-back bathrooms. (D) Square tower provides most corner guestrooms and minimal circulation. (E) Circular tower offers minimum area and perimeter but substantially smaller bathrooms. (F) Triangular tower has less efficient core, but more variety in room shape.

(facing page – far left)
Slab configurations
(A) Single-loaded plans, while more costly, are sometimes necessary for narrow sites or to take advantage of views. (B–D) Double-loaded plans show shared back-to-back bathrooms, and the most efficient options for elevator cores, egress stairs, and service functions. (E) Offset slab plans offer efficiency of interior core and more variety in the building massing.

(facing page – left)
Atrium configurations
(A) Typical atrium features scenic elevators and single-loaded balcony corridors. (B) Hybrid atrium plan combines visual excitement of atrium space with more efficient double-loaded slab extension.

The high degree of efficiency of the slab plan is based primarily on the double loading of the corridors; single-loaded schemes require 5 to 8 percent more floor area for the same number of rooms. Therefore, only where external factors are present—a narrow site dimension or spectacular views in only one direction—should single-loading be considered.

While slab plans as a category are the most efficient, experienced hotel architects and management company staff have found approaches to further tighten the layout of the typical floor. Configurations that bury the elevator and service cores in interior corners have several advantages. They slightly reduce the non-guestroom area, substantially reduce the amount of building perimeter, and increase the opportunities for creating architecturally interesting buildings. The "offset slab" plan, for example, is especially economical because the public and service elevator cores share one area and, in addition, they do not displace any guestrooms from the building perimeter. The "knuckle" configuration, which bends at angles, creates the potential for interestingly shaped elevator lobbies, provides compact service areas, and breaks up the slab's long corridors.

The core design is complicated by the need to connect the public elevators to the lobby and the service elevators to the housekeeping and other back-of-house areas. This often necessitates two distinct core areas at some distance from each other, although in many hotels they are located side-by-side. One common objective is to position the elevator core in the middle third of a floor in order to reduce the walking distances to the farthest rooms. Most often, the vertical core is fully integrated into the body of the tower but, occasionally, the designer may, for planning reasons, add the core to the end of a compact room block or extend it out from the face of the façade.

The actual layout of the core is another determining factor of efficiency in the typical plan. In most slab-plan hotels, the vertical cores require space equivalent to two to four guestroom modules. If one goal is to keep the core to a minimum, then the efficiency of the plan is improved when the core displaces the fewest number of guestroom bays. The comparison of many projects shows that the vertical core displaces fewer guestroom bays when the service areas are located behind the public elevators, rather than beside them or at some distance. Many of the more efficient configurations also feature a distinct elevator lobby. Such a foyer space helps to isolate the noise and congestion of waiting people from nearby guestrooms. Also, those plans which incorporate an elevator lobby tend to have fewer awkwardly shaped rooms, thereby providing a more uniform guestroom product.

Building codes generally require egress stairs at opposite ends of the building. Each stair tower might simply replace the last guestroom on the corridor. But, instead, the architect may be able to integrate the stairs within the building, as part of an elevator core, at an "inside corner" where the building turns, or within the usual bathroom zone of a guestroom bay (where it is part of an oversized room or suite). Careful placement of the stairs provides one more opportunity to create a more efficient overall plan by reducing gross floor area, compared with simply attaching the stair tower to the end of the building.

One limiting factor to the number of rooms on the guestroom floor is the typical building code requirement for hotels with automatic sprinklers that there be no more than, say, 300 ft (91 m) between egress stairs. Therefore, another goal in planning the repetitive guestroom floor is to create a layout that does not require a third fire stair. Experienced hotel architects have established techniques for maximizing the number of rooms per floor and manipulating the stairs and corridors to increase the building's overall efficiency.

Tower Configuration

A second major category of guestroom-floor plans is "tower" plans, generally organized with a central core surrounded by a single-loaded corridor and guestrooms (see accompanying plans). The exterior architectural treatment of the tower can vary widely as the geometric shape of the plan changes from square to cross-shaped, circular to triangular. The tower plan exhibits very different characteristics than the slab, but raises a similar series of questions for the designer:

- *Number of rooms:* How many guestrooms economically fit a particular layout?
- *Shape:* Which shape is most efficient and permits the desired mix of rooms?
- *Corridor:* How is hallway access to corner rooms arranged?
- *Core layout:* How are the elevators, linen storage, and stairs organized?

Unlike the other plan configurations, selection of the tower shape creates specific limitations on the number of rooms per floor. For the most part, towers contain between 16 and 24 rooms, depending on the guestroom dimensions, the number of floors, and the optimum core size. With only 16 rooms, the core is barely large enough for two or three elevators, two egress stairs, and minimum amounts of storage. On the other hand, designs with more than 24 rooms become so inflated and the core so large that the layout becomes highly inefficient.

For most guestroom configurations, the efficiency is improved by increasing the number of rooms on a floor, with little or no increase in the core or building services. With the tower plan, the opposite is true. The analysis of a large sample of hotel designs shows that, surprisingly, the fewer the number of rooms per floor, the more efficient the layout becomes: the core by necessity must be extremely compact and, as a result, the amount of corridor area is kept to a bare minimum. The more *inefficient* layouts often result from *adding* rooms and from extending single-loaded corridors into each of the building corners.

The shape of the tower has a direct effect on the appearance of the structure and on its perceived scale. The efficiency of the plan is also a direct result of the shape, because of the critical nature of the corridor access to the corner rooms in the rectangular towers and because of the design of the wedge-shaped guestroom and bathroom in the circular towers. Those plans that minimize the amount of circulation and, in addition, create unusual corner rooms exemplify the best in both architectural planning and interior layout.

For circular tower plans, the measures of efficiency are judged by the layout of the room as well as the core design. Typically, the perimeter of the wedge-shaped guestroom is about 16 ft (4.9 m), whereas the corridor dimension may be less than 8 ft (2.4 m), thus challenging the designer's skill to plan the bathroom, entry vestibule, and closet.

While the design of the core in both rectangular and circular towers is less critical than the arrangement of guestrooms, certain specific issues have to be resolved. Generally, the core is centrally located, and the vertical elements are tightly grouped. The smaller hotels, those with only 16 rooms per floor, usually do not feature an elevator lobby, and the guests in rooms opposite the elevators must tolerate noise from waiting guests. In a few cases, the core is split into two parts, creating a roughly H-shaped circulation zone, and effectively providing an elevator lobby on each floor. The two fire stairs can be efficiently arranged in a scissors configuration (if permitted by code) to conserve space.

In the larger tower plans, those with 24 or more rooms per floor, the central core becomes excessively large. Some hotel architects have introduced a series of multi-story "skylobbies" to make this wasted space appear to be a positive feature, or they add conference rooms on every guest floor. Unfortunately, these solutions only show up the problems resulting from poorly conceived and designed guestroom-floor planning. The efficient design of hotel towers requires the simultaneous study of both the core layout and the ring of guestrooms around it, with attempts to compress both as much as possible.

Atrium Configuration

A third major category of guestroom-floor plans is the "atrium" design, which was reintroduced by architect John Portman for the Hyatt Regency Atlanta hotel in 1967. The atrium prototype had been used late in the nineteenth century in both Denver's Brown Palace, still in operation, and San Francisco's Palace Hotel, destroyed in the 1906 earthquake and fire. The true atrium configuration has the guestrooms arranged along single-loaded corridors, much like open balconies overlooking the lobby space (see accompanying plans). The following issues must be addressed by the architect:

- *Shape:* What configuration of rooms best fits the site and can be integrated with both public and back-of-house area needs? Should any guestrooms look into the lobby volume?
- *Public elevators:* How are scenic (glass-sided) or standard elevators best arranged?
- *Corridor:* How can the amount of single-loaded corridor effectively be reduced?
- *Service core and stairs:* Where are these best located and integrated into the overall building design?

Practically all atrium hotels feature glass-enclosed "bubble" elevators that provide the guest with an ever-changing perspective of the lobby activity as well as adding animation to the space itself. Often these are located on a bridge or platform extension, thereby increasing the amount of circulation on each floor. In some cases, scenic elevators are placed opposite conventional ones, creating the anomaly of two very different experiences for the guest. The location of the service

elevators, housekeeping support functions, and egress stairs, while needing to be integrated into the plan and the lower service levels, aren't particularly critical to the efficiency of the guestroom floor.

In addition to the open lobby volume, each atrium hotel is distinguished by the plan of the guestroom floors. While the basic prototype is square, many of the more recent atrium designs are irregularly shaped to respond to varying site constraints. This sculpting of the building contributes to creating a unique image for the hotel, a primary goal of those developers and architects who select the atrium configuration and who accept the fact that, because of the single-loaded corridors, it is by far the least efficient of the plan types. Recently, architects have sought ways to gain the prestige benefits of the atrium while increasing its efficiency. One technique that has been successful in several hotels is to combine a central atrium with extended double-loaded wings, as was done at the Hyatt Regency hotels in Cambridge, Massachusetts, and Dallas, Texas. This effectively and appropriately draws together the architectural excitement of the atrium space— usually on a smaller and more personal scale than in the larger atrium volumes—with the desirable economies of the double-loaded plan. However, many developers and architects believe that the atrium design has become a cliché—and also recognize its tremendous cost premium (both in construction and operations)—and seek other means to create a memorable building and guest experience.

Defining the Guestroom and Suite Program

After the architect establishes the conceptual design, including a basic configuration for the guestroom floors, the team needs to refine and modify the earlier thumbnail guestroom program to fit the architectural concept—or shape the building to accommodate the nuances of the program. The room mix is based on the initial market study and, more importantly, on the advice and experience of the hotel operating company. The guestroom program defines the typical room module (principal overall dimensions and bathroom configuration) and the room mix (number of rooms furnished with a king bed, with two double or queen beds, or suites). The proposed room mix is intended to reflect the estimated demand from the individual business, group, and leisure market segments. The details of guestroom and suite design are discussed in the next chapter.

Design development of the guestroom floors to meet the specific requirements of the program is among the earliest steps in refining the conceptual design. The design team studies a wide range of possible modifications, including changing the width of the guestroom module, the number of bays per floor, the location and layout of the elevator and service cores, and the arrangement of suites. Frequently, misunderstandings arise over the actual number of separate rentable guestrooms in a particular project. To avoid this, the following vocabulary should be used consistently:

- *Key:* A separate, rentable unit
- *Guestroom bay:* The typical guestroom module
- *Structural bay:* The dimension between two structural columns,

323

Table 15.3 Typical guestroom program for 300-room hotel

Room type	Unit area*		Keys	Bays	Total bays	Total net area*		Comment
King	350	(32.5)	120	1	120	42,000	(3,900)	
Double-double	350	(32.5)	160	1	160	56,000	(5,200)	
Parlor	350	(32.5)	6	1	6	2,100	(195)	Wet bar; connects to K and DD
Hospitality suite	700	(65)	6	2	12	4,200	(390)	Kitchen; connects to K and DD
Conference suite	700	(65)	4	2	8	2,800	(260)	Boardroom; connects to K and DD
Deluxe suite	1,050	(97.5)	3	3	9	3,150	(295)	Connects to K and DD
Presidential suite	1,400	(130)	1	4	4	1,400	(130)	Connects to dedicated K and DD
Concierge club	1,400	(130)	0	4	4	1,400	(130)	Include pantry and conference room
Total			300		323	113,050	(10,500)	

* Unit area and total net area in sq ft (sq m).

typically equal to the width of one or, sometimes, two guestrooms

- *Suite:* Combination of living room and one or more bedrooms

Generally, the hotel management thinks in terms of "keys," which represent the total number of individual guestroom units available to sell. A suite containing a living room that connects to two bedrooms totals three keys if the parlor has a full bathroom and convertible sofa and if the bedrooms can be locked off, but only two keys if the living room and one bedroom must be sold together. Large suites often are described in terms of the number of guestroom bays they equal, so a hotelier may refer to a four-bay suite containing a two-bay living room and two connecting bedrooms. Architects, on the other hand, refer to the individual rooms and to structural bays, the former being the basis of the contract documents and the latter a chief component of cost estimates for the guestroom portion of the hotel.

During the early development phases, the feasibility consultant projects revenues and expenses, occupancy percentages, and average room rates based on the number of guestroom keys and the anticipated occupancy percentage. In addition, both parking requirements and zoning ordinances (used to control project size and density) are usually based on the key count. However, clarification is essential in order to avoid possible misunderstandings and delays. Table 15.3 illustrates an example of a typical guestroom and suite program and the use of the terms "key" and "bay."

Documenting the Guestroom Mix

Throughout the later design phases the architect and other design team members continually modify details of the guestroom structure, perhaps in response to the owner's or operator's input or as the result of changes in the public and service areas on the lower floors. But often it is the result of the impact of a fuller design of the building's mechanical and electrical distribution systems, elevator cores, or stair towers. Because it is important that the team be able to keep an accurate count of the total bays and keys, the architect or interior

designer should prepare and regularly update a "guestroom mix analysis."

Table 15.4 illustrates one typical approach for documenting the guestroom mix. This technique forces the architect or interior designer to make a number of conscious decisions:

- *Architectural shape:* Identify each room that has a different shape or configuration
- *Bed type:* Label each room by its bed type (king, queen, double-double, etc.)
- *Connecting rooms:* Indicate adjoining guestrooms
- *Suite locations:* Position and label any suites
- *Guestroom numbers:* Assign final room numbers
- *Key and bay analysis:* Develop and maintain a summary table of keys and bays by architectural shape or bed type

There are many advantages for documenting the room count. First, at the earliest conceptual design phase the design team can test the schematic design against the major element in the space program—the required number of guestrooms—and initiate any necessary changes. Second, a format is established so that, as the project proceeds through the later design phases, the designers can readily analyze the guestroom mix and maintain a precise record of the guestroom count. Third, details of the repetitive guestroom block can be considered at a relatively early phase. For example, the architect can study possible pairing of rooms to increase the number of back-to-back bathrooms and to establish a repetitive pattern of set-backs at the guestroom corridor doors. Fourth, the interior designer can identify any potential problems such as unusually shaped guestrooms that might not easily accommodate the necessary furnishings and amenities. In addition, other members of the team can offer better input when changes to the guestroom tower are fully documented through the different design phases. For instance, the engineering consultants can review the major systems in the guestroom tower—the elevators, HVAC, and communications systems, for example—in the same context as the rest of the design team. And, later, when suites are added to the top floor, or offices or breakout meeting rooms displace guestrooms on a low floor, the room mix analysis offers the design team a way to quickly confirm the total room count.

Table 15.4 Guestroom mix analysis

The guestroom floor plans illustrate the procedure for analyzing the architectural planning and room layout for a hypothetical hotel. The two plans show the typical and suite floors, the latter with five different room types—not unusual as the standard room bay is modified to fit around elevators, stairs, or support areas; the number of different room types is increased further by disabled-accessible bathrooms and by various suites. The following discussion describes the necessary steps, including key plans for each floor, labeled with room shape (I, II, etc.), bed type (K, DD, etc.), room number, and connecting doors, and a comprehensive tally of the guestroom mix.

- Architectural shape: Identify each room of a different shape or configuration (primarily different dimensions or bathroom layout) and assign it a number. Identify different room types by a Roman numeral in the top half of the circular code in each room. Room I is the most typical unit; room II is the corner guestroom with a wider bay, different bathroom and entry; room III is the disabled-accessible room (in the corner, where the bathroom can be easily enlarged); room IV is a three-bay VIP suite (one key, with a dedicated king bedroom); and room V is a two-bay conference suite that connects to two standard guestrooms.
- Bed type: Label each room by its bed type (king, queen, double-double, queen-queen, king-studio, parlor, accessible room, etc.) and place a simple abbreviation (K, Q, DD, etc.) on the plan. Note that the standard room shape may be furnished in a variety of ways.

- Room numbers: Assign room numbers to the bays to meet the management company's operating standard. Determine room numbers to simplify directional signage. Maintain corresponding numbers on different floors (leave out numbers if necessary so that consecutive odd/even room numbers are directly opposite each other). Doing this in schematic design aids communication among the various design professionals and reduces later confusion if the operator were to modify the room numbering.
- Connecting rooms: Mark interconnecting rooms with an open circle, for example between rooms 17 and 19. Operating companies seek a specific number of connecting pairs of particular types (for example, half the pairs connect K to DD).
- Suites: Position all suites, combinations of a living room and one or more adjoining bedrooms within the typical room configuration. Three suites are shown in the example: a two-bay conference suite that connects to both a king and double-double room (the conference suite also counts as a "key," or rentable unit, because it has a full bathroom and a convertible sofa); and a three-bay VIP suite with a dedicated king bedroom that also connects to a DD room. Often, the suites are grouped together on the top guestroom floors.
- Key and bay analysis: Develop a summary table to tally the number of rentable "keys" and room modules for each floor by bed type. Also, the table visually represents suites with a dark border around multiple bays. The chart shows the stacking of typical and suite floors, connecting rooms, and provides the total number of rooms for each type.

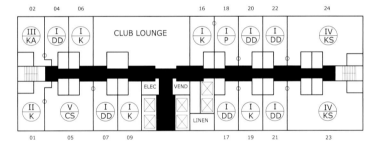

SUITE FLOOR

TYPICAL FLOOR

Fl\Bay	01	03	05	07	09	11	13	15	17	19	21	23	25	27	02	04	06	08	10	12	14	16	18	20	22	24	26	28	K	DD	S
8	K	○KS-CONF○		DD	K				DD○	K	DD○	KS-VIP			KA○	DD	K	CLUB LOUNGE				K○	P	○DD	DD○	KS-VIP			6	6	3
7	K	K	K○	DD	K				DD○	K	K○	K	K	K	K-A○	DD	K	○DD	K	DD	DD	K○	P	○DD	DD○	DD	K	K	15	8	1
6	K	K	K○	DD	K				DD○	K	K○	K	K	K	K-A○	DD	K	○DD	K	DD	DD	K○	P	○DD	DD○	DD	K	K	15	8	1
5	K	K	K○	DD	K				DD○	K	K○	K	K	K	K-A○	DD	K	○DD	K	DD	DD	K○	P	○DD	DD○	DD	K	K	15	8	1
4	K	K	K○	DD	K				DD○	K	K○	K	K	K	K-A○	K	K	○DD	K	DD	DD	K○	P	○DD	DD○	DD	K	K	15	8	1
3	K	K	K○	DD	K				DD○	K	K○	K	K	K	K-A○	K	K	○DD	K	DD	DD	K○	P	○DD	DD○	DD	K	K	15	8	1
2	K	K	K○	DD	K				DD○	K	K○	K	K	K	K-A○	K	K	○DD	K	DD	DD	K○	P	○DD	DD○	DD	K	K	15	8	1
																										Total by type			96	54	9

Guestroom and Suite Design

Many hotel operators believe that the guestroom and guest bathroom make a more lasting impression on the lodging guest than does the exterior architecture, or the lobby, or any other single interior space. Design of the individual guestrooms and suites, while clearly more an interior layout problem than an architectural one, is still an important part of the architect's responsibility. Along with design of the public spaces, it is also one of the two major areas of focus for the interior designer. Because of the guestroom's residential character, such irritating deficiencies in layout or equipment as a non-working light switch at the room entry, inadequate mirror or counter area in the bathroom, or chair arms that won't fit under the desk, are especially obvious to the traveler. These design details call for the coordinated attention of the entire team: architect, engineer, interior designer, other design consultants, building contractor, and hotel manager.

The evolution of the hotel guestroom over the past two centuries shows how design and management professionals collaborated to design a better room. Until the Tremont House opened in Boston in 1829, no major hotels with private rooms existed; guests were content to share rooms—even beds—with whatever other travelers were staying at a particular roadhouse. The Tremont House's innovative use of private and lockable guestrooms—still without private bathrooms—became an overnight success and set the standard for a burgeoning new industry in North America.

Throughout the nineteenth century, in order to remain competitive, the industry quickly introduced technological advances: gas—then electric—lights, voice annunciators, then telephones, and eventually elevators, central heating, and running water. These innovations culminated in the construction of the sumptuous Hotel Statler in Buffalo, New York, in 1908 where, for the first time in a major hotel, all the guestrooms included private baths: "A room and a bath for a dollar and a half," the ads proudly proclaimed. Other design innovations of the Statler guestrooms included bathrooms designed back-to-back for economy of the vertical plumbing runs, and such features in each room as circulating ice water, a full-length mirror, a light switch inside the entry door, a bedside telephone, a built-in radio, and the "servidor"—a shallow, garment-sized compartment constructed within the guestroom door to facilitate pickup of soiled—and delivery of laundered—clothes.

Four Seasons Guangzhou, China
The straightforward uncluttered layout of the Four Seasons Hotel and its bathrooms belies the luxuriousness of the accommodations.

Establishing Design Criteria

The layout of the hotel guestroom is intertwined with decisions that the design team makes during the schematic design, when they establish the dimensions of the guestroom module and the structural bay, accept a variety of non-typical room configurations, and approve a final room mix (see previous chapter). These decisions provide the interior designer with the framework to creatively plan the individual spaces and to give the hotel guestrooms a character consistent with the public areas.

Guestroom design entails a series of orderly steps, some of which are defined during the architectural planning of the guestroom structure. The designer should establish or confirm the following points:

- Define the major market segments that the hotel will attract.
- Confirm the principal guestroom dimensions.
- Confirm the room mix, including the number and type of suites.
- Design the typical guestroom.
- Design each suite type and any special rooms (disabled-accessible, etc.).
- Propose an FF&E budget for the guestrooms, suites, and corridors.

The best designers recognize the specific needs of the target markets and identify features and amenities that these groups most want and expect. In general terms, the transient business person looks for single accommodations, the convention and group markets need double rooms, and the leisure market requires one bed for two guests or, for families, sometimes multiple beds or adjoining rooms. For example, many of the hotel rooms around Walt Disney World in Florida are furnished with two queen beds and a convertible sofa, to accommodate a vacationing family of four to six. Also, because each of these market groups uses the room differently, the designer must consider work and meeting functions in one case and family activities in another. The principal market characteristics that influence the layout and furnishing of hotel and resort guestrooms are identified in Table 16.1.

Room Dimensions and Configurations

The guestroom design decision which most influences the room layouts and much of the guest reaction to a hotel is the choice of three critical room dimensions: the inside or net width, the length of the room from the exterior wall to the bathroom wall, and the length of the bathroom. The net width establishes the structural module throughout the building (equal to the width of either one room or two rooms), which carries through to the public and service areas on the lower floors. The most common room width in the United States at the end of the twentieth century was 12 ft (3.7 m),

Table 16.1 Hotel guest characteristics

Market	Guest characteristics	Purpose for travel	Guestroom design factors
Business			
Group	Single or double occupancy; 2–4 night stay; 55% men, 45% women; somewhat price insensitive	Conventions, conferences, professional associations, sales and training meetings	King or double-double; bathroom with dressing area; lounge seating with good work area
Individual	Single occupancy; 1–2 night stay; 50% men, 50% women; price insensitive	Corporate business, sales, conventions, conferences	King; bathroom with separate stall shower; lounge seating with good work area
Leisure			
Family	Multiple occupancy (including children); 1–4 night stay, longer in resort areas; budget or mid-price	Family vacations, sightseeing, sports, family activity	Double-double, queen-queen, or adjoining rooms; lounge seating and television; large compartmentalized bathroom; balcony, outside access
Couples	Double occupancy; 1–7 night stay; mid-price to upscale	Tours, clubs, associations, sightseeing; theater, sports, weekend packages, shopping, vacation	King; dining area, writing surface; moderate storage; large compartmentalized bathroom
Singles	Single occupancy; young professionals to seniors; mid-price to upscale	Tours, clubs, associations; culture, arts, theater, sports/recreation, shopping	King or queen; lounge/entertaining area; standard bathroom

Table 16.2 Minimum guestroom dimensions

	Living area*		Bathroom		Total guestroom	
	Dimensions ft (m)	Area sq ft (sq m)	Dimensions ft (m)	Area sq ft (sq m)	Dimensions ft (m)	Area ft² (m²)
Budget	11'6" x 15 (3.5 x 4.5)	172 (16)	5 x 5 (1.5 x 1.5)	25** (2.3)	11'6" x 20'6" (3.5 x 6.2)	236 (21.9)
Mid-price	12 x 18 (3.6 x 5.5)	216 (20.1)	5 x 7'6" (1.5 x 2.3)	37 (3.4)	12 x 26 (3.6 x 6.6)	312 (29)
First-class	13'6" x 19 (4.1 x 5.8)	256 (23.8)	5'6" x 8'6" (1.7 x 2.6)	47 (4.4)	13'6" x 28'6" (4.1 x 8.6)	385 (35.8)
Luxury	15 x 20 (4.5 x 6.1)	300 (27.9)	7'6" x 9 (2.3 x 2.7)	68 (6.3)	15 x 30 (4.5 x 9.1)	450 (41.8)

* Living area is the principal room space, excluding the bathroom, closet, and entry/dressing area.

** Budget guestroom bath may include only tub/shower and toilet; the sink often is part of the dressing area.

initially adopted in the mid-1950s by the Holiday Inn chain as a standard for all of their roadside properties. It was sufficient to comfortably accommodate two double beds against one wall and a desk/dresser/luggage stand/television against the opposite wall, with an adequate aisle between. While the typical room layout has evolved slowly over the last half-century, the industry's standard guestroom layout today is little different from the one pioneered in 1953 by Kemmons Wilson, the founder of Holiday Inns. To be sure, though, style, comfort, and guestroom technology have seen major advances.

Until this development, even the newest and largest convention hotels built in the post-World War II period incorporated a variety of room sizes, including a large percentage that were narrower than the new 12 ft (3.7 m) standard width. These hotels, many of them still operating and competing with properties thirty to sixty years newer, are greatly limited by the smallness of their guestrooms. In the United States and Canada, no first-class or chain-affiliated hotels (except for the budget inns) are built today with rooms less than 12 ft wide. Occasionally, when older downtown or resort properties are acquired and fully renovated, the size of some rooms may be smaller where they are limited by unavoidable architectural constraints. (See the discussion on updating existing hotels, Chapter 12.)

In the past few years, guestroom dimensions have become generally standardized for different quality levels of hotels or resorts (Table 16.2). While a few hotel operators have tried to provide noticeably larger rooms than their direct competitors, the guestroom size, quality of furnishings and finishes, and room rate remain closely linked, because of the overriding influence of the initial cost of construction and furnishings.

The guestroom layouts on page 331 illustrate typical room design alternatives as well as a number of more innovative and luxurious layouts. The budget chains have reduced slightly the size of the 12 x 18 ft (3.7 x 5.5 m) mid-price room in order to lower construction costs, shortening it to between 14 and 16 ft (4.3 to 4.9 m), still sufficient to accommodate two double beds, and reducing the width by 4–6 inches (10–15 cm)—although a few operators of "pod

hotels" are building even smaller units. On the other hand, companies which are selling a more luxurious room have experimented with larger guestroom spaces and, especially, have created innovative bathroom layouts. Increasing the width of the room module to 13 ft or 13 ft 6 in (4.0 to 4.1 m) permits one major change in the room layout: a king-size bed can be positioned against the bathroom wall instead of the side wall, allowing for a variety of other furnishing arrangements, or the bed can "float" in the room against an open wall/headboard.

Generally, there is little advantage to increasing the guestroom width beyond 13 ft 6 in. Even this slightly larger space does not improve the interior arrangement, and construction costs increase dramatically because of additional corridor and exterior wall area. However, at a room width of 16 ft (4.9 m) or more, a new set of design alternatives arises: the bed or beds can be positioned against one side wall and the lounge and work area against the opposite wall. Also, the greater width permits unusually luxurious bathroom arrangements, often with four or five fixtures, as well as a larger entry vestibule and dressing area.

Architects HKS have pioneered another common arrangement, with short dead-end corridors leading to a pair of rooms, rather than providing a separate entry hallway for each guestroom. In this case (see room F, page 331), the bathroom becomes wider, yet the room module still contains an entry zone with dressing area. Also, corridor doors can be closed off to create a pair of adjoining rooms, rather than providing a doorway in the common wall between two rooms.

The wedge-shaped guestrooms characteristic of circular towers present their own design problem in the layout of the guest bathroom. The smaller towers have a corridor frontage of only 6–8 ft (1.8–2.4 m), the larger-diameter tower a more reasonable 10 ft (3 m). Although many of these room plans show such positive features as compartmentalized bathrooms (out of necessity), compact foyer space, a large lounge area, and expansive window wall, today's increasing competition in room size and upscale furnishings has made the small-diameter cylindrical towers virtually obsolete.

Designing the Individual Guestroom

The definition of the market determines not only the most appropriate bed combinations, but also the other guestroom furnishings for a particular hotel. But the bed is the primary defining characteristic. Generally, hotels include a mixture of rooms with one oversized bed (most often a king), two beds (generally double or queen beds), and suites of various types. Table 16.3 lists many of the more common bed sizes. The selection of a proper room mix is important because it influences the hotel's ability to rent 100 percent of its rooms and to generate the maximum revenue. For this reason, rooms which offer more flexibility are popular with the management companies. A room with two double beds is more flexible than a king (it can accommodate one to four people); a king-size bed plus a convertible sofa is attractive to a single business person but can be converted to family use. Table 16.4 illustrates typical room mix percentages for the different types of hotels and resorts.

Typical King and Double-double Rooms

The full list of furnishings can be determined by analyzing the guestroom functions—sleeping, relaxing, working, entertaining, dressing—and their space requirements. The plan of a typical hotel room clearly shows these several zones: the bathroom and areas for dressing and clothes storage are grouped next to the corridor entrance; the sleeping area is in the center of the guestroom space; and the seating and work areas are located near the window. New layouts

Table 16.3 Guestroom bed types

Room type	Bed types and sizes	Bed dimensions in inches (meters)
Twin	2 twin beds	39 x 80 (1 x 2)
Double-double	2 double beds	54 x 80 (1.35 x 2)
Queen	1 queen bed	60 x 80 (1.5 x 2)
King	1 king bed	78 x 80 (2 x 2)
California king	1 king bed	72 x 80 (1.8 x 2)
Oversized twin	2 twin beds	45 x 80 (1.15 x 2)
Queen-queen	2 queen beds	
Double-studio	1 double bed and convertible sofa	
Queen-studio	1 queen bed and convertible sofa	
King-studio	1 king bed and convertible sofa	
Parlor	1 convertible sofa	
Wall bed ("Sico room")	1 wall bed (queen or king)	

Table 16.4 Guestroom mix for different hotel types

Type of hotel	Percent of total guestrooms				Comments
	Double-double	King	King-studio	Suites	
Urban (business)	30	60	3	7	Limited double occupancy
Boutique hotel	10	75	3	12	Suites depend on market and building configuration
Suburban/airport hotel	50	40	5	5	Full range of potential market segments; needs flexibility
Roadside inn	70	30	5	0	Trend away from all double-double; increasingly kings
Budget inn	80	20	0	0	Often queen instead of king bed
Resort/family	75	10	10	5	Some queen-queen; provide room for cots
Resort/couples	20	70	5	5	Increasing emphasis on suites
Convention hotel	55	35	0	10	Continuing reliance on double-double
Conference center	30	60	5	5	Single occupancy, except for weekend social business
All-suite hotel	30	70	0	0	All keys include living room with dedicated bedroom
Super-luxury	20	70	0	10	Double-double replaced with oversize twins
Mega-hotel	50	40	5	5	Double-double flexible for family/group/business markets
Casino hotel	50	40	0	10	Double-double or queen-queen count depends on strength of tour market

A

FEET
0   5   10
METERS
0 .5   1   3

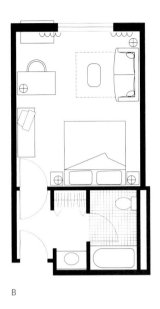

B

C

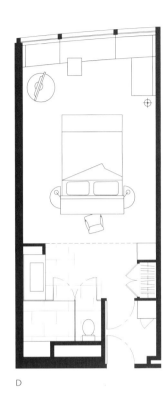

D

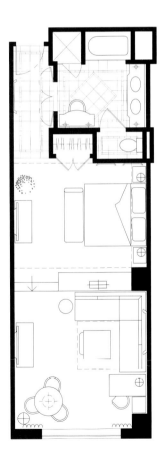

E

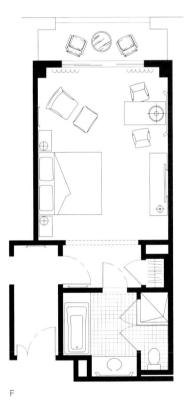

F

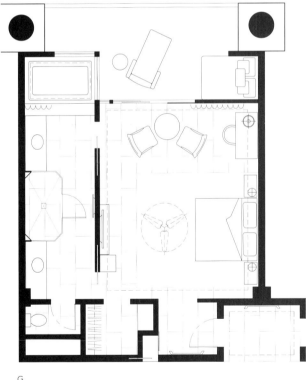

G

Guestroom plans

(A) Economy pod room uses very little space but, at 200 sq ft (18.5 sq m), includes a window; even smaller rooms do not (Yotel, London, United Kingdom). (B) Midscale king room, 320 sq ft (30 sq m) shows how placing the bed against the bathroom wall increases usable space. (C) Typical double-double room, also 320 sq ft (30 sq m) with typical furnishings. (D) An unusual layout, with the bed in the middle of the room, its head against a desk, 470 sq ft (43.5 sq m), also features an oversized bathroom (W Barcelona, Barcelona, Spain). (E) Luxury casino-hotel room, 600 sq ft (55 sq m) features a large bathroom and a separate living area, two steps lower (Venetian, Las Vegas, Nevada). (F) Architects have experimented with short dead-end corridors providing a more direct entry experience, 420 sq ft (39 sq m) (Terranea, Rancho Palos Verdes, California). (G) Greatly oversized resort room, 700 sq ft (65 sq m), with elegant outdoor lanai and huge bathroom, pampers the guest (St. Regis Sanya Yalong Bay Resort, Sanya, China).

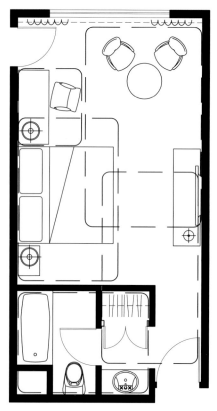

Guestroom Activity Zones
The hotel guestroom accommodates one to four or more people, sometimes with several activities occurring at one time (for example, bathing and dressing, working and watching TV). The designer needs to be aware of techniques for separating some activities while combining others, in both cases increasing the flexibility and adaptability of the room to different users. The plan illustrates the five principal guestroom activity zones: sleeping, working, lounging, bathing, and dressing.

combine the several functions in different ways or find techniques for separating them more fully. For example, the designer can provide suite-like characteristics in a standard room by adding a screen to separate the sleeping and sitting portions of the space. Or the team may create a compartmentalized bathroom by isolating the tub/shower and toilet area from the sink and dressing function. The plan on this page shows how the functional zones in a room may overlap.

With the continuing increase in construction and furnishing costs, as well as increasing competitiveness among hotel brands, it becomes more important to develop innovative layouts for guestrooms—designs that combine function and comfort within realistic budgets. Basic approaches include using fewer individual pieces of furniture, sometimes combining several functions, or scaling them slightly smaller to give the perception of a larger or more luxurious room. The designer might include the following:

- *Queen- or 72 inch (1.8 m) king-size bed:* Beds smaller than the 78 inch (2 m) king create more open space.
- *Convertible sofa or wall-bed:* These provide more open space and flexibility, either as the second bed in a queen or king room, or as the only bed in a parlor.

- *Adequate luggage and clothes space:* Sufficient drawers, luggage stand, and closet space reduce the clutter of clothing and personal items throughout the room.
- *Wall-mounted TV:* Provide a flat-screen television mounted to the wall to eliminate unnecessary counter space. Hide power and cable connections behind the television.
- *Desk:* A wheeled computer stand that rolls under the main desk offers a better height for a guest's laptop computer and provides additional work surface.
- *Lounge and desk chairs:* Lounge chairs designed at a height appropriate for the work desk may eliminate the need for a desk chair.
- *Mirrors:* Mirrors enlarge the space visually.
- *Wall-mounted bedside lamps:* These permit a smaller bedside night table.
- *Bathroom:* Designs should increase lighting and enlarge the countertop and mirror surfaces; compartmentalize the toilet and/or tub/shower.

Several details in the room arrangement and furnishing do not have any best solution, although there are more common ones for different types or categories of hotels. For example, many operators of economy properties insist that the telephone should be located next to the beds, whereas others prefer that it be placed at the work area. Most first-class hotels have solved the question by providing two phones—or three, with an additional one in the bathroom. Often, one is cordless—with the base unit a speakerphone—which enables guests to roam around their room while talking on the phone. Similarly, the lower-priced budget inns often prefer drapes which combine the decorative drapery and blackout into a single unit, to reduce the number of drapery tracks, whereas others insist on separate sheer, blackout, and overdrape to allow easy cleaning and maintenance. Guests in upscale hotels—and even at mid-level hotels in Asia—can control the several drapes by pushing a button at the bedside. Throughout the room, the designer must balance the conflicting needs of function, safety, maintenance, comfort, aesthetics, and budget, and, at the same time, consider the varying requirements of the several different guest markets that a single hotel tries to attract. (See Table 16.5.)

Not every operator is trying to provide the smallest possible room or find ways to combine functions with multi-purpose furnishings. The 3,000-room Venetian Hotel in Las Vegas opened in 1999 with standard guestrooms of 665 sq ft (61.8 sq m), including a five-fixture guest bathroom of 110 sq ft (10.2 sq m). In floor area, this room is larger than many hotel suites, yet the room is only one bay wide. It features, in addition to the generous bathroom, clearly separated sleeping and living areas (see plan E on page 331).

The wide adoption of flat-screen televisions has nearly eliminated the reliance on the armoire in guestroom design. This allows the guestroom module to be slightly narrower, although designers may need additional floor space as they explore alternatives to the traditional desk, offering more work surface, perhaps a computer cart, better lighting, and ergonomic seating. Also, exercise equipment may find its way into business-oriented hotel guestrooms.

A

B

C

D

E

Guestroom Interior Views

Guestrooms must readily accommodate different market segments. (A–B) In high-rise hotels, the view can be especially dramatic (W Barcelona, Barcelona, Spain; Hard Rock Casino, Macau, China). (C–D) Smaller hotels and resorts often have a more residential feel (The Study at Yale, New Haven, Connecticut; JW Marriott Ihilani, Hawaii). (E) Hotel themes may predominate; here, the Obama Room (President Hotel, New York, New York).

Suites

The principal way that a hotel provides different qualities of accommodations is to include a variety of guestroom suites in the room mix. A suite is defined simply as a living room connected to one or more bedrooms. Larger hotels frequently provide a hierarchy of suites, from single-bay living rooms with a sleeping alcove to multiple-bay living rooms with connecting rooms, including dining/conference rooms and one or two bedrooms (Table 16.6). Some management companies have gained a well-earned reputation for the overall quality of their suites. Four Seasons, the Toronto-based luxury hotel chain, offers a standard two-bay suite consisting of a one-bay living room with powder room, connecting through double French doors to a bedroom with oversized guest bathroom.

Table 16.5 Elements required for complete guestroom design

Furnishings

Casepieces	Desk, dresser, tables, chairs, nightstands, headboard, and TV
Soft goods	Bedspreads, drapes, and upholstery fabrics; carpet sometimes included
Lighting	Lamps at the bedside, desk, and lounge seating areas
Accessories	Framed mirrors, art, planters, other amenities. (Wastebaskets, coffee maker, iron and ironing board, and other miscellaneous items are provided by the hotel operator)

Guestroom finishes

Floor	Generally carpet over padding, although resorts may have tile (warm climates) and suites may have wood parquet with area rugs
Wall	Vinyl wall-covering preferred, or paint; baseboard and moldings if budget permits
Ceiling	Acoustical paint
Doors	Wood, pre-finished, or painted—all solid core
Door frames	Painted to match doors, walls, or accent color

Bathroom finishes

Floor	Porcelain, ceramic, or marble tile
Walls	Porcelain, ceramic, or marble tile around tub; vinyl wall-covering or paint elsewhere
Ceiling	Paint

Electrical/mechanical

Outlets	Minimum of five duplex outlets: two at the beds, one each at desk, dresser, and lounge area; require outlets convenient for guest computer and for housekeeper
Cable	Television, dual telephone lines, internet, fire alarm, or other communications system
Mechanical	HVAC integrated with room layout; bathroom exhaust
Fire protection	Minimum of one heat or smoke detector and one sprinkler in each guestroom; some areas require additional sprinklers in closet and bathroom. All interior furnishings should be carefully checked for fire-retardant and nontoxic finish.

Table 16.6 Suite types

Suite type	Size	Count	Comment
Junior suite	1.5 bays, 1 key	<2%	Not programmed; the result of planning that yields oversized guestrooms.
Parlor suite	2 bays, 2 keys	<5%	One-bay parlor; connected to a typical king bedroom. The parlor is a rentable key, with a sofa-bed and full bathroom.
Hospitality suite	3 bays, 2 keys	1–2%	Two-bay parlor/lounge, with pantry; connected to a typical king bedroom. The living room (with lounge furnishings) is a rentable key, with sofa-bed and full bathroom.
Conference suite	3 bays, 2 keys	1–2%	Two-bay meeting room, with pantry; connected to a typical king bedroom. The meeting room (with conference table and limited lounge furnishings) is a rentable key, with a sofa-bed and full bathroom.
Deluxe suite	3 bays, 1 key	1–2%	Two-bay parlor, with powder room and pantry; connected to a one-bay dedicated king bedroom. The parlor is furnished as a living room with a small conference/dining table; the king bedroom has a four-fixture bathroom.
Executive suite	4 bays, 1 key	1%	Two-bay parlor, with powder room and pantry, similar to above; connected to a two-bay dedicated king bedroom, with a four-fixture bathroom.
Presidential suite	4–6 bays, 1 key	Only 1	Two- to three-bay parlor, plus an additional conference/dining bay, powder room, and pantry; connected to a two-bay dedicated king bedroom, with a five-fixture bathroom.

Generally, each parlor also connects to a typical double-double guestroom;
provide one or more accessible suites of each type with an accessible powder room.

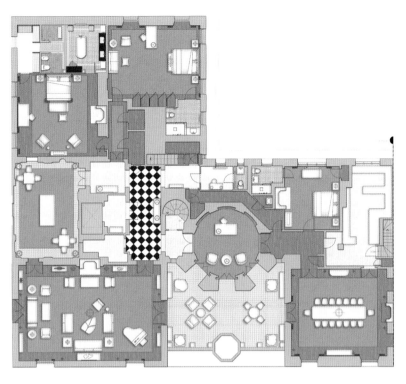

Guestroom Suite Views

The penthouse suite at the Fairmont San Francisco, originally built in the 1920s and designed by Moorish scholar Arthur Upham Pope, rivals many of the richly detailed mansions built in the city's heyday. The restored space, covering the entire eighth floor of the original hotel building, is intended to host VIP leaders and as a site for celebrity weddings. The suite includes three oversized bedrooms, living room, formal dining room, two-story rotunda library, a dramatic billiard room covered with Persian tiles, and an expansive terrace with sweeping views of the city skyline.

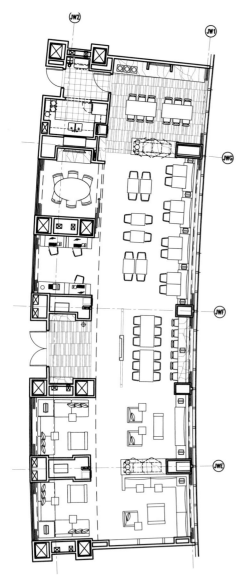

Concierge-Floor Lounge

Luxury and convention-oriented properties often provide a concierge or club-floor lounge, covering three to six bays (or more) on an upper floor, providing such VIP services as express check-in and check-out, Continental breakfast, all-day beverage and snack service, and normal concierge services. This six-bay example includes a reception area, large permanent buffet with adjoining pantry, small guest conference room, computer workstations, and guest lounge and dining space (JW Marriott, Indianapolis, Indiana).

The number or percentage of suites varies among hotel types. Most hotels have no more than 2–5 percent of their keys allocated to suites; first-class and convention hotels, on the other hand, provide up to 10 percent of the total guestroom count in suites. These most likely are positioned on the upper floors of the tower, where the suite rooms have better views, but may be stacked vertically where unusual conditions occur. For example, suites may be used to fill any larger structural bays on the typical floor, grow into additional area behind stairs or elevators, or are located where the building form provides uniquely shaped rooms.

At the beginning of the 1980s, several companies in the United States recognized the growing need of the extended-stay market and established chains of all-suite hotels. But the operators found that these small suites also held great appeal to the traveling businessperson and family, both of whom appreciated the separate living room and bedroom and the provision of a small kitchen. At the time, operators such as Residence Inn, Embassy Suites, and Guest Quarters were successfully converting apartment buildings or building new structures with suites of approximately 450 sq ft (42 sq m). In the late twentieth century, a number of franchise companies established innovative all-suite brands, many of them with entries in the "economy suite" segment, with accommodations no larger than a conventional hotel guestroom, but with a small kitchenette.

Many hotels now offer concierge or club-floor levels to offer a higher-quality room and additional amenities at a premium price. Usually representing 10–20 percent of the total room count, the club-floor rooms are identical in size to typical guestrooms, but feature better-quality finishes, furnishings, and bathroom amenities. More important to most guests are the additional services available in the club-floor lounge, including express check-in and check-out, complimentary breakfast, tea, cocktails, and evening snacks, and the more personal services of a concierge on the guest floors. The lounge space usually is equal in size to at least three guestrooms, and in major convention hotels, with their private conference rooms and additional business services, may displace as many as six to eight rooms. See the plan on this page for an example of a club-floor lounge in a convention headquarters hotel.

Guest Bathroom

Nowhere in the room is planning and design more important than in the guest bathroom. In the mid-twentieth century, with the great surge in the development of chain properties along the new interstate highways, bathrooms grew from about 30 sq ft (2.8 sq m)—hardly big enough for the standard three fixtures—to at least 40 sq ft (3.7 sq m). This growth in the bathroom paralleled the huge expansion in roadside inns to serve the family market. This standard bathroom still is used today, and the 5 x 8 ft (1.5 x 2.4 m) dimensions still comfortably accommodate the standard three fixtures. But competitive pressure, and marketing, and guests' eagerness for something no less than they have at home, have pushed the first-class and luxury operators to add fixtures and other amenities. By 2010 it was common for downtown hotels, catering to a single business traveler, to offer a bathroom with a large sink/counter, bathtub, separate shower

A

B

C

D

Bathroom Interior Views
(A) Successful guest bathrooms incorporate a strong sense of arrival, with an axial focus on the sinks or whirlpool tub (Four Seasons Marrakech, Morocco). (B) Hyatt developed several hotels with a wet-room, combining tub and rain shower in one space (Hyatt Regency Mainz, Germany). (C) Resort hotels often allow the bathroom to flow outdoors, sometimes including a plunge pool (Four Seasons Seychelles). (D) Upscale hotel bathrooms increasingly incorporate a separate stall shower and compartmentalized toilet (Rosewood Sand Hill, Palo Alto, California).

stall, and compartmentalized toilet: all for one person. Resort and super-luxury properties go one better, adding a second sink and plenty of open floor space.

Designers need to study the market data to understand what features and amenities will be most important. Is the market predominantly men or women? Single travelers or couples or families? What are their demographics, and do they expect unusual levels of luxury in the bathroom? Several management companies took to heart the research that showed that nearly 90 percent of travelers staying in their properties preferred showers. As a result, in newer hotels they have omitted the tub/shower combination and replaced it with an oversized stall shower, but still provide the tub/shower in double-double or queen-queen rooms intended for the family segment. In the late twentieth century, Global Hyatt opened several hotels in Germany and Japan with unusual bathrooms, featuring a wet-room—a space about 5 x 5 ft (1.5 x 1.5 m) with a normal tub, plus overhead rain shower—a compartmentalized toilet, and a spacious sink counter and make-up area. The bathroom is separated from the bedroom by sliding panels or a glass partition. The photographs on the previous page suggest how designers can use the guest bathroom to give the guest a truly memorable overnight experience.

Accessible Guestroom/Universal Design

All hotel operators must provide accommodation and other services for guests with physical disabilities. In the United States, the federal government in 1992 passed the Americans with Disabilities Act (ADA), which mandates equal access to all public accommodations—not only lodging properties but retail stores, restaurants, theaters, museums, airports, transportation services, etc. Hotels before this time had made some token efforts to provide rooms for disabled guests, most frequently those in wheelchairs. But the ADA broadened the definition to those with other disabilities, such as arthritis, or those who are hearing- or sight-impaired. For twenty years these laws remained unchanged, but the government recently made changes which took effect in March, 2012. All areas of the hotel or resort must meet the guidelines of the ADA, not only the public areas and guestrooms but the employee areas as well. A recent U.S. Census Bureau study indicates that over 22 percent of the U.S. population have some sort of disability—defined as difficulty performing normal activities of daily living (or as many as 53 percent of those over age 50).

One area where accessible design is most evident is in the "handicapped-accessible guestrooms," a small number of rooms which feature larger bathrooms with somewhat different fixtures—a roll-in shower stall, for example—and a number of features intended to improve the accommodation for a person with specific disabilities. Interestingly, many of these features are a great boon to the able-bodied traveler: lever handles on doors and faucets, a hand-held shower, grab bars in the bathroom, large buttons on the telephone, and more accessible outlets and switches—that is, design features which have "universal" appeal. Hotel interior designers have begun to realize the value of *universal design* and are adopting as many of these features as make economic and functional sense.

In a recent study, one franchise company surveyed some of the 20 million people with disabilities in the United States who travel regularly, asking them what they most want from their hotel. The respondents (73 percent wheelchair users, 5 percent sight- or hearing-impaired, and 22 percent "other") in particular listed many characteristics of the guestrooms (along with other comments dealing with the hotel providing accurate information, helpful staff, and more accessible parking):

- Accessible showers
- Large bathrooms
- Enough space for easy maneuverability

- Suitable beds
- Aesthetically pleasing guestroom
- Refrigerator in guestroom
- Easy access to guestroom controls

Guestroom Technology

The early decades of the twenty-first century have seen incredible innovations in technology, much of it appearing in hotel guestrooms. At the turn of the century, because nationwide nearly 60 percent of all roomnights were generated by business travelers, most major management companies adopted internet access in all their hotel guestrooms, initially hard-wired Ethernet connections, which offered connection speeds 50 times faster than normal phone lines and, further, didn't interfere with telephone use. Increasingly, business travelers carried laptops with them on trips, the great majority to stay in e-mail contact with their office or family. A side benefit was that adoption of the high-speed cable networks freed up the existing PBX (telephone) trunk lines, lessening the burden on another essential piece of the communications network.

But, with the advent of "smartphones," the need in guestrooms has changed. Guests want to customize their experience by integrating their own technology with the hotel systems. Guests now travel with their own video content and need to connect with the television for both business computing and entertainment. Their personal devices, increasingly, will be able to control or access room temperature, television, high-speed Internet—even the guestroom door lock. ARIA Hotel and Casino, part of the CityCenter development in Las Vegas, which opened late in 2009, allows guests to connect their laptop or game console to the 42 inch LCD high-definition television. In addition, the ARIA guestrooms offer simple touch-screen control of such features as dimmable lighting, room temperature, television/video systems, music, wake-up calls, draperies, and requests for services. Today, major hotels provide wireless service throughout their properties, enabling communication and e-mail service over a wide range of products. These new systems, some incorporating radio frequency identification (RFID) technology, easily control door locks and energy usage, among others. As technology becomes more fully integrated over the next few years, we can expect to see faster adoption of innovations for such systems as:

- door locks
- door bells; hallway "privacy" and "service" indicators
- high-definition televisions
- wireless internet
- telephone
- bedside controls (clock, draperies, temperature, fan, etc.)
- energy management
- in-room safe

Of course, it is important to provide conveniently located power outlets in the room, as well as the wiring to connect the many in-room devices and control panels. Luxury hotels look for every way to pamper their guests, and technology plays a role here, too. Several hotels have introduced iPads to their concierge staff, or put them into guestrooms. One, the Hotel Beaux Arts Miami, developed a proprietary tablet application (app) for the several dozen iPads it placed in guestrooms, used primarily for ordering room service and making spa reservations; the tablets also replace the printed portfolio that had previously been in every room. The apps are important in helping to position the innovative brand to the tech-savvy guest. According to the hotel's sales and marketing executive, their guests "have gone beyond use of the phone." Many hoteliers prefer to provide power and bandwidth, rather than try to stay ahead of the guests in terms of changing technology.

that affect the room design and guest comfort. In addition, the model room is used as a promotional tool to interest business or convention groups in the hotel and to provide them with assurances of the quality of the final room product before the hotel opens.

In addition, the largest management companies may build model rooms for each separate brand at their headquarters, and regularly update them as the markets evolve and change. Marriott, for example, has sample guestrooms for nearly every brand in its Maryland headquarters, using them as a sales tool to interest potential franchisees.

Proposing the Guestroom FF&E Budget

Early in the process, after preparing the initial guestroom mix, the interior design firm proposes a budget for the furnishings and interior equipment for the guestrooms and suites, representing about half of the hotel's total interior design budget. Generally, the designer accomplishes this in several stages, each one more focused and detailed, as the design becomes more specific:

- *Concept design:* Budget based on $ per guestroom or suite, $ per key for corridor finishes.
- *Schematic design:* Budget based on an allowance for each furniture item ($ per bedset, nightstand, desk, etc.) prior to selecting the individual item.
- *Design development:* Budget with exact $ figure for most specified FF&E items, but with allowances for artwork, signage, and accessories.
- *Contract documents:* Figure for each item, including input from purchasing agent to obtain competitive pricing from vendors.

By 2010, costs for hotel guestroom interiors in the United States ranged from about $3,000 to well over $20,000 per room, depending primarily on the quality level of the property. While the size of the room is a factor, it has relatively minor significance. The lower-priced rooms have extremely basic furnishings, base-grade carpet and fabrics, painted walls, inexpensive light fixtures, and casegoods with a plastic-laminate finish. The higher-priced rooms have a more sumptuous feel, with luxurious fabrics, wood-veneer casepieces, overstuffed furnishings, triple-matted and framed artwork, and extra lighting to enhance the visual atmosphere. Each individual item may be at least twice as expensive, and designers often include a number of additional accessories or extra amenities.

The sheer number of guestrooms requires that the designer be particularly conscious of seeking economies in the layout of the rooms and the selection of the furnishings and finishes. Because of the importance of these factors in influencing the guest's perception of the hotel as well as cost, hotel developers often will build a full-scale mock-up to test the design before purchasing the furnishings. This model room provides the perfect setting for the final coordination of many furnishing, room finish, and engineering-system decisions

339

Public Space Design

While the hotel guestrooms take up the majority of the floor area in virtually all hotels, it is the public space that defines the differences among the various types. Because the lobby, restaurants and lounges, meeting and banquet space, and recreation facilities vary so greatly (from only 5 percent in a budget inn to 25 percent in a conference center), understanding the distinctions among the different hotel types is crucial to programming and designing a successful project.

Table 17.1 (overleaf) identifies the key differences in public space for the different hotel types. Convention hotels and conference centers, for example, have relatively more meeting and banquet space; resorts and, often, conference centers include major recreational components; urban and luxury hotels, among others, have fewer but generally high-quality food operations.

In addition to providing the appropriate mix of facilities for each type of hotel, the architect must create an organization that meets the functional requirements of the developer and the hotel management company. The budget and mid-price companies insist on tight and economical layouts overall, and the limited public areas tend to be multi-purpose. The first-class and luxury-hotel operators, while they, too, strive for some efficiency, are more concerned with the visual qualities of the building and in providing a level of amenity; these companies frequently will accept a less economical layout in order to accommodate more appealing and saleable architectural and interior design features.

Whatever the type of hotel, an overall objective for the planning and design of the public areas is that they be clustered around the lobby. This arrangement assures that the hotel guests can find the various facilities with a minimum of difficulty and provides the opportunity for functions to overlap. Hotel atrium lobbies, especially, exhibit such characteristics, where the guest registration area, multiple restaurants and lounges, meeting pre-function space, guest elevators, and upper-floor corridors all occupy the same volume.

A second major objective in high-rise projects is to organize the public areas with an understanding of their location in relation to the guestroom structure. This is important for two reasons. One, the architect needs to plan the lobby floor so that the major guest circulation from the entrance to the front desk to the elevators is convenient and logical. Two, the designer must position any long-span spaces, primarily the ballroom and other larger meeting rooms, so that they are not directly under the guestroom tower, in order to simplify the structural design of the hotel and reduce construction costs.

Renaissance Arlington Capitol View, Arlington, Virginia
The lobby of the Renaissance Hotel combines many of the features prevalent in today's lobby layouts: registration podiums, comfortable seating, quick-service food and beverages, large-screen televisions, and space for guests to socialize.

Table 17.1 Public space matrix

Hotel type	Lobby	F&B areas	Function spaces	Recreation	Retail	Parking
Urban (business)	Moderate	Small	Varies	Moderate	Moderate	Small
Boutique hotel	Moderate	Small	Small	Small	Small	Small
Suburban hotel	Moderate	Moderate	Moderate	Moderate	Small	Large
Airport hotel	Moderate	Moderate	Large	Small	Small	Moderate
Roadside inn	Small	Moderate	Small	Small	Small	Moderate
Resort (golf/beach/tennis)	Moderate	Large	Moderate	Large	Large	Large
Resort (other)	Small	Moderate	Small	Large	Large	Moderate
Convention hotel	Large	Large	Large	Moderate	Large	Moderate
Conference center	Moderate	Moderate	Large	Large	Small	Large
Condominium hotel	Small	Small	Small	Moderate	Small	Moderate
All-suite hotel	Moderate	Moderate	Moderate	Moderate	Small	Moderate
Super-luxury hotel	Small	Moderate	Small	Small	Moderate	Moderate
Mega-hotel	Large	Large	Large	Large	Large	Moderate
Mixed-use hotel	Large	Large	Large	Moderate	Large	Moderate
Casino hotel	Moderate	Large	Large	Large (casino)	Moderate	Moderate

Key: "Small" means lobby <6 sq ft per room (0.55 sq m); food and beverage areas <0.7 seat per room; function spaces <2 seats per room; recreation area = small pool or health club plus limited other facilities; parking <0.7 car per room.

"Moderate" stands for lobby 6–10 sq ft per room (0.55–0.93 sq m); food and beverage areas 0.7–1.2 seats per room; function spaces 2–4 seats per room; recreation area = pool and spa/health club plus other facilities; parking for 0.7–1.2 cars per room.

"Large" indicates lobby >10 sq ft per room (0.93 sq m); food and beverage areas >1.2 seats per room; function areas >4 seats per room; recreation areas = extensive facilities including full spa; parking >1.2 cars per room. Some types of hotels require additional parking for buses.

Exterior Approach and Entrances

The architectural aspects of the building, of course, are best observed on the approach to the hotel entrance, and the details of the site and exterior design—the landscaping, the night illumination, the entry drive, and canopy—all contribute to the guests' anticipation of their stay. Larger hotels may develop a number of different entrances to help separate overnight guests and visitors, to reduce the amount of unnecessary traffic through the lobby, to establish a distinct identity for a restaurant or other facility, or to provide increased security. Resorts may focus on the landscaping at the entry driveway and the approach to the hotel. The designers should assess the relative need for the following entrances:

- Main hotel entrance
- Ballroom/banquet entrance
- Restaurant/bar/nightclub/casino entrance
- Health club/spa entrance
- Tour bus/airport bus drop-off
- Suite or condominium entrance.

Centara Grand at CentralWorld, Bangkok, Thailand
Many city hotels feature a canopy extending over the sidewalk to protect arriving guests from inclement weather.

JW Marriott San Antonio, Texas
Where hotels have sufficient space, the preferred arrival arrangement is to provide a covered porte cochère extending across the driveway.

Morongo Casino, Cabazon, California
Often, a hotel will create a dramatic porte cochère to signal the arrival point.

Each entrance needs to be clearly marked according to its function with a canopy, signage, special illumination, or other architectural treatment. Some entrances require space for waiting taxis or buses, others require temporary luggage storage, and the condominium entrance requires special security. Some city hotels may succeed with no more than a drop-off at the curb, but in destinations such as Orlando or Las Vegas, the largest hotels often have four to six lanes at the porte cochère to handle the heavy volume of arrivals and departures. The design requirements for the hotel entrances can be summarized briefly:

- *Canopy:* Provide a porte cochère or covered drop-off at the main entrance and principal secondary entrances (ballroom or restaurant) to protect guests from inclement weather; include lighting, signage, and heat, if necessary; ensure sufficient height for buses and emergency vehicles.
- *Driveways:* Predict the amount of traffic and provide a sufficient number of aisles and queuing space for waiting taxis, loading and unloading of passengers and luggage, and short-term standing, including valet-delivered cars and tour or airport buses.
- *Parking:* Make garage access convenient to and from the main hotel entrance; if there is valet parking, establish a location for the valet office near the main entrance.
- *Sidewalks:* Design pedestrian areas that are sufficiently wide for handling baggage, storing baggage carts, and providing a doorman or bellman station; at bus locations, provide space for groups to assemble.
- *Doors and vestibules:* Develop a weather vestibule with revolving or automatic doors to limit temperature differences; include access into luggage-storage room from curb; provide ramps as necessary for both disabled guests and luggage carts.

Lobby

Among the many public areas of the hotel, the lobby makes the single greatest impact on the guest and on visitors to the hotel. Its design—whether intimate or expansive, formal or casual—sets the tone for the hotel or resort. Therefore, the planning of the major lobby elements and the design of the details are crucial to making a positive and lasting impression on the guest. The most successful designs carefully balance two key factors: visual impact and function.

For most of the twentieth century, until the Hyatt Regency Hotel opened in Atlanta, Georgia, in 1967, most hotel lobbies were relatively small, designed along the same economical principles as the rest of the hotel. However, in the 1970s emphasis shifted toward larger lobbies, not only in convention hotels and mixed-used complexes, but also in smaller hotels built in suburban areas and at airports. The beginning of the twenty-first century, with its increase in hotel specialization, shows evidence of a return to more intimate interior spaces, especially in the super-luxury, all-suite, and conference-center categories. Thus, among the initial questions facing the developer and architect is to decide what should be the scale, atmosphere, and

Hotel Public Space

John C. Portman, Jr.
Chairman, John Portman & Associates
Atlanta, Georgia

A century ago, the world experienced a transition from an agrarian to an industrial society. Now, early in the twenty-first century, the world is in the throes of another transformation, into an age of technological innovation. Design in this period will continue to reflect not only changing social views, but also evolving technology. We have only begun to sense the impact of technology and innovation on human endeavor and its effect on work, play, travel, and perceptions of "place."

These perceptions are influenced by the art and architecture of the environment, the natural surroundings, and the times. It is the architect's responsibility to integrate these elements to create an enhanced human experience. In hotels, for example, the resurgence of the hotel lobby as an active place to see, be seen, and participate has changed from a time when it was less multi-dimensional. Public space is becoming a public-happening place. Lounges and restaurants, shops and libraries, and special seating groups all interact to create comfortable and convenient, yet active, environments.

Public space today is a place in which people linger as well as move into, out of, and through. The challenge to designers is to create architecture that by its expression acknowledges the many varied activities.

The architect must integrate public spaces, both indoors and outdoors, in such a way that people are drawn to the space. Today, you must immerse people in an evolving diversified world. Whether the desired effect is to calm or excite, the architect must organize guests' sequence through the hotel. From the building approach, to entering the front door, to moving through the lobby, to continuing to their room, guests must anticipate a build-up of the experience largely created by the hotel's design.

image of the lobby. Many hotel companies today are making the lobby into much more of a social center, combining the traditional functions into one space where guests register, eat, meet, and socialize; Marriott calls it the "great room."

Program and Planning Objectives

The space program for the lobby must recognize the type of hotel and the amount of circulation within the public areas. Larger hotels, such as convention properties and those located within mixed-use

Westin Minneapolis, Minneapolis, Minnesota
The adaptive reuse of the 1941 Farmers & Mechanics Bank space creates a dramatic lobby for the Westin Minneapolis. The 214-room hotel features a three-story multi-purpose lobby space complete with elegant wood carvings and details.

Renaissance Arlington Capitol View
The "great room" lobby of the Renaissance hotel illustrates the multi-purpose design of today's hotel lobby.

projects, require tremendous amounts of space to accommodate the number of guests and visitors drawn to the variety of facilities. Smaller hotels, and those that cater to few outsiders other than hotel guests, require relatively little floor area. Most hotels provide between 6 and 10 sq ft (0.6–0.9 sq m) of floor area per guestroom in the lobby, not including circulation to remote functions (see Chapter 14). Convention and mega-hotels, and those developed as part of a mixed-use project, may require 10–15 sq ft (0.9–1.4 sq m) per room.

Locating bars, restaurants, and retail kiosks within the lobby is one way to increase the apparent size of the space without adding additional gross area. Atlanta architect John Portman refers to this concept as "shared space," in which additional lobby functions create variety, not only in scale but in relative level of activity, with fluctuating usage throughout the day. In order to accomplish this diversity successfully, the best plans provide a clear definition of the several functions that occur within the lobby and make their organization obvious to the guest.

The planning requirements of most hotel lobbies are similar, regardless of the type of hotel (see Table 17.2). In addition to establishing the image of the hotel, the lobby serves as the main circulation space, directing guests to the front desk, elevators, food and beverage outlets, meeting and banquet facilities, health club, and other public areas; as guests linger, it serves as an informal gathering space. It also functions as a security control point, where the staff can visually supervise access to the building. The several planning objectives for the lobby include:

- *Entrances:* Consider additional exterior entrances for the main lobby, banquet facilities, restaurants, health club, or other high-traffic areas.
- *Front desk location:* Locate the desk so that it is immediately visible to the entering hotel guest and so that desk personnel can visually oversee access to the passenger elevators.
- *Office access:* Provide entrances to the front office, safe-deposit area, executive offices, and sales and catering offices.
- *Guest elevators:* Locate elevators close to the front desk and the main entrance and provide sufficient elevator lobby space for handling luggage.
- *Seating area:* Provide a seating area near the desk and entrance, including some private seating groups; locate additional seating contiguous with the lobby bar.
- *Circulation:* Establish clear paths to the front desk, elevators, restaurants and bars, meeting and banquet areas; where possible, separate hotel-guest traffic from convention-oriented visitors.
- *Retail areas:* Provide lease space convenient to the guest circulation areas or with exterior frontage.
- *Bellman/luggage:* Position bellman station near the front desk, elevators, and front entrance; locate luggage storage nearby.
- *Support functions:* Locate such accessory functions as toilets, coats, house phones, public phones, meeting directory, and assistant manager's desk conveniently in relation to other areas.

Table 17.2 Lobby design checklist

Front desk area
- ❑ Stations for registration, cashier, information
- ❑ Assistant manager's desk
- ❑ Bellman station, cart storage
- ❑ Luggage storage
- ❑ House and pay phones

Seating area
- ❑ Seating capacity and type
- ❑ Food and beverage service
- ❑ Water feature or other visual focus

Circulation
- ❑ Access to public elevators
- ❑ Access to restaurants and lounges
- ❑ Access to function rooms
- ❑ Access to recreation facilities
- ❑ Access to retail shops and other public areas
- ❑ Access to parking garage

Retail areas
- ❑ Sundries shop (newsstand, toiletries, souvenirs)
- ❑ Travel services (city tours, airlines, rental cars)
- ❑ Clothing (men, women, specialty shops)
- ❑ Gifts (jeweler, florist, toys, books)
- ❑ Other services (bank, copy center)

Successful lobby planning requires the designer to carefully consider the relative layout of several major functional elements (front desk, public elevators) and many additional details (house phones, seating areas, etc.). Some relate to the lobby space itself, others to adjacent areas, and yet others to movement through the space. The checklist identifies the essential elements of good lobby planning.

(facing)

The Nines, Portland, Oregon

Top: The adaptive reuse of the upper floors of the Meier & Frank department store included a seven-story atrium cut into the building to accommodate the lobby, bar, and restaurant.

Bottom: Semi-private seating alcoves are arranged throughout the atrium in the 333-room hotel.

Design Objectives

The written design objectives for the lobby should provide a detailed description of the front desk, seating area, circulation, and secondary functions. To a large extent, the architect and interior designer must first study each area individually, solving a multitude of design and functional issues, and then put them together. Some issues are more related to the back-of-house (front desk), others to food and beverage (lobby bar), and others to organizing the public flow. The design of the front desk and related activities, just one aspect of the lobby, requires making conscious decisions on each of the following features:

- *Size of desk:* Provide individual workstations, each 6 ft (1.8 m) long, for registration and cashier; assume two stations for the first 150 rooms, one more for each additional 100 rooms; alternatively, provide dual registration pods for the reception staff.
- *Queuing space:* Provide sufficient space in front of the desk for guests to line up; for convention hotels, provide at least 20 ft (6.1 m) clear of circulation.
- *Assistant manager's desk:* If required, provide a desk, seating, and storage near the front desk for a concierge or assistant manager; consider making the desk a major decorative feature within the lobby.

- *Bellman station:* Provide a bellman station near the front desk and main entrance.
- *Luggage storage:* Provide a lockable storage area adjoining the bellman station, with shelving for checked luggage; provide direct access to the curb.
- *Telephones:* Include house phones close to the front desk and public phones convenient to the lobby, approximately one per 100 rooms.
- *Furniture and fixtures:* Establish ambience of lobby area by providing special millwork detailing and finishes, front desk, bellman station, assistant manager's desk, and furnishings (lounge seating, decorative lighting, artwork) to establish the image of the hotel.

The design of the other areas of the lobby deals with fewer functional elements but requires more manipulation of the space. The definition of circulation, seating, and retail areas usually is advanced by such standard design techniques as level changes, floor materials, varying ceiling heights, special lighting, signage programs, articulation of decorative details, and custom millwork. Many of these are evident in the illustrations of hotel and resort lobbies throughout Part 1.

Westin Boston Waterfront, Boston, Massachusetts
The dual reception podiums are a requirement for most Starwood hotels.

St. Regis Atlanta, Atlanta, Georgia
The chandeliers, curving grand stairs, and small seating areas exemplify the luxurious St. Regis look and feel.

Westin Warsaw, Warsaw, Poland
The 361-room hotel features a glazed vertical atrium at the corner of the structure, holding the glass observation elevators typical of Portman-designed projects.

Qasr Al Sarab, Abu Dhabi, United Arab Emirates
Located in the legendary Liwa Desert, one of the largest uninterrupted sand deserts in the world, the Qasr Al Sarab Desert Resort features stunning desert views from the lobby and guest suites.

Baronette Renaissance Hotel, Novi, Michigan
The Renaissance Hotel, located in a Detroit suburb, features a lobby with a reflective stone and glass hearth and seating clusters for small groups to work and socialize.

Food and Beverage Outlets

The hotel's restaurants and lounges offer the potential to give the property an individual identity and to make a business or vacation trip memorable. Generally, at least one restaurant and one cocktail lounge are clustered conveniently around the hotel lobby. These and other more specialized types of food and beverage outlets—specialty or theme restaurants; deli and coffee/pastry shops; lobby bar and entertainment or sports lounges—form a second, more complex category of public spaces. However, these vary so widely in quality and character that the program and design of each outlet must be developed individually, based on a survey of the total market and the existing competition.

Hotel food service has gone through frequent cycles of popularity with the public. Until late in the twentieth century, and then only in the better hotels, most U.S. hotel restaurants had a reputation for poor food and uninspired design. Their mediocrity may have been due to the fact that hotel restaurants often were only profitable at breakfast, when the overnight guests could be depended on to fill the more casual outlet; guests scarcely used them at lunch and hardly more at dinner. In the 1970s, in a climate of increased competition, the industry began to recognize the marketing opportunities of improved restaurant and lounge operations. They found that well-conceived food and beverage outlets increased the demand for guestrooms and meetings, attracted the general public, especially at the low-volume lunch and dinner periods, and had the potential to generate additional profits. But the cyclic nature of the industry and resultant downsizing of staff at many hotels in the 1990s forced a new series of economies, and challenged designers and operators again to seek creative solutions.

Some companies decided, instead, to outsource their F&B operations, selecting a local or national brand to occupy space in the hotel, rather than run the outlet themselves. Such branding became a major theme in the 1990s and should continue to flourish. However, it does have some downsides. Leased operations remove the hotel operator from direct control over the product quality, introduce non-hotel staff into the property, and greatly complicate room service and back-of-house functions such as receiving and storage. Where it works, outsourcing can be a great success: Heartbeat, the restaurant in the W New York, serves over 180 dinners and about 300 room-service meals each day.

Designing successful restaurant and bar operations must recognize the public's changing attitudes toward food. For example, more people now eat outside conventional mealtimes, forgoing breakfast but taking a larger morning coffee break or putting off dinner for a late-evening meal or snack. Travelers appreciate restaurants that provide self-service elements—an elaborate buffet set up, or more traditional salad bar—from which they can select items, control portion size, and better manage the time spent dining. These considerations should be part of the market analysis, which defines both the hotel guest and the local customer, so that the hotel's food and beverage facilities can enjoy the largest possible audience.

Food and Beverage Concept Development

The high visibility of hotel restaurants suggests that both management and designers should think through their detailed operations early in the development phase. However, in smaller and midscale hotels, restaurant menus often are not developed until a few months before the hotel opens. As a result, the restaurant may not be designed until well after the building shell is complete, when modifications to the public area or kitchen access, or the addition of level changes, display features, or special ceiling treatments, are impossible. The result, too often, is an unexceptional restaurant.

Experienced hotel management companies evolve food and beverage concepts in two ways. Some, like Marriott and Hyatt International, define the operations early in the development process and establish the type of food and service, the hours of operation, the theme and general atmosphere, including even the outlet's name and logo. The architect and interior designer then develop a schematic building design that accommodates these themes. Before considering the detailed planning and design issues of hotel restaurants and lounges, designers should become familiar with such operational aspects of food service as marketing, menu-planning, service, and food-preparation techniques. This enables them to communicate better with the managers who establish detailed restaurant and lounge criteria:

- Market characteristics
- Concept (type of menu, style of service, entertainment)
- Design elements (atmosphere, tabletop, display elements)
- Operations (hours open, staffing, seating mix)
- Financial projections

The designer should address the components of restaurant or lounge design identified in the food and beverage concept checklist; see Table 17.3.

The other procedure is to establish only rough space requirements at the program phase, and to develop the food and beverage concepts after the architect has conceived the organization of the hotel, in light of the actual location and type of space provided. For example, the three-meal restaurant might have one theme if it is within an atrium space, another if it overlooks the pool or a garden courtyard. This was carried even further at the Seaport Hotel in Boston, where the developer decided to delay establishing any restaurant concept until six months before the hotel opened. He reasoned that many hotel restaurants are redesigned every three to five years in order to remain current. Therefore, the hotel plan included a generic kitchen and restaurant space that was not finally designed or detailed until the hotel was nearly complete and almost ready to open.

A recent approach to hotel food service has been to develop a single restaurant with several distinct moods that are appropriate to the different meal periods and levels of informality. This is especially appropriate in smaller properties, where one three-meal restaurant must have a bright and airy feel and include a buffet setup at breakfast, a balanced, casual, yet business atmosphere at lunch, and an intimate or formal mood at dinner time. This can be accomplished partly by the larger design elements: placing some

Table 17.3 Food and beverage concept checklist

General
- ❏ Name of outlet
- ❏ Location
- ❏ Capacity
- ❏ Operating hours
- ❏ Market description
- ❏ Financial projections
- ❏ Staffing

Food or beverage concept
- ❏ Menu
- ❏ Style of service
- ❏ Food/wine display
- ❏ Bar/lounge emphasis
- ❏ Exhibition cooking
- ❏ Atmosphere
- ❏ Entertainment

Layout (general)
- ❏ Entry sequence
- ❏ Seating mix
- ❏ Orientation (interior display, exterior views)
- ❏ Level changes
- ❏ Entertainment area
- ❏ Kitchen or back-of-house access

Layout (food outlets)
- ❏ Host/maître d'
- ❏ Cashier
- ❏ Self-service buffet
- ❏ Service stations
- ❏ Food/wine display
- ❏ Exhibition cooking
- ❏ Service bar

Layout (beverage outlets)
- ❏ Bar
- ❏ Bar storage
- ❏ Stage
- ❏ Dance floor
- ❏ Special entertainment

Design/décor
- ❏ Atmosphere
- ❏ Finishes
- ❏ Seating types
- ❏ Feature elements
- ❏ Window treatment
- ❏ Lighting
- ❏ Tabletop
- ❏ Artwork

Uniforms
- ❏ Uniform design

Special equipment
- ❏ Exhibition cooking area

Centara Grand at CentralWorld, Bangkok, Thailand
The gourmet dining room, Fifty five, near the top of the slim guestroom tower, overlooks downtown Bangkok and offers diners the best in Thai cuisine.

Centara Grand at CentralWorld, Bangkok, Thailand
With more than 200 interior seats, Ginger, featuring Chinese, Japanese, and Thai foods, offers hotel guests a variety of Asian cuisines in a modern setting overlooking the city; additional outdoor seating provides an alternative venue for the typically warm, tropical evenings.

Table 17.4 Opportunities for food merchandizing

❑ Multiple themes: Several small restaurants, capacity of 30 to 80 seats, with distinct ethnic or other themes operate from a single commissary (English pub, French bistro, Italian trattoria, etc.).

❑ Exhibition cooking: Food is prepared in the restaurant or at an area visible from the seating areas, and is used as the source for many menu items (pizza oven, grill, bakery, pasta-making, rotisserie, Chinese wok, etc.).

❑ Food display: A display area, either at the entrance or located near the center of the outlet, serves either as a source for food or as decoration (appetizers, carved roasts, desserts, wines, special coffees, etc.).

❑ Buffet: Display area is used for guest self-service.

❑ Tableside service: Service carts are rolled to each table with the presentation or preparation of individual entrees (specialty appetizers, Caesar salad, desserts, liqueurs, etc.).

❑ Takeout: In downtown hotels, especially in shopping and tourist areas, fast service and informal outlets with takeout counter (ice cream, pastries, deli sandwiches, coffee, other specialty foods, etc.).

❑ Lobby breakfast: Temporary cart or kiosk service in the lobby to sell coffee, juices, and pastries during peak breakfast hours.

❑ Atrium restaurant: Exposed and visible food outlet, such as a sidewalk café in the lobby, increases awareness of the restaurant and encourages guest use, whatever the theme.

seating near windows, some around the buffet, some on hard flooring, some in an adjoining semi-private alcove, and so forth. In addition, the operator may adjust the atmosphere from one meal to the next by closing window blinds or dimming the room lights, modifying the use of food displays, adding music, changing the tabletop, or dressing the staff in different uniforms.

However, larger hotels and resorts still have several restaurants, requiring individual and distinctive themes. If a property includes only two outlets, they usually are a three-meal restaurant (the former "coffee shop")—and a specialty restaurant. A third operation might be a casual deli or a coffee/pastry outlet. Few hotels today attempt to compete with local restaurateurs with a fine-dining room. Each restaurant has its own image and, while attracting hotel guests, attempts to compete for different groups of outside diners.

Many food and beverage concepts include conscious attempts to merchandize the food in novel ways, such as through an elaborate display or an exhibition kitchen. Increasing the visibility of the food choices and developing unusual food combinations can greatly increase revenues. Some of the many opportunities for better food merchandizing are shown in Table 17.4.

Bar operations are similarly varied. While nearly every type of property except budget inns and the smallest hotels (under 50 rooms) includes a small lounge of some type, larger hotels offer a lobby bar, a sports bar or entertainment facility, and, occasionally, a rooftop lounge, where the view warrants it. Additional small outlets for food and beverages may complement and support a hotel's recreation facilities, such as the pool bar, marina bar, or the grill room at the resort's golf or tennis clubhouse.

Program and Planning Objectives

The optimal number of restaurant and bar outlets varies with the size, type, and location of the hotel, and with the relative emphasis that the operator gives to that part of the operation. Convention hotels, at which the breakfast meal creates the largest peak demand, usually have a large three-meal restaurant, at least one specialty restaurant, and substantial demand for room service. Remote-destination resorts, where the typical length-of-stay is longer and all the guests must be served three meals, plan for the flexible use of outdoor areas—breakfast terraces and pool snack bars, for instance—in addition to two or more outlets. Cruise ships (the ultimate destination resort) plan the capacity of the main dining room to accommodate all passengers in two sittings for the formal "captain's dinner," but include several additional theme outlets for the bulk of the dining. At extended-stay hotels, where many guests stay several weeks or longer and where they often prepare their own breakfast and dine out in the evening, only minimal food and bar service is needed.

In Asia, where the tradition is to dine out at hotels more than at independent restaurants, the hotel F&B operations become a major revenue generator. A hotel with 300–400 rooms may have a half-dozen or more different-themed dining rooms and lounges. Table 17.5 illustrates the variety of ethnic or other distinctive outlets that are common in business hotels, such as the Centara Grand in Bangkok (505 guestrooms) and the Sheraton Incheon in Korea (319 rooms).

Experienced hotel operators approach the food and beverage program with an instinct about the relative size of the several outlets. Operators vary in their standards, but a good starting rule-of-thumb in North America and Europe is to provide restaurant seats equal to 0.6 times the number of guestrooms, and lounge seats equal to 0.3 times the number of rooms. This initial program objective can be increased or decreased according to the consultants' market study and the hotel operator's further financial analysis. Thus, a 400-room hotel might feature, instead of a 240-seat restaurant (0.6 times the number of guestrooms), a moderate-priced food outlet for 160 people and a specialty restaurant with about 80 seats. Table 17.6 gives guidelines on restaurant and bar capacities for different-size hotels; however, these generally need to be modified to recognize site and local market conditions, as well as regional attitudes toward hotel dining—such as just described in Asia.

The planning requirements for restaurants and lounges are as critical as for the other public areas, but, to a large extent, each outlet is independent of the others. Nevertheless, the following points are essential to an effective organization:

- Provide each food outlet with direct, convenient access to the kitchen; those outlets with minor food service may be served from pantries
- Provide each beverage outlet with service backup, from either the kitchen or the bar storage area

Centara Grand at CentralWorld, Bangkok, Thailand
The 170-seat Globe Bar provides trendy late-night cocktails and music in a contemporary setting complete with a nightly disc jockey.

Table 17.5 International hotel F&B outlets

Hotel	Cuisine	Seats	Comment
Centara Grand at CentralWorld, Bangkok, Thailand (505 rooms)	International	204	Dining inspired by the five continents; open 24 hours
	Pan-Asian	208 (60)	Japanese, authentic Thai, and trendy Chinese fare; open lunch and dinner
	Gourmet dining	90	Gourmet dining; open lunch and dinner
	Urban bistro	81 (149)	Chic urban bistro, plus wine bar and martini bar; open evenings and late nights
	Lobby lounge	68	Cocktails, desserts and cakes, and British tea; open all day
	Whiskey bar	170	Cocktail lounge with DJ; open evenings and late nights
	Café/deli	30	Quick-service outlet; open all day
	Juice bar	10	In-spa outlet, offering fresh fruit and vegetable juices; open all day
	Poolside bar	30	Light meals and cocktails; open all day
Sheraton Incheon, Songdo City, Korea (319 rooms)	International	148	Open kitchen with à la carte and buffet menus; open lunch and dinner
	Italian	86	Authentic Italian with antipasti; open lunch and dinner, and Sunday brunch buffet
	Japanese	98	Four private rooms; adds options for business meetings; open lunch and dinner
	Cantonese	138	Seven private rooms cater largely to groups; open lunch and dinner
	Lobby lounge	48	Cocktail bar with live entertainment
	Cocktail bar	40	Refined cocktail bar; open afternoons and evenings

Seats are indoors (outdoors).

Table 17.6 Restaurant and bar capacities for different size hotels (number of seats)

	Number of guestrooms					
	200	**300**	**400**	**500**	**750**	**1000**
Three-meal restaurant	120	180	160	180	225	250
Specialty restaurant			80	80	100	150
Theme restaurant					75	125
Grab'n'go				40	50	75
Lobby bar	60	30	40	50	60	60
Cocktail lounge		60	80			80
Restaurant holding bar					20	20
Entertainment lounge/sports bar			100	140	140	

Centara Grand, Bangkok, Thailand
The Red Sky is the rooftop bar, situated behind the dramatic lotus-flower feature at the top of the guestroom structure, featuring mostly outdoor seating overlooking the city skyline.

- Locate each outlet so that it is accessible from public flow areas; make the café visible from the lobby.
- Pair each food outlet with a nearby bar or include a small holding lounge.
- Plan larger restaurants and bars so that sections can be closed during slow periods.
- Locate restaurants and bars, where appropriate, with exterior frontage and direct outside access.

Restaurant Design Objectives

Design objectives follow directly from a clear and well-researched operational and marketing concept. Based on the menu and such operational aspects as the type of service, method of beverage service, check handling, and use of entertainment, designers create the desired mood, function, layout, finishes, lighting, and furnishings.

Each restaurant outlet, depending on its type and quality level, must have a very different design treatment. For example, the hotel's main three-meal restaurant needs a theme that will permit the mood to vary from light and casual at breakfast to more formal at dinner. This may be accomplished by providing variable lighting, changing the tabletop from placemats to table linen, closing the counter seating, presenting a food display, or extending room dividers to make smaller and more intimate dining areas. The design of a three-meal restaurant should include the following considerations:

- *Cashier/hostess station:* Provide a combined station to control access to all sections of the room, handle guest checks, and supervise coat-check area.
- *Separate sections:* Divide the restaurant into two or more areas so that sections can be closed during periods of low occupancy.
- *Flexible arrangement of tables:* Provide paired deuces, flip-top fours (table leaves convert a square table into a larger circular one), to provide for large parties.

- *Counter seating:* Provide about 10 percent of total seats at counter for singles.
- *Buffet/display areas:* Provide an area for self-service buffet or food display.
- *Service stations:* Provide wet service stations for every 80 or so seats, to supply water and coffee; store linen and cutlery; and hold soiled dishes.
- *Adaptable lighting:* Provide dimmable lighting to change the mood from breakfast to lunch to dinner.
- *Background music:* Consider including soft music.
- *Uniforms, tabletop, graphics, and signage:* Design the accessory elements to complement the outlet or hotel theme.

Similarly, design objectives can be established for a hypothetical higher-priced restaurant. The specialty or signature restaurant may be open daily only for dinner, although lunch service is profitable in urban locations, as is Sunday brunch in the suburbs. Its mood and décor may reflect a theme, developed primarily around the menu or style of service. Decorative touches in materials, detailing, furnishings, planting, artifacts, artwork, and tabletop design further reinforce the theme. The design objectives, modified and refined by analyzing the market and developing a unique food concept, include the following:

- *Entry sequence:* Establish a foyer space to set the mood for the restaurant.
- *Maître d':* Provide a host station at the entrance to the restaurant.
- *Focal point:* Organize all seats to take advantage of some focal point, either inside the dining room (food display, water feature, and entertainment) or outside it.
- *Seating areas:* Incorporate screens or level changes to create more intimate, semi-private groups of tables.
- *Table seating:* Provide clear definition to the seating areas, separating them from the aisles, service, buffet, and host areas. Each table should have some privacy from other tables.
- *Food display:* Arrange a food display either near the entrance or central to the seating.
- *Exhibition cooking:* Based on the food concept, consider providing an open area for food preparation, such as a wood-fired oven, grill, or Japanese teppanyaki feature.
- *Entertainment:* Provide a small stage and dance floor, or consider how the plan might be modified to accommodate entertainment in the future; tables should be organized with views toward this focal point.
- *Service stations:* Develop inconspicuous wet and dry service stations without compromising staff efficiency.
- *Bar or holding bar:* Provide beverage service from an adjacent cocktail lounge, or a separate holding bar designated for the specialty restaurant, or from a kitchen-service bar.
- *Intimate lighting:* Design the variable lighting to create a more intimate mood at dinner; allow for brighter levels at lunch and for cleaning (fluorescent lights should not be used in any area).
- *Uniforms, tabletop, graphics, and signage:* Select all design accessories to complement and reinforce the specialty theme of the room.

Table 17.7 Restaurant and bar area requirements

Outlet type	Casual	Formal
Three-meal restaurant	16 (1.50)	18 (1.70)
Specialty restaurant	18 (1.70)	20 (1.85)
Fine dining	—	25 (2.30)
Chinese-theme restaurant	20 (1.85)	25 (2.30)
Grab'n'go restaurant	16 (1.50)	—
Ice cream/fast food	12 (1.10)	—
Lobby bar	20 (1.85)	25 (2.30)
Sports bar	15 (1.40)	—
Cocktail lounge	16 (1.50)	20 (1.85)

Approximate area requirements per seat in sq ft (sq m).

Most other restaurant outlets feature aspects of these two dining types. The more casual theme restaurants may combine the counter seating and cashier functions—a "diner" outlet, for example—or introduce some variation on a native cuisine. A deli operation might be open 24 hours in an urban hotel and feature imaginatively designed display cases with pastries and other specialty items, sandwich preparation areas, high lighting levels, and easily maintained finishes.

Restaurant designers need to understand the influence of different types of seating on creating efficient layouts. Booth and banquette configurations, which reduce the amount of flow space around a table, are more efficient but are not always popular with customers. Larger tables, say for six diners, are more efficient overall than are deuces (tables for two), which need to be spaced for a modicum of privacy. In addition, the type of service and general quality level influences the space programming, which, in general, requires 15–20 sq ft (1.40–1.85 sq m) per person, or up to 25 sq ft (2.3 sq m) for formal settings (see Table 17.7).

Lounge and Bar Design Objectives

Similar to the way the design team conceives restaurants, the hotel operating company establishes bar and lounge concepts, the architect prepares preliminary plans to accommodate these requirements, and the interior designer more fully develops these themes, including their furnishings and fixtures. Even more than the restaurants, the lounge areas vary extensively among different types of hotels. In a small downtown property, the primary beverage outlet may be a quiet and luxuriously furnished lobby bar, whereas in a convention, casino or resort property, it may be an action-oriented sports bar or entertainment lounge, adding a major nighttime focus for the hotel. Variation among these active bar/lounges is usually based on the opportunities of the local market and on the expected hotel clientele. Therefore, it is especially important that the designer be given a clear set of design objectives for each outlet.

Le Meridien, Philadelphia
Placing Le Bar in the lobby of the former YMCA building, adaptively renovated to Le Meridien standards, both creates energy and provides revenue to the operation.

The lobby bar developed in the 1970s as a way to create activity and excitement in the open atrium spaces in large hotels. After it proved itself as a popular meeting place and revenue-generator, the lobby bar became standard in most types of hotels and locations. Fully open to the lobby space, separated only by planters, railings, a water feature, or level change, the lobby bar offers additional public seating when it isn't used as a beverage outlet. Operators discovered, too, that they also could utilize the space for continental breakfast or for merchandizing late-evening snacks. The designer should attempt to include the following features in the lobby bar:

- *Visibility:* Provide an open area that is obvious to hotel guests and visitors.
- *Seating:* Furnish the bar primarily with lounge seating—sofas, lounge chairs, end tables—or with a combination of lounge and bar seating; provide a few seats at a service bar.
- *Bar:* Feature a small bar for beverage service, with nearby storage or backup from the kitchen.
- *Entertainment:* Specify a location for a piano or other entertainment.
- *Food service:* Consider back-of-house access for limited food service, especially Continental breakfast, hors d'oeuvres, and snack service.

The second beverage outlet often is some type of active bar or lounge, usually featuring a sports/video theme or entertainment, sometimes with dancing. Quite different from the more subdued lobby bar, the entertainment lounge is completely enclosed to reduce high noise levels, and features lower light levels and more closely spaced seating. The designer, in developing the layout and design of entertainment lounges, should consider the following:

- *Entry sequence:* Develop an enclosed entrance, to maintain acoustic and visual separation between the lounge and the hotel circulation areas.
- *Separate sections:* Establish distinct zones for the bar, the video/games area or entertainment/dancing area, and the quieter lounge area.
- *Bar (about 10 to 25 percent of the lounge area):* Provide a large bar that is visible from the entrance and is situated so that guests can view the video screens or entertainers; provide pick-up stations for the staff, provide close-by bar storage.
- *Entertainment area (50 to 65 percent):* Develop an integrated section to accommodate at least half of the guests—provide multiple video screens and display of sports paraphernalia, or create stage and dance-floor area; add platforms to provide better sight lines throughout the space.

- *Lounge area (20 to 30 percent):* Design a separate lounge area, where guests can sit outside but within reach of the active zone; consider soft lounge seating.
- *Lighting:* Install flexible lighting, controlled at the bar, including stage and dance-floor lighting, as appropriate.
- *Video and sound system:* Provide control of all video screens at the host stand or bar; or provide integrated sound system with speakers focused on the dance-floor area.

Developing the restaurant and lounge concepts and establishing design goals are only part of the process. Often, the constraints of the building's schematic design greatly influence, for better or worse, the success of the food and beverage areas. The designer needs to combine the programmatic requirements with the operational standards to create a workable scheme. Hotel restaurants and bars, because they face such severe outside competition, create the greatest of all interior design challenges. While guestrooms and meeting spaces include their own important pragmatic requirements, the dining experience—combining food, service, and design elements—or the bar scene—with its new focus on entertainment—require more imagination.

Function Space

The third principal category of public space includes the meeting, banquet, reception, and exhibit spaces, which form a major core in many medium and large hotels and in conference centers. Variously referred to as "function space," "meeting and banquet area," or "convention complex," the cluster of individual spaces generally includes a large ballroom, intermediate-size banquet rooms, and smaller meeting and breakout rooms. In fact, the principal distinctions among types of hotels often focus on the size and mix of the function space.

Introduced in the late nineteenth century to accommodate important civic and social gatherings, hotel function space has more recently been incorporated to meet the needs of corporations and professional associations. The two create very different demands. The corporate group market mainly requires a variety of relatively small but high-quality spaces for sales and management meetings, launches of new products, and continuing-education programs for executives. The association market primarily needs facilities for large group meetings, smaller general-purpose rooms for seminars and workshops, and extensive exhibition space. In addition, local organizations and the public in general use hotel meeting space for a variety of meetings, banquets, and reception functions.

Program and Planning Objectives

Generally, the hotel feasibility study recommends a mix of function space that is based on an analysis of the demand for different types of business and social uses. Small-town hotels and chain-franchise properties, for example, commonly offer a single multi-purpose ballroom, simply decorated, which is intended to accommodate the full range of small meetings, civic lunches, wedding receptions, and local product displays. It usually is not intended to attract business to fill the hotel guestrooms. On the other hand, convention hotels and conference centers provide a wide range of facilities—large and small, simple and elegant, with and without high-tech audiovisual equipment—as the principal attraction to the hotel. Meeting planners select the hotel, to a large extent, for its ability to provide complete meeting facilities, which, in turn, sells large blocks of guestrooms.

At resort hotels where seasonal fluctuations in demand create low periods for several months of the year, properties have added conference wings to increase the demand for guestrooms throughout the shoulder and off-season periods. In super-luxury hotels, which have relatively fewer rooms and which place an important emphasis on intimacy and exclusivity, developers include small but elegantly finished meeting rooms; the function areas tend to be used for receptions and banquets, and to cater to the surrounding community rather than to the hotel guests.

In all but the smallest properties, function space is an essential ingredient of the successful hotel. The earlier chapters on convention hotels (Chapter 9) and conference centers (Chapter 10) illustrate a number of successful properties of those types. But for each type of hotel or resort, not just these, the development team must carefully establish the appropriate mix of function space, and detail the equipment and features needed to meet the expectations of the market. Table 17.8 identifies the typical size for different function spaces and highlights many of the key features which the designer must incorporate into the design.

Once the program is established, the architect, interior designer, consulting engineers, and operator must cooperate in planning the function space in order to create a saleable property. The success of meeting and banquet sales depends on a number of functional planning considerations—which meeting planners have learned to seek out—as well as interior décor, proper lighting, acoustical and mechanical engineering, and other technical requirements. The key planning requirements include:

- Group all function areas together (in major convention hotels, some separation may be desirable).
- Provide a separate function entrance from the street or parking area.
- Locate the function space close to and easily accessible from the hotel lobby.
- Locate additional function areas, such as an exhibit hall or audiovisual theater, so that they are convenient, but not adjacent, to the ballroom foyer.
- Include adjacent public support areas: toilets, coatrooms, telephones, and a convention-services office.
- Provide direct food-service access to the ballroom and all banquet rooms; locate the banquet pantry on the ballroom level.
- Include essential meeting and banquet storage adjacent to the ballroom.
- Design the ballroom and other larger rooms to be independent of the guestroom tower so as to simplify the building structure.
- Plan pre-function space to enhance wayfinding; provide dramatic visual elements at major foyer intersections.

Table 17.8 Function room characteristics

Space and uses	Principal planning requirements	Program (capacity) for hotel types	
Ballroom			
Meetings, banquets, receptions, exhibits	Divisibility, high ceiling, direct food access, no columns	Typical, most types: Resort: Convention:	2 x GR 0.5–1.5 x GR 2–4 x GR
Ballroom foyer			
Reception, meeting registration, flow	Access to all ballroom sections and support functions, access to terraces	Typical: Resort: Convention:	0.2 x BR 0.3 x BR 0 25–0.3 x BR
Banquet rooms			
Banquets, meetings, receptions	Divisibility, direct food access, natural light	Typical: Convention:	0.2–0.6 x BR 0.4–0.6 x BR
Meeting rooms			
Meetings, limited banquets	Permanent audiovisual systems, limited divisions	Typical: Convention: Conference center:	0.2–0.4 x BR 0.4–0.6 x BR 0.5–0.8 x BR
Boardroom			
High-level meeting	Separate from other meeting rooms, built-in audiovisual, superior finishes	All hotel types:	12–20 people
Exhibit hall			
Exhibition	Display access, floor loading, high ceiling, high lighting level	Convention:	# booths = market need
Auditorium or amphitheater			
Lectures, audiovisual presentations, case discussions	Sloped floor or tiered levels, fixed theater seats or permanent work-counter, permanent AV	Convention Conference center	0.2–0.4 x GR 0.4–0.8 x GR

Key: GR = number of guestrooms; BR = capacity of ballroom.

Renaissance Arlington Capitol View
The ballroom pre-function area features a dramatic ceiling element to help orient guests.

Blackstone Hotel, Chicago, Illinois
The historic "hotel of presidents" recently underwent a complete restoration, including the Crystal Ballroom.

AT&T Executive Education and Conference Center, University of Texas, Austin, Texas
The ballroom in the university conference center is the site for frequent campus events and festive dinners.

Waldorf=Astoria, New York
Since the Waldorf opened in 1931, one of its most iconic rooms has been the Starlight Room, originally a nightclub with a retractable roof, where the wealthiest New Yorkers dined and danced. But more recently, the room has been reconfigured as a meeting and banquet space overlooking Park Avenue. In this image, stacking chairs are arranged in a semi-circle facing a podium, beneath an ornate ceiling, now permanently fixed.

JW Marriott San Antonio, Texas
Among the many ballroom design tasks is to coordinate the ceiling design. Here, the ballroom features floating ceiling panels, curving in opposite directions below a painted-out void.

The first item in this list of planning requirements identifies the need to decide on the relative clustering of the function areas. Convention hotels, especially those which serve as the headquarters for a major meeting, may attract one major group or no more than four or five smaller groups at one time. For the occasions when a single major convention is in the hotel, it is convenient to have the ballroom, junior ballroom, and several meeting rooms immediately adjacent to each other, perhaps sharing a foyer or pre-function area. This is the usual and preferred arrangement in small and midsize hotels of 250 to 400 guestrooms.

When multiple functions need to be accommodated, it may be preferable to separate the principal meeting and banquet areas so that several groups can assemble simultaneously, without interference or distraction. The 900-room Grand Hyatt Washington has function space arrayed over three levels (see exploded plan): the main ballroom (17,500 sq ft; 1,625 sq m) and junior ballroom (8,500 sq ft; 790 sq m) are on separate levels well below grade, and the 90-seat conference theater (5,000 sq ft; 465 sq m) is on the lobby floor. At the 1,400-room Sheraton Centre in Toronto, the largest convention hotel in Canada, the main ballroom and exhibition hall are on a basement floor, whereas two junior ballrooms are in separate areas on a mezzanine level; three different organizations can easily meet without interference or direct contact with each other. For the same reason, although at a very different scale, small conference centers arrange their meeting rooms and breakout areas in several clusters, so that each group is assured privacy.

Design Criteria

The coordination among the design team is especially important in the evolution of the details for the function space. The architectural aspects (proportions, divisibility, and access), the interior design considerations (finishes, furnishings, and lighting), and the engineering requirements (ventilation, sound system, and fire protection) are clearly related and heavily influence each other.

Connecting these facts are several overall issues. One is the relative specificity of the various function areas: that is, the degree to which each is designed as a multi-purpose room or, instead, is intended particularly for a single purpose, say a board meeting or film presentation. The principal considerations include size, divisibility, complexity of services, and quality of finishes. The better defined the use of a particular room, the more specific the interior design can be. Larger hotels, and those with a clear market orientation, such as luxury properties and conference centers, can afford to provide very specific meeting and banquet rooms and further assure their use by groups with individual needs. The suburban hotel, however, must use its single ballroom for so many different functions that, too often, none is particularly well served. Table 17.9 identifies the type of architectural, decorative, and engineering decisions that the design team must make to create a successful large function room, such as the hotel ballroom. Many similar issues arise in designing the smaller rooms, as well.

A second consideration is planning the divisibility of ballroom and larger function rooms. Practically all hotel ballrooms are divided

Table 17.9 Design criteria for large function space

Architectural	
Divisibility	Number of subdivisions and proportions of each, storage of dividing walls, acoustic rating of dividing walls
Proportions	Location of and views to head table or stage
Structure	Full span, no columns
Ceiling height	Projection booth, use for exhibitions, chandeliers, cost of divisible walls, implications for second floor
Floor load	Use for displays and exhibits
Access/egress	Public and service access to each subsection, storage, display access, emergency exits
Windows	Desirability, blackout requirement

Interior design	
Floor	Carpet, patterned to assist furniture placement, portable dance floor
Walls	Various finishes (paint, vinyl, fabric panels), chair rail, folding wall finish to match perimeter, doors to cover wall storage compartments
Ceiling	Complicated design needs downlights, chandeliers, track lighting, emergency lighting, HVAC diffusers and air return, sprinklers, smoke detectors, sound system, wall tracks in integrated pattern
Windows	Full blackout capability
Lighting	Combination of functional, decorative, display, and accent lighting
Furniture	Round banquet and rectangular meeting tables, stacking chairs, risers, lectern, audiovisual equipment for function rooms; seating in foyer areas

Mechanical/electrical	
All	Fully separate controls in each room and subdivisions of larger rooms
Lighting	Fully dimmable, control at podium, flexible track lighting where required
Electrical	208 volts available in ballroom and exhibition areas
Sound	Television, telephone, microphone jacks in each area, control from sound and light booth
Mechanical	Full air-conditioning, fire protection
Plumbing	Wet utilities available near ballroom and exhibition areas

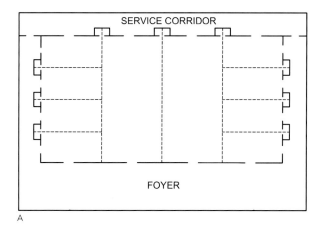

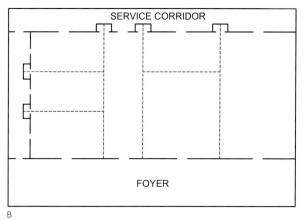

Ballroom schematics
Subdividing the hotel ballroom adds functionality: (A) Small rooms at the ends of the ballroom are reached by a combined public/service corridor outside the ballroom. (B) Larger rooms require dedicated service access, with the public reaching the spaces through the ballroom itself.

into several sections, so that a smaller group is in an appropriately sized space, two or more groups can use the room simultaneously, or a group can use one part for a meeting and the adjoining section for meals. Two typical approaches for subdividing the ballroom are illustrated in the accompanying diagram.

A third aspect of function room design is matching the room layout to the space. The larger multi-purpose rooms usually are furnished either banquet or theater style—or are essentially unfurnished when used for an exhibition or reception. But the midsize and smaller rooms will be furnished and equipped in a variety of ways to meet the particular needs of a group. The designers must test the actual capacity of each room under different furnishing configurations. Table 17.10 illustrates typical area requirements for different seating configurations over a range of large and small function rooms.

Many designers and hotel operators have found that the single most critical element in the meeting and banquet rooms is the design of the ballroom ceiling. When a hotel ballroom is set up for a banquet or meeting, the tables and attendees obscure most of the floor and the lower part of the walls. The ceiling, though, is totally visible and contains down lights, chandeliers, and track lighting, as well as mechanical diffusers and return grilles, sprinklers, sound-system speakers, smoke detectors, and movable wall tracks. All must be integrated into a single, cohesive, organized, and attractive pattern.

Another design aspect that too often is ignored during design development is provision for sufficient electrical and communication services to the ballroom, meeting rooms, and, especially, the exhibit hall. Not only electrical outlets, but telephone, television, and microphone jacks, controls for various projectors, projection screen, and lights, and, in some cases, a wet utility panel, must be provided. Exhibit halls, for example, should contain electrical outlets every 10 ft (3 m) in the floor, ceiling-mounted spotlight tracks 30 ft (9 m) on centers, and convenient water and drain connections for exhibitors.

Table 17.10 Area requirements for hotel function rooms

	Reception	Theater	Banquet	Classroom	Boardroom
Ballroom >10,000 (930)	7 (0.6)	8 (0.7)	10 (0.9)	—	—
Ballroom >3,000 (280)	8 (0.7)	8 (0.7)	11 (1.0)	12 (1.1)	—
Banquet room <3,000 (280)	9 (0.8)	10 (0.9)	12 (1.1)	14 (1.3)	—
Meeting room	9 (0.8)	10 (0.9)	12 (1.1)	14 (1.3)	16–20 (1.5–1.9)
Boardroom	12 (1.1)	—	15 (1.4)	—	20–25 (1.9–2.3)
Auditorium	—	8–10 (0.7–0.9)	—	—	—
Amphitheater	—	—	—	15–20 (1.4–1.9)	—

The approximate area requirement per seat in sq ft (sq m).
Conference centers often provide much more generous spacing, increasing these figures by 20 to 40 percent.

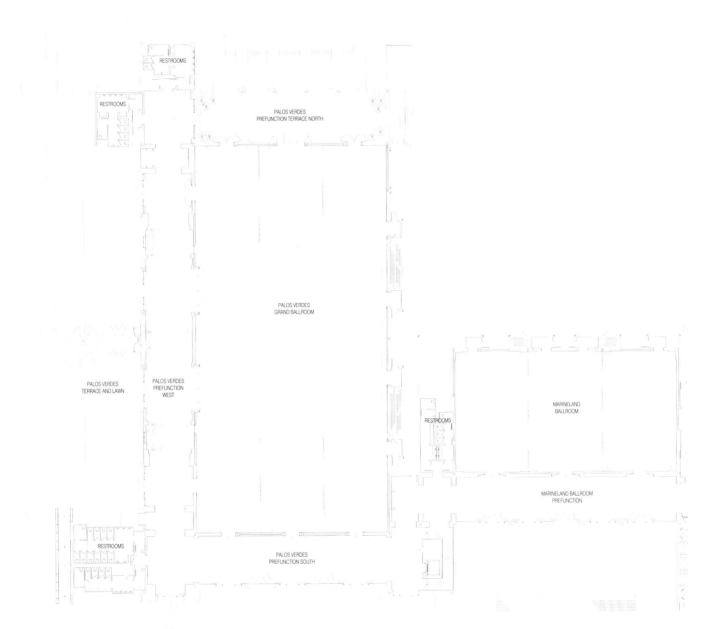

Terranea, Rancho Palos Verdes, California

The ocean-front Terranea Resort is a popular location for meetings and weddings in Southern California. The 18,000 sq ft (1,670 sq m) ballroom has its own guest entrance and function lawn.

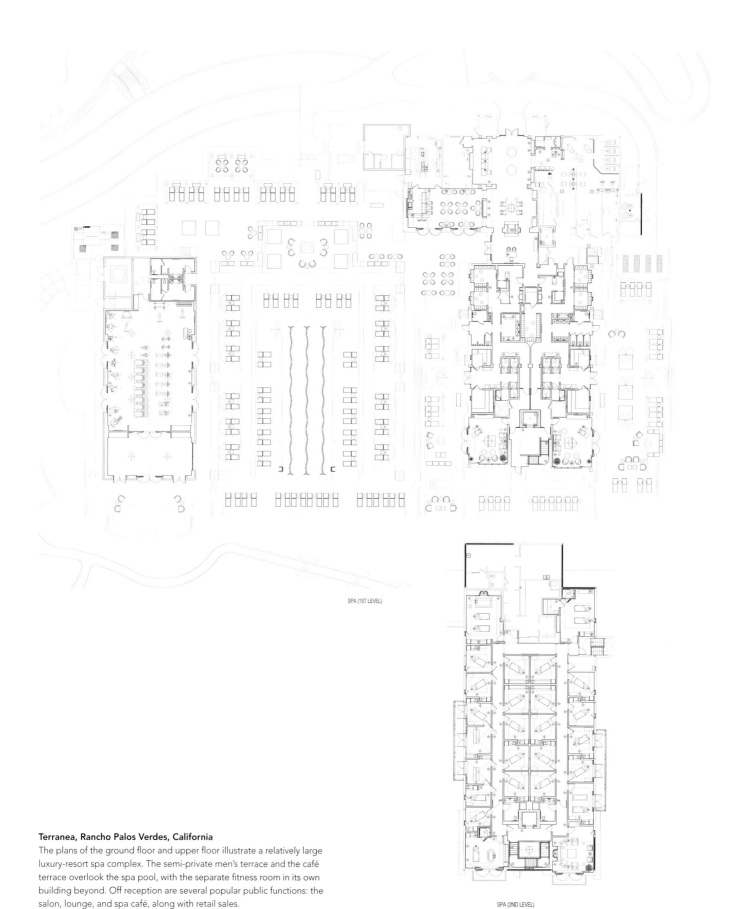

SPA (1ST LEVEL)

SPA (2ND LEVEL)

Terranea, Rancho Palos Verdes, California
The plans of the ground floor and upper floor illustrate a relatively large
luxury-resort spa complex. The semi-private men's terrace and the café
terrace overlook the spa pool, with the separate fitness room in its own
building beyond. Off reception are several popular public functions: the
salon, lounge, and spa café, along with retail sales.

Table 17.11 Fitness facilities checklist

Activity	Minimum overall floor area sq ft (sq m)	
Swimming pool		
Pool surface	800	(75)
Total including deck area	2,400	(220)
Health club		
Reception	300	(28)
Hair salon	300	(28)
Lockers and toilets	20 per person	(1.9)
Whirlpool/hot tub (single)	50 per person	(4.7)
Whirlpool/hot tub (group)	20 per person	(1.9)
Sauna	20 per person	(1.9)
Exercise room		
Exercise room	600	(56)
Nautilus circuit	400	(37)
Exercise equipment	50 per unit	(4.7)
Spa		
Reception	1,000	(93)
Office	400	(37)
Café	600	(56)
Pantry	300	(28)
Hair salon	800	(75)
Lockers/toilets	30 per person	(2.8)
Steam and sauna	200 per gender	(18.5)
Lounge	400 per gender	(37)
Lounge, coed	600	(56)
Treatment room, single	120	(11)
Treatment room, couples	200	(18.5)
Other		
Aerobics room	800	(75)
Gym	2,000	(185)
Steam bath	20 per person	(1.9)
Loofah bath	100 per person	(9.3)
Herbal wrap	100 per person	(9.3)
Massage	100 per person	(9.3)
Hairdresser/barber	70 per person	(6.5)

These are minimum areas; many spa/pool/fitness centers are considerably larger.

Recreation Facilities

Increasingly, hotels provide recreational facilities, ranging from an outdoor pool at a roadside inn, to a major spa or health club in downtown hotels, to extensive golf, tennis, marina, or ski complexes at destination resorts. While surveys show that relatively few guests actually use the swimming pool and other recreational facilities at most hotels, nonetheless, many guests expect them and it is essential that the developer provide these amenities in some form.

To counter low use, some operators expand rather than minimize their recreational features and profitably promote them to the community, in addition to the hotel guests. In a highly competitive market, this is one more area in which a hotel can gain an edge over other properties. The developers of a downtown hotel, for example, may include a full-size spa or health club to complement the property's other business-oriented facilities; for a suburban hotel, provide an enclosed pool and related amenities as a swim club for the community; or for a conference center, add extensive outdoor jogging, tennis, or golf facilities to attract the high-level executive retreat. The checklist in Table 17.11 shows the principal types of recreational facilities that a developer or operator might program into a property.

The hotels discussed in Part 1 of this book illustrate the kinds of recreational facilities that are commonly found at different types of properties. Generally, the smaller, budget, and mid-priced motels and hotels—those which attract a large number of price-conscious family travelers—include little more than an outdoor swimming pool and a game room or small fitness center. Larger hotels, and especially those with a business market or strong leisure orientation, frequently add an extensive spa or fitness center. Resorts and other lodging types catering to longer-staying guests, and hotels in outlying areas, where land costs are less, feature additional outdoor facilities.

Swimming Pool

Nearly all hotel management companies require the developer to include a swimming pool, although minimum sizes vary. The pool area should be separated from other public spaces, so that guests dressed in bathing suits need not pass through the hotel lobby. Other key planning considerations include:

- *Location:* Place the pool so that guests can reach it from guestroom elevators without passing through the lobby; provide some guestrooms with views of the pool; screen any exterior views toward the pool.
- *Orientation:* Position the pool so that it receives unobstructed sunlight from mid-morning to late afternoon.
- *Size:* Provide a pool of sufficient size to accommodate the swimming and sunbathing needs of the guests, but no smaller than about 20 x 40 ft (6 x 12 m), with at least 10 ft (3 m) of deck space on all sides.
- *Support functions:* Provide toilets and lockers where required, towel-issue area, snack bar or vending, equipment room, and furniture storage.

Terranea, Rancho Palos Verdes, California
The spa relaxation room is located in one corner of the second floor of the spa building, with fabulous views of the Pacific Ocean.

Terranea, Rancho Palos Verdes, California
The second floor of the spa building includes 21 individual treatment rooms, many with expansive views of the Pacific.

Terranea, Rancho Palos Verdes, California
In the other west corner, opposite the relaxation room, is the water therapy room, dramatically placed with a balcony and views of the ocean.

Peninsula Spa, New York, New York

The 30,000 sq ft (2,787 sq m) spa by ESPA fills the entire 21st floor of the hotel; guests are first greeted in the reception area, then move to the men's or women's locker rooms, before passing behind the reception area to the treatment rooms. The elegant swimming pool, fitness area, and rooftop cocktail lounge are one floor above, connected by a handsome curved stairway.

① 21ST FLOOR PLAN

Peninsula Spa, New York, New York

The curved shapes and figurative tree elements of the reception area set the mood for the invigorating spa experience; natural materials and warm colors reinforce the concept of purity and balance and spa amenities are available for purchase.

Peninsula Spa, New York, New York

One of twelve massage rooms, the VIP treatment room, isolated and insulated from other rooms, offers two tables for couples and a soaking tub.

- *Safety:* Do not provide a diving board; include slip-free deck surface, depth markings, underwater lighting, safety or "pool rules" signage.
- *Wading pool, whirlpool:* Include additional pools within view of the swimming pool but slightly separated.
- *Indoor pool:* Design either operable roof or glass walls to provide direct sunlight and ventilation.

Spa and Health Club

A second major component of hotel recreational facilities is the spa or, in smaller properties, the health club, a feature that for many types of hotel has become more central than the pool. The focus of the spa is on the guest's experience, and introduces unique images, sounds (flowing water or music), scents (aromatherapy), and more to soothe and relax the individual. At a destination resort, there might be as many as one treatment room for every five guestrooms, dropping to one to every 50 or 100 in urban locations. In contrast, a simple health club may feature little more than a combination of exercise equipment (such as Nautilus or Universal machines) and such specialized facilities as whirlpool baths, steam rooms, and saunas. Larger complexes may add a unisex hair salon, a multi-purpose room for aerobic exercise—even racquetball courts. The spa at the Terranea Resort in Southern California is representative of how a medium-size, upscale resort property can cater to guests and the local community. Its 20,000 sq ft (1,850 sq m) spa, not including the adjoining fitness center and pool, has 23 treatment rooms for about 380 hotel guestrooms, plus many casitas and golf villas. See the

further discussion of spa facilities in the discussion of resort hotels in Chapter 7. The following items should be considered during the planning phase:

- *Location:* Plan the spa so that guests can reach it directly from the guestroom elevators, and local members have access from the street or parking area, without passing through the hotel lobby.
- *Program:* Include the following, depending on the market:
  - Reception area with attendant
  - Retail sales area
  - Salon
  - Lockers, showers, and toilets
  - Exercise room
  - Sauna, steam room, and whirlpool
  - Treatment rooms
  - Relaxation lounges
  - Spa café and support areas
- *Adjacencies:* Plan the complex with the control area and lounge most visible, and with the private functions either shared (exercise room) or back-to-back (saunas and restrooms).

Parking

The provision of sufficient parking can be a crucial element in both the budgeting and conceptual planning, for a hotel or motel. And its design often influences the guest's first and last impressions of the property. Roadside inn developers know they must provide

Table 17.12 Parking needed for different types of hotel

Hotel type	Number of spaces/room	Comment
Business (downtown)	0.4–0.8	Assumes limited function space
Boutique hotel	0.3–0.8	Higher factor in resort areas
Suburban hotel	1.2–1.4	Heavy local meeting and banquet use
Airport hotel	0.6–1.0	Moderate rental-car use
Roadside inn	1.0–1.2	Very limited local banquet and F&B use
Resort (all types)	0.2–1.4	Varies by market, location, and proximity to urban centers or major attractions
Convention hotel	0.8–1.4	Regional convention hotels need more parking
Conference center	1.0–1.3	If full house, minimum local use
Condominium hotel	1.2–2.0	May need two spaces/condominium
All-suite hotel	0.8–1.2	Limited F&B and function areas
Super-luxury hotel	1.0–1.2	Limited function areas
Mega-hotel	1.0–1.2	Limited local business; high rental-car use
Mixed-use hotel	0.6–1.2	Highly variable depending on other activities
Casino hotel	0.8–2.0	Varies by location (for example, Atlantic City requires extensive bus parking)

Table 17.13 Parking analysis

The following steps describe an approach to calculating parking requirements based on the changing needs of the guestrooms and other hotel facilities throughout the day. The maximum parking demand in most properties is created not by the rooms but by the meeting and banquet space. The provision of parking must recognize the sum of the various components and the interrelationship of the peaks and valleys over a 24-hour period.

1. Determine the components of the parking requirement: overnight guests, restaurant and bar patrons, meeting attendees, and other visitors (see Step 3).
2. Calculate the maximum number of cars that might be reasonably anticipated, planning to accommodate full demand on 80–85 percent of all days, but not peak demand for each component. The overnight guest calculation is illustrated by the following example:

Number of rooms	400
Percent occupancy	85
People per room	1.4
Percent arriving by car	40
People per car	1.5

Each calculation will be slightly different; the equation for calculating the overnight guests' parking requirement is:

$$\frac{(Rooms) \times (\% \ occupancy) \times (people/room) \times (\% \ by \ car)}{(People/car)}$$

Example: $\dfrac{400 \times 0.85 \times 1.4 \times 0.40}{1.5} = 127 \ cars$

The calculation for the other components includes similar factors as appropriate, such as food and beverage covers, percentage of diners arriving by car, and number of employees by shift.

3. Develop a table (see below) showing hourly parking use factors (example shows four-hour periods). For example, the parking facility needs to accommodate all (100 percent or 1) overnight guest cars from midnight to 4:00 A.M. but, because of checkouts, only 60 percent (0.6) during the midday periods.
4. Combine the parking requirements for each component (Step 2) with the use table (Step 3) to calculate the total amount of parking necessary during each time period. In this example, hotel guests would require 127 parking spaces (1 x 127) at midnight but only 76 spaces (0.6 x 127) at noon. Recognize that high evening demand, for example, might be partially met by available parking nearby.

User	Morning			Afternoon		
	Midnight–4:00	4:00–8:00	8:00–noon	Noon–16:00	16:00–20:00	20:00–midnight
Hotel guests	1.0	0.95	0.6	0.6	0.9	0.95
Restaurant and bar patrons	0.05	0.1	0.1	0.1	0.2	0.25
Meeting/banquet attendees	0.05	—	0.1	0.1	0.4	0.4
Health club members	—	0.2	0.1	0.2	0.2	0.05
Visitors	—	0.1	0.2	0.1	0.2	0.4
Employees	0.25	0.25	0.4	0.4	0.35	0.35

one space per room; full-service hotels need additional spaces for employees and for any public areas—restaurants, bars, meeting space, or recreational facilities—that attract guests from the community. An otherwise successful hotel can be seriously affected—especially its ability to attract local banquet business—by insufficient or inconvenient parking.

The key objective should be to provide optimum but not excessive amounts of parking. Unless unusual conditions (sports complex, large banquet facility, retail center) exist, the parking provision for different types of lodging properties falls within the ranges shown in Table 17.12. Land cost is an increasing problem in suburban and rural locations, where parking usually is on grade, often covering more land than the building itself, making it necessary for developers to program their parking requirements more carefully. However, the more

critical concern is at downtown hotels, and at those other properties where high land costs preclude extensive amounts of surface parking or require the construction of a garage, often below the hotel. It is not uncommon for the developer and architect to appeal zoning regulations, if justified, based on an analysis by traffic experts. One technique is to project hourly parking requirements, recognizing that hotel guests, conferees, banquet guests, and employees create peak demands on parking at different periods of the day (see example, Table 17.13).

In addition to programming the parking, the design team must consider the impact it makes on the lasting impression the guest has of the hotel. Designers need to address concerns about convenience, safety, and possible claustrophobia:

- *Garage entrance:* Locate the entrance so that it is readily accessible to the guest drop-off area.
- *Hotel access:* Provide a secure and convenient interior route, usually an elevator, from the garage directly to the hotel lobby.
- *Safety and security:* Design the garage to be visually open, with wide aisles; provide security cameras to scan area.
- *Guest comfort:* Find solutions to reduce feelings of claustrophobia, by increasing lighting levels; raising ceiling height; painting surfaces light colors; providing art, murals, or music.
- *Signage:* Provide clear signage, both for drivers (to enter/exit) and pedestrians (to lobby or street).

In mixed-use projects, the hotel should negotiate its own parking spaces, perhaps behind an access gate, to assure that parking is available to hotel guests. Also, this permits the hotel to set up security for that dedicated portion of the garage. Many hotels choose to offer valet parking as a guest amenity. Equally often, though, this decision is made because of space and budget limitations: hotel staff can park many more cars in the same amount of space and don't require the wide aisles or other design features that guests expect.

Signage and Iconographics

The perception of a hotel goes well beyond its architecture and interior design. Such small yet critical details as signage, graphics, tabletop items, and uniform design complete and reinforce the desired image and marketing goals of a hotel. These elements, which should be conceived of as an integral part of the design process, require the collaborative effort of the architect, interior designer, lighting designer, and such specialists as a graphic consultant or uniform designer.

Signage and Graphics

The signage and graphics program not only provides guests with immediate information and orients them to the project, but it also may help to reinforce the branding of a particular hotel. The major components include directional and destination signage, and printed graphics. The corporate or property identity, which later may be embedded in the signage throughout the hotel or resort, often is introduced to the public in the advertising and promotional literature prior to the opening. Hyatt revised its corporate logo in the mid-1990s and frequently uses elements of the design, not only in the printed graphics but in much of the interior signage throughout the hotel. Starwood Hotels' W brand successfully incorporates the logotype into both signage and graphical images throughout its hotels. The elements most commonly included in a signage and graphics program are listed in Table 17.14.

Architects and designers often have challenges in creating a meaningful image for the property. For example, frequently, the first identification that a guest may see, the building's exterior signage, is restricted in its placement, size, color, and lighting by

Table 17.14 Signage and graphics

Exterior signage	
Brand and building identification	
Vehicular directional signs	Guest entrance and exit, receiving and service area, employee entrance; guest parking, disabled parking, staff parking; taxi and public transportation
Pedestrian directional signs	Lobby entrance, restaurant entrance, ballroom and meeting room access; outdoor amenities including beach, pool, spa, tennis, golf, and boating
Interior signage	
Event directory	
Directional signage	Lobby, retail shops, food and beverage outlets, ballroom and meeting rooms, recreational amenities, etc.; floor identification and room direction, emergency exiting
Destination signage	Front desk, guestroom numbers, function rooms, toilets, coats, elevator identification, F&B outlets
Printed graphics	
Marketing materials	All hotel advertising, marketing, sales brochures, and related items
Guestroom amenities	Room-service and guest information books; bathroom soap/shampoo and related packaging; robe and towel logos; stationery items such as note pads, letterhead, envelopes, and pencils; also guestroom card-keys
Menus and restaurant/bar supplies	All food and beverage menus, wine lists, tabletop merchandizing, etc.; related paper products such as matchbooks, coasters, napkins, etc.
Front office and accounting forms	Registration materials, guest receipts, invoices, etc.

local ordinances. At more expansive resorts, especially, arriving guests depend on directional signs to guide them to the hotel lobby, or to restaurant or banquet entrances. Signs identify staff and receiving areas or highlight disabled routes or parking spaces. These all may be subject to local regulations. Once inside the hotel, guests rely on signage to find their way from the lobby to guestrooms, F&B outlets, function space, recreational amenities, and so forth. Some architects at the schematic design phase test the hotel organization by imagining the future signage—if it is difficult to conceive how directional signage can orient guests and lead them through the property, then the entire architectural organization needs to be rethought and clarified.

Both exterior and interior signage should be integrated with the hotel's architecture and interior design, so that the design elements reinforce the theme and style of the property. This commonly is achieved through the consistent use of color, shape, or pattern, and by repeating the same typeface and materials that are found in the architecture and hotel interiors. At The Beverly Hills Hotel, the signage and graphics package draws from the lush banana plants that flourish in the grounds around the hotel. This banana-leaf motif is repeated throughout the interior decoration on wallpaper, drapery and upholstery fabrics, and even on printed items, consistently applying the theme through a multitude of visual elements.

The American Hotel and Lodging Association (AH&LA) has approved over 100 universal symbols to represent such common hotel areas or services as check-in, information, restrooms, and luggage check. These standard graphics are a good starting-point for the design of signage, since the symbols are easily recognized internationally, but most operators wish to make their signage and graphics programs unique and more reflective of the character of their property. The destination signage throughout the hotel—at individual guestrooms as well as at each function room—or the identity graphics at each restaurant or lounge are especially important.

Uniforms and Tabletop Design

Uniforms and restaurant tabletop design are two additional visual elements to which guests are directly and constantly exposed. For many years, the hotel management company designed and specified uniforms for the front-of-house staff, to reflect the corporate image. Increasingly, today, for first-class and luxury hotels and resorts, companies retain an independent uniform designer to complement and reinforce the hotel theme, service style, and local customs in the design of the uniforms. Once

again, the designers creatively manipulate color, pattern, fabric, and shape to coordinate the uniforms—or "costumes"—with the hotel's architectural and design style. The uniforms may vary as much as does the style of the property, ranging from formal attire—even top hat and tails at some luxury properties—to beachwear at more casual resorts. The operators of some urban boutique hotels have established uniform design as a statement of high fashion: the sight of doormen clad in black Armani suits instantly identifies the genre.

Tabletop design is another integral part of the guest's experience that should be conceived as part of the overall theme of the property. The tabletop items appear in many areas outside the normal F&B outlets: the several restaurants, lobby lounge, sports bar—even in-room dining. Consider that food and beverage sales occur in the lobby itself, in function rooms and pre-function areas, around the pool, and in the guestrooms and suites. The style and complexity of the tabletop often is reflective of the design and formality of the hotel. Some of the tabletop items are standardized within each hotel company. However, designers or corporate management, or occasionally the executive chef or the food and beverage manager, may custom-design individual pieces for the particular hotel and its setting. Table 17.15 identifies the most common items included in the hotel tabletop program.

Art and Artifacts

Art plays a growing role in the styling of a hotel. The development of an art program is a service frequently provided by the interior designer or an independent art consultant, and should be conceived as an integral thread throughout the design. Art, artifacts, and antiques can create the "feeling of home" for the business traveler or the "element of fantasy" for the leisure traveler.

Artwork appears in nearly every hotel. Budget properties certainly have framed prints in the guestrooms and in the hotel lobby, if nowhere else. Midscale hotels introduce art and artifacts into the food and beverage outlets and the meeting pre-function areas, and may place a framed mirror in each guestroom-floor elevator lobby. These mid-market hotels may be able to incorporate original art fairly economically by commissioning a local artist to create pieces, which they then reproduce in quantity for the guestrooms or other areas. Larger hotels may incorporate sculptures throughout the public space.

Among the most lavish art programs—which sometimes approach museum quality—are those found in traditionally styled luxury properties. The Ritz-Carlton chain, as an example, has collected eighteenth- and nineteenth-century European and American art and antiques—paintings by renowned artists, sculptures, tapestries, decorative accessories, oriental carpets, and a variety of unique furniture pieces—which are displayed throughout the hotel public areas. The Ritz-Carlton Hotel in San Francisco keeps a fine-arts advisor and curator on staff to document, maintain, and conserve its art and antiques collection. In addition, staff are trained to answer the most common questions that guests have regarding the collections.

Table 17.15 Uniforms and tabletop design

Uniforms

Front of house	Doorman, bellman, concierge, front desk staff
Food and beverage	Hostess, wait staff, bartender, bus staff, room service
Back-of-house	Food and beverage, security, housekeeping, maintenance, parking

Tabletop

Linen	Tablecloths, table runner or placemats, napkins
Place setting	China, glassware, tableware
Tabletop accessories	Flower or bud vases, salt and pepper cellars, tea service, cream and sugar, wine buckets, ashtrays, etc.

Renaissance Arlington Capitol View, Arlington, Virginia
The hotel introduces a tree-like sculpture to separate the lobby from
flow space.

The traditional art and antiques program has expanded to include new and creative uses for art, and the term "antiques" has been redefined to include twentieth-century decorative objects, furniture, and art from many cultures. Once just the accents which completed the feel or look of a property, art and antiques are now often used to create the overarching theme of a hotel and have become integral to the marketing of a property. The boutique Claris Hotel in Barcelona displays on the lobby mezzanine the hotel owner's private collection of Greek and Roman antiquities; the guestroom art program features additional ancient artifacts, placed in carefully lighted niches, which are a dramatic contrast with the hotel's strikingly original and very contemporary interiors. Drawing from the neighborhood context of New York City's many fine art galleries along 57th Street and Fifth Avenue, Chambers West 56 Hotel features "art walls" in its public space. The entire hotel theme is expressed by the paintings, prints,

and etchings, set in a custom system of horizontal tracks of blackened steel that exhibit constantly changing artwork.

The designer may need to consider how the art will be installed in order to prepare the space. Even small and midsize pieces may require structural support, lighting, security, water connections, or other preparation:

- Sculpture may require additional structural support (floor or ceiling) and coordination for accent lighting.
- Water features require additional structural support, plumbing connections, and power for underwater lighting.
- Paintings and mirrors may require blocking inside walls for support, power connections to security systems, and coordination for accent lighting.

New uses for art are everywhere. In addition to incorporating a museum within the property as an amenity or celebrating art through changing exhibitions, designers have used overscaled art as headboards, and museum postcards as guestroom art. Today, we find art even in elevators, restrooms, exercise rooms, and parking garages. A growing number of cities require the developer to invest 1 percent or more of the construction cost in public art. This has resulted in the commissioning of art from major exterior sculptures for the hotel's arrival courtyard to large-scale murals, water features, or other art for the hotel lobby.

Administration and Back-of-house Design

The planning and design of the administration offices and other back-of-house or service areas of the hotel, most of which the hotel guest rarely sees, are equally critical to the eventual success of the hotel. Generally comprising between about 10 and 15 percent of the total floor area in all lodging types—somewhat less in motels and budget inns and occasionally more in luxury hotels and resorts—the organization of the offices and service areas greatly influences the staff's ability to meet overall administrative needs and to provide efficient food and beverage, housekeeping, repair, and engineering services to the hotel. The main functional areas include the following:

- Administration offices
- Food preparation and F & B storage areas
- Receiving, trash, and general storage areas
- Employee areas
- Laundry and housekeeping areas
- Engineering and mechanical areas

The provision and sizing of these spaces varies considerably from property to property, depending on the type of hotel or resort and on its size and location. Larger hotels and resorts have extensive administrative staffs and require substantial office suites to accommodate the complex office functions, whereas small properties may be run out of little more than a single office. Resorts in remote areas may need to provide their own engineering services, including the supply of electricity and fresh water, as well as employee housing and extensive grounds-keeping facilities. In contrast, motels that don't include a restaurant or meeting space may need no more than sufficient storage for guestroom linen, operating supplies, and maintenance equipment.

It is essential not only to provide adequate back-of-house areas but also to plan them appropriately, so that, for example, staff can reach all areas of the hotel without passing through the lobby and other public spaces. Basic planning objectives include clustering the major service functions around the receiving area and employee entrance or along a major service corridor, and grouping the food outlets close to the kitchen or at satellite pantries, where required. The following sections discuss the operational characteristics and planning and design criteria for each area.

Peninsula Shanghai, Shanghai, China
The front desk of this 235-room luxury hotel is configured to allow both a high level of service and adequate privacy for guest transactions.

Administration Offices

The effective layout of the front desk and administration offices influences the guest's impression of the hotel. While many guests will have contact only with the front desk, others may need to meet with the sales and catering staff or with assistant managers. Therefore, the proper planning, design, and equipping of the hotel's office space deserves no less attention than that given to the guestrooms and public areas. The planning and interior design of the workplace and its equipment are essential, not only to the morale and productivity of the staff, but also to the public's perception of the quality of the hotel.

Administrative office areas generally are divided into five clusters:

- Front desk and front office
- Executive office
- Sales and catering office
- Accounting office
- Information technology offices

Other office components, such as the human resources and purchasing functions, typically are placed in the back-of-house close to related service areas. While locating offices together has substantial advantages—shared reception and support areas, closer communication among the staff, and better visibility to the guest—most hotels of over a few hundred rooms separate the administrative offices into two or three clusters. This is done, in part, in order to locate the sales and catering offices near the ballroom and other function space. More than anything else, though, such arrangements should not be the result of unclear programming and hastily conceived schematic designs. Often, space near the front desk that initially was designated for offices must be reallocated for other support functions that had not been sufficiently recognized in the program and early design phases. Where office suites are located on separate levels, the architect should consider adding a dedicated stairway connecting the floors.

Front Desk and Front Office

The front office, which supports the guest registration and cashier functions at the front desk, is often the largest of the five clusters and the one with which the casual guest is most familiar. The key elements in terms of layout are the front desk itself (or reception pods) and the work area behind it, around which most of the other offices are clustered. It includes the following areas:

- *Front desk:* Provide dual-function registration and cashier stations. Alternatively, provide free-standing pods for reception and cashiering.
- *Concierge desk:* May be located either near the front desk or somewhat apart. In smaller properties, front desk staff may also serve as concierge.

Table 18.1 Front office area planning

Program
- ❏ Provide 3–5 sq ft (0.3–0.5 sq m) per guestroom for the front desk and related front office functions.
- ❏ Allow 6 linear ft (1.8 m) per workstation; provide two stations for the first 150 rooms plus an additional one for each 100 rooms.

Planning
- ❏ Locate the desk so that it is easily visible from the entrance.
- ❏ Locate the desk in sight of the guest elevators.
- ❏ Locate self-service kiosks in sight of the desk.
- ❏ Allow sufficient queuing space to accommodate high-volume periods.
- ❏ Position the luggage storage and bellman nearby, or with good visual connection with the desk.
- ❏ Provide a fire control room near the front desk or hotel main entrance.
- ❏ Position the front desk where it is not constrained by structural columns.
- ❏ Plan the front office so that both reservations and telephone operators are near the guest registration area.
- ❏ Place the safe-deposit room so that a cashier can handle guest requests.
- ❏ Consider placement of luggage carts before and during service.

Design
- ❏ Design the front desk so that the cashier and registration functions can be staffed flexibly.
- ❏ Screen guests' views into office work areas.
- ❏ Recognize requirements for support functions: brochure display, house telephones, concierge or assistant manager, and bell station close to front desk.
- ❏ Provide decorative focus at the desk: counter material, lighting, treatment of back wall, and signage.
- ❏ Consider design elements to assist with queue management: floor finishes, temporary or permanent queuing guides.

- *Front office work area (includes printing, copying, mail, etc.):* Provide work area immediately adjacent to the front desk, with built-in work counter and files.
- *Front office manager:* Provide private office convenient to the work area.
- *Reservations and telephone:* Provide space with counter work area and acoustic partitions for telephone operators and reservations staff, convenient to the front desk; include security and alarm monitoring systems.
- *Reservations/revenue manager:* Provide semi-private office adjoining the reservations work area.
- *Safe-deposit area:* Provide secure space with safe-deposit boxes and, adjoining, a small guest viewing room with counter and chair.
- *Counting room:* Provide secure space where F&B outlet and retail managers count receipts and place the deposit in a drop-safe or pass it directly to cashier.
- *Fire control room:* Provide space next to the front entrance with dedicated alarm panels for use by the fire and life-safety personnel in responding to fire and other emergency situations.
- *Support functions:* Provide for such accessory needs as toilets, storage, coats, and pantry.

In smaller hotels, where employees may be cross-trained to perform a variety of duties, such functions as telephone and reservations need to be convenient to the front desk, because on the night shift only one person may be on duty. Increasing payroll costs in all types of hotels and resorts have made it more important for management to rethink how they staff departments. Smaller hotels, for example, may locate a modest sundries shop or F&B outlet immediately adjacent to the reception area, so that the desk clerk can double as the shop cashier. Also, instead of locating a business center at some distance from the lobby and needing to staff it throughout the day, companies increasingly place it next to the front desk, enabling further sharing of staff duties. Even in hotels where self-service kiosks or other technologies streamline the registration and check-out process, some form of front desk is still recommended to provide information and assistance.

In planning the front desk, as with many other areas in the hotel, collaboration among the members of the design team is necessary. First, the brand or operator specifies the hotel's front desk requirements (full desk, podiums, self-service kiosks, or seated check-in); second, the architect establishes the general location of the desk and the offices; third, the interior designer may modify the details of the plan for design or functional reasons and propose a series of finishes and lighting; fourth, the technical staff from the operator specifies and locates the information technology in the workspace. See Table 18.1 for an outline of the front office planning and design issues.

Executive Office

The executive office is the smallest of the five administration clusters. In smaller hotels, the operator may choose to combine it with the front office, the general manager assuming the duties of rooms-division manager. In larger hotels, the executive office includes the following:

- *Reception area:* Provide reception/waiting area for visitors; include receptionist desk, visitor seating, and appropriate display.
- *General manager:* Provide large private office for the general manager, appropriate to the size of the hotel.
- *Executive assistant managers:* Provide private offices for the senior staff, including the rooms-division manager, food and beverage director, marketing director, revenue manager, etc.
- *Administrative support:* Include space for one or more administrative assistants with necessary support functions (copying, printing, etc.).
- *Conference room:* Include private conference room for 8–12 people for use by the senior staff or for meetings with visitors; include small pantry for coffee/refreshment service.
- *Support functions:* Provide space for storage, toilets, coats, pantry, etc.

The general manager in large hotels may be highly visible, greeting dignitaries and hosting special visitors. Thus, this office and its adjoining conference area may begin to resemble public reception and lounge areas. Where this is the case, the offices need to be larger and should be located where guests can readily find them and where security can be assured. Some senior managers prefer that their office is located near the receptionist, whereas others insist on it being more remote, even on another level, away from the distractions of the office routine. The rooms-division and food and beverage managers, who share in policy decisions, usually are clustered with the general manager rather than with their respective departments.

Sales and Catering Office

The third administrative group, the sales and catering office, is responsible for attracting meetings and group business and for servicing events once they are in the hotel. The sales and catering staff deal with many outside visitors, and the offices should be designed to be easy to locate and to present the best public image of the hotel. The cluster includes the following:

- *Reception:* Provide separate reception/greeting function or combine with executive office reception.
- *Director of sales:* Provide large private office.
- *Sales representatives:* Provide semi-private cubicles for additional sales staff adjacent to printers and work counter.
- *Catering manager:* Provide private office for staff member responsible for arranging details of banquet functions.
- *Banquet manager:* Provide small office for supervisor of banquet staff; this may be located in the back-of-house.
- *Convention-services manager:* Provide private office for person who serves as liaison for all non-banquet functions; this may be combined with conference concierge service in larger convention properties or conference centers.
- *Conference room:* Provide dedicated conference room (may be combined with executive office) for sales and catering meetings.
- *Administrative support:* Provide space for several administrative assistants for the senior staff and for all sales, catering, and banquet representatives.
- *Support functions:* Provide necessary space to accommodate usual support functions: storage, toilets, coats, and pantry.

Since the sales staff show prospective guests the available meeting and banquet facilities, the office suite frequently is located near the function area rather than off the lobby. As with the other clusters, the most common arrangement is to group the private offices around a centralized work area. The sales and catering office becomes fairly large in convention and other properties that cater predominantly with groups rather than individual guests. The space requirements, which vary depending on the type of hotel, usually fall between 2 and 4 sq ft (0.2–0.4 sq m) per guestroom.

Accounting Office

The accounting office, while best located as part of the main complex near the front desk, can operate satisfactorily at some distance. Its main connection to the front office is the need to coordinate any cash-handling functions. The accounting cluster includes the following requirements:

- *Controller:* Provide private office for the hotel's senior financial officer.
- *Assistant controller/auditor:* Provide a semi-private office for the assistant controller who is the day-to-day manager of the accounting activities.
- *Cashier:* Provide secure room with pass-through window similar to bank teller; provide large floor safe and alarm system.
- *Accounting staff offices:* Provide work areas for payroll, accounts receivable, and accounts payable managers.
- *Accounting work area:* Provide cubicle workspace for additional accounting staff, depending on the size of the hotel. Include work counter with files and space for copying, printing, etc.
- *Other (storage, toilets, coats, pantry):* Provide for accessory functions, especially if the accounting area is remote from other office suites.

The layout of the accounting area is not complicated by special operating requirements or technical equipment other than the standard office computer systems. The architect should allocate approximately 3 sq ft (0.3 sq m) per room for the accounting offices.

Information Technology Office

Management of the hotel's information technology (IT) infrastructure requires offices and work space that, while generally located in back-of-house areas, primarily support administrative functions. Placement of the IT cluster should be a reflection of the hotel type and size. IT staff who are on call may need to quickly access other back-office areas, whereas in a large convention hotel they may need to be close to high-demand locations like the business center. The IT cluster includes the following requirements:

- *IT director:* Provide a private office for the hotel's senior IT officer.
- *Tech support work area:* Provide cubicle workspace for tech support and programming staff, with the number depending on the size of the hotel. Include a deep work counter and bench storage space for component servicing.
- *Help desk:* Provide one or more cubicles equipped with workstations for managing service requests.
- *Server room:* Provide a climate-controlled, raised-floor space with good lighting. May not be required if the hotel uses off-site or "cloud" services.
- *Other:* storage, toilets, coats, and pantry. Storage needs tend to be high for this cluster.

Food Preparation and Storage Areas

Of all the service areas in a hotel, the kitchens and related food-preparation and F&B storage areas require the most design attention, in part because of the integration of the mechanical, electrical, and plumbing systems with the layout of the kitchen equipment. More importantly, the design of the kitchen and related areas critically influences labor and utility costs for the life of the building. The design team must plan the kitchens so that all food-related activities are located close together, distances between the kitchen and the several outlets are as short as possible, and the individual layouts are flexible in order to accommodate changes in the future. Therefore, the planning and design aspects of the kitchens require the coordinated attention of a variety of specialized kitchen and engineering consultants.

Program and Planning Objectives

The amount of floor space required in the kitchen and food and beverage storage areas depends on the number of meals served, the complexity of the menu, the degree of in-house production, and vendor delivery schedules. Because of the high cost of equipment, energy, and labor, the goal should be to design the smallest kitchen that meets operational objectives while still offering flexibility. For example, in many downtown hotels, where space is at a premium because of high land costs and where most foods are readily and frequently available, food storage areas are kept to a minimum. In smaller properties, having all food-handling facilities close at hand promotes operational efficiencies that cannot be obtained in large hotels, where the presence of multiple food and beverage outlets necessitates widely dispersed finishing kitchens. In this case, it is common to have centralized receiving, storage, and bulk production, and to push final preparation and warewashing to satellite kitchens close to the point of service.

It is imperative that the general concepts for the hotel's food and beverage offerings are determined before any sizing or placement of the kitchen takes place. Today's wide range of production methods and equipment types means that there is no such thing as a "standard kitchen" that can be installed somewhere in the back-of-house to support restaurants and bars that will be defined later. Close communication between the architect and the hotel management company about the food and beverage concepts and operating parameters early in the project is the best way to ensure an effective and cost-efficient outcome.

Rules-of-thumb for space allocation vary depending upon the quality level of the hotel. However, a typical starting point is to base the kitchen size on the number of restaurant and banquet seats and hotel guestrooms, and to refine it as the food and beverage concepts are better defined. The accuracy of these rules-of-thumb is affected by the size of the hotel; smaller hotels (fewer than 200 rooms) and satellite restaurant pantries require a larger allocation per seat in order to equip even a minimum kitchen. Food-preparation areas for representative types of hotels are included in the sample space programs in Chapter 17. Table 18.2 provides the initial space

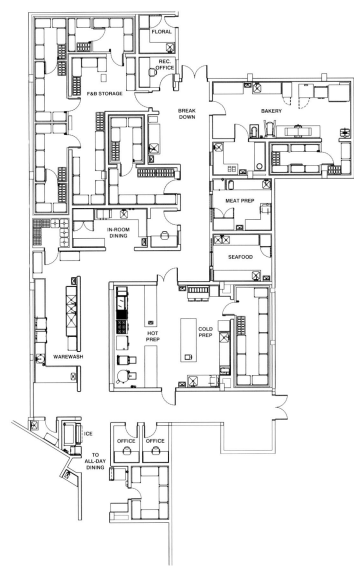

Raffles Praslin Seychelles, Republic of Seychelles
Grouping refrigerated storage together as much as possible saves on equipment cost and simplifies materiel handling. To protect food from cross-contamination or unsafe temperatures, dedicated areas need to be created for meat and seafood preparation, baking, and warewashing. Adequate office space, often overlooked in kitchen planning, allows the hotel's management to more effectively control costs and coordinate food production.

requirements for hotel kitchens and lists overall planning and design objectives.

Among the many planning goals that the architect should address during conceptual design, the most important is to locate the receiving area, food storage, kitchen, and all outlets (restaurants and banquet areas) on a single floor. When this goal is not possible, as is often the case in downtown hotels and other properties over 400 rooms, the designer must assess the relative merits of alternate groupings of service and public functions. Table 18.3 identifies the critical adjacencies in the food-service areas.

Table 18.2 Kitchen planning for full-service hotels

Program (kitchen)
- 4–6 sq ft (0.4–0.6 sq m) per restaurant seat, plus
- 1.5–2 sq ft (0.14–0.2 sq m) per ballroom and banquet seat, plus
- 1–1.5 sq ft (0.1–0.14 sq m) per lounge seat, plus
- 1–1.5 sq ft (0.1–0.14 sq m) per hotel guestroom

Program (F&B and smallwares storage)
- 15–30 percent of main kitchen area

Planning
- Provide forward flow of food from storage to serving; eliminate cross-traffic and backtracking
- Minimize distance between kitchen serving area and restaurant seating
- Arrange compact work centers
- Locate secondary storage near each workstation, as required
- Place shared facilities centrally
- Plan for the efficient use of utilities
- Group all walk-in refrigerators and freezers together to share common walls and compressors
- Group all equipment that requires ventilation
- Locate the soiled-dish drop-off immediately inside the doors from each restaurant, feeding a single warewashing area
- Provide service vestibules between the kitchen and all outlets, banquet pantry, and ballroom; baffles between service corridors and banquet rooms

Design
- Select multi-functional equipment with locking casters
- Use indirect wastes wherever possible
- Provide for security in all storage areas and at the kitchen service bar
- Depress floor slabs for refrigerated storage so that the refrigerator and freezer floors are level with the kitchen floor
- Place floor drains in front of tilting equipment and in wet areas
- Consider sanitation and employee safety in the selection of all equipment and materials
- Plan aisles on the cooking lines to be about 3 ft 6 inches (1.05 m) wide or 4 ft (1.20 m) where employees must pass

Table 18.3 Food-service adjacencies

Critical
- Food storage to main kitchen
- Main kitchen to restaurants
- Room-service area to service elevators
- Banquet pantry to ballroom

Desirable
- Receiving to food storage
- Main kitchen to banquet pantry
- Banquet pantry to smaller banquet rooms
- Banquet pantry to pre-function area
- Kitchen to room-service area
- Kitchen to bars and lounges
- Kitchen to garbage/trash holding
- Kitchen to employee dining

Main Kitchen

Once the kitchen area program is set and the architect has established its location and general plan in the schematic design phase, the food-service consultant tests the appropriateness of the space and proposes a preliminary equipment layout. If major planning criteria are met, such as providing a single main kitchen close to the restaurant outlets and function rooms, the overall design is greatly simplified and the duplication of equipment eliminated. While the food-service consultant is responsible for preparing the detailed kitchen plan, the architect must understand in general the flow of food and personnel through the kitchen and related support areas. Table 18.4 identifies the individual kitchen areas that must be integrated into a workable layout, and includes the area breakdown of F&B storage areas. Large properties will include most or all of these functions but many hotels will not do any butchering or baking in-house.

The kitchen planner usually approaches the design in two stages: first, to locate each department (such as the bakery or the warewashing area) within the larger kitchen space, and second, to develop each

Table 18.4 Kitchen checklist

Food and beverage storage
- ❑ Dry food storage   30%
- ❑ Refrigerated food storage   25%
- ❑ Frozen food storage   10%
- ❑ Beverage storage   15%
- ❑ Refrigerated beverage storage   5%
- ❑ Nonfood storage (china, silver, paper)   15%

Preparation areas
- ❑ Butchering
- ❑ Bakeshop
- ❑ Vegetable preparation area
- ❑ Meat preparation area
- ❑ Salad and dessert preparation area

Cooking areas
- ❑ Restaurant cooking line
- ❑ Banquet cooking line
- ❑ Room-service cooking line
- ❑ Employee cafeteria

Sanitation
- ❑ Warewashing
- ❑ Pot washing
- ❑ Garbage and trash removal
- ❑ Compost and recycling

Serving areas
- ❑ Restaurant(s) pickup
- ❑ Banquet pickup
- ❑ Room-service area
- ❑ Employee servery

Other
- ❑ Chef's office
- ❑ Service bar
- ❑ Staff toilets

workstation by selecting and arranging the specific pieces of equipment. The food-service consultant also must incorporate a wide range of details—some mechanical, electrical, or plumbing; some related to precise dimensions; others to particular finishes or features of the kitchen space—coordinating them with the architect and engineers so that the space can accommodate the equipment as designed and specified.

F&B Storage Areas

The food and beverage storage areas in most cases are located adjacent either to the receiving area or to the kitchen, the latter being preferable. The storage and control requirements for hotels require that supervision and security be available at all times. A key feature in planning kitchen storage areas is to cluster all the refrigerated storage together. Walk-in refrigerators and freezers require a depressed floor slab (to accommodate floor insulation) and share common insulated walls. Such grouping also allows efficiencies in the refrigeration system, with compressors best located in a mechanical room slightly away from the storage. The closely grouped storage areas are clearly designated in the accompanying kitchen plan.

Receiving, Trash, and General Storage Areas

The hotel's receiving and trash areas, while sharing the loading dock, require clear separation of incoming and outgoing goods. Only in smaller hotels are the two functions typically combined into a single area. The receiving area connects directly to the main back-of-house corridor and, eventually, to each major service area. In some properties, the receiving area is immediately adjacent to the kitchen. This is a great boon to the F&B department but may necessitate an unusually long route to move goods to the laundry, housekeeping, maintenance, or general storage areas. The security of any incoming items is controlled at the receiving dock.

Equally important to the layout of the receiving and trash area is its integration with the site plan, so that it accommodates the necessary movement of trucks without disrupting guest parking yet is hidden from the hotel guestrooms and such public areas as restaurants, lounges, and recreational areas. An otherwise well-designed hotel can be severely downgraded by the poor location of its receiving and trash areas. The overall planning requirements are listed in Table 18.5.

The receiving and trash areas require between 2 and 3 sq ft (0.2–0.3 sq m) per guestroom, but the size of the area is determined only in part by the number of guestrooms. More important is the relative amount of restaurant, lounge, and function space—reflecting the volume of food and beverage operations—and the quality level of the hotel.

Hotels require considerable amounts of storage area. Most of this space is associated with specific activities: food storage near the kitchen, function storage near the ballroom and banquet rooms, linen storage on each floor and adjacent to housekeeping, and records

Table 18.5 Receiving and trash area planning

Receiving

❑ Provide an elevated loading dock large enough to accommodate two trucks at one time (three trucks if 400 or more rooms); screen area from public view; provide roof overhead; confirm size of trucks and height clearance.

❑ Provide enclosed receiving area for inspection and temporary holding of incoming goods.

❑ Include windows between the loading dock, receiving area, and receiving office.

❑ Arrange access to the area to avoid cross-traffic between incoming goods and outgoing items.

Trash, garbage, and holding area

❑ Separate the trash/garbage holding area from receiving, and provide space for one vehicle.

❑ Provide refrigerated area for garbage and a space for can washing, if needed.

❑ Enclose compactor area, yet allow staff accessibility at all times.

❑ Provide adequate space for storage and recycling of paper, cardboard, glass, and other items.

❑ Provide additional space for temporary holding of soiled and clean linen if the hotel uses an outside laundry service.

storage close to administration offices. However, in addition, two categories of storage often are located near the receiving area: outdoor equipment and general storage. The first, generally requiring a few hundred square feet but more in resorts, is for building and grounds maintenance equipment and outdoor furniture. The second, often occupying an area as large as the entire receiving and trash area, is for extra furnishings and equipment, archived financial records, printed material, and various unassigned items.

While ideally near receiving, these storage areas have different requirements. Space for outdoor equipment for landscaping or snow removal, often omitted from the program, should be located at grade level. The general storage area needs to be secure, perhaps comprising several distinct areas separated by wire fences, so that different operating departments control particular sections of the space. Although the general storage area is necessary for a variety of miscellaneous items, it does not replace the need for adequate storage at each of the back-of-house or administrative functions discussed previously.

Employee Areas

The staff areas form a third major part of the hotel's back-of-house areas. While in smaller and economy properties these areas may be limited, adequate space for the hotel staff is essential to a full-service hotel. In a few cases, primarily resorts and overseas hotels, the developer may even include large-scale staff housing. The usual components—human resource offices, men's and women's lockers, and employee dining—are somewhat independent from each other and relate to other back-of-house areas as much as they do to each other. For example, the personnel function is related closely to the employee entrance, the lockers to the uniform

issue area and to the timeclock, and the employee cafeteria to the main kitchen.

The area requirements total between 6 and 10 sq ft (0.55–0.9 sq m) per room. Security, circulation, and equipment requirements for the employee areas are less rigid than for other back-of-house functions, allowing greater flexibility in their location within the service block. The architect, nevertheless, must incorporate important operational features into the planning and design of the employee areas (see Table 18.6).

Many major hotel chains require that their general manager live in the hotel. Often, this unit is the equivalent of a five-bay suite, including a two-bay living room, one-bay dining room and kitchen, and two bedrooms. In destination and some highly seasonal resorts, as well as hotels in many developing regions where no community is close enough to provide housing for the full staff, hotel developers often build their own employee housing. For example, in much of the Middle East, where virtually all hotel employees are from other countries, the developer must construct a major housing complex—effectively a second hotel. While entailing substantial capital cost, such housing complexes can be justified in terms of lower payroll

Table 18.6 Employee area planning

Human resources office

❑ Provide office suite for HR director, assistant director, and administrative support, with sufficient space for job applicants.

❑ Include additional private office for interviewing and counseling employees.

❑ Provide a training room for staff meetings and education.

❑ Provide small first-aid room.

Employee entrance, timekeeper, and security

❑ Provide employee entrance separate from receiving area.

❑ Locate timekeeper and security office immediately inside the employee entrance, with visual control of the main service corridor.

Employee lockers and toilets

❑ Provide separate facilities, sized according to the staff program and shift schedules; estimate staffing at 60 percent male, 40 percent female unless local experience differs.

❑ Consider separate lockers for banquet staff.

❑ Plan separate access to toilets without passing through locker areas.

Employee dining/break room

❑ Plan cafeteria near kitchen or, if on different floor, near employee locker rooms.

❑ Design cafeteria to contain service line, seating, and soiled-dish holding area; include vending machines.

❑ Provide sufficient capacity for peak periods; consider numbers at shift change.

Employee housing/other

❑ Provide manager's apartment as part of guestroom program.

❑ Where necessary, include two-bedroom apartments for senior management and one-bedroom apartments for junior staff; plan dormitory units for other employees.

❑ Provide appropriate commons areas such as recreation room, self-service laundry, pool, and lounges.

❑ Provide religious facilities in international locations where local custom dictates.

costs and such operating advantages as reduced absenteeism, lower turnover, and greater employee productivity and promptness. It may be necessary, in Muslim and some other countries, to provide prayer rooms or other accommodation for religious practice.

Laundry and Housekeeping

The laundry and housekeeping areas create the fourth key element of the service facilities of a major hotel. Even the smallest roadside property provides some space for storage and control of guestroom linen. In larger hotels, the amount of space required for linen storage is substantial and, in addition, most developers invest in a full in-house commercial laundry. This is different from smaller properties, say up to 150 rooms, where a recurring question is whether or not to include an in-house laundry. In small inns, the cost of building and equipping the laundry, plus its ongoing operating expenses, causes many operators to either rent linen or send the hotel's laundry to a commercial service. On the other hand, virtually all upscale hotels operate their own laundry in order to control quality and assure the availability of linens—as well as to reduce overall laundry expense.

The laundry and housekeeping areas are closely related and should be adjacent, even though they are managed separately. But when the laundry space is omitted, extensive space is still required for collecting and loading soiled laundry and receiving and storing clean linen. The main function, of course, is to clean and distribute guestroom (bed and bath) linen, restaurant and banquet table linens, uniforms, kitchen linens, and guest clothing. Resort hotels may have additional laundry demands, such as for towels at the swimming pools. The laundry and housekeeping areas have key adjacency requirements, related to servicing the guestrooms and providing staff uniforms and other linen throughout the hotel.

Table 18.7 Laundry and housekeeping area planning

Laundry
- ❑ Provide a linen chute, including provisions for smoke control, venting, and locked access.
- ❑ Plan continuous flow of linen and uniforms through the laundry cycle.
- ❑ Consider energy conservation approaches such as heat recovery for all equipment.
- ❑ Provide dry-cleaning services in upscale and luxury hotels.
- ❑ Provide locked storage for laundry chemicals.

Housekeeping
- ❑ Locate offices with visual control of the laundry and housekeeping areas.
- ❑ Locate uniform issue area off main service corridor, convenient to locker rooms.
- ❑ Establish separate locked linen storage for particular departments, such as food and beverage or spa/health club.
- ❑ Provide locked room for guestroom amenities; provide lost-and-found storage room.
- ❑ Create separate area for night shift to access cleaning equipment and supplies.

The area requirements are fairly standard—from 10 to 14 sq ft (0.9–1.3 sq m) per room—because the great majority of laundry demand is generated by the guestrooms. Two very different types of hotels, smaller roadside inns and larger transient business hotels (over 600 rooms), are at the low end of the range. On the other hand, resort hotels, properties with extensive food and beverage or function facilities, and first-class and luxury properties reach toward the high extreme. The necessary space is about equally divided between the laundry and housekeeping areas, including their respective support spaces.

The laundry layout often is designed by the technical-services staff of the hotel management company or by a laundry design consultant, sometimes associated with a major commercial equipment manufacturer. The hotel laundry preferably should be located on the hotel's lowest floor to lessen the chance that noise and vibration from the laundry might interfere with any public or guestroom areas. Table 18.7 identifies the principal planning requirements for the two areas.

Engineering and Mechanical Areas

The final back-of-house area contains three related functions supervised by the hotel's chief engineer: engineering offices, repair and maintenance shops, and mechanical and electrical equipment rooms. Too often these activities are given insufficient space. While the architects and engineering consultants provide more than enough space in the mechanical and electrical areas, they may allocate only leftover space to the offices and shops.

The mechanical equipment areas do not need to be immediately adjacent to the other service areas, although they should be close to the laundry, kitchen, and other high-energy use areas for most economical operation. In fact, the equipment rooms can be organized along a separate service corridor for better control and supervision. However, the maintenance and engineering function operates 24 hours a day, and therefore must directly connect to back-of-house areas and to the service elevators. It should be convenient to the loading area in order to receive equipment and materials needed for engineering activities.

The offices and shops require between 3 and 5 sq ft (0.3–0.5 sq m) per guestroom; the extensive area required for the mechanical and electrical rooms varies considerably, depending on such factors as climate, size of hotel, type of construction, orientation, and operational objectives, but may approach 4 percent of the total gross hotel area. Most often the architect and engineers together determine the necessary space requirements for the building systems. The engineering and mechanical spaces should accommodate the basic planning requirements identified in Table 18.8.

Loews Atlanta, Atlanta, Georgia

An efficiently planned hotel back-of-house is organized around a single circulation "spine" that connects major support functions to the loading dock and to vertical circulation for staff and goods. This plan for a 414-room convention hotel groups related functions together to reduce circulation time, improve communication, and increase employee productivity. Personnel offices are located close to the employee entrance; engineering and IT areas are co-located; uniform pick-up, employee locker rooms, and the staff cafeteria are adjacent to one another; and housekeeping and laundry have clear access to the service elevators and linen chute.

Table 18.8 Engineering and mechanical area planning

Engineering offices

- ❑ Locate the secretarial area to control all access to the shops and mechanical areas.
- ❑ Group engineer, assistants' offices, and record and drawing storage around central work area.
- ❑ Provide energy management computer room as required.

Maintenance shops

- ❑ Position the carpentry, upholstery, and paint shops adjacent to each other.
- ❑ Provide exhaust system from paint shop (fumes) and carpentry shop (airborne sawdust).
- ❑ Provide additional electrical service to all shops.
- ❑ Locate grounds maintenance space convenient to the outdoors.

Mechanical, electrical, and plumbing equipment areas

- ❑ Locate mechanical areas in high-ceiling space (16 ft or 5 m) where noise and vibration will not disturb guests or public activities.
- ❑ Provide secure rooms for telephone switch, and for television antenna system and associated video/movie functions.
- ❑ Locate rooms where large equipment can be replaced reasonably easily.

Technical Coordination and Construction

The mid-point of the twentieth century marked the beginning of the most dramatic increase in worldwide education and mass travel in history, as two young architects, at the famed Chicago firm of Holabird and Root, planned the first new group of hotels to be built after two decades of depression and war. William B. Tabler and Richard E. Smith developed studies demonstrating that advanced technology would make hotels more viable. Thus began a new era for one of the most complex building types, led by pioneering hotel operators such as Statler-Hilton, the largest chain of its day, and InterContinental, the first major chain created by an airline (PanAm). A system of teamwork was developed at this time, between hotel companies, architects, interior designers, and other consultants (see Table 19.1), which continues to flourish.

The process begins at the project level, with the initial guidance by the developer and operator to ensure that the hotel will comply with the latest standards. To this end, hotel companies offer their technical data and assistance in such areas as specialized hotel information and review of design, as well as new prototype concepts, if desired. As market strategies are developed, feedback from the operator is essential in areas ranging from trend research to detailed space requirements, special hotel systems, food- and beverage-service requirements, and typical layouts for the back-of-house and other applicable service areas. Because hotel operators have an important stake in the project's success, they participate in the design process.

One developer compared the coordination required on major hotel projects to other building types as follows: "It's like developing apartments, offices, and a mall, rolled into one, with all the tenant trimmings." The procedures outlined below are intended to maximize efficiency on these complex development projects, based on their applicability to the requirements of the specific hotel. To this end, the key consultants and a synopsis of their typical agreements, containing special hotel provisions, are discussed in this chapter. For example, one of the main procedures on hotel projects is to organize the consulting agreements so that:

- all necessary services are covered;
- duplication and overlapping of responsibilities is avoided;
- primary cost responsibility for each budgeted item is assigned by mutual agreement.

Methods of organization vary with the size and complexity of the project, required scheduling, and construction contracting system to be selected, as well as existing procedures of the various team

Shangri-La Hotel at the Shard, London, United Kingdom
The concrete elevator core of the 72-story mixed-use tower leads the construction progression with floor slabs, curtain wall, and interior build-out to follow in sequence. The construction schedule anticipates 38 months of construction. When completed it will be the tallest building in the United Kingdom and one of the tallest buildings in Europe.

Table 19.1 Typical development and design team

❑ Owner	The owning company which also may be the developer, an equity investor, operator, government, or a combined joint-venture of any of the above.
❑ Developer	The entity actively managing the overall development process for the owner.
❑ Operator	The hotel company that holds a management agreement and, normally, a technical services agreement with the owner. The operator also may be an owner or joint-venture partner or developer.
❑ Franchiser	The hotel company that holds a franchise agreement with the owner, as franchisee.
❑ Lender or funding source	Institution or entity providing primary debt financing; may also be an owner or joint-venture partner.
❑ Construction lender	Institution providing temporary financing until construction is complete.
❑ Feasibility consultant or appraiser	Independent accounting, appraisal, or similar professional firm recognized in the field of hotel development and finance.
❑ Design consultants	Architect, engineers, and additional specialty consultants, such as interior design, food service, landscape, etc.
❑ Lender's architect	Architect independently reviewing design and construction for the lender.
❑ Contractor	General construction contractor experienced in hotels, who holds agreement with owner to build the project as described in the program for a stipulated sum (lump sum) or on a guarantee maximum price basis.
❑ Construction manager	Consultant employed by the owner to manage the construction and equipping of the hotel when not managed directly by the owner.

Table 19.2 Types of consultants and contractors

Consultants to owner/developer
- ❑ Architect
- ❑ Interior designer
- ❑ Food-service consultant
- ❑ Theming consultant
- ❑ Golf course architect
- ❑ Site surveyor
- ❑ Geotechnical engineer
- ❑ Construction manager (CM)
- ❑ Project manager.

Consultants to architect
- ❑ Structural engineer
- ❑ Mechanical engineer
- ❑ Electrical engineer
- ❑ Life-safety consultant
- ❑ Landscape architect
- ❑ Water-feature consultant
- ❑ Traffic/parking consultant
- ❑ Acoustical consultant
- ❑ Elevator consultant
- ❑ Laundry consultant
- ❑ Cost estimator
- ❑ Building code consultant.

Consultants to interior designer
- ❑ Lighting consultant
- ❑ Graphics consultant
- ❑ Art consultant.

Contractors and specialty suppliers
- ❑ General contractor (or CM)
- ❑ Separate trades contractors
- ❑ Purchasing agent (for FF&E)
- ❑ FF&E installer
- ❑ Landscape contractor
- ❑ Artwork supplier
- ❑ Sign contractor
- ❑ Printed materials supplier
- ❑ Uniform supplier
- ❑ Inventory suppliers (china, linen, miscellaneous supplies, etc.)
- ❑ Systems suppliers (computer, data, phones, audiovisual)
- ❑ Field representative.

members involved, and should be modified accordingly wherever possible, consistent with the basic objectives.

The many consultants and contractors usually required on hotel projects are summarized in Table 19.2.

Types of Professional Services Agreements

Hotel projects include more consultants than most building types because of the variety of special operational and technical requirements (e.g., kitchens, laundry, audiovisual, water features, etc.) that are a part of many lodging projects. Among the first contracts the owner signs, before the architect or interior designer

or construction agreements, for instance, is the technical services agreement with the future hotel operator, who provides continuing advice and input throughout the planning and construction phases. Although the following agreements are discussed in quasi-legal terms, the material should not be excerpted or used without consultation with an attorney.

Technical Services Agreement

Through technical services agreements, hotel companies provide such additional design information and guidance as agreed, including facilities and area programs (number, size, and type of guestrooms and suites; seating capacities for food, beverage, banquet, and meeting areas; recreation; retail; parking; and other special requirements); technical guidelines; circulation flows; layouts for special systems (communications and computer equipment, back-of-house service areas, kitchens, laundries, front desk); operating and design themes for food and beverage areas; staffing requirements (offices and employee back-of-house areas); required office layouts and equipment; signage and room numbering; and other detailed hotel requirements affecting the design and budget.

Coordination review is provided in all phases of design, from initial program and concept to final documentation, field inspection, and acceptance, to ensure that the operator's and owner/developer's needs are fully met. A capital budgeting checklist indicates the stages at which facilities programming information and other hotel technical data are incorporated into the architectural and interior design documents, as well as their review and approval by the owner/developer and operator. Technical services fees vary by chain and are often based on a fixed amount per room, with a minimum total sum per hotel.

Architect's Agreement

The architect's agreement should contain the following special provisions: The architect shall perform the following professional services pertaining to the hotel [list] and be responsible to the owner. The hotel operator's approval shall be obtained on all matters required by the management agreement. Often, the question of whether the owner or architect owns the design and the drawings becomes an issue during the negotiation of the contract; generally, all documents should be the property of the owner.

The architect's fees for the scope of services described below are normally a lump sum amount, based on a percentage of the agreed estimate of the construction cost of the work designed by the architect and related consultants. The exact fee depends greatly on the size and complexity of the project, but normally ranges between 5 and 8 percent of the construction budget. If full technical services are not provided by the hotel company, the architect's fees may be increased by up to 1 percent. Fees may vary from the above averages through unique conditions. But more than any other factor, the client's ability to provide information, decisions, and approvals rapidly saves time and expense for the consultants and enables them to reduce their fees accordingly.

Basic Services

Basic services shall consist of the following six phases, including normal structural, mechanical, electrical, fire protection, elevators, civil engineering, landscaping, sitework, parking, acoustical, audiovisual, standard lighting, security, estimating, and coordination of all required consultants as approved by the owner. The architect shall provide value design and value-engineering services consisting of evaluation of all reasonable design components, systems, and methods for efficiency, economy, life safety, and adaptability to the site. The architect warrants that documents shall be in full compliance with all applicable codes and regulations. All construction estimates shall be prepared by a qualified estimator in adequate detail to evaluate the work at each phase, according to the following schedule, not to be exceeded, except for reasonable cause, by either the architect or owner [insert agreed completion dates for each phase here]. The owner shall have the right to require modifications to achieve its desired goals with respect to overall design and operation of the hotel.

- *Schematic design*: Based on the hotel facilities list and design program, technical guides, construction budget, and other data furnished by the owner, the architect shall prepare single-line plans and variations of buildable schemes, indicating the relationships of all hotel components. The architect shall further refine the concept selected by the owner, presenting all floor plans, exterior elevations, building sections, exterior color perspectives, and cost estimates.

- *Design development:* Based on the approved schematic design documents, the architect shall prepare further detailed drawings and outline specifications describing all aspects of the hotel's size and character, including architectural, structural, mechanical, electrical, and fire-protection systems, materials, and an updated cost estimate. In compliance with energy conservation codes and standards, the architect shall prepare a comparative analysis of capital costs and operating expenses of alternate mechanical, electrical, and energy-saving systems so that the owner can select among them.

- *Construction documents phase I (50 percent complete documents):* Based on approved design development documents, the architect shall prepare final detailed drawings and specifications of all construction requirements for the hotel, coordinating in the documents all data provided by the owner and consultants on guestroom layouts, kitchen, bars, and laundry equipment layouts, exterior signs, and other standard details. The architect shall provide the interior designer with drawings of fixed interior elements of the hotel, but not including movable furnishings or other work directly provided by the owner's consultants. The architect shall refine engineering subsystems and advise the owner of any adjustments to the cost estimate.

- *Construction documents phase II (90 percent complete documents):* The owner and their consultants shall give the architect material and color selections and data on any additional systems or equipment to be incorporated in final documents including front desk, communications, and computer equipment. The architect shall submit updated drawings and specifications, advise of any adjustments to the cost estimate, and assist the owner in preparing necessary bidding documents.

- *Construction documents phase III (100 percent complete documents and bidding):* The architect shall finalize drawings and specifications and file them on behalf of the owner with appropriate regulatory agencies for issuance of the building permit, with the owner paying all associated fees. The architect will submit an updated cost estimate and assist the owner in clarifying documents during bidding. Where mutually considered necessary to ensure that the budget is met, the architect will organize specified portions of the design as bid alternates.

- *Construction phase:* The architect shall promptly review and take appropriate action on the contractor's submittals to make sure they conform with the design concept and construction documents and forward them to the owner. The architect shall visit the site as appropriate, but not less than once each month, to make recommendations to the owner about progress of the work, evaluate the contractor's applications for payment, endeavor to guard against defects in the work, but not to guarantee performance by the contractor or supervise construction means, methods, or safety precautions. The architect shall interpret all documents and provide certificates of substantial and final completion of the work.

Construction Budget

The architect agrees that the construction budget is a maximum of [insert amount here] and its best efforts shall be made to delineate a design biddable within this sum, but if exceeded by lowest *bona fide* bids, the owner shall: (1) approve increase; (2) authorize rebidding; or (3) cooperate in revising the scope, materials, or details to reduce the cost. In such case, the architect, without additional charge, shall modify final documents to bring the cost within the construction budget.

Compensation to the Architect

The owner's payments shall be made on approved invoices at the completion of each of the following phases:

• Schematic design	10 percent
• Design development	35 percent
• Construction documents phase I	55 percent
• Construction documents phase II	70 percent
• Construction documents phase III	80 percent
• Construction (final phase payable monthly in accordance with construction progress)	100 percent

If the scope of the hotel is changed substantially after approval of the schematic design phase, or the architect's services, through no fault of the architect, have not been completed within six months after the originally scheduled completion date, the architect's compensation for the then uncompleted portion shall be subject to renegotiation.

Insurance

The architect shall maintain during service, and for a minimum of five years after their completion, professional liability insurance specifically covering errors and omissions, as well as during service, workers' compensation, employer's liability, and comprehensive general liability insurance [specify amounts here]. The architect shall submit certificates of insurance naming the owner and operator as additional insureds to the extent permitted by the carrier. Such insurance shall not limit the architect's liability. The architect shall hold the owner and operator harmless from the liability, loss, or property damage resulting from the architect's acts or omissions.

Interior Designer's Agreement

In hotel work the interior designer generally is hired directly by the owner, rather than the architect, as is done for some other building types. The interior designer works collaboratively with the architect and other design consultants to prepare a cohesive concept for the hotel or resort. The agreement should include phrasing that the operator's approval shall be obtained on all matters required by the management agreement between the owner and operator. Also, it should define clearly the complete scope of work: that is, a detailed listing of the spaces to be designed. Besides all guestroom areas and the hotel public spaces, the interior designer's scope usually includes the elevator cab interiors, public restrooms, administration offices, and occasional outdoor areas such as dining and pool terraces. In addition, the designer may be called on to design interior signage, uniforms, the restaurant tabletop, and other special items.

Basic Services

Basic interior design services shall consist of the following six phases including normal interior design services for furniture, fixtures, and equipment (FF&E), accessories, special finishes, graphics, uniforms and tabletop items, and coordination of consultants approved by the owner. The designer shall coordinate with the architect and other consultants. The designer warrants that documents shall be in full compliance with all applicable codes and regulations. All interior design estimates shall be prepared by a qualified estimator in adequate detail to evaluate the work at each phase, according to the following schedule, not to be exceeded, except for reasonable cause, by either the designer or the owner [insert agreed completion dates for each phase]. The owner shall have the right to require modifications to achieve the desired goals with respect to overall design and operation of the hotel.

- *Concept phase:* Based on the hotel facilities list and design program, technical guides, room mix, suggested operating and design themes for food and beverage areas, budget for FF&E and special finishes, available architectural plans, and other data furnished by the owner, the designer shall prepare preliminary floor plans and variations indicating proposed furniture layouts for public areas and guestrooms; sketch perspectives of overall design concepts; provide colors and samples of proposed materials, photos of furnishings, and alternate selections; and provide cost estimates.
- *Design development:* Based on approved concept documents, the designer shall prepare preliminary room layouts for all public areas, guestrooms and suites including furniture, ceiling and lighting designs, electrical outlet locations, with color perspective renderings and presentation boards containing color, fabric, and material samples of floor, wall, and ceiling finishes, window treatments, furniture and furnishing fabrics and materials including drawings and photos of standard and custom-fabricated furniture, fixtures, and accessories, for presentation to the owner. The designer shall present a preliminary design direction for graphics,

uniforms, and artwork to the owner and submit a preliminary line-item estimate of interior FF&E and special finishes.

- *Documentation phase I (working drawings of furniture and special finishes and mock-up room specifications and review):* The designer shall prepare complete working drawings, including floor plans showing all furnishings identified by type, size, and total number of each item, coded on the drawings and cross-referenced to all other specification data. Drawings shall include elevations, sections, and ceiling plans identifying all wall and window treatments, location of special finishes and materials, variations in ceiling heights and floor levels, location of lighting and outlets for electricity, communications, and TV. The designer shall prepare specifications for a mock-up of a typical guestroom and assist in installation and adjustments to meet the owner's approval.

- *Documentation phase II (millwork and special finishes drawings, complete specifications, and confirmation of budget):* The designer shall prepare final working drawings and bid specifications for all millwork and special finishes, including floor and ceiling plans, sections, elevations, and details of all fixed furniture, furnishings, fixtures, and finishes including floor, wall, and ceiling decorative elements and level changes and coordination of all engineering outlets. Each decorative item shall be detailed and identified by manufacturer. The designer shall provide a finish schedule and specification books of swatches illustrating all materials, fabrics, colors, details, or catalog cuts of interior FF&E, cross-referenced to drawings and specifications; carpet and fabric designs including color tufts or samples; itemized schedules and bid specification sheets including alternate sources of supply; design and procurement coordination for artwork and special accessories; and a final estimate breakdown conforming with the budget for FF&E and special finishes for approval of the owner, operator, and their designated purchasing agent.

- *Documentation phase III (graphics, uniforms and tabletops):* The designer shall provide a graphics program throughout the hotel, including specialty signage for each food and beverage area and required drawings, specifications and color samples for all interior signs for the owner's approval. Estimates shall be included in the budget for FF&E. The designer shall assist the owner in reviewing uniform design and selections of tabletop items including glassware, china, linen, and related service pieces, menus, and accessories designed by others.

- *Construction and installation phase:* The designer shall verify that construction and installation of interior spaces conform to documents; review and approve color and material samples, shop drawings, and manufacturers' detail submittals of furniture, fixtures, and millwork; provide on-site coordination with the installation contractor to approve furniture arrangements; locate decorative materials, artwork, and accessories; and prepare a final punch-list of defective items.

Cost of FF&E and Special Finishes

The designer agrees that the budget for FF&E and special finishes is a maximum of [insert amount here] and best efforts shall be made to delineate a design biddable within this sum, but if exceeded by

lowest *bona fide* bids, the owner shall: (1) approve increase; (2) authorize rebidding; or (3) cooperate in revising scope, materials, or details to reduce cost. In such case, the designer, without additional charge, shall modify final documents to bring costs within the FF&E and special finishes budget.

Compensation to the Designer

The owner's payments shall be made on approved invoices at completion of each of following phases:

• Concept design	25 percent
• Preliminary design	40 percent
• Documentation phase I	50 percent
• Documentation phase II	70 percent
• Documentation phase III	80 percent
• Construction and installation (final phase payable monthly in accordance with progress of services)	100 percent

Provisions for renegotiation of compensation, ownership of documents, and insurance should be similar to those discussed under the architect's agreement above. The interior designer's fees for the scope of services defined in the above agreement are normally a lump sum amount, ranging from 6 to 10 percent of the agreed cost estimate of the work designed and specified by the interior designer and their consultants. The exact fee depends on the size and complexity of the hotel (for example, the number of restaurants or special suites). But, for extensive renovation services, fees may range as high as 12 percent.

Budgeting, Estimating, and Cost Control

The foremost goal of budgeting and estimating systems is to establish a reliable capital budget that works throughout the entire development and construction program, beginning with appropriate allowances and adding detail as the design takes shape. A fully detailed facilities outline and area program based on the market demand study (see Chapter 14, Programming and Development) enables the developer to set initial project budgets and a carefully prepared 10-year business proforma and financial forecast for the project.

The complexity of many hotel developments demands that the developer estimate and monitor a budget with hundreds of individual line items. The earliest budgets, based on preliminary plans and sketches, and before undergoing value design, value engineering, or substantial interior detail, are too preliminary to use for sound budgetary purposes. Therefore, the most reliable preliminary budgets during the schematic phases are generated through fair-market unit-price estimates, based on hands-on experience on comparable developments.

However, the developer should make certain that the budget estimates are (1) complete and do not omit any category or item, and (2) properly indexed to the local area—not based on broad regional or national indexes averaging all types of hotel construction. In addition, it is important, where the hotel structure or concept might be unusually costly, that the construction manager (CM) offers value design and ensures that the market concept is strong enough to carry the extra initial cost as well as debt service.

Maintaining the budget control requires careful monitoring of the project during both the design and construction phases. Throughout the design period, the owner needs be confident of having accurate estimates for all categories, updated monthly or at the end of each documentation phase. In addition to the budget estimates submitted by the architect and other consultants for architecture and engineering, site development, interior design, kitchen equipment, and operating supplies, the project manager or, where applicable, an outside quantity-estimating firm should prepare a second estimate, with any differences in the budget estimates resolved by mutually agreed revisions to the drawings and specifications. Design consultants must be held responsible for redesigning, revising, and respecifying to meet the initial agreed budget without an additional fee.

Technical Guides

The major management companies provide technical design and engineering guides to hotel developers and their consultants. These manuals assist the team in developing imaginative, efficient, and marketable design solutions as well as ensure a safe and environmentally sound structure. The comprehensiveness of the guides, which have been developed over many years and through the experience of scores of projects, often worldwide, is evident in their typical outline. A typical corporate standard may have a first volume containing proprietary planning and technical standards and a second volume covering the recommended systems and procedures (checklists, reference documents, and coordination methods) used during the development and construction period. The guides also may include other volumes, such as one covering "prototype" plans and typical details customized for internal use. These technical guides are frequently available on-line through the hotel company's website and can be accessed with a user name and password provided to the owner during or after franchise negotiations. Many hotel company websites provide prototypical room layouts, public space layouts, and even typical kitchen and laundry layouts, complete with equipment specifications in CAD formats that can be easily incorporated into the project construction documents. (See Table 19.3.)

Architectural and Engineering Systems

Whether the hotel is a high-rise urban tower or a luxury resort with the guestrooms arranged in scattered villas, its market type and program help to determine appropriate solutions to the myriad architectural and engineering alternatives. These involve a number of structural issues, many based on differing requirements of the guestroom areas versus the public and support facilities. For example, by their nature the guestrooms utilize a short-span structure while the public areas, especially the ballroom, require medium to long spans. These areas

Table 19.3 Technical guides

Volume 1 Design, planning, and development standards
- ❏ Introduction, purpose, and intent
- ❏ General requirements, reviews, and approvals
- ❏ Site planning, zoning, massing, and exterior design considerations
- ❏ Building codes, including structural, life-safety, and accessibility requirements
- ❏ Facilities and space programming standards
- ❏ Site and environmental planning requirements, including parking and roadways, recreation, and landscape
- ❏ Guestroom, suite, and villa standards
- ❏ Public space standards, including restaurants and lounges, function and conference areas, indoor recreational amenities, themed shopping, and entertainment features
- ❏ Back-of-house service requirements
- ❏ Furniture, fixtures, and equipment (FF&E) standards
- ❏ Special systems requirements, including fire-protection, security, communications, television and in-room entertainment, audiovisual, property management, and guest service systems
- ❏ Keying and guest security standards
- ❏ Building systems including electrical, mechanical (heating, ventilating, and air-conditioning; energy conservation), plumbing, vertical transportation (elevators and escalators), and fire-protection systems

Volume 2 Technical services
- ❏ General description: scope of technical services, types of agreements, list of consultants, and development sequence
- ❏ Market surveys and feasibility studies: scope of surveys and analysis, types of agreements, and proforma development software
- ❏ Facilities programming systems: area matrix and programming software, and facilities checklists
- ❏ Budgeting and estimating systems: budget estimating software, progress confirmation cost reviews, and value engineering by CM, architectural and engineering firm, or cost consultant; definitive estimate format; and operations pre-opening expense budget format
- ❏ Progress scheduling and reporting systems: critical path method for scheduling, reporting, and approvals; design and construction phase scheduling formats; checklist of early areas for FF&E installation and training; and project manager's coordination checklists
- ❏ Design requirements: selection process format and agreements for architect, interior designer, food service, site survey, geotechnical report, and other required consultants; environmental, location, and parking checklists, including circulation diagrams, parking analysis, and basic building configuration alternatives; checklists for life-safety, security, audiovisual, and special hotel systems; checklists for guestroom types, food and beverage, recreation and health spa amenities, conference, lobby, front office, administration, and back-of-house services; checklists for renovations and additions; and formats for prototype and protopart concepts
- ❏ Construction contracting, bidding and negotiation process: selection format for alternate construction contracting systems
- ❏ Construction contracts and field supervision requirements
- ❏ Construction contracts and general conditions, including provisions for inspection, testing, reporting, and insurance guarantees; and construction management agreements as required
- ❏ FF&E procurement and installation requirements: purchasing agent's agreement, checklists of required FF&E items; and format for preliminary FF&E information and estimate
- ❏ Required inspections, permits, and approvals: format for local checklist of permits and licenses
- ❏ Confirmation of staff training and early occupancy requirements
- ❏ Soft opening and building acceptance procedures: checklist for construction closeout
- ❏ Opening

Volume 3 Prototype plans and typical details
- ❏ New prototype hotel plans
- ❏ Recommended protopart plans: guestroom and suite layouts, health club plans, back-of-house layouts
- ❏ Typical details: brand logos, standard and selected details developed for specified applications

also have different needs for mechanical systems and ceiling heights, and fall under different sections of the building code.

The number of general planning and design issues continues from these larger conceptual aspects to the smallest detail. Where the hotel is based on a prototype, it needs to adapt to the site and the surrounding environs. In addition, the architect should consider how many areas in the hotel will need to adapt to future changes—certainly the restaurants and lounges will undergo frequent re-theming to keep them current—and all areas will be regularly updated and refreshed. Meeting-room technology will change, fitness-center equipment must follow health trends, and guestrooms may need to adapt elements of an office or spa. Therefore, the building infrastructure needs to be highly adaptable to future innovation and change.

While the architect and engineers may evaluate different structural and mechanical systems, the nuances of hotel design tend to limit available choices. There are a number of common building system alternatives, which have different but direct application to guestroom and public/support areas. For example, depending on the location and type of hotel, it may be appropriate to use a frame structure, bearing-wall system, or even pre-fabricated guestroom modules. The decision is based not only on available technology and skills of the building trades, but more on issues related to bay-spacing and the need to integrate mechanical and other systems into the structure.

Structural Systems

The principal structural system for all mid- and high-rise buildings is the steel or reinforced concrete frame structure. Office buildings, which require an open-plan design and suspended ceilings, generally utilize the steel frame. However, the guestroom portions of a hotel are more easily built with flat-plate concrete or precast concrete floor slabs. With no need for HVAC ducts or extensive recessed lighting, the underside of the slab can easily be given an appropriate ceiling finish. Steel-frame buildings require a dropped ceiling which, therefore, results in additional cost owing to increased floor-to-floor height and additional fireproofing demands. All high-rise buildings must be designed to resist wind loads, which often requires diagonal bracing, sheer walls, or other accommodation within the structural system.

Steel is sometimes more suitable for long-span spaces, and therefore commonly is used for public spaces that require large column-free areas, such as ballrooms. Post-tension concrete can also achieve long spans, so the project team will need to assess the current material cost trends when deciding on the most economical structural system to use.

There are a number of structural systems that apply to low-rise buildings, including load-bearing concrete block with spanning metal-deck floors and conventional load-bearing wood or light-gauge steel framing. These systems are easily applied to guestroom wings where the spans are relatively short, but a hybrid system might be called for in long-span column-free spaces by incorporating steel framing.

Modular structural systems, where guestroom units are factory built and assembled on site with precast structural elements, continue to have relevance for hotel projects owing to the repetitious nature of the guestroom modules. The main advantages of these systems are in the speed and quality control of their assembly-line production, but they also reduce material waste and therefore are considered a sustainable technology.

Mechanical Systems

HVAC systems for hotels and resorts vary widely, depending on the building type, location, and configuration. They also vary according to the functional component of the building. For example, the guestrooms of a typical upscale mid-rise or high-rise urban hotel are most often heated and cooled by a two-pipe or a four-pipe fan coil system tied to a central cooling and heating plant. Each guestroom is equipped with an air-handling unit, with a fan that blows air across a copper coil which, depending on temperature setting, is circulating heated or chilled water, thereby transferring heated or chilled air into the room. The four-pipe system (two for supply, two for return) allows heating or cooling to occur at the same time in different rooms, facilitating individual guest control of room temperature. During the spring and fall you could have a warm day followed by a cool night, or you could have guestrooms on one side of the building exposed to the sun's warmth with the other side in cool shadow. The four-pipe system accommodates both needs. A two-pipe system is more economical to build and to operate but only allows heating or cooling to occur at one time, depending on whether the central chiller or the boiler is operating.

Guestrooms in limited-service mid-rise to low-rise hotels often choose through-wall packaged terminal air-conditioner (PTAC) units as the most economical system. They permit individual temperature control, can introduce fresh air, and do not require the expense of a central plant. The downside to PTAC units is that they tend to be noisier than fan coil units and are less able to deal with extreme humidity. In high-humidity climates, PTAC units can be the source of maintenance problems because of the large exterior wall penetration.

Public spaces in most hotels and resorts have special requirements that require dedicated HVAC systems for their specialized needs. The heating or cooling load of a ballroom must be able to provide a comfort level for each of its various uses; conferences, banquets, weddings, etc. When a ballroom is divided, different sections might require different air-conditioning loads. A variable air volume (VAV) system allows individual thermostats in each division to control a damper system that will deliver the appropriate cooling volume to each area.

Sustainable Building Systems

More than any other industry for which real estate development is an essential part of their operation, the hotel industry has embraced the principles of environmental responsibility and sustainability with fierce conviction. Every major hotel company now proffers a mission statement detailing elaborate corporate goals to achieve zero-carbon

Green Design for Sustainable Operations

Sara Schoen
Hospitality Sector Manager
U.S. Green Building Council
Washington, DC

"Sustainability" may be on this year's list of overused words. We hear it in the context of FF&E purchasing, landscaping, lighting—even bedbugs. We have emerged from the phase when many hotel designers and developers were ambivalent about LEED (the U.S. Green Building Council's Leadership in Energy and Environmental Design green building certification program) into a new era in which sustainability is valued for its ability to augment guest experience.

One of the next frontiers in hotel development is building a stronger connection between green design and operations. We are tasked with finding ways to ensure that the benefits of green elements can be drawn into a hotel's operational phase, beyond its grand opening. Performance after the ribbon cutting should be top of mind throughout the development process: projects designed with an eye on energy efficiency, ongoing waste management, indoor environmental health, and alternative transportation will better support the imperative of sustainable operations throughout their lifetimes.

Developers can investigate local recycling systems and build recycling infrastructure into back-of-house spaces and guestroom casegoods. An integrated design process that includes playing with building shape, orientation, and fenestration in the earliest stages can permanently maximize a hotel's efficiency and daylighting. Installing geothermal energy systems, efficient mechanical equipment, or a solar water-heating system will reduce a property's reliance on costly off-site energy production and cut energy bills significantly. In addition to giving a hotel some local flavor, installing native species eliminates landscaping water and fertilizer use and reduces maintenance and other ongoing costs associated with groundskeeping.

Permeable paving on a hotel's grounds will reduce its heat island effect, lowering cooling energy use year after year and minimizing effects on local microclimates and wildlife habitats. Such pavers can also enhance a hotel property's aesthetics, giving it a novel, more natural and relaxed look, and improve guest comfort by eliminating the need to walk on overheated concrete or asphalt on a hot summer day. A sometimes overlooked benefit of permeable paving is its ability to allow natural stormwater collection and drainage to continue even after a site is developed. This can improve local water quality and significantly lower stormwater management costs by reducing runoff and shifting the burden back to the natural system for stormwater filtration, detention, and storage.

A lobby that is designed so that guests and staff choose to climb stairs more often instead of taking an elevator every time will yield sustainability benefits throughout the hotel's life. Such behavioral shifts not only reduce energy usage but also improve occupant health. The idea is not to compromise guest experience by removing amenities, but to make the green choice easier and more appealing.

The most important new initiative of USGBC is Building Performance Partnership, a platform for tracking and benchmarking the ongoing environmental performance of LEED-certified buildings. Any hotel pursuing green design should also keep an eye on this program and how it might perform in tracking the hotel's ongoing energy and water consumption, indoor air quality, waste management, and use of alternative transportation.

Staying focused on sustainable operations throughout the design process ensures that the return on a hotel's green design will not end with the achievement of a LEED for New Construction certification and a plaque on the wall. Choosing green features that impact the life of a hotel and planning for sustainable operations during the design phase can help bridge the gap between green design and the lifetime environmental footprints of our hotels.

footprint and environmental conservation. The motivation is not only for achieving valued public relations credentials for helping save the planet: through research and development, the hospitality industry is setting the bar in realizing demonstrable economic benefit from sustainable initiatives. Hotels, with their multiple and varied functions, provide fertile ground for the application of green technology. The application of sustainable technology applies broadly to the program elements of a hotel, whether seen as a commercial business, a residential accommodation, an entertainment venue, a culinary establishment, a recreational amenity, a conferencing center, or a service facility. Some of the sustainable building systems applications hotels regularly employ are listed in Table 19.4 (overleaf).

As commitment to sustainable principles takes on new importance to the hospitality industry, many hotels and resorts seek to measure and demonstrate to travelers their achievements in fulfilling their obligation to be environmentally responsible by obtaining LEED (Leadership in Energy and Environmental Design) certification through the United States Green Building Council (USGBC) or BREEAM (Building Research Establishment Environmental Assessment Method) certification through the World Green Building Council (WorldGBC). (See Appendix A for LEED certification checklist.) In achieving LEED Platinum certification, the highest score in the rating system, the Proximity Hotel in Greensboro, North Carolina, employed a wide array of environmental principles, both in the design of its building systems and in its operations and services to guests.

LEED-NC
NEW CONSTRUCTION

PURPOSE The Leadership in Energy and Environmental Design (LEED) Rating System was designed by the US Green Building Council to encourage and facilitate the development of more sustainable buildings.

LEED CREDITS The environmental categories are subdivided into the established LEED credits, which are based on desired performance goals within each category. An assessment of whether the credit is earned or denied is made and a narrative describes the basis for the assessment.

CREDITS ACHIEVED The applicant has provided the mandatory documentation which supports the achievements of the credit requirements, achieving the associated points. Currently the project has scored the adjacent points in this category.

55

RATING **Platinum**

OFFICIAL SCORES Official LEED v2.2-2008 Scores: **Certified:** 26-32 **Silver Rating:** 33-38 **Gold Rating:** 39-51 **Platinum Rating:** 52+

SUSTAINABLE SITES   POSSIBLE POINTS 14

CONSTRUCTION ACTIVITY POLLUTION PREVENTION — PREREQUISITE
The project has followed local erosion and sedimentation control standards and codes, which are more stringent than the NPDES program requirements.

SITE SELECTION
The hotel site does not meet any of the prohibited criteria.

DEVELOPMENT DENSITY; COMMUNITY CONNECTIVITY
The project has been renovated or constructed on a previously developed site within 1/2 mile of a residential zone or neighborhood with an average density of 10 units per acre net and within 1/2 mile of at least 10 Basic Services.

ALTERNATIVE TRANSPORTATION; PUBLIC TRANSPORTATION ACCESS
The project is located within 1/4 mile of one or more stops for two or more public or campus bus lines usable by building occupants.

ALTERNATIVE TRANSPORTATION; BICYCLE STORAGE; CHANGING ROOMS
Secure bicycle racks/storage has been provided for at least 5% of all peak building users within 200 yards of a building entrance and shower/changing facilities have been provided within 200 yards of the building entrance for at least 0.5% of Full-Time Equivalent occupants.

ALTERNATIVE TRANSPORTATION; LOW EMITTING; FUEL EFFICIENT VEHICLES
Preferred parking has been provided for low-emitting and fuel-efficient vehicles for 5% of the total vehicle parking capacity of the site.

ALTERNATIVE TRANSPORTATION; PARKING CAPACITY
The parking capacity has been sized to meet, but not exceed, the minimum local zoning requirements, and that preferred parking has been provided for 5% of the total provided parking spaces.

SITE DEVELOPMENT; PROTECT OR RESTORE HABITAT
A minimum of 50% of the site area that does not fall within the building footprint has been restored with native planting.

SITE DEVELOPMENT; MAXIMIZE OPEN SPACE CREDIT
Local zoning requirements do not require open space, so an area of open space has been allocated which is equal to or greater than 20% of the total site area.

STORMWATER MANAGEMENT; QUANTITY CONTROL
Existing Imperviousness less than or equal to 50%. A stormwater management plan or stream channel protection strategy has been implemented that protects receiving stream channels from excessive erosion.

ENVIRONMENTAL TOBACCO SMOKE (ETS) CONTROL — PREREQUISITE
No smoking is allowed in the building and designated exterior smoking areas are located at least 25 feet away from entries, outdoor air intakes and operable windows.

OUTDOOR AIR DELIVERY MONITORING
A CO_2 monitoring system has been installed.

INCREASED VENTILATION
Outdoor air ventilation rates have been increased to all occupied spaces by at least 30% above the minimum rates required by ASHRAE Standard 62.1-2004.

CONSTRUCTION INDOOR AIR QUALITY MANAGEMENT PLAN; DURING CONSTRUCTION
The project developed and implemented a construction IAQ management plan that followed the referenced SMACNA Guidelines. A copy of the project's IAQ Management Plan and photos highlighting the implemented IAQ measures have been provided.

LOW-EMITTING MATERIALS; ADHESIVES; SEALANTS
All adhesive and sealant products comply with the VOC (Volital Organic Compounds) limits.

LOW-EMITTING MATERIALS; PAINTS; COATINGS
All indoor paints, stains, and clear finishes comply with the VOC (Volital Organic Compounds) limits of the referenced Green Seal and SCAQMD standards.

LOW-EMITTING MATERIALS; CARPET SYSTEMS
Installed carpet systems comply with the VOC (Volital Organic Compounds) limits of the CRI Green Label Plus Testing Program.

CONTROLLABILITY OF SYSTEMS; LIGHTING
Sufficient lighting controls have been provided for all shared multi-occupant spaces and that at least 50% of the individual workstations have been provided with lighting controls.

CONTROLLABILITY OF SYSTEMS; THERMAL COMFORT
Individual comfort controls have been provided.

THERMAL COMFORT; DESIGN
The project has been designed to maintain indoor comfort within the ranges established by ASHRAE 55-2004.

THERMAL COMFORT; VERIFICATION
A post-occupancy survey will be conducted to determine occupant thermal comfort satisfaction.

DAYLIGHTING; VIEWS; DAYLIGHT 75% OF SPACES

DAYLIGHTING; VIEWS; VIEWS FOR 90% OF SPACES
97.15% of critical visual task areas have direct access to views of the outdoors.

INNOVATION; DESIGN PROCESS   POSSIBLE POINTS 5

INNOVATION IN DESIGN
Achieving views for 97.15% of critical visual task areas.

INNOVATION IN DESIGN
Green Building Education efforts.
1. Poster board narratives
2. A series of "Sustainable Practices Symposiums" available to the public
    (a) Outreach to the education community
    (b) Providing speakers (in the first year, over 70 speaking engagements were fulfilled by team speakers)
    (c) Sustainable Practices tours (over 9,000 in the first year)
3. NC A&T State University collaboration program with their Center of Energy Research and Technology

INNOVATION IN DESIGN CREDIT
Restoration of 700 linear feet of stream to the NC Department of Water quality standards.

INNOVATION IN DESIGN
Over 40% of the building materials sourced locally.

LEED ACCREDITED PROFESSIONAL
A LEED AP has been a participant on the project development team.

STORMWATER MANAGEMENT; QUALITY CONTROL

HEAT ISLAND EFFECT; ROOF CREDIT
Reflective roofing materials have been used for at least 75% of the project's roof surface.

LIGHT POLLUTION REDUCTION
The maximum candela value from interior fixtures does not intersect transparent or translucent exterior building surfaces OR automatic lighting controls turn off non-essential lighting during non-business hours and the Lighting Power Density is within the LEED Allowable threshold and the percentage of site lamp lumens above 90 degrees from nadir is no greater than 2%.

WATER EFFICIENCY   POSSIBLE POINTS 5

WATER EFFICIENT LANDSCAPING
The landscaping and irrigation systems have been designed to reduce irrigation water consumption from a calculated baseline and the irrigation water used on site is supplied by a non-potable source.

WATER USE REDUCTION
Water use has been reduced by 33.5% through the use of low-flow fixtures.

ENERGY; ATMOSPHERE   POSSIBLE POINTS 17

FUNDAMENTAL COMMISSIONING — PREREQUISITE

MINIMUM ENERGY PERFORMANCE — PREREQUISITE

FUNDAMENTAL REFRIGERANT MANAGEMENT — PREREQUISITE
The project's HVAC & Refrigeration systems do not contain CFC-based refrigerants.

OPTIMIZE ENERGY PERFORMANCE
The energy modeling output indicate a 39.2% savings between the design case and the budget case based on ASHRAE 90.1-2004.

ON-SITE RENEWABLE ENERGY
Calculations indicate that 8.49% of the building's regulated energy cost is provided by on-site renewable energy.

ENHANCED COMMISSIONING

ENHANCED REFRIGERANT MANAGEMENT
The base building HVAC & Refrigeration equipment does not exceed the LEED Ozone Depletion and Global Warming maximum threshold formula.

MEASUREMENT; VERIFICATION
The project has developed and implemented a measurement and verification plan consistent with Option (D) of the IPMVP.

GREEN POWER
35% of the Electricity is from renewable sources.

MATERIALS; RESOURCES   POSSIBLE POINTS 13

STORAGE; COLLECTION OF RECYCLABLES — PREREQUISITE
Appropriate facilities for recycling have been provided.

CONSTRUCTION WASTE MANAGEMENT
The project diverted 1,535 tons (86.9%) of on-site generated construction waste from landfill.

RECYCLED CONTENT
22.4% of the total building materials content, by value, have been manufactured using recycled materials.

REGIONAL MATERIALS
45.9% of the total building materials value is comprised of building materials and/or products that have been extracted, processed and manufactured within 500 miles of the project site.

INDOOR ENVIRONMENTAL QUALITY   POSSIBLE POINTS 15

MINIMUM INDOOR AIR QUALITY PERFORMANCE — PREREQUISITE
The requirements of ASHRAE 62.1-2004 have been met.

Proximity Hotel, Greensboro, North Carolina
Dozens of sustainable features contributed to the hotel achieving LEED Platinum certification, the highest score in the rating system. The most visible feature is the 100 rooftop solar panels that provide 60 percent of the hot water needed for the hotel and restaurant. The LEED checklist shows how the project was scored with other sustainable features and operations.

Table 19.4 Sustainable building systems applications

Energy reduction
- ❑ Solar energy systems
- ❑ Geothermal energy
- ❑ Green roofs
- ❑ Solar shading
- ❑ Insulated building envelope
- ❑ Reflective roofing materials
- ❑ Energy-efficient appliances
- ❑ Energy-efficient lighting
- ❑ Modular construction
- ❑ Energy-recovery technology
- ❑ Energy-efficient glazing
- ❑ Efficient HVAC systems
- ❑ Enhanced guestroom controls
- ❑ Regenerative drive elevators
- ❑ Local material usage

Water conservation
- ❑ Rainwater harvesting
- ❑ Recycled water
- ❑ Green roofs
- ❑ Low-flow plumbing fixtures
- ❑ Stormwater management/bio-swales
- ❑ Restricted irrigation systems

Renewable resources
- ❑ Natural carpets
- ❑ Recycled materials
- ❑ Shower-gel dispensers
- ❑ Restorative landscaping
- ❑ Native planting

Healthy environment
- ❑ Low VOC (volatile organic compounds) finishes
- ❑ Day-lighting
- ❑ Natural ventilation
- ❑ Noise reduction
- ❑ Convenient stairs
- ❑ Sustainable transportation
- ❑ Light pollution control
- ❑ Wellness centers

Hotel Technology Systems

Rapidly expanding technological advancements in hotel systems are transforming the way lodging properties are operated and guest services provided. High-speed internet, broadband WiFi/WLAN wireless networks, biometric cellular smartphones, intelligent cameras, and high-definition 3-D touch-screen interactive television are defining how guests interface with hotel services. These new advancements are augmenting what have become conventional technologies such as computerized check-in, automatic wake-up calls, electronic guestroom locks, satellite television, and teleconferencing. Few buildings have a greater variety of computerized or other specialized systems than do today's lodging properties. These fall into five broad categories:

Property Management Systems

Computerized reservations systems were first centralized by Sheraton in 1956, further developed by Holiday Inns in the early 1960s, and since then have gone through many generations of refinement. Practically every major hotel chain has its own computerized international reservation system, which integrates internet-based inquiries with the more typical telephone ones.

Central to computerized hotel operations today is the property management system (PMS). These information technology (IT) systems tie together the several operational areas of the hotel, and feature components to access the hotel reservations networks and accept credit card authorization. At the individual hotel, the PMS integrates a wide range of potential guest charges, such as restaurant point-of-sale terminals, guestroom movie purchases, and long-distance phone charges, with a number of in-house recording tasks and general office systems, such as word processing or internet access. Among the most important features are front office requirements that clearly identify room inventory and can track guest history information, including room preferences or membership in airline frequent flyer programs. The most common functions of today's PMSs include:

- Guest reservations
- Guest registration and folio accounting (the record of guest charges for room, food and beverage, and telephone)
- Accounting, including night audit, city ledger, accounts payable, and general ledger
- Guest history and other marketing reports
- Daily and monthly operating reports
- Payroll and related reports
- Inventory

Among the most visible systems may be the point-of-sale units that have become ubiquitous in most retail operations and certainly are common in hotel restaurants and lounges. The system allows the server to place an order at a terminal located in the dining room; the system then prints out the order in the kitchen, where the production staff begins to prepare the food. In addition to saving steps and time, the restaurant systems reduce errors in calculating and totaling the final check, immediately post the charge to the guest's room account, and provide a variety of analyses, including daily accounting and food inventory reports.

The choice of a PMS vendor depends on the type of hotel and what functions are most important. Part 1 of this book describes the incredible variety of lodging properties; consider how these place very different demands on the choice of technology:

- Smaller hotels such as roadside and suburban properties need straightforward reservations and accounting systems.
- Convention hotels need a flexible system to handle special functions and such features as group billing.
- Resorts need to track a variety of guest-related activities such as golf club or spa use.
- Super-luxury hotels need to maintain detailed guest history files.

Communication Systems

Gone are the days of the traditional hotel switchboard. Personal cellular phones and smartphones have rendered conventional guestroom telephones all but obsolete as few guests wish to incur unnecessary charges for their use; rather, the in-room phone has been more or less relegated to calls for room service, valet parking, concierge services, or to other guestrooms or the front desk. Further inexpensive internet telecommunications services provide guests with long-distance capabilities through their laptop computer or iPad. Revenues from telephone switchboards have been largely replaced by sales of in-room internet connectivity, either through a hard-wired USB port or, more often, via a WiFi network.

Provision of high-speed internet connectivity has become an essential service that hotels must provide to remain competitive. WiFi access through a broadband antennae network should provide guests with connectivity not only in their guestrooms but throughout the public spaces as well. Hotel management also benefits, as the use of mobile devices permits efficient operations in administration and back-of-house areas. WLAN (wireless local area network) "heat-sensitive" technology can read the density of activity on the network, and add WiFi muscle to parts of the grid that require more bandwidth. Similarly, everything from support and integration of mobile devices, such as smartphones and tablet computers, to the delivery of hotel services has become paramount. With the security of biometric fingerprint recognition, guests can now safely make purchases and guestroom charges through their mobile devices. By downloading special apps provided by the hotel, which convert a smartphone to a super remote-control device, guests can activate do-not-disturb signs, open or close window curtains, adjust light and temperature levels, order room service from a menu display, make golf tee-time reservations—even select music and TV channels. For added security it is important that multiple levels of encryption and data protection are provided to prevent fraud and privacy violations.

Life-safety Systems

Fire-protection systems in hotels were greatly enhanced in the 1980s and 1990s because of a number of devastating hotel fires that raised public awareness to life-safety issues. Among those with the most fatalities were fires at the MGM Grand Hotel in Las Vegas, Nevada, the DuPont Plaza in San Juan, Puerto Rico, and the Stouffer's Hotel in Westchester, New York. Testing and research on the causes of these and other hotel fires have improved design methods and standards, and new technology has advanced the quality of detection, alarm, and fire-extinguishing systems. As a result, most hotels in Western countries incorporate state-of-the-art fire-protection systems; those without these systems should not be considered safe.

One issue that affects the provision of life-safety systems is the mandate of building codes. For example, an electrical fire at a Boston hotel caused the city to modify its standards for the protection of emergency generators. Other hotels under construction at that time upgraded their plans even though they had complied with previous codes. A serious fire at a Fort Worth, Texas, hotel was the impetus for requiring sprinklers even in low-rise guestroom wings. Concern

after a fire in an atrium hotel near Chicago resulted in code changes that required increased exhaust systems to draw smoke away from atrium guestroom corridors.

As a result of these and several other fires, the National Fire Protection Association (NFPA) and the AH&LA have urged developers to incorporate new technology even where codes don't require it. The ultimate goal, of course, is to install fail-safe protection in all hotels worldwide. Life-safety technology includes the following:

- Automatic fire-detection and alarm systems
- Fully sprinklered building
- Central annunciator panels
- Guest evacuation sound systems
- Firefighters' voice communication system
- Smoke-proof and pressurized exit stairs
- Emergency generator (alarm systems, lighting, smoke exhaust)

Also, building codes specify numerous construction details to further protect the building occupants as well as the property. The United States has several building codes in addition to the NFPA life-safety code on which most individual city or state codes are based. The United Kingdom, France, Germany, and many other nations also have precise building regulations. Although similar, the detailed requirements vary somewhat from code to code—the number of sprinklers required in a hotel guestroom, for example, varies from one to four depending on the code in force, with even more in such special situations as rooms looking into an atrium—so that hotel standards must be designed to meet the most stringent requirements of all codes.

Because of the high priority given to fire safety by the hotel industry, large national and international hotel companies have established their own fire-safety standards that exceed most local codes, thereby reducing the problem of satisfying varying regulations in different localities. Up-to-date, consistent company standards that go beyond codes are also becoming the key to legal safety as well. Today, owners who fail to apply the latest safety or security measures throughout a hotel or chain may risk liability. For example, after a hotel in Washington, DC, installed electronic locks in its new addition, it was held liable for a theft in the older building because locks there were less secure. Attempts have been made to apply this legal principle also to life-safety issues; therefore, operators and designers must carefully consider safety standards and consistently implement them in all hotels under the same ownership or management.

Smoke or heat detectors are now required by most codes in all hotel guestrooms as well as public areas. These usually are placed above the bed and at regular intervals along the guest corridors. Additional heat detectors in such service areas as kitchens, laundries, and mechanical areas are set to recognize the usual high temperatures in these spaces. A critical factor is how any alarm is recorded: In addition to sounding a local alarm, an integrated system automatically notifies the local fire department; sends a signal to a fire-control panel near the hotel entrance, which is easily accessible to firefighters; and alerts hotel staff in the telephone PBX room—the main point from which directions can be quickly communicated to hotel guests.

A major issue in hotel fires is the approach taken to notify guests of the emergency. Some hotels have attempted to put out a local fire without evacuating the building. Often, in emergencies, guests have been uninformed about whether they should try to leave their room or remain there until the emergency is over. Various approaches to establishing sound systems connected to hotel guestrooms have been implemented, including corridor speakers loud enough to be heard in the guestrooms. Some regulations insist that a guest evacuation sound system be carried over the telephone system, master television antenna (MTV), or independent low-voltage systems.

Recognition that much of the danger from fires comes from smoke rather than the fire itself has created an increased awareness of the importance of controlling the spread of smoke. This goal is accomplished horizontally by automatic closers on guestroom and other doors and by the installation of fire doors at elevator lobbies, which are held open magnetically but which close automatically when detectors sense a fire. The problem is more severe vertically because of elevators, stairs, mechanical ducts and shafts, and numerous small penetrations through the floor slabs. Any vertical openings must be protected with fire-rated automatic dampers to isolate smoke and fire between adjoining floors. These dampers, adding substantially to the capital costs of a project, can be designed to also help control energy use.

Vertical stair towers present a similar smoke problem. Two common solutions are to pressurize the stairs, so that when any door is opened the higher air pressure keeps the stair clear of toxic smoke, or to provide for smoke evacuation in stair vestibules. Elevator shafts require similar specialized systems. In Germany codes require pressurization of elevator shafts, while in France all elevator openings are further protected by automatic fire shutters. In the United States many jurisdictions require automatic smoke doors between the elevator lobby and the guestroom corridor.

Security Systems

While improved life-safety systems protect the public against fire or such other emergencies as earthquakes, new security systems protect guests, employees, and the physical property from crime. The systems and the procedures set up by management may be developed, at least in part, to meet the requirements established by the hotel's legal and insurance advisors and to help ward off lawsuits. To protect people and property against theft, physical assault, vandalism, arson, and terrorism, the hotel security system has three principal components: locking systems, television surveillance cameras, and various types of alarms.

The keying system is the largest element in hotel security and has undergone the most change over the past few years. Mechanical locks have practically disappeared from guest areas, where electronic card-key systems now are standard. Before the card-keys became common, hotels were under intense pressure to physically change each lock after a key had been lost or stolen. However, owing to the time and expense involved this wasn't done sufficiently often. The same card-key systems are becoming more common in back-of-house areas because of

the ability to generate a record of what card—that is, which employee—attempts entry.

A second major part of the hotel's security systems is closed circuit television (CCTV). The television surveillance system is controlled and monitored in larger hotels at a security office and in smaller properties at the receiving office or telephone PBX. Cameras can be used to scan outdoor areas and specific indoor locations where theft or unauthorized access is a problem. They may be programmed to run only when an alarm is sounded or when a particular door is opened; in other cases, especially in casinos, the CCTV systems monitor areas continuously. The hotel areas most often protected by closed circuit television include the several hotel entrances, storage rooms, and areas where large amounts of cash are handled.

The third element in a security plan, in addition to effective employee training, is the installation of intrusion alarms at critical points. These incorporate various types of electrical circuits, light beams, and motion detectors. Obviously, these depend on standby or emergency power systems to protect the hotel completely. Intrusion detectors can be used for all areas of the hotel: grounds, doors and windows, unoccupied rooms including guestrooms and storage areas, and selected locations such as the safe and safety deposit boxes. Connecting these alarms to a security console permits the operator to notify authorities of the exact location of the alarm, before he or she takes action.

All these security systems increase the safety of the guests and employees and help reduce the hotel operator's insurance premiums. As with other specialized systems, the security components generally are available as part of an overall, integrated package, including life-safety and energy management.

Enhanced Security Systems

The attacks on The Taj Mahal Palace Hotel in Mumbai and on the North Caucasus ski resorts in Russia emphatically demonstrate that certain hotel and resort security systems need to focus not only on petty criminals and intruders bent on theft, vandalism, arson, or personal assaults, but must apply cutting-edge technology in early threat detection of potential terrorist attacks. Politicians, celebrities, captains of industry, military personnel, and other potential political targets of terrorists are particularly vulnerable when away from the protective cover of their dependable home or workplace security networks. Hotels and resorts that cater to this clientele must consider going beyond conventional hotel security systems and employ real-time intrusion-detection and threat-assessment technology. Conventional magnetic card access can be augmented by radio frequency identification (RFID) technology, facial geometry/recognition and such biometric access applications as retinal scanning. A system of long- and short-range pan-tilt-zoom (PTZ) cameras enabled with video intelligent-convergent technology can employ an integrated tag-and-track network in providing real-time detection, and real-time, or immediate, assessment of a threat.

Applications that can convert incoming data to three-dimensional displays of the facility and its environment further enable understanding and assessment of a menacing situation and help in establishing an interactive virtual barrier. Images can be streamed live to portable devices supporting a deployed response to a threat. On waterfront properties, a virtual electronic "bubble" of security can secure approaches up to 7 miles (11 km) out to sea, using ground-based radar and all-weather, day–night laser illuminated PTZ cameras integrated to automatically vector in, and track on approach, unknown targets. This enhanced electronic surveillance intelligence-enabled camera network should be operated from a centrally located command and control center, ideally within a hardened perimeter.

Construction Services

Managing the construction of a hotel or resort requires a well-organized system. The owner's project manager and other financial and operational members of the project team now take on major leadership roles, closely follow the progress of construction, and, especially, pay particular attention to any modifications of the project scope, budget, schedule, or quality. They must establish a methodical control system that tracks each change and continually measures expenditures against a variety of construction and line budgets, and updates the project schedule. Once the building is largely completed, the owner needs to purchase and install literally thousands of furniture, fixtures, and equipment (FF&E) items, followed by training staff and testing special systems, all well before the anticipated opening date.

The first step in establishing an effective control system is to fully plan the construction project well in advance. Each aspect of the work must be reduced to a group of tasks and subtasks that will allow adequate monitoring and timely reporting at any sign of schedule delays or potential cost overruns. The owner/developer's project manager must carefully identify and diagram the scope and priority of all tasks. Just as marketing and design are crucial to the project's image, so, too, are the construction methods critical to its schedule and budget, and its eventual success.

Construction completion dates generally are more critical for hotels than for most other types of buildings. Hotels under construction—even those late in the design phase—sell large blocks of guestrooms and meeting space to convention groups several years before the hotel opens. Any delay not only entails lost revenue but can negatively affect the hotel's reputation among travel agents, corporate groups, and disaffected guests. In addition, staff payroll, training, and other fixed pre-opening expenses are further extended. To help ensure that opening dates are met, the construction contract may include liquidated damage and bonus clauses to penalize or provide incentives for the contractor.

An essential step is to define clearly the roles of the project team, to avoid potential overlapping—or gaps—in key areas of responsibility. While the "general conditions" part of the construction contract establishes a legal relationship between the contractor or construction manager and the owner, additional roles and detailed work descriptions should be prepared to better tie the design professionals, consultants, subcontractors, and suppliers to the project.

Project Delivery

The complexity of the mixed-use aspects of hotels—lodging, assembly, commercial, and other uses combined in one facility—presents significant challenges in construction as well as operation. Therefore, the choice of the construction contract form can greatly influence the quality, timeliness, and cost of the final product. While there are various ways to combine the typical contract types, the most common arrangements are (1) the traditional design/bid/award contract, (2) construction management, often including fast-track elements, and (3) design/build. Generally, the owner or developer designates a staff executive or consultant to act as the overall project manager, with clear authority and appropriate staff for the size and complexity of the project. Table 19.5 (overleaf) illustrates the key advantages and disadvantages of each type of project delivery method.

Among the three most prevalent variations, the design/bid/award contract separates each of the roles: the architect completes the design and construction documents, contractors review these and submit a lump sum bid, the owner and architect select a contractor, who then completes the building expressly as designed and specified. Construction management integrates these elements more fully by offering construction and cost-estimating advice throughout the design process. Also, the process may provide the option to fast-track the schedule and deliver the project earlier by overlapping the design and construction phases. In the design/build variant, the owner pre-selects a contractor who directs the design effort, seeking techniques that offer greater potential for cost savings and design improvements during construction. The final selection will depend on the unique special conditions of the project but, generally, design/bid/award best establishes a firm price, construction management offers greater flexibility and the potential to shorten the schedule, and design/build offers a "turnkey" solution appropriate for less complex lodging types. The availability and productivity of skilled labor also may affect the choice of contract and delivery options.

Design/Bid/Award Contract

The traditional design/bid/award contract is widely used by the hotel industry. It may require the most time: several months for the architect and design team to prepare full drawings and specifications, then time to allow several general contractors (GC) to calculate their bids and the owner to analyze these before awarding the contract. In this contract form, the emphasis is on tight construction documents from the architect and independent management by the general contractor, who takes full responsibility for managing and scheduling the construction. Allowing the architect sufficient time to produce clear, complete, and concise documents provides the owner with the best opportunity to purchase the entire project at a competitive cost and reduces the risk of price overruns. While some people feel that the GC and, in turn, the many subcontractors, may submit a low bid expecting to recoup money later through change orders, the owner/developer and project manager should accept bids only from qualified and reputable contracting firms to minimize that possibility.

Table 19.5 Construction contract options

	Design/bid/award	Construction management/fast track	Design/build
Client/owner			
Advantages	Professional advice on contract and construction quality issues Good industry understanding of how method operates Budgets most accurately resemble actual costs Easier guaranteed maximum price negotiations Clear penalties for cost overruns Unambiguous chain of responsibility	Shorter project delivery time Lower project costs Builder is agent to the owner Professional advice on contract and construction quality issues Clearly defined sharing of cost overruns and savings	Shorter project delivery time Lower project costs Single responsible party Inventive design/construction solutions Reduced project-management workload Reduced number of claims Single fee to pay
Disadvantages	Longer start-to-finish time Inability to negotiate subcontractor costs Multiple fees to pay	Project management increases workload Decision-making responsibilities unclear	No independent professional design advice
Contractor/construction manager			
Advantages	Definitive plans and specifications on which to base bids Role clearly understood by all parties	Reduced financial risk Early completion bonuses Easier to recommend substitutions	More control over project Minimum risk and uncertainty Improved design Direct communication with design professionals Opportunity to increase profits
Disadvantages	Less flexibility for substitutions of materials, equipment and systems Adversarial relationships with design professionals	Difficulty in establishing guaranteed maximum price Coordination failures result in delays Penalties Gaps in insurance coverage	Responsibility for design errors and omissions
Architect/designer			
Advantages	Greatest control over design and construction quality Role clearly understood by all parties	More involvement in the field Quick decisions by all parties Input from builder during design process	More control over project quality Opportunity to increase profits Field experience Greater credibility with clients Reduced number of claims from contractor
Disadvantages	Adversarial relationships with contractors	Decision-making responsibilities unclear Priorities blurred Timeliness more important than quality Coordination workload increased	Responsibility for errors and omissions of the contractor

In the design/bid/award form, the GC takes more risk in that its bid must anticipate future material and labor costs and depends on the timely work of countless subcontractors and suppliers. This contract form makes it more difficult for the owner or architect to make scope or design changes—which require negotiating price and schedule changes—but helps to keep the project on budget and on schedule.

Construction Management

The construction management method, developed over the last half of the twentieth century, draws together and integrates the construction, cost-estimating, architecture, and engineering traditions.

The construction manager (CM) acts, in effect, as both the owner's agent and project manager, providing a continuous involvement from early conceptual design to hotel opening, during which he or she is responsible for the overall budget and schedule, creating value in the design, and value engineering. The main advantage is that the owner, early in the project, has access to advice on construction methods and costs. Also, the owner has greater flexibility to make modifications in scope or design during the project, and can easily work with subcontractors and suppliers to seek out equivalent but more competitive systems and products.

Construction management often assumes some degree of fast-tracking, in which construction may begin before the full drawings and specifications are complete. Consider that the contractor can begin the excavation, even the foundations and lower floors, before the architects, engineers, and designers specify every detail of the guestroom systems and finishes. While reducing the overall construction schedule is a great boon, and may allow the hotel to open and generate revenues earlier, the owner must recognize the risk in beginning a project before the design is complete and final costs are known.

Generally, the architect completes the schematic design and, with the construction manager, agrees on the major design elements, including structure, principal materials, mechanical systems, and vertical circulation. For example, they may establish the column spacing based on the garage bay or the guestroom module and choose between, say, steel and reinforced concrete structural systems. This sets a number of key elements that should not be changed and allows the contractor to order long lead-time items in advance of the completion of the design. While early construction proceeds, the architect and design consultants complete the documentation of the remaining details. The owner must carefully analyze the benefits of an accelerated construction timetable and earlier opening versus the potential increases in project cost due to deferring important design and construction decisions.

Without complete drawings it is impossible to agree on a lump sum. The CM process, instead, often utilizes a "guaranteed maximum price" (GMP) based on a clear definition of the scope of the work and outline specifications detailing the quality levels of finishes and systems. The contract usually is structured so that owner and contractor share any savings below the GMP, giving the contractor a clear incentive to lower construction costs.

The construction manager may select a general contractor but usually manages separate contracts with individual subcontractors. Therefore, the CM plays a strong on-site role coordinating many diverse trades, but has the flexibility to go back to the owner or architect as he or she sees opportunities to add a feature or modify a design, within reasonable constraints. Sometimes, where subcontractors are rushed to complete a task, the quality of workmanship may become an issue. Thus, the CM needs to balance the owner's objectives for quality against the real needs to keep to a schedule and budget. The major difficulty with fast-track projects is that there is the potential for costs to rise when the design isn't fully documented until toward midway in the construction process. An experienced CM should be able to shorten the construction period, particularly if he or she uses subcontractors and building components with which he is familiar, without jeopardizing the quality of the finished hotel.

Design/Build

The design/build format was developed to reduce the delivery time of a project and centralize the design and construction responsibility in a single entity. This approach is best used where the project has fairly simple design requirements and all parties recognize a range of appropriate solutions. Full responsibility is placed in the design/build team, generally headed by the construction side. In this variation, the design aspects usually are secondary to simplifying construction and reducing costs, which, while not unattractive to hotel owners, may not fully meet the needs and expectations of the hotel guest.

The design/build method has a useful application where the project can be defined very narrowly and the owner benefits from the guaranteed price and schedule. For example, a turnkey approach may be suitable to a guestroom renovation, where the owner approves a particular design direction and leaves it to the contractor to complete the renovation, replacing bathroom fixtures and finishes, adding new electronic locks, upgrading electrical and data lines, and purchasing and installing the guestroom FF&E, all for an established price.

Owners without in-house project management experience may hire a for-fee developer to represent them throughout the process. Or the developer may initiate the project, investing some funds but seeking joint-venture partners for the majority share, while managing the entire process. Whichever, the project manager performs the following tasks:

- Represents the owner at project meetings
- Applies for required approvals from city agencies
- Reviews applications for payment
- Prepares minutes of meetings
- Organizes planning information for the owner; and
- Guides and organizes the project team

Construction Schedule

Most contractors and construction management firms use the critical path method (CPM) to schedule a construction project. These, now, are computer programs (e.g., Primavera or Microsoft Project) that identify each separate task and its relationship to others in the project. The CPM requires that the contractor carefully organize the project ahead of time, making these precise decisions:

- Identify each discrete task or subtask.
- Determine its duration in days or weeks.
- Identify the task's dependence on other, earlier, steps.

The program calculates the relationship among all the tasks and prepares a graphical representation, highlighting milestones or major events, such as topping out of the structural frame or completion of the enclosure. The diagram clearly shows each step of the process, the amount of time each one requires, and the task's dependency upon other activities. The graphical organization of the staging and sequencing of tasks helps to identify the importance of long-lead items to the entire schedule. Integrated programs add other features; for example, if each task includes an estimate of the required labor, the program will generate work schedules. Or another module ties the owner's cash flow to the schedule.

As the project moves forward, the program monitors the real-time performance against the schedule and helps to organize and track the work flow. Its overriding advantage is to alert project managers to a potential problem or delay so that they can solve it before one becomes critical.

A key skill brought to the project by the right general contractor or construction manager is an ability to organize the site so that the work proceeds in an orderly manner. For example, work can be completed more efficiently when the several trades work separately from each other, rather than share space. Materials need to be delivered in sufficient quantities and stored, sometimes under cover, convenient to their final placement. Similarly, equipment needs to be available when it is needed and the site kept clean and free of debris and potential hazards. In the United States, the Occupational Safety and Health Act (OSHA) places very specific rules on the construction site, such as temporary railings on above-ground areas, which must be fully enforced and obeyed. Where the supervisors manage the project in all its details, work flow, efficiency, and, ultimately, the quality of the project all are enhanced.

Furniture, Fixtures, and Equipment

At the completion of the design phases of a hotel project, the architect and interior designer have detailed designs and specifications describing the fixed décor and the furniture, fixtures, and equipment (FF&E) for the hotel. Other FF&E items include carpets and rugs, artwork and accessories, window treatments, decorative lighting, decorative hardware, bathroom accessories, and planters. The hotel operator also specifies and purchases operating supplies and equipment (OS&E), such additional items as linens, china, glassware, uniforms, and banquet equipment. The specifications include all the information required to prepare the purchase orders, tracking forms, and installation schedules required to buy and coordinate FF&E and OS&E items. For each project these come from hundreds of sources, and frequently one vendor is dependent on another's product to complete his work. For example, before a lobby sofa can be delivered to a site, the purchasing agent orders fabric from one source, has it sent to another vendor for flame- and soil-treatment, if applicable, and shipped to the sofa manufacturer to be upholstered. Each step must be completed on schedule for the manufacturer to meet the timetable for the project. The architect, interior designer, purchasing company, or in-house staff may send the specifications to various manufacturers for competitive pricing or, alternatively, may send the packages directly to vendors with whom they already have a good relationship.

The construction manager or FF&E installer must develop a systematic approach to assure the developer and operator that the property will be complete and ready for occupancy before the scheduled soft opening. Once vendors have been selected, the management team uses purchase orders, tracking forms, delivery schedules, and punch-lists to document the process. The number of FF&E purchase orders can be in the thousands for a large-scale hotel project. For example, one style of sofa might be ordered in several sizes and with a variety of fabrics and trims, each one intended for a different location. Properly documenting all of these details, if they are coordinated at the specification and purchase order stage, not only sets up a smooth installation but also helps protect the owner and consultants from manufacturing and delivery mistakes. Table 19.6 identifies the type of detail required to adequately purchase and track FF&E items.

The purchasing company typically develops a tracking system to catalogue and chart all items that have been purchased and create a

Table 19.6 Purchase order information

- ❑ Project name and location
- ❑ Purchase order number, coded for easy reference such as 'f' for fabric, 's' for sofa, etc., and number for each different item
- ❑ Order date
- ❑ Delivery date required
- ❑ Product manufacturer's name, address, telephone, and contact person
- ❑ Item number, description, and quantity
- ❑ Unit price, extended price, and total price (including applicable taxes and shipping)
- ❑ Deposit required and balance due after receipt and/or installation
- ❑ Special requirements (e.g. finish sample, dye-lot cutting, shop drawings, or mock-up required for approval; field measurements required prior to manufacturing)
- ❑ "Ship to" address (vendor to vendor, vendor to storage warehouse, vendor to hotel site)
- ❑ Side-mark (indicate on the outside of the shipping package the final destination of the item, such as lobby, guestroom type, etc.)
- ❑ Specification (attach full spec, often with catalog photo or physical sample of fabric or wood finish)

simple form for follow-up. The architect, interior designer, or in-house personnel make frequent calls to check whether a particular product is on schedule. The tracking forms help ensure that all items are delivered on schedule—or identify potential shipment problems in a time frame that allows the team to react. New computerized systems make this information readily available on the internet to members of the team, allowing them to find almost instantly the status on any particular item.

The FF&E installation is part of the overall project schedule, and included in the CPM matrix. Typically, the FF&E is phased to follow construction completion, but as the opening date approaches contractors, delivery people, and installation crews often are working in the same areas—and vying for use of the loading dock, delivery entrance, and freight elevators—making schedule coordination critical. Architects and interior designers prepare FF&E plans and

Table 19.7 Order for FF&E installation

Contractor-installed items
- ❑ Back-of-house equipment
- ❑ Decorative light fixtures (chandeliers and wall sconces)
- ❑ Special hardware
- ❑ Bathroom accessories
- ❑ Floor coverings
- ❑ Window treatments

Guestroom items
- ❑ Wall-mounted items (headboards, framed mirrors)
- ❑ Large furnishings
- ❑ Small furnishings
- ❑ Art and accessories
- ❑ Public-space items (lobby, restaurants and bars, meeting rooms, corridors)
- ❑ Large furnishings
- ❑ Small furnishings
- ❑ Art and accessories (rugs, throw pillows, interior planting)

elevations, coded to the specifications and purchase orders, indicating the precise location for each specific item.

Depending on the schedule, furniture and other items may be delivered directly at the site or arrive, first, at an intermediate warehouse facility where they are received, inspected, and stored until needed. When the FF&E arrives directly at the site, it is important for the designer or another person to inspect the delivery for damage and to match the items to the tracking forms. Often, the hotel ballroom is the last space to be completed, so that it can be used as a staging area for temporary storage of other items during the FF&E installation phase. As the construction project nears completion, contractors, furniture installers, pre-opening staff, inspectors, and others all need access to the same spaces. Therefore, it is important that the delivery and installation proceed in an orderly way, as identified in Table 19.7.

After the FF&E are installed, the team prepares a punch-list, identifying missing or damaged items that need to be replaced or repaired. Often, there hasn't been time to complete a separate punch-list of deficiencies in each room before the furniture is placed, so the same list identifies paint and electrical items, for instance, which need correcting. Only after all items have been properly installed, and operate as designed, should the construction manager or designer authorize final payment.

Future and Fantasy Development

The twenty-first century began with aggressive expansion of hotel development into hundreds of new markets worldwide. This rapid growth has demonstrated that the commonplace is no longer acceptable: new hotels in urban and luxury resort areas need to be dramatic, timeless, and unique, while more humble properties still need to reflect high style and current technological advances to meet the ever-higher expectations of travelers. Massive mixed-use projects that combine hotels with residential, office, retail, and entertainment continue to be a factor in major city-center development, but innovative approaches to urban hotel design are rapidly gaining favor and visionary architects are exploring new ways to create exciting, sustainable leisure and business hotel concepts that may transform the industry. This chapter describes some of the major trends and fantastic ideas for hotels of the future.

Innovative Trends

The earlier sections of this book have detailed the constant innovation taking place throughout the hotel and resort industries. Developers and operators are marketing to increasingly narrow segments, finding success in fine-tuning their design and services to the needs of particular guests in each market they serve. Owners are identifying new sites for development, long overlooked by traditional builders. And designers are imagining incredible resorts that float in the air, hug the bottom of the sea, or orbit the earth.

The program mix at many of the newer hotels has gone through a substantial change as well. Of course, most hotels focus on the lodging component but many place an equal emphasis on the public assembly facilities or, in Asia, on the extensive and celebrated food and beverage outlets. Spa facilities, once a special amenity for destination resorts, are now a de facto requirement for any hotel with four stars or more. Many properties aim to appeal to multiple affluent markets concurrently by incorporating ever more elaborate concierge or club levels and in-hotel residences with their own dedicated lounges and services. The "one size fits all" program for a given hotel brand is no longer viable, particularly in new and emerging markets that have distinct customs and expectations regarding privacy, social activity, and alcohol use.

Here are the dominant hotel development and design trends that are likely to become more prevalent in the next decades.

Cliffhanger Resort,
Grand Canyon, Arizona
Dangling the building over the edge of the canyon's West Rim allows guests to enjoy a fantastic sense of engagement with the surrounding landscape while at the same time having minimal environmental impact on the delicate site. HKS Architects designed the building system to be fully modular and transportable so that the 27 stacked hotel rooms and their supporting functions can be re-installed in other dramatic locations worldwide.

Increased Emphasis on Technology

Far from a panacea, technology will need to be applied when and where it is most appropriate. Guests will still need and desire human interaction when technological solutions don't meet their needs or when they crave contact with a real person after hours of dehumanizing travel. Hotels that have tried to move toward kiosk-only check-in have found that having some kind of personal service by well-trained employees is important to guest satisfaction.

Technological advances will continue to influence the design of guestrooms. Just as flat-screen televisions have altered FF&E selection, newer consumer electronics such as tablet computers may reduce the need for dedicated workspace in many hotels. Universal wireless access allows guests to work on multiple devices anywhere in the property, so guests are using public spaces as communal offices where they can perform their jobs alone but in company. E-readers and tablets take a bit more room on the bedside table than a classic paperback, space that will be freed up by the elimination of in-room telephones. Looking further out, digital window treatments may obviate the need for draperies and will offer the guest the chance to customize the room's ambient light. Guestroom walls can incorporate digital screens so that entertainment can be streamed from the guest's own devices, and the hotel can provide in-room controls and information without having to mount thermostats or print brochures. Smartphones and other devices will serve as room keys and will streamline the check-in and check-out process. And real-time displays of how much energy and water are being used by guests will encourage participation in sustainable initiatives.

New construction techniques, materials, and systems will speed the development process and greatly reduce hotel carbon footprints.

Philips Ambient Window Prototype
This innovative approach to controlling daylight and guestroom ambience uses transparent LCD technology to give guests functional and artistic control over the window treatment in their rooms. Simple hand gestures spread a selection of animated patterns across the window to block some or all of the outdoor view, and a variety of background colors and gradient patterns can be chosen to filter incoming daylight.

This will include further advances in HVAC and lighting controls, water reduction and reuse systems, naturally-occurring power and heat sources, and accelerated composting. Centralized construction of building components or entire rooms will continue to develop, encouraging the creation of transportable hotels that can follow hotel demand while minimizing environmental impact on the site.

Experience Customization

While technological tools offer ways for guests to customize their guestroom entertainment and ambience, there will still be a major role for personalization with a human touch. Customer relationship management (CRM) systems will continue to grow in sophistication such that the operator will have ever more detailed information about guest preferences and can offer travelers precisely the mix of services, amenities, and care that they want or have grown accustomed to during previous stays. As hotels that have adopted customized bedding programs have found, offering multiple choices of pillow means more storage space and a bit more time in the guestroom for housekeeping staff, requiring design solutions that speed the cleaning of other parts of the room to balance the extra time being spent on customization. These "trickle-down" effects of experience customization programs will need to be carefully considered by planners and designers during design development.

Non-brands

The strength of well-known lodging brands will continue to drive much of the world's hotel development. But the rise of dozens of new hotel brands in recent years has led to a very crowded field in almost all segments. A natural response to this heavy emphasis on branding is the "non-brand," groups of affiliated hotels that downplay or hide altogether their connection with one another or with a parent company. The Autograph Collection is a group of independent hotels with unique design, cultural, or historic value that operate as a subset of the Marriott Corporation but celebrate their individualism and distinct identities through their own websites and marketing initiatives. Hyatt is the guiding light behind the 88-room boutique Hotel Victor in Miami, but this corporate provenance is kept largely in the background. "Stealth" brands like the Victor will allow hotel companies to test radically new ideas and the viability of small, discerning markets without diluting the existing brand image.

Increased Sustainability

"Green" as a distinguishing feature of some hotels will disappear: all new projects will be expected to incorporate sustainable technologies and practices as a matter of course. The challenge for hotel designers will be to make green initiatives relatively transparent to the guest, particularly in the North American market, which has been slow to accept key-controlled guestroom power and other sustainable strategies that are common elsewhere in the world.

Increased Security

Unfortunately, in recent years some hotels have become targets for terrorist activity. Guests routinely rate security as a growing concern when they travel, particularly in large urban markets and in locations

Envision Green Hotel, Miami, Florida
Adopting a dramatic and unorthodox shape, the Envision Green Hotel mimics a living organism by literally breathing: atmospheric conversion systems would allow air to flow to the building's interior without mechanical intervention. Building energy would be supplied by the hotel's skin of photovoltaic sheathing supplemented by massive wind turbines, while indoor vertical gardens would create mini-microclimates to filter the air and act as added insulation.

Hospitality Design in the Near Future: Radically Practical Innovations

Howard J. Wolff
Senior Vice President
WATG
Honolulu, Hawaii

The hospitality design world has not been known for embracing dramatic structural changes. But the future could be different. Take a look at the winners and finalists of the Radical Innovation in Hospitality Awards, an international design competition co-sponsored by the John Hardy Group and *Hospitality Design* magazine.

Challenge 1: How to Tame Fluctuating Hotel Occupancies and Operating Inefficiencies

Every night, more than one third of the hotel rooms around the world are empty. But a week later, at any given property, hoteliers may have to turn guests away.

One design solution is a hotel that can expand and contract in sync with its occupancy, so that only occupied spaces would need to be heated, cooled, and lit. This could spawn a new generation of responsive architectural spaces that react to the changing needs of their users, owners, and operators.

Addressing the issue of fluctuating occupancies at the scale of a destination, a city, or an entire region, several Radical Innovation in Hospitality Award finalists have proposed solutions that revolve around eco-friendly portable nomadic structures that could be erected during times of high demand—whether it's for an event or a season—and then taken down and moved to the next destination.

One such concept, called "Bucket List Lodging," is envisioned specifically as a modular kit of parts that could fit into an aircraft's cargo hold or a ship container.

Challenge 2: How to Create Authentic Urban Guest Experiences While Conserving Resources

Tomorrow's urban travelers—and even today's, for that matter—will spend the majority of their time away from the hotel, exploring the attractions of the city.

Architects and designers from WATG created an award-winning concept for a network of hotels called "elmerse" that would use the surrounding city as its amenities, allowing each location to offer an array of guest experiences without having to duplicate what is already available in the community.

The reduction in public space within the hotels enables the elmerse network to inhabit existing buildings in virtually any community and grow almost anywhere. If 30 guestrooms aren't enough for one location, the hotel can expand to another floor, or to a building down the street. To keep each location as efficient and economical as possible, housekeeping and maintenance are proportionally sized to match the number of guestrooms.

Think of this as the first social-networking hotel. Using a guest profile, the hotel can help travelers find local businesses, restaurants, and clubs to fit their interests and needs; create opportunities to network with other guests; and provide feedback on places they've visited and activities they've experienced.

Hoteliers have not only taken notice but have also been implementing many of these concepts. The winner of the Radical Innovation Award two years after elmerse was an actual operating luxury hotel: the Pixel Hotel serves the now-thriving city of Linz, Austria.

Challenge 3: How to Create Shelter in a Fiscally and Environmentally Sustainable Manner

The organic, geometric-shaped Prisms of the award-winning Mosaic PATHWAY (Portable Adaptable Temporary Hotel With Alternative You-ses) system are collapsible for ease in transportation, are pre-fitted with built-in fixtures and furnishings, and come with self-contained energy, plumbing, and lighting systems and self-leveling foundations.

The individually configured modular Prisms can be outfitted as needed as spas, salons, or guestrooms. Grouped together, Mosaic Prisms are attached organically to Mosaic Hubs that comprise and contain lobbies, restaurants, bars, lounges, and other amenities. The pop-up concept allows for accommodations at existing properties to capture additional peak-season business. Mosaic Hubs and Prisms accommodate adventure travelers and "voluntourists" and can remain in place as housing for local communities.

This concept incorporates many eco-friendly technologies, including: a methane digester; geothermal heating and cooling; hydroponic greenhouses; rainwater cisterns; wind and solar power; and a reverse osmosis plant for fresh-water generation.

The real-world challenges facing hotels—fluctuating occupancies, operating efficiencies, environmental sustainability—require innovative thinking and technology that is at-hand today.

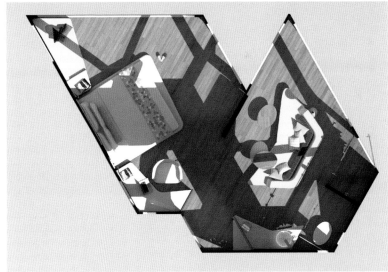

Mosaic PATHWAY (Portable Adaptable Temporary Hotel With Alternative "You-ses")

Mosaic is a concept developed by architects WATG to address demand variation in the hospitality industry by providing a mechanism to allow a hotel to expand or contract its room count as circumstances dictate. The Mosaic modular system is comprised of organic, interlocking prisms constructed from a highly durable polymer which retracts and folds to a rectilinear shape, making the units easily stackable and able to be packed tightly for easy shipment around the world. "Pop-up" hospitality like Mosaic is perfectly suited to supply additional accommodations that might be needed through seasonal demand peaks, cultural festivals, major sporting events, or even to provide shelter and facilities for disaster relief in times of crisis.

with a history of unrest. Design interventions to control access to entrances, guestroom areas, and key back-of-house functions are common now but will need to be even more stringent. Architects and interior designers will have great challenges devising ways to incorporate scanning and explosive-detection systems into hotel entrances and parking areas, and will need to consider security facilities and staff support in a much broader range of spaces in the hotel than has been the norm.

Visions of the Future

Hotels continue to capture the imagination of architects and visionaries worldwide. Here are just a few of the innovations being proposed for the coming decades.

Songjiang Hotel, Shanghai, China
Built into the steep stone banks of a 328 ft (100 m) deep water-filled quarry, the 400-room resort designed by Atkins Design Studio combines environmentally sensitive planning with unique climbing and water sport amenities. The guestroom floors wrap around a naturally lit internal atrium, built against the rock face and draped with lush vegetation and waterfalls. In addition to the resort's green roofs and geothermal energy extraction, the quarry site provides natural heat control and shelter from wind and weather.

Poseidon Undersea Resort, Fiji

Forty feet (12 m) below the surface of a private Fijian lagoon will be twenty-four 550 sq ft (51 sq m) guestroom pods, each with over 70 percent of its surface made of plexiglass for unobscured underwater viewing. The pods will be flanked by underwater public spaces, all connected to a pressurized central spine that allows comfortable guest access without the need for dive gear or even a swimsuit. Much larger beach villas along the lagoon's edge will supplement the undersea guestroom pods and allow guests to vary their experience during the weeklong stay at the resort.

Aircruise Luxury Airship

The pioneering design and innovation company Seymourpowell has introduced a visionary transportation concept with its 2,852 ft (265 m) solar- and hydrogen-powered vertical airship, designed to carry travelers in style and luxury. Promoting a view of travel where "slow is the new fast," Aircruise will appeal to travelers looking for a more reflective journey where abundance of time and space define the luxury experience. Featuring only 10 units, Aircruise would offer guests magnificent cloud-top views without the intrusive effects of engine noise.

New Orleans Arcology Habitat (NOAH), Louisiana
In response to the recurring severe weather patterns that
affect the Gulf Coast and New Orleans in particular, Schopfer
Associates has designed NOAH, a 30 million sq ft (2.79 million
sq m) urban "ark" that serves as a self-contained floating
habitat for 40,000 people. NOAH would contain three hotels,
20,000 residential units, 1,500 time-share units, casinos, retail,
office and cultural facilities, and public amenities like schools,
health clinics, and administrative offices, making the structure
socially self-sufficient. Sustainable features will include secured
wind turbines, freshwater recovery and storage systems, a
passive glazing system, sky garden heating/cooling vents,
graywater treatment, and solar arrays and river-based water
turbines for power generation.

Research by the British government has shown that space architecture is likely to be a fast-growing industry by 2030. Space tourism is a primary driver of this activity, with significant investments by companies like Richard Branson's Virgin Galactic, the Sasakawa International Center for Space Architecture (SICSA), and Barcelona-based Galactic Suite forging ahead developing detailed concepts for space hotels and other space tourism projects.

Forward-looking projects like these chart an exciting course for an unbridled industry so free that it advances in a multitude of dynamic directions at once.

Virgin Galactic Spaceport, New Mexico
Virgin's SpaceShipTwo, the world's first commercial spaceline, will offer daily space tourism flights from the proposed Virgin Galactic Spaceport in New Mexico. Designed by Foster and Partners, the spaceport will include a 10,000 ft (3,050 m) runway. Once in space, Virgin Galactic guests will use a moon-orbiting hotel as a base for forays in a two-man spaceship to within a few hundred feet of the lunar surface.

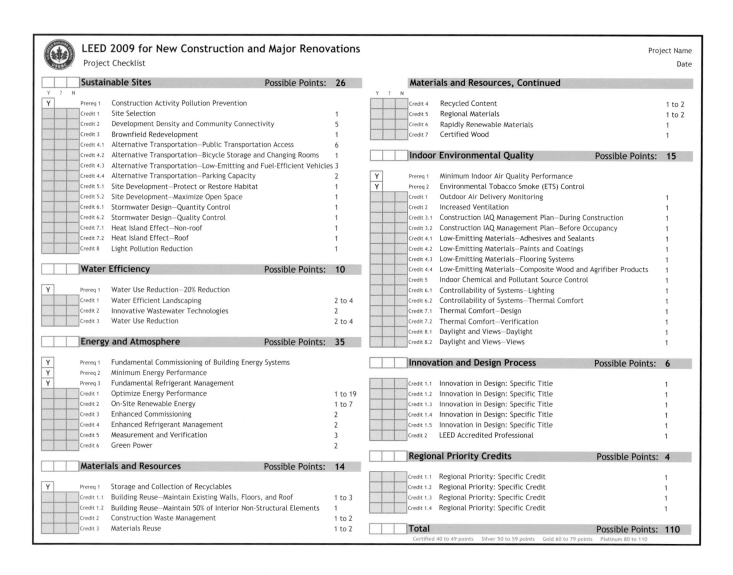

LEED 2009 for New Construction and Major Renovations

Project Checklist

Project Name

Date

Sustainable Sites — Possible Points: 26

Y	?	N			
Y			Prereq 1	Construction Activity Pollution Prevention	
			Credit 1	Site Selection	1
			Credit 2	Development Density and Community Connectivity	5
			Credit 3	Brownfield Redevelopment	1
			Credit 4.1	Alternative Transportation—Public Transportation Access	6
			Credit 4.2	Alternative Transportation—Bicycle Storage and Changing Rooms	1
			Credit 4.3	Alternative Transportation—Low-Emitting and Fuel-Efficient Vehicles	3
			Credit 4.4	Alternative Transportation—Parking Capacity	2
			Credit 5.1	Site Development—Protect or Restore Habitat	1
			Credit 5.2	Site Development—Maximize Open Space	1
			Credit 6.1	Stormwater Design—Quantity Control	1
			Credit 6.2	Stormwater Design—Quality Control	1
			Credit 7.1	Heat Island Effect—Non-roof	1
			Credit 7.2	Heat Island Effect—Roof	1
			Credit 8	Light Pollution Reduction	1

Water Efficiency — Possible Points: 10

Y	?	N			
Y			Prereq 1	Water Use Reduction—20% Reduction	
			Credit 1	Water Efficient Landscaping	2 to 4
			Credit 2	Innovative Wastewater Technologies	2
			Credit 3	Water Use Reduction	2 to 4

Energy and Atmosphere — Possible Points: 35

Y	?	N			
Y			Prereq 1	Fundamental Commissioning of Building Energy Systems	
Y			Prereq 2	Minimum Energy Performance	
Y			Prereq 3	Fundamental Refrigerant Management	
			Credit 1	Optimize Energy Performance	1 to 19
			Credit 2	On-Site Renewable Energy	1 to 7
			Credit 3	Enhanced Commissioning	2
			Credit 4	Enhanced Refrigerant Management	2
			Credit 5	Measurement and Verification	3
			Credit 6	Green Power	2

Materials and Resources — Possible Points: 14

Y	?	N			
Y			Prereq 1	Storage and Collection of Recyclables	
			Credit 1.1	Building Reuse—Maintain Existing Walls, Floors, and Roof	1 to 3
			Credit 1.2	Building Reuse—Maintain 50% of Interior Non-Structural Elements	1
			Credit 2	Construction Waste Management	1 to 2
			Credit 3	Materials Reuse	1 to 2

Materials and Resources, Continued

Y	?	N			
			Credit 4	Recycled Content	1 to 2
			Credit 5	Regional Materials	1 to 2
			Credit 6	Rapidly Renewable Materials	1
			Credit 7	Certified Wood	1

Indoor Environmental Quality — Possible Points: 15

Y	?	N			
Y			Prereq 1	Minimum Indoor Air Quality Performance	
Y			Prereq 2	Environmental Tobacco Smoke (ETS) Control	
			Credit 1	Outdoor Air Delivery Monitoring	1
			Credit 2	Increased Ventilation	1
			Credit 3.1	Construction IAQ Management Plan—During Construction	1
			Credit 3.2	Construction IAQ Management Plan—Before Occupancy	1
			Credit 4.1	Low-Emitting Materials—Adhesives and Sealants	1
			Credit 4.2	Low-Emitting Materials—Paints and Coatings	1
			Credit 4.3	Low-Emitting Materials—Flooring Systems	1
			Credit 4.4	Low-Emitting Materials—Composite Wood and Agrifiber Products	1
			Credit 5	Indoor Chemical and Pollutant Source Control	1
			Credit 6.1	Controllability of Systems—Lighting	1
			Credit 6.2	Controllability of Systems—Thermal Comfort	1
			Credit 7.1	Thermal Comfort—Design	1
			Credit 7.2	Thermal Comfort—Verification	1
			Credit 8.1	Daylight and Views—Daylight	1
			Credit 8.2	Daylight and Views—Views	1

Innovation and Design Process — Possible Points: 6

Y	?	N			
			Credit 1.1	Innovation in Design: Specific Title	1
			Credit 1.2	Innovation in Design: Specific Title	1
			Credit 1.3	Innovation in Design: Specific Title	1
			Credit 1.4	Innovation in Design: Specific Title	1
			Credit 1.5	Innovation in Design: Specific Title	1
			Credit 2	LEED Accredited Professional	1

Regional Priority Credits — Possible Points: 4

Y	?	N			
			Credit 1.1	Regional Priority: Specific Credit	1
			Credit 1.2	Regional Priority: Specific Credit	1
			Credit 1.3	Regional Priority: Specific Credit	1
			Credit 1.4	Regional Priority: Specific Credit	1

Total — Possible Points: 110

Certified 40 to 49 points   Silver 50 to 59 points   Gold 60 to 79 points   Platinum 80 to 110

International Hotel and Travel Organizations

AH&LA	American Hotel & Lodging Association Washington, DC, USA www.ahla.com		**GBTA**	Global Business Travel Association Alexandria, VA, USA www.gbta.org
ARDA	American Resort Development Association Washington, DC, USA www.arda.org		**GHA**	Green Hotels Association Houston, TX, USA www.greenhotels.com
ASTA	American Society of Travel Agents Alexandria, VA, USA www.astanet.com/		**HAC**	Hotel Association of Canada Ottawa, ON, Canada www.hotelassociation.ca
ATME	Association of Travel Marketing Executives Washington, DC, USA www.atme.org		**HCIMA**	Hotel & Catering International Management Association London, UK www.instituteofhospitality.org
BEUC	Bureau Européen des Unions de Consommateurs Brussels, Belgium beuc.org/index_e.htm		**HHA**	Historic Hotels of America—National Trust for Historic Preservation Washington, DC, USA www.historichotels.org
BHA	British Hospitality Association London, UK www.bha.org.uk/		**HOTREC**	Hotels, Restaurants & Cafés in Europe Brussels, Belgium www.hotelstars.eu
CE	Council of Europe Strasbourg, France www.coe.fr		**HSMAI**	Hotel Sales and Marketing Association International McLean, VA, USA www.hsmai.org
CHTA	Caribbean Hotel and Tourism Association Barbados www.caribbeanhotelassociation.com		**IATA**	International Air Transport Association Geneva, Switzerland www.iata.org
CTO	Caribbean Tourist Organisation Barbados www.onecaribbean.org		**ICCA**	International Congress & Conventions Association Amsterdam, The Netherlands www.iccaworld.com
EHMA	European Hotel Managers Association Ahrensburg, Germany www.ehma.com		**IH**	Institute of Hospitality Surrey, UK www.instituteofhospitality.org
EHMA	European Hotel Managers Association Rome, Italy www.ehma.com		**IH&RA**	Independent Hotel and Restaurant Association Lausanne, Switzerland www.ih-ra.com
ETC	European Travel Commission Brussels, Belgium www.etc-corporate.org		**IHEI**	International Hotels Environment Initiative London, UK www.ihei.org
FTO	Federation of Tour Operators London, UK www.fto.co.uk		**IHRA**	International Hotel & Restaurant Association Paris, France www.ih-ra.com

LHW   Leading Hotels of the World
New York, NY, USA
www.lhw.com

PATA   Pacific Asia Travel Association
Bangkok, Thailand
www.pata.org

SITE   Society of Incentive & Travel Executives
Chicago, IL, USA
www.siteglobal.com

SLH   Small Luxury Hotels of the World
London, UK
www.slh.com

TIA   U.S. Travel Association
Washington, DC, USA
www.ustravel.org

TIES   The International Ecotourism Society
Washington, DC, USA
www.ecotourism.org

TTRA   Travel and Tourism Research Association
Lake Orion, MI, USA
www.ttra.com

UNWTO   World Tourism Organisation
Madrid, Spain
www.unwto.org

WATA   World Association of Travel Agencies
Geneva, Switzerland
www.wata.net

WTTC   World Travel and Tourism Council
London, UK
www.wttc.org

Development Budget
(typical 500-room hotel)

Typical budget summary for a 500-room mid-rate hotel

Summary budget	Amount ($)	Percent of total	Amount per room
Hard costs			
Land	0	varies*	0
Hard Construction & Sitework	$68,400,000	60.0%	$136,800
Furniture, Fixtures, and Equipment (FF&E)**	$20,520,000	18.0%	$41,040
Soft costs			
Architecture & Engineering Fee	$4,560,000	4.0%	$9,120
Design Review Fee	$2,280,000	2.0%	$4,560
Project Management Fee	$1,140,000	1.0%	$2,280
Development Fee	$3,420,000	3.0%	$6,840
Pre-opening and Operating Inventory	$4,560,000	4.0%	$9,120
Capitalized Interest and Cost of Issuance	$3,420,000	3.0%	$6,840
Contingency	$5,700,000	5.0%	$11,400
Total	**$114,000,000**	**100.0%**	**$228,000**

* Land costs vary dramatically (5 to 15% of total project cost) depending on location (country, urban vs. rural) and new-build vs. renovation.

** FF&E includes interior design furniture and fixtures; kitchen, laundry, and back-of-house equipment; purchasing agent's fee; and special systems.
Operating supplies are included in the Pre-opening figure.

Hotel Cost Indices

Hotel classification	Cost index	Total cost (500 rooms)	Cost/room
Luxury	1.33	$151,620,000	$303,240
Upscale	1.20	$136,800,000	$273,600
Mid-rate	1.00	$114,000,000	$228,000
Economy	0.80	$91,200,000	$182,400

Dollar estimates approximate and subject to location.
Courtesy of Frank F. Homiah, Global Development Consultants.

Ten-year Forecast of Net Operating Income

Calendar year	2013		2014		2015		2016	
Number of keys	270		270		270		270	
Number of occupied roomnights	64,058		67,014		68,985		71,150	
Occupancy	65%		68%		70%		72%	
Average daily rate (ADR)	$135.50		$143.57		$146.44		$149.37	
Revenue per available room (RevPAR)	$88.08		$97.63		$102.51		$107.55	
	$000	%	$000	%	$000	%	$000	%
Revenue								
Rooms	$8,680	64.5%	$9,621	66.0%	$10,102	66.0%	$10,628	66.0%
Food and beverage	$3,903	29.0%	$4,082	28.0%	$4,286	28.0%	$4,509	28.0%
Other operated departments	$673	5.0%	$656	4.5%	$689	4.5%	$725	4.5%
Rentals and other income	$202	1.5%	$219	1.5%	$230	1.5%	$242	1.5%
Total revenue	$13,457	100.0%	$14,578	100.0%	$15,306	100.0%	$16,103	100.0%
Departmental expenses								
Rooms	$2,482	28.6%	$2,646	27.5%	$2,627	26.0%	$2,763	26.0%
Food and beverage	$3,040	77.9%	$3,061	75.0%	$3,214	75.0%	$3,382	75.0%
Other operated departments	$486	72.3%	$459	70.0%	$468	68.0%	$493	68.0%
Rentals	$20	10.0%	$22	10.0%	$23	10.0%	$24	10.0%
Total departmental expenses	$6,009	44.7%	$6,166	42.3%	$6,309	41.2%	$6,638	41.2%
Undistributed operating expenses								
Administrative and general	$1,278	9.5%	$1,385	9.5%	$1,378	9.0%	$1,449	9.0%
Sales and marketing	$1,077	8.0%	$1,254	8.6%	$1,148	7.5%	$1,127	7.0%
Property operations and maintenance	$659	4.9%	$714	4.9%	$689	4.5%	$725	4.5%
Utilities	$579	4.3%	$596	4.1%	$614	4.0%	$632	3.9%
Total undistributed expenses	$3,593	26.7%	$3,949	27.1%	$3,828	25.0%	$3,933	24.4%
Gross operating profit	$3,855	28.6%	$4,462	30.6%	$5,169	33.8%	$5,532	34.4%
Management fees	$404	3.0%	$437	3.0%	$459	3.0%	$483	3.0%
Income before fixed charges	$3,451	25.6%	$4,025	27.6%	$4,710	30.8%	$5,049	31.4%
Fixed charges								
Property and other taxes	$484	3.6%	$525	3.6%	$551	3.6%	$580	3.6%
Reserve for replacement	$269	2.0%	$437	3.0%	$459	3.0%	$644	4.0%
Insurance	$161	1.2%	$146	1.0%	$153	1.0%	$161	1.0%
Total fixed charges	$915	6.8%	$1,108	7.6%	$1,163	7.6%	$1,385	8.6%
Net operating income	$2,536	18.8%	$2,917	20.0%	$3,546	23.2%	$3,664	22.8%
NOI per key	$9,394		$10,804		$13,135		$13,570	

	2017		2018		2019		2020		2021		2022	
	270		270		270		270		270		270	
	72,927		72,927		70,956		73,127		72,927		72,927	
	74%		74%		72%		74%		74%		74%	
	$152.36		$155.40		$158.51		$161.68		$164.92		$168.22	
	$112.74		$115.00		$114.13		$119.65		$122.04		$124.48	
	$000	%	$000	%	$000	%	$000	%	$000	%	$000	%
	$11,111	66.0%	$11,333	66.0%	$11,247	66.0%	$11,823	66.0%	$12,027	66.0%	$12,267	66.0%
	$4,714	28.0%	$4,808	28.0%	$4,772	28.0%	$5,016	28.0%	$5,102	28.0%	$5,204	28.0%
	$758	4.5%	$773	4.5%	$767	4.5%	$806	4.5%	$820	4.5%	$836	4.5%
	$253	1.5%	$258	1.5%	$256	1.5%	$269	1.5%	$273	1.5%	$279	1.5%
	$16,835	100.0%	$17,172	100.0%	$17,042	100.0%	$17,914	100.0%	$18,223	100.0%	$18,587	100.0%
	$2,889	26.0%	$2,947	26.0%	$2,924	26.0%	$3,074	26.0%	$3,127	26.0%	$3,190	26.0%
	$3,535	75.0%	$3,606	75.0%	$3,579	75.0%	$3,762	75.0%	$3,827	75.0%	$3,903	75.0%
	$515	68.0%	$525	68.0%	$521	68.0%	$548	68.0%	$558	68.0%	$569	68.0%
	$25	10.0%	$26	10.0%	$26	10.0%	$27	10.0%	$27	10.0%	$28	10.0%
	$6,939	41.2%	$7,078	41.2%	$7,025	41.2%	$7,384	41.2%	$7,511	41.2%	$7,662	41.2%
	$1,515	9.0%	$1,545	9.0%	$1,534	9.0%	$1,612	9.0%	$1,640	9.0%	$1,673	9.0%
	$1,178	7.0%	$1,202	7.0%	$1,193	7.0%	$1,254	7.0%	$1,276	7.0%	$1,301	7.0%
	$758	4.5%	$773	4.5%	$2,000	11.7%	$806	4.5%	$820	4.5%	$836	4.5%
	$651	3.9%	$671	3.9%	$691	4.1%	$712	4.0%	$733	4.0%	$755	4.1%
	$4,102	24.4%	$4,191	24.4%	$5,418	31.8%	$4,384	24.5%	$4,469	24.5%	$4,565	24.6%
	$5,793	34.4%	$5,902	34.4%	$4,599	27.0%	$6,146	34.3%	$6,243	34.3%	$6,360	34.2%
	$505	3.0%	$515	3.0%	$511	3.0%	$537	3.0%	$547	3.0%	$558	3.0%
	$5,288	31.4%	$5,387	31.4%	$4,088	24.0%	$5,608	31.3%	$5,696	31.3%	$5,802	31.2%
	$606	3.6%	$618	3.6%	$613	3.6%	$645	3.6%	$656	3.6%	$669	3.6%
	$758	4.5%	$859	5.0%	$852	5.0%	$896	5.0%	$911	5.0%	$929	5.0%
	$168	1.0%	$172	1.0%	$170	1.0%	$179	1.0%	$182	1.0%	$186	1.0%
	$1,532	9.1%	$1,648	9.6%	$1,636	9.6%	$1,720	9.6%	$1,749	9.6%	$1,784	9.6%
	$3,756	22.3%	$3,739	21.8%	$2,452	14.4%	$3,889	21.7%	$3,947	21.7%	$4,018	21.6%
	$13,911		$13,848		$9,082		$14,403		$14,617		$14,882	

Coordination Matrix

To avoid duplications or omissions in the budget, responsibility should be assigned on the design, construction, purchasing, and installation costs of all structures, equipment, and furnishings by using the following, or an equivalent system, often referred to as the budget "differentiation document."

Basic Budget Categories

C	Building construction and sitework
FD	Fixed décor, millwork, and special finishes
FFE	Furniture, fixtures, and equipment
OP	Operating supplies, inventories, and consumables
SS	Special hotel systems

Design Team Members and Consultants

A	Architect
AC	Acoustical consultant
AV	Audiovisual consultant
CE	Construction estimator or cost consultant
CIV	Civil engineer
EE	Electrical engineer
EV	Elevator consultant
F	Fire-protection consultant
G	Graphics designer
GC	General contractor
I	Interior designer
IN	Installation contractor for FF&E items
K	Kitchen, bar, and food-service consultant
L	Laundry consultant
LS	Landscape architect
LT	Lighting consultant
MC	Millwork contractor
ME	Mechanical engineer
O	Operator's purchasing department
O*	Subject leasing option
PA	Purchasing agent for FF&E items
S	Systems consultant
ST	Structural engineer
V	Vendor

	Areas of responsibility	Budget category	Estimated by	Designed by	Contract documents by	Purchased by	Installed by
1	General construction	C	CE	A/ST/AC/F	A/ST	GC	GC
2	**Furniture (seating, casepieces, etc.)**						
	a. Movable	FFE	I	I	I	PA	PA/IN
	b. Fixed/millwork	FD	I	I	I	GC/MC	GC/MC
3	**Artwork and artifacts**	FFE	I	I	I	PA	PA/IN
4	**Flooring**						
	a. Carpeting and pad	FFE	I	I	I	PA	PA/IN
	b. Marble, decorative tile, and wood	FD	I	I	I	GC	GC
	c. Concrete, resilient tile, ceramic tile (bathrooms), quarry tile (kitchens and pantries, etc.)	C	CE	I/A	A	GC	GC
5	**Wall-covering**						
	a. Vinyl in guestrooms	C	CE	I	A	GC	GC
	b. Vinyl in public areas	FD	I	I	I	PA	GC
	c. Paneling/marble/other decorative finish	FD	I	I	I	GC/MC	GC/MC
	d. Masonry and plaster, drywall, and paint or ceramic tile in bathrooms, kitchens, and pantries	C	CE	I	A/I	GC	GC
6	**Ceiling finish**						
	a. Paint or acoustic tile	C	CE	I/A	A	GC	GC
	b. Coffered or other decorative treatments	FD	I	I/A	I/A	GC/MC	GC/MC
7	**Doors (finishes, hardware, door frames, etc.)**	C	CE	I/A	A	GC	GC
8	**Moveable partitions (ballrooms and meeting rooms)**	C	CE	I/A	A	GC	GC
9	**Lighting**						
	a. Plug-in decorative fixtures	FFE	I	I	I	PA	PA/IN
	b. Fixed decorative fixtures	FFE	I	I/LT	I/A/EE	PA	PA/IN
	c. General lighting	C	CE	I/A/EE	A/EE	GC	GC
	d. Conduit, wiring, dimming systems	C	CE	A/EE	A/EE	GC	GC
10	**Mechanical, electrical, life-safety, and security systems (sprinklers, standpipes, fire hoses, smoke detectors, alarms, fire extinguishers, etc.)**	C	CE	A/ME/EE/F	A/ME/EE	GC	GC
11	**Elevators and escalators**						
	a. Equipment	C	CE	A/EV	A/EV/EE	GC	GC
	b. Cab interiors, doors, and frames	C	CE	I/A	A	GC	GC
12	**TV system**						
	a. Conduit	C	CE	A/EE/S	A/EE	GC	GC
	b. Equipment and wiring	SS	S	S/V	S/V	O*	V
13	**TV surveillance systems**						
	a. Conduit	C	CE	A/EE/S	A/EE	GC	GC
	b. Equipment and wiring	SS	S	S/V	S/V	O*	V
14	**Telephones**						
	a. Conduit	C	CE	A/EE	A/EE	GC	GC
	b. Equipment and wiring	SS	S	S	S	O*	V
	c. Public phones	SS	O	O/V/I	V/I/A	O*	V

table continued overleaf

419

	Areas of responsibility	Budget category	Estimated by	Designed by	Contract documents by	Purchased by	Installed by
15	**Computer, internet, and reservations systems**						
	a. Uninterrupted power supply (UPS) and conduit for computer systems	C	CE	A/EE/S	A/EE	GC	GC
	b. Equipment and wiring	SS	S	S/V	S/V	O*	V
16	**Audiovisual systems**						
	a. Fixed equipment and wiring	SS	S	A/S/AV	A/AV	GC	V
	b. Movable equipment	SS	S	S/AV	S	O*	V
	c. Conduit	C	CE	A/S/EE	A/E	GC	GC
	d. Built-in projection screens	C	CE	A/AV	A	GC	GC
17	**Food-service equipment**						
	a. Kitchen, bar, and pantry equipment set in place	FFE	K	K	K	PA	GC
	b. Ice and vending machines	FFE	K	K	K	O*	GC
	c. Mechanical and electrical rough-in, final connections, and ventilation	C	CE	K/A/ME/EE	K/A/ME/EE	GC	GC
	d. Food-service carts	FFE	K	K	K	O	O
18	**Laundry and dry-cleaning**						
	a. Equipment (set in place)	FFE	L	L/A/ME/EE	L/A/ME/EE	PA	GC
	b. Mechanical and electrical rough-in, final connections, and ventilation	C	C	L/A/ME/EE	L/A/ME/EE	GC	GC
	c. Linen chute	C	CE	A	A	GC	GC
19	**Housekeeping and maintenance equipment (vacuum cleaners, maids' carts, floor polishers, tools, maintenance shop equipment, etc.)**	FFE	O	O	O	O	O/V
20	**Storage shelving**						
	a. Fixed wood	C	CE	A	A	GC/MC	GC/MC
	b. Metal movable	FFE	O	A/O	A/O	O	IN
21	**Office and front desk equipment**						
	a. Office furniture, files, vaults, business machines, copiers, etc.	FFE	O	O	O	O	O
	b. Safe-deposit boxes	FFE	O	O	O	O	GC
	c. Baggage carts	OP	O	O	O	PA	PA/IN
22	**Meeting-room equipment (movable stages, dance floors, lecterns, easels, etc.)**	FFE	O	I/O	I/O	PA	PA/IN
23	**Recreation facilities**						
	a. Pools, tennis courts, etc.	C	CE	A	A	GC	GC
	b. Equipment	FFE	O	O/A	O/A	O	O
24	**Window coverings**						
	a. Draperies, tracks, and blinds	FFE	I	I	I	PA	PA/IN
	b. Valances	FD	I	I	I	GC/MC	GC/MC
25	**Shower curtains**	FFE	I	I	I	O	IN
26	**Shower rods/door assemblies**	C	CE	I/A	A	GC	GC
27	**Vanities**	C	CE	I/A	A	GC	GC

	Areas of responsibility	Budget category	Estimated by	Designed by	Contract documents by	Purchased by	Installed by
28	**Mirrors**						
	a. Public areas and guestrooms	FD	I	I	I	GC/MC	GC/MC
	b. Bathrooms	C	CE	I	A/I	GC	GC
29	**Accessories**						
	a. Towel bars and shelves, tissue dispensers, paper holders, robe hooks, etc.	C	CE	I/A	A	GC	GC
	b. Closet shelving and clothes rods	C	CE	I/A	A	GC	GC
	c. Luggage racks	FFE	I	I/O	I	PA	PA/IN
30	**Bedspreads**	FFE	I	I	I	PA	PA/IN
31	**Mattresses and boxsprings**	FFE	O	O	O	O	IN
32	**Linens, bedding, and terry**	OP	O	I/O	I	O	O
33	**Uniforms**	OP	O	I/O/V	O	O	O
34	**Tableware (china, glassware, flatware, holloware, table linen, etc.)**	OP	O	I/O	I	O	O
35	**Kitchen and bar utensils and smallwares**	OP	O	O	O	O	O
36	**Food and beverage consumables**	OP	O	O	O	O	O
37	**Working inventories**						
	a. Office supplies; cleaning, laundry, and maintenance supplies; guestroom and bathroom supplies (wastebaskets, soaps, tissues, etc.)	OP	O	O	O	O	O
	b. Menus and printed forms	OP	O	O	O/G	O	O
38	**Interior signage**	FFE	I	I/G	I	GC	GC
39	**Exterior signage**						
	a. Building identification signs	SS	O	O/A	O/A/V	O	V
	b. Directional, traffic, and parking signs	C	CE	A/G	A	GC	GC
40	**Interior landscaping**						
	a. Fixed planters	C	CE	I/A/LS	A	GC	GC
	b. Movable planters	FFE	I	I/LS	I	PA	PA/IN
	c. Plants	FD	I	I	I	O*	V
	d. Water features	FD	I	I/A/ME	I/A/ME	GC	GC
41	**Exterior landscaping**						
	a. Planters	C	CE	A/LS	A	GC	GC
	b. Irrigation and drainage	C	CE	A/CIV/LS	A/CIV	GC	GC
	c. Planting, water features, and hardscape	C	CE	A/LS	ALS	GC	GC
42	**Roadways, parking, and walks**	C	CE	A/CIV/LS/SS	A/CIV	GC	GC
43	**Vehicles (vans, golf carts, grounds care trucks, etc.)**	OP	O	O	O	O*	O

APPENDIX F

Chain Brands

	Accor	Carlson/Rezidor	Choice	Hilton
Luxury	Sofitel			Conrad Waldorf=Astoria
Lifestyle	M Gallery	art'otel Missoni Radisson Blu		
Full-service	Mercure Novotel Pullman	Park Plaza Radisson	Ascend Collection Clarion Quality	DoubleTree Hilton
Select-service	Formule1/f1 Ibis Ibis Budget Ibis Styles Motel 6	Country Inn and Suites Park Inn	Comfort Inn EconoLodge Rodeway Sleep Inn	Hampton Hilton Garden Inn
Suites and extended-stay	Adagio Grand Mercure Studio 6 Suite Novotel		Comfort Suites Cambria Suites MainStay Suites Suburban	Embassy Suites Homewood Suites Home2 Suites
Vacation ownership				Hilton Grand Vacations

Hyatt	IHG	Marriott	Starwood	Wyndham
Park Hyatt	InterContinental	Autograph Collection Bulgari JW Marriott Ritz-Carlton	Luxury Collection St. Regis	
Andaz	Hotel Indigo	Autograph Collection Edition Renaissance	element W	Dream Night
Grand Hyatt Hyatt Regency	Crowne Plaza Holiday Inn Holiday Inn SunSpree Resorts Holiday Inn Garden Court Holiday Inn Select Parkroyal	Marriott	Le Meridien Sheraton Westin	Planet Hollywood Ramada Ramada Encore Wyndham
Hyatt Place	Centra Forum Holiday Inn Express	Courtyard Fairfield Inn	aloft Four Points	Days Inn Howard Johnson Microtel Ramada Inn Ramada Plaza Super 8 Travelodge Tryp Wingate Wyndham Garden
Hyatt House	Candlewood Suites Staybridge Suites	ExecuStay Marriott Executive Apartments Residence Inn SpringHill Suites TownePlace Suites		Baymont Suites Hawthorn Suites
Hyatt Vacation Club		Grand Residences Marriott Vacation Club Ritz-Carlton Destination Club		ClubWyndham WorldMark Wyndham Vacations

Bibliography

Hotels and Resorts—Development and Planning Guidelines

Baucom, Alfred H. *Hospitality Design for the Graying Generation*. New York: Wiley, 1996.

Baud-Bovy, Manuel and Fred Lawson. *Tourism and Recreation: Handbook of Planning and Design*. Oxford: Architectural Press, 1998.

Berens, Carol. *Hotel Bars and Lobbies*. New York: McGraw-Hill, 1997.

Conservation International. *Sustainable Hotel Siting, Design and Construction*. London: Conservation International, 2005.

Curtis, Eleanor. *Hotel Interior Structures*. London: Wiley-Academy, 2001.

Davies, Thomas D. and Kim A. Beasley. *Accessible Design for Hospitality*. New York: Nichols, 1994.

Gee, Chuck Y. *Resort Development and Management*. East Lansing, MI: Educational Institute of AH&MA, 1988.

Henderson, Justin. *Casino Design: Resorts, Hotels, and Themed Entertainment Spaces*. Gloucester, MA: Rockport, 1999.

Hillier Group. *A Conference Center by Design*. St. Louis: International Association of Conference Centers, 2000.

Huffadine, Margaret. *Project Management in Hotel and Resort Development*. New York: McGraw-Hill, 1993.

Kaplan, Michael. *The New Hotel: International Hotel and Resort Design 3*. Glen Cove, NY: PBC International, 1998.

Kaplan, Michael. *Resort Design: Planning Architecture, and Interiors*. New York, McGraw-Hill, 2000.

Lawson, Fred. *Hotels and Resorts: Planning, Design and Refurbishment*. Oxford: Butterworth Architecture, 1995.

Penner, Richard H. *Conference Center Planning and Design*. New York: Whitney Library of Design, 1991.

PKF Consulting. *Hotel Development*. Washington, DC: Urban Land Institute, 1996.

Portman, John and Jonathan Barnett. *The Architect as Developer*. New York: McGraw-Hill, 1976.

Raleigh, Lori E. and Rachel J. Roginsky (eds). *Hotel Investments: Issues and Perspectives*. East Lansing, MI: Educational Institute of the AH&MA, 1999.

Rushmore, Stephen, Dana Michael Ciraldo, and John M. Tarras. *Hotel Investments Handbook*. New York: West Group, 1999.

Rutes, Walter A. and Richard H. Penner. *Hotel Planning and Design*. New York: Whitney Library of Design, 1985.

Rutes, Walter A., Richard H. Penner, and Lawrence Adams. *Hotel Design, Planning, and Development*. New York: W. W. Norton, 2001.

Schwanke, Dean, et al. *Resort Development Handbook*. Washington, DC: Urban Land Institute, 1997.

Stipanuk, David M. *Hospitality Facilities Management and Design*, third edition. East Lansing, MI: Educational Institute of the AH&LA, 2006.

Suchman, Diane R., et al. *Developing Timeshare and Vacation-Ownership Properties*. Washington, DC: Urban Land Institute, 1999.

Hotels and Resorts—Projects Illustrated

Avermaete, Tom and Anne Massey (eds). *Hotel Lobbies and Lounges: The Architecture of Professional Hospitality*. New York: Routledge, 2012.

Bahamon, Alejando. *New Hotels*. New York: Harper Design International, 2003.

Bangert, Albrecht and Otto Riewoldt. *Designer Hotels*. New York: Vendome Press, 1993.

Beng, Tan Hock. *Tropical Retreats: The Poetics of Place*. Singapore: Page One Publishing, 1996.

Black, Wendy. *International Hotel and Resort Design 2*. New York: PBC International, 1991.

Borras, Montse. *Hotel Spaces*. Beverly, MA: Rockport, 2008.

Broto, Carles. *Stylish Hotel Design*. Barcelona: LINKS, 2010.

[no author] *Clubs and Resorts: Designing for Recreation and Leisure*. New York: PBC International, 1993.

de Vleeschouwer, Olivier. *New Hotel Designs*. Paris: Telleri, 1998.

[no author] *Hotel Facilities: New Concepts in Architecture and Design*. Tokyo: Meisei, 1997.

Knapp, Frederick. *Hotel Renovation Planning and Design*. New York: McGraw-Hill, 1995.

Kretschmar-Joehnk, Corinna and Peter Joehnk. *101 Hotel Rooms*. Hamburg: Braun, 2011.

Kunz, Martin Nicholas (ed.). *Cool Hotels: Spa and Wellness*. Kempen, Germany: teNeues, 2008.

Moreno, Elena Marcheso. *Hotels: International Design Portfolios*. Gloucester, MA: Rockport, 1998.

Mostaedi, Arian. *Design Hotels*. Barcelona: LINKS, 1998.

[no author] *New Hotel Architecture: Modern Hotel Design, a Pictorial Survey*. Tokyo: Meisei, 1993.

Newson, Veronica. *Ultraluxe Hotels: The Experience Awaits …* New York: Wiley, 2009.

Phillips, Alan. *The Best in Lobby Design: Hotels and Offices*. London: Quatro, 1991.

Radulski, John P. and William Weathersby, Jr. *Pleasure Paradises: International Clubs and Resorts*. Glen Cove, NY: PBC International, 1997.

Riewoldt, Otto. *Hotel Design*. Corte Madera, CA: Gingko Press, 1998.

Riewoldt, Otto. *New Hotel Design*. London: Lawrence King, 2002.

Schmid, Anne M. *International Hotel Redesign*. New York: PBC International, 1990.

Schmid, Anne M. and Mary Scoviak-Lerner. *International Hotel and Resort Design*. Glen Cove, NY: PBC International, 1988.

Tackach, James. *Great American Hotels, Luxury Palaces and Elegant Resorts*. New York: Smithmark, 1991.

Tikos, Bill. *The World's Coolest Hotel Rooms*. New York: Collins Design, 2008.

WATG. *The Hospitality and Leisure Architecture of Wimberly Allison Tong & Goo*. Gloucester, MA: Rockport, 1997.

WATG. *Designing the World's Best Resorts*. Mulgrave, Australia: Images, 2005.

WATG. *100 Hotels + Resorts: Destinations that Lift the Spirit*. Mulgrave, Australia: Images, 2008.

Wilson, Trisha. *Spectacular Hotels: The Most Remarkable Places on Earth.* Dallas: Signature Publishing, 2004.

Yee, Roger. *Hotel and Restaurant Design.* New York: Visual Reference, 2005.

Yee, Roger. *Hotel and Restaurant Design, No. 2.* New York: Visual Reference, 2008.

Ypma, Herbert. *Hip Hotels: City.* London: Thames & Hudson, 1999.

Ypma, Herbert. *Hip Hotels: Escape.* London: Thames & Hudson, 2000.

Hotels, Motels, and Resorts—History

Allegrini, Robert V. *Chicago's Grand Hotels.* Charleston, SC: Arcadia, 2005.

Belasco, Warren James. *Americans on the Road, From Autocamp to Motel, 1910–1945.* Cambridge, MA: MIT Press, 1979.

Berger, Molly W. (ed.). *The American Hotel.* Cambridge, MA: MIT Press, 2005.

Berger, Molly W. *Hotel Dreams: Luxury, Technology, and Urban Ambition in America, 1829–1929.* Baltimore: Johns Hopkins University Press, 2011.

Braden, Susan R. *The Architecture of Leisure.* Gainesville, FL: University Press of Florida, 2002.

Corbett, Theodore. *The Making of American Resorts.* New Brunswick, NJ: Rutgers University Press, 2001.

Curl, Donald Walter. *Mizner's Florida: American Resort Architecture.* Cambridge, MA: MIT Press, 1996.

Donzel, Catherine, Alexis Gregory and Marc Walter. *Grand American Hotels.* New York: Vendome Press, 1989.

Hirsh, Jeff. *Manhattan Hotels: 1880–1920.* Charleston, SC: Arcadia, 1997.

Kramer, J. J. *The Last of the Grand Hotels.* New York: Van Nostrand Reinhold, 1978.

Lapidus, Morris. *An Architecture of Joy.* Miami: Seemann, 1979.

Liebs, Chester H. *Main Street to Miracle Mile.* New York: Graphic Society, 1985.

Limerick, Jeffrey, Nancy Ferguson, and Richard Oliver. *America's Grand Resort Hotels.* New York: Pantheon, 1979.

Ludy, Robert B. *Historic Hotels of the World: Past and Present.* Philadelphia: David McKay, 1927.

McGinty, Brian. *The Palace Inns.* Harrisburg, PA: Stackpole, 1978.

Meade, Martin and Jean Larteguy. *Grand Oriental Hotels.* New York: Vendome Press, 1987.

Pevsner, Nikolaus. *A History of Building Types.* Princeton, NJ: Princeton University Press, 1976 (Chapter 11, pp. 169–192).

Sandoval-Strausz, A. K. *Hotel: An American History.* New Haven, CT: Yale University Press, 2007.

Sterngass, Jon. *First Resorts: Pursuing Pleasure at Saratoga Springs, Newport and Coney Island.* Baltimore: Johns Hopkins University Press, 2001.

Tolles, Bryant F., Jr. *The Grand Resort Hotels of the White Mountains: A Vanishing Architectural Legacy.* Boston: David R. Godine, 1998.

Tolles, Bryant F., Jr. *Resort Hotels of the Adirondacks: The Architecture of a Summer Paradise, 1850–1950.* Hanover, NH: University Press of New England, 2003.

Watkin, David. *Grand Hotel.* New York: Vendome Press, 1984.

Wharton, Annabel Jane. *Building the Cold War: Hilton International Hotels and Modern Architecture.* Chicago: University of Chicago Press, 2001.

Williamson, Jefferson. *The American Hotel: An Anecdotal History.* New York: Alfred A. Knopf, 1930.

A=Architect; ID=Interior Designer;
LA=Landscape Architect; P=Photographer; R=Renderer

10 Trinity Hotel, London, United Kingdom. A: Woods Bagot; P: Courtesy of
Woods Bagot.

21c Museum Hotel, Louisville, Kentucky. A and ID: Deborah Berke and
Partners; P: Catherine Tighe.

47 Park Street—Marriott Grand Residence Club, London, United Kingdom.
A: Wimperis and Simpson; ID: WATG; P: Courtesy of Marriott Vacation Club
International.

Abu Dhabi Golf Club Resort Hotel, Abu Dhabi, United Arab Emirates. A: GREC
Architects; ID: The Gettys Group; P: Courtesy of Starwood Asset Library.

Abu Dhabi Mirage Hotel, Abu Dhabi, United Arab Emirates. A and R: KA3
Design Group.

Ace Hotel & Swim Club, Palm Springs, California. A: o2 Architecture;
ID: Commune in association with Atelier Ace; P: Douglas L. Thompson and
Jon Johnson, Courtesy of Ace Hotel.

Aircruise Luxury Airship. A: Seymourpowell; R: Courtesy of Seymourpowell.

The Alexander, Indianapolis, Indiana. A and ID: Gensler; R: Neoscape.

The Algonquin Hotel, New York, New York. ID: Champalimaud Design;
P: Jesse Harris.

Alila Villas Uluwatu, Bali, Indonesia. A and ID: WOHA; P: Patrick Bingham Hall.

The Alluvian, Greenwood, Mississippi. A: Foil-Wyatt Architects & Planners;
ID: ForrestPerkins; P: Bruce Wood.

Aman Hotel, New Delhi, India. A and ID: Kerry Hill Architects, Mohit Gujaral
and Design Plus Architecture; P: Courtesy of Aman Resorts.

Amangiri, Canyon Point, Utah. A: I-10 Studio; ID: CSR Design; P: Ken Hayden.

Ames Hotel, Boston, Massachusetts. A: Cambridge 7 Associates; ID: Rockwell
Group; P: Kwesi Arthur.

**Anantara Desert Islands Resort & Spa by Anantara, Abu Dhabi, United Arab
Emirates.** A: WOHA; ID: Andrea Graff; P: Felix L. Steck.

Anantara Golden Triangle Resort & Spa, Golden Anantara Triangle, Thailand.
A: Mom Luang Tridhosyuth Devakul; ID: John Lightbody; LA: Bill Bensly;
P: Peter Malinowski.

Anantara Xishuangbanna Resort & Spa, Xishuangbanna, China. A: Architectural
and Engineering Design Institute of Yunnan Povince; ID: P49 Design and
Associates; P: Courtesy of Anantara Resorts.

Andaz and Langham Xintiandi, Shanghai, China. A: KPF and Leigh & Orange;
ID: Remedios Siembieda and Super Potato; P: Courtesy of KPF.

Armani Hotel, Burj Khalifa, Dubai, United Arab Emirates. A: Skidmore Owings
and Merrill; ID: Armani; P: James Steinkamp.

Arrabelle at Vail Square, Vail, Colorado. A: 4240 Architecture; ID: Silfer Designs;
P: Jack Aflect, Robert Miller, Todd Winslow Pierce.

Arrebol Patagonia Hotel, Puerto Varas, Chile. A and ID: Harald Opitz Jurgens;
P: Francisco Negroni.

**AT&T Executive Education and Conference Center, University of Texas, Austin,
Texas.** A: LakelFlato and HKS Hill Glazier Studio; ID: Wilson Associates;
P: Blake Marvin.

Atlantis Dubai Resort Hotel, Dubai, United Arab Emirates. A: WATG, Archavision
International and NORR Limited; ID: Wilson Associates; P: Courtesy of WATG.

Banyan Tree Sanya, Sanya, China. A+ID: Architrave Design & Planning;
Courtesy of Banyan Tree Hotels & Resorts.

Bardessono Hotel and Spa, Yountville, California. A: WATG; ID: Marta Salas-
Porras; LA: Girvin & Associates; P: Sammy Todd Dyess.

Bella Sky Hotel, Copenhagen, Denmark. A+ID: 3XN Architects; P: Adam Mark.

Bethesda Marriott Suites, Bethesda, Maryland. A and ID: Marriott International
and Cauhaus Design; P: Cristian Molina.

Binh Tien Resort, Nha Trang, Vietnam. A: WATG and Bensley Design;
ID: Bensley Design; LA: Bensley Design; P: Courtesy of WATG.

Blackstone Hotel, Chicago, Illinois. A and ID: Gettys Group; P: Courtesy of
Gettys Group.

The Boundary Hotel, London, United Kingdom. A: Conran + Partners; ID:
Terrance Conran; P: Paul Raeside.

Burj al Arab, Dubai, United Arab Emirates. A: Atkins; ID: KCA International;
P: Courtesy of Jumeirah Hotels & Resorts.

Casino Public Area Schematic. A/R: Hnedak Bobo Group.

Centara Grand, Bangkok, Thailand. A and ID:BBG-BBGM; P: Benoit Laboup.

Chambers Hotel, New York, New York. A: Adams Soffes Wood; ID: Rockwell
Group; P: David Joseph.

City of Dreams Resort, Macau, China. A: Arquitectonica, P: Courtesy of Melco
Group.

Cliffhanger Resort, Grand Canyon, Arizona. A: HKS Hill Glazier Studio; P: Blake
Marvin.

Coeur Mediterranée, Marseilles, France. A: MAP; P: Courtesy of Constructa.

Connexion Integrated Health Centre, Singapore. A: DP Architects; R: Courtesy
of Connexion at Farrar Park.

Cosmopolitan of Las Vegas, Las Vegas, Nevada. A: Arquitectonica and
Friedmutter Group; ID: Rockwell Group and The Digital Kitchen; P: Courtesy
of Cosmopolitan Las Vegas.

Courtyard by Marriott "Refreshing Business" lobby design. A and ID: CR
Architecture + Design; P: Jim Burnett, Courtesy of Marriott International.

Courtyard by Marriott and Springhill Suites, Indianapolis, Indiana. A and ID:
PFVS Architects; P: Courtesy of White Lodging.

Courtyard by Marriott, Portland. Oregon. A and ID: SERA Architects;
P: Michael Mathers.

Crown Casino, Macau, China. A: Arquitectonica; ID: Remedios Studio;
P: Courtesy of Melco Group.

Crown Plaza and Staybridge Suites, Abu Dhabi, United Arab Emirates.
A and ID: Kann Finch Group; R: Courtesy of InterContinental Hotels Group.

Crowne Plaza Changi, Changi Airport, Singapore. A: WOHA Architects;
P: Patrick Bingham-Hall.

Crystal Towers Hotel & Spa, Cape Town, South Africa. A: Vivid Architects;
ID: Plan 1 and Les Harbottle: P: Marc Hoberman.

The Dolder Grand Hotel, Zurich, Switzerland. A: Foster & Partners; ID: United Designers of London; P: Simon Vogt, Stefan Schmidlin, and Courtesy of The Dolder Resort.

Dream Downtown, New York, New York. A and ID: Handel Architects; P: Bruce Damonte and Philip Ennis.

Enchantment Resort and Mii Amo Spa, Sedona, Arizona. A: Gluckman Mayner; P: Courtesy of Enchantment Group.

Envision Green Hotel, Miami, Florida. A: Michael Rosenthal Associates; R: Richard Moreta Castillo.

Estrel Hotel & Convention Center, Berlin, Germany. A: Karl Waldemar Tilemann and Heiner Hennes; ID: S & S GmbH; P: Manuel Frauendorfer.

Exclusive Resorts, Papagayo, Costa Rica. A and ID: Exclusive Resorts; P: Courtesy of Exclusive Resorts.

Fairmont Hotel, San Francisco, California. ID: Champalimaud Design; P: Mathew Millman.

Fairmont Pacific Rim, Vancouver, Canada. A: James KM Cheng Architects; ID: B+H and Robert Baily; P: Courtesy Fairmont Hotels & Resorts.

Fairmont Peace Hotel, Shanghai, China. A: Allied Architects International (AAI); ID: HBA Hirsch Bedner Associates; P: Ken Hayden, Courtesy of Fairmont Hotels & Resorts.

Finca Prats Hotel Golf & Spa, Lleida, Spain. A and ID: Pampols Arquitecte SLP; P: Courtesy of Finca Prats Hotel Golf & Spa.

Flamingo Hotel, Las Vegas, Nevada. ID: Cagney & Tanner; P: Courtesy of Las Vegas News Bureau.

Four Acres Hotel and Residences, Scottsdale, Arizona. A: Ronnette Riley Architect and Mathes Brierre Architects; R: T.W. Schaller.

Four Seasons Firenze, Florence, Italy. A: Studio Noferi and Magris & Partners; ID: Pierre Yves Rochon; P: Courtesy of Four Seasons Hotels & Resorts.

Four Seasons, Guangzhou, China. A: Wilkinson Eyre; ID: HBA Hirsch Bedner Associates; P: Ken Seet, Courtesy of Four Seasons Hotels & Resorts.

Four Seasons Marrakech, Morocco. A: Hill Glazier and Didier Lefort; ID: GA Design; P: Richard Waite, Courtesy of Four Seasons Hotels & Resorts.

Four Seasons Resort, Bora Bora, Tahiti. A: Didier Lefort and Pierre-Jean Picart; ID: BAMO; P: Courtesy of Four Seasons Hotels & Resorts.

Four Seasons Resort, Hualalai, Hawaii. A: HKS Hill Glazier Studio; ID: Wilson Associates; P: Blake Marvin.

Four Seasons Resort, Langkawi, Malaysia. A: Bunnag Architects and Bensley Design Studios; ID: Bensley Design Studios, Underwood Co. and Lim Teo+ Wilkes Design Works; P: Courtesy of Four Seasons Hotels & Resorts.

Four Seasons Resort, Republic of Seychelles. A: Area Architects and Locus Architects; ID: HBA Hirsch Bedner Associates; P: Peter Vitale, Paul Thuysbaert, Courtesy of Four Seasons Hotels & Resorts.

Four Seasons Resort, Vail, Colorado. A: HKS Hill Glazier Studio/Hill Glazier; ID: Brayton Hughes; P: Courtesy of Four Seasons Hotels & Resorts.

Four Seasons Tented Camp, Golden Triangle, Thailand. A and ID: Bill Bensley Design; P: Courtesy of Four Seasons Hotels & Resorts.

Gansevoort Hotel, New York, New York. [Meatpacking District] A: SBJ Group; ID: Andi Pepper; P: Courtesy of Gansevoort Meatpacking NYC.

Gansevoort Hotel, New York, New York. [Park Avenue] A: SBJ Group; ID: Andi Pepper; P: Magda Biernat, Courtesy of Gansevoort Hotel Group.

Gaylord National Resort and Convention Center, National Harbor, Maryland. A and ID: Gensler; P: Courtesy of Gaylord National Resort and Convention Center.

Gaylord Texan Hotel, Dallas, TX. A: Hnedak Bobo Group; ID: Wilson Associates: P: Wes Thompson, Courtesy of Hnedak Bobo Group.

Goldenkey Kartalkaya, Bolu, Turkey. A: LEA Invent; ID: Barbara Pensoy; P: Courtesy of LEA Invent.

Gramercy Park Hotel, New York, New York. A: BBG-BBGM; ID: Philippe Starck; P: Courtesy of Gramercy Park Hotel.

Grand Hyatt Chengdu, Chengdu, China. A: Goettsch Partners; ID: Tony Chi; P: Courtesy of Goettsch Partners.

Grand Hyatt Tokyo at Roppongi Hills, Tokyo, Japan. A: KPF; ID: Remedios Siembieda and Super Potato; P: H.G. Esch, Courtesy of KPF.

Grand Hyatt, Washington, DC. A: RTKL; ID: HBA Hirsch Bedner Associates; P: Courtesy of the Grand Hyatt Hotel.

Great (Bamboo) Wall, Beijing, China. A and ID: Kenzo Kuma; P: Satoshi Asakawa.

Great Wolf Lodge, Grapevine, Texas. A: GSBS Batenhorst; P: Courtesy of Great Wolf Lodge.

Hampton Inn and Homewood Suites, Toronto Airport, Canada. A: Chamberlain Architects; ID: Robert Chaban & Associates; P: Courtesy of Homewood Suites by Hilton.

Hard Rock Hotel, Chicago, Illinois. A: Lucien Lagrange; ID: Yabu-Pushelburg; P: Courtesy of Hard Rock Hotel.

Hard Rock Hotel, Macau, China. A: Arquitectonica; ID: Gettys Group; P: Courtesy of Melco Group.

The Heldrich, Rutgers University, New Brunswick, New Jersey. A and ID: CMMI; P: Creative Sources Photography.

Hersham Golf Club Hotel, Walton-on-Thames, United Kingdom. A: ReardonSmith Architects; P: Courtesy of ReardonSmith Architects.

Hilton Garden Inn and Homewood Suites, Bossier City, Louisiana. A: Mathes Brierre Architects; ID: Peggy Dye & Associates; P: Courtesy of Mathes Brierre Architects.

Hilton Garden Inn and Homewood Suites, Jacksonville, Florida. A and ID: Bounds and Gillespie Architects; P: Courtesy of Bounds and Gillespie Architects.

Hilton San Diego Bayfront Hotel, San Diego, California. A: John Portman Associates; ID: HBA Hirsch Bedner Associates; LA: Sasaki Associates; P: Jim Brady, HeliPhoto, Courtesy of Hilton San Diego Bayfront Hotel.

Hilton Sanya Resort & Spa, Sanya, China. A: WATG and Shanghai Institute of Architectural Design and Research; ID: Chhada Siembieda Leung; LA: Belt Collins; P: Courtesy of WATG Architects.

Homewood Suites and Hampton Inn, Silver Spring, Maryland. A: A.R. Meyers and Associates; ID: Guest Purchasing Services; P: Courtesy of Hilton Hotels & Resorts.

Hope Street Hotel, Liverpool, United Kingdom. A: Falconer Chester Hall; ID: Basia Chlebik; P: McCoy Wynne.

Hotel del Coronado, San Diego, California. A: Hornberger + Worstell; ID: HBA Hirsch Bedner Associates; P: Courtesy of Hotel del Coronado.

Hotel Habita, Monterrey, Mexico. A: Landa Arquitectos; ID: Joseph Dirand & Associates; P: Undine Pröhi.

Hotel Marques de Riscal, Elciego, Spain. A and ID: Frank Gehry; P: Courtesy of the Luxury Collection, Starwood Hotels & Resorts Worldwide.

Hotel Missoni, Edinburgh, United Kingdom. A: Allan Murray; ID: Matteo Thun and Missoni Design Team; P: Courtesy of Hotel Missoni.

Hotel OMM, Barcelona, Spain. A: Juli Capella; ID: Tarruella and López; P: Courtesy of Design Hotels.

Hotel Palomar, Philadelphia, Pennsylvania. A: Gensler; ID: Dayna Lee; P: Courtesy of Gensler.

Hotel Remota, Patagonia, Puerto Natales, Chile. A and ID: Germán del Sol; P: Francisco Negroni.

Hotel SnowWorld, Landgraaf, Netherlands. A: Ton Vanderburgh Architekten; P: Courtesy of SnowWorld.

Hotel Therme Vals, Vals, Switzerland. A: Peter Zumthor; P: Courtesy of Hotel Therme Vals.

Hyatt Regency McCormick Place, Chicago, Illinois. A: TVS Design; ID: HBA Hirsch Bedner Associates; P: Brial Gassel.

Hyatt Regency Tamaya Resort & Spa, Santa Ana Pueblo, New Mexico. A: HKS Hill Glazier Studio; ID: Carlson Joyce Interior Design; P: Blake Marvin.

Hyatt Regency, Dusseldorf, Germany. A: SOP-Architekten; ID: FG stijl; P: Courtesy of SOP-Architekten.

Hyatt Regency, Mainz, Germany. A: JSK Architects; ID: HBA Hirsch Bedner Associates; P: Ken Kirkwood.

Ibis and Mercure Salvador Rio Vermelho Hotel, Salvador, Brazil. P: Roberto Borella and Mac Bertrand, Courtesy of Accor Hotels.

IBM Palisades, Palisades, New York. A and ID: Mitchell-Giurgola; P: Mick Hales.

India Tower, Mumbai, India. A: Foster and Partners; R: Courtesy of Foster and Partners.

Inn at Middleton Place, Charleston, South Carolina. A: Clark & Menefee Architects with Charleston Architectural Group; ID: Dian Boone; P: Brianna Stello and Tim Hursley–The Arkansas Office.

Innside Premium Hotel, Munich, Germany. A: Helmut Jahn; ID: Jahn Lykouria Design; P: Courtesy of Melia Hotels International.

InterContinental Paris Avenue Marceau, Paris, France. A and ID: Bruno Borrione; P: Courtesy of InterContinental Hotel Paris.

James Hotel, SoHo, New York, New York. A: Perkins Eastman Architects with ODA–Architecture; ID: ODA–Architecture and Amanda Sullivan, Piet Boon (Penthouse); P: Courtesy of The James New York.

The Jefferson, Washington, DC. A and ID: ForrestPerkins; P: Stirling Elmendorf, Courtesy of ForrestPerkins.

Jumbo Stay, Arlanda Airport, Stockholm, Sweden. A+ID: Monsen Arkitekter AB; P: Lioba Schneider, Jumbo Stay.

Jumeirah Frankfurt Hotel, Frankfurt, Germany. A: KSP Engel und Zimmermann; R: Courtesy of PalaisQuartier GmbH.

Jumeirah Himalayas Hotel, Shanghai, China. A: Arata Isozaki; ID: KCA International; P: Zhu Shaoci, Courtesy of Jumeirah Himalayas Hotel.

Jupiter Hotel, Portland, Oregon. A and ID: Skylab Architecture; P: Courtesy of Jupiter Hotel.

Juvet Landscape Hotel, Alstad, Norway. A and ID: Jensen & Skodvin; P: Courtesy of Juvet.

JW Marriott and Ritz Carlton at L.A. LIVE, Los Angeles, California. A: Gensler; ID: Barry Design Associates; P: John Edward Linden and Ryan Gobuty, Courtesy of Gensler.

JW Marriott Ihilani, Hawaii. A: WATG; ID: Wimberly Interiors; P: Courtesy of WATG.

JW Marriott, Indianapolis, Indiana. A: HOK Chicago and CSO Architects; ID: Simeone Deary Design Group; P: Dan Ham Photography; Steve Hall and Tony Soluri.

JW Marriott San Antonio Hill Country Resort & Spa, San Antonio, Texas. A: HKS Hill Glazier Studio Architects; ID: ForrestPerkins; P: Barbara Kraft.

Kimber Modern Hotel, Austin, Texas. A and ID: Baldridge Architects; P: Courtesy of Casey Dunn and Baldridge Architects.

Kimpton Palomar, Chicago, Illinois. A: GREC Architects; ID: Orlando Diaz-Azcuy; P: Greg Murphy, Courtesy of GREC Architects.

Kingdom Tower, Jeddah, Saudi Arabia. A: Adrian Smith and Gordon Gill, design architects; R: Adrian Smith + Gordon Gill Architecture.

Kruisherenhotel, Maastricht, Netherlands. A: Satijn Plus; ID: Henk Vos Maupertuus; P: Roel Vink.

Le Germain Hotel at Maple Leaf Square. Toronto, Canada. A and ID: Lemaymichaud; P: Tom Arban.

Le Meridien, Philadelphia, Pennsylvania. A: Blackney Hayes; ID: Forchielli Glynn; P: Jeffrey Totaro, Courtesy of HEI Hotels & Resorts.

Le Royal Monceau Raffles, Paris, France. A and ID: Philippe Starck; P: Courtesy of Mango Public Relations.

Liberty Hotel, Boston, Massachusetts. A: Cambridge 7 Associates; ID: Champalimaud Design; P: Kwes Arthur and Peter Vanderwarker.

Lied Lodge, Nebraska City, Nebraska. A: Alley Poyner Macchietto Architecture; P: Luis Peon-Cassanova.

Linked Hybrid, Beijing, China. A and ID: Steven Holl Architects; P: Shu He, Courtesy of Steven Holl Architects.

Lodge at Woodloch, Hawley, Pennsylvania. A: Cooper Carry; ID: Jinnie Kim Design; P: Robert Miller.

Loews Atlanta, Atlanta, Georgia. A: Rule Joy Trammel & Rubio; ID: Daroff Design; P: Zach Rolen.

Loisium Wine & Spa Resort, Langenlois, Austria. A and ID: Stephen Holl Architects; P: Hauke Dressler, Courtesy of Design Hotels.

London NYC, New York, New York. (RIHGA Royal Hotel) A: Frank Williams and Associates ID: David Collins.

Mandarin Oriental Dellis Cay, Turks and Caicos Islands. A: Oppenheim Architecture + Design; ID: David Chipperfield, Zaha Hadid, Kengo Kuma, Pierro Lissoni, Shigeru Ban, Chad Oppenheim, and Carl Ettensperge; P: Carl Ettensperge.

Marina + Beach Hotel, Dubai, United Arab Emirates. A: Oppenheim Architects; R: Courtesy of Oppenheim Architects.

Marina Bay Sands, Singapore. A: Safdie Architects; ID: Safdie Architects and CL3, HBA Hirsch Bedner Associates; P: Tim Hursley.

Marriott Marquis, New York, NY. A: Acheson Doyle Partners Architects; ID: ForrestPerkins; P: Jeff Goldman.

Marriott Marquis, Washington, DC. A: Cooper Carry; R: Courtesy of Cooper Carry.

Marriott Vacation Club Grande Vista, Orlando, Florida. A: Helman Hurley Charvat Peacock; ID: Design Continuum; P: Jay Jenks, Matteo Thun, Courtesy of Marriott Vacation Club International.

Marriott World Center, Orlando, Florida. A and ID: TVS Design; P: Courtesy of Marriott International.

Mayakoba, Riviera Maya, Mexico. A: Three Architecture; P: Courtesy of OHL-Mayakoba.

Meydan Grandstand and Hotel, Dubai, United Arab Emirates. A: TAK Architects; P: Courtesy of Meydan Hotels.

Miraval, Tucson, Arizona. A: Mithun Architects; ID: Clodagh; P: Robert Reck.

Missoni Hotel, Edinburgh, United Kingdom. A: Allan Murray; ID: Matteo Thun; P: Graven Images.

Morongo Casino, Cabazon, California. A and ID: Jerde Partnership; P: Doug Park, Courtesy of the Jerde Partnership.

Montana Trails Lodge, Big Sky, Montana. A: Bitnar Architects; R: Courtesy of Bitnar Architects.

Mosaic PATHWAY. A and ID: WATG; P: Courtesy of WATG.

Motel 6 "Phoenix" Design Scheme. A and ID: Priestmangoode; P: Courtesy of Accor North America.

New Orleans Arcology Habitat (NOAH), Louisiana. A: Schopfer Associates; R: Courtesy of Tangram 3DS.

Nhow Hotel, Berlin, Germany. A: NPS Tchoban Voss Architects; ID: Karim Rashid; P: Courtesy of Nhow Hotels.

Nine Zero Hotel, Boston, Massachusetts. A: Tsoi/Kobus & Associates; ID: Wilson Associates; P: Courtesy of Tsoi/Kobus & Associates.

Nines Hotel, Portland, Oregon. A: SERA Architects; ID: ForrestPerkins; P: Bruce Buck and Basil Childers.

Oberoi Udaivilas, Udaipur, India. A: Abhikram; ID: Lim, Teo + Wilkes Design Works; P: Courtesy of Oberoi Hotels & Resorts.

Omni Hotel, Dallas, Texas. A: BOKA Powell and 5G Studio Collaborative; ID: Waldrop+Nichols studio. R: Courtesy of 5G Studio Collaborative.

Paradisus Resort, Punta Cana Dominican Republic. A: Alvaro Sans; P: Courtesy of Paradisus Hotels.

Park Hyatt Hadahaa, Republic of Maldives. A and ID: SCDA Architects; P: No Limit Fotodesign and Yaeko Masuda.

The Peninsula Hotel, New York, New York. A: Stonehill & Taylor; ID: Champalimaud Design; P: Mark Weiland, Courtesy of The Peninsula New York.

Peninsula Shanghai, Shanghai, China. A: BBG-BGM; ID: Pierre-Yves Rochon; P: Andrew J. Loiterton.

Planet Hollywood, Las Vegas, Nevada. A: COLAB Architecture and Urban Design with Sotto Studios LA; R: Courtesy of COLAB Architecture.

Poseidon Undersea Resort, Fiji. A: U.S. Submarine; P: Courtesy of L. Bruce Jones.

President Hotel, New York, New York. A and ID: Stonehill & Taylor; P: Gregory Goode.

Princesse Bora Lodge & Spa, Sainte Marie Island, Madagascar. A and ID: Patrice Alexis Mayer; P: Courtesy of Princesse Bora Lodge & Spa.

Proximity Hotel, Greensboro, North Carolina. A: Mark File; ID: Bradshaw Orrell Interiors; P: Courtesy of Quaintance-Weaver Hotels.

Qasr Al Sarab Desert Resort by Anantara, Abu Dhabi, United Arab Emirates. A: Northpoint; ID: HBA Hirsch Bender Associates; P: Durston Saylor, Courtesy of Anantara Resorts.

Radison Blu Hotel, Chicago, Illinois. A: Studio Gang Architects; ID: Jim Hamilton; P: Craig Skorburg.

Raffles Praslin Seychelles, Republic of Seychelles. A: WATG; Kitchen Design: Innovative Foodservice Design Team.

Ramada Encore, London West, United Kingdom. A: Hamilton Associates; ID: Young & Gault and Occa Design; P: Courtesy of Wyndham Hotel Group.

Renaissance Arlington Capital View, Arlington, VA. A: Cooper Carry; ID: ForrestPerkins; P: Kenneth M. Wyner.

Renaissance Clubsport Aliso Viejo, Orange County, California. A: Dahlin Group; ID: Barry Design; P: Courtesy of Leisure Sports.

Renaissance Paris Arc de Triomphe Hotel, Paris, France. A: Atelier Christian de Portzamparc; ID: ERA; P: Courtesy of Marriott International.

Residence Inn and Courtyard, New York, New York. A: Nobutaka Ashihara Architect; R: Courtesy of Nobutaka Ashihara Architect.

Resorts World Sentosa, Singapore. A: Michael Graves; P: Courtesy of Resorts World Sentosa.

Revel, Atlantic City, New Jersey. A: Arquitectonica; P: Courtesy of Revel Entertainment.

The Ritz-Carlton at ICC, Hong Kong, China. A: KPF Associates and Wong & Guyang; ID: LTW Design Works; P: Christopher Cypert, Grische Ruschendorf, Tim Griffith, Courtesy of KPF Associates.

The Ritz-Carlton Bachelor Gulch, Avon, Colorado. A: HKS Hill Glazier Studio; ID: Wilson Associates; P: Blake Marvin.

The Ritz-Carlton Club and Residences, San Francisco, California. A: Charles F. Bloszies and Associates; ID: Forrest Perkins; P: Courtesy of Marriott International.

The Ritz-Carlton Club, Aspen Highlands, Colorado. A: Robert A.M. Stern Architects; P: Joe Aker.

The Ritz-Carlton Hotel and Residences, Guangzhou, China. A: WATG and R&F Design; ID: HBA Hirsch Bedner Associates; LA: Cicada; P: Courtesy of WATG.

The Ritz-Carlton Lake Tahoe, Truckee, California. A: Hornberger + Worstell and OZ Architecture; ID: Brayton Hughes Design Studio; P: Courtesy of Hornberger + Worstell.

The Ritz-Carlton Sanya, Sanya, China. A: WATG and Shanghai Institute of Architectural Design and Research; ID: Chhada, Siembieda & Associates; LA: Belt Collins; P: Christopher Cypert, Courtesy of WATG.

Roosevelt New Orleans, New Orleans, Louisiana. A: Steven J. Finegan Architects; ID: Paradigm Design Group; P: Courtesy of Dimension Development.

Rose Rotana Hotel, Dubai, United Arab Emirates. A: Khatib & Alami; P: Courtesy of Rotana Hotel Management.

Rosewood Sand Hill, Menlo Park, California. A: HKS Hill Glazier Studio; ID: BAMO; LA: SWA Group; P: Matthew Millman.

Saffire Resort, Coles Bay, Australia. A: Circa Architecture; ID: Chhada Siembieda; P: George Apostolidis.

Savoy, London, United Kingdom. A: ReardonSmith; ID: Pierre Yves Rochon; P: Courtesy of Fairmont Hotels.

Semiramis Hotel, Athens, Greece. A and ID: Karim Rashid; P: Courtesy of Karim Rashid.

Shanghai Tower J-Hotel, Shanghai, China. A: Gensler; P: Courtesy of Gensler.

Shanghai World Financial Center, Jin Mao Tower, and Shanghai Tower, Shanghai, China. A: KPF, SOM and Gensler; P: Courtesy of Gensler.

Shangri-La Hotel at the Shard, London, United Kingdom. A: Renzo Piano; P: Aurelien, Hyaes Davidson, and John McLean, Courtesy of Renzo Piano Building Workshop.

Sheraton Milan Malpensa Airport Hotel and Conference Centre, Malpensa, Italy. A and ID: King Roselli Architetti and Saporiti Hotel Design; P: Santi Caleca, Courtesy of King Roselli.

Sheraton Tianjin Hotel, Tianjin, China. A: Woods Bagot; P: Courtesy of Woods Bagot.

Signature at MGM Grand, Las Vegas, Nevada. A: Bergman, Walls & Associates; P: Courtesy of Bergman, Walls & Associates and MGM Resorts International.

Silken Puerta America, Madrid, Spain. A: Jean Nouvel; ID: Arata Isozaki, Norman Foster, Marc Newson, Ron Arad, Richard Gluckman, Javier Mariscal, Victorio & Lucchino, Zaha Hadid, and others; P: Rafael Vargas.

Singita Pamushana Lodge, Malilangwe Wildlife Reserve, Zimbabwe. A: OMM Design Workshop; P: Courtesy of Singita Game Reserves.

Solis Hotel, Shenzhen, China. A: Steven Holl; ID: Jaya Ibrahim; P: Iwan Baan.

Songjiang Hotel, Shanghai, China. A and ID: Atkins Global; R: Courtesy of Atkins Global.

Southern Ocean Lodge, Kangaroo Island, South Australia. A and ID: Max Pritchard Architect.

The Standard, New York, New York. A: Ennead Architects; ID: Roman & Williams and Shawn Hausmann; P: Jeff Goldberg/ESTO and Nocolas Koenig.

St. Pancras Renaissance Hotel, London, United Kingdom. A: RHWL Architects and Richard Griffiths Architects; ID: GA Design International, and David Collins Studio; P: The Photographers Gallery.

St. Regis, Atlanta, Georgia. A: Rabun Architects; ID: HBA Hirsch Bedner Associates; P: Durston Saylor.

St. Regis Deer Valley, Park City Utah. A: IBI Group; ID: Linda Snyder Associates; P: Bruce Buck.

St. Regis Hotel and Residences, Singapore. A: WATG and RSP Architects, Planners, & Engineers; ID: Wilson Associates; LA: Cicada; P: Courtesy of WATG.

St. Regis Sanya Yalong Bay Resort, Sanya, China. A: BBG-BBGM; ID: DiLeonardo; P: Courtesy of BBG-BBGM.

Statler Hotel, Cornell University, Ithaca, New York. A: The Architects Collaborative; ID: Kenneth E. Hurd & Associates; P: Robert Barker.

Steigenberger Golf Resort El Gouna, El Gouna, Egypt. A: Michael Graves; ID: Michael Graves and Lina Bamyeh; P: Courtesy of Stigenberger Hotel Group.

The Study at Yale, New Haven, Connecticut. A+ID: Kuwabara Payne McKenna & Blumberg; P: Tom Arban, Courtesy of Hospitality 3.

Taj Mahal Palace, Mumbai, India. A: Lissoni Associati; ID: BAMO, LTW Design Works, James Park Associates; P: Courtesy of Taj Hotels, Resorts and Palaces.

Terranea Resort, Rancho Palos Verdes, California. A: HKS Hill Glazier Studio; ID: BAMO; LA: Burton and Associates; P: Matthew Millman.

Tierra Atacama Hotel & Spa, San Pedro de Atacama, Chile. A: Rodrigo Searle & Matias Gonzalez; ID: Alexandra Edwards and Carolina Delpiano; P: Courtesy of Tierra Hotels.

Umstead Hotel and Spa, Cary, North Carolina. A: Three Architecture of Dallas; ID: Frank Nicholson; P: Courtesy of Umstead Hotel and Spa.

Vdara, Las Vegas, Nevada. A: Rafael Viñoly; P: Courtesy of MGM Resorts International.

Venetian, Las Vegas, Nevada. A: WATG and TSA of Nevada; ID: Dougall Design and Wilson Associates; LA: Lifescapes International; P: Courtesy of WATG.

Viceroy Miami Hotel, Miami, Florida. A: Arquitectonica; P: Courtesy of Viceroy Hotel Group.

Viceroy, Anguilla, British West Indies. A: WATG; ID: Kelly Wearstler; LA: Girvin & Associates; P: Christian Horan Photography.

Vigilius Mountain Resort, San Vigilio, Italy. A and ID: Matteo Thun; P: Courtesy of Vigilius Mountain Resort.

Virgin Galactic Spaceport, New Mexico. A: Foster & Partners; R: Courtesy of Foster & Partners.

W Barcelona, Barcelona, Spain. A and ID: Ricardo Bofill, Taller de Arquitectura.

W Dallas, Dallas, Texas. A: HKS Hill Glazier Studio; ID: Shopworks; P: Blake Mavin.

W Hollywood, Los Angeles, California. P: Courtesy of W Hollywood.

W London, London, United Kingdom. A+ID: Jestico + Whiles; P: James Newton.

W Minneapolis-Foshay, Minneapolis, Minnesota. A: Elness Swenson Graham Architects; ID: Munge Leung; P: Bobak Ha'Eri, Heinrich Photography.

W Mumbai at Namaste Tower, Mumbai, India. A: Atkins Global; P: Courtesy of Atkins Global.

W Retreat Kanai & Spa, Riviera Maya, Mexico. A: Richard Meier & Partners; R: Vize.com, Courtesy of Richard Meier & Partners.

W Singapore Sentosa Cove, Singapore. A: WATG; ID: AXIS.ID Pte.

Waldorf Astoria Maldives, Republic of Maldives. A and ID: Mohamed Shafeeq–GX Associate; P: Courtesy of Hilton Hotels & Resorts.

Waldorf=Astoria Hotel, New York, New York. A and ID: Kenneth E. Hurd & Associates; P: Edward Jacoby.

Water Cay Resort, Turks and Caicos Islands. A: Tropical Architecture and Mathes Brierre Architects; ID: Yabu Pushelberg; LA: EDSA; P: Courtesy of Tropical Architecture.

WaterColor Inn & Resort, Santa Rosa Beach, Florida. A and ID: Rockwell Group; P: Paul Warchol, Courtesy of Rockwell Group.

Waterhouse at South Bund, Shanghai, China. A and ID: NHDRO; P: Derryck Menere and Thomas Uusheimo.

West 57th Street by Hilton Club, New York, New York. A: HKS Hill Glazier Studio; ID: Alexandra Champalimaud & Associates; P: Courtesy of Hilton Hotels & Resorts.

Westin Beach Resort and Spa, Ft. Lauderdale, Florida. A: Mathes Brierre Architects; ID: ForrestPerkins; R: Courtesy of FSM&Y and Mathes Brierre Architects.

Westin Book Cadillac Hotel, Detroit, Michigan. A: Kaczmar Architects; ID: ForrestPerkins; P: Courtesy of Westin Hotels & Resorts.

Westin Boston Waterfront, Boston, Massachusetts. A: Arrowstreet; ID: BBG-BBGM; P: Peter Vanderwalker.

Westin Elbphilharmonie, Hamburg, Germany. A: Herzog & de Meuron; ID: Tassilo Boer; R: Courtesy of Herzog & de Meuron.

Westin Hotels (Farmers & Mechanics Bank Building), Minneapolis, Minnesota: A: Elness Swenson Graham Architects; ID: Moncur Design Associates; P: George Heinrich.

Westin, Warsaw, Poland. A: John Portman & Associates; ID: HBA Hirsch Bedner Associates: P: Jaime Ardilles-Arce.

Yas Viceroy, Abu Dhabi, United Arab Emirates. A: Asymptote Architecture; ID: Jestico + Whiles, Richardson Sadeki, De8 Architetti; LA: Cracknell Landscape Architects; P: Gerry O'Leary.

Yotel, Heathrow Airport, London, United Kingdom. A and ID: Priestmangoode; P: Courtesy of Yotel.

YOTEL, New York, New York. A: Arquitectonica; ID: Rockwell Group; P: Courtesy of Yotel New York.

About the Authors

Richard H. Penner, a professor emeritus of Cornell University, taught hotel planning, development, and interior design at the School of Hotel Administration for over forty years. He brings together experience in architecture and hotel management, having spent year-long sabbatical leaves with international designer Hirsch Bedner Associates (Santa Monica, CA) and the architecture group of Starwood Hotels & Resorts (White Plains, NY). He graduated from Cornell with bachelor's and master's degrees in architecture, and is an author of four books, two of which were co-authored with the late Walter Rutes, the lead author of the first edition of *Hotel Design, Planning, and Development*. In 1992 *Hospitality Design* magazine honored him with its Platinum Circle Award for his contributions to hospitality design as an author and teacher. His research has focused on planning criteria for different types of lodging properties, including the detailed comparative space allocation standards that have become benchmarks for measuring the efficiency of new hospitality projects. He has presented seminars on hotel development and planning throughout the world. A former director of graduate studies at the Hotel School, he also organized design seminars at the European Meeting on Hotel Interior Design in Rimini, Italy, and chaired five hospitality design roundtables sponsored by the Center for Hospitality Research at Cornell.

Lawrence Adams, AIA, a vice president of ForrestPerkins, is a global authority on hotel and resort design. He earned a bachelor of architecture degree from Louisiana State University. He has managed and directed the design of large-scale development projects at major architectural and planning firms for the past thirty-five years. With a specialty in hotel design, Mr. Adams served as adjunct faculty at New York University for nine years teaching master's degree courses on Hotel Design and Development. He co-authored the first edition of *Hotel Design, Planning, and Development* with Richard Penner and the late Walter Rutes. His projects include the Four Seasons Hotel New York, the RIGHA Royal Hotel, the Chambers Hotel, The Westin Ft. Lauderdale Beach Resort, and the national headquarters of the Marine Corps Reserve. Mr. Adams, who is certified by NCARB, is also a registered architect in New York, Massachusetts, Kansas, Mississippi, and Louisiana.

Stephani K. A. Robson holds three degrees from Cornell University: a bachelor of science and doctorate in hotel administration and a master of science in facilities planning and management. Her professional career has included design work on a number of large hotel and hospitality projects in her native Canada. She joined the full-time faculty at Cornell University's School of Hotel Administration in 1993. A specialist in hospitality design psychology, she has numerous research publications in academic journals, including the *Journal of Environmental Psychology* and the *Cornell Hospitality Quarterly*, and frequently contributes to trade journals on topics related to design and development. She has taught and presented her research on hospitality environments worldwide.

Index